P9-APE-331

DISCARDED

University of Winnipeg, 515 Portage Ave., Winnipeg, MB. R3B 2E9 Canada

A HISTORY OF ENGLAND

From the Defeat of the Armada
to the Death of Elizabeth

VOLUME II

DA
355
C54
1948
V.2
C.2
Rutherford

A History of England

From the Defeat of the Armada to the
Death of Elizabeth

With an Account of English Institutions
During the Later Sixteenth and
Early Seventeenth Centuries

BY

EDWARD P. CHEYNEY

PROFESSOR OF EUROPEAN HISTORY IN
THE UNIVERSITY OF PENNSYLVANIA

IN TWO VOLUMES

VOLUME II

NEW YORK
PETER SMITH
1948

COPYRIGHT, 1926, BY
LONGMANS, GREEN, AND CO.

Reprinted 1948 by
special arrangement with
ALICE A. CHEYNEY

PRINTED IN THE UNITED STATES OF AMERICA

PREFACE TO VOLUME II

THE long period that has intervened between the appearance of the first and the present volume of this work is due in part to causes connected with the war, in part to more personal exigencies. It has brought one partial compensation, the opportunity to make use of other studies in the period published during the decade, for which acknowledgment is here duly made. There has been, unfortunately, no possibility of utilizing that which has appeared on subjects covered in the first volume.

The absence in this volume of the Bibliography promised in the Preface to Volume I is due to the anticipated early appearance of the general Bibliography of English History of the Tudor period being prepared by a group of American scholars parallel to the Bibliography of the Stuart period in preparation by a group of British scholars. This larger work will make a special bibliography of materials used in this book of relatively little value. The promise of the subtitle and the Preface, also, that this work will include a description of English institutions in its period, would seem to have been but poorly carried out when the organization of the church, the universities and schools, the Inns of Court, and so many aspects of intellectual and social life have not been described. The author can only plead the limitations of time, the extent of the task, the need of a larger canvas on which to paint a picture including so much detail.

EDWARD P CHEYNEY

UNIVERSITY OF PENNSYLVANIA
Thanksgiving Day, November 26, 1925

CONTENTS

PART V

THE YEAR 1596

PART VI

THE LEAGUE AGAINST SPAIN

PART VII

THE LAST FOUR PARLIAMENTS OF QUEEN ELIZABETH

PART VIII

LOCAL GOVERNMENT

PART IX

THE FALL OF ESSEX

PART X

THE LAST DAYS OF THE REIGN

Part V
The Year 1596

Part V   The Year 1596

CHAPTER XXV

SCARCITY

ALTHOUGH in the former volume of this work we have occasionally passed beyond the midpoint of our period, and in this will sometimes recur to earlier events, we have been engaged in the main with the years from 1588 to 1595, and have now to complete the narrative down to the death of the queen in 1603. It may be of interest therefore to make a somewhat detailed study of the occurrences of the year 1596, the middle year of the period, both as a typical year and as a point of departure for the remainder of our history. It was a critical year, a year of privation, high prices and threatened internal rebellion, of much military recruiting and naval conscription, of an aggressive campaign against Spain which won ample glory but little profit, of threatened revenge by a new armada and a still further spread in Ireland of the native struggle for independence. It was also a year of crisis in Elizabeth's relations with her allies of France, the Netherlands, Germany and the North. The calling of a parliament was avoided by the collection of a loan on privy seal but extreme poverty was not lessened thereby and indeed was so apparent this year as to become the principal subject of legislation in the parliament that met in 1597.

In another domain, that of literature, which must here, unfortunately, be alluded to only, not discussed, 1596 was an important year; for although it was not marked by the actual publication of so many conspicuous works as some years that preceded or followed, it lay midway in a period of great activity, and much that has been read ever since was then either brand new or approaching completion. Most of Shakespeare's comedies were new pieces on the stage, A Midsummer Night's Dream was within the first twelvemonth of its perennial popularity, his chronicle plays had all been the product of the last three years or were to be the fruit of the next. Spenser, an absentee for the time from his Irish estates, spent this year in England and brought the Faerie Queene into its final form. Bacon was polishing his Essays for their first appearance in the succeeding year. It was the heyday of Elizabethan satire, and the best of Elizabethan songs were being collected for publication the next year. Ralegh and Donne, Dee, Hakluyt, Harvey, Hooker and the long list of representatives in their respective fields of literature and thought, — poets, essayists, scholars, university men, statesmen, lawyers, historians and geographers, could be found at no time probably during the whole Elizabethan period more actively and effectively at work than in the year 1596.[1]

Of all these varied interests the two which made the deepest impression on the minds of men living in that year, if we are to judge from surviving records, were, in internal affairs, the scarcity and consequent high price of food; in external affairs, the expedition to Cadiz. It was the third and hardest of a series of five continuous years of dearth. The main cause is abundantly indicated in the literature of the time. It was the rain. In 1594, the first of these five years, it was declared, on contemporary authority,

> " The ox hath therefore stretched his yoke in vain,
>   The ploughman lost his sweat, and the green corn
>   Hath rotted ere his youth attained a beard."

In 1595 the pious Churchyard testifies that

[1] F. E. Schelling, *English Literature in the Lifetime of Shakespeare;* C. T. Onions, Ed., *Shakespeare's England.*

" A colder time in world was never seene;
  The skies do loure, the sun and moon wax dim,
  Summer scarce known, but that the leaves are greene,
  The winter's vaste drives water o'er the brim . . .
  Nature thinks scorn to do his dutie right
  Because we have displeasde the Lord of Light."

A preacher at York reminds his hearers that " Our July hath been like to a February, our June even as an April, . . . our years are turned upside down, . . . our summers are no summers, our harvests are no harvests. . . . For a great space of time scant any day hath been seen that it hath not rained upon us." The chroniclers tell the same story. Camden speaks of continual rains in summer, and Stow reports that " this summer, by reason of much raine and great floods, corne waxed scant." Other causes of distress were undoubtedly present; wet summers were not unprecedented in England, nor have they been unknown since. Still it is evident that whatever other troubles there may have been in these years the wheat, rye, barley and oats that were garnered were insufficient for the nation's needs. The seasons were likewise unfavorable to cattle, and a deficiency of meat accompanied the shortage of grain. Potatoes, the great resource of modern times, were as yet unknown, except as a curiosity, and other vegetables at best played but a small part in the food supply of the sixteenth century, which was meat and wheat for the upper, rye for the lower classes. For a while at the beginning of August 1596 seasonable weather gave hopes of a better harvest for this year, but these hopes were soon disappointed, there were autumn and winter rains and the scarcity was unrelieved. " This time of dearth " remained an expression of constant recurrence.[2]

As the summer of 1596 wore on and last year's supplies were more and more depleted grain rose to famine prices.

[2] *Midsummer Night's Dream*, Act 2, Sc. 1; Churchyard, *Charities;* Strype, *Annals, Sermon of Dr. King*, iv, 294–5; Camden, *History of Elizabeth*, Ed. 1688, 506; Stow, *Annals* Ed. 1631, 782; *Acts of the Privy Council*, xxvi, 381.

The average price of wheat for the year, calculated from many examples, was more than seven shillings a bushel. This price corresponds to something like seven dollars a bushel in modern value. Rye cost scarcely less than wheat, oatmeal frequently cost more. These prices were greater even than in the two preceeding and the two succeeding years; they were more than twice the prices of a period only three years before and a few years later. They are from five to eight times prices normally prevailing in modern times.[3]

In certain parts of the country and at certain seasons of the year prices rose still higher. In Devonshire in mid-summer, just before harvest, wheat was selling at nine shillings a bushel, and there was but little reduction after harvest. In London in December wheat was ten shillings a bushel, oatmeal eight and rye six. In Bristol wheat was sold at twelve and fifteen shillings; at Shrewsbury, somewhat farther north, wheat rose to eighteen shillings, rye to fifteen shillings and beans to thirteen shillings a bushel. In all these values dollars may be safely read for shillings to obtain a modern equivalent. Even at these extreme rates grain could in many places scarcely be obtained. At Barnstaple in Devonshire we hear that " but little cometh to the market, and such snatching and catching for that little and such a cry that the like was never heard." At Shrewsbury, where the town authorities took charge of the sale of bread, the poor " were so unruly and gredie to have it that the baylyff's six men and other officers had much adoe to serve them." In Hertford although from 1200 to 1500 bushels of wheat and rye were offered each market day the demand was so great that after the market bell was rung it was generally gone within the hour. In the far north the dean of Durham declares that poor people had sometimes to travel sixty miles to buy bread.[4]

[3] *Acts of the Privy Council*, xxv, 153, 206, xxvi, 81, 113, 380; J. E. Thorold Rogers, *History of Agriculture and Prices*, v, 180, 182, 268.
[4] *Wyot's Diary*, pub. in *North Devon Herald*, June 3, 1880, quoted

Suffering was correspondingly great. A contemporary chronicler testifies that " many in all counties in England die and goe in great numbers myserably begginge." A preacher at Oxford said of the famine that " it maketh the poor to pinch for hunger and the children to cry in the streets not knowing where to have bread." In Newcastle the town accounts through spring and early summer include payments for burying poor folk who died for want in the streets, and for " victualles for the relefe of the seke folke afielde and within towne." In the Midlands, in Oxfordshire and Norfolk, there is the same report of scarcity, prohibitive prices and consequent widespread suffering of the poor. A pamphlet of the next year says, " The complaint of the poore through penurie in Englande hath continued long, Christian reader, and yet it appeareth the want groweth greater." These conditions are of course true only of the lower classes, and it is also true that poverty and distress were familiar enough to the mass of the English people during the whole of Queen Elizabeth's time; but the tide of suffering among them rose measurably higher in these years of poor crops, difficulty of distribution, warlike policy and social change.[5]

The problem of public need could according to sixteenth century belief be solved only by public means. In the absence of shops or other places of private sale always open, it was a large part of the work of the municipal authorities to foresee and provide for the food supply of the towns. During times of dearth this was especially necessary and many of them now acted with vigor. The

---

in E. M. Leonard, *Early History of the English Poor Law*, 120–4; *Cal. State Papers, Dom.* 1595–7, 126, 347; Seyer, *Memoirs of Bristol*, ii, 255; Owen and Blakeway, *History of Shrewsbury*, i, 400; Stow, *Annals*, Ed. 1631, 783; Camden, *History of Queen Elizabeth*, 506.

[5] *Wyot's Diary;* George Abbott, *Lectures upon Jonah*, 104, quoted in Strype, *Life of Whitgift*, Ed. 1822, ii, 337; Owen and Blakeway, *Shrewsbury*, ii, 400; *Accounts of Newcastle on Tyne*, 1514–1688, in M. H. Richardson, *Reprints of Rare Tracts*, iii, 43, 44; H. A., *Provision for the poore*, C; *Cal. State Papers, Dom.* 1595–7, 316.

bailiffs and aldermen of Shrewsbury after long negotiations with the authorities of London bought there 3200 bushels of rye which had come in from Dantzig and Denmark, and sold the greater part of it in their own town at four shillings a bushel below the market price. The remainder they had baked by the town bakers in amounts of forty bushels a week in penny, twopenny and fourpenny loaves for the poor who could not buy in larger amounts. The council of Barnstaple sent an agent to London to buy corn for that town. The authorities of Ipswich borrowed enough money from their fellow townsmen to buy 800 bushels of rye and 1200 bushels of barley to be sold to the poor.

The officials of Bristol made a good venture of their provisioning of that city. They sent one of their number, John Whitson, to London. At the close of the year 1595 he contracted with Thomas Offley, a well-known merchant, to deliver 24,000 bushels of Dantzig rye in Bristol by the end of May at about three and a half shillings a bushel. By the time it arrived the market price was already five and a half shillings and much of it was soon afterward sold to townsmen who were glad to pay six shillings a bushel. After paying all Whitson's expenses and a fee for his services and after giving away many pecks and half bushels to the very poor, the town authorities nevertheless made a profit of more than £700. A similar purchase was made in August by the gild merchant of Exeter of 3200 bushels of rye from abroad to be paid for by contributions of the members, each contributor to receive in kind on the arrival of the grain one half of what his contribution would pay for and to allow the other half to be sold to the poor. Seventy-one members subscribed £550 toward the purchase and the rye was eventually procured and distributed at a cost of four shillings six pence a bushel.[6]

[6] Ashley, *English Economic History*, ii, 33–38; Owen and Blakeway, *Shrewsbury*, i, 400; Bacon, *Annals of Ipswich*, 385; Seyer, *Memoirs of Bristol*, ii, 254–6; *Acts of the Privy Council*, xxvi, 83–1; *Additional MSS.* 32092, fo. 145, quoted in Leonard, *History of English Poor Law*, 121; *Barnstaple Records, ibid.;* Cotton, *An Elizabethan Guild*, Appendix, xliv.

It was, however, not the town officials but the active and
paternalistic privy council that took the principal responsibility for solving the food problem. They like the queen
were loth to believe that any serious problem of supply
existed, or that the high prices of grain had other than an
artificial origin. " Her highness doth verily think," they
declare " the fault thereof, in parte, to be the covetous
disposition of such as are farmers and corn masters, that
not acknowledging God's goodness, do seek immoderate gain
by enhancing the prices of corn and grain, to the great
oppression of the poorer sort." The high prices were mainly
due, in their estimation, in the first place to the cupidity of
those who possessed the grain and refused to sell it till
it had risen still higher, and in the second place to the
unfair action of the grain dealers who went to the farmers'
homes to buy grain on speculation to sell again, rather than
let it be brought for sale directly to the consumers in the
open market. These were the two greatest violations of
commercial morality, engrossing and forestalling, popularly
believed to be the principal causes of excessive prices.

Familiar precedent existed for the punishment of these
offenses. Some ten years before this time a complete code
had been worked out which was expected to prevent them
entirely, so far as concerned grain. The sheriff and justices of the peace of each county were ordered to meet, to
divide themselves into as many groups as there were distinct sections of the county, to call before them in these
divisions the constables and substantial men of the section
and appoint from them a local board or jury for each
parish or small group of parishes. This board or jury
was put upon its oath and required to hand in a list of all
persons who raised grain in their neighborhood, the amount
each had stored in his barn or had growing in his field and
the number of souls in his household. The justices of the
peace of the district then, after allowing to each grain
raiser an amount sufficient for the consumption of his household until next harvest and for seed for the next season,

required him to take all the surplus regularly in specified amounts to the nearest weekly market. There he must
sell it in as small quantities as any one chose to ask and
at a price considered by the justices to be reasonable.
Farmers could buy no grain to sell again, and bakers,
brewers and grain dealers could buy only the amounts for
which they held a license from the justices, only in the
open market, and must keep a record showing what they
had bought or sold, where and at what price. It was the
duty of the justices to attend at the market towns on market
days to see that these regulations were carried out and to
exert whatever pressure they could for the sale of grain at
moderate prices.

One may doubt whether such formidable requirements
had ever been enforced, but such as they were they had
been renewed in 1594 and again in 1595, and now August 3,
1596 they were reissued in still more detailed and stringent
form.

Letters enclosing the regulations were sent by messengers
to the sheriff and justices of the peace of each county in
England and Wales declaring the queen's compassion for
her suffering subjects, reprobating the " wilful increase of
prices of grain," and making requirement for its compulsory
sale at reasonable rates. The justices should assist the
poor in purchasing at reasonable prices, and if necessary
over-rule the prices asked by the possessors of grain and
distribute it to the poor at a more moderate price. If
any sellers should " murmur or repyne," against these
orders, they should be committed to prison till they would
conform; and instances are not lacking of such vigorous
action by local authority. Recalcitrant possessors of grain
bold enough to refuse obedience to local officials were disciplined in the Star Chamber. A man named Mison declared in opposition to the action of the justices of the
peace in his district " My goodes are myn owne, they, nor
the queene, nor the Councelle have to do with my goodes,
I will doe what I like with them." But this degree of

individualism was not good sixteenth century doctrine, and Mison was fined £100, imprisoned, forced to confess his fault, to wear a paper declaring his offense, and to give bonds for future good behavior.[7]

To require that grain should be sold only in the nearest market, and only by the immediate producer to the actual consumer was unpopular with all the parties most closely concerned, always difficult and in many cases impracticable of enforcement, and the privy council was therefore engaged in an unending and hopeless attempt to carry out its regulations. In some cases, where they were obviously inapplicable it suspended them, in others their policy was inconsistent. In September, for instance, letters were sent to the lord lieutenant, sheriff and justices of the peace of Gloucestershire complaining of their dereliction in not carrying out rigorously the requirements of the proclamation, but less than a month afterward the council writes again to the same officials directing them to permit the bakers and brewers of Bristol to buy grain anywhere in Gloucestershire or Worcestershire and transport it down the Severn, notwithstanding the proclamation, because there was not sufficient raised in the vicinity of Bristol to furnish both its inhabitants and the shipping fitted out there. When there was still trouble, the privy council ordered a number of gentlemen of Gloucester to meet them in conference on October 22 immediately after dinner, in the Star Chamber, to arrange the matter independently of the regulations. The authorities of the home counties were ordered to allow the bakers of London to buy throughout their limits considerable amounts of grain for the use of the great city, at the same time that the lord lieutenant of Hampshire, one of those counties, was ordered rigorously to enforce the proclamation against selling for distant markets.

[7] *Acts of the Privy Council*, xxv, 8, 25, 80, xxvi, 81–3; Bland, Brown and Tawney, *English Economic History, Select Documents*, 374–80; *Lansdowne MSS.*, xlviii, fo. 128, No. 54, quoted in Leonard, 318–320; *Egerton MSS.*, 2644, fo. 55, quoted in Leonard, 119; Hawarde, *Reportes del Cases in Camera Stellata*, 76, 104.

The authorities of Colchester, York, Hull, Tenderden, the county of Somerset and others were allowed to buy grain for their needs by special license through the whole counties of Norfolk, Rutland, Northamptonshire and elsewhere. It was found necessary to grant permission to obtain a supply for London from almost anywhere it could be obtained. It becomes difficult to say whether the enforcements or the dispensations from enforcement are more extensive.[8]

Sometimes prohibition of transport from one district to another worked only too well. About a thousand bushels of wheat which had been bought up by representatives of a London baker and brought to Sandwich to be sent by water to the city was impounded by the authorities there and ordered to be sold to their own people. The dealer offered to sell a hundred bushels on the spot at a shilling a bushel less than he paid for it or to give outright thirty bushels to the poor of the city, if the authorities would let the rest go, but relying on the proclamation they refused. The dispute lasted more than six months, drew in the lord mayor and aldermen of London and the privy council itself, but has left us no record of its eventual settlement. Later repetitions of these regulations, the need for frequent exceptions, and new devices to reach the same end alike testify to the failure of the council in its efforts to regulate the grain market so strictly and minutely. Nevertheless evidence exists of the appointment of juries of investigation, of the regulation of prices by the justices and of the punishment of growers and dealers for engrossing and forestalling. Payment to a man " for his paynes being clarke to the 12 men appoynted to sertche for corne according to the Councell's orders," appears on the records of Leicester, and among the papers of many country gentry are the detailed instructions which they at least attempted to carry out.[9]

[8] *Acts of the Privy Council*, xxv, 25, xxvi, 80, 96, 226–7, 269, 331, 503, 523, 541, xxvii, 359.

[9] *Ibid.*, xxvi, 534, 549, 559; *Hist. MSS. Comm., Rutland MSS.*, i, 332–3; *Montague House MSS.*, i, 229, *Cal. Hatfield House MSS.*, vii, 496, 497–8; Bateson, *Records of Leicester*, iii, 326–330.

In addition to regular sales in the open market, the queen and council believed that much of the distress might be relieved by the exercise of hospitality on the part of the country gentry. The ideal country gentleman of the time was a man who lived in his own manor house, helped to defend the country from attacks from without and to repress disorders within, kept up a liberal but not wasteful household, entertained his friends, provided for his dependents and gave from his abundance to the relief of his poor neighbors. One of the constant preoccupations of the government was the effort to enforce this ideal upon a by no means assenting gentry. July 1, on the last day of Trinity term, in Star Chamber, the lord keeper of the great seal, in giving his instructions to the justices going on circuit, declared to them that it was the queen's will that all gentlemen who had forsaken their country dwellings to live in cities or towns should go back to their country homes. A public proclamation to the same effect was issued. But obedience was hard to enforce. In addition to the evergrowing attractions of the city, the burdens of expenditure while living in the country were beyond precedent. At the very time that the gentry were being urged to remain in their country homes and offer an abundant hospitality, they were being required to pay the double subsidies of the last parliament, to pay for the musters and support the trained bands, to meet the expense of levying troops for Ireland, to furnish the government with cattle at reduced prices or pay composition money and to keep a burdensome watch upon their recusant neighbors.

Hospitality as a means of lessening suffering therefore though constantly insisted upon was but slightly effective. In October the earl of Bath writing from Tavistock, complains that the gentlemen of Devonshire are leaving their country houses to go to Exeter, and begs that in this time of extremity and dearth they be required to come home again. Repetitions of such complaints and orders are constant. On Christmas day the privy council order the lord mayor and aldermen of London to send them a list of all gentlemen of ability having houses in the country but now remaining in the city, and this order was repeated shortly afterward.[10]

In the effort to diminish the sufferings of the poor the government was not likely to neglect its ecclesiastical officials, who formed a civil army which might by organized precept and example accomplish much. Five days after the circular instructions to the officials of counties of August 3 had been sent out the privy council wrote to the archbishop instructing him to require all preachers to point out in their sermons that " that gaine is moste ungodly that is gotten by pinching and starving of poore people." All possessors of grain were to be admonished to bring it to market to sell in accordance with the proclamation, and all persons of position were urged to " keep hospitality " for the relief of the poor. It was to be urged upon the well-to-do that they should be satisfied with a sober diet and cut off all forms of waste. These instructions were repeated two months later, with still more stress upon abstinence and upon giving of alms and with a reminder that they apply to the clergy themselves as well as to the laity.

Plans were worked out by the archbishop for the administration of this ecclesiastical oversight of clerical and lay frugality. The parish clergy must report to the bishop monthly who observed and who failed to observe the requirements of the council. Each bishop must report for his diocese quarterly to the archbishop, and the archbishop from time to time to the queen. Circular letters with these instructions were sent out to the bishops in Christmas week. Among the specific appeals the clergy were to make to well-to-do people was that they should go without suppers on Wednesdays, Fridays and other fast days, partly that the food of the country might be conserved, partly that they might bestow the price of it on the poor. The same

---

[10] *Hist. MSS. Comm., Somerset Papers,* 15 Rep. app. vii, 20; *Rutland MSS.,* i, 332; *Acts of the Privy Council,* xxvi, 381.

plan, along with general plainness of diet, was urged by the
privy council upon the masters, wardens and members of
the city companies. Much efficacy was attributed to this
form of economy. A writer in a midland town commends
the archbishop's appeal and expresses the belief that if
everyone would " let the poore have the full benefit of their
sayde suppers, there should not one person have cause to
begge there for all this deare yeare." The privy council
ordered the lord mayor of London to make the same requirement for all " men of the better sort " in the city. It
was calculated that the price of the supper of four able-
bodied persons would serve for the relief of " one poor
body " for a week. The voluntary sacrifice of Sunday supper and the gift of its price to their own poor is said
to have been the regular plan by which the companies of
foreign Protestants in London succored their poor.[11]

The use of barley for ale and beer among a people who
drank these beverages instead of wine and largely instead
of water was a serious diminution of the available food
supply. A careful estimate showed that the alehouses of
the city of Wells used in the year 1596 some 12,000 bushels
of barley, an amount which it was calculated would have
provided ten bushels weekly to every market town of the
shire for the year. Although there was no thought of prohibiting brewing, the privy council took steps to limit its
amount. An old order of 1586 had required the use of
oats instead of barley for malt where possible and enjoined
the restriction by the justices of the number of alehouses
and the amount of food and drink consumed in them.
Special orders were now sent to the authorities of London,
Norwich, Gloucester and certain of the counties not to
allow so much beer to be brewed nor of such great strength
" in thes deere and hard tymes," and many brewers who
violated this requirement were summoned before the coun-

---

[11] *Acts of the Privy Council*, xxvi, 95, 96, 380–383; Strype, *Whitgift*,
ii, 336–7, iii, 348–50; H. A., *Provision for the poore now in penurie*,
B. 3, C.

cil. Nevertheless this restriction was not construed too rigorously, for the deputy lieutenants and justices of the peace of Devon were allowed by special license to send an agent through the country to buy malt, each purchase to be entered upon his commission till he should have secured 24,000 bushels.

In the same direction of limiting consumption of the higher grains, the council tried to make available a greater amount of cheaper food; at one time forbidding farmers to feed their sheep on peas, which might be brought to market and sold to poor people, at another requiring bakers to bake loaves of barley, peas and beans for the use of the poor; at still another time authorizing the justices of the peace of three midland counties to buy peas, rye and barley in their own counties to send down to Somersetshire which was in dire need. Even in the days of Elizabethan ruffs no grain was to be spent in making of " a stuff called starch, as of late there hath been discovered great quantity expended in that vain matter." [12]

But none of these provisions actually increased the supply of food for the English people. That must come either by retaining within the country what would under other circumstances have gone abroad or by bringing more into the country. The desirability of prohibiting the export of food during these times of scarcity was obvious. The requirement that grain should be sold directly from producer to consumer and in the nearest local market should automatically have produced this result. None could have gone abroad. But this was, as has been seen, hard to enforce and there were many exceptions. More specific prevention of export was therefore provided by special orders and prohibitions. This kind of regulation was a familiar form of policy. The existing corn laws placed the granting or withholding of licenses to export in the hands of the queen's officers. Such licenses were now regularly denied. Specific

[12] *Acts of the Privy Council*, xxv, 7, 19–21, xxvi, 149, 152, 154, 226, 259, 269, 276, 323, 327, 335, 358, 505, 539.

orders were issued for the enforcement of the law; the port officers of Lynn were ordered to be watchful in preventing the export of grain brought secretly by night from the adjacent wheat-growing counties. Two gentlemen of Northumberland were brought before the lord warden of the Middle Marches in January for smuggling butter and cheese through Berwick to Scotland. Chester was warned by the privy council to allow no grain to be exported on pretense of being taken to Ireland or the Isle of Man, except such as government officials themselves should take out. The Council of the North were ordered to prevent exports from York, and in November officers of the ports of Yorkshire were under careful observation to see whether they were performing their duties. Scotchmen were forbidden to furnish their ships with victuals for outward voyages at English port towns and allowed to buy only enough grain for their use while in port.[13]

Notwithstanding all these well-meant efforts of the government to prevent speculation, to enforce frugality and to conserve the national supply, it was certainly desirable to bring more food into the country. Some came automatically as a result of the attraction of high prices in England. From the Baltic coasts of Germany and Poland, known in England as the East Countries, was regularly exported a vast amount of grain which was carried by vessels of the Hanse towns to those countries where the best prices or the most advantageous trading conditions were offered. London was, under the conditions of this year, a profitable market, even though a bitter dispute between England and the Hanse towns was in progress, and though Spain and Italy offered still more attractive conditions of sale, if those countries could be safely reached. The Netherlands and Denmark also exported a certain amount of grain in favorable seasons. From time to time during the year 1596 fleets from one or other of these regions arrived in the Thames.

---

[13] *Acts of the Privy Council*, xxv, 87, 133, 137, 153, 180, 206, xxvi, 151, 257, 328.

In August a number of shiploads arrived from Zealand. In October when twenty ships laden with corn from the East Countries came into the Thames, the privy council wrote to the lord mayor of London ordering him to see that it should not get into the hands of engrossers but be sold so that poor men might be relieved, and yet that the price be not so depressed as to discourage other foreigners from bringing in grain. For further encouragement of importation many of the usual restrictions were withdrawn. Some 6000 bushels of rye, for instance, were brought in through Harwich for London by a special dispensation, and Shrewsbury was allowed by a special license to import corn from whatever country it could be obtained. The Muscovy Company was allowed to send to Russia in contravention of the usual rules against the export of bullion £500 in Spanish reals and dollars toward payment for 3,000 bushels of wheat to be imported from that country. Within less than a week, between October 26 and 30, seventeen well known London merchants brought into that port some 5,000 bushels of wheat and 48,000 bushels of rye. The government contracted with merchants to bring in wheat and rye from abroad for the queen's service, £1,500 being put into their hands by way of imprest in December.

Finally, December 5, the queen, troubled by the rising prices and believing that merchants of the port towns would be willing to import wheat and rye abundantly " in this time of want and dearth " if they could be relieved of the usual import duties, gave under her sign manual orders that all port officers should permit grain to enter free of duty until they received further orders. This was a considerable sacrifice for the treasury, but along with the previous series of licenses it opened the floodgates to importation, for in the last three months of the year more than one hundred cargoes were unloaded in the London Custom House amounting to almost 450,000 bushels of grain. These importations were by both English merchants and foreigners, from many ports and in all sorts of amounts from a cargo of 10,000 bushels imported by such a great merchant as William Offley, down to one or two quarters transshipped in a small boat from some other English port. The largest amounts were from the German ports Dantzig, Slade and Emden and from such Netherlands ports as Middleburg and Flushing. From October 1596 to March 1597, a period of seven months, 888,660 bushels of grain were brought into the port of London, about four fifths being imported by native, one fifth by foreign merchants.[14]

That vessels from the north laden with grain should be allowed to sail through the Narrow Seas past English harbors on their way to more southern ports when their cargoes were so sorely needed in England, when they were suspected of carrying contraband to her enemies and when there was an English fleet on the water, was hardly to be expected. Early in the year, therefore, orders were sent to the fleet to watch for vessels of Easterlings or others suspected to be on their way to Spain; to take them into some port of England and force them to unload there and sell their cargoes. Later in the year Sir Harry Palmer, vice admiral, was ordered to stay all vessels from the East Countries claiming to be on their way to Rochelle or elsewhere to the southward and to send them with prize crews directly to Dublin or Waterford in Ireland, where the English forces needed supplies. There if proved to be on the way to Spain, they were to be confiscated, ship and all, otherwise their cargoes were to be discharged and paid for, costs of carriage paid, and the vessels allowed to go on their way. These were simply applications of England's policy of contraband, with all its complications, as they have already been described.

Just at the end of this year a more striking if inconclu-

14 *Cal. Hatfield House MSS.*, vi, 507, vii, 192, 206; Murdin, *State Papers,* 811; *Cal. State Papers, Dom.,* 1595-7, 307, 314-5, 431; *State Papers, Dom., Elizabeth,* cclx, 79, cclxi, 30, 31, 32; *Acts of the Privy Council,* xxvi, 223, 281, 374; Owen and Blakeway, *Shrewsbury,* i, 400; Seyer, *Bristol,* ii, 254-6; Overall, *Remembrancia,* ii, 31, 571, *Index to Remembrancia,* 63; Camden, 506.

sive example of this policy occurred. Two hundred sail of ships from the north loaded with provisions, claiming to be on their way to southern France and driven by stress of weather, put into Flushing, the English garrison town in Zealand. The queen sent orders to Sir Robert Sydney, the English governor, to stay the vessels and urge them to come to England to dispose of their cargoes, offering them as good prices as they could get anywhere. If they refused, he was to borrow some warships from the Council of Zealand and force the grain ships to come to England. Sydney had to report his inability to secure the agreement of the shipmasters or to obtain the necessary warships from the Netherlanders to prevent them leaving the harbor. The vice-admiral was thereupon ordered to lie in wait for them off the mouth of the Scheldt. Unfortunately the outcome is unrecorded. Another instance was that of a great Venetian " argosy," the St. Agatha, which put into the harbor of Portsmouth late in the year. It had come from Amsterdam laden with grain and, according to its master, Francisco Morosini, and its purser, Constantine Patriano, was destined rather indefinitely southward. Lord Mountjoy, captain of Portsmouth, stayed her and ordered her cargo of grain to be unloaded and placed in the government storehouses, at the same time giving her purser assurances that the cargo would be well paid for. The customhouse officers ordered enough to be sold at three shillings four pence to four shillings a bushel to pay the cost of freight, so that the vessel herself might leave. This was a slender price for the times; there were disputes and protests and correspondence with the signory of Venice, as a result of which the officers of Portsmouth were ordered to retain 12,000 bushels for the use of the government, paying the agents of the owners the much higher price of six shillings a bushel, since the queen wanted, as she said, to deal with them as she would want Englishmen to be dealt with in a friendly state. Three vessels were sent down from London to carry the 12,000 bushels to Ireland for the army, and the keys of the Portsmouth storehouses were turned over to the factors so that they might sell the remainder for whatever they could get for it in the public market. From December to May the great ship lay in the harbor, the dispute got into the admiralty court and the whole affair was a matter of much public interest.

Sometimes friendly relations with foreign rulers prevented such high-handed measures. A " hulk " from the East Countries came into the harbor of Plymouth for refuge from a November storm, laden with corn consigned to the duke of Tuscany. The officials of Plymouth asked that it be stayed and its cargo sold on account of the dire need for food in that part of the country. The privy council sent word that the queen had " passed her worde " to the duke that this grain should be suffered to pass without stay. The local authorities however were allowed to take from the ship before she sailed some six or eight hundred bushels and sell it to the people, paying over to the English agents of the duke the amount received. A gift of a little box of oil, drugs and conserves sent by the duke of Tuscany to the earl of Essex earlier in the year perhaps gives a clue to the favorable treatment of the Italian ship.[15]

Notwithstanding all these efforts of the government to lower prices and bring about a better distribution of the food supply, its own requirements this year acted in an exactly contrary direction. The privy council and treasury records from the very beginning of the year are filled with instructions to local authorities to purchase or to provide ready for the government purchasing agents on their arrival grain, bacon, beef and other food supplies needed as provision for the garrisons of Ireland and the Channel Islands and for the troops and crews upon the queen's ships preparing for the defense of the coasts and for the great

[15] *Acts of the Privy Council*, xxv, 39, 387; xxvi, 393-7, 441, 445, 454, 466, 503, 545, 550; Cheyney, *International Law under Queen Elizabeth*, *Eng. Hist. Rev.* xx, 659; *Cal. Hatfield House MSS.*, vi, 59, 67, 82, 100, 190.

expedition being equipped against Spain. In January, for instance, the local officials of Devonshire are ordered to have ready at Plymouth for sale to Marmaduke Darrell and James Quarles, surveyors of victuals for the navy, 3200 bushels of wheat, 200 oxen and 200 flitches of bacon, at a price apparently somewhat below what was then current. Within the next few weeks orders of approximately the same character were sent to every county in England. In April the same navy officials were provided with £700 with which to buy food for 300 men going to Guernsey for the next four months as a garrison under Sir Thomas Leighton, since the island could not supply victuals for any more than its usual inhabitants. A similar garrison was similarly supplied somewhat later for Jersey. Grain was bought for use in the Isle of Man. In October food is purchased in six northern counties for the garrison of Berwick. In November the treasurer of war for Ireland is authorized to spend £5000 for victuals for the troops there. There was widespread protest. Petitions for exemption came pouring in. A number of the shires insisted that they must be relieved altogether from the grain requirement and allowed to furnish meat instead. The justices of Leicester declare that the 2400 bushels of wheat demanded of them could hardly be found in the whole shire. The privy council acknowledges the difficulties and makes many concessions, but the demands were still heavy and the concentration of this demand at certain places and at certain times intensified the shortage.[16]

If the efforts of the government to lessen the evil effects of the food shortage of 1596 be compared with similar efforts in more modern times, when insufficiency of food threatens, it will be seen that for all the autocracy of that period the administration did not carry out so stringent a policy as that of its modern successor. It did not establish

[16] *Historical MSS. Comm., Somerset Papers*, 13; *Acts of the Privy Council*, xxv, 107–9, 136, 138, 143, 158, 164, 178, 196; *Cal. State Papers, Dom., Addenda*, 1580–1625, 375, 377, 383.

a legal price for food, it did not subsidize production, it did not actually control food supplies, it did not itself purchase or import food, it did not ration the population. Its pressure was all indirect. Moreover the hiatus between the high assertions and the ineffective results of Tudor government is no less marked in this than in other fields. Its failure was due largely to the same general cause, the lack of trained and paid instruments for carrying out its aim. The gentry were too unskilled, too little under the control of the central government and too much interested in the continuance of the conditions being attacked to carry out effectively any policy of strict regulation. The privy council had in this case too narrow a view of the source of the difficulty with which it was contending, but quite apart from this, inertia was too strong to allow much effect to its limited power.

CHAPTER XXVI

TURBULENCE

THE effort of the privy council and of county and town authorities to secure food for the populace was not due entirely to a sense of their responsibility for the livelihood of the people or to sympathy with their sufferings. It sprang partly from fear of popular insurrection. Privation acting upon the restless masses disinherited in the country districts by recent enclosures and evictions, impoverished in the towns by the industrial changes of the period and, in the case of soldiers, discharged from the armies after campaigns on the continent without other support, was a constant incentive to disorder. They " stick not to say boldly, they must not starve, they will not starve." The privy council, lords lieutenant, justices of the peace and town officials were perpetually apprehensive of bread riots or worse. One of the reasons given by the lord lieutenant of Devonshire for asking that country gentlemen be compelled to remain on their estates was " to stay the fury of the inferior multitude, if they should happen to break out into sudden outcry for want of relief, as, without good circumspection, many suspect they may and will do." The clergy were ordered by the archbishop to warn the people " to beware how they give ear to any persuasions or practises of discontented and idle brains, to move them to repine or swerve from the humble duties of good subjects." The possibility of insurrection was never long out of the minds of the authorities.

The previous year there had been bread riots in London, and in Wiltshire grain dealers hauling wheat across the country were set upon at one time by sixty, at another time by a hundred rioters, who seized their stock. It was the same in the year that followed. In April, 1597 at three places in Norfolk, the people assembled riotously and attacked pack trains carrying grain to the harbors, and near Lynn they seized and unloaded a vessel laden with corn. Rumors spread that the " poor were up " in the west country and the people thereabouts " only waited for a drum." In the same region disorder was feared early in 1596 because of the poverty of the spinners and weavers. The chronicler of Bristol describes how during the worst part of the year every burgess of any means was ordered to give one meal per day to eight, six, four or two poor people, according to his ability, " whereby the poor of the city were all relieved and kept from starving or rising." The Council of the North writing from York in May draw a breath of relief when they can close their report with the words, " the country, God be thanked, is in reasonable good quietness; the Lord long continue it." [1]

Although these were only food riots and the authorities were perhaps unduly fearful, apprehension of general disorders was by no means unwarranted. A justice of the peace in Somerset named Hext draws a somewhat lurid picture this year of the lawlessness which had come to his notice. A group of thieves in his county acknowledged on their trial that they had lain in an alehouse for three weeks, stealing a sheep each night, cooking and eating it. In a certain remote haybarn from forty to sixty vagrants had gathered, stealing and cooking all kinds of food. When the inhabitants complained of them to the justices of the peace at Easter sessions the justices ordered the neighboring township officers to arrest the outlaws, but the constables declared they were afraid to adventure against them. On another occasion, when a sturdy man who had once been a traveler abroad but was now a vagrant in England was ordered at quarter sessions to be whipped, he threatened before the whole bench, with an oath, that it would be a

[1] *Acts of the Privy Council*, xxv, 43; *Cal. State Papers, Dom.* 1595-7, 401; *Cal. Hatfield House MSS.*, vi, 35, 204; *Hist. MSS. Comm. Rep.*, 15 Rep. vii, *Somerset Papers*, 20; Seyer, *Bristol*, ii, 256; Camden, *Hist. of Elizabeth*, 506; Strype, *Annals*, iv, 407, *Whitgift*, iii, 348-50.

dear whipping to some if the order was carried out, and the local justice who ordered his arrest, in fear of revenge, asked that the case be adjourned to the assizes, where the queen's judges would have the responsibility. The man was eventually discharged without punishment. According to Hext's estimate there were three or four hundred nondescript vagabonds in the shire, besides gypsies, tinkers, pedlars, wandering soldiers, thieves and receivers of stolen goods.

In the year 1596 in the county of Somerset according to an unofficial statement forty persons were executed, thirty-five branded on the thumb and thirty-seven whipped for felony. Besides these, one hundred and twelve who had been committed to prison were discharged, having been acquitted by the trial juries, or their indictments having been ignored by the grand jury. Yet it is claimed that not one criminal in five in the county was indicted. In March the country justice who makes this report to Lord Burghley, on arresting and examining a company of vagrants whose passports and licenses to beg proved to be counterfeit, discovered, or believed he had discovered, that they were members of a secret confederacy extending through many parts of the kingdom and reported the matter to the privy council. Orders were immediately given to the justices of assize, who were about to leave on their southwestern circuit, to bring these men to trial and if they thought best to send some of them up to Westminster to be tried in Star Chamber. Similar orders were sent to the deputy lieutenants of Norfolk and Suffolk, to which the confederacy was believed to extend.

In April a body of rioters in Kent stopped and plundered some carts loaded with grain, and the council gave orders that they should be tried and punished at the Easter sessions for fear others on the same plea of hunger might commit further and more serious outrages. In Somerset sixty vagrants seized a cart-load of cheese being taken to a fair and divided it among themselves, for which those captured were fined and imprisoned at the next quarter sessions. Later in the year a band of gypsies wandering through Northampton were arrested and some of their number sent up to London, examined and finally sent to the torture at Bridewell in the effort to discover their objects and ringleaders.[2]

The London authorities seem likewise to have been panicky. In July a ballad by Thomas Deloney, a popular ballad writer, appeared in which the queen was made to speak " dialogue-wise " with the people on their sufferings on account of the great scarcity of food. The Mayor, fearing the poem might " aggravate their grief and take occasion of some discontentment," suppressed the ballad, imprisoned the printer, and sought, though in vain, for the author. Later in the year another unauthorized ballad on the same subject appeared.[3]

It was not only among the lower classes that restlessness existed, nor was the dearth and high price of grain the only cause of dissatisfaction and threatened sedition. The hand of the government was laid this year with even more than its usual weight upon the gentry and middle classes, and some of its claims were old objects of resistance. Forced military service outside of the realm was of at least dubious legality, and was more than once during this year openly challenged. Doubt was even expressed whether men could be forced merely by the queen's orders to drill, or to pay the expenses of military equipment and training. Neither the queen nor her council nor her law officers would listen for a moment to such claims; nor did they pay any regard to 'them in their administrative action, although a chance jotting, partly in Burghley's hand, dated August, 1596, to the effect that 17,800 pressed soldiers had been sent to foreign parts and 3,293 to Ireland since 1589, indicates that the most thoughtful of Elizabeth's ministers at

[2] *Acts of the Privy Council,* xxv, 312, 314, 316, 333, 334; xxvi, 325; Strype, *Annals,* Ed. 1824, iv, 404-12.

[3] Lodge, *Times of Queen Elizabeth,* ii, 462, 464; *Lansdowne MSS.,* lxxxi, 28, 30, 32.

least had these matters in mind. In fact there had been a serious mutiny of the drafted men of Norfolk, Suffolk and Essex at Ipswich, the year before, on this very point, the men " utterly refusinge to goe beyond the seas," disembarking after they had been put aboard, threatening to march on London, and stirring up the discontented masses of that old rebellious district. It was only with considerable effort that they were persuaded to reëmbark and to do their duty.

Men of the lower classes were regularly drafted for service in the Netherlands, France, Ireland and the Channel Islands and under the shadow of threatened invasion from Spain compulsory musters and drills were frequent. The gentry were required by the queen's prerogative to pay assessments for this training and for arms and armor for the equipment of expeditions sent abroad. Townsmen and even countrymen were forced to pay ship-money. These sums were often considerable. The lord lieutenant and deputy lieutenants of Devonshire report that in nine months of the year 1596, payments required for the crown from that county amounted to £7,876, 6s., 9d. It is no wonder that even the rigorous government of Elizabeth did not prevent occasional murmurs or protests. The deputy lieutenants of Dorset report that they cannot collect the £700 required in aid of the port towns without grave discontent and the necessity of arresting a multitude of the people, and beg to have the sum remitted. Just at the opening of the year 1596 the earl of Bath, lord lieutenant of Devonshire, reports that some gentlemen and captains in his county have expressed doubt whether he has authority to train men or to impose any increase of arms and weapons by the queen's patent of lieutenancy, seeing that the traditional form of that document does not include the word training. The council, however, reassure the lord lieutenant as to his powers, and order him to enjoin any objectors to appear before them.[4]

[4] *State Papers, Dom.*, cclix, 16, 19, 27, 127, cclx, 42; *Cal. Hatfield House MSS.*, vi, 35, 36, 137; *Acts of the Privy Council*, xxv, 236; *Hist. MSS.*

A certain lawyer named Nicholas Ridgeley, of the Inner Temple, denied the queen's power to order her subjects to go abroad on military service, and stated that English kings of former times did not claim the right to send their subjects abroad to fight except by their own consent, but after having been committed by the council to the Fleet prison he lost heart and made a full and humble recantation, declaring that not only was the queen's prerogative not to be disputed, but that both by common and statute law the queen had power to compel her subjects to serve her beyond the seas wherever it should please her, and that no learned lawyer would or could maintain the contrary. A few weeks later a certain Robert Tailboys of Durham in a letter to the bishop of that diocese declared that the queen had no right to levy money of her own motion for her military service. He was ordered to come to London, kept in attendance for six weeks under a bond of £500 and only allowed to go back to the north when he had made a complete and abject apology. A Robert Tayllard of Huntingdon had a somewhat similar experience in this same year.

The pressure exercised by the council through its power to put men under bonds and cause them to waste their time and substance in daily attendance until they were dismissed was more influential than argument and more effective than indictment for a questionable offense. The constant stream of men "making appearance" before the council, sometimes for using "lewd and disobedient words" sometimes without charge, testifies to the amount of more or less openly expressed dissatisfaction, and to the government's quiet but effective means taken to suppress it. No occasion was lost however to insist on the arrest and indictment of violators of law, of those who threatened the peace or of those who refused their military duties. On the very last day of the year the magistrates of Nottingham, who had pleaded their chartered right not to be taxed for any

---

Comm. Rep., Somerset Papers, 27; Sir Thomas Smyth to Burghley, Letters of Eminent Literary Men, 93.

military service out of their corporate limits, were denied
exemption from their share of expenses of the troops going
to Ireland, on the ground that the charge was a public one
and it would be unreasonable for them to be freed from
a proportionate payment, notwithstanding the wording of
their charter.[5]

In the middle of the summer the council was suddenly
confronted with what seemed for the moment to be a threat
to put criticism into practice. This was the more important
because it was initiated by a man of sufficiently prominent
position to give the threat some weight. Sir John Smythe,
an Essex gentleman, author of two standard works on military science, in his earlier days a traveler and volunteer
soldier on the continent, now a disappointed and embittered
ex-official of the queen, gave a striking exemplification of
the proverb *in vino veritas*. During the musters at Colchester on the morning of June 12, after eating oysters
and partaking rather freely of white wine and sack, Smythe
rode out in front of the pikemen of Sir Thomas Lucas's
company who were being drilled on Windmill Field and
cried out " the common people have been oppressed and
used as bondmen too long, but if you will go with me, I
will see a reformation and you shall be used as freemen."
He also declared that two lawyers had told him that no man
was bound to go out of the realm on military service without parliamentary requirement, and spoke disparagingly of
Lord Burghley, boasting at the same time of the royal connections of Thomas Seymour, second son of the earl of
Hertford and brother of Lord Beauchamp, who was his
companion at the time. When none of the soldiers left their
ranks, with his companions he rode off the field. In the
afternoon hours a servant of his named Wendon used similar expressions in the open street of Colchester. These
occurrences were immediately reported to the privy council
and Smythe was arrested by a queen's messenger, brought

[5] *Acts of the Privy Council*, xxv, 302, etc., xxvi, 3, 138, 231, 318, 407;
Cal. State Papers, Dom., 1595–7, 238, 281.

to London and lodged in the Tower. The next day he was examined, avoided answering for a while, then when indisputable testimony was brought forward, acknowledged his speech. He excused his disrespect to the lord treasurer by his over-indulgence in wine, denied some details, but insisted that he was right in his statement of the law and therefore justified in advising the people not to allow themselves to be commanded to go out of the realm for military service. He declared that Sir Roger Manwood, lord chief baron of the exchequer, had remarked that it had not been usual in former ages to levy men by commission to send beyond seas, and that according to the old records the armies which Edward III and other kings took to France were all voluntary men.

Smythe was second cousin to Lord Beauchamp, who was one of the only possible competitors with the queen for the crown; he was known to be a sympathizer with the Catholics, though himself Protestant and always loyal, and to be widely connected in Essex. The council therefore took the matter up seriously, sent him back to the Tower, asked the law officers of the crown to examine him further, ordered his dwelling places to be searched for incriminating documents, his adherents to be discovered if possible and his advisers to be sought for and arrested. On the other hand, he was an old man, known to be querulous and faultfinding. He had been knighted by the queen's own hand, and had performed valuable diplomatic service in France and Spain; his writings were standard works, and nothing was found to indicate any intention of actual rebellion. Moreover, he had only said in intoxication what many men thought when they were sober. The gentlemen who had dined with him and ridden with him to the musters were arrested and examined but not shown to have had any share in his outbreak. He made a humble submission, remained in the Tower for two years, barely escaped Star Chamber, oscillated between servile and railing letters to Burghley. His servant, doctor and lawyer were soon admitted to attend him, and he was eventually allowed by the queen to return to his native village of Baddow in Essex under bonds not to go more than a mile away from it without special permission.[6]

There was little substance in the affair of Sir John Smythe, and most of the other threatened disorders seem to have been false alarms or exaggerated fears. But in November a rising was actually planned by some poor laborers and tradesmen in the western part of Oxfordshire. Rumors were current through all that countryside that a rising would soon take place on account of the high price of food and the extension of enclosures. Men said that rather than famish for want of corn they would take it from other men's houses. It was asked whether there were no good fellows about who would knock down the gentlemen and rich men who enclosed the commons and made corn dear. A certain Bartholomew Steere, a carpenter, moved, as he declared, by the misery of the poor people, in November began to urge a rising. He said to Roger Symonds, another carpenter, who had a wife and seven children and complained that by his hard work he could hardly feed them on bread and water, "care not for work, for we shall have a merrier world shortly; there be lusty fellows abroad and I will get more." He declared he would not always live like a slave, and that servants in England were so held in and kept like dogs that they would be ready to cut their masters' throats; that it would never be well until the gentry were knocked down, and that it would only be a month's work to overrun the realm. Steere said he knew a man who had a device for making balls of wildfire and with them and a sling he could set fire to houses at his will. Moreover, he knew a farmer who had 600 bushels of corn that he would give to them or sell cheap to feed their company until they could demand supplies from the govern-

---

[6] Strype, *Annals*, Ed. 1824, iv, 413–8; *Lansdowne MSS.*, lxiv, 43, 45, 52, 65; lxv, 62, 64; *Letters of Eminent Literary Men, Camden Society*, 48–65; 88–97; *Cal. State Papers. Dom.*, 1595–7, 421–4, 1598–1601, 2, 17, 208, 417; *State Papers. Dom.*, ‸ ‸6, 19, 21, 22, 26, 27, 33–5, 49, 51, 54–9.

ment, and an armorer who could direct them to all the
stores of arms in Oxfordshire.

Steere drew into his company two brothers named Brad-
shaw who were sons of a miller and as they traveled through
the country purchasing grain they persuaded others to join
them. One of the Bradshaws reported that wheat was selling at nine shillings a bushel, and that poor men could no
longer live, and that he knew a hundred good fellows who
would rather rise than starve. Roger Ibill, another miller,
Thomas, a carter of Lord Norris, Sir William Spencer's
baker, Edward Hoffer, a servant, and others became the
nucleus of a body of rebels believed by themselves to number 200 or 300 men. They arranged to meet on Enslow
Heath, the rendezvous of an earlier popular rising, on the
night of Monday after St. Hugh's Day, November 25.
Their plan was to attack the houses of six or eight of the
neighboring gentry, most of whom were known to be away
at the time, and seize their horses, armor and victuals.
There was some talk of cutting off gentlemen's heads and
tearing down the hedges that enclosed the old open fields
and cut off the old cross-country roadways. They would
go to Rycot, to the house of Lord Norris, lord lieutenant
of Oxfordshire, where they could get weapons for 100 men,
take two brass cannon which he had there, place them on
the wheels of his coach and so go their ways. If they
found themselves still weak, they would march to London
where they believed the 'prentices, whose restlessness could
always be depended on, and was now greater than usual
because of the barbarous punishments of the preceding
year, would join them.

The fate of the Londoners, however, was a bad omen. A
few young men had seized butter in Southwark market,
offering only threepence a pound when its owners asked
fivepence. They were punished by whipping, the pillory
and imprisonment. Angered by this some others rioted and
led by a trumpeter, one Sunday afternoon in June, threw
stones at the warden of the Tower on Tower Hill. The

queen issued a proclamation against rebellion, appointed a provost marshal, and on the twenty-second of July five youths were arraigned for this offense, convicted of high treason and two days later, hung, drawn and quartered.

Further than the wild talk, the march to Rycot, the vague references to the London hangings and the rendezvous on Enslow Hill the Oxfordshire men do not seem to have made plans, and it is no wonder that most of those who were approached paid no heed to the hopeless project. When one of those who heard the talk of the workmen told the whole story to his employer it was at first disregarded. Later this gentleman made some inquiries, became convinced that there was something in the stories, and while the leaders with a handful of men waited in vain in the cold and darkness for the gathering of their followers on Enslow Hill from nine to eleven on the appointed night, one of the neighboring justices of the peace, Sir William Spencer, was taking measures that soon led to the arrest and examination of some twenty of the ringleaders of the movement. The results of the inquiries were sent to Lord Norris, and by him reported to the privy council. The council took the matter up as usual with much energy, gave orders for four of the leaders to be sent up to London under charge of the sheriff, "their hands pynnioned and their leges bound under the horse bellys." Others were to be sent up later and in the meantime all concerned were to be arrested and strictly examined. The principal culprits soon arrived in London and were carried to different prisons, interrogatories were prepared, and on the 19th of December the council ordered that they should be taken to Bridewell to be examined under torture by the law officers of the crown. Within a few days the examinations in London and Oxfordshire were over and everything that could be learned about the wild scheme was fully "boulted oute." The lack of adequate records has left us without knowledge of what was ultimately done to these Oxfordshire plotters, but the promptness, persistency and harshness with which the council followed up this, like all other threats of disorder, indicates how insecure this powerful body felt internal peace to be.[7]

It is evident that under the surface of the carefully regulated Elizabethan administration, there was deep discontent and constant danger of revolt. Along with sincere loyalty to the queen and pride in their country, there was much reluctance to yield submission to constituted authority, much dissatisfaction with prevailing policy, and much practical disobedience. There was, besides, the whole miserable mass of distress, crime and vagabondage that crowded the gallows, prisons, streets and highways of the time. Unemployment was frequent, poverty was everywhere, enclosures were depriving the small farmer of his livelihood, the great poor law of the next year had not yet been enacted and the problem of feeding the people and keeping them orderly was, although intensified in these years of scarcity, a constant and largely an unsolved problem. Many contemporary observers believed that England had entirely too much population. A writer of this very year declares that " if some speedie order be not taken for the removal of the surplusage or at least the basest and poorest sort of them into some foreigne place of habitation the realm cannot possiblie long maintaine them."

Steps were taken to remove one intrusive element July 11, 1596. An order was given to an agent named Baines, declaring that the queen had heard that divers " blackamoores " had recently been brought by Sir Thomas Baskerville's ships into the realm, where there were too many already; God had blessed England with an abundant population, of whom many were even now without occupation and in misery. It was her majesty's pleasure therefore, that these " negros and blackamoores " should be sent away, and Baines was given authority to transport ten of them out

[7] Stow, *Annals,* Ed. 1605, 1279–81; *Cal. State Pap., Dom.,* 1595–7, 316–20, 322–5, 342–5; *Acts of the Privy Council,* xxvi, 364, 365, 373, 383, 398, 412, 455, 483, 548.

of the country, with authority to call on the officers of London and other towns for help in doing so. A week later a German merchant, Casper Van Zenden, was granted his request to take up eighty-nine negroes in England and carry them to Spain and Portugal there to be exchanged for the same number of English prisoners whose release he had secured in these countries and whom he had brought to England and freed. The queen hopes that the masters of these negro servants, considering that she wishes to have them sent out of England, will consent. This foreign merchant deserved credit for his kindness to English prisoners, and it is a Christian and charitable thing to be served by their own countrymen rather than by " those kind of people." [8]

No sovereign remedy was devised at that time or has been yet for human poverty and misery, but the introduction the next year of a more enlightened system of poor relief, the recurrence two years later of a series of better harvests, and the gradual adoption of a peace policy reduced the suffering of the mass of the people measurably from its high-water mark of the year 1596.

[8] *Acts of the Privy Council*, xxvi, 16, 20–1; Hakluyt, *Voyages*, vii, 286; viii, 111–2, 143; *Discourse on Western Planting*, 36–7; Sir Henry Knyvet, *Defense of the Realme; Cal. Hatfield House MSS.*, xi, 569.

CHAPTER XXVII

*ADVENTURES AT SEA; THE EXPEDI-
TION TO CADIZ*

ALTHOUGH three or four small garrisons were kept up regularly on the continent and in Ireland, and some thousands of English troops were engaged from time to time in warfare on land, England's natural sphere of fighting was on the sea. As a matter of fact, seven warlike fleets, large and small, performing one naval service or another, were on the sea within the twelve months of 1596.

The expedition of Drake and Hawkins to the West Indies had at the opening of the year, although this was not yet known in England, already failed of its object, its two commanders had been successively buried at sea, an indecisive naval battle had been fought off the Isle of Pines, and the scattered ships with their sick and starving crews were in March and April making their way slowly homeward. The main body of the fleet was still together under the command of Sir Thomas Baskerville, though the Elizabeth Bonaventure under Troughton, the Foresight under Winter, the Hope under Nicholas Baskerville and some other vessels had detached themselves and arrived in various ports. The privy council sent messengers to the port towns and a pinnace along the coast to warn the main fleet not to go into Plymouth, where the land and sea forces of Essex and Howard were already gathering, and where the shattered remains of one expedition could not but discourage the hopeful advance guard of another.

May 8 Baskerville himself reported his presence off the Scilly Islands and confirmed the already rumored death of the two commanders and the practical failure of the expedition. Within the next few weeks all the queen's ships were finally collected in the Downs and at Chatham and the dismal process of identifying and securing such plunder as it had obtained and of paying off the surviving soldiers and sailors ran its usual course. The scanty harvest of gold and silver bars and pearls from La Rancheria and elsewhere on the Spanish Main was mainly kept safely in locked chests of which the keys were in the possession of the officers of the fleet, but several sailors and servants in the early days of shore leave showed while in their cups jewels and gold the results of their private peculation. There were some efforts to discover and seize these and thus to reduce the deficit in the cost of the expedition. There was long delay in paying the returning captains and soldiers though there were a scanty four hundred left alive. An attempt was made to allocate to them a proportionate share of the plunder instead of wages, but they insisted they had been pressed into the service without any share in its adventurous side and clamored for the pay due them. A month after the return of the fleet the Chancellor of the Exchequer writes to Cecil: " If you saw the numbers, being 200 poor miserable creatures, hanging at my gate, who neither have meat nor clothes, it would pity your heart." The 600 sailors on the queen's ships had been paid up to July 8, 1595. The navy officers at Chatham now proposed that the remainder of their pay should be calculated as beginning August 1, thus saving the queen £300, though incidentally it cheated the sailors out of three weeks' pay. Over £3000 would be required to settle in full. This was still slow in coming down and on the last day of the year, December 31, 1596 some of the mariners are still using " hard speeches " to the navy treasurers who are not yet in a position to pay their wages. Baskerville himself was soon despatched to France as colonel general of the 2000 men whom the queen sent in the autumn of that year to support the king in Picardy. Early in the next year he died.[1]

---

[1] *Cal. Hatfield House MSS.*, vi, 152, 163, 172, 192, 201, 213, 215, 543; *Cal. State Papers, Dom.*, 1595-7, 209, 222, 291, 435; *Acts of the Privy Council*, xxv, 365, 367.

University of Winnipeg, 515 Portage Ave., Winnipeg, MB. R3B 2E9 Canada

As the shattered remnants of the Drake and Hawkins expedition crept into the southern harbors, a much smaller but a fresh little fleet started away on an adventure which ultimately followed the route over which they had come. This was a privateering expedition sailing under the leadership of Sir Anthony Sherley, equipped at his private expense and that of his father, Sir Thomas Sherley, who was for the moment receiving a large income from his position as Treasurer at wars. The Sherleys had collected and manned this fleet in the later months of 1595 and the early months of this year, but lacked an adequate commission. Sir Anthony had a certain claim on Essex from his recent marriage with a lady who was a distant cousin of the earl, as well as for his service with his father in Ireland and with himself in Normandy. He therefore sought and ultimately obtained from Essex and Howard a commission for exercising subordinate powers to those which they had recently received from the queen, empowering him to act as commander of all such ships as he and his father should set out at their own expense, and to levy and arm a number of men not to exceed 1500.[2]

Sherley had had no experience at sea and his adventure was looked upon with some dismay by his friends. It may have been in exchange for his commission or in doubt of his ability to handle his considerable fleet of ten ships and 900 men, that he left three of his ships and 500 men with Essex and Howard at Plymouth, to take part in their greater expedition, and sailed away on the 2nd of May with the remainder. Their first objective was St. Thomé on the coast of Guinea and they followed the coasts of Spain, Portugal and Morocco down to its latitude; but calms, pouring rains, midsummer heats, disease, attacks of negroes when they attempted to get water, and finally the troublesome shoals, put them out of heart, and they buccaneered

---

[2] Rowland Whyte to Sir Robt. Sydney, Collins, *Sydney Papers,* i, 359; Birch, *Memoirs,* i, 455–8; *Cal. Hatfield House MSS.,* vi, 162; *Cal. State Papers, Dom.,* 1595–7, 44.

for a while through the Cape Verde and Canary Islands, then sailed across the Atlantic to San Domingo. The usual story of sickness, " so vile that men grew loathsome unto themselves, frantic and desperately raving," was only ameliorated by an October stay in San Domingo. From October to May they sailed about through the West Indies along the Main, to Jamaica, coasting Cuba, Honduras and Guatemala, occasionally capturing a not over-rich Spanish prize or occupying for a while a poor Spanish town. But all this time they were losing men by death and ships by flight or by acquiescence of the commander, until there was only the admiral of the fleet left, with the commander and a handful of men not one of whom had been in the Indies before. Yet with the indomitable enterprise of the time, Sherley planned to sail north to the Newfoundland Banks to revictual and reman his ship, then sail for the Straits of Magellan, go to the other side of the world and continue his privateering in the East Indies. With his little crew he reached Newfoundland June 5, 1597, " not having one hour's victuals to spare." Notwithstanding refreshment among their fellow countrymen, however, after days of waiting for the possible return of any of their other vessels, they gave up the voyage and reached Plymouth fifteen months after they set out.[3]

While in the West Indies, Sherley had joined forces for a while with a still less formally organized expedition, that of Master William Parker of Plymouth, with two vessels sent out at his own adventure, haunting the waters lying between the South American coast and Cuba. They met while Sherley was in his temporary occupation of Jamaica, arranged a consortship, and while they were together an attempt was made on Truxillo on the shore of Honduras, Cavallo was captured and a plan was formed to cross the isthmus and harry the Pacific coast. They separated at the point of Yucatan and Parker had certain further adventures along the coast of Central America, including the capture

[3] Hakluyt, x, 266–76.

of Campeche by sending fifty-six of his men ashore in one of the long Indian canoes of that region and their escape from its reassembling population by tying their prisoners together and using them as a living barricade while they made good their retreat. But one of Parker's ships was captured by the Spaniards and her captain and crew hung; no booty was secured though he watched for weeks outside of Havana, so he soon followed the course of Sherley to the Banks and reached England scarcely later than he.[4]

There were few years during this period when the earl of Cumberland did not have a privateering fleet on the sea, and 1596 was no exception. The year before he had built at his own expense at Deptford the largest privately owned vessel of her time, the Malice Scourge, of 900 tons, later sold to the East India Company, and as the Red Dragon, sent out on their first voyage. On her Cumberland started out in person in February, 1596, accompanied by the Dreadnaught of the royal navy and some smaller ships, making up what according to the traditional calculation was his tenth voyage. But they encountered such a storm at sea that they returned, and Cumberland suffered from such another storm at court that he contented himself for the rest of the year with sending out one other ship, the Ascension, well armed and manned, under one of his own captains, to watch for shipping off Lisbon. The Ascension also suffered from storms and came still nearer destruction, as they lay on and off La Roca, from an attack by the Spanish admiral Zubiaur with six ships. The English fought themselves free and continued for some time on the Portuguese coast, till, their provisions exhausted, they made their way homeward without a capture to reimburse the earl for his expenditure on their equipment. Without tracing in detail the other voyages of this year it may be noted that it was in the year 1596 that Sir Walter Ralegh sent out that second expedition to Guiana which fixed in his mind the

[4] Hakluyt, x, 277–80; Thomas Lediard, *Naval History of England*, i, 318.

belief in the existence of a gold mine in that region which lured him long afterward on his last voyage, and led him ultimately to the scaffold. In this year also sailed the ill-fated expedition of Benjamin Wood to the East Indies, of which nothing but the vaguest rumors were afterward heard.[5]

However characteristic of the age and however con-tributory to the distress of the scattered possessions of Spain, these were all expeditions of but minor rank com-pared with the combined military and naval attack on Cadiz that formed the most famous warlike adventure of the year 1596, and perhaps of the age. An observer of the next reign remarks of Queen Elizabeth's military and naval policy, " Her warres were a long time more in the auxiliary part, in assistance of forraign Princes and States, than by invasion of any, till common policie advised it for a safer way to strike first abroad than at home to expect the war." [6] An early exception to this defensive policy had been the Portugal expedition of 1589. Its plan consisted of sending a fleet transporting a considerable army instructed to carry out three objectives, to destroy Spanish warships, to capture merchant prizes and to invade some part of the coast of Spain or Portugal. A repetition of this project though postponed had never been definitely given up. The results of the expedition of 1589, notwithstanding its meas-urable failure under the walls of Lisbon, its losses, its costs and its disappointments, had no more seriously discredited the policy of carrying the war into the enemy's country, than had the failure of the Armada of 1588 convinced the Spaniards that England could not be successfully invaded. It was rather a lack of decision and of funds than any definite abandonment of a line of policy that had prevented during the intervening years alike the sending of another English fleet and army to Spain and another Spanish

---

[5] Purchas, *His Pilgrimes*, xvi, 5–27; *Cal. Hatfield House MSS.*, vi, 14, 102, 145, 231; Hakluyt, *Voyages*, x, 452–95, xi, 1.

[6] Naunton, *Fragmenta Regalia*, Ed. 1901, 101–2.

armada to England. By the autumn of 1595, influenced
by the repeated reports of a Spanish invasion and by the
urgency of some of her most trusted advisers, Elizabeth had
given a reluctant and doubtful consent to the resumption
of that policy.

There was good reason for her doing so. The Spanish
raid on the coast of Cornwall in July, 1595, insignificant as
it had been, had brought the war home to the English people, and made actual a possibility always in the minds of
the queen, the great officers of state and the local authorities, that is to say, the invasion of England. Spaniards
were still established at Blavet in Brittany, from whence
last year's little fleet of galleys had made its incursion, and
there were frequent, if in most cases unfounded reports,
either directly from France or by way of Jersey or Guernsey, of the reinforcement of these troops and their strengthening for a more serious attack upon England or English
possessions. An invasion directly from Spain seemed likely
to occur at any time. Queen and people lived in an atmosphere of rumor. There were constant reports of spies
and news received through sailors, merchants and travelers
of the preparation and dispatch from Spain of a new and
greater armada than that of 1588. An unusually trustworthy correspondent reported in July, 1595, that the
bishops, lords and principal men of Spain had collected
9,000,000 crowns as a gift to Philip to help him invade
England. The long struggle of Spain to put down the Dutch
rebellion, in which England was so deeply involved, had
been lately stiffened by the arrival of a new army under
the archduke Albert overland from Italy. In France Henry
was threatening to make peace with Philip and before the
year was over, in order to avoid this contingency, English
troops had to be sent to face those of Spain. Letters from
Philip to the Irish rebels in alliance with him were intercepted, in which they were urged to continue their resistance
to the queen and promised early reinforcements. The English government had good reason to prosecute the war with

vigor or else to make peace, and no proposal for peace was now under consideration.[7]

This plan was to organize an expedition under the joint command and largely at the private expense of Lord Admiral Howard and the earl of Essex. Divided authority, the fruitful source of dispute and failure, as exemplified in the Portugal expedition of Drake and Norris and the West Indian expedition of Drake and Hawkins, was to be tried once more in the persons of two of the most highly placed men of their time. The project seems to have been the special proposal of Howard, though the restless and ambitious spirit of Essex grasped at an opportunity to substitute a more active and possibly more lucrative occupation for the life of court and council to which he had perforce devoted the four years since he had returned from Normandy.[8]

The main outlines of the plan were familiar enough, but just as the Portugal expedition had included a special additional project, that of placing Don Antonio on the Portuguese throne, so this expedition included, in the mind of Essex at least, the further plan of holding some spot which they should conquer in Spain, probably Cadiz, fortifying it, and using it for a base for further " annoyance of the Spaniard." This part of the plan, however, Essex kept carefully to himself, neither the queen, the council nor his partner, apparently, having had knowledge of such a design. Indeed the whole expedition was a state secret for some months after it had been decided upon. The earliest intimations of the project seem to have been made to foreign allies. On the 12th of November, 1595, the queen wrote from Richmond to the king of Denmark complaining that Philip was planning to send an immense fleet against England the next year, and asking him, in accordance with the old friendly relations between the two countries, to lend her eight of his largest vessels, and to forbid his subjects to furnish any

[7] Birch, *Memoirs*, i, 263; *Acts of the Privy Council*, xxv, 129–30, 149.
[8] Devereux, *Lives of the Devereux, Earls of Essex*, i, chaps. x–xi.

ships to Spain. This letter, sent through Thomas Ferrers, deputy governor of the English merchants at Stade, did not reach Christian for three months. He then replied declining to lend the ships, partly on the ground that he had no more than enough to protect Denmark, partly on the ground that it would be an infraction of his treaties with Spain.[9]

Early in the same month, November, 1595, Caron, the representative in England of the Estates of the Netherlands, was told by Lord Burghley that if his masters would grant some help in shipping and men to be used against the Spaniards, say thirty of their best ships, the queen would probably be less insistent than she had been lately on the repayment of their debt to her. The same communication was made through Bodley, the queen's representative there, directly to the Estates. The authorities of the Netherlands were more amenable to such a suggestion than the king of Denmark. Ready as always for war on the water, they intimated that they were willing to send practically as many ships as the queen might require. As to men they were not quite so ready, although even to the sending of these they made little objection. In the middle of January, the queen gave orders that Vere should be summoned to England for conference on the plans, and although the Estates made some protest against one of the principal military commanders in the field leaving the country at such a critical time, they restricted their opposition to begging that he be returned as soon as possible. Vere was found at Duisburg by the messenger, with Count Maurice; he came to The Hague on the first of February and by the tenth was on his way to England. There was little time lost. He was in England but two weeks. While there he attended at least one conference with the two commanders at the lord admiral's house, where the requirements for the expedition

[9] Bodley to Cecil, Nov. 26, 1595, Birch, *Memoirs of Elizabeth,* i, 331; Elizabeth to Christian IV, Nov. 12, 1595, *45 Rep. Dep. Keeper Pub. Records,* App. ii, 32; Christian IV to Elizabeth, Feb. 10, 1596, *46 Rep., App.* ii, 35; *Acts of the Privy Council,* xxv, 83-4; *Cal. Hatfield House MSS.,* vi, 69.

were discussed. By February 22 he was again at Margate awaiting a favorable wind, and before the end of February had returned to The Hague with letters from the queen. She demanded, in addition to a Dutch contingent, 2000 men from the English garrison in the Netherlands, part to be taken from the troops in the field, part from those in the cautionary towns. On the 4th of March Vere delivered his letters, reminding the Estates of their promise of ships and adding a further request that 2000 Dutch soldiers should accompany the expedition. On the 7th of March Vere writes to Essex that he has presented the plan and has no doubt of its acceptance, and on the 9th that the Estates have agreed to the queen's request. As a matter of fact they were in no position to refuse, though the withdrawal of the land forces was most unwelcome. Within a few weeks, with his usual vigor, Vere had gathered his troops, and brought them, on the 16th of April, at the same time with the Dutch fleet and its contingent of infantry to Boulogne, ready to be sent to Plymouth to the rendezvous.[10]

Long before this time preparation for the expedition had been taken up in earnest in England, though it was still put on the ground of protection against an anticipated invasion by a Spanish fleet and the consequent necessity for setting the queen's navy in readiness. As early as the middle of December orders were sent to the sheriffs and justices of the peace of most of the shires requiring them to supply specified amounts of provision for the navy at prices to be announced and paid by the regular provisioning officers. A week later orders were sent to a number of seaboard towns requiring them, as in 1588, to provide at their own expense a given number of vessels, with crews, victuals and munitions, equipped for a period of four months, to be ready by the end of March and to appear where the lord

[10] *Cal. Hatfield House MSS.*, vi, 25, 43, 52, 67, 70, 75, 86, 90; Birch, *Memoirs*, i, 387-9, 468; *Acts of the Privy Council*, xxv, 199, 273, 289; Vere, *Commentaries*, 106; *Sydney Papers*, i, 367; Corbett, *Successors of Drake*, 43.

admiral should require them. These ships were, according to the proclamation, to attend upon her majesty's fleet, and were in fact intended primarily to serve as transports of men and supplies, but also on occasion to do some fighting for themselves and possibly to gain some plunder. The city of London was so prompt in sending its quota of twelve ships and two pinnances that the queen ordered a special letter of thanks and appreciation to be written the lord mayor and aldermen. Many towns, however, yielded reluctantly, even when they were assured that the expenses should be shared by neighboring coast and even by inland towns and the surrounding rural districts. Heavy pressure was necessary to secure obedience, and protests long continued to trouble the council. On the 18th of January orders for supplies and shipping were more clearly defined, Quarles and Darrell, official victualers, were given their commissions, and thenceforward through January, February, and March, amid much protest, petition, delay and readjustment of burdens, all the heavier because of the prevailing scarcity, the various counties and towns provided their quotas to the expedition, which it was now generally known was to be one of invasion of Spain. In February the gunfounders of Sussex were busy making new ordnance and shot for the fleet.[11]

The queen as usual hesitated to commit herself definitely to the enterprise. On the morning of the 17th of March, it is true, letters authorizing the preparation of the commissions of Essex and Howard were signed by the queen, and she told Essex she had signed them, while Cecil sent similar word to Lord Admiral Howard. But later in the day she half repented of her decision. In the midst of sermon time she called Conway, one of the gentlemen ushers, to her and sent a message to Windebank, clerk of the signet, bidding him to stay the document she had just signed.

[11] *Acts of the Privy Council*, xxv, 107–9, 122–5, 152, 157, 161, 167, 177, 178, 198, 212, 223, 227, etc.; *Cal. Hatfield House MSS.*, vi, 6; Birch, *Memoirs*, i, 387.

After dinner she told Windebank to write to Secretary Cecil ordering him to come to court that night, and in the meantime had the proposed commission read over and ordered some of the wording changed. However, the next day, March 18th, it was sealed with the great seal and somewhat later their instructions were drawn up and sent to the two commanders. They were authorized to levy 5000 troops and engage the same number of mariners to man the ships. Vere and Clifford representing the land forces, Sir Thomas Howard and Ralegh representing the navy, and Sir Thomas Carew, Lieutenant of the Ordnance, were appointed a council of war, and carefully drawn provisions required the two commanders to accept the advice of a majority of these councillors. The plans for the expedition, as they remain to us in a draft of the instructions in Burghley's handwriting, were more definite than usual, requiring the commanders, first, to destroy warships and stores in Spanish harbors, second, to capture and destroy towns on the coast, third, to secure booty from captured towns and to watch for prizes, as they should find practicable.

There were also a series of enlightened and humane prohibitions of unnecessary slaughter of their enemies or the killing under any circumstances of women and children and aged men unable to bear arms. Due, perhaps from the military point of view an undue, regard was imposed upon the commanders for the safety of their ships and men.

The financial plan seems to have been that the queen should provide ships fully equipped for war and transport purposes, supply food and pay the expenses of the actual voyage, including the wages of the sailors, but the preliminary costs of the levy of soldiers and sailors, advance wages to them, and the expenses of loading the ships and assembling them at the rendezvous should be paid by Essex and Howard. Who should in the last resort pay the wages of the land troops seems to have been left unsettled. Probably the wages of the soldiers, and in fact the whole expense, it was anticipated with the optimism of the time, would be repaid from the profits of the expedition. The initial expense for the navy and shipping, food and equipment for the voyage, to be paid from the royal treasury, was estimated at £78,000, a sum considerably larger than the whole cost of the Portugal expedition, exclusive of the expenses of the coast towns in providing their contingents of ships. The actual sum spent by the queen was much less, probably not more than £48,000, or even £38,000; the existing accounts of the government are too confused to be clear which. It is not probable that Howard and Essex kept careful enough accounts to know exactly what they spent, but there is no difficulty in accepting the statement of Essex that he was engaged more deeply than his estate was worth.[12]

During the remainder of March and much of April, Howard, Essex and their subordinate commanders were busy with the multiplicity of duties which were required by the Elizabethan policy of organizing each campaign of the war against Spain as if it were an entirely new and detached adventure. Commissions were issued to trusted officers to recruit the men required, and the privy council supported their efforts by letters sent to the county authorities. Essex wrote personal letters to the lords lieutenant, deputy lieutenants and sheriffs of all the counties and to his many personal friends and followers in various parts of the country, urging their assistance in filling up the levies.[13] The privy council seems to have planned to reach two ends at the same time in obtaining recruits by utilizing condemned criminals against whose wholesale execution men's feelings revolted. They ordered the sheriffs of all the counties to send in com-

---

[12] Wright, *Queen Elizabeth and her Times*, ii, 457; *Cal. Hatfield House MSS.*, vi, 101–2, 162–3, 172, 180; *Cottonian MSS.*, Otho E. ix; Lediard, i, 320–2; Camden, *History of Elizabeth*, Ed. 1675, 515; *State Papers, Dom., Elizabeth*, cclvi, 107, cclxv, 68; *Cal. State Papers, Dom.*, 1595–7, 160, 188–90, 192, 554; *Acts of the Privy Council*, xxv, 307; Birch, *Memoirs*, i, 452.

[13] *Acts of the Privy Council*, xxv, 307, 323; *Cal. Hatfield House MSS.*, vi, 14, 117, 121, 125–7.

plete lists of prisoners then in the jails, with a statement of their age and condition of body, the offenses with which they were charged or of which they had been convicted, and the prospects for their execution or pardon. Later the council sought, in the case of London at least, advice as to which of the condemned prisoners might as a matter of mercy be " bestowed in her majesty's service of the warres with hope of theire good demeanour hereafter," and such a list was evidently sent in. Convicted criminals had been used to fill up the crews of vessels going on exploring and maurauding expeditions; it had been repeatedly proposed to use them as colonizing material; and there was ancient precedent for sending them to the wars. There is but little indication of the actual use of criminals at this time, although orders to proceed with the execution of those in London not pardoned intimates that the others were sent to the wars. Some fifty masterless men in London were by permission of the privy council taken up forcibly by Sir Ferdinando Gorges to garrison the new fort at Plymouth. But there seems to have been no very serious difficulty in obtaining voluntary soldiers for this expedition; and more than a thousand gentlemen joined on their own account.[14]

The greatest difficulty was met, as usual, in obtaining supplies and in engaging mariners. The lord admiral writes to Cecil that he cannot take time to come to court because along with Ralegh and Lord Thomas Howard he is busy every day from early till late up and down the river. He has more than two hundred men engaged at his own expense in victualing ships, but even then he doubts whether they will be ready at the appointed time. Mariners had to be pressed into the service, and even under the authority of government could be secured only with difficulty. The sailors of the seaport towns hearing that the press was about to be issued slipped away and took refuge in the parts of

---

[14] *Acts of the Privy Council*, xxv, 121, 171, 182, 233, 250; Hakluyt, *Voyages*, vii, 286, viii, 111–12, 143; Hakluyt, *Discourse on Western Planting*, 36–7.

their shires most distant from the sea, hoping to remain unobserved till the fleet had departed and then to engage in merchant voyages. The privy council hearing of this sent proclamations to the officers of seaport towns, threatening the sailors with death by court martial if they fled and ordering them to return to their native ports and await the usual press officers.

There seems to be almost no distinction in the usage of this period between the words " press " and " prest." This confusion was due no doubt to similarity in sound. Etymologically there was no relation between the two words. The former intimated compulsory service, the latter or its other form " imprest " meant payment in advance. An order of the council in this year requires the justices of the peace " to take up and imprest suche soldiers or other voluntary men as shall be willinge of themselves to serve," they are to be punished " when they have taken prest money if they run away." But since men were frequently forced to serve, and also were regularly given money beforehand for necessary expenses, or to bind the bargain, the two words came to be used almost interchangeably. " Press money " and " prest money " was put in the hands of the recruiting officers. Soldiers were habitually " pressed " or " prest " or " prested," the words being used indiscriminately, and giving small clue to the voluntary or involuntary nature of their service. For this expedition the soldiers served voluntarily, sailors served under compulsion. According to the order for a press for the latter in April 1596 warrants were sent to the vice-admirals and other officers, dividing the southeastern, southern and southwestern coasts of England into ten districts, in each of which two " presters " were appointed. It became then the duty of the local officials of each district, on being notified, to cause all mariners and seafaring men between eighteen and fifty years of age to appear at a suitable time and place. The presters then chose such as were required, and sent them to the ships. Ralegh complains that he has been " dragging in the mud from one alehouse to another " hunting runaway mariners. " As fast as we press men one day they run away another, and say they will not serve." There was even a rumor that 700 English sailors had deserted from Plymouth with a ship stored with ordnance and taken it to the king of Spain.[15]

The first two weeks of the month of April were occupied in playing out the interlude of the Spanish siege of Calais, the futile English preparations for its rescue and its fall, all of which will be described in another connection.

Bitter as was the disappointment of Essex at his failure to relieve Calais, at least one of his advisers had from the beginning considered it an undesirable diversion from his main task, the invasion of Spain. Sir Francis Vere, trained soldier as he was, looked upon the relief of Calais as hopeless from the time the harbor mouth was blocked, and wrote from the Netherlands urging that the other expedition should be so much the " more royally set forward," that Essex should give his undivided attention to it, since if it succeeded it would " make him famous forever," and that the queen should merely strengthen the French king in the field with 4000 or 5000 men added to his general army. Henry himself evidently anticipated a long campaign for he had already asked that when troops were sent over they should be provided with instruments for digging and for laying a regular siege, judging with a foresight that was justified again in the same region more than three hundred years later, that " spades will be of as much use as swords there." Vere as he wrote was just about to leave Middleburg to join Essex and Howard at Dover. All the principal leaders of the expedition were in that seaport by the 17th of April. Immediately afterward Howard, after appointing Burghley his deputy to exercise the office of lord admiral in his absence, and leaving Ralegh and Sir Thomas Howard to gather the rest of the supplies and bring up the rear guard, set sail with the fleet for Plymouth, which was to be,

[15] *Cal. Hatfield House MSS.*, vi, 86; Birch, *Memoirs*, i, 440, 448; *Acts of the Privy Council*, xxv, 253, 275, xxvi, 140.

as usual, the general rendezvous. Essex accompanied the fleet as far as Rye, then went with Vere to court for last instructions and farewells.

These were not pleasant. Essex speaks afterward of missing the words of encouragement that he would so gladly have had and writes to the queen " Your unkind dealing the very day of my departure doth stick very deeply in my heart and soul." The queen, it is not unlikely, resenting his readiness to leave her, expressed doubts of the success of the expedition, and spoke with sarcasm of his knight errantry. There were others who thought Essex might after the diversion of Calais be induced to give up the larger project or that the queen might forbid it. But his determined spirit and impetuous activity would not hesitate or delay or yield to any commands except those of absolute prohibition, and these the queen did not give. In fact she sent after him an affectionate letter written with her own hand, and expressing the hope that all evil might fall elsewhere than on the earl and her " good Charles." [16]

Essex left the court at Greenwich on April 25; at four o'clock in the morning of the 27th he was riding out of Andover in Hampshire and made the next hundred miles to Honiton by eight o'clock that night. The next day he rode the remaining fifty miles to Plymouth, and reported from thence to Cecil and his secretary that he was " weary in body and mind," but impatiently looking forward to the arrival of the main fleet. He urged haste in sending forward the remaining supplies and the rearguard of ships that still lay in the Thames.[17]

The weeks of delay while awaiting belated equipment, the queen's decision or a fair wind, from which scarcely an expedition of this period escaped, covered in this case almost exactly the month of May. The month was spent by the

[16] *Cal. Hatfield House MSS.*, vi, 171; *Cottonian MSS.*, Otho. B, ix; Lediard, i, 322.

[17] *Cal. Hatfield House MSS.*, vi, 140, xiii, Add. 566; *Cal. State Papers, Dom.*, 1595–7, 205–10; Devereux, *Lives of the Devereux, Earls of Essex*, i, 338, 339; Birch, *Memoirs*, i, 467–8, 474.

commanders in such labors, preparations and correspondence as were required, and in such patience as they could summon up. The main fleet arrived almost immediately, the other ships and men were gradually all collected, Ralegh arriving with the last on the 21st of May. The ships were organized into squadrons, the men formed into regiments and drilled. The fleet consisted of forty-eight fighting ships, accompanied by about a hundred vessels used as transports or victualers, making in all, according both to English and the Spanish observers, who later had only too good opportunities of counting its numbers, about one hundred and fifty sail. Of the fighting ships, eighteen were from the queen's navy, twelve were the ships provided by the city of London and armed as warships, the remaining eighteen the war fleet sent by the Estates of the Netherlands.

Of the transports and victualers, some seventy were directly in the service of the queen or the Estates, and regularly attached to the squadrons of war vessels; the others were provided irregularly by the coast towns or private persons at their own expense. A considerable number of the last class attached themselves to the fleet, hoping to be hired to bring home the plunder gained by the adventurers, or themselves to share in it. The whole fleet was divided into four squadrons, respectively under the lord admiral, Essex, Lord Thomas Howard and Sir Walter Ralegh. The lord admiral carried his crimson flag on the Ark Royal, the same flagship he had used in the Armada fight in 1588. Essex on the Due Repulse carried the " orange-tawney " colors he regularly used as livery for his followers. Lord Thomas Howard and Ralegh, both with new ships, the Mere Honour and the Warspite, carried blue and white respectively. Van Duvenvoord, the Dutch admiral, had also a new ship, the Neptune, of 400 tons. One who saw the fleet in Plymouth harbor speaks of it as " our navy beautiful to behold."

The army, which consisted of something over 6000 men levied directly by the commanders or withdrawn from the

Netherlands, besides those which were in the Dutch squadron and perhaps a thousand " gentlemen voluntaries," accompanying the expedition on their own account, numbered nearly 10,000 men. It was divided into eight regiments. Each of the generals commanded one, the others were under Vere and Clifford, the two military members of the council, Gerard, Blount and the two Wingfields. The army was unusually well equipped and, composed of volunteers instead of pressed men, was of better material than the average English forces of the time. It consisted of " as tall, handsome men as ever I set eyes on," according to one observer. According to another the adventurers accompanying the army were " covered with feathers, gold and silver lace." [18]

Sharp discipline was kept at Plymouth. Two soldiers were hanged on the Hoe with papers pinned on them declaring, in one case that the victim had drawn his sword and made a mutiny against his commander, in the other that he had deserted his colors. A Dutch soldier who had killed one of his companions was tied to the body of the man he had murdered and they were thrown together into the sea. A Sussex gentleman named Gildridge was suspected of spying on the forces, and on the complaint of Essex and Howard summoned to London by the privy council and examined, but released. A lieutenant who had taken bribes was dishonorably discharged from the army by proclamation; and Arthur Throckmorton, who quarreled violently with Vere in the presence of the two generals, although he was a relative of Sir Walter Ralegh was nevertheless ordered from the table, dismissed from the army and forbidden to go on the voyage, though he seems later to have made his peace and ultimately secured his knighthood on the expedition.[19]

[18] Birch, *Memoirs*, i, 480, 484, 487, ii, 7, 10, 14–17; Slyngsbie, *Voyage to Cadiz*, Ed. J. S. Corbett, *Navy Records Soc., Naval Misc.*, i, 41–50; *Monson's Tracts*, Ed. Oppenheim, *Navy Records Soc.*, i, 344, 358–61; Stow, *Annals*, Ed. 1605, 1282–93; *Cal. Hatfield House MSS.*, vi, 201, 202, 305–6.

[19] Anthony Standen to Bacon, May 23, Birch, *Memoirs*, ii, 10–11, 50; Stow, *Annals*, Ed. 1600, 1284; *Acts of the Privy Council*, xxv, 449.

Three formal documents drawn up, or at least promulgated, at Plymouth by the two commanders during this month awakened much interest in their own time and have had some permanent influence on the development of international law and military organization. One was a " Declaration of the causes moving the queen's majesty to prepare and send a navy to the seas for defense of her realms against the king of Spain's forces." It was stated contemporaneously that this document, like many others of the time, was drawn up by the old lord treasurer, and it may well have been so. There is still in existence a draft in his handwriting. It declares that the queen is sending this fleet out only in defense of her realms against the mighty forces reported to be in preparation by the king of Spain for an invasion of her dominions, such as had been attempted treacherously during discussion of peace in 1588. Since the queen is in perfect amity with all kings and princes of Christendom except the king of Spain, her commanders declare that they have orders to avoid injury to any except the subjects of that monarch or such strangers as give that king manifest aid in men, ships, munitions or victuals. To show their good faith and to conform to this prohibition of contraband trade all such persons are urged to withdraw from the ports of Spain and Portugal and return to their own harbors, or else to seek protection with the English fleet. Any who refuse to do so and persist in aiding the king of Spain with contraband goods the commanders of the English fleet will treat, " as by the law of arms we may," as manifest enemies, and their princes or lords will have no just cause to solicit from the queen amends for their losses or injuries.

The commanders announce that they have signed and sealed this proclamation to be seen by any who wish, that they have caused the same to be printed in French, Italian, Dutch and Spanish, and have caused it to be distributed as widely in the ports of Spain and Portugal as possible. An Italian translation was made by an English agent at Venice, and on the 5th of June he was busy securing a private printer by whom it might be printed and disseminated among the princes of Italy. There is testimony to the fact of its distribution, translated into the other languages mentioned. This proclamation came as near to being a declaration of war on Spain as did any public document or announcement during that anomalous conflict between two great nations that continued for eighteen years without declaration or acknowledgment of war by either of the parties concerned. It contained also the traditional English doctrine of contraband in its most uncompromising form, the persistent effort of a naval power to prevent supplies from being carried to her enemies in war time.[20]

The second proclamation was a series of articles defining the duties and rights of each officer of the army and of the field. It was drawn up by Essex, with the advice of Vere, who had had long experience in various fields of warfare, and was intended to prevent controversy among a group of nobles and gentlemen naturally jealous of their claims to precedence and independence and not too well trained in military subordination. As a matter of fact the articles seem to have been effective for their purpose and as far as external conformity extended there was no breach of them during this journey. They were frequently referred to in subsequent instructions to officers.[21]

The third document was a body of rules for general discipline in the fleet, which seem to have been based on a body of " notes for sea service " drawn up by John Young, an old captain who had seen much sea service and was now seeking occupation in the expedition. These rules extend from the nature of the signals to be used at night and the care that must be taken about fire and the cleanliness of the ships to the requirement that common prayer should be

[20] Slyngsbie, *Naval Misc.*, i, 38–41; Birch, *Memoirs*, ii, 17, 26, 85; Stow, *Annals*, Ed. 1605, 1282–3; Speed, *Chronicle*, Ed. 1632, 1194–5; Strype, *Annals*, iv, 362–4.

[21] Birch, *Memoirs*, ii, 20–1; Vere, *Commentaries*, 107–8.

read twice a day, and " that no man, soldier or mariner, do dispute of matters of religion, unless it be to be relieved of some doubts." In the latter case he should inquire of some of the clergymen on the voyage, " for it is not fit that unlearned men should argue of such mystical matters." This was no meaningless requirement, since Essex took with him four chaplains, the lord admiral three, and Ralegh, Howard, and the earl of Sussex, a volunteer, each one.

Still another piece of writing may be included in this list. It is a prayer accompanying that to be regularly used on the fleet, said to have been written by the queen. If actually the work of Elizabeth, it has a logical organization and an easy eloquence much beyond her other compositions, which are frequently confused to the verge of incomprehensibility. It pleads, " Thou that by Thy foresight dost truly discern how no malice or revenge, nor quittance of injuries, nor desire of bloodshed, nor greedieness of lucre hath moved the resolution of our new-set-out army; but a needful care and wary watch that no neglect of foes or oversurety of promise might breed either danger to us or glory to them . . . we humbly–beseech Thee with bended knees prosper the work, and with the best forewinds guide the journey, speed the victory, and make the return the advancement of Thy glory, the triumph of their fame and surety of the realm, with the least loss of English blood." Cecil thought the prayer not entirely of human origin. It was " divinely conceived by her majesty . . . conceived in the depths of her sacred heart . . . an invocation unto the Lord purposely indicted by His spirit in His annointed queen." At any rate it made its way into Italy, was translated into Italian by an Englishman in Venice, read aloud in the Piazza and several copies dispersed there. The translator considered himself in danger of trial by the Inquisition for impiety and falsehood, as it was generally believed in Venice that people in England did not pray and knew nothing of Christ or indeed of any religion. In the meantime there were at

London less inspired prayers "ecclesiastical, noble and popular for his lordship's success."[22]

In addition to watching for a favorable wind and aside from activities connected with the completion of equipment, the organization of the army, and the drawing up of these formal documents, two difficulties only too familiar complicated this month of waiting, dissension between the commanders, and the queen's inveterate tendency to change or even abrogate her plans. The division between Howard and Essex extended back to their stay at Dover, if not before. Relations could hardly help but be somewhat strained. Howard was sixty years of age, holding the great office of lord admiral; Essex was less than thirty, holding no office, except the minor honor of captain of the horse, yet owing to the personal attachment of the queen, possessing a consideration in the privy council and in state and military affairs far beyond that of the admiral. When Elizabeth had momentarily determined to send troops to the relief of Calais, instead of simply diverting a part of the expedition then under organization to France under the same joint command, she had given a separate commission to Essex, leaving Howard only the labor of providing shipping. The fact that his predecessors as lord admiral had more than once gone to France in command of armies gave point to the slight, and there still remains a "passionate letter," as Cecil calls it, written by Howard from Dover, April 13, 1596, in which with his usual vigor he wishes he had been drowned before receiving such a letter as that just sent him, complains of being used simply as a drudge, and threatens not to go on the expedition to Spain and to give up martial affairs for ever. Placated for the time, apparently by the youthful good feeling and good sense of Essex and by the abandonment of the Calais diversion, some bitterness seems to have remained.

[22] Slyngsbie, *Naval Misc.*, i, 51–8; Birch, *Memoirs*, ii, 18–19, 23, 85–6; *Cal. Hatfield House MSS.*, vi, 194, 201, 211; Stow, Ed. 1605, 1284; *State Papers Dom., Elizabeth*, cclix, 45.

All through the stay at Plymouth there are indications of this obscure jealousy. The insistent reports to London of the continued outward amity of the two generals suggest the expectation on the part of the writers that this unity might at any time cease to exist. The lord admiral's physician, Dr. Marbecke, a good observer, reports that the "strife and contention" between the two generals had already showed itself while they were ashore, but became much more manifest after they were on shipboard. The difficulty was partly no doubt the usual friction between army and navy, partly due to the embarrassment of double control, but there were also some personal jealousies. Even as late as May 24, Essex has to explain the absence of his signature on a joint letter to the queen by the fact that his name had originally been written higher than Howard's and had therefore been cut out by "her unruly admiral." [23]

The danger that the queen would hold back the expedition also extended back to its rendezvous at Dover, or even earlier. On March 20, only two days after the commissions had been signed, Burghley in a secret memorandum directed "To her majesty's only most fayre Hand from a simple weak Head" expressed not only his doubts of the wisdom of the voyage, but apparently his suspicions of the commanders. He suggests that they be made to declare to the queen just what parts of Spain and Portugal they expect to go to, and how far to the south or west they have any intention of going themselves or sending any of their ships or men. There can be little doubt that Burghley deprecated the journey. Before it had sailed for Plymouth had come renewed appeals from the French king for aid, and Essex either met or just escaped meeting the messengers bringing that appeal. Such aid could without doubt most easily be given by diverting this English army from Spain to France. It was obviously more to the advantage of Henry that the English troops should remain in the Nether-

---

[23] *Cal. Hatfield House MSS.*, vi, 144, 146, 194, 195–6; Birch, *Memoirs,* i, 491; *Stowe MSS.*, clix, p. 353.

lands and that others be sent to France than that they should be sent in a maritime campaign to a distant part of the coast of Spain, and he begged the queen in his letters so to use them. Notwithstanding the declaration of the French ambassador that he personally took no active steps to dissuade the queen from her Spanish plans, there is no doubt that there was a steady pressure upon Elizabeth and her advisers from the French side against the plans of Essex and Howard. It was the gossip of the English court that the expedition to Spain would be given up. Even at Madrid it was believed that the capture of Calais, the dispersal of the fleet of Drake and Hawkins and the death of those two great seamen, the news of which came close upon that of the loss of Calais, would cause the queen to give up her plans for an invasion of Spain. The advice of the French king fell in with the queen's general disinclination to let her favorite courtiers, especially Essex, go out of her sight, her dread of a bold policy, and her recurrent fear that England might be attacked during the absence of the fleet and admiral. Essex himself declared privately in vexation that " the queen wrangles with our action for no cause but because she has it in hand; if this force were going to France, she would then fear as much the issue there as she doth in our intended journey. I know I shall never do her service but against her will." " Yet," he continued almost in the spirit of a later and even more Puritan commander, " if I be not tied by the hand, I know God hath a great work to do by me." [24]

There was no doubt that the queen's interest in the expedition was cooling. Essex writes to Cecil on May 7 complaining that although he and Howard have asked the queen for no money with which to levy troops or to take them to the place of their rendezvous, have sought no authority to press men into the service, and are now keeping them on land at Plymouth at their own cost, without spending the

[24] Birch, *Memoirs*, i, 467, ii, 4–6; Oppenheim, *Monson's Tracts, Navy Rec. Soc.*, i, 377; *State Papers, Dom., Elizabeth*, cclvi, 99.

sea victuals; although they are advancing vast sums, maintaining poor captains and relieving many of the queen's poor adventurers who have just come back from the West Indies, and although Essex has " a little world eating upon him " in his own house, he receives no word from the queen other than he would if he had lost her troops instead of preserving them. He gets confidential word at the same time that the queen has spoken of him to the French ambassador as rash and wilful, and has threatened to bridle and stay him.

This condition of affairs came to a climax about the 18th of May when private letters reached Plymouth indicating that the queen had practically decided either to give up the whole expedition or at least to revoke Essex and Howard from its command, placing it under other generals and changing its character. Instead of expostulating to the queen directly, Essex showed his good judgment by writing to the privy council a letter which would surely reach the queen's eyes, in which he used just those arguments which would appeal to her most effectively, the waste of the money already used in the preparations, the loss of credit with the coast towns which have been pressed so hard to furnish ships and men and will now see that " our alarms are but false and our journies but dreams," the trouble in settling accounts with the Low Countries, the danger that the king of Spain will send help to Ireland, and that the insolent rebels there will perceive that the English preparations are only smoke, and so extend their revolt. A still more definite protest came from the commanders next in rank below Essex and Howard. In a round robin addressed to Howard, they stated their unwillingness to serve under any one but the earl and himself and their belief that calamity will follow any attempt at this late day to change the leadership and the character of the expedition.[25]

[25] Essex to Cecil, May 7, 12, *Cal. Hatfield House MSS.*, vi, 164, 172, 174-5; Lord Thomas Howard, Sir George Carew, and others, to Cecil, May 18, *Ib.* 188-90; Birch, *Memoirs*, ii, 5, 8-9.

The queen was angry and wrote a sharp letter to the two generals criticizing the arguments of Essex; but she did not insist on her intention. Either convinced by the reasons given or dreading the dissatisfaction that would have followed, she yielded to the storm of protest, and sent Sir Fulke Greville down to Plymouth with a second letter to the two commanders close after the first giving them the necessary license to depart. This letter arrived on the 23d of May; both the generals immediately went aboard, and the embarkation of the troops began the next day. Essex spent some of his last hours on shore writing a long letter to the privy council, but he provided against its bringing about any change in his plans by sending it back to London by Sir Fulke Greville, under cover to his secretary, with orders not to deliver it till the wind had served to carry them toward Spain for at least a week, and then only when there was a full meeting of the council. As a matter of fact, it was put in the hands of the privy councillors at Greenwich on the 7th of June, just a week after his departure.

In this argumentative and at the same time eloquent letter Essex quoted classical and all other expert authority for the wisdom of attacking an enemy in his own country rather than awaiting him in one's own, defended the former expedition against Portugal on the grounds that it tended, like the present voyage, to " cut the sinews " of the king of Spain by intercepting his treasure from the Indies, pointed out that the relative geographical positions of England and Spain indicated that Elizabeth should " become mistress of the sea, which is the greatness that the queen of an island should most aspire to," pleaded with the council to use their influence with the queen to allow her soldiers to retain the part of Spain which they should capture so as to injure the king by making " a continuous diversion, and to have lefte as it were a thorne stickinge in his foote," and finally apologized if in the eagerness of his protests to the queen against giving up the expedition he had " forgot those reverend forms which I should have used." [26]

By the first of June everything was on shipboard and the wind came around to the north sufficiently to allow them to work their vessels out; the master gunner shot off a piece as a signal and the whole fleet sailed bravely out of Plymouth harbor, the lord admiral leading. A temporary change of weather kept them a while in Cawsand Bay, but June 3 they got away with a northeast wind, crossed the Channel and keeping well off the coast of Spain did not see land again till they rounded Cape St. Vincent. The objective point of the journey, undecided or kept secret by the generals until after their departure from Plymouth, and their immediate proceedings after their arrival, were discussed and decided upon at a series of meetings of the council of the expedition held during the journey, the last the very day before reaching Cadiz. In contrast with the carelessness of the scout vessels in the fleet of Drake and Hawkins the year before, a careful watch was kept so that no knowledge of the whereabouts of the fleet should reach the Spanish authorities; and although its equipment and departure from Plymouth was known to them, Philip was ill, the government was in much confusion, a poor watch was kept off the coast, and it was commonly believed both in Spain and on the fleet that its destination was Lisbon. When it appeared therefore far to the southward, the news reached Medina Sidonia, the old commander of the Invincible Armada, now Governor of Andalusia and in command of the adjacent seas, only twelve or fifteen hours ahead of the fleet. Early in the morning of Sunday, June 20, they dropped anchor off the mouth of the harbor of Cadiz. Illustrations of the time, conventionalized as they are, corroborate the narratives in showing that fleets at sea then habitually kept well together. As the eastern sun fell

---

[26] Birch, *Memoirs*, ii, 11, 20; *Cottonian MSS.*, Otho E. ix; Devereux, *Lives of the Devereux*, i, 344–5, 348–56. Lediard, i, 323–4; *State Papers, Dom., Elizabeth*, cclix, 13, 14.

on the white sails of a hundred and fifty English ships only half a league from the point of land beyond Cadiz on which the monastery of St. Sebastian was built, even the Spaniards, to whom the sight was a most unwelcome one, confessed that it was " the most beautiful fleet that ever was seen." [27]

On the journey the English fleet had picked up three Dutch flyboats two weeks out from Cadiz and later an Irish bark, which had left but twenty-four hours before, from which they had the welcome news that no word of their coming had reached Cadiz and that the harbor was full of unsuspecting vessels. In the harbor lay, as a matter of fact, four great galleons of a thousand to twelve hundred tons apiece of the group of the " Twelve Apostles," which Philip had built the year before at Genoa, eighteen galleys, armed but of no great size, and some forty or fifty merchantmen, altogether probably some sixty vessels. Thirty of the merchant ships, including three which had been in the engagement with Drake and Hawkins off Dominica the year before, belonged to the West India fleet, the remainder were from the north, Portugal, Italy or the Levant. Several of the Indian ships had but recently arrived, the galleon St. Philip having come in from the Indies and unloaded five millions of treasure less than a month before. A few of the ships were armed for purposes of war, but for the most part they were quite unarmed. In any case the English fleet was overwhelmingly superior. Many of the Spanish merchantmen were already laden with cargoes of oil, wine, silk, quicksilver, ammunition and other supplies for the American colonies or for Lisbon or Brittany. The city, almost surrounded by the sea, was partially fortified though, as in all Spanish administration of the period, the plans that had been made were far behind their fulfilment. There was no lack of officials present, but none of them was in a position of supreme authority and the defense suffered accordingly.[28]

[27] Slyngsbie, 59–61; Stow, Ed. 1605, 1285; *Cal. Hatfield House MSS.*, vi, 226; Oppenheim, *Monson's Tracts*, i, 344, 381.

[28] Stow, 1285; *Sydney Papers*, i, 384; *Monson's Tracts*, i, 344–7;

In accordance with the plan decided upon by the council on the fleet, that the town should be attempted first, the English proceeded immediately, when daylight disclosed the situation, to place their warships in such a position that no Spanish vessels could leave the harbor, and to make ready to land their troops at the Caleta, an open beach in front of the city, hastily and inadequately fortified by the inhabitants with casks of sand, and permitting easy entry, if captured, directly into the city. The ships' boats were loaded with men, and Essex proceeded to carry out the landing. But the wind was high, the waves rolled in almost unbroken from the sea, two boatloads of eighty men were capsized and most of their occupants drowned. Ralegh, returning in the Warspite from a scouting trip along the main shore, urged a change of plan, pointing out that many men would be sacrificed in the high waves and that those who landed would be for the time at the mercy of the Spaniards. He was asked by the other captains to go and persuade the admiral to agree to the change of plan. As he came back with the admiral's agreement that the fleet in the harbor should be attacked first and called from his boat to Essex, " *Intrabimus!* " Essex threw his hat into the sea for joy and turned with enthusiasm to the new project. It took, however, all the rest of the day to get the troops back from their boats into the ships, and it was not until after sunset that the English ships weighed anchor and entered the bay. All the Spanish craft, after some futile cannonading, retired further up the harbor, which extends some miles inland beyond the city. A puritanic chronicler who was present attributes the foul weather, the high seas and the sinking of the two boats to the displeasure of God, — not with the whole undertaking, as its later success proved, but with the initiation of the attack on " His day of rest." Another observer, the admiral's physician, found a better omen in the alighting of a

---

Slyngsbie, 68–9; *A Libel of Spanish Lies*, Hakluyt, x, 254; Marbecke, *Ibid.* iv, 241, 249; *Confessions of Certain Spaniards, Cal. Hatfield House MSS.,* xiii, Add. 607–9.

dove on the main yard of the admiral's ship, where it sat quietly three or four hours undisturbed by the confusion aboard.[29]

During the night the new plan of attacking the Spanish fleet first, the town later, was discussed at a council held on Essex's ship. If this were done Essex claimed the honor of sailing ahead into the inner harbor and leading the attack, but Howard had been especially charged by the queen to look out for Essex's safety, and he and all the other commanders well knew what awaited them if any mischance should happen to the queen's favorite. So the whole council withstood the plan. The channels in the harbor were narrow, but few vessels could take part in the actual fighting at best, and Howard was almost as careful of the queen's beloved ships as of her beloved courtier. Ralegh and Lord Thomas Howard were therefore ordered to lead the attack. The lord admiral and Essex were to be under sail but not to come into danger unless the others were in actual peril. "At peep of day," therefore, Ralegh and Lord Thomas sailed forward with a group of the English warships accompanied by the Dutch squadron, while the whole English fleet followed them as best they could, taking the places in the open harbor that the Spaniards had occupied the day before. They found the four Spanish galleons at anchor stretched across a narrow part of the harbor, broadside on, the galleys supporting them, while the merchant ships had withdrawn to Puerto Real, a deep indentation across the bay from the long promontory on which Cadiz stands. A battle of five or six hours ensued, each of the more prominent English commanders, including Essex himself, successively forcing his ship far to the front in order to obtain a more prominent part in the fighting. It did not diminish the interest of the fight that two of the galleons, the St. Philip and St. Andrew, had been in the fleet against which Sir Richard

[29] Stow, Ed. 1631, 773; Speed, 1196; *Monson's Tracts*, i, 347; Ralegh *Relation, Works*, Ed. 1829, viii, 668–70; Slyngsbie, 65; Marbecke, *Hakluyt*, iv, 245; Purchas, *Pilgrimes*, xx, 8.

Grenville had fought five years before. Ralegh declared that he was resolved " to be revenged for the Revenge or to second her with mine own life." There was indeed some unseemly and dangerous rivalry for the "point of honor."

Even a soldier as familiar with warfare as Ralegh was impressed with the continuous battery. " Volleys of cannons and culverins came as thick as if it had been a skirmish of musketeers." At last the English made ready to board; the galleons, in no condition to resist, cut their cables and in the effort to manoeuver in the narrow channel ran aground, where two, the St. Philip and St. Thomas, were set on fire by their commanders and burned to the water's edge. The burned and blackened soldiers and sailors tumbled into the sea: " as if any man had a desire to see hell itself it was there most lively figured," as an observer remarks. The other two ships, the St. Matthew and St. Andrew, were captured by the English and eventually taken safely to England and added to the queen's navy. The galleys made their way up channel and watched for an opportunity to pass the bridge that obstructed the narrow passage-way to the sea.[30]

Resistance on the water was now broken. The few cannon on the fortifications of the town toward the harbor, badly placed and badly served, had either dismounted themselves in action or exhausted their ammunition. The commanders passed on to the attack on the city by land. The Dutch regiments disembarked first and captured the outlying fort of Puntal, two miles back from the town, while Essex landed some 2000 soldiers on a sandy beach nearer the city. A detachment under three of the colonels was sent inland to seize the bridge which led from the island promontory to the mainland, and Essex himself set forward across a stretch of deep sand to the town. There was no very serious resistance. Some companies of cavalry and foot-soldiers, 600 horse and 500 foot, according to one of the English captains, were brought out from the town and en-

[30] *Monson's Tracts*, i, 349; Stow, Ed. 1631, 773-4; Slyngsbie, 69-72, 78; Hakluyt, vi, 248; Ralegh, *Relation, Works*, Ed. 1829, viii, 669, 670-2.

gaged in a skirmish with the English, but soon broke and
retreated in confusion. As they rushed in through the gate
they closed it, leaving forty or fifty of their men on the outside. The walls on this side of the town were under repair
and such heaps of débris were piled up against them that
the abandoned Spanish soldiers climbed their own wall from
the outside and thus set an example that the English soon
followed. Essex himself with many of his men climbed the
wall and set the English ensign on it; the soldiers jumped
down inside, opened the gates to their comrades, and soon
all were rushing through the narrow streets to the market
place, hindered by little more than the occasional stones
thrown down from the flat oriental roofs of the houses.
The losses of the English had been small, probably not more
than two hundred altogether, in both the sea and land fighting. In the market place, however, Sir John Wingfield,
colonel of one of the regiments and brother of Sir Anthony
Wingfield who was killed at Crozon two years before, a
conspicuous figure riding on a captured Spanish horse because of a slight wound he had just received outside the
wall, was shot and killed.[31]

Before landing Essex had sent two officers to suggest to
the lord admiral that while the land attack was in progress
he. proceed with the naval contest by seizing the fleet of
merchant ships across the bay. Howard, however, either,
as so often, feeling his responsibility for Essex's personal
safety, or himself longing for glory and plunder where they
seemed for the moment to offer themselves most conspicuously, followed Essex into the city with his own regiment
and a number of the other naval men and joined his fellow
commander in the centre of the town. Ralegh and some
other seamen also refused the offer of two captains to take
some boat loads of soldiers across the bay to attack the
merchant fleet, and claimed this as their service, but post-

[31] Slyngsbie, 73–6; Vere, *Commentaries, Stuart Tracts,* 108–17; *Monson's
Tracts,* i, 352; *Documentos Ineditos,* xxxvi, 240, 249; Gyfforde to Southampton, July 5, 1596, *Cal. Hatfield House MSS.,* xiii, 577–9.

poned it until the next day and meanwhile joined Howard and Essex in the city. All fighting was soon at an end. Fort St. Philip, the City Hall, the Priory and other points of resistance surrendered. A guard with a drum was sent through the city announcing that all who would yield and come to the City Hall should have mercy, but others should expect no favor. The populace generally yielded on the spot, though a considerable body of the more well-to-do citizens, 8000 or 10,000, it was claimed, fled to the citadel or old city, where, temporarily protected from the reckless soldiers by the ancient walls, they begged respite till the next morning. That night, Monday the twenty-first of June, the two generals lodged at the priory and the fort respectively, their ensigns floating above them, and the city was with small restraint given up to the plunder of the soldiers. Even the ships were deserted, " all running headlong to the sack." The massacre does not seem to have been bloody, though the Dutch showed greater bitterness than the English, re-prisals perhaps for recent occurrences in the Netherlands. Ralegh says that the Netherlanders " used merciless slaughter till they were by myself and afterward by my lord admiral beaten off."

Next morning a flag of truce hung from the walls of the citadel, and a parley resulted in the signature of an agreement for the ransom of the lives of all in the old city for a large sum, to be paid in twelve days, fifty principal men to be held as hostages in the meantime, though five or six should be allowed to go to Seville to collect the ransom. The keys of the castle were thereupon put in charge of one of the English officers and everything in the city was surrendered to the mercy of the generals. This surrender according to the testimony of all concerned, English and Spanish alike, was not misused by the victors. Essex and Howard were both high-minded men, and there was no reason of war or state for undue severity. A proclamation was issued declaring that no more blood should be shed and that in accordance with the positive instructions of the queen no violence should be done to men, women or children. All the Spanish population was ordered to leave the city, the common people by land over the bridge that connected the promontory with the mainland; the better sort, except the hostages and some personal captives of the English officers, were sent by boat seven or eight miles across the bay to St. Mary Port. Essex and Howard themselves stood at the waterside to prevent any ill usage of the fugitives. Ladies were treated with respect, allowed to put on as much of their wearing apparel as they could carry, and take with them even their jewels and ornaments. Sir Amias Preston was sent over in one of the boats in special charge of one hundred or more elderly gentlewomen and merchants' wives. The bishop of Cuzco who was about to sail with the fleet to take charge of his South American diocese, was treated with deference, troubled with nothing more serious than some theological discussions with Essex's chaplain and allowed to depart for Seville promising that he would do what he could to secure in return the release of all English captives there. The city was then given over to the systematic sack of the English and Dutch soldiers and sailors.[32]

In the meantime the conquerors were by their own negligence losing the most valuable part of their booty. On Monday as has been said, the attack on the forty or fifty merchant ships gathered at Puerto Real had been postponed till the next day. Negotiations for their ransom were entered upon with the Spanish civil and military officials on Tuesday morning. Representatives of the fleet and port officers offered a payment of 2,000,000 ducats for the ships and cargo. Howard was inclined to accept money for the merchandise but not for the ships. In the meantime he gave orders to the vice-admiral with some of the smaller warships and merchant vessels drawing little water to make preparations for going across the bay to capture or if necessary to sink the merchant fleet. The Spanish merchants were at

[32] Stow, 1288–9; Slyngsbie, 76–8; Hakluyt, vi, 253, 258, 261; Ralegh, *Relation, Works,* viii, 673; Lediard, *Naval History,* i, 322.

the same time surreptitiously unloading some of the most valuable of their cargoes on the mainland. Negotiations, preparations and salvage were brought to a sudden close by the outbreak of fire through the whole merchant fleet. It was deliberately fired, apparently by the orders of Medina Sidonia who had now reached Saint Mary Port, was taking general charge of all operations, and was credited with having no kindly feeling toward the merchant city which was now in such dire straits. As a matter of fact a great part of the merchandise in the fleet was the property of Dutch not Spanish merchants. Although English merchant ships hurried across the bay and some merchandize and a few pieces of ordnance were saved, nevertheless the value of ten or twelve million ducats was lost. Moreover the losses thus inflicted upon the enemy at Cadiz were declared to have made it impossible for the representatives of the hostages in Seville to obtain the ransom required for their pardon.[33]

One piece of good fortune fell to the Spaniards. News came of the escape of the fleet of galleys which had rowed far up the harbor. An English guard had been placed at the bridge, but its officers slipped away to take part in the sack of the city. The few soldiers who had remained, drunk with native country wine, had their throats cut, the bridge was broken down and the galleys made their way into the open sea, and were able later to harry the rear of the English fleet.[34]

In the annals of plunder the capture of Cadiz was a striking exploit. Within two days from the appearance of the English fleet before the city all the king's war vessels in the harbor had been destroyed, captured, or damaged and driven into flight, all naval materials in the storehouses there were in the possession of the captors; the city had been captured, denuded of its inhabitants and was being system-

---

[33] Stow, 1289; Slyngsbie, 79-80; *Monson's Tracts,* 353; Ralegh, *Works,* viii, 674; Pieter Bor, *Chronicle,* quoted in Motley, *United Netherlands,* iii, 391.

[34] Slyngsbie, 78-9.

atically pillaged; the merchant ships and their cargoes, instead of being on their way to the Indies or to European ports had been burnt and sunk, and the most distinguished men of the city were prisoners held to ransom. If the primary object of the expedition was to inflict loss and humiliation upon the Spanish government, this had been attained as completely as was possible by the capture of one city.

Reports of the chivalry and moderation of the commanders, especially of Essex, made their way to the court of Spain and into general Spanish tradition. If the testimony of a Catholic Englishman then living at Toledo is to be believed, every one, from the king to the common people, had a good word to say for the gallant earl who had stood in conversation with eight or nine Spaniards at Cadiz alone and unarmed, who had given his protection to all the religious, and freely dismissed the bishop of Cuzco and the president of the Casa de Contratacion; who had shown himself courteous and modest to nuns, virgins and honorable ladies, and had given his hand to kiss to the populace. The exiled Englishman adds to his report the statement of his opinion that this readiness of the Catholic Spaniards to acknowledge honorable treatment should show to his fellow-countrymen the error of blemishing their heroic acts by the foul process of beheading, hanging and disemboweling their poor Catholic fellow-countrymen at home. The same tradition of good treatment is reflected in the pretty story by Cervantes, who was then living in Seville, of the " Española Inglessa." She was a little Spanish maid who was captured in 1596 " among those many spoils which the conquerors from the famous northern island, governed by a most noble queen, carried away from Cadiz." Taken to England, she was brought up in the family of her captor, who were " Christians in heart, although in public they made show to follow the religion of that country." Her audience with the great " Isabella " and kindly treatment by her, the gallantry of her betrothed at sea, and their marriage and happy life, restored to her native city, make, like the acknowledgement of Essex' generosity, a pleasant oasis in the desert of contemporary hostility and brutality. It was perhaps a part of the same impression made at Madrid that led to a plan for sending an English Catholic emissary from the Spanish court to Cadiz to see whether Essex would consider a change of religion or would favor the Infanta's title to the English throne, and to discuss the exchange of Calais for Flushing, thus establishing terms of peace, naming his own price for these services. The lord admiral at Cadiz and the earl of Shrewsbury in France were also to be sounded. But all this was probably mere rumor.[35]

For two weeks the pillage of the city continued, while the commanders waited for the emissaries of the hostages to return, collected and loaded on their ships captured cannon and stores and discussed their further plans. An English captain, sure of the present whatever might happen in the future, dated his letter home " From her majesty's city of Cales, not in fancy, but won and yet held by her soldiers' swords." Essex was all for refortifying and holding this city of her majesty. This had been his real intention from the beginning. Vere had surmised and encouraged the plan before he left the Netherlands, and Essex had described and advocated it in the letter he had left behind him for the privy council, though his care to be well away before his letter was delivered showed his fear that the project might be forbidden by the queen. At first he carried the council of officers with him. It was pointed out that there was rice, corn, sugar, wine, rusk and oil in the Spanish government storehouses in the town. With these and their own victuals they could provision a competent garrison of 3,000 or 4,000 men for four months, during which time new supplies could be obtained from England, the Low Countries or Barbary. It was, therefore, proposed that the two commanders should go back to England with their own ships, that the weakest of the vessels and men should follow them, that Lord Thomas Howard and Ralegh with six ships should go to

---

[35] Birch, *Memoirs*, ii, 124–5, 307; *Cal. Hatfield House MSS.*, xiii. 577–9.

the Islands to watch for Indiamen and the rest of the expedition should remain at Cadiz. Orders were prepared to unship cannon from the fleet to be used in fortifying and defending the walls; Sir Anthony Ashley was to be dispatched to England at once to obtain the consent of the queen, and a message was to be sent to the king of Morocco asking for assistance with galleys, men and food. But when Essex insisted that he himself should remain in command of the occupied city, no one was bold enough to contemplate returning to England without him; excuses of lack of supplies and other deficiencies were made, and all the council, the lord admiral leading, declared against the project of retaining the city. It was most reluctantly, at least on the part of Essex, given up. The choice of the less bold rather than the more bold policy was a matter of regret to many observers and English sympathizers in France, Italy and the Netherlands then and long remained a matter of recrimination in England. Essex insisted that he had been overruled in the matter and that the plan could and should have been carried through. In its default Essex proposed a march inland before they left but this too was disapproved by the council.[36]

On Saturday, the 26th of June, Sir John Wingfield was buried in the cathedral with all the honors of war, "the drums and trumpets sounding dolefully," the generals with the ready symbolism of the age throwing their handkerchiefs "wet from their eyes" into the grave. On Sunday the Anglican morning service was read without compunction in the abbey church; later in the day a sermon was preached by Master Hopkins, the earl's preacher. Between these two functions, a great ceremony of knighting, as always occurred when Essex had opportunity or excuse, took place. The candidates included, according to a somewhat unsympa-

[36] Slyngsbie, 80–82, 85; Stow, 1290; *Monson's Tracts*, i, 352; Devereux, i, 353–5; Carew to Cecil, June 30, 1596, *Cal. Hatfield House MSS.*, vi, 229; Vere to Essex, *Ib.* 86–8; Bongars to Camerarius, Aug. 27, 1596, *Lettres de Bongars*, Ed. 1695, 499.

thetic eyewitness, " all who deserved it or affected it or did not neglect and refuse it, as some did." Essex knighted thirty-three, Howard twenty-seven, including Don Christopher, Prince of Portugal, youngest son of Don Antonio, Count Louis of Nassau, son of the head of that house, William Howard, young son of the lord admiral, and other adventuring gentlemen and officers of the expedition. With two who had been knighted at the entry into the city, and a few others knighted later, altogether sixty-five men dated their new and somewhat questionable knighthood from the Cadiz expedition.[37]

An exchange of formal Latin letters and messengers between Howard and Medina Sidonia led to a promise by the latter to release fifty English captives from the Spanish galleys. In due time a galley appeared from Saint Mary Port, carrying a white flag and bringing to the fleet thirty-nine Englishmen who had been serving at the oar in Spain, some for six, others for eight, ten and even twenty years. They were delivered aboard the lord admiral's flagship with a promise that the other eleven should be forthcoming as soon as they could be found and brought from their places of service. At the same time some thirty or forty " Turks " who had long been prisoners in the Spanish galleys jumped overboard and swam to the English fleet. They were given a bark and a pilot and allowed to sail away to Morocco. The monotony was also broken by a foray on the mainland and a night attack made by Essex with a body of soldiers to seize some provender and to scatter a body of Spaniards reported to be secreted near the bridge. More than twelve days had passed and the envoys had not returned from Seville. The commanders thereupon decided to carry the hostages to England, and, as a matter of fact, took nine Spanish gentlemen and officers with them and ultimately secured their ransom.[38]

[37] Stow, 1289; Slyngsbie, 81–2; *Cal. State Papers, Dom.*, 1595–7, 263; Birch, *Memoirs*, ii, 49.

[38] Hakluyt, iv, 262, 263–6; Stow, 1291; *Cal. Hatfield House MSS.*, vi, 241–2; Slyngsbie, 85.

By this time the work of pillage had been brought practically to an end. The forms of plunder might be considered as five; merchandise in ships and in storage, ransom of distinguished persons, naval stores, money, jewels and plate, and miscellaneous loot. The first and second of these have already been discussed. So far as the official duty of transferring Spanish stores to the English vessels was concerned there was certainly much neglect. The ordnance was taken from the forts and walls and some salvaged from the burned ships, but there is little evidence that the arms for 5000 men, the 1500 pipes of wine, the 2000 chests of sugar, the rice and other stores which they found at Cadiz ever reached England or served as subsistence for regular troops. Private plunderers fared more successfully, though there was much disappointment and a vast amount of wanton careless destruction. One man who took part in the sack speaks of wine, oil, almonds, raisins, olives and spices thrown out and trampled under foot in every common highway; another of silks, carpets and furniture similarly wasted. But sugar, hides, steel, Spanish iron, tin, lead, armor, quicksilver, wine, church bells and tapestries made lading for many English vessels. Some of the captains and even higher commanders loaded sugar and other commodities into the merchant ships that had followed the fleet and dispatched them privately for England. Coin, jewels and objects of portable value were stored in seamen's and soldiers' chests, and there was much talk of enrichment of individuals and much recrimination. One ship's captain tells how rich prisoners worth ransoms of 20,000, 15,000 or 10,000 ducats were given to land officers, "besides great houses of merchandise."

Each plunderer took what appealed to him. One of the chaplains of the army, Rev. Edward Doughtie, appropriated eighteen volumes of recently published books from the Jesuit college there, seventeen of which can still be seen in their delicate white vellum bindings in the library of Hereford cathedral and one in the Bodleian. A chest of books also came into Ralegh's possession, and a certain Captain Edward Wilton acknowledged that he had secured a chest of books on the civil law. The Rev. Samuel Purchas in his *Pilgrimes* told long afterward, when the story perhaps had had time to grow, how his old sexton, still living in 1625, had taken from a jeweler's store when a young soldier at Cadiz, a hatful of rubies and sold them for a song. It was said that even after two weeks of plundering, much treasure buried in the graves in the cathedral and in other places remained undiscovered. The English talked of staying long enough to pump the wells dry in the town for treasure supposed to have been thrown into them. There must have been a busy market among the plunderers, the instinct for a bargain competing with the instinct for loot, for scarcely a piece of testimony concerning the sack fails to speak of purchases and sales among the English officers, soldiers and sailors, exchanges of the most bizzare description sometimes taking place. Arthur Savage who obtained possession of a physician's house " which no one had asked for " sold its contents as they stood for £65 and eight small pieces of plate. Other articles changed hands by the familiar way of play, Sir Walter Ralegh for instance entering in his list of acquisitions " five little peces of wrought plate got at play."

Although the soldiers and sailors were still reluctant to leave the city the leaders decided that there was no further reason for staying, so after a final meeting of the council to which five or six other officers were called, held at the Munitions House on Friday, the 2d of July, on Sunday, the 4th, two weeks after their arrival, thirty soldiers from each regiment were told off to burn the city except the cathedral and the priory. This work was not very effectively done, since a Spanish government commission which came to Cadiz two weeks afterwards reported that they found 328 buildings inhabited, 685 uninjured and fit for habitation, although not actually occupied, and only 290 burned. The stone of which the city was so largely built did not of course lend itself easily to such crude means of destruction.[39]

The army was reëmbarked under the oversight of Essex, he himself being the last man to leave the shore. That night they lay at anchor in the roads of Cadiz, the wind being scant, and the council met on the admiral's ship to decide on their next movements. As a result of the conference the next day Ashley was sent to England to report to the queen on all occurrences so far, and with him were taken the sick and wounded soldiers. The remainder of the expedition set sail westward with the object of resuming their pillage at Faro, the nearest city of any size on the coast. A week later the fleet anchored off the shore of the Portuguese province of Algarves near that port and on the 14th of July the army disembarked on a little island and went into camp not far from their landing-place. Although Howard had deprecated this attack, once it was determined upon he claimed the honor of leading it. The July sun was, however, at his age and in his condition of bad health, intolerable, so at the urgency of the other officers he returned to the ships and left the landing at Faro like that at Cadiz to Essex. The next day they prepared to attack but found the city abandoned: the inhabitants had fled to the mountains taking their valuable goods with them, and leaving an almost empty town to the invaders. One piece of furniture left behind to the mercy of the English was however of more than passing interest; this was reported at the time to be the famous collection of books and manuscripts made by Bishop Ossorius, but seems rather to have been that of his successor Mascarenhas. These books were carefully packed by Essex, carried in the fleet to England, and given in 1600 to the newly founded Bodleian Library, where a number of them are still recognizable bound in black calf and marked with the coat of arms of their original possessor. This literary booty, a little wine

---

[39] Stow, 1289–90; *Eng. Histor. Review*, xxxi, 606–10; *Cal. State Papers, Dom.*, 1595–7, 264–8, 269, 273–6, 278; Purchas, *Pilgrimes*, xx, 16, 17.

and fruit, some stuff from a nunnery and six or eight brass cannon from the fort was the sum of the plunder of Faro. The English army remained there two days while troops foraged industriously through the surrounding country up to the base of the mountains. A captain with a detachment of 800 soldiers was sent six or eight miles inland to a little town named Lotha in pursuit of fugitives from the coast city, but all they obtained was about a hundred oxen, sheep and hens, while they paid heavily for these by finding some of their comrades who had fallen out on the way up piti-fully mutilated, their hands chopped off and their throats cut by the peasantry. On the sixteenth of July Faro was burnt to the ground and the troops marched back through the heat and the sand " three great Spanish leagues " to their ships, Essex insisting on going on foot with the sol-diers. The next day the troops were embarked and the fleet passed on to further exploits.[40]

Essex wished to attack Lagos some twelve miles west-ward from Faro, but it was known that it had been newly garrisoned and fortified and Howard, supported by a num-ber of the officers, declared that its capture would require the unshipment of the cannon and would certainly cause the loss of many lives; that it was but a fishing town at best and would yield neither wealth nor glory after Cadiz; and that after all the Portuguese were England's friends and should not be attacked unnecessarily. A serious lack of fresh water, the most constant deficiency in the seafaring of the time, an asserted lack of food, notwithstanding the opportunities for revictualing and insistence by many of the captains that there was still plently in the fleet, some disease, much desire to realize on their lately acquired plun-der, and a growing homesickness that exaggerated the diffi-culties of all routes except that leading homeward, intro-

<hr>

[40] Stow, 1291–3; Slyngsbie, 88–90; *Monson's Tracts*, 354; *English His-torical Review*, xxxi, 608–10; Carew to Cecil, *From her Majesty's good ship the Mary Rose here on the coast of Algarvia, this 18 July, 1596, Cal. Hat-field House MSS.*, vi, 268; *Cal. State Papers, Venetian*, 1592–1603, 224–7, 232.

duced depression into the discussions of the council, and
they rounded Cape St. Vincent without any determinate
plan of what to do next. It is a curious fact that no proposition seems to have been made by any of the leaders during the expedition to extend their attacks to Lisbon. No
mention of such a project is made in any of the records, no
discussion of its practicability or impracticability. It is
difficult to see any reason for this. Lisbon had been repeatedly attacked before and not without success; the primary object of destroying the king's ships would have been
better attained there than elsewhere. The Spaniards seem
to have anticipated such an attack both when the fleet left
England and after the sack of Cadiz. The Adelantado hastened overland from Toledo to Lisbon to prepare its defense
and a meeting of the Portuguese council was held for the
purpose. Moreover the unpreparedness and confusion there
was so great that it seems altogether probable that such an
attack could have been quite as successful as at Cadiz. The
disregard of Lisbon at this time still remains a mystery.[41]

At Cape St. Vincent a strong wind from the eastward,
driving them eighty leagues to sea, for a while determined
them to go on to the Azores to water and watch for the
carracks and the West Indian fleet, and they sent Sir Arthur
Savage to England to report this movement to the queen.
But a change of wind brought a change of plan, and they
soon were at The Rock, or Cape Roca, a familiar place for
watering. Even here Essex and Lord Thomas Howard asked
to be allowed to stay with twelve ships, revictualed and
manned from the rest of the ships, and with the Hollanders,
who volunteered to stay with them, to watch for Spanish
ships as long as their supplies held out. But the opinion of
the council went against them. The arrival of the Spanish
treasure fleet from the West Indies two days after they had
left gave bitter point to this decision. However, they had
left the Rock and another messenger was sent to England

[41] Cal. State Papers, Dom., 1595-7, 301-2; Hist. MSS. Comm. Somerset
Papers, 23-4; Birch, Memoirs, ii, 126; Cal. Hatfield House MSS., vi, 226-7.

to say that the fleet would sail along the coast of Spain looking into Ferrol and Corunna and so home. The generals expressed their regret that they were at an end of doing her majesty service but rejoiced " to think we shall so soon come to see your fair and sweet eyes." On the first of August they were off Finisterre and Howard sent into Corunna a caravel with a crew of English sailors dressed as Spaniards to look for Spanish ships. They reported none there or at Ferrol. Sir Edward Conway was sent forward to prepare the queen for their speedy return; two days afterward they left the Spanish coast. Each vessel made its own way across and landed where it best could. Howard hastened on with the largest division of the fleet and arrived in Plymouth harbor August 8. Essex held back to convoy the St. Andrew, one of the captured galleons, became separated from the rest of his division, and might have been seriously endangered had not Duvenvoord stayed by him and come into Plymouth with him on August 10. This chivalry on the part of the Dutch admiral was rewarded with a special letter of appreciation from Elizabeth. He had already been knighted on shipboard on the journey home, the two generals giving him his accolade with one sword. The fleet had been away two months and ten days.[42]

The commanders had a poor reception. Since July 18 by various routes confused and exaggerated reports had been reaching England of the attack on Cadiz. Some Bristol mariners set ashore by a Flemish vessel at Salcombe and examined at Exeter; a naval messenger sent by one of the captains; vague rumors by way of France and even from Spain; letters from men in the fleet to friends at court sent by chance opportunity had brought their varying news. In the first flush of early reports of brilliant success the queen prepared, as in 1589 after the Portugal expedition, a letter of approval, thanks and congratulation. It was written in

---

[42] Stow, 1293; Slyngsbie, 89–92; *Monson's Tracts*, 355–6; Pieter Bor, *Chronicle*, iv, 235, quoted in Motley, *United Netherlands*, iii, 389; *Cal. Hatfield House MSS.*, vi, 310.

the best Elizabethan manner. " If my Pen had as many Tongues as the Flock of Owners had Feathers they shall scarce express the Lauds that my soul yieldeth to the Highest for this great Victory which His Graceful Hand hath given Us. . . . You have made me famous, dreadful and renowned, not more for your Victory than for your Courage, nor more for either than for such plentiful Life nor of Mercy which may well match the better of the two." [43]

The first official report, that brought by Ashley, reached the queen July 31. On the basis of this and later reports, as they arrived, the queen wrote less and less gracious letters, which probably, however, reached the commanders only after their return. In these she expressed her surprise that notwithstanding their promise that in case of the sacking of any town, its spoil should be carefully preserved to pay the charges of the expedition, she nevertheless learned there had been much disorderly pillage by common soldiers and sailors. She recommended therefore that while the ships were still at sea there should be a thorough search for and listing of all plunder. August 7 the privy council forwarded a long letter, which they hoped but scarcely anticipated would reach the generals before they left the coast of Spain, transmitting the queen's criticism of their operations, based partly on the report of Ashley, partly on the news that had come still later describing the return voyage of the fleet as far as Bayonne in Galicia. She reminds the commanders of the original object of the expedition, laying much more stress upon the intercepting of the Indian fleets than had actually been done in their written instructions, blaming them for not performing it, and requiring them even still, after sending the bulk of their land forces and shipping home, to dispatch a body of good shipping under suitable captains to watch for the ships from the Indies. The council, in view of the queen's determination, are in-

---

[43] *Cottonian MSS.*, Otho. E. ix; Lediard, i, 335; *Cal. State Papers, Dom.*, 1595–7, 257–8, 271.

clined to believe that even if the commanders shall have returned to Plymouth before they receive this letter they had better send back some of the ships, remanned and revictualed for that service. As to the land army which was being returned the queen expressed her wish that the troops from the Netherlands should be returned thither immediately, where the Estates were in great need of them; and that from the remainder a thousand or fifteen hundred men should be immediately drafted off to Limerick or Galway to help put down the rebellion which had broken out in Connaught.

The queen's ill temper grew. Close upon this letter came another from the council dated two days later, recognizing that the commanders were already ashore or would be by the time it reached them, expressing the queen's high dissatisfaction that instead of securing a profit from the whole transaction, for herself, London, the port towns and the adventurers, as those who had pressed the expedition upon her had assured her would be its result, she had now been given to understand she might be called upon to pay further wages to soldiers and sailors before the army and fleet were dissolved. She reiterated her commands that the troops should be dispatched promptly to the Netherlands and Ireland, their officers carefully searching all men and shipping for plunder before they were sent forward.[44]

Essex hurried up to court immediately on landing; partly to greet and placate the queen, partly to induce her to grant him permission to take a part of the ships and troops now returned with him and make an attempt at the rescue of Calais. But although this expedition returned with fewer losses and with its men in better health, probably, than any other warlike expedition of this period, no Elizabethan fleet or army was ever able to start out again immediately after its return to port, nor did the queen

---

[44] *Cal. State Papers, Dom.*, 1595–7, 244, 246, 255–6, 257; *Acts of the Privy Council*, xxvi, 84–9, 102–5; Birch, *Memoirs*, ii, 68–95, *Cal. Hatfield House MSS.*, xiii, 577–9; Lediard, i, 342–4.

approve of a further French venture. Vere and the troops for the Netherlands were sent over with the Dutch squadron and some men were shipped to Ireland but all further projects fell and Howard took the fleet to the Downs.

At first, on favorable news, at the request of the archbishop of Canterbury the queen ordered a general popular thanksgiving for the victory to be celebrated on the 8th of August, but afterward, as her dissatisfaction developed, she restricted the services to London. At this celebration nevertheless one of the archbishop's chaplains in his sermon at Paul's cross compared Essex successively with all the greatest generals of the world's history, and complimented him on his wisdom, justice and noble carriage in this action. The popular repute of the earl undoubtedly stood the highest then of any period of his career. There was a strong desire on the part of all concerned in the voyage to make the expedition as a whole and their own share in it appear well not only to the court but to the world. So far as the court was concerned, the disputes about preëminence and priority that blemish great achievements in all ages were intensified at this time by the petty jealousies which increasingly characterized these later years of the queen. Essex, constantly worried by detraction during his absence by those desirous to diminish his influence with the queen, and anxious that his part in the occurrences at Cadiz should not be disparaged, authorized his secretary, Henry Cuffe, who was with him and an eye witness of its events, to prepare a narrative of the expedition which Essex corrected with his own hand.

This " True Relation " was to be taken by Cuffe to London, to be delivered to Essex's secretary there with instructions to have it transcribed by some unknown hand. It was to be signed R. B. or some other such initials purporting to be those of a gentleman of good standing with the expedition, directed to Fulke Greville or some other gentleman at court who would connive with them and put in the hands of a printer for immediate publication. Unfortunately for this plan Cuffe fell sick, Friday, July 30, on his way up from Portsmouth, while Sir Anthony Ashley with whom he had come from Spain reached London on Saturday the 31st, spent all Sunday morning with the privy councillors and the afternoon with the queen, giving a verbal account of the expedition and no doubt betraying to the queen and council that Essex had sent home a personal narrative for publication. A day or two afterward when the " True Relation " arrived and the secretary of Essex took it to one printer after another, they all declared that they had been forbidden by the archbishop in the name of the privy council to print any account of the expedition without special permission, and the queen sent Fulke Greville to Cuffe to tell him not to publish any account of the expedition without her approval on pain of death. When every effort had been made by those to whose hands this narrative had now come to get it into print without success, by means of members of their own faction they secured a tolerably wide circulation of manuscript copies in England and Scotland and sent a French translation to Henry IV. Bodley secured its transmission to the Netherlands and Hawkyns its appearance in Venice in an Italian translation, but the element of promptness which Essex had so much desired was of course lost.

Even before Cuffe had left Plymouth a messenger from Lord Thomas Howard, a relative of Sir Arthur Throckmorton, brother-in-law of Ralegh, began to spread reports especially favorable to that commander. An " official " account was promptly issued. It was drawn up by Secretary Cecil principally from the information brought by Ashley but utilizing also a letter of description from Howard to Lord Hunsdon written July 8, and no doubt oral information which was now available. After the fleet returned to England the events of the voyage soon became matters of common knowledge or gossip, and charges and countercharges against the various commanders survived long in public interest. Many participants later prepared formal narratives, Essex his " Censure of the Omissions of the

Cales Voyage," Sir Francis Vere a vigorous chapter in his
" Commentaries," Sir William Monson long afterwards in
his " Naval Tracts," Ralegh's " Narration," published post-
humously, and many others, some of known authorship,
some anonymous.[45]

In the meantime the remainder of August and much of
September were spent in a somewhat unseemly series of
efforts on the part of the government to extract from the
coffers of the officers, the holds and cabins of the merchant
shipmasters and the sea chests and boxes of the soldiers and
sailors the plunder which they had in many cases so un-
worthily obtained and now struggled so hard to get into an
English port and to retain in their own hands. A somewhat
tenuous distinction was drawn by the government between
matter of " lawful pillage " which might be retained or
would be returned to those who had it, consisting of apparel, household stuff, small pieces of plate and such articles; and, on the other hand, money, jewels, plate and all
manner of merchandize, which were the proper possession
of the queen and ought to go to defraying the charges of
the journey. Commissioners were appointed in London and
in the western ports to examine all possessors of spoil from
Cadiz, following it up even in the hands of those to whom
it had been sold.

Proclamations were issued forbidding small boats to approach any vessels lately from Spain lying in the harbors.
Twenty-eight ships on the Thames disgorged Cadiz freight
of £2,959 value, but £1,299 worth of this was not openly
declared, but discovered in secret hiding-places on the
vessels. Other vessels had sold parts of their cargoes in
Plymouth, Dartmouth or Portsmouth and thus eluded the
commissioners; two slipped into Bristol harbor and unloaded
part of their contents into little boats before the port officers found they were there. Essex, Howard and one or two
other officers had " disdained plunder," but Ralegh, Vere

---

[45] Julian S. Corbett, *The Successors of Drake*, 439–445; Birch, *Memoirs*,
ii, 95–102.

and twenty-one other officers acknowledged during the first three days after the arrival of the fleet goods which had come into their hands adding up to the value of £12,838. These included Turkey carpets, tapestries, 1325 chests of sugar, quicksilver, ornaments of gold, objects made of silver and other contents of a wealthy and luxurious city. Sir Francis Vere, marshal of the forces, who had succeeded perhaps best, had obtained 12,570 ducats in coin, £60 worth of plate, a gold chain worth £30, and a suit with silver buttons worth 40 shillings a button, altogether amounting to the value of £3,638 15s. Ralegh had £30 value of silver royals, 37 ounces of wrought plate, 110 chests of sugar, which he gave to various captains, 1250 India hides, a half-worn Turkey carpet, 9 pieces of gold hangings, some " Quis-shions and other household stuff " that he had bought, and the chest of books, all valued at £1,769 5s.[46]

Sir Anthony Standen told a friend how he had gotten together £100 which would enable him at least to pay back what he had borrowed to go on the expedition. Sir Matthew Morgan tells how he has obtained £25 in plate, 20 pieces of tapestry, one third of all the bells in Cadiz, four chests of red caps, a chain bought from a sol-dier for £14 10s., a crystal bracelet, and three butts of Spanish wine. If everything he has obtained is allowed him he thinks he will be richer by £400 or £500. Much of the spoil in money was handed directly over to the queen's treasury; a hundred and twenty bags of money were deliv-ered by Darrell and Ashley and seventy-nine bags by Mon-son; another sum of £1,500 was taken directly from the citadel, these three items amounting to £7,150. Of £12,700 brought in the Dutch vessels and taken from them, much to their discontent, £4,000 was given to the queen, the remainder kept by Essex and Howard toward their ex-penses. Curious stories of occurrences at Cadiz come out

[46] *Acts of the Privy Council*, xxvi, 98, 109, 113–14, 120–2, 125–6, 135; *Cal. State Papers, Dom.*, 1595–7, 264–6, 274; Birch, *Memoirs*, ii, 49, 52; Devereux, *Lives of the Devereux*, i, 380–5.

in the investigation; the division of the houses with their contents among the adventurers and officers; eleven rich houses near the Castle not parceled out but left for anyone to go in and take what he found; the plunder of the custom house by the Spanish mob before the English got possession of it, and again by English soldiers and sailors before a guard could be placed over it; handfuls of coin given to satisfy objectors; purchase and sale on speculation; and the whole series of difficulties usually found in the division of plunder among thieves.

Examinations before appointed boards and disputes between officers ran on for weeks. Five of the Spanish hostages were summoned before the privy council to tell what the English soldiers had captured, and their exuberant account of the former wealth of the pillaged city must have stirred anew the cupidity of the queen. Early in September the council complains that even brass ordnance has been embezzled, and as late as the 18th of that month a curious collection of almost worthless materials is seized at Rye, though finally handed back to the captor, who had " deserved well and been at great charge." The repeated protests of the Dutch at the summary removal of all plunder from their ships was at last heeded and a part at least returned to them in October. One estimate of the total value of goods taken at Cadiz is 621,500 ducats, which would amount to about £170,000.[47]

It was doubtless almost impossible then and would be quite so now to tell just what had been the net cost of the Cadiz voyage to the crown, to the two main adventurers, Essex and Howard, to the lesser adventurers, and to London and the seaboard cities which had sent ships at their own expense. The dissatisfaction of all concerned, so far as money was concerned, is testimony to its unprofitableness from that point of view. It is doubtful whether any expedi-

---

[47] *Acts of the Privy Council*, xxvi, 120, 136, 141, 185, 188, 221, 247, 263, 311; *State Papers, Dom., Elizabeth*, cclix, 94–6; *Cal. State Papers, Dom.,* 1595–7, 274–90; *Cal. Hatfield House MSS.*, xiii, 577.

tion of the time really paid its own expenses, and indeed whether warfare can ever be waged at a money profit even to the victor. It is difficult to make destruction profitable. Judged from a military and political point of view, however, an anonymous critic of the time made out for this venture even a better case than that which was given by Wingfield for a somewhat similar expedition against Lisbon seven years before, which has already been quoted, an estimate which, making some allowance for sixteenth century amplification, was not an unfair judgment upon this campaign.

" First, of honor, when threatened with invasion the queen gave battle to the enemy at his own door, defeated and destroyed a war and merchant fleet in one of his harbors, captured and pillaged the fairest town in that part of Spain, remained fourteen days on land unattacked, forced the Spaniards to give up the queen's poor subjects captive in their galleys, and in mercy herself gave up thousands of the poor subjects of the king who were her captives. Secondly, for profit, she strengthened her navy by two goodly ships worth £15,000 apiece, and enriched and encouraged for further service her soldiers and mariners. Thirdly, of annoyance and loss to the enemy, he lost several of his most valuable ships of war and suffered damage to the others, he lost forty merchant-men of his West Indian fleet and four other ships bound for the Levant. He lost the strongest and richest town he had ever lost, and was deprived of supplies and munitions it would take years to replace. His merchants lost in the fleet that was burnt twelve million ducats, and many of the traders with the Indies were made bankrupt. Above all he lost most in being not only partially disarmed at sea but discovered to be so weak at home."

As a matter of fact the king of Spain himself, largely as a result of the losses at Cadiz, found himself in November unable to repay to the bankers in Florence the money he had borrowed from them. The regular report was made on the exchange "*Il re d'Espagne e fallito,*" a number of bankers failed as a consequence, comforting themselves, as it is recorded, by the fact that they might subsequently speak of 1596 as the year in which they and the king of Spain became bankrupt together.[48]

Two more results of the Cadiz voyage must be noted. The active participation of the United Netherlands in this expedition made final and irremediable the break between those provinces and the king of Spain. Now for the first time they attacked their overlord in his own ancient dominions, without the claim of defense of their own liberties. or excuse of the support of a rival for the Portuguese throne. The savagery of the Dutch soldiers at Cadiz and the bitterness against them shown through the whole of Spain made it certain that the Netherlands would go permanently a different path from that country, and therefore necessarily be thrown into closer alliance with England and France. The second result was the provocation of Philip into the preparation and dispatch of a new armada against England.

[48] Vol. I, 187; *Cal. State Papers, Dom.*, 1595-7, 290; Duro, *Armada Española*, iii, 131-2; Birch, *Memoirs*, ii, 47, 270; Oppenheim, *Monson's Tracts*, ii, 14.

CHAPTER XXVIII

THE SPANISH ARMADA OF 1596

EVER since the failure of the Invincible Armada of 1588 the Spaniards had planned and the English had dreaded a repetition of that adventure. The Portugal expedition of 1589 had been intended to head off such an attack. In 1590 special musters of troops were held in anticipation of an invasion, and when the summer passed safely reports of ships being built in the Indies and in northern Spain were considered to indicate preparation for an attack in 1591. The large Spanish fleet which was collected in April caused much apprehension in England though actually intended as a convoy for Philip's second instalment of Spanish troops for Brittany. The occupation of Blavet in that province by Spain created a base for a possible direct invasion of England and compelled the queen to fortify Plymouth. Each fleet prepared in Spain to send reinforcements to Brittany or the Netherlands was reported by spies as an armada against England. In 1592 and again in 1594 rumors were rife of a great fleet in preparation. The Spanish efforts in 1592 to corrupt the French governor of Calais were for the purpose of making that city a still more advanced base for an attack on England.[1]

The foray of July 1595 was a small affair and had little importance beyond the fact that it was the only time in the whole war that Spaniards actually set foot on English soil. Nevertheless in 1596 a tax collector complained of his difficulty in making collections because his part of the country was so much burnt by the Spaniards; and the possibil-

---

[1] *Acts of the Privy Council*, xix, 414–16, 480; *Cal. State Papers, Dom.*, 1591–4, 38, 82–94, 196, 208, 220, 251, 256, 291, 451, etc.

ity of a repetition of the raid, "to the dishonor of the realm," during the absence of the fleet at Cadiz, in June and July, 1596, led to the issue of orders to the maritime counties to put everything in a state of defense during the summer.

The dispatch by Philip of an armada against Elizabeth which actually occurred in 1596 was due to the appearance of two new causes, one the desire for reprisals for the sack of Cadiz; the other the ripening of certain old plots in Ireland. Stung beyond measure by the humiliation at Cadiz, urged to action by the nobles who surrounded him at Toledo, and convinced by Diego Brochero de Anaya of the practicability of a diversion against England in Ireland, Philip determined on a prompt revenge. He acted with unusual resolution and energy. It was reported by one of the spies of Essex at the Spanish court that the saying ran there that the king's forces had been doubled by the loss of Cadiz; the news had cured him of his sickness. Many of the nobles, it was said, thanked God on their knees for the coming of Essex and Howard to rouse up their dulled spirits in those parts. " The king himself that languished before and slept and died living . . . was so nettled with the news of your success that presently he awaked out of his dream and dispatched more in three days at that time than was done in three years before." As a matter of fact, the second armada against England that had for years been talked about, half determined upon, half prepared, then procrastinated, and ultimately abandoned, was now organized, equipped and sent to sea within a few weeks in the autumn months of 1596.

Any active policy against England was popular in Spain. The libels and abusive verses attacking the king and his council which were found so frequently tacked to the posts at the street corners in Madrid and Toledo disappeared when it was announced that a new armada was to be sent out. Of the 12,000,000 gold crowns brought by the Indian fleet which arrived soon after the English fleet had left the coast, 4,000,000 belonged to the king. The chapter of the cathedral of Toledo offered him 6000 crowns for a holy war against the English, and the clergy generally were ready to help. The cortes of Castile was called and made an extraordinary grant for the same purpose. In conversation with the prince and infanta, Philip pointed to one of the silver candlesticks on his table and declared he would sell it rather than want for money to send an expedition against England.[2]

The plan as it was entered upon seems to have been practically that long advocated by Diego de Brochero, one of the best of the Spanish commanders. It was to be directed rather against Ireland than England itself. Philip had long played with the idea of making trouble for Elizabeth by giving aid and encouragement to the half-hostile chieftains in Ireland, and had entered into correspondence with them with this object. Their restiveness had developed during the years 1594, 1595 and 1596 into full rebellion, a series of events which will be more fully described in another connection. Now however the native forces already fighting against their English rulers, if strengthened with Spanish troops, provided with munitions and other supplies, encouraged by the return of the Irish exiles in Spain and protected by a Spanish fleet, might give to Philip another kingdom and one from which he might exert overwhelming pressure upon England.

When once determined upon the plan was followed up promptly. Before August was over preparations had begun in earnest in Lisbon and other ports under Spanish control. All foreign vessels in harbor that could be used as transports and all mariners of all nationalities were stayed. The vessels that had escaped destruction at Cadiz by being at San Lucar, farther up the river, and those which had subsequently come home from the Indies, eluding Essex and

[2] *Sydney Papers*, i, 343, 345; Birch, *Memoirs*, ii, 109-10, 117, 120, 123-4, 126; Duro, *Armada Española*, iii, 129-131; *Cal. State Papers, Venetian*, 1592-1603, 219-26, 232, 245; *Cal. State Papers, Dom.*, 1595-7, 77-81.

Howard and slipping into harbor early in September, were ordered to join the main armada at Lisbon, guarded by a fleet of galleys. Some other ships then at Vigo were ordered to join them later, and the completion of still others at Guipuzcoa was hastened. The larger part of the troops in Brittany, where there was still a truce, were sent for, forces recently sent against the Turks were recalled, and it was said that every fifth man in Spain was summoned to serve as a soldier in the fleet. The expedition was put under the command of Don Martin de Padilla, Conde de St. Gadea, admiral of Castile, with Diego de Brochero as vice admiral. Padilla had won distinction in Flanders, had been captain general of the galleys at Lepanto, had defended the entrance to the Tagus against Drake in 1589, and had just been appointed adelantado, the highest official under the king in Castile. Brochero was a well-trained and competent commander.[3]

The fleet was not gathered without difficulty. Among the ships commandeered in Lisbon for transports were some twenty Netherlands vessels. The Dutch sailors protested against the interference with their voyage and complained of their wages and their victuals, but the adelantado drove them back by force into their ships. When he tried, however, to force the Portuguese in the port of Lisbon to serve they told him frankly that if he wanted to man the fleet he must do it from Spain; and when he threatened with hanging those who refused, there was a riot in which muskets were aimed at the commander himself and he was glad to find refuge in a church. Twenty-three Hanse ships from Hamburg and Dantzig, some small French vessels, and several larger Portuguese and Biscayans were secured for transports, and gradually a sufficient number of sailors was obtained; foreign merchants and travelers in many cases,

[3] Duro, *Armada Española*, iii, 129–30; Birch, *Memoirs*, ii, 119–20, 156, 174; *Somerset Papers, Hist. MSS. Comm. Rep.*, 15 *Rep.*, pt. vii, 22–4; *Cal. State Papers, Dom.*, 1595–7, 261, 277, 297–8, 301–2; *Cal. State Papers, Ireland*, 1596–7, 120, 141; Kelso, *Die Spanier in Irland*, 38–42.

to avoid the press, making their way overland or by different sea routes to their homes.[4]

By the early part of October, three months after the sack of Cadiz, Padilla had gathered at Lisbon a fleet of ninety-eight sail, great and small. Of these some twenty were men of war, ranging from small armed merchant ships of 100 tons or less up to the admiral of the Levant fleet, of 1200 tons, and the Santiago of 1400. There were also several galleys of about 1000 tons each. Artillery was provided by stripping some of the coast fortresses, and a certain amount of food was obtained from the ill-filled royal store-houses. Forty ships and galleys from Andalusia, provided with wine and other supplies, were daily expected to join them at Lisbon, and a fleet of vessels from Vigo, twenty-five in number, under Captain Zubiaur, was to meet the main armada off Cape Finisterre. The army on shipboard was estimated at numbers varying from 15,000 to 40,000, but for the most part it was made up of what one of the witnesses describes as " simple and ill-appareled boys." Aboard were, besides, a considerable number of Irish gentry and clergy, taking the opportunity of these favorable circumstances to return from exile. If the armada had therefore all been drawn together it would have consisted of a hundred and fifty or more vessels, with a very considerable army aboard, approximately as large as either the Spanish armada of 1588, the English fleet which invaded Portugal in 1589, or the Cadiz expedition of Essex, the three greatest fleets of this period. Examined more closely the equipment, personnel and plan of operations of this hurriedly organized expedition were incredibly deficient, even for that country and that period of defective naval organization.[5]

[4] Duro, *Armada Española*, iii, 132; *Cal. State Papers, Dom.*, 1595-7, 273, 301-3; *Cal. State Papers, Ireland*, 1596-7, 173; *Hist. MSS. Comm. Somerset Papers*, 22-4; Birch, *Memoirs*, ii, 12; *Cal. Hatfield House MSS.*, vi, 438-9.

[5] *Cal. State Papers, Dom.*, 1595-7, 277, 297-8, 301-2; *Cal. State Papers, Ireland*, 1596-7, 175; *Cal. State Papers, Venetian*, 224-7, 233; *Hist. MSS.. Comm. Somerset Papers*, 22-43; Birch, *Memoirs*, ii, 174.

Of all these details and of the objective of the fleet the English for some time knew little. They only knew that Philip " wounded with the late enterprize happely achieved against him at Cadiz," as the privy council expressed it, was gathering a great armada which might strike at any moment on any part of the coast of the queen's dominions. It seemed unlikely, it is true, that it would sail so late in the season. On the other hand, the Spaniards knew the English fleet had been dismantled since its return from Spain, and a surprise attack might well be, as indeed it actually was, a part of the Spanish plan. Reports of the preparation of the fleet began to reach England by the beginning of September, a letter having been sent by a private correspondent from Spain to Essex on the last day of August, followed by another from a still more secret observer written shortly afterward. By the middle of October the composition of the Spanish fleet was well known, but whether it was for Ireland or England, for the west coast, the Isle of Wight or the Thames was a pure matter of guesswork.

There was reason to suspect the fleet was intended for Ireland. Through September and October reports from Irish spies and English officials of some eager anticipation on the part of the restless Irish chieftains and of the arrival of Spanish messengers among them reached the English court. The queen and council thought it wise, therefore, to strengthen the Irish garrison. On September 10th, 1000 men were ordered to be gathered and shipped from Chester by the end of the month. Later, in October, when news of another Spanish envoy and the rumor of Spanish reinforcements reached England, 2000 more men were levied in Wales and the western counties and some of them shipped to Ireland. The usual delays kept others back and December 2nd, when the immediate threat was withdrawn, those who had not yet embarked were sent back to their homes.

Other rumors were that the armada was intended for Jersey; still others that it was for England. An attempt was made to secure news of the movements of the Span-

iards by sending out three scout vessels from Plymouth, one
to the coast of Portugal, another to Cape Finisterre, and a
third to the Scilly islands; but no news was brought by
these vessels until fuller information had reached England
by other means. Such serious preparations as were made
to meet the danger were therefore made in England itself,
and with but scant knowledge of the situation.[6]

Early in November news of the advanced state of preparation of the adelantado's fleet having been received from
both English sailors and Portuguese captives, the earl of
Essex, doubtless with the assent of the queen, drew up and
submitted to the principal military and naval men of the
time and to some other officials a series of ten questions.
In this paper they were asked to give their opinions as to
the probable time and place of attack by the Spaniards and
to make suggestions as to the best means of meeting it.
This informal and documentary council of war, as it practically was, consisted, besides Essex, of Burghley, Willoughby, Borough, Norris, North, Ralegh, Clifford, Knollys,
Vere and Carew. The fact that a group of such well-known
men, including at least eight veteran officers, could be called
into consultation indicates how completely England had
within the last few years become a military nation.

There was great diversity of views among those consulted.
An almost unanimous judgment was expressed, however,
that an attack might be anticipated shortly in the nature of
a surprise. There was also a quite general agreement, although as we know wide of the truth, that it would be
directed in the first place against the Isle of Wight and
surrounding ports and later come into the Thames. In
both questions and answers the example of 1588 was referred to, though as a result of recent experience all agreed
that the danger was not so great as it had then been thought.
Yet the proposals for defense were not particularly bold.

[6] *Cal. State Papers, Dom.*, 1595–7, 302, 307; *Acts of the Privy Council*,
xxvi, 161–5, 178–80, 190–1, 238–44, 343–6; *Hist. MSS Comm. Somerset
Papers*, 15–17, 23.

Burghley, who was not a military man, suggested that all cattle and food be removed from the seacoast where the enemy landed, that the roads be blocked up, the drinking water made unusable, and the grindstones taken from the mills; that devices be arranged to burn their ships in the harbor, a general and other officers of defense be appointed, and the local forces put into better order. Lord Borough, such was the prestige of the Spaniards and the distrust of local defense, also suggested that the " first fury " of the invaders should be shunned, that there should be constant skirmishes but no battle, that guides should be kept away and the region of their descent deserted.

Other suggestions were scarcely less Fabian in their character. Stress was laid on the desirability of more shipping, even if it were not heavily armed, on the ground that so many of the Spanish king's fleet were pressed foreign vessels that his admiral would probably not venture a battle, and that these foreign merchantmen would come over to the English fleet if it were conspicuously superior and within sight. Ralegh's opinion, as might have been anticipated, had more distinction than that of most of the councillors. He was in the first place rather skeptical as to the coming of the Spanish fleet this year or perhaps at all. Essentially a naval man as he was, however, he urged the preparation of a sufficient fleet to watch the mouth of the Channel. If the Spaniards came to land at all, he thought it would probably be on the banks of the Thames. These might and should be guarded by a sufficiently large land army, though Ralegh draws on his knowledge of military history to show by a dozen or more examples how nearly impossible it has always proved to stay an enemy at a passage over a stream, and advocated greater reliance on the fleet.[7]

By the time these suggestions were returned the government was thoroughly alarmed and proceeded to take active

---

[7] Ralegh, *Works*, Ed. 1829, viii, 675, 676-9; *Monson's Tracts, Navy Records Soc.*, ii, 15; Corbett, *The Successors of Drake*, 445; *Cal. State Papers, Dom.*, 1595-7, 299-300, 303, 305; Birch, ii, 174, 187, 189, 194.

measures for defense more or less in accordance with them. Letters were sent from the privy council to various knights and gentlemen ordering them to proceed immediately to their dwellings near the coast and put them in a state of defense; to the lords lieutenants of Hampshire and Wiltshire ordering them each to send 450 men as a garrison for the Isle of Wight; to officers of the southwestern towns reminding them to have all their " fireworks " prepared for defense, as in 1588; to the lords lieutenants of the eight maritime counties to hold musters of the 41,000 men in the trained bands, and to have all equipment ready; and to the ten counties adjacent to these to have 24,000 of their militia ready to march to the seacoast when called upon. London was ordered to have 3000 men from the 10,000 of its trained bands selected, equipped and ready to go into Kent or Essex when ordered. The new fort at Plymouth was garrisoned, and extra defenses were placed in Southampton and Portland, " in these troublesome tymes, when the ennemye doth so greatlie thyrst after revenge." [8]

The navy was also called into service. Five vessels were already in commission in the Channel, two others were commissioned for service during October and November. On November 2nd the naval authorities were authorized to equip and provide with food sixteen of the ships lately brought back from the Spanish coast and more ships were apparently fitted out a month later.

Especial attention was given to the defense of the Thames. At the beginning of November the mayor of London was ordered to send three or four of the best ships of the city to Tilbury Hope to watch for the appearance of the enemy. A week later Borough was ordered to repair and place in the Medway two unused galleys, to carry ordnance and to be sufficiently manned for defense. Minute provisions were made for a series of watch vessels from Sheerness to

[8] *Cal. State Papers, Dom.*, 1595–7, 301, 304, 314; *Acts of the Privy Council*, xxvi, 281–90, 294, 296–7, 306, 309, 323, 327, 363; *Monson's Tracts*, ii, 16.

Chatham navy yard, and it was arranged that on notification of the approach of an enemy by gun from the vessels or by beaconfire more than a thousand men from the surrounding country should meet at Chatham Church under their captains to protect the fleet. Upnor Castle was defended by fifty soldiers. The lord admiral, perhaps remembering what had happened at Cadiz, showed a real dread of the destruction of the fleet and wanted Ralegh sent down to defend it. Orders were sent to the county authorities to seize the horses and arms of all recusants, holding them until the danger should be over. Some time afterward further action was taken against recusants, all those who had formerly been arrested and confined to Ely but released on bail now being rearrested and confined. In especially hard cases the oldest son was allowed to represent his parents in the burden and honor of imprisonment.[9]

By the time these arrangements had been completed the need for them had been averted by the natural agency that has so often defended the English shores. Again, as in 1588, " He blew with His wind and they were scattered." Lateness of the season had been recognized to be a daily increasing danger to the Spanish fleet. Impressed with this fact, weary of waiting for the ships from Andalusia and urged by Philip's commands, on the 13th of October the adelantado set sail from the Tagus with his fleet of ninety vessels. Prayers for the success of the armada were said in the churches throughout the kingdom and the psalm *Contra paganos* was sung. For four days the fleet made its way slowly northward; then on the 17th of October, off Cape Finisterre it was suddenly struck with an equinoctial gale from the southwest. The whole fleet was scattered. Many of the vessels were driven on the sands and banks of the lee shore of the gulf of Cantabria and wrecked; others were forced into such shelter as they could find. Between thirty and forty were lost including some of the best of the war-

---

[9] *Acts of the Privy Council*, xxvi, 282, 297, 305–6, 312, 322–3, 327, 361, 363–4; *Cal. Hatfield House MSS.*, vi, 482.

ships. The Santiago, a galleon of 1400 tons, carrying a great part of the military equipment, and another galleon, the Levant admiral of 1200 tons, two galizabras, three ships of 300 tons each built for the king by Lambert, an Englishman, and an Irish ship, the San Domingo, were totally wrecked. The losses added up to more than 7000 tons burden of shipping. Between 2000 and 5000 men were drowned. Among these were eight captains and six other officers of the fleet and many of the Irish. Cahill O'Connor, his wife, mother and children, Viscount Baltinglass, John and Robert Lacy, sons of one of the Desmonds, the bishop of Killaloe, several other clergymen and a number of other Irishmen of note were drowned, as well as common men. Some of these had been long in Spain, others had but lately arrived, having come over from England secretly on the fleet of Essex and Howard and escaped while in the harbor of Cadiz.[10]

When the admiral gathered his shattered fleet at Corunna, it amounted to less than fifty vessels of all sorts, but few of which were warships. Moreover many of the crews of the vessels which had been driven to places of shelter on the coast had deserted, the plague broke out in the fleet, and the troops when put ashore to escape infection went home; they were short of provisions, and death was fast depleting the already reduced numbers. Zubiaur brought his contingent from Vigo to Ferrol later, but even he suffered some losses on the way. The Andalusian fleet reached Lisbon but remained there instead of following the adelantado. The vessels from the Biscayan coast never got to the rendezvous. The losses and discouragements had been so overwhelming and the season was now so impossibly late that the great attack on England was again put off, as so often before, and consolation for failure was sought in the making of plans for a still more extensive expedition the next year.

[10] Duro, *Armada Española*, iii, 130–1 n.; Kelso, 40–1; *Documentos Ineditos; Cal. State Papers, Venetian,* 1592–1603, 233, 234, 239–41; *Cal. State Papers, Ireland,* 1596–7, 173, 175; *Cal. Hatfield House MSS.,* vi, 125, 499, 513.

Although the catastrophe occurred in October, it was not until November that the knowledge of it reached England, nor were details certainly known until late in December or even in January. But more and more definite rumors came in, and as the vessels sent out from Plymouth finally came back with stories of disaster and chance captures of Spanish prizes, the troops were withdrawn from the Thames and the Isle of Wight, the ships were discharged, reinforcements for Ireland were countermanded, and the panic was again over.

Philip, however, seems to have made one more plan within the year for revenge for Cadiz. Writing to the cardinal archduke Albert, governor of the Netherlands, he suggests that he should gather a body of troops at his new conquest of Calais, transport them across the Channel in light vessels and thus invade England. But no action followed; it is probable that no knowledge of the project reached England, and the year closed with the dread of further Spanish invasion suspended, at least for the time.[11]

[11] *Cal. State Papers, Dom.*, 1595–7, 323, 326, 342, 350–1; *Cal. State Papers, Ven.*, 1592–1603, 242, 245, 253–4; Birch, *Memoirs*, ii, 209, 215; Oppenheim, *Monson's Tracts*, ii, 16–20.

Part VI

The League Against Spain

Part VI
The League Against Spain

CHAPTER XXIX

*GROWTH OF NATIONAL POLICY IN FRANCE
AND THE NETHERLANDS*

A T first glance the relations between England and her
nearest neighbors across the Channel might seem to
have been much the same during the years 1595 and at the
beginning of the year 1596 as they were during the diplomatic and military occurrences of the later months of the
year 1594, when we last had them under consideration, and
indeed as they had been since the formation of the alliance
with the United Netherlands in 1585 and with France in
1589. With the Netherlands the series of disputes on
financial and commercial questions still continued, and the
support of the garrison and cautionary towns still gave
occasion for reluctant expenditures on Elizabeth's part and
dissatisfaction with their inadequacy and overchargeable-
ness on the side of the Netherlands. A repetition of the
familiar requests for men and money by Henry and denials
of these requests by Elizabeth was still the most marked
feature in the relations between England and France.

Considered more carefully, however, two important
changes will be seen to have taken place; the king of France
was much more a national ruler and the United Netherlands
were much nearer to national independence. Henry was no
longer merely a claimant for the crown, supported by a
party in his own country and given precarious aid by the

English queen. Now, his capital established at Paris, most of the national domain obedient, in religious conformity with the great body of his subjects and opposed only by a constantly diminishing group of obstructionist nobles, he was really the king of France. He represented French national feeling and was in turn controlled by it. He was neither so enforced as before to seek personal support, nor was he so free to follow his personal policy. Since January, 1595, he had been formally at war with the king of Spain. The question had arisen, was it still in conformity with French interests to continue that war or was it not? Henry was able, indeed he must contemplate the alliances of France in Europe independently, and consider whether he should remain in antagonism with Spain or make peace.

This new factor in the international situation affected England deeply, because a treaty between Henry and Philip at this time almost inevitably meant a break between Henry and Elizabeth, and at best would leave England that much more nearly isolated in her war with Spain. Such a separate treaty had been looked upon by English statesmen as a dangerous possibility ever since Henry's conversion in 1593. It is true that he had entered into a formal agreement with Elizabeth, under the great seals of the two monarchs, in August of that year at Melun not to make a treaty with Spain except by mutual consent; but such agreements are necessarily modified by later events, and English statesmen could not feel that such a barrier could be trusted implicitly. An approximation between the two Catholic kings was necessarily to be dreaded.[1]

As time passed the danger to England became more threatening. The probability of a Spanish alliance was largely dependent upon Elizabeth's willingness or unwillingness to give the French king further military and financial aid. Henry did not want to make peace with Spain yet. The boundaries of France were too deeply indented by Spanish territories, too many provinces were under the

---

[1] Birch, *Memoirs,* i, 252. Camden, Ed. 1688, 496–9.

practical control of nobles or cities long pledged to the Spanish interest, the domination of Spain in Europe was still too threatening for Henry to be really ready to enter into a Spanish alliance if he could find the means and the support to carry the contest further. But that support, it would seem, must still come largely from England. It will be remembered that at the close of the year 1594 or within the next few weeks, all English troops were withdrawn from France. The year 1595 was largely a test of Elizabeth's willingness to resume support in men and money or of Henry's ability to keep up the struggle without it.

At the beginning of that year Henry gathered and organized the forces he possessed, material and moral, for a great struggle. That part of his plan of campaign which especially involved the English alliance was an invasion of the three provinces still under Spanish control nearest his eastern border, Franche Comté, Luxemburg, and Artois. But the Spanish forces from the Netherlands partly repelled this attack, partly forestalled it by a counter invasion of Picardy, that region fated so often to bear the shocks of war, which occupied the upper valleys of the Somme and Oise and, in its more extended sense, reached to the Channel and included Boulogne and Calais. The population of Picardy, war weary and apathetic, could be counted upon to do little to help in resistance to the invaders. The king was not in a position to take charge personally in that province. Military requirements continually urged him further east, political requirements further south. From the middle of May to the end of August he was absent on what was then called his " journey to Lyons," an expedition made at the urgent request of the citizens of that city and intended largely for the political consolidation of the obedient south, but much extended in time by incidental efforts for the military conquest of the southeastern frontier, still largely in the possession of his enemies.[2]

[2] A. Poirson, *Histoire du Règne de Henri IV*, Ed. 3, ii, 4–16; Standen to Bacon, Nov. 21, 1593, Birch, *Memoirs*, i, 133.

From the political point of view this journey was of great value to Henry in the pacification of his kingdom, but on the military side it was calamitous. With his inadequate army he accomplished but modest results in the field, the arrangements which he had hoped would keep conditions in Picardy at least stationary in his absence broke down, and the Spanish invaders began a series of operations which filled the annals of two years with events most detrimental to Henry and to France. Le Catelet was captured by them in June, 1595; in July the French suffered one of the most disastrous defeats of the whole war under the walls of Dourlens. That city was then captured and its citizens put to the sword. Montreuil and Boulogne were threatened, and a siege of Cambrai, the great barrier of France to the northeast, was begun in August. All France was impressed with the impending danger. The loss of Cambrai would open Picardy and Champagne to the troops of Spain in that region and would enable those in Flanders to take more active steps against Henry's northern allies. The king, warring in Franche Comté and bound by his engagements in the south, could not come to the rescue and would require reinforcements when he came. There was only one direction in which to look for relief, that was to England. Henry had already, early in the year, sent an ambassador, Morlant, to Elizabeth complaining that her withdrawal of Sir John Norris with all the English troops had broken his measures for war and asking for their return. The queen had refused, harking back to the French failure to deliver Morlaix to her troops according to promise, and declaring that she needed Norris and her troops in Ireland. The king was reluctant now to risk another rebuff, but the danger of Cambrai gave him no choice, so on the 5th of August, he called Edmonds, the English resident, who had accompanied him on the southern journey, and sounded him as to the probability of the queen yielding him 2000 or 3000 men for three months. The fact that they were needed to defend cities so near the Channel the king thought would make the request an easy one to grant. Although Edmonds, knowing the queen's state of mind, gave him little encouragement, Henry determined to send a Huguenot gentleman, M. de la Barrauderie, to Elizabeth with the request.[3]

The French commanders in Picardy had already written directly to the queen, begging assistance in troops, money and powder. The sudden intensification of their need also spurred the King's council at Paris to a formal request for help from the same source. They sent to the queen on their own account a Paris lawyer, Étienne Chevalier, who arrived in England August 19th. He was ordered to describe to the queen the lamentable losses at Dourlens, the serious condition of affairs at Paris, and to ask that 4000 foot soldiers be sent over within fifteen days, the city of Paris giving security for payment of their wages and the expenses of their levy and transportation. Still a fourth French official M. de la Chatte, governor of Dieppe, fearing a sudden raid of the Spaniards, asked that some English troops be made ready for the succor of that city if it were attacked, and finally a similar request came at almost the same time from the Estates of Brittany.[4]

Elizabeth may well have taken satisfaction in so many-sided an appeal for so small a boon and one the granting of which lay so close to her own interests. It was certainly the flattery of power, but she was in no mood for giving, certainly not for giving without an equivalent. It is true she ordered some levies of troops to be made in the southern shires to be ready to defend against sudden attack either of the cities across the Channel whose capture would immediately endanger her own shores. Courtiers who were near the queen also believed that, as usual, if she could add a French cautionary town to those she already held in the Netherlands she would be more amenable. They even be-

---

[3] Poirson, ii, 74-83; *Lettres Missives de Henri IV*, iv, 308-13; Birch, *View of the Negotiations between the Courts of England, France and Burgundy*, 273, 275-6, 289; P. Laffleur de Kermaingant, *Mission de Jean de Thuméry*, 6-8.

[4] Birch, *Memoirs*, i, 267-8, 268-9, 278-80; *Sydney Papers*, 344.

lieved the necessities of the French might drive them to it.
But nothing of this appeared on the surface. To the requests contained in the letters from the field and the messages brought by Chevalier, she gave a negative answer;
and she dismissed Barrauderie with the bare promise to
send a messenger of her own to the king with a fuller explanation of her plans. She chose as this messenger, Sir
Roger Williams, an old soldier friend of Henry. Williams
received his instructions both in writing and in a private
interview with the queen and Burghley, hastened across the
Channel, and on the 15th of September met the king near
Paris on his way from Lyons. The letters and messages he had to deliver carried small comfort. He was
instructed to say, and the letters had the same import, that
the queen would send the reinforcements asked for on one
condition only, that Henry would grant her old request for
the occupation of Calais.[5]

Henry was disappointed and angry, for he had no intention of risking Calais in Elizabeth's hands; but learning
that Cambrai was still holding out, and realizing that help
must be obtained if in any way possible, he avoided a break
with the queen. He took Williams with him to Paris, and
from there a few days later sent him back accompanied by
a special ambassador of his own, M. de Loménie, each
carrying long explanations, expostulations and appealing
letters to the queen, Burghley, Essex, Howard and La Fontaine, the minister of the French church in London.
Loménie was besides entrusted with oral messages, and
apparently given more latitude in the time and manner of
delivery than ambassadors are usually allowed by the governments that send them. Williams and Loménie reached
England together early in October. Neither in letters nor
messages was there any definite reply to the queen's request

[5] *Sydney Papers*, i, 343–4; Birch, *Memoirs*, i, 296–7; *Instructions to
Sir R. Williams, State Papers, Foreign*, xxvi, 5, 8, quoted in Black, *Elizabeth
and Henry IV*, 92; Gaillard, *MSS. de Brienne*, No. 37, *Notices et Extraits*,
ii, 109.

for Calais or an open refusal by the king to grant it, though that request was in the minds of all concerned. Loménie was told in his instructions that the king could not believe that the queen had asked for that city, which his majesty would no more give up than any other place in his kingdom; and although we do not know the actual contents of Williams' verbal report, it evidently included his opinion that the king was unwilling to grant Elizabeth's request.

In his letters the king described recent occurrences, deplored his losses, regretted the queen's failure to send him succor, hinted at the possibility of a separate peace, and renewed his general appeal to the queen for a common struggle against their common enemy. To secure this end he proposed an early conference of plenipotentiaries to draw closer the bonds of their alliance, suggesting Calais, St. Valéry, Dieppe or some other city on the French side of the Channel as a place for the conference. In the meantime he begged for troops. Loménie, a man of somewhat sharp temper, laid before the queen in plain terms Henry's position; unprovided with an army adequate to resist the Spaniards in Picardy, unable to collect taxes sufficient to enable him to levy troops, urged by many of his council, by four visiting cardinals and by the populace to make peace with Spain. The ambassador delivered " with very stout speeches," as an English chronicler reports, his personal belief that if the queen refused assistance now the king would provide for himself as best he could, even if he had to withdraw his agreement of 1593 not to make a separate peace. He " wrote very roundly " also to the queen from his lodgings advising against her proposed withdrawal of her troops from the Netherlands, declaring that in case of a break between France and England or a separate peace between France and Spain, the Netherlands would certainly follow Henry's lead rather than hers. Elizabeth was offended with these brusque threats and Loménie was soon allowed to leave London and return to France with an intimation that the queen would agree neither to the dispatch of troops nor to the proposed conference. The discourtesy of the French ambassador long remained an object of complaint on the queen's part when she wished to reproach the king or to divert discussion from more difficult matters.[6]

In the meantime, however, her decision was not absolutely final. As Loménie lay windbound through all October and part of November at Dover and Rye, messages and letters reached him from Essex, La Fontaine and others at court indicating the possibility of the grant of all he had asked. As one of these correspondents observes, " the business of this court is not the gospel, for there is often both yea and nay." Conflicting influences were being brought to bear upon the queen. It is almost certain that Burghley opposed giving further aid to the king at this time; it is quite certain that Essex favored it. However, whatever part in the queen's inclinations these influences took, no more favorable decision was actually made, and in November Loménie was back in France reporting his failure to the discouraged king. In the meantime, without means to relieve Cambrai Henry had been forced to see it fall on September 29th. In the effort to check the further progress of the Spaniards, he soon afterwards laid siege to La Fère which they had occupied and were using as their principal garrison and arsenal town in Picardy. The siege endured the whole winter and far into the spring.[7]

Elizabeth compounded for her ungracious treatment of Loménie by sending by messenger a long, friendly, almost apologetic letter to Henry, dated November 12th and presented to the king in his camp before La Fère by the English resident in France, November 30th. The queen excused herself for not sending troops on the ground that her people were demanding " some respite from war."

[6] Instructions to Loménie, MSS. de Brienne, quoted in Gaillard, Notices et Extraits, ii, 110; Lettres Missives de Henri IV, iv, 417–21, 422–4. Sydney Papers, i, 354; Birch, View, 27.

[7] Birch, Memoirs, i, 294, 297, 327, 345; Notices et Extraits, ii, 106, 111, 112; Lettres Missives de Henri IV, iv, 417–24; Sydney Papers, i, 354.

Although she had no fear of disaffection among her people she felt that she must use moderately their lives and fortunes; especially as mothers, infants and relatives were calling upon her to send no more men abroad. She had continued to attack their common enemy the king of Spain vigorously on land and sea in addition to the help she had given Henry, as she reminded him, at Dieppe, Paris, Rouen, Brest and elsewhere in Brittany. She promised that somewhat later she might accept the king's suggestion of a meeting of deputies to arrange for joining forces more effectively, and offered in the meantime to send some person of quality as an ambassador to communicate more freely with him. She then expressed surprise " that the king after his many vows and her many services to him could consider making so odious, dishonourable and dangerous a resolution " as to negotiate separately with Spain. She declared that she was not averse to a general peace in Christendom, if it were proposed at a proper time and contained honorable provisions, " having regard likewise to the reparation of past injuries." Henry on having this letter read to him by Edmonds answered briefly that he was not able to sustain the burdens of the war alone, that he would consult with his council as to what resolutions to take, and that if necessity should force him to change his course the fault would not be his. The queen, in such a case, might, instead of excuses and justifications, have cause only for sorrow.[8]

The possibility of a peace between Henry and Philip was brought closer by the formal grant of absolution by the pope to the penitent monarch for his earlier disobedience to the church, August 20th, the completion of the ceremony with much pomp at Rome, September 7th, the bishop of Rouen representing the king, and the conveyance of the information of this action with the pope's blessing to Henry, later in September. The general depression in England and in France at the failure of Elizabeth to grant

---

[8] *Notices et Extraits*, ii, 113; Birch, *Memoirs*, i, 315-16, 328-9; Birch, *View*, 29-36.

support to Henry at this time, the vexation in the latter country at the demand for Calais, " which doth so much touch the heart of France," and at the refusal to join in a formal conference, are all reflected in the correspondence of the English ministers as the year 1595 approached its end.

The danger of a separate peace between France and Spain that would leave England to bear the brunt of the war alone, or at most with the help of the Netherlanders, had thus emerged into full recognition during these autumn months of 1595. The pressure exerted upon the king at home and the repellant attitude of Elizabeth seemed likely to raise this possibility into a certainty. Statesmen of various countries looked forward to such a break with dread or anticipation as the case might be. Essex who deplored the queen's chaffering policy and would gladly have again led troops across the Channel in support of the French king, with or without payment, intimated to a friend on the continent as early as September 12th his expectation that Henry would transfer his alliance from England to Spain. Somewhat later the whole privy council met at Burghley's house in the Strand in much trouble of mind about news of an approaching separate peace. The English resident in France fully expected it. Correspondence from The Hague indicated Dutch anticipation that an accommodation would soon be made between France and Spain, and an English fugitive in Antwerp reported that thousands of ducats were being wagered by the Flemish nobles that they and the Spaniards would be at peace with France and perhaps with their northern Netherlands enemies within a twelvemonth. Henry himself wrote to La Fontaine that the queen's good will toward him had evidently diminished, that it would be more honorable and more advantageous to him to compound with his enemies than to purchase friends too dear, and indeed that he must either lose his kingdom or make an accord with Spain. Thus the year 1595 drew to its close with every indication that the insistent national interests

of France, left unsupported by England, would force Henry
to an early separate peace with Spain and that England
would thus be isolated.[9]

A second factor which had entered into the international
relations of England since 1594 was the vastly increased
strength of the United Netherlands. Without acknowledgment of their independence by their Spanish master, with
but partial and grudging recognition of their right to fight
for it by the English queen, with only precarious military
success, the Netherlanders of the northern provinces had,
nevertheless, become, largely by their economic development,
virtually a nation. Little submissive as their tone had ever
been toward Elizabeth, it became constantly less so. When
Bodley, the English representative, brought across in
August, 1595 the queen's demands for the repayment of
£700,000 of her long standing loans and her proposal that
the English contingent should now be withdrawn, the leading Dutch statesmen, even those well inclined to the project,
feared to bring it before the more popular provincial Estates
or the people themselves. These believed that they were assisting the queen in her war against Spain on approximately
equal terms, and felt little occasion for gratitude to her or
willingness to have her troops withdrawn. The queen
stormed at her representative, Bodley, when he came home
with an unsatisfactory reply, threatened to revoke her
troops and to expose the illdoing of the Estates to all Europe. Bodley was able to name to the Netherlands authorities the many provinces, districts, towns and forts they had
recently brought into obedience, to call to their attention
the great augmentation of their customs and tolls by means
of their fishing and traffic by sea, which was now expanding
to all regions, the populousness of their country and the
resort to it of foreigners. He used this as an argument for
their ability to pay the queen what they owed and to fight
their own battles, but their pride grew with their power and

[9] Birch, *Memoirs*, i, 297, 301, 305, 222. *Sydney Papers*, i, 375, 378;
Birch, *View*, 25–6.

he discovered that these facts rather called to their attention their country's growing strength and independence than inclined them to yield payment or advantages to their great neighbor.[10]

The clearest indication, however, of the larger part the Netherlands were playing in international affairs was the help in money, men and supplies they were now able to give to Henry. At the very beginning of Henry's campaign of 1595 the States General had sent 2000 men under Philip of Nassau to aid him in expelling the Spaniards from Luxemburg. This contingent did valuable service under the duke of Bouillon in that rather unsatisfactory campaign, but in April, under the claim that they could not endure the air of that country any longer, and moreover that their time had expired, they were suddenly withdrawn into Zealand. Somewhat later partial amends were made by the Estates by sending to Bouillon some money and 30,000 weight of powder. When the news of the collapse of the French invasion and the rapid advance of the Spaniards into Picardy came, Henry, at the same time he sent his appeal for aid to Elizabeth, wrote from Lyons to the United Provinces, asking them to send 3000 men to meet him at the frontier to help raise the siege of Cambrai. He declared he would do the same for them in similar circumstances and that their refusal would indicate less affection between them than he believed to exist. In this letter he addressed the Estates in a tone of confidence and equality, referred to his ambassador resident with them, and used all the forms of courtesy and recognition usual in diplomatic correspondence. It is evident that he looked upon the United Netherlands as already an independent power in Europe. In this particular case their assent to the king's request was prompt but its fulfilment dilatory. Although he sent fresh messages of appeal from Paris, and although it was reported in the middle of September that the Estates had arranged to send twenty companies to the king, no troops reached him till

[10] Birch, *Memoirs*, i, 285–6, 288–9; *Sydney Papers*, i, 346.

after Cambrai had fallen. In fact the Netherlanders, though successful in some other fields, during this summer suffered continuing bad fortune in the aggressive military operations they had undertaken in the south and were in no position to spare troops for Henry's defense.[11]

Late in October, however, the promised supplies came. Two thousand Netherlands troops, money enough to pay two thousand more of Henry's own troops levied in France, and a considerable amount of provisions reached the king in time to be used during the long winter siege of La Fère. Before the end of November the Estates had spent £20,000 in his aid and he spoke of them as " the best of all his friends." The troops under La Noue that the Estates were paying for were especially well armed and disciplined and formed the best part of Henry's rather nondescript army before La Fère. In December the king's ambassador assured the Netherlands leaders, what he had secretly avoided assuring Elizabeth, that under no circumstances would he make peace or an agreement with the king of Spain without their knowledge and liking; he consulted them about future campaigns; and continued to urge a closer and closer union. He was unable to refrain in his letters to Elizabeth deploring her unwillingness to give him any help from speaking of the comfort he had obtained by the assistance sent him by the Estates. The queen's comment on this was that if the Estates were rich enough to send supplies to Henry they ought to be able to afford to pay her what they owed her. But her ill-humor at this diversion of funds, like her anger at their neglect of her request for settlement of the old accounts, gradually yielded to her satisfaction with their readiness to further her plans for the Cadiz expedition.[12]

The exigency of the queen's demands for repayment and

[11] *Lettres Missives,* iv, 311, 403-5, 416; Birch, *Memoirs,* i, 240-1, 261, 278-9, 289, 299; *Sydney Papers,* i, 346; Poirson, ii, 11, 13, 15, 17, 131.

[12] *Sydney Papers,* i, 378; Murdin, *Burghley Papers,* 715; *Lettres Missives,* iv, 432, 486, 494; Birch, *Memoirs,* i, 212, 328-9, 330, 334; Meteren, xviii, 383, DuVair, *Advis sur la Constitution de l'Estat d'Angleterre,* 1173.

her desire for release of her garrison troops in the Netherlands, however, indicate an embryonic or instinctive recognition on her part and that of her ministers that a free, independent and ambitious nation directly across the Channel might ultimately be a source of danger to England's commercial ambitions. Henry, on the other hand, less in dread of such a conflict of interests and more generous and enlightened in his general policy, not only treated the Low Countries in a more friendly spirit but warned Elizabeth against bringing pressure upon them at this time to repay her loans for fear of strengthening their already existing dislike.

During the discussions connected with Henry's unsuccessful appeals for help from Elizabeth and but partial and delayed reinforcements from the Netherlands, there gradually developed the proposition which especially characterized the year 1596; that is to say, a plan for a definite alliance of the three countries in their opposition to Spain, to which other opponents of Spain should also be admitted if they could be so persuaded. In October 1595 an English courtier pointed out that a separate peace between France and Spain would as surely divide France from the Netherlands as from England, and that the king could best be upheld not by either of those countries alone but " by a concurrency of both their forces." Henry, he believed, would gladly make an agreement to bind all three powers, so that " holding always together they might be a balance against the Spanish greatness." There was another inducement to such a close alliance. The Huguenots in France, now that the king was a Catholic, naturally turned their eyes abroad, and one of the most influential of their number expressed to Cecil his hope for a league of the Netherlands, England and France that would guarantee the safety of Protestantism against the rising tide of conformity. When Vere was in England at the beginning of the year Essex confided to him his intention of urging the queen to agree to such a league, and when the English general returned to the

Netherlands and mentioned the project to the French minister and Dutch statesmen he found universal approval.[13]

There was of course little that was new about this plan. The countries were already allied two by two, England and France, England and the Netherlands, the Netherlands and France. A single alliance would simply join the three sides of the triangle. It was besides an old project of Henry's, suggested when he made his first treaty with Elizabeth, in September, 1589, and it always remained a part of his policy. To whatever extent Henry may have been responsible for the traditional "great design," the plan of a general alliance of as many European states as possible for large common ends was always as attractive to him as it was antipathetic to the somewhat provincial mind of Elizabeth. Just at this time, however, the plan of a definite triple alliance among the three adjacent states could hardly fail to appeal to them all.

[13] Birch, *View*, 27; *Sydney Papers*, i, 344–5; *Cal. Hatfield House MSS.*, vi, 6, 90; Birch, *Memoirs*, i, 397.

CHAPTER XXX

THE SECOND EMBASSY OF SIR HENRY UNTON

WHEN the year 1596 opened, therefore, the new conditions of the problem of the relations of England, France and the Netherlands were comparatively clear. The likelihood of a separate alliance of France with Spain was recognized by both the English and the Dutch governments; the growing power, indeed the practical independence of the United Netherlands, made them a more important factor in all negotiations than they had been in the past; the possibility and the value of a union of the three countries on something like equal terms was in the minds of statesmen of all three lands. It was the work of the year to attempt a practical embodiment of these conditions, to substitute for the former alliances a single alliance which should bind all three at least formally in one common opposition to Spain and should, it was hoped, become the nucleus of a larger league.

Circumstances were such as to demand some prompt action. The new governor of the Spanish Netherlands, the cardinal archduke of Austria, was slowly making his way northward from Geneva through Savoy and the border provinces, with reinforcements of men and money for the Spaniards in Flanders, and Henry was already in the second month of the long and doubtful siege of La Fère in Picardy not far from the Flemish border. No means exist for tracing changes in Elizabeth's mind, but even before the end of 1595, as indicated in the letter she had sent to Henry after Loménie's embassy, she had begun to see the necessity of placating the king, although she had not as yet decided to send him succor. She now determined to send again to

France perhaps the ablest and best trained ambassador in her service, Sir Henry Unton. One of the English ministers writes to a friend, " We are now dispatching Sir Henry Unton to the French king hoping to direct him from a course with Spain." The effort was to dissuade him " from making peace with Spain, which most of his council, doubting English help, persuade him to." Another declares, " I pray God he come not too late to do good." In addition to Unton's instructions from the queen Essex intrusted him with a series of suggestions that, in view of the close relations of patron and follower between them, amounted almost to another set of instructions, though secret and unauthorized. Unton according to these, was to discover Henry's real intentions and to impress upon him the desirability of forcing the queen's hand by a continued show of dissatisfaction. But this doubly secret diplomacy lay so much in the line of Henry's own inclinations and indeed of the queen's intentions that it had little real importance. Early in January Unton arrived in the camp of the king before La Fère, instructed to give assurances of the queen's friendship, to ward off the danger of a separate peace and to arrange for a conference of English and French plenipotentiaries.[1]

He had a difficult task. Within five months Elizabeth had twice denied succor to the French king, had refused the proposed conference of ministers of the two powers, had offended the national feeling of the French by asking again for the occupation of Calais, and had dismissed the French ambassador Loménie with what both he and his sovereign felt to be scant courtesy. Moreover he had no concessions to offer except a belated agreement to hold a joint conference of envoys. It is no wonder he approached his work without enthusiasm and was " sorry he had nothing more agreeable to say " to the French councillors. He made his residence at Coucy near La Fère for the next three months so as to be near the king. Henry was away on a short

---

[1] *Sydney Papers,* 378, 396; Birch, *Memoirs,* i, 353, 392, 394.

journey at his arrival but returned January 9th, and Unton succeeded, with some difficulty, in obtaining an audience the next day. He found the king surrounded with considerable state; guards ranged in order about the hall, with numerous councillors and nobles present, all very different from the old rough and simple camp life when Unton had attended him five years before at the siege of Rouen. The ambassador presented the queen's letters and then proceeded to make the best and fullest statement of the English position practicable. He explained the necessity for the withdrawal of the English troops from Brittany the year before and the inability of the queen to grant the succor for Picardy recently asked through Barrauderie and Loménie; he described the queen's offense at the ." insolent carriage " of the last named ambassador, and her surprise and incredulity at the news that had come to England through an Italian pamphlet that the king was contemplating a private peace with Spain. He stated his belief that the queen would now be willing to enter into a conference as the king had formerly suggested, and doubtless to give him any other satisfaction in the power of an affectionate ally, who was however too much surrounded by dangers and burdened by expenses to send troops out of her own country. Henry read the queen's letters and listened to the ambassador's speech patiently, but replied that he was sorry the queen could not help him, that he had hoped there would be something more substantial in the message the ambassador brought, that such a fruitless assurance seemed rather intended to do him a scorn than anything else, and that he could not allow himself to be amused by mere words when he looked daily to be attacked by a new Spanish army.

Notwithstanding Henry's personal regard and even fondness for Unton, he spoke to him with a " countenance far different " from of old, mentioned that he was treating him with more respect than his ambassador had received in England, adverted sarcastically to the little honor Unton enjoyed in bringing such a hollow message, and finally referred him to his council, and "so dismissed him." The next day's conference with the five members of the king's council deputed to meet with him was no more satisfactory. To their complaints that he had nothing to offer except a proposal for further discussions and a possible new treaty, which would cause delay while the circumstances of the king called for immediate action, he had nothing to reply.

The next day the council sent him the king's formal answer to his messages. Henry simply recapitulated his causes of complaint; that although the treaties between France and England bound them to help one another in need, Elizabeth had refused to send help the last summer though his need was so great and Picardy was so near her own dominions that he had expected she would be the more ready to fulfill her engagements. He pointed out that the queen need not have sent over another ambassador, as he had nothing new to say except to suggest a conference of their ministers, which the queen had declined when he proposed it some months before, and which looked suspicious now as tending only to delay and keeping the king in hope, while what he needed was immediate succor in men and means, not conferences, treaties and delays. As the queen says she cannot help him, he will desist asking her, and seek another plan to relieve the desperate straits of his country. If the queen appeals to the promise of 1593, that neither will make peace without the other, he can only say that he will do his best to keep it, but since it provided for mutual assistance, and the queen has left him now for some time with the whole burden of the war, he is not bound to do things beyond his strength. The safety of his realm is the first consideration.[2]

Unton transmitted this formal reply of the king directly to the queen, but feeling somewhat humiliated by the tone used by the councillors in his meeting with them, pressed for a more private and personal interview with Henry. This he finally obtained a week after the first presentation

[2] Murdin, 701–6; *Cal. Hatfield House MSS.*, vi, 11–12, 17.

of his letters. After the king had sent all others out of his cabinet he made Unton sit down by him, dropped his formality, recalled occurrences of his previous embassy, fell into the cordial manners of his old soldierly days, and proceeded to make his own complaints against the queen, and give Unton an opportunity to say what he wished. The former were the familiar ones; the queen had treated his last ambassador unkindly, she had uttered contemptuous words about the king himself, she had recalled all her troops in Brittany and Normandy, she had demanded Calais, she had refused the conference Henry had proposed, she had never fully accepted the treaties between England and France, signed before Henry's time. He admitted that he had about decided to make peace with Spain and hoped the queen would not condemn him if his miserable state forced him to an unpleasing yet necessary remedy. Unton hinted, as he had lately been instructed in a letter from Cecil, that the queen might be included in this treaty if the king really made it. Henry said he had urged this project already, but that the pope who was the special instigator of the treaty, would not hear of it. The king declared that he did not really want to make a treaty with Spain but " desyred a streight counter league with her Majesty and the States of the Low Countryes and with the Princes of Germany and Italye, whereby better to bridle the ambition of Spayne." But the pressure for peace was great, the new governor of the Netherlands was " bringing warre and peace with him," and the king, like the French generally, believed that the English proposals for a further conference were merely dilatory. After two hours of this somewhat intimate intercourse, the king ended wearily but without passion, and Unton withdrew, " much cast down in mynd " and " infynytely discontented," as he wrote to Essex the same evening.[3]

A call by the ambassador the next day on the king's sister only made it more clear how constantly Henry was

[3] Murdin, 706, 707–11; *Cal. Hatfield House MSS.*, vi, 16–17.

solicited by his councillors to make peace with Spain. This lady was a Huguenot and dreaded the bad effect of such a peace on those of " the religion," and therefore favored a continuance of the alliance with England. This attitude was even more strongly represented by the duke of Bouillon, with whom Unton had a private conference at about the same time. Bouillon acknowledged to him that his fellow Protestants were sorely troubled at their prospects. A treaty of peace between the Catholic kings of France and Spain, negotiated through the influence of the pope, would leave the Protestants of France but slight hope of a continuation of their present liberty. He disclosed to Unton a determination on their part that if they were not better treated by the council than at present and if freedom of worship was not guaranteed to them by the king, they would " stand upon their strength," recommence the old religious wars, and try to secure separate support from Elizabeth and the other Protestant princes and states of Europe. Rather than do so, however, he appealed to Unton to use all his influence with the queen to help the king with her forces so that Henry might avoid entering into a treaty with Spain. This policy would be " more honorable and more safe for the queen and less chargeable " than to aid the Huguenots later against the king.[4]

It is just possible that this obscure negotiation was only one of the schemes of Henry to put pressure on the queen to send troops to his assistance. His policy was sometimes even more tortuous than Elizabeth's, and the course of events prevented either the disclosing or the ripening of any such plan. But Unton was thoroughly convinced of the probability, indeed the almost inevitable forming of a separate peace. Everything combined to force the king to it. All but six of his council urged it, the pope guaranteed honorable terms from Spain, the country was weary of war and clamored for peace, there was great misery in all France, the king had borrowed on all the taxes and the

[4] Murdin, 705.

bonds for these loans were overdue, the expenses of keeping up garrisons and troops in the field were crushing, the siege of La Fère was a doubtful one, and a new Spanish army was approaching whose arrival would probably cause the withdrawal of the Dutch contingent then with Henry. An English visitor in Paris remarks that " The prattlings of the people are generally to desire peace, be it with never so dishonorable conditions, their present necessities urging them to leave the boast of their ancient valor, and to seek capitulation with their greatest enemies." [5]   In the meantime a new French ambassador to the Netherlands was waiting for some possible favorable outcome from the English mission before going to The Hague to see how the Estates would take the proposition of a peace between France and Spain that might obtain some favorable terms for them.   The Dutch resident at Paris was being sounded at the same time by the Spanish party as to the terms of peace the Netherlands would accept.   The intensification of any one of these difficulties in January and February of 1596 would, at least in the opinion of the king's secretary Villeroy, make all France rise against the king unless he made peace with Spain.   Unton was in despair, yet he received no encouraging decision from home; — indeed for almost six weeks he had no instructions of any kind, and feeling became constantly more bitter in France at the English coldness and delay.   The king doubts whether he ought to wait longer and fears that if he is forced to give up La Fère he will get poorer terms from Spain and from England, but declares he does not intend to send an ambassador again to England to be despised as others have been.   Villeroy warns a Frenchman in England that if the queen is holding back till she can make profit by their necessity and force them to receive Englishmen into their cities as masters, she is much mistaken.   One would rather be injured by a foe than a friend.   The English ambassador writes to Essex from Coucy February 4, " If the queen

does not in time apply a remedy, *actum est*." Henry even
loses faith for a while in the good feeling of Essex toward
him, and believes that he also is waiting till the affairs of
the king become still worse to obtain Calais and Boulogne.
In the efforts to ward off this possibility, Henry wrote to
the Estates again declaring his intention of uniting himself
with them more closely than ever and urging them to continue their contingent and the pay of the two Dutch supported French regiments at least till the fall of La Fère.
To this, after the usual delay, he received a favorable
reply.[6]

A letter from Cecil sending a picture of the queen which
Unton was to use in such a way as to impress the king with
her good feelings toward him, and one from the queen to
Henry suggesting, apparently, that he come to England to
visit her, led to an interview in which Unton presented the
queen's letter; but this brought no result except a sudden
outburst of anger on Henry's part and a tirade against the
English ministers whom he believed to be blocking his
plans. Unton learned from some of the council that the
king had momentarily thought well of going to England, but
had been dissuaded by the assurance that the English would
in all probability seize his person for objects of their own.
During an hour's walk in the king's garden, at another time,
in which Henry placed Unton on one side of him and his
mistress, Gabrielle d'Estrées on the other and chatted on
all subjects, Unton showed the queen's picture and Henry
captured it after some playful wrestling. Unton sent to
the queen a pleasant description of this garden scene, in
which, remembering to whom he was writing, he did not
fail to depreciate the fair Gabrielle, but the interview had
no other outcome.[7]

At the end of February, Unton at last received a batch
of long delayed letters from England including the queen's

[6] Murdin, 705; *Cal. Hatfield House MSS.*, vi, 54–5; Birch, *Memoirs,*
i, 404; *Lettres Missives*, iv, 486.
[7] Murdin, 717–19, 724; Birch, *Memoirs*, i, 422.

reply to the king's letter handed him at the beginning of his mission. There followed a repetition of the experiences of that time. He obtained a private interview with the king in his chamber, in which all left the room except four or five councillors who gathered at its lower end. The queen's letter was very long and Henry called his secretary to read it to him, but as she dilated on her own troubles and necessities, Henry showed more and more discontent, and finally interrupted to say that he did not desire to contend with his good sister, that these were mere words, while his necessities were real. Unton urged him to listen to the latter part of the letter where the queen speaks more at large of a conference, and pointed out to the king that if a stricter amity were in this way tied the queen would afterward hardly allow him to receive hurt for want of help. Henry gave little evidence of acquiescence or satisfaction and Unton remained discouraged. Afterwards, however, the king seems to have made up his mind to accept the queen's suggestion, and to have told Unton of his intention and suggested Abbeville or Boulogne as the place of meeting of a conference, since to meet at Calais was too closely bound up with rumors of English ambitions.

Unton's health, however, was poor, and he was soon afterward attacked by the prevailing camp fever. He received the best of medical attention from the king's own physicians. They gave him "*confectio alcarmas*, compounded of musk, amber, gold, and unicorn's horn, with pigeons applied to his side." Nevertheless he died on the 23d of March at Coucy. On his very deathbed, the ambassador assured the king, who visited him to comfort him in his sickness and to find the real intention of the queen, that he believed the queen was in earnest and really meant to draw the bonds of mutual help closer.[8]

Unton could have had little else than his loyalty to serve as a basis for such an asseveration at such a time, for he had just received news which he did not disclose to the

[8] *Cal. Hatfield House MSS.*, vi, 80, 81-4, 103, 112; Murdin, 729, 730-3.

king that the queen was to withdraw 2000 of the English troops from the Netherlands for the Cadiz voyage. Scarcely had the decision to postpone negotiations with Spain and to resume them with England been made by the king after this conference when this news almost drove Henry and his councillors again to the belief that the queen was luring them on only to deceive them at last. To send an English army to Spain, especially to withdraw English troops from the Netherlands to form it, seemed to the French king merely a betrayal. It made his own supply of troops from England much less likely, it made more probable the withdrawal of the Dutch troops in his own service in order to protect their own territories from the Spaniards, and it would set free Spanish-Flemish troops to work their will in his border provinces. All this Henry recited to Elizabeth in a letter, primarily sent with condolences on the death of Unton but directed largely to the dissuasion of Elizabeth from sending an army to the distant shores of Spain. Henry had nevertheless by this time fully determined to draw what advantage he could from the more conciliatory attitude of the queen. He had decided upon this policy at least as early as his interview with Unton on his death-bed, though from consideration for his councillors he did not declare it till they had discussed and agreed to it. It was a decision of some moment since it meant putting an end, at least for the time, to all plans for a peace with Spain. On the 28th of March Henry announced that he intended within four or five days to send an ambassador, Sancy, over to " open his heart " to the queen on the subject of a conference.

Before more than two of these days had elapsed, Sancy had another message to take to England. The Spaniards unexpectedly established themselves before the walls of Calais, and threatened by a sudden attack to wrest it from the French, much as the French themselves had seized it from the English thirty-eight years before. The danger to Calais put a whole new face on the negotiations between Henry and Elizabeth. The immediate mission of Sancy was transformed from the preparation for a formal and deliberate conference to be held at some later time, to an immediate and pressing demand for succor to prevent the fall of the city in which both sovereigns took such an intense interest.[9]

[9] *Lettres Missives,* iv, 355–9; Birch, *Memoirs,* i, 450.

CHAPTER XXXI

THE CAPTURE OF CALAIS

A N attack upon Calais from the Spanish Netherlands had been anticipated by careful observers for some time, though it had not led to any adequate preparation of the city to withstand a siege. The actual attack was due to the arrival of the Spanish governor of the Netherlands with the reinforcements which had been so many months on their way overland from the Mediterranean. Archduke Albert of Austria, the new governor, the same prince who as governor of Portugal had with such inadequate forces faced Drake and Norris at Lisbon in 1589, arrived at Brussels on the first of February, 1596. He left the army he had brought with him for the time back of the Meuse, and there during the next six weeks he collected all available troops from Flanders and Hainault, concentrating them at Valenciennes. Henry, still engaged with his main force in the siege of La Fère in Picardy, took it for granted that the archduke with his reinforced army would attack him there and was making strenuous efforts to capture that city before it was relieved.

The Spanish commander, however, suddenly struck north instead of south and an advance detachment appeared, March 30th, before the walls of Calais. By the end of the next day the Spanish general had brought up his artillery and seized the fort of Rysbank controlling the entrance to Calais harbor, making it difficult, if not impossible, to introduce reinforcements from either of Henry's maritime allies, England or the Netherlands. A new danger to France, to England and the Netherlands threatened, a base for a Spanish fleet on the Narrow Seas. The English could not

fail to be most deeply interested. The news reached England immediately. Essex, who, it will be remembered, was
already engaged in the levy and equipment of men, ships
and supplies for the Cadiz expedition, hastened down from
London to Dover, and early in the morning of the 3rd of
April sent his friend, Sir Conyers Clifford, across the Channel in a small vessel to see whether the harbor of Calais
could still be entered. One of his ensigns promised to swim
in if it could be entered no other way. Howard had already
sent orders to Sir Henry Palmer, vice admiral, to draw up
the Channel and obtain information of the state of affairs.
Palmer was outside the harbor by midnight.[1]

The Dutch were equally prompt. The danger from Spanish possession of Calais was perhaps greater for them than
for England, for it would interfere seriously with the passage of their merchant ships to the southward through the
Channel. They had long feared just such a Spanish surprise. Orders were therefore immediately sent from The
Hague to get supplies and ammunition to the garrison of
Calais, plans were made to send reinforcements of troops,
and the French ambassador in Holland sent an encouraging
reply to Vidosan, the governor of Calais, in answer to his
hurried letter of information of his straits. The English
messengers from Essex and Lord Howard, therefore, found
twelve Dutch ships already lying in Calais roads, but like
themselves unable to enter the harbor. They got into communication, however, with the governor, and secured his
statement of the position of the enemy, his appeals for help
and promise to admit into the city whatever succors should
be sent.

It seemed but a natural plan to make use of the shipping already prepared, the commissions already in the hands
of Essex and Howard, and the English soldiers who could
be so quickly gathered to aid the French in resisting the

[1] *Cal. Hatfield House MSS.*, vi, 52, 124, 132; *Sydney Papers*, i, 379;
Birch, *Memoirs*, i, 405; Murdin, 722; Demotier, *Annales de Calais*, 120-5,
149-55.

common foe. It was the first thought of the French ambassador in the Netherlands that the Cadiz preparations would be diverted to this end. Even Burghley, normally disinclined to bold action, after lying awake all night suffering from the gout and worrying about the news which had just come from Calais wrote to Cecil in the morning saying that troops ought to be taken over immediately by Essex and Howard, " for England may not endure this town to be Spanish." [2]

Henry, his army too far away and too deeply engaged in the siege of La Fère to be moved as a whole, hastened to Boulogne with his own regiment and 500 horse, hoping to throw reinforcements into the city either by sea or land. But when with a group of nobles he embarked hoping to get into the town, he was driven back by the wind. Two small detachments of troops succeeded in getting into the town by way of the dunes. While Sancy was pressing Elizabeth with appeals for immediate succor, Essex, all on fire with anxiety to lead English troops across the Channel and promising to transport in some way or other as many as the queen will send or the governor admit, was sending one letter on the heels of another to the council, Burghley, Cecil, Howard, Henry. On the 4th of April, he hurried to court at Greenwich, intending to plead in person with the queen for haste, but met just before Canterbury letters indicating, as he believed, that the queen was " nobly resolved " to send her troops to the relief of the beleaguered city. He therefore returned to Dover to go on with the work of collecting supplies, appointing officers, studying the map of Calais, and " preparing stratagems " for getting his men into the city. The queen in fact seemed at first inclined to proceed promptly. The need for promptness was certainly great. On Wednesday, April 7, the governor having but 600 men and being on bad terms with the burghers at best, abandoned the city itself to the besiegers, agreed

[2] Lodge, *Times of Queen Elizabeth*, ii, 459, 460; Birch, *Memoirs*, i, 335, 373, 398.

to take no hostile action for six days unless help should come, and retired to the citadel, sending word to Henry that he could hold out there several days and might still preserve the fortress if help were sent him. But the queen, although apparently she intended to send the troops, could not resist the temptation to gain an advantage from the sudden exigency and utilize the opportunity to obtain the entrance of her troops into the long coveted city across the Narrow Seas. When Sancy arrived in London, therefore, Saturday, April 10, he was received by the council with a half-promise to send troops, but his interview with the queen was postponed till the next day, Sunday, at Greenwich. In the meantime, Saturday night, she sent Sir Henry Sydney with a letter across the Channel to Henry, to say as so often before that she would send the troops if Calais when rescued should be left for the time in her hands.[3]

Sancy's interview with the council on Saturday had its own difficulties, for coincident with his arrival had come a story that Calais had surrendered. Taking his reputation for truthfulness in his hands, the envoy, according to his own story, assured the ministers of the queen that it was only the town that had fallen, that he had certain news that the citadel was still holding out and that the captain had promised to hold it till succors arrived. This statement, so far as Sancy's knowledge went, was a deliberate falsehood, but as a matter of fact, a French messenger, De Champers, arrived at court that evening, having been sent from the French king from St. Valéry on Thursday with a message to that very effect. At the next day's interview Sancy got the impression from the queen, as he had from others, that troops were being embarked and that Sydney had been sent over to assure the king of that fact. The queen said nothing about the conditions she had imposed on the king, but remarked casually that when she had asked for Calais some

[3] Devereux, *Lives of the Devereux, Earls of Essex*, i, 335; *Cal. State Papers, Dom.*, 1595-7, 196-201; *Cal. Hatfield House MSS.*, vi, 132, 134; Demotier, *Annales de Calais*, 150-2.

months before it was with no intention of keeping it but only to prevent seizure by the Spaniards while the French king was so far away that he could not protect it. The ambassador, having blundered into the truth the day before, blundered out of it again by sending a messenger to cheer the king with the news that succors were already on their way.[4]

In the meantime, the queen's changeableness was maddening to all concerned. On Thursday, the 8th, she gave orders for the levying of 6000 men from the trained bands of the five southeastern counties and London, to be ready at Dover on Sunday night, the 11th, at the latest. Before this levy could be made in the usual way, on Friday, the 9th, Good Friday, while the lord mayor and aldermen were listening to a sermon at Paul's Cross, they were suddenly summoned by messengers from the privy council and ordered to press into the service 1000 men to be sent immediately to Dover. This was done before evening, and by Saturday morning the London contingent were all under arms. In the afternoon of Saturday, however, they with those that had been levied in the counties were discharged and sent to their homes, on the ground that news had come that Calais had fallen and they would therefore be too late.

Even Burghley is shocked at the sudden decision to withdraw the troops and fears that " these so many changes will breed hard opinion of counsell." On Sunday morning the court wind at Greenwich had changed and the troops were summoned again. The orders to London would seem to have come at very inopportune times from a devotional point of view, though the task of the press officers was certainly made easier thereby, for at ten o'clock on Easter morning when all good people in London were in their parish churches about to receive communion, the aldermen of the various wards with their deputies and constables were

---

[4] *Oeuvres de Messire Guillaume DuVair*, Ed. 1625; 3–4; *Negotiations de MM. de Bouillon et de Sancy en Angleterre en 1596, MSS. de Brienne*, 37, quoted in Gaillard, *Notices et Extraits*, ii, 116, 118–19.

ordered to close the church doors and proceed to select the necessary men for the impressment. This was done by twelve o'clock, and the soldiers proceeded to equip themselves and start for Dover again, while the remainder of the population returned to their church services or their Sunday dinners.[5]

On the same day Essex seems to have come up from Dover, spent the afternoon and evening at court, and started back at midnight provided with the queen's reluctant but definite orders to take 6000 men across with him to the relief of Calais. There were now at Dover nine transports; shortly afterward six more appeared and anchored in the road and troops soon began to gather from London and the nearby counties. Tuesday the 13th, a commission was made out and sent to Essex. His instructions, however, included many restrictions. Calais must be delivered to the queen to be held until she was repaid for her expenses in assisting Henry during the last seven years. The English troops must be used for no purpose except the succor of Calais; and only then on the king's providing an army of some strength so that the English might be used as auxiliaries not as principals. Essex must also leave behind him the eager group of court nobles who had been gathering at Dover, except such as could show special permission from the queen to go on the expedition. It is no wonder that Essex complained that the queen's instructions " bound his hands behind him." Another difficulty soon appeared. In making these arrangements the queen had overestimated Henry's appreciation of his difficulties and willingness to come to her terms. When Sydney delivered his message, the king turned his back on the ambassador and replied in an epigram that has come down to us in various forms, no one of which may be authentic, but any one of which fairly enough described the case. He " would as leave be bitten by a dog as scratched by a cat "; " It would be no worse to

[5] *Acts of the Privy Council*, xxv, 338–9, 340;. Stow, *Annals*, Ed. 1605, 1281–2; *Cal. Hatfield House MSS.*, vi, 138, 141.

be bitten by a lion than a lioness "; " It would be more disgraceful to be plundered by friends than by enemies." [6]

The eagerness of Elizabeth to regain Calais and the shifts to which she had gone to obtain control over it have been repeatedly adverted to. In 1563 an attempt had been made to bribe the French governor and his councillors to deliver Calais into English hands, and thirty of the conspirators had as a result been hung by the French king from the windows of the city hall. In 1595, as already mentioned, another attempt had been made to obtain it in return for help to be given by English troops. In the meantime, Brest, St.Malo, Paimpol, Morlaix, Hourdel, Harfleur, Rélane, had been spoken of or utilized at one time or another as English cities of occupation; but Calais was after all the special object of English desire, and attempts to secure it were not to cease even with this occasion. Henry, on the other hand, shared to the full the fear widely felt in France that a city on the French side of the Channel once in the hands of the English could with difficulty be recovered. When the report of Sydney's demands got back to England or were disclosed there in the instructions of Essex, Sancy was bold enough to point out to the queen that it would be better for the French king to let the Spaniards capture Calais than to hand it over to the English, for he could hope to win it back from the former, but if he demanded its return from the queen, she would be offended and then instead of having one enemy he would have two. [7]

Henry, however, with his usual diplomatic address, sent Sydney back on Tuesday with a letter to the queen in which he gently expresses his inability to believe, whatever Sydney might say, that the queen would be willing to measure their friendship by the advantages that might accrue from it to her. He begs her not to bring shame upon him and even

[6] *Cal. State Papers, Dom.*, 1595–7, 509; Birch, i, 465.

[7] *Cal. State Papers, Dom.*, 1597–7, 202–3; *Lambeth MSS.*, 250, quoted in Corbett, *Successors of Drake*, 40–43; Demotier, *Annales de Calais*, 153, 157; Birch, *Memoirs*, i, 465; *Notices et Extraits*, ii, 120–2.

lay some touch on her own reputation by refusing him succor in a case of such extremity except on terms that he could not honorably grant; and he closes by asking again for the immediate dispatch of Essex with the troops, " very humbly kissing your beautiful and happy hands which hold the keys of my good fortune." [8]

Whatever the beauty and the power of the queen's hands, those of Essex, while she awaited the return of Sydney, were still tied behind him. Although his commission had been signed, although the troops were at the seaside and the transports ready, although from Dover, and even from the court at Greenwich, the cannon could be heard all day battering the citadel at Calais, although Sancy at Greenwich was assuring the queen that his " hair stood on end " to think of the evils if Calais should fall, although a message came from Boulogne that the king was standing on the quay watching for the coming of the English and had sent word to the governor of the citadel that he would hang him if he surrendered before succor came, yet the queen for twenty-four hours more held back permission to sail. Essex writes at ten o'clock on Tuesday morning, at noon, and again at nine o'clock in the evening, and again on the morning of Wednesday, in desperation at lying inactive almost in sight of the French king and, as he declares, to the scorn of all Christendom and to his own lasting personal disgrace.

At midnight, he writes in deep depression that although Sir Robert Sydney has come back to plead with the queen and he himself is forwarding new letters from the French king, and although he can still hear the cannon from Calais, he has almost given up hope. This continued through Wednesday, but before Thursday morning the queen had decided to yield, and at last was delivered to Essex on his ship, the Due Repulse, the queen's letter, written in her own hand, permitting him to start, but warning him to be more than careful and not to peril so fair an army for another prince's town. By daylight the embarkation of the

[8] *Lettres Missives*, iv, 573-4, 575.

troops began and long before Thursday night they were ready to weigh anchor.

But since ten o'clock in the morning there had been an ominous silence from Calais, and in the afternoon a French gentleman brought over word that on that very day, Thursday, the 15th, the citadel had been surrendered. There was nothing to be done. The next day Essex himself carried the news to the queen, and on Saturday the troops were ordered to their home counties and discharged. The Dutch fleet, which during the whole siege had been lying in Calais roads with a thousand soldiers aboard ready to help in the relief of the city, sailed away and landed its troops in Zealand. Calais was occupied by a Spanish garrison and placed under a Spanish captain. Ardres near by was soon afterward captured, and these towns remained in Spanish hands for two years till in 1598 they were returned to France by the fourteenth article of the Treaty of Vervins.[9]

The populace of London, panic-stricken by the proximity of a permanent Spanish force, threatened to rise in revolt. Their reproaches of the councillors of the queen for indolence or treachery form one of the few recorded instances of popular criticism of the actions of government during this time. The same events roused an old soldier, Sir Henry Knyvett, to write a little book, *The Defense of the Realme*, which he finished on the 19th of April, 1596, five days after the surrender of Calais, according to his own note, but which lay unprinted for three hundred and ten years, until in 1906 a similar threat of danger from across the Narrow Seas awakened sufficient interest to lead to its publication. The queen herself apparently realized that she owed some explanation to her people, for she ordered the lords lieutenants of the southeastern shires to thank their counties for their readiness to send troops and to give them the following lucid explanation of the course of recent events;

[9] *Cal. Hatfield House MSS.*, xiii, Add. 570; *Lambeth MSS.*, 250, quoted in Corbett, *Successors of Drake*, 43; *Lives of the Devereux*, i, 336; Du-Vair, 4.

that her action had been taken upon information sent by the French king, which had proved to be variable and inconsistent with her majesty's intention. In France, Catholics and Huguenots alike bitterly reproached the English for their failure to come to the rescue of Calais, declaring that Essex had deserted them and that " the queen of England was making a mock of the king." On the other hand, the Spaniards, they said, had fought fairly, for after their capture of the city they had not slain a man. Indeed, French nobles and common people alike declared that they would rather the Spaniards had the town than the English, and that the king would do well to make peace with the king of Spain.[10]

[10] Birch, *Memoirs*, i, 466–70; Camden, Ed. 1688, 516; *Acts of the Privy Council*, xxv, 352; *Cal. State Papers, Dom.*, 1595-7, 203-5; DuVair, 4, 7.

CHAPTER XXXII

THE TRIPLE ALLIANCE

THE king had determined, notwithstanding the loss of Calais, not to make peace with the Spaniards, but to proceed with the conference in England, which had been arranged for partly by correspondence, partly through Sancy. On the 16th of April, the day after the fall of Calais, the duke of Bouillon, the principal personage in the French deputation, landed at Dover and passed on to Greenwich. There were now gathered in England an impressive group of French gentlemen and officials. Besides Sancy, the ambassador proper, who had already been in England for a week holding daily conferences with the queen and her councillors concerning the succors for Calais, and the Duc de Bouillon, the special envoy, conspicuous for his high rank, his title of marshal of France, and his leadership of the Huguenots, were the Sieur DuVair, one of Henry's council, to whose spirited narrative of the negotiations we owe most of our knowledge of their detail, the Sieur d'Ancel, who was later to go on from England to Germany to extend the league, the ex-ambassador Loménie, who came this time as little more than an adviser and messenger, and La Fontaine, the trusted pastor of the French Church in London. The English representatives were Burghley, Hunsdon, Cobham, Fortescue and Cecil. Essex and Howard, who would naturally have taken part, were, at least after the first few days of the negotiations, at Plymouth organizing the Cadiz expedition and hoping that the conclusions of the conference would not interfere with their projects. The conferences between these representatives of France and the English councillors extended over the whole month lying between the middle of April and the middle of May, and took place almost altogether at Greenwich, largely in a little pleasure house in the park.[1]

At the first session, Tuesday, April 20th, the French negotiators called attention to the fact that it was Elizabeth who had first proposed this closer alliance, though their coming now was due to the condition of the king's affairs which required a speedy decision. They then proposed an offensive and defensive alliance. Burghley adopted from the beginning and retained to the end a critical and even obstructive attitude. He reverted frequently to the king's desertion of Protestantism and the lessened interest in his fortunes this gave the queen and to the king's failure to repay the loans the queen had already made him. He dilated on the extent of the war the queen had already made on the king of Spain in the Netherlands, in France, in Ireland, in the West Indies, and was even then preparing to wage on the coast of Spain. He counted up the queen's expenditures and pointed out that Henry's risk of loss was less than hers. He expressed his surprise that the French envoys, instead of coming to thank her for what she had done, came to ask her to do more. When Sancy pointed out that the queen would have the use of the French harbors and their ships, Burghley murmured aside to his fellow councillors, "They are trying to sell us the bear's skin before they have killed the bear." The other English negotiators were completely subordinated to the old treasurer and took but little part in the discussions. It is evident that back of Burghley stood the queen, at least for the early part of the negotiations. In her formal interviews she pressed her questions of what Henry had to offer her from his side in the alliance and what reason she had to expect his promises would be better kept this time than on earlier occasions. The opportunity was taken to lay before the envoys detailed statements of earlier loans to the king still owing.

The Frenchmen controlled their resentment at the atti-

[1] *State Papers, Foreign, France,* xxxvii, 185, 190.

tude of queen and council, avoided so far as possible
answering specific objections, and put the claims of the
desirability of an alliance on more general grounds. To
allow the king of France to be forced to make terms with
the king of Spain would leave England defenseless against
his subsequent attacks; the real object of Spanish attack
was not France but England and the Netherlands, and the
retention of France as a bulwark against this would be in
itself enough profit from the alliance; in matters of offense,
the territory and harbors of France could be advantageously
used by England in an attack on Spain. It is quite evident
that the French had in mind a much broader scheme than
the English queen or her councillors were willing to consider.
The ideal of a far-extending alliance, to include not only
England, France and the Netherlands, its original members, but the Protestant princes of Germany and even
some Italian states, a league whose members should deliberately move their joint forces against Spain, the common
enemy, and attack him with a powerful combined army,
was included in the proposal put forth at the very beginning
by the French negotiators.[2]

So much of the negotiation on the part of the English
was devoted to recrimination, the expression of doubts as
to the advantages of such an alliance, the question of
guarantees for its enforcement, and paring down of the
amount of help to be given that general principles or plans
got scant consideration. The queen also objected to the
inclusion of the Estates of the Netherlands on equal terms
with sovereign princes, and wished to deny them freedom to
make treaties except with her consent, since they were under
her protection. The French tried to force the fighting. At
the third regular session, April 29th, Sancy rose and said
that if the English were not able to give any assistance
in the proposed plan, it might be as well to know it at once

[2] *State Papers, Foreign, France,* xxxvii, 214–15; *State Papers, Dom.,*
cclix, 113; *Propositions faites à la Royne par les sieurs de Bouillon et de
Sancy, ambassadeurs de Henri IV, Oeuvres de DuVair,* 1155, quoted in
Poirson, *Henri IV,* 3 Ed., ii, 315.

so that the king might be relieved of the expense of keeping his ambassadors in England uselessly and might know that he would have to arrange his affairs in a different way. "We see that we are too poor; you do not consider that you can deal with us."

This produced the result of at least initiating definite proposals. Burghley drew from his pocket a little paper and read from it memoranda of the old English-French treaty of 1571, and a statement that the queen had authorized them to offer to the king 3000 men if he would, before they left England, provide the money for the cost of levying them and one month's pay in advance. If when parliament met, however, there were objections, the queen should not be bound to allow these troops to go. The envoys gave this proposal the compliment of consideration over the dinner hour, but then explained that if the king had the money he could readily obtain soldiers in his own country, in Switzerland or in Germany, and that the reference to parliament seemed simply to offer an opportunity for non-fulfilment of the agreement. A treaty on such conditions was meaningless. At another time it was proposed to postpone succor to the Greek Kalends by declaring that the treaty should come into effect when Essex and Howard had returned from the sea and the Irish rebellion was over.[3]

Letters of complaint to the queen, ceremonious good-byes to the council, and preparations for departure became almost a regular part of the negotiations. Tuesday, May 4th, Bouillon declared that he would return to France immediately and asked to have a vessel prepared for his departure. The queen, however, did not intend to let the meeting break up ineffectually. There is no evidence that at this time she was seriously considering a peace with Spain, nor did she deliberately wish to weaken France or to prevent the freedom or a reasonable commercial advance of the Netherlands. Yet she and her councillors were as usual invincibly opposed to a bold policy, and apart from

[3] DuVair, 17-18.

her reluctance to take active steps the minds of the negotiators on both sides were so obsessed with suspicion, the curse of all diplomacy, that a common ground was hard to find. The French suspected the English of planning to hand over their cautionary towns in the Netherlands to Spain in return for Calais and a favorable peace, the English attributed to the French plans to make a more favorable treaty immediately with Spain when they should face her strengthened by English and Dutch reinforcements.

New questions came up. When news came that after the capture of Calais the Spaniards were besieging Ardres and threatening Boulogne and Montreuil directly across the Narrow Seas, Sancy awaited Elizabeth as she took her afternoon walk in Greenwich park and begged her to send 25,000 crowns immediately for their succor irrespective of the signature of a more extensive treaty. The queen remarked that " so much has been drawn from the well that it is dry," but on Wednesday the council offered £6,000, that is to say, 20,000 crowns, if Bouillon and Sancy would make themselves personally liable for the debt, secure the guarantee of Rouen bankers and promise that the money should be used only for the defense of the two Picardy towns. On the 7th of May this sum was duly paid over to the two ambassadors and their receipts accepted, and the thrift of Burghley took occasion to include again with the receipt a note of all bonds due from the French king up to that date.[4]

This loan seems to have been part of a definitely more conciliatory policy decided upon by the queen. Tuesday afternoon, May 4th, when there had been a particularly warm session of the negotiators, she took occasion, as she returned from a ride, to pass the lodgings of the French deputies at Greenwich, and said to them that she understood they were ill content with the progress of their affairs, but that she did not intend they should remain so and expected to send them away satisfied. Little occurred for

4 *Cal. Hatfield House MSS.*, vi, 171, 191-2, xiii, 581; DuVair, 16.

the next few days, but on the 10th she invited the envoys
to meet her alone in her " gallery " in the palace at Greenwich and told them she had decided to yield to the wishes of
the king to authorize the Netherlanders to enter into the
league, and on other points had sent her councillors to London to draw up the treaty in regular form. She declared she
would call back Essex and Howard and send them with the
whole army into France if it were not for the criticism it
would cause. The next three days were spent in London in
a series of disputes and interchanges of views as to wording
and significance of the treaty that was now being drawn up.
Burghley endeavored to introduce an article at the end of
the document providing that the king should at the request
of the queen grant to his Protestant subjects the exercise
of their religion as freely as it had ever been granted to
them by Henry or any of his predecessors. The French
ambassadors proudly refused, on the ground that the king
would never agree that another than himself should be the
protector of any of his subjects; and cut off further discussion by asking what the queen would think of an intervention in behalf of her Catholic subjects. When, on the
other hand, the French ambassadors brought up some antiquated pretensions to the precedence of the king of France
over other monarchs, the English minister drily suggested
that they might take the treaty as it was or leave it altogether. May 14th the whole document, drawn up in formal
Latin, was signed at Greenwich by all parties. At the very
last the French envoys claimed the meaning was tampered
with in the translation and the Latin had to be changed.
The seals were attached and their copy delivered to the
French plenipotentiaries on Sunday, May 16th, at five
o'clock in the afternoon.[5]

The treaty consisted of twenty-three articles. Its early

[5] DuVair, 19–25, Ed. 3, 213–41; Prévost-Paradol, *Elisabeth et Henri IV,*
1595–8, 23–40; P. P. Laffleur de Kermaingant, *L'Ambassade en Angleterre
sous Henri IV, Mission de Jean de Thuméry, sieur de Boissise,* 1598–1602,
1–46.

clauses provided that all former treaties should remain in force, that this should be considered an offensive and defensive treaty against the king of Spain, and that other princes and states whose position led them to oppose the machinations of the king of Spain should be invited to join the league. So far as England and France were concerned, neither was to be at liberty to treat for peace with Spain nor even to enter into a truce with any lieutenant of that king for any longer period than two months without the formal consent of the other party given in writing. The fourth article was the most extensive. It provided that as soon as circumstances should permit a united army should be formed from contingents provided by all members of the league and that these combined forces should make an overwhelming attack upon the dominions of the king of Spain. This was for the future; the more immediate object with which Henry was concerned was prestige in the eyes of his own people and succor for his still hardly pressed outposts in France. To meet this need the queen agreed that as soon as possible after the signature of the treaty 4000 foot soldiers should be levied and sent to France, to serve for six months, their pay being advanced by her, on condition that they should be called on to fight only in the provinces of Picardy and Normandy and the adjacent parts of the Netherlands, within fifty miles of Boulogne, and on further condition that the cost of their levy and wages should be repaid within the six months. Four thousand men should be sent to France for a similar period of six months in each subsequent year if it should prove convenient to the queen to send them. Detailed provisions were made for the muster and payment of these troops and the repayment of the queen's loans, much as in the treaty of Greenwich made with the Netherlands in 1585. Hopes were given that after the settlement of the Irish troubles and in the absence of disorder in any other parts of the queen's dominions, additional troops might be sent. In the meantime the king was to be allowed to levy 3000 or 4000 more men in England at his own expense if he had the money and if they were not needed by the queen. Four hostages of suitable rank and means were to be left with the queen as gages for the repayment of the loans, in lieu of cautionary towns such as were given by the Netherlands and as the queen would have required if France had been a weak group of rebellious provinces instead of a proud and independent kingdom.

Provisions for succor of the queen by Henry with the same number of troops and with the same restriction upon service more than fifty miles from the coast were introduced to meet the possibility of England being invaded and in order that the league should be reciprocal in character. Two general provisions closed the document. The king and queen will mutually protect each other's merchants so that they can carry on their commerce in both countries without impediment; the king of France agrees that no subject of the queen when in his country will ever be vexed by inquisitors or others on account of his adherence to the religion now received in England.[6]

Such was the treaty of Greenwich of May, 1596, as it was proclaimed to the world then, and as it was supposed by all but a few on each side of the Channel to be. But moderate as were its terms, they were more than Elizabeth was willing actually to conform to. The alliance was highly desirable for its effect on the international relations of both parties, and its terms should be generous, " to give credit and reputation to the league," as the French expressed it; " for the advantage of the Kinge and his estate in the sight of the worlde," in Elizabeth's words. But the queen only agreed to sign this public treaty after the French negotiators had agreed on their part that certain articles should be privately " retrenched and abridged." Bouillon and Sancy therefore immediately afterward signed a secret

[6] Dumont, *Corps Diplomatique du Droit des Gens*, V, i, 525–6; Friedr. Leonard, ii, 652–5; *A General Collection of Treaties*, 1732, 97–102; Pieter Bor, *Nederlandsche Hoorlogen*, Ed. 1679–84, iv, 262–5; *Cal. Hatfield House MSS.*, vi, 180.

agreement that whereas the treaty required the queen to provide 4000 men immediately as succor to the king, with pay advanced for six months, nevertheless, in consideration of the queen's needs in Ireland and at sea, the king would be satisfied with 2000 men, with pay advanced for four months, and these 2000 men should be employed only to garrison Boulogne and Montreuil or to fight under the king himself in person in Picardy and near the seacoast. Nor should the queen be asked to send any other succors to the king until the next year. The French envoys agreed also that the 20,000 crowns recently advanced should be repaid in September instead of the next May, as the treaty called for, though as no loans to the king of France had ever yet been repaid at all, this point must have gratified the queen's business instincts rather than guaranteed the replenishing of her exchequer. Finally, as concerned the only large proposal, that an army of the allies should be put into the field to invade the dominions of the king of Spain, the envoys agreed that this should be looked upon as having been inserted in the treaty " for the reputation of the league and not to obligate the queen to any expense for organizing at present the said army corps." [7]

This annexed convention, signed May 26, two days later than the treaty, practically formed a second, secret treaty, modifying the first. The two treaties were so described immediately afterward by the queen in her private instructions to her ambassador going to France, the differences between them pointed out, and her claim that she was bound by the former only as modified by the latter made clear; and so the three French negotiators who knew the circumstance and the king himself understood it. It is no wonder that Bouillon, on leaving England immediately afterward, expressed his doubts of ratification and wrote of the league that it was " much less in my judgment than the greatness of the persons and the kingdoms merit, less than our affairs

[7] P.R.O. *State Papers, France,* Bundle 116, quoted in Kermaingant, *Mission de Jean de Thuméry, Pièces Justicatives,* 256-8.

required to be solaced by, and infinitely less than my hope." [8]

Yet the treaty, meagre as it was, was by no means without significance. It made fruitless, at least for the time, Spanish projects for peace with France and the Netherlands. Along with the sack of Cadiz, which took place within the same month, it prevented peace between England and Spain. It encouraged a somewhat more vigorous series of campaigns in the fall of 1596 and in the next year. It prevented that entire alienation between England and France that had seemed probable at the beginning of the year. It gave, as will be seen, fuller recognition to the United Netherlands and carried them one step nearer to full recognition as an independent European state.[9]

The conference bade fair at one time to help in the settlement of certain questions somewhat outside of the political sphere which were troubling Europe. Among the scattered state papers of this time are two memoranda or lists of recommendations which seem to have been brought before this conference of plenipotentiaries, but upon which no action was taken, or which left but a slight impress on the treaty as it was actually adopted. One of these, apparently emanating from the French commissioners, consists of ten articles intended to secure greater freedom and security of commerce for the subjects of the king of France and the queen of England. The greatest obstacle to security at sea at this period was the connivance of the officials of port towns in both France and England with violations of the law, and the inability of the rulers to give adequate protection to the sufferers. These regulations proposed that no vessels armed or unarmed should be allowed to go out of any port in either country without first putting in bonds with the authorities to refrain from any damage to the subjects of the other country. Judges should be appointed in each seaport to settle any suit brought before them sum-

---

[8] *Ibid.*, Bundle 117; *Cal. Hatfield House MSS.*, xiii, Addenda, 573–4.

[9] Birch, *Memoirs*, ii, 10, 33, 110.

marily and finally. In case of failure to put a vessel under bond or to carry out the judgment of a court, the officials of the towns should themselves be responsible for the damage committed or the judgment claimed; and if there was any delay, claims should be enforced by the grant of letters of marque and reprisal against citizens, vessels or merchandize of the offending towns. Vessels driven by stress of weather into a port should not be compelled to sell their goods there unless they wished. If they were required to do so, losses might be made good by the grant of letters of marque and reprisal against the town. If there were any so cruel and barbarous as to kill, drown or sell any subjects of either sovereign, the inhabitants of the town of which such offenders were natives should be required to pursue and punish the criminals at their own expense; and if they did not do so should be held liable for civil damages. Without effect as these propositions seem to have been, they give an interesting glimpse into the prevailing barbarity of sixteenth century commerce, the inefficiency of central administration, and the cumbrous methods relied upon to secure better conditions. Indeed six months had not passed before there were, as so often before, bitter complaints by French merchants in England, letters of marque and reprisal granted to them by Henry, and a royal dispute on the subject.[10]

The other suggestions were apparently of English origin and were even more directly commercial in their interests. They provided for the establishment within four months of an English staple of cloth and wool in one or more towns in France, as English staples had been kept in Antwerp, Bruges and Bergen. When such staple towns had been appointed and acknowledged by the French king, English merchants should be permitted to live there in their own dwellings, under their own governors and officers, subject only to their own rules for trading, and at liberty to dis-

---

[10] *Bibliotheque Nationale, MSS.,* 15,980, No. 93, Kermaingant, *Mission de Jean de Thuméry, Pièces Justicatives,* 258–60; *Cal. Hatfield House MSS.,* vi, 528, vii, 16.

pose of their personal belongings by gift, sale, or bequest without impairment by the French laws of property. French taxes, tolls, and customs should be set down once for all and notified to English merchants. They should then never be increased nor should new impositions be laid. Considering that France was a rising commercial country just on the eve of the great national industrial movement that characterized the reign of Henry IV as a whole even more than the adventurous wars of his early years, it is not a matter of surprise that proposals to establish in the heart of France a foreign commercial monopoly like the medieval Steelyard in London, the house of the Merchants Adventurers in Bruges or the *fondachi* of the Mediterranean cities found no place in the completed treaty. Nor was it likely that France would yield to alien restrictions on her freedom of taxation.

Still further proposals were that in case of war between the two nations, two months should be allowed to the merchants of each country to withdraw themselves and their goods; that the sections of the old treaty of 1515, prohibiting the reception of foreign ships of war in any port of either country or sale to them of munitions or supplies, should be renewed; and that a new agreement should be entered into declaring that during the existing war with Spain, no Hanseatic or other merchants should be permitted to " make any staple " of grain in France for transport into Spain. These proposals were all still-born.[11]

The formalities involved in the final ratification of any treaty are many and varied, and the completion of those between England and France in this case may be described here before passing to the next stage of the formation of the alliance, the adherence to it of the United Netherlands. Bouillon and Sancy left London immediately after the signature to return to France, and although, as so often occurred, they were detained some days on the English side of the Channel by bad weather they were with the

[11] *Cal. Hatfield House MSS.*, xiii, 574–5.

king again at Abbeville, to which he had come after the
surrender of La Fère, by the 7th of June. The king if he
was disappointed at the terms of the new treaties, as he
could hardly fail to have been, dissembled his chagrin, expressed satisfaction, and spoke vaguely about accepting an
invitation of the queen to cross the Channel to visit her.
He secured the reluctant approval of his council to the
treaties, told La Fontaine to let the queen know of his intention of ratifying them, and as a matter of fact signed and
sealed both of the treaties at Amiens July 9. During June
and the early part of July letters were going to and fro
arranging for places for the exchange of ratifications as
nearly as possible simultaneously, for persons to represent
their respective sovereigns at these ceremonies, and for
permanent ambassadors in the two countries who should
represent the closer relations which were now to exist. It
was soon announced from the French side that Bouillon
would be sent back to England with full authority to swear
to the treaty in his sovereign's name and to be present when
the queen should take her oath to it. The king would in
turn give his oath at Rouen, where he was to be given a
reception of honor by that long rebellious city. Antoine de
Moret, sieur de Reaux, should be permanent ambassador
in England. Henry, along with news of these arrangements,
sent his thanks to the queen for her somewhat barren assurances of immediate help to succor Boulogne if it should be
attacked and equally perfunctory offers to help her if she
needed help in England.[12]

Several English noblemen were considered, and even summoned, to take over the queen's ratification; but the earl
of Northumberland excused himself because he was too deaf
and too poor, Lord Cobham because he was of too low rank
and because of his " weakness and unaptness." Before the
end of July this duty had been committed to the earl of
Shrewsbury, and Sir Anthony Mildmay, the son of an old

---

[12] *Cal. Hatfield House MSS.*, vi, 192, 221, 281; xiii, 573; *Lettres Missives*, iv, 598–9, 614–16.

courtier and official of Elizabeth, had been chosen to accompany him and to remain as permanent ambassador. Diplomatic honors were laborious and expensive under Queen Elizabeth, and Mildmay pleaded ill health, unfamiliarity with the language and present customs of France, since he had not been there for twenty-one years, and an involved and insufficient estate, as good reasons why he should not be sent. His ultimate lack of success justified his doubt of himself; he was a very unsatisfactory successor to Sir Henry Unton.[13]

Bouillon arrived at Dover with La Chatte, governor of Dieppe and other attendants on this second visit of the year, on the 25th of July, was taken in great state to the court at Greenwicn, and remained in England six weeks. After some slight dispute between Burghley and Bouillon as to reservations, due to the queen swearing to the treaty before the king had taken his final oath, difficulties were removed by mutual promises and concessions. On Sunday, the 29th of August, in the royal chapel at Greenwich, the queen swore to the treaty in the presence of the duke and of an impressive group of English prelates, ministers, noblemen and gentlemen, " the bishop of Chichester holding to her the book of the gospels." The actual form of ratification to which the queen took her oath, after all explanations remained somewhat ambiguous. It was quite certain that she agreed to an offensive and defensive alliance against the king of Spain. According to her interpretation, not denied by the king, though questioned by statesmen then and historians since, each sovereign was also bound under no circumstances to make a separate peace with the monarch of Spain without the consent of the other, an agreement which in due time Henry disregarded as completely as if it had no place in the treaty. But this has been the general practice of nations.[14]

---

[13] *Cal. Hatfield House MSS.*, vi, 260–1; Birch, *Memoirs*, ii, 68.

[14] Dumont, V, i, 526; Camden, Ed. 1688, 525; Kermaingant, i, 46–56; Poirson, *Henri IV*, Ed. 3, ii, 242–4; *Acts of the Privy Council*, xxvi, 136.

Immediately after the ceremonies the queen gave a great state dinner to the ambassadors and presented Bouillon with a collection of plate amounting to almost half the value of the loan to the king so grudgingly given at the treaty. Two days later the earl of Essex gave a banquet to the ambassador and his train at Essex house which was estimated to cost half as much more.

Two weeks later Shrewsbury, Mildmay and the English lords who accompanied them left for France, the special ambassador bearing not only instructions as to the witness of the ratification and a large packet of letters to various French nobles and dignitaries, but the order of the Garter to be bestowed upon the king. The journey from Dover to Dieppe took them, because of a calm followed by unfavorable winds, from the 14th to the 22nd of September. On the 28th they were at Rouen, and after an infinity of visits and delays at last on the 6th of October they watched from a window on the High Street the great cortège by which Henry was accompanied on his entrance to the city. The king saluted them as he passed. There were two or three days of entertainments and exchanges of courtesies, and on the 9th, in the Church of St. Ouen, in the presence of the English representatives and a great gathering of peers and marshals of France and lieutenants of provinces, the king swore to all the articles in the two treaties. The next day, which was Sunday, the king invited the English lords to dinner and to supper. Between these two functions took place with vast ceremonies, carefully prepared beforehand, the investment of the king with the ancient English order.[15]

A few days afterward Henry wrote to the queen from Rouen a letter full of praise of Shrewsbury, thanks for the Garter and congratulations on their alliance. He hoped " that our friendship will be judged by all to be so perfect that it will serve as an example to posterity, as a consolation to us and our good subjects and terror to our enemies

[15] Dumont, V, i, 526–7; Kermaingant; 57–63; Birch, *Memoirs,* ii, 121, 154–5.

so long as we shall live." He wrote at the same time to Essex that he trusted the queen would not " regret her old friendship or new confederation." All was rejoicing when Shrewsbury early in November sailed for England.[16]

It is now necessary to change the scene to the Netherlands. In May, immediately after the signature of the treaty in England, Bouillon, Sancy and Du Vair returned to France, while Ancel with the Dutch ambassador to France, Laevinus Calvart, left for The Hague to report the agreement at Greenwich and to prepare for the conference in Holland. Three weeks after the signature of the treaty, Henry himself wrote from Abbeville to the States General. He congratulated them on the alliance, both because of the advantage to the common cause it promised and because of the agreement that the Netherlands should enter it as a sovereign state. He refers them to their ambassador and his own for the knowledge of his necessities, and begs them to assist him with further succors while awaiting the completion of the alliance and their formal inclusion in it.[17]

It was considered that final ratification between England and France should be completed before negotiations with the Netherlands for the extension of the treaty were begun. It was not till three months afterward, therefore, till Bouillon's second visit to England had been completed, and the queen had sworn to the treaty at Greenwich, that he passed over to the Netherlands, accompanied, by the queen's appointment, by Lord Borough. Bouillon arrived at The Hague on Wednesday the 16th of September and was entertained by his sister, the Princess of Orange, though, by agreement, at the expense of the States. In an audience with the States on the succeeding Saturday, he presented a full statement of his experiences in England and the requests of his own sovereign for their action. A few days later all these matters were put before them in writing, with the letters of credence of Henry, signed and dated July 9 and

[16] *Lettres Missives,* iv, 652–3.
[17] Birch, *Memoirs,* ii, 122; *Lettres Missives,* iv, 598–9.

August 16. George Gilpin, the English member of the Council of State and representative of the queen, presented a new letter from the queen, dated September 11, urging the States to accept the opportunity to join in the league now offered to them.

All these suggestions, the general advice of the queen as well as the specific proposals brought by the duke, seem to have been welcome to the States, and the letter from the queen handed them by Gilpin was so friendly to the king of France that they thought by it to excuse any degree of generosity to him on their part. The cumbrous organization of the Dutch government, however, involved as much delay as the complications of French politics, the hesitations of English policy or the vagaries of the Channel winds, so that it was not until the last day of October, new style, that the treaty which was to complete the negotiations entered upon in France in January, and carried one stage further in England in May, was signed in the Netherlands. The year 1596 had expired and it was not until January 1, 1597, that it was finally ratified.[18]

The main treaty consisted of a statement of the çircumstances of its original formation, a recapitulation of its general provisions and a declaration of adhesion to it by the States General, the Council of State, and Count Maurice of Orange on the part of the United Netherlands. It recited the continuance of all old treaties with England and France, the offensive and defensive character of the new league, the invitation to other princes and states opposed to the king of Spain to join in it, the agreement to form as soon as practicable a combined army to invade the king of Spain's dominions, the promise not to make a separate peace with him nor any lengthened truce, the grant of liberty to purchase warlike supplies in one another's countries, of reciprocal freedom of trade to merchants, and of exemption from persecution for religion in France. The

[18] Birch, *Memoirs*, ii, 148, 170, 176; Dumont, V, i, 536–7; *Cal. Hatfield House MSS.* vi, 344, 391; *Lettres Missives*, iv, 670, 682.

treaty was signed by Bouillon and Buzenval for France, by Gilpin for England, and by Aerssen, as secretary for the Estates.[19]

The treaty was now complete so far as creating an offensive and defensive league of the three countries involved was concerned. It bound them all reciprocally to a few somewhat general requirements, and by it they pledged themselves to friendly relations and presented a united front to Spain. The provisions of the original treaty, by which Elizabeth agreed to furnish certain specific aid to Henry, were not repeated in the general alliance. In their place, signed only by the representatives of France and the Netherlands, certain " capitulations," conditions and articles were agreed on between those two countries. These were fifteen in number. Through them runs a spirit of greater boldness, more complete confidence and closer amity than in the somewhat restricted and suspicious clauses of the English treaty, even in its fullest and most public form.

The vague invitation to other rulers and states to join the alliance was now extended specifically to the kings of Scotland and Denmark and the princes of the Holy Roman Empire. The actual time and manner of sending envoys to them was to depend on the judgment of the king of France. A great general congress of all who entered the alliance should be assembled as soon as possible, and at latest before the end of the year 1597, to deliberate on means for carrying out the plan of a joint attack on the king of Spain and other objects of the confederacy; the time and place of this congress to be at the convenience of the king of France and the queen of England. Independent of this larger project, the next spring the army of the States, consisting of 9000 or 10,000 men, should join the army of the king of France on the frontiers of Picardy to make such a joint campaign as should then seem wise to Bouillon and Prince Maurice, the two principal commanders. The States would continue their subsidy of men and money to Henry

[19] Dumont, V, i, 531-7.

through the next year to the value of 450,000 livres. Henry on the other hand promised to keep continuous war or ravaging on the borders of the Spanish Netherlands, and if the States were hard beset, to send some of his troops into the Netherlands. The French king also promised to do his best to recover the confiscated estates in Brabant and Flanders of the widow and children of William of Orange.

The commercial clauses indicated an even closer union between France and the United Netherlands. Not only were all letters of marque and reprisal issued by either government against subjects of the other to be withdrawn and none issued for the future, and complete freedom of trade granted in both countries on the same terms, but the French government promised to protect the Netherlands and aid them in getting the same immunities and privileges as they themselves possessed in all countries to which Netherlanders should go for traffic. The French agreed also that Dutch ships might trade in all their possessions, especially in the western world. A promise that would secure to Dutch traders access on equal terms with the French to the lands of the Sultan and the shores of the St. Lawrence was no slight proof of their desire for friendship. Finally, it was agreed that French ships on the way to or from North-western Germany, the Baltic or other parts of the North, might sail past the Netherlands without being required to touch at any port there, and if driven into a Dutch harbor by storm should not be required to unload or sell any of their merchandize. Netherlands' ships passing the French coast eastward or westward should have the same exemption. Thus the whole body of practice of seizure of contraband and local right of preëmption was abolished, so far as the relations between these two countries were concerned.[20]

The signing of the treaty caused great public rejoicing in Holland. It furnished an occasion to gratify the national fondness for pageants; banquets were held, bonfires lighted,

---

[20] Dumont, V, i, 537–41; *A General Collection of Treaties,* 2 Ed., London, 1732, 103–19.

the French arms were set up " in every corner." The duke of Bouillon´was presented with six coach horses and several chests of the fine and costly linen of the country. There were also rumors that he had been given by the States a casket of gold, a chest of silver and an annuity of a thousand pounds, but these reports, if true, were carefully denied to the English, partly for fear of impressing the queen with such a belief in Dutch wealth as would induce her to demand repayment of her debts, partly for fear of arousing jealousy between English and French. It is to be remembered also that Bouillon was through his sister almost a member of the well-loved house of Orange. The duke left The Hague for home by way of Brielle a week or two after the signature of the treaty, accompanied at his departure by his sister, Count Maurice and a great train of nobles, ladies and gentlemen as far as Maesland Sluys where they took leave of him, " the men affectionately, the women passionately." But changes of weather and of plans brought him back from Brielle to The Hague, and it was not until late in November that he joined the king again at Rouen.[21]

The network of treaties and special_engagements thus woven among the three countries was made up for the most part of detailed provisions, but it was broadened by the conception of an extended league of states which should be its ultimate outcome. Toward the fulfilment of these larger ends England and the Netherlands took but languid steps. At Secretary Cecil's request, Dr. Beale drew up a " Discourse " as to how the princes of Germany might be dealt with for the league. There was an exchange of ambassadors between Elizabeth and the Emperor and various princes in Germany in 1596 that might have served this purpose. The earl of Lincoln was sent to represent the queen at the christening of the infant daughter of the landgrave of Hesse and to carry letters to the dukes of Brunswick and Holstein and the count of Friesland; but he left England in July before the league was consummated; he was back

[21] Birch, *Memoirs,* ii, 199, 200, 210, 213.

again in London, " glad to tread once again on English
ground," in October, before Ancel had started for Germany
on his mission, and there is no indication that he or other
English envoys mentioned any closer alliance to their
German hosts.[22]

The French government on the other hand instructed
Ancel, who had been in Germany before he went to England
with Sancy and Bouillon in April, 1596, to go to the Netherlands, and thence to make a journey into Germany, to draw
its Protestant princes into the proposed league. He was
provided with letters of credence, dated August 6th, but did
not actually leave on his mission till the very close of 1596.
In January, 1597, Henry, in returning to the Netherlands
his formal ratification of the treaties of October, urged them
to send someone to accompany his envoy to Germany for
the extension of the league, but the States took no action.
Ancel's mission was therefore as unsupported as it proved
to be futile. On the 23rd of December he was with Bongars,
the French resident at Nuremburg, and left soon afterward,
with but small encouragement from his colleague. He visited in all ten rulers of the petty states of the Empire, the
elector Palatine, the dukes of Wurtemburg and Brunswick,
the landgrave of Hesse, the margraves of Anspach, Baden-
Durlach and Brandenhurg, Anhalt, Newburg and Magde-
burg. He seems to have argued boldly and well for what he
considered the common duty of all Protestant states, especially the small states of Germany, to oppose the efforts of
Spain for universal monarchy and Catholic orthodoxy and
urged the greater strength to be obtained by union. As in
England and the Netherlands, here also Henry sought along
with the league immediate succors, asking for 4000 foot and
1000 horse from the German princes for two years. But
Ancel could not overcome the preference of these states for a
strict neutrality, a preference strengthened by the influence

---

[22] *Cal. Hatfield House MSS.*, vi, 189, 212, 425, vii, 16, 17; *Acts of the
Privy Council*, xxvi, 8, 13, 66; Murdin, 809; Nichols, *Progresses of Queen
Elizabeth*, iii, 380.

of the Spanish ambassador, Mendoza, who more than once crossed his path. The German princes alleged that the laws of the empire forbade alliances with outside powers, and that all their strength was needed to protect themselves from the possible advance of the Turk, now firmly established in Hungary. The landgrave of Hesse doubted the wisdom of awakening the resentment of Spain when they had no better protectors than England, governed by a notoriously capricious and selfish woman, Holland, scarcely able to protect herself, and France, weakened by thirty years of civil war.

Henry's recent conversion to Catholicism naturally did not strengthen his position with Protestants. Nor did the Lutheran states feel much sympathy for Protestant countries which rejected the Confession of Augsburg. As Bongars wrote from Frankfort to his friend Camerarius at Nuremburg concerning the Lutheran clergy, " I fear God has sent the Turks into Germany for their punishment, for these theologians think them no worse than the Calvinists." The alternative plan of an independent league, altogether of German states, against Spain, which was ultimately realized in 1599, was already under discussion and deterred some of the princes from joining the triple alliance. Ancel returned from his journey without any fruits of his efforts.[23]

There still remained Scotland and Denmark; but there was a strong Spanish faction at each court, and England was jealous of the approximation at this time between the two northern powers, and rather opposed than favored any efforts including them both. Ancel therefore made no attempt in that direction, although it was a common question in the Netherlands why when the king of France had secured two confederates for himself he did not go on and engage " all five fingers," meaning a quintuple alliance of Scotland and Denmark, besides his own country, England and the Netherlands. Still another combination was urged

[23] Anquez, L., *Henri IV et l'Allemagne*, 45–7; *Lettres de Bongars*, Ed. Hague, 1695, 505; Poirson, A., 3d Ed. ii, 290–2; Birch, *Memoirs*, ii, 247. Dumont, V, i, 596–8.

by Lord Willoughby, who, out of service since his campaign of 1589, had been traveling in Germany and now wrote to Essex from Venice urging an alliance between England, the king of Denmark and the duke of Wurtemburg. He suggested the permanent engagement of 1000 horsemen from Germany and offered to lead them himself. Later Willoughby recommended a still more ambitious plan and one more in consonance with the treaty. A great force should be gathered against the archduke to consist, first, of the French troops under Biron; secondly, of those of the Netherlands under Count Maurice and Vere, marching from Ostende; and thirdly, of 10,000 men from England under Essex or some other popular leader who should land under color of recapturing Calais or attacking Dunkirk but should immediately join the other forces in their grand attack. But nothing came of either of these suggestions. Nor were any steps taken to draw into the alliance Venice or any other Italian state, as had been suggested.[24]

The fruits of the treaty seemed to ripen slowly. It is true that immediately after its signature in May, rumors spread in England that the queen was to take Boulogne and Montreuil into her hands, and at least one ambitious knight begged to be made captain of one or the other town. Troops were actually levied to be held ready to be taken across the Channel if the Spaniards should attack other seaboard cities besides Calais. But the archduke, after capturing Ardres and threatening the Channel and Picard cities, carried his troops far to the north, and to overawe the southernmost districts under the control of the independent Netherlands, laid systematic siege to Hulst. Count Maurice followed him there and tried to force him to raise the siege. During this period of immobilization, the Dutch contingent in Henry's service took leave of the king and returned to their own country. Henry, from motives of economy, also dismissed for two months in the middle of the summer the greater part

[24] Birch, *Memoirs*, i, 322-5, ii, 164-8, 199; *Lettres de Bongars*, 501; DuVair, 20.

of his cavalry. Neither strong enough of himself to attempt any great action nor in danger of immediate attack from the local Spanish garrisons, he occupied his troops with ravaging the parts of the Flemish provinces adjacent to France. A more active campaign would have been preferable if he had been able to induce Elizabeth to yield to the wishes of her more warlike subjects to grant his requests for larger forces or even to anticipate the fulfilment of the secret treaty before the completion of the formalities of its ratification. To neither of these, however, would she agree, and Henry was not keen for an inconclusive campaign.

On the 10th of August, in the midst of this period of comparative calm, Essex, back from Cadiz, came posting up to court hot to bring his fleet and army to the regaining of Calais, which he had never accepted as irrecoverable. He had written from the fleet on his way home, ordering his secretary to visit Caron, representative of the States, and La Fontaine, representing Henry, suggesting to them the advisability of asking the queen to use his services with the returning fleet and army to capture Calais or to carry on some campaign in its vicinity. The city authorities of London were incited to make the same request. It seems to have been generally expected also that Bouillon would on his return urge the recapture of Calais and even " make it English." Little enthusiasm for this project, however, seems to have been shown by anyone but Essex. The arrival of Bouillon was delayed, and while Essex was going from fleet to court and from court to fleet, the lord admiral and both sea and land captains were sending up testimony that the fleet was incapable of being sent out without refitting, and the sailors and soldiers were deserting from the ships as they lay in the Downs. Henry also intimated that he would rather do the regaining of Calais from the Spaniards himself.[25]

[25] Monson, *Naval Tracts, Navy Records Society,* i, 357; *Cal. Hatfield House MSS.,* vi, 186, 193, 281, 285, 396; Birch, *Memoirs,* ii, 29, 38, 75, 77, 84–5, 97, 99–100, 101, 102–3, 148.

The English government was, however, not insensible of the absolutely essential military needs of the situation. In July, while Essex and Howard were still away, 500 men were sent to Flushing to reinforce the cautionary garrison there which had been weakened by the withdrawals for Cadiz, and Sir Robert Sydney early in August was ordered to resume his post as governor. The queen also intimated to Caron that the States might recruit 1000 or 1200 volunteers in England, at their own expense, if they wished.

About the middle of September, ratification being now practically certain, orders began to go out to the county authorities for the levy of troops for France for the fulfilment of the treaty. On the 23rd of September, general orders for a levy of 2000 men were sent to twelve of the southeastern counties. They were not to be drawn from the trained bands, but were nevertheless to be serviceable men; one half of them must be musketeers. They were to be shipped from London, Harwich and Southampton to St. Valéry in Picardy. They were to be dressed in russet coats, but London might use some special uniform if she wished. Sir Thomas Baskerville, who had brought home with conspicuous skill the remains of the Drake and Hawkins expedition, was commissioned as colonel of one of the two regiments and to have charge of the whole body. He was instructed that he and his troops should take their oath to the king's service, saving their allegiance to the queen, that they were to serve only at Boulogne and Montreuil, except when the king was present in person, when they might serve anywhere in Picardy; that they were not to go where they were in danger of the plague, where the French did not go, nor where the danger would be overwhelming; they were not to be separated, nor should they misuse the French, nor seize their goods without payment, nor desecrate their churches in any way. Moreover they must use the English form of prayer, if possible, every day. They were to be governed by martial law, including the code drawn up by Essex and Howard at Plymouth a few months before. They were to serve for six months, at the longest, and musters were to be taken once a month. October 8th was appointed for their sailing, but on the 5th the inevitable stay was ordered while the queen consulted with the king of France. The next day, however, it was announced that they might go as originally planned. On Sunday, a restraining order was sent from Richmond for such as had not yet embarked, but on Monday this was again reversed.[26]

On the 5th of November, Baskerville was able to report that his troops had all arrived safely in Picardy, but that he had immediately met difficulty in following out his orders. His own vessel had been driven by adverse winds into Dieppe and he had gone to see the king at Rouen. Henry was of course glad to have the English allies within his own borders, although less enthusiastic than if they had come at one of the more critical periods through which he had recently struggled. He did not like Baskerville's instructions. He had called a meeting of the Estates General at Rouen and could not leave them. He wanted to send the English troops to the border of the Spanish Netherlands to assist in the ravaging operations there, but could not go there in person to conform to Elizabeth's requirement. He complained, not quite ingenuously, that the queen constantly wrote him not to hazard his person, but now would not let him send his lieutenants to war in his place. The queen, two weeks later, after some correspondence and negotiations and the active interposition of the earl of Essex, made the necessary concessions, so long as the troops remained in Picardy or Artois. For the remainder of the year 1596 and the early months of 1597 the little English army shared with the French an inactive, inglorious and ineffective campaign in that war-cursed region.[27]

---

[26] *Acts of the Privy Council*, xxvi, 192–200, 208, 216–21, 224, 225, 244–7; Birch, *Memoirs*, ii, 75, 99–100; *State Papers, Dom., Elizabeth*, cclx, 54; *Cal. Hatfield House MSS.*, vi, 387, 390, xiii, 585, 588.

[27] *Acts of the Privy Council*, xxvi, 324; Birch, *Memoirs*, ii, 192–3, 198.

Part VII

The Last Four Parliaments of Queen Elizabeth

Part VII

The Last Four Parliaments of Queen Elizabeth

CHAPTER XXXIII

THE PARLIAMENT OF 1589: PROCEDURE

ALTHOUGH much of the narrative of our period has been traced nearly to its close we must now return to its beginning to make a consecutive study of parliament, an essential and perennially interesting institution, even if not comparable in influence at this time with the administrative side of government. September 18, 1588, but six weeks after the defeat of the Armada, and even before the Thanksgiving service in St. Paul's, the queen issued writs for a parliament to meet November 12. It was perhaps the expected success of the loan on privy seal that was being issued at the time that led to the postponement of this meeting. October 14 a writ of prorogation was issued; on the day originally appointed an empty ceremony of meeting and adjournment took place in the presence of a few officials and members, and it was not until February 4, 1589, that the first parliament after the great victory actually opened. Writs of summons had been sent, as usual, to the archbishops, bishops and guardians of spiritualities of such bishoprics as were vacant, to the lord chancellor, to the one marquis, fifteen earls, two viscounts and thirty-seven barons who made up the nobility of the period; to the three chief justices, their six colleagues, the attorney and solicitor general, to two serjeants at law and Sir Francis Walsingham, principal secretary. Those below the nobles were summoned in a subordinate capacity, but, like the lord chancellor and the nobles, by separate writs. Writs were also directed to the sheriffs of thirty-five counties, and to those of London and fourteen other cities and boroughs which were also counties, ordering them to secure the election of the usual number of knights of the shire, citizens or burgesses.[1]

During October and November the elections took place. We have but few glimpses left to us of the sixteenth century meetings in the county towns in which the forty shilling freeholders in accordance with the old law and in obedience to the queen's writ elected two knights to represent the shire, and we have scarcely more knowledge of the action of the voters who chose their representatives from the cities and boroughs. Yet in the records connected with this parliament and with others shortly before and after we have quite enough to show that the privy council kept its hand on parliamentary elections as on every other phase of government. The writs which were sent to the sheriffs were issued by the queen " with the advice and assent of my council." In October, 1588, a letter was sent from the council to the sheriff of Essex warning him that by ancient custom he must hold the assembly to elect knights of the shire for that county at Chelmsford and not elsewhere. When in 1593 by some mischance the writ did not reach the sheriff of Shropshire till the day after the " countie day," and he doubted the legality of holding the election a month later, after parliament would be actually in session, the council reassured him and instructed him to proceed with the election. When Sir Thomas Lucy, sheriff of Warwickshire, on the other hand, postponed the election from the first county court after he received the writ, ostensibly in order to secure a better attendance of electors, the privy council sent him

[1] Public Record Office, *Parliament Pawns, No. 13;* Sir Simonds D'Ewes, *Journals of all the Parliaments of the Reign of Queen Elizabeth,* 419; Sir William Dugdale, *Summons of the Nobility to Great Councils and Parliaments,* 533–7; Robert Steele, *Tudor and Stuart Proclamations, 1485–1714,* No. 806; Adair, E. R., and Evans, Miss F. M. Grier, *Writs of Assistance, 1558–1700, Eng. Hist. Rev.,* July, 1921, 356–72.

a sharp rebuke, ordered him to hold an election at the very
earliest opportunity and expressed their suspicion that he
had a factious object, seeking to block the election of a
certain candidate, in the council's opinion entirely suitable.
A similar reprimand was administered to Sir Francis
Palmer, sheriff of Hampshire, on the same ground. As a
matter of fact the privy council frequently urged their
choice upon the electors, notwithstanding their repeated
asseverations that a " tender consideration is had of the
free election by the corporations." They warned the electors of Worcestershire not to let religious faction prevent
them from electing Sir Thomas Leighton whose choice
" would be very agreeable to her Majesty," and when they
heard that Lord Rich was using his influence in Essex to
oppose the proposed election of Sir Thomas Heneage, vice-
chamberlain of the queen, and Sir Henry Gray, captain of
the band of Gentlemen Pensioners, they required him to
forbear his effort to get a large number of freeholders together at the county court to oppose such worthy nominees.[2]

In 1586 the council wrote to the sheriffs praising the
choice of representatives in the last parliament and requiring them to call three or four influential men into consultation with them and arrange for the choice " in their free
elections " of the same men to the parliament about to meet,
or if they were dead or abroad to nominate suitable successors. When one of the sheriffs, Henry Hugon of Norfolk,
disregarded these letters and carried on the election " in-
orderly," the council secured from the lord chancellor a new
writ for that shire and while insisting that they did not
mean to impeach the free election by the freeholders required the sheriff to hold a new election with the deputy
lieutenants assisting to see that " fit men should be chosen
known to be well affected to Religion and the present es
tate." [3]

[2] Sir Thomas Smith, *De Republica Anglorum*, Book ii, chap. 2 ; *Acts of
the Privy Council*, xvi, 298, 318, xxiv, 48.

[3] *Acts of the Privy Council*, xiv, 227, 241-2.

There is little doubt that as the reign of the queen grew older this pressure became stronger. In August, 1597, the privy council sent out, along with the chancellors' writs fifty-two letters to all the sheriffs and some of the towns reciting the queen's desire to have representatives chosen for the approaching parliament who will not only know local conditions but be of discretion in discussion of matters of general policy. She has no doubt of the sufficiency of those who will be chosen as knights of the shire but is more doubtful of the borough representatives. The cities and towns are therefore to be warned to be careful in their choice. It is possible that this warning was preliminary to a more specific naming of candidates, for Sir Robert Cecil, who had become principal secretary the year before, followed it up almost immediately with a series of requests to a number of the boroughs to allow him to name the candidates whom they would elect. Promptly as this request was made it was in most cases too late. The town councils had chosen their representatives between the time of the receipt of the writ and Cecil's letter. East Grimstead, Colchester, Stockbridge sent him their regrets; they would have been glad to pleasure him but they had already proceeded to an election. The archbishop of York, however, secured him one of the appointments from Ripon and Lord Cobham from Romney; the two burgess-ships from Poole were given him, and doubtless others were at the service of the government as evidenced by the appearance as members of this parliament of all members of the privy council and many other officials.[4]

In the last parliament of the reign this pressure was even more marked. Many burgess-ships are either claimed by or offered to Cecil by their burgesses or patrons who have control of their elections. The under-sheriff of Yorkshire brings a signed indenture with one line blank for Cecil

[4] *Acts of the Privy Council,* xxvii, 361–2 ; *Hatfield House MSS.,* vii, 361. 385, 396, 404, 410, 415, 429, 432 ; xi, 405 ; Mary Bateson, *Records of the Borough of Leicester,* iii, 331 n.

to write in the name of the man he wants; Jonathan Trelawney of Poole again presents him with the appointment of two burgess-ships for the coming parliament; Viscount Bindon offers him one or two appointments out of several which have been given him by various towns. The growing interest of the government in parliament is also indicated by its watchfulness over the progress of legislation and the activity of the privy councillors in its debates, as will be indicated later.[5]

Local influence on elections exercised by noblemen or other influential persons was even more conspicuous than that of the queen and council, though as these noblemen were often courtiers, it was in many cases an indirect exercise of the same influence. The effect of such mixed pressure can be well seen in the parliamentary experiences of Leicester. In the elections for the parliaments of the earlier part of the reign of Elizabeth, there is no evidence of outside interference. In 1584, however, the mayor received letters from various gentlemen of the county asking for their own election and from Sir George Hastings, brother of the earl of Huntingdon, asking to be allowed to name one of their representatives. The earl of Huntingdon had a town house in Leicester, his principal country house was at Ashby-de-la-Zouch nearby, and he was lord lieutenant of the county. His family influence was therefore almost overpowering. At the same time came a letter from Sir Ralph Sadler, chancellor of the duchy of Lancaster, within the administrative control of which Leicester lay, and who therefore spoke in a certain sense in the name of the government. He asked for the nomination of both members. The town authorities under this triple demand hesitated and procrastinated, but eventually yielded to pressure, granted one appointment to Sir Ralph Sadler, who promised that he would appoint Henry Skipwith, originally a Leicestershire

[5] *Hatfield House MSS.*, xi, 401, 405, 409, 443; *State Papers, Dom., Eliz.*, cvii, 59, 63, 86; cxlviii, 1; ccxxiii, 17; J. R. Tanner, *Tudor Constitutional Documents*, 518–27.

man, though now one of the queen's gentlemen at court; and for the other elected Thomas Johnson, the nominee of Sir George Hastings, who was also originally from Leicestershire though now a sergeant-at-arms of the queen. In 1586 not only did the privy council urge the reëlection of the two members of the preceding parliament, as already stated, but the earl of Huntingdon wrote asking, as his brother had done two years before, for one appointment   The two requirements were not incompatible, as the earl's nominee was one of the old members, and both were reëlected.   There are no details of the election of 1588, but in 1593 Sir Thomas Heneage, newly appointed chancellor of the duchy of Lancaster, demanded as a right attached to his office and accepted as precedent that he be allowed to name the burgesses of Leicester.   This time the mayor and alderman resisted; they denied there was any precedent, except as a matter of grace in a single instance, and although the minority proposed to give him both his appointments the majority refused the chancellor's nominees, declared that they would have no outsiders, eliminated the names of two country gentlemen, and elected two of their own number. In 1597, although two townsmen were in nomination, the earl of Huntingdon urged upon the electors a country gentleman named Beaumont and the principal town officials were willing to grant his request, but again the majority resisted on the ground that Beaumont was an incloser and would not support the principal measure of reform they anticipated from the coming parliament, so they again elected two townsmen, Parkins, son of the Recorder, and Stanford, son of a prominent alderman who had himself formerly represented the town.

The bitterest contest of the period came in the elections for the parliament of 1601.   On one candidate, William Heyricke, there was no contest.   He was of a type well known in romance and in real life.   His father had left Leicester many years before, had become rich as a London goldsmith, had served the queen in various capacities and the son had now come back to take a share in local interests as lord of a Leicestershire manor. He was supported alike by the earl, the mayor and the alderman. For the other position there were two prominent candidates, both, like Heyricke, county gentlemen. One, Bromley, was approved by the earl; the other, Belgrave, violently opposed by him. The majority of the town council evidently wanted Belgrave. By a sudden and dramatic appearance in the streets and at the guildhall of Leicester on the day of the election, clothed in a blue coat of the Huntingdon livery, wearing the bull's head crest of that family on his sleeve and asserting that the earl had withdrawn his opposition and now favored him, Belgrave secured his election, though at the cost of the anger of the earl against himself and the town, a long suit in Star Chamber, and a dispute between the House of Lords and the House of Commons on the question of parliamentary privilege.[6]

In some boroughs appointment by a patron or official was more direct and constant. The town of Colchester passed a resolution in 1584 granting to Sir Francis Walsingham the nomination of both members for the future. Appointment of one of the members of Christchurch " belongs by ancient right " to the earl of Huntingdon. One of the representatives of Wickham is regularly appointed by Lord Windsor, steward of the town, but in 1601 he asks for both, though he finds that a certain privy councillor has already claimed the appointment of one. Elizabeth added thirty-one new boroughs with sixty-two members to the list of represented towns, and although these additions were all made in the earlier part of her reign it seems probable that their representatives were regularly appointed not only at first but regularly afterwards by courtiers or the crown.[7]

[6] James Thompson, *History of Leicester*, 271–8, 294–5, 299–301, 314–19; Bateson, *Leicester*, iii, 207–11, 227–8, 289–90, 331, 336, 435–6; *Acts of the Privy Council*, xiv, 227, xxvii, 361.

[7] Merewether and Stephens, *History of Boroughs*, ii, 1346, 1348–50, 1393–4; John Hatsell, *Precedents of Proceedings in the House of Commons*, Ed. 1818, ii, 411–13.

The elections for knights of the shire were almost equally under outside influence. Sir John Gray in 1601 appeals both to Cecil and the earl of Rutland to secure his election as one of the knights for the county of Leicester, and there are indications that Warwickshire, Worcestershire, York and other counties sent representatives to this parliament named by the government or neighboring lords.[8]

The loss of control by boroughs and counties over the selection of their members was closely connected with the cessation of the practice of paying them for their services. It is true that by the old law every knight of a shire had a right to receive from his constituents four shillings per day and burgesses two shillings, including the time spent in going and coming, usually estimated at a day for each thirty miles in summer and twenty in winter. Such payments are occasionally recorded, as when the two representatives of Leicester are paid £7 14s. each for their service in the parliament of 1576, or when one representative in 1593 was paid £6 6s. Moreover a later law threatened absentees with loss of their wages, and as late as 1580 an order of the House of Commons forbade the clerk of the crown to deliver any writ for the levy of wages to any member who had departed before the end of the session without permission of the House.[9]

But this practice of payment of members by their constituents had been long disintegrating under the influence of the attractions of membership in parliament. There were always well-to-do gentlemen willing and anxious to serve for the sake of the distinction, without money payment. Readiness to serve without pay was a regular form of appeal for election. The earl of Leicester, for instance, in asking

[8] *Hist. MSS. Comm., Rutland MSS.*, i, 380; *Acts of the Privy Council*, xxxii, 251, 271, 342; Merewether and Stephens, 1223–1386; *Cal. State Papers, Dom.*, 1581–90, 208.

[9] 16 Ed. II; 12 Rich. II, c. 12; 23 Henry VI, c. 10; 6 Henry VIII, c. 16; Porritt, *The Unreformed House of Commons*, i, 157; *House of Commons Journals*, i, 136; D'Ewes, 309; Mountmorres, *Ancient Parliament of Ireland*, i, 87.

the borough of Andover to allow him to nominate one of their members makes the further offer that if for the purpose of saving expense they intend to name for the other burgess some one outside of the town he will see that a sufficient man is provided who will make no charge, and suggests that they send the indenture of election to him in blank and he will fill in the two names. Northampton in 1601 elects two men on condition that they agree to bear their own charges. Payment of one of the Leicester members was objected to on the ground that he had agreed not to ask for pay " except he did good to the Towne," and it was ordered that unless he did something of special advantage to the town in the next parliament he should return his wages. Another member, who had quarreled with his constituents, brought suit against them for his wages. They testified that he had agreed to serve without wages, was not a freeman of their town and had not attended the parliament. Payment of some members long continued, certainly into the next century, but in the main the contemporary historian of parliament was correct when he declared " of late times the knights, citizens and burgesses of the House of Commons for the most part bear their own charges." They were of a class of society that could well afford to do so.[10]

Elections were usually made by small numbers of voters, but there were occasional instances of large gatherings. In the election for knights for the county of Norfolk in 1586, 3000 persons were present. In 1597 election for Yorkshire was sought by Sir John Stanhope, a land owner and *custos rotulorum* of the North Riding, and also treasurer of the queen's chamber, master of the posts, and long resident at court, and Sir Thomas Hobby, a nephew of Lord Burghley and also a courtier. They had great support, especially

---

[10] Merewether and Stephens, ii, 1223, 1393–4; Bateson, *Leicester,* iii, 188; *Northampton Borough Records,* ii, 493; D'Ewes, 80, 407; *List of all Cities . . . sending burgesses to Parliament, State Papers, Dom., Eliz.,* cclxv, 28.

from the northern nobility and gentry and the officials of the Council of the North, and believed they could count on some 3000 votes if they needed them. Shortly before the election, however, Sir John Savile, a Yorkshire gentleman backed by the earl of Shrewsbury, announced himself a candidate, sought support among the clothiers and artisans of the West Riding, and secured as a fellow candidate a representative of another old Yorkshire family, Sir William Fairfax. On the evening of Sunday, October 2, the day before the meeting of the county court the city of York was full of the partisans of the opposing candidates, led by the candidates themselves. The Archbishop of York and other members of the Council of the North issued a proclamation enjoining good order and summoned Sir John Savile to appear before them early next morning to promise an orderly election. He did so reluctantly and only on the ground that it was the "queen's business." He wished to have the election adjourned from the Castle, where it regularly took place, to a neighboring moor on account of the numbers expected, but finally agreed to the regular procedure, including reading of the writ and of the laws restricting voting to forty shillings freeholders, but insisting on the reading also of the law requiring that representatives should be residents of the county.

When the election was opened by the under-sheriff, the writ and statutes read and the nominations made, there was a great clamor from the many hundred present, each shouting for his candidate. This lasted for two hours until the parties agreed to draw off into two groups, each marshaled under a leader. Then the sheriff and five gentlemen from each party went up to a window in the castle where they could look down on the crowd. They all agreed that the supporters of Savile and Fairfax were the more numerous by two or three hundred. The other party, however, declared that in the crowd were women and children, artisans and others who were not freeholders and should not therefore be counted, and demanded that everyone should be polled and sworn as to his right to vote. There was some dispute as to how this should be done and while it was being attempted, with the gate shut, Sir John Savile and his followers opened the gate and rushed out with the claim that they were victorious. They carried the under-sheriff off with them to dinner.

The Stanhope party, who claimed that if only freeholders were counted they had a majority of at least three hundred, protested and tried to induce the sheriff to hold a new election, but he did not return to the Castle till two hours later, then declared the court open again and immediately signed the credentials of Savile and Fairfax. The protests of Stanhope, being the official candidate, were more influential at court than among the mixed population of York. A series of orders from the privy council for the punishment of Savile followed and although he had left for London before he could be arrested, when he arrived there he was sent to the Fleet and kept in prison three weeks, until after parliament had actually opened. Nevertheless he and his companion remained the representatives from Yorkshire in the parliament of 1597.[11]

On October 20, 1601, when the election for the next parliament was in progress at Denbigh in Wales there was a sudden outcry that two knights and their followers had their swords drawn against another knight and his followers in the churchyard. The tumult grew till the sheriff was forced to adjourn the election to avoid bloodshed, and as a matter of fact Denbighshire went without a representative through the whole of this parliament.[12]

These election questions had to do with the Commons; the most familiar echo of the writs sent to the Lords, both temporal and spiritual, was a series of requests for permission to remain away. Absence was possible because of the practice of giving proxies in the House of Lords, which of

11 *Hatfield House MSS.*, vii, 411–17, 425–6, 435–6; *Acts of the Privy Council*, xxviii, 46, 114; D'Ewes, 396.
12 *Acts of the Privy Council*, xxxii, 342; D'Ewes, 627.

course did not exist in the House of Commons. Nobles permitted to stay away sent a proxy to act and vote for them to some one who would be present; frequently Burghley and other great officials held a number of such proxies. The Bishop of Carlisle writes to Cecil that he has no robes ready to wear in parliament and must either stay away or sit in his rochet. Archbishop Hutton of York is old and feeble; Lord Darcy asks Shrewsbury to procure him a license to stay away because he is sick and old, and sends him his proxy. Viscount Bindon, Lord Morley and the earl of Bath are sick and offer Cecil the disposal of their proxies. Excuses ran all the way from the bishop of Worcester's dread that travelling on horseback at a bad season of the year would bring on a fit of the stone to the earl of Pembroke's sulking in his tent because a much desired sinecure office had gone to Sir Charles Blount not to himself, and he would under the circumstances feel disgraced to come into the presence of the other nobles. The three nobles who were pardoned for their participation in the Essex rebellion in the spring of 1601 were summoned to parliament in the fall but ordered to send proxies rather than come in person, as their presence might, in the view of the government at least, be distasteful to their more loyal colleagues. Yet excuses were not lightly made nor readily accepted, and as a matter of fact an almost unbroken body of the peerage of England were found in their places when parliament opened, or sent explanations of their delay and presented themselves later.[13]

The official instructions for the ceremonies on the opening of the parliament of 1589 by the queen are still preserved, and from them the scene can be pictured. Tuesday, February 4, in the morning she emerged from her palace of Whitehall and, preceded by a long train of gentlemen, esquires, knights, judges, lawyers, household and heraldic

[13] D'Ewes, 3-9, 422; *Cal. State Papers, Dom.*, 1581-90, 575; *Hatfield House MSS.*, xi, 409, 442, 443, 456-7; *Histor. MSS. Comm. Rep.*, Rutland Papers, i, 379.

officers, the lord chancellor, lord treasurer, lord admiral, and lord chamberlain, archbishops, bishops, nobles, servitors carrying her cloak and hat, her sword and cap of honor, riding while all others walked and followed by the ladies of her court and her guard, she passed across the few hundred yards to Westminster Abbey and entered by the north door of the transept, where hundreds of worshippers, sightseers and idlers enter daily now. She was received at the door by the dean and chapter and by the officers of her own chapel, presented with the sceptre, which was then kept in the abbey, and led to the choir. While she waited the lord steward went to the parliament house and brought back the mace. After service, in which the queen alone took communion, and a sermon, the procession left by the south door of the transept, where the sceptre was handed back to the dean, passed across Old Palace Yard, and the queen with the most distinguished of her train entered through a passageway not far from the present royal entrance, to the parliament buildings, then on practically the same site as now, though far different in construction. The Commons meanwhile were gathering in their own house.

While the queen put on her robes in her robing room the lords did the same in theirs and took their seats according to their degrees in the long room which served them as a meeting place and which was almost identical in location with the present outer lobby common to the two Houses. The queen then emerged from her robing room, took her place in her " seat royal," the lord chancellor at her right hand, the lord treasurer at her left, other high officials ranged in their proper positions and the emblems of majesty placed before her. The names of the nobles were then called in order by the clerk of parliament, the knights of the shire and burgesses advised of the queen's presence and permitted to enter, and the lord chancellor in a formal oration declared in her name the reason of their summons. Then the queen was reminded that she should direct the Commons to retire to choose their speaker, which she did.

As they left she rose from her seat, disrobed in her room and returned to Whitehall, some of her train following her by land, others going by the river.[14]

The entrance of the Commons to listen to the lord chancellor's address and to receive permission from the queen to withdraw to choose their speaker holds but a minor place in the official arrangements for the ceremony of the opening day of parliament, but it was this which distinguished it from a score of other contemporary processions and which gave it a significance far beyond them. It is the representatives of the shires and the boroughs that we must follow to understand the organization and trace the history of parliament Before and immediately after the royal progress to the parliament house the lord steward, in 1589 the earl of Derby, sitting in the great room of the Court of Requests administered to such privy councillors as had been elected to parliament the special form of the oath of supremacy ordered to be taken by its members. They in turn called the roll of members and gave the oath to groups of them as they appeared. The knights, gentlemen and burgesses then took their places in their own house, which was at this time St. Stephen's Chapel, separated only by a lobby and a single turn from the House of Lords.

It was apparently in the midst of these proceedings that the summons came to attend the queen. In response they thronged into the House of Lords crowding around the rail or bar at its lower end. There was not room there for all the members of the Lower House and there was much crowding and disorder before the door was closed and many were necessarily left outside. At a later parliament of this period the gentleman usher of the House of Lords closed the doors so promptly that all but a very few of the Commons were excluded. When they clamored outside he opened the door far enough to call out a threat to have them

---

[14] *State Papers, Dom., Eliz.,* ccxxii, 59; *Harleian MSS.,* 6849, p. 79; Josef Redlich, *Parliamentary Procedure,* Trans. from German by E. Steinthal, i, 26–43; Tanner, 541–5.

all put in the stocks.   The exclusion and the insult alike were bitterly resented by the Commons and protested against when they returned to their own House, and were subsequently apologized for by the privy councillors present.[15]

The privy councillors who were members of the House of Commons were in a peculiar and interesting position.   All the members of the privy council were members of one House or the other.   Those who were not nobles or prelates, and therefore not in the House of Lords, secured by one means or another seats in the House of Commons in each successive parliament as knights of one or other of the shires. In the parliament of 1589 of the privy councillors who were not peers Sir Francis Knollys, treasurer of the household, sat for Oxfordshire, Sir Walter Mildmay, chancellor of the exchequer, for Northampton, Sir Thomas Heneage, vice chamberlain, for Essex, Sir James Croft, comptroller, for Hereford, and Secretary John Wooley, for Dorset, besides Sir Francis Walsingham, who was knight of the shire for Surrey although he did not attend, and died before the end of the session.   In 1593, Heneage, Knollys and Wooley were again members.   Sir John Fortescue was chancellor of the exchequer and a member, and Sir Robert Cecil, who was now a privy councillor, sat as knight of the shire for Oxford. In the House of Commons of the parliament of 1597 there were but three privy councillors, Cecil, now secretary, Fortescue, chancellor of the exchequer, and Sir William Knollys, son of Sir Francis, comptroller.   In 1601, there were four, Cecil, Knollys, Sir John Stanhope, vice chamberlain, and Sir John Herbert, second secretary.   There were thus always three, four or five privy council members. They formed a sort of embryo ministry.   They evidently sat near together, for they are spoken of at one time as " talking one with another."   Their place was near the speaker for they were more than once referred to as " the honorable that sit about the chair."   The expression " honorable " seems to have been already applied in a special

15 D'Ewes, 205, 332, 422, 456, 468, 535, 548.

sense to the privy councillors. The speaker mentions them once as " the Honorable persons which do assist this Chair "; at another time there is a reference to two of the privy councillors as " those two Honorable Persons that sit above." Again when Secretary Cecil was annoyed at an interruption from a member sitting near the door he challenged him to change position and office with him, evidently referring to his own place in the House.

It was quite natural that the privy councillors should be in a certain sense leaders in the House of Commons. Their daily duties and presence at court as well as in parliament made them a link with the queen; the prestige of their membership in the permanent administrative council of the realm necessarily gave them prominence in this still more dignified though less continuous council; and they were familiar with many affairs of state of which other members of parliament knew nothing. Indeed on one occasion the queen rebuked the House for treating those whom she honored with her permanent confidence as if they were ordinary members of parliament, councillors for but a season. At another time, when she wished to be especially gracious at the close of a session it was " Mr. Comptroller and Mr. Secretary and you of my council " that she addressed among the throng of members of the House of Commons present, asking them to bring their fellow members to kiss her hand before departing to their homes. Their fellow members, on the other hand, appealed to them to induce the queen not to dissolve parliament immediately after it had passed the subsidy and before it completed the legislation on which it was engaged. At another time one of the privy council members offered, if the House wished him to, to communicate privately with the queen about certain doubtful matters they had before them. They were placed on all important committees, one or other of them frequently took the initiative in bringing matters before parliament and they all spoke frequently in debate. It is possible from a study of their speeches and actions in parliament to formulate their position somewhat as follows: they took a leading part in debate, they opposed any action that would be distasteful to the queen, they protected her prerogative, they pushed through the subsidies, they acted as spokesmen for the queen and in a less formal way than the Speaker as intermediary between her and the House. It will be noted that in the House of Lords the lord chancellor who opened and closed parliament, the lord steward, who swore in the members, the lord treasurer, who was an active participant in its actions, were all privy councillors.

Yet there is no indication of the joint action of the privy councillors in the two Houses, and the solidarity of the little group of privy councillors in the House of Commons must not be exaggerated or their influence overestimated. They frequently took different sides in debate and even the most influential of them were often outvoted. They were special councillors of the queen, heads of branches of her official household, influential members of parliament but not leaders of a party, much less members of a cabinet.[16]

One of the most definite parts played by the privy councillors in parliament was the initiative they or some one of them took in nominating the Speaker. Although it is intended that this chapter should be devoted primarily to the parliament of 1589, its special subject, parliamentary organization and procedure, can be made more clear by supplementing its records by those of 1597. When in 1589 Lord Chancellor Hatton after his address to the Lords and Commons bade the latter retire to their own House and complete their organization by naming for the queen's approval one of their own number to represent them, it is recorded only that they did so, electing George Snagg, a London lawyer, as their Speaker. The ceremonies connected with the election of Serjeant Yelverton in the parliament of 1597 are recorded in much greater detail and are doubtless equally

---

[16] *Return of Names of Members of Parliament, Blue Book,* 1878, i, 422–41; Townshend, *Historical Collections,* 249, 337–50; D'Ewes, 176, 466, 471–4, 488, 632, 652, 660, 663–5, 675–6.

typical. In this parliament after listening at the bar of the House of Lords to the opening address of Lord Keeper Egerton and being commanded by him in the name of the queen to retire and choose their Speaker, the Commons withdrew as usual to their own House. After they had sat for some time in silence, Sir William Knollys, comptroller of the household, stood up and with considerable circumlocution and occasional pauses, during one of which, according to the Journal, " the House hawked and spat," presumably to show their impatience, he declared that according to his judgment Mr. Serjeant Yelverton was the fittest of their number to be Speaker, and asked the members to show their approval or disapproval of his nomination; " after which words Mr. Yelverton blushed and put off his hat and after sat bare-headed." Amid a chorus of ayes, the comptroller then " made a low reverence and sat down " and Mr. Yelverton rose and " after a very humble reverence " stated his deficiencies. He pointed out that " he that supplieth this place ought to be a man bigg and comely, stately and well spoken, his voice great, his carriage majesticall, his nature haughty and his purse plentiful and heavy," that " contrarily the stature of my body is small, myself not so well spoken, my voice low, my carriage lawyer-like and of the common fashion, my nature soft and bashful, my purse thin, light and never yet plentiful." Especially did he shrink from appearing before " the unspeakable majesty and Sacred Personage your dread and dear Sovereign; the terror of whose countenance will appall and abase even the stoutest heart, yea whose very name will pull down the greatest courage. For how mightily doth the estate and name of a Prince deject the haughtiest stomach even of their greatest subject!"

Notwithstanding all this modesty and half-humorous self-depreciation on the part of the candidate and his appeals to the House to choose some one else, Sir John Fortescue, chancellor of the exchequer, proceeded to second the nomination, there was general acclamation, Knollys put the ques-

tion of his election, and when a storm of ayes responded and
there were no nays the two privy councillors placed the
nominee in the Speaker's chair. A similar ceremony was
apparently performed in each of the parliaments of Elizabeth. In the parliament of 1584 the Treasurer of the
Household named Sir John Pickering, and when the members, most of whom were new, remained silent, a court
lawyer called to those near him " Cry ' Pickering,' " which
they did. In the parliament of 1589, as already intimated,
we are told only that the House chose George Snagg, serjeant
at law, and that he was placed in the chair and subsequently
led to the bar of the House of Lords by two of the most
eminent personages in the House of Commons. In the
parliament of 1593, Sir Francis Knollys, treasurer of the
household, and Sir Thomas Heneage, vice-chancellor, nominated Solicitor General Coke, and in the remaining parliament of Elizabeth, that of 1601, Sir William Knollys,
comptroller of the household, and Sir John Stanhope, vice-
chancellor, similarly nominated and supported John Crooke,
Recorder of London. In each case the nomination was
made by one of the privy council, seconded by another and
carried by acclamation of the House. There is no recorded
election of a Speaker in the reign of Elizabeth who was not
nominated by a privy councillor. The nominee was in each
of the eleven parliaments of Elizabeth a lawyer, either one of
the law officers of the crown, as in the cases of Solicitors
General Onslow and Popham in the early parliaments and
Coke in 1593, or, as in the cases of Puckering in 1586 and
1587 and Yelverton in 1597, serjeants of the law who were
destined to early further promotion under the crown.

Under these circumstances it can hardly be seriously
doubted that the nominee was regularly selected by the
queen beforehand and notified of his approaching election,
and that all this ceremonious deference to the general opinion
of the House, like the surprise and self-disparagement of the
nominee, were an empty form. For the parliament of 1589
we have proof. September 2, 1588, five months before par-

liament met, but only two before its original summons, Lord Chancellor Hatton writes from court to Serjeant Puckering, " I have thought good to let you understand how the world goes here touching the Speaker of the Lower House, which charge her Majesty hath now resolved to lay on Mr. Serjeant Snagge." This doubtful relation between form and reality troubled contemporaries as much as it has modern scholars. One of the best known and most learned books of the period, Sir Thomas Smith's *De Republica Anglorum,* in its first edition, in 1583, describes the election of the Speaker as if it were entirely in the hands of the members; the same book in its third edition, published in 1589 and stated, but probably untruly, to be revised by the author, declares that the Speaker " is commonly appointed by the King or Queene, though accepted by the assent of the House." [17]

The second meeting, usually two days after the first, was regularly devoted to the completion of the process of organization. The queen again appeared in state, the Lords took their formal positions, wearing their parliament robes, " sitting still in their great estates very solemnly," as Sir Walter Ralegh once described them, and the Commons again came thronging to the bar of the House of Lords, this time bringing with them their nominee for Speaker. He was presented to the queen by his sponsors, the two privy council members who had originally nominated him. In the case of Serjeant Snagg, Speaker of the parliament of 1589, Coke of the parliament of 1593, Yelverton in 1597, and Crooke in 1601, the ceremony was the same. The Speaker-elect addressed the queen, " disabled himself," according to the contemporary expression, with even more logic and eloquence than that which he had used to his fellow members, and asked to be excused from duties to which he was so

[17] D'Ewes, frontispiece, 3, 79, 121, 156, 205, 281, 333, 421, 428, 469, 548, 621 ; Thomas Wright, *Queen Elizabeth and her Times,* ii, 243–4; Sir Thomas Smith, *De Republica Anglorum,* Book ii, chap. 2, Ed. 1906, 51, 148, 154; Sir Harris Nicolas, *Life and Times of Sir Christopher Hatton,* 482.

unequal. But the lord chancellor, after a private colloquy with the queen, declared her acceptance of him, in more than one instance pointing out that the very speech in which he had described his deficiencies showed by its form and content his special capacity to fill the office. The candidate now yielded, thanked the queen for her acceptance of him and made a set speech, closing with a request for the usual privileges of the Commons.

These time-honored privileges were that members might have liberty of speech in their debates in the House, that they, their servants and attendants might have freedom from suits and arrests, that they might have access to the queen " on all urgent and important occasions," and, for the Speaker himself, that if he mistook his instructions or his duty he should be pardoned. These were the " ancient liberties " of the Commons, as they were regularly claimed. Though they were of very different degrees of ancientness, by 1589 they had become stereotyped; they were always the same and were always granted.

It is noticeable, however, that Elizabeth seldom failed to make some reservation or restriction upon her grants. In 1589, according to the Journal, " Her majesty was graciously pleased to grant all his said Petitions, and that he the said Speaker and the House of Commons should use and enjoy all such liberties and privileges as others before them had been accustomed to use and enjoy in the times of her Majesties most noble progenitors, and withal admonishing them not to extend the said privileges to any unreverent and misbecoming speech, or unnecessary accesses to her Majesty." In the next parliament, Lord Keeper Puckering explained that " For libertie of speech her majestie commandeth me to tell you, that to saye yea or no to Bills, God forbid that any man should be restrained or afrayde to answer accordinge to his best likinge, with some shorte declaracion of his reason therin, and therin to have a free voyce, which is the verye trew libertie of the house, not as some suppose to speake there of all causes as he listeth and to frame a forme of Relligion or a state of Government as to their idle braynes shall seeme meetest. She sayeth no king fitt for his state will suffer such absurdities." Similarly they were warned that the freedom of their attendants as well as themselves from arrest should not protect their servants' ill doings or failure to perform their duties. Access to her person was to be " onlye on matters of the greatest exigencie and weight." This opening speech of the lord keeper in 1593, quoting the verbal instructions of the queen and delivered in her presence, as we now have it in a more authoritative form than that given by D'Ewes, was an alternation of concessions that " her majestie graunteth you liberall but not licentious speech, libertie therefore but with dew limitations," and warnings " that each man of you conteyne his speech within the bounds of loyaltie and good discrecion." [18]

In 1597 the Commons received admonition " that the said Liberties and Priviledges should be discreetly and wisely used, as was meet." In 1601 they are warned that the freedom from arrest of their attendants should not be so used as to allow them to protect " notorious persons either for life or behaviour and desperate Debtors, Pettifoggers and vipers of the Commonwealth." Queen Elizabeth's conception of the government of England was far from including a parliament independent of the crown. Parliament must, like everything else, be under her constant supervision and the Speaker and parliament itself in the last resort subject to her control; though fortunately neither she nor they so acted under usual circumstances.

After obtaining approval of his election and these promises and making three low bows to the queen, the new Speaker was escorted back to the Commons House by the serjeant with the mace, the members following, and placed in his chair. The queen then withdrew from the House of

---

[18] D'Ewes, 460, 526, 602; Smith, *De Republica*, Book ii, c. 2; *Harleian MSS.*, 6265, fos. 111–4, edited by E. M. Neale, *The Lord Keeper's Speech to the Parliament of 1593, Eng. Hist. Review*, Jan. 1916, 134–7; Tanner, 550–65.

Lords, first directing the lord chancellor to bid the Lords proceed with their labors.[19]

The last four parliaments of Queen Elizabeth, those which fall within the period of this work, were held at intervals of almost exactly four years, in 1589, 1593, 1597 and 1601. The sessions were not long. Each lasted for a period of seven weeks only, except the third, which ran on for almost twice that long, though three of its fourteen weeks were devoted to a Christmas holiday. The House of Lords would have included some seventy members, if all the peers of England, lay and spiritual, had been present, but the actual attendance was between forty-five and fifty-five. In the House of Commons were four hundred and sixty members. The type of men who made it up were country gentlemen, brothers or younger sons of noblemen, rural landowners, well-to-do town merchants, a sprinkling of lawyers and officials, a few men of lower rank who had become famous as military or naval men. The names on the roll of parliament are often well known elsewhere. Francis Bacon, Sir Walter Ralegh, Fulke Greville, Sir Francis Drake, Sir Henry Unton, Sir Thomas Baskerville, Doctor Caesar, Jerome Horsey, John Lyly, John Chamberlain, Thomas Cavendish, Sir Robert Sydney, Sir John Norris, Sir Richard Lovelace, Humphrey and Adrian Gilbert, Carew Ralegh, Sir William Monson, John and Thomas Sherley and many more appear familiarly in the records of parliament as they already have in other chapters of this book as men of learning, poets, ambassadors, explorers, commanders of expeditions by sea or land. There were Blounts, Moores, Fortescues, Gawdeys, Wentworths, Cromwells, Howards, Wingfields, Careys, Norrises, Trelawneys, Godolphins, Courtneys, Brookes, Seymours and other possessors of well-known patronymics each characteristic of some English or Welsh shire. Sometimes there were four or five of the same family name in the same parliament.

There were, besides the group of privy councillors already

[19] D'Ewes, 97, 116, 141, 421, 428, 440, 459. 460, 478, 536, 548.

named, such lower officials as Dr. Dale, master of the Court
of Requests, Sir George Carey, marshal of the household,
Thomas Hesketh and later James Morrice, attorneys of the
Court of Wards and Liveries, Thomas Fanshawe, remem-
brancer of the Exchequer, Thomas Fleming, solicitor general, the lieutenant of the Tower, the attorney of the Duchy
of Lancaster and others. The knights of the shires and burgesses in the House of Commons were of the same classes,
rural gentry, officials, lawyers and substantial merchants, as
we constantly meet carrying on the local government and
most of the central administration of Elizabethan England.
Forty out of the four hundred and sixty members of the
parliament of 1589 were knights, though, as we have frequently observed, this is not an important distinction, since
many others were of the same social class and personal
prominence, though they might be simple esquires or gentlemen. There were some twenty lawyers in the same parliament, all representing town constituencies. When other
burgesses can be identified they are either town officials,
merchants, nearby gentry or, in a large number of cases,
government officials. As one looks over the lists of well-
known names representing obscure boroughs and distant
counties, the inference cannot be avoided that this last class,
those who obtained their position directly or indirectly by
the influence of the government, was overwhelmingly large
and another evidence of the ubiquity of Tudor administration.[20]

As in all assemblies some members were active, others
less so. Certain names are constantly met with serving on
committees, taking part in debate, appointed to confer with
the Lords. If Sir Walter Ralegh, Francis Bacon and Sir
Robert Cecil had not been eminent in any other sphere
they would still have been famous as the most active parliament men of their time. Ralegh was a member of the

[20] *Return of Names of Members of Parliament, Blue Book,* 1878, i, 422–
41; Heywood Townshend, *Historical Collections . . . of the Proceedings of
the Four Last Parliaments of Queen Elizabeth,* 337–50.

last three parliaments of the period, appointed on almost every important committee, speaking again and again in debate and indefatigable. Bacon was a member of all four parliaments and his many speeches are noticeable even in the arid official records from their sententiousness, originality of simile and fertility of suggestion. Cecil was strenuous beyond the activity already mentioned as characteristic of the privy councillor members of parliament. He was a member of the last seven parliaments of the reign. Though he announced early in the parliament of 1601 that he intended to take but little part in the proceedings he spoke practically every day of the session and was more than once engaged in a prolonged and somewhat acrid wrangle. The lawyer members were also usually active, as were in one or more of the parliaments Sir Thomas Hastings, brother of the earl of Huntingdon, George Brooke, brother of Lord Cobham, Sir Thomas Hobby, nephew of Lord Burghley, Sir Roger North, Francis Moore and many others. In contrast with these were the " silent members," familiar in all periods and parliaments.[21]

The parliaments of the time as a whole were hard-working bodies, meeting almost if not quite every day, usually at eight o'clock in the morning, sometimes at seven or even half past six. The House of Commons sat till noon, the afternoons being usually given over to committee meetings. On one occasion when the debate dragged on till quarter of one it was spoken of as " very late " and the House became so restless that they passed an important bill without a division, though a division had already been announced. Doubtless the midday dinner customary at the time was making its appeal, especially as committee meetings were usually appointed for two o'clock. Perhaps also the fact that it was not till half a century later that the innovation of providing seats with backs was introduced had something to do with the desire of the members to adjourn. The House

---

[21] *Return of Members*, i, 422–41; D'Ewes, 428–689; Porritt, *The Unreformed House of Commons*, i, 427; *House of Commons Journals*, i, 141.

was also much overcrowded if all members were present. In the later weeks of the session the House often held two sessions a day, in the afternoon as well as morning, leaving the committees to meet as best they might.

Although parliament as a whole was industrious, many of the individual members neglected their duties. The parliament of 1589 had only been in session five days when one of its members called attention to the poor attendance; the matter was referred to a committee, which recommended that the roll should be called from time to time and that members absent should be fined. Two weeks later the matter was again brought up and still later in the session it was declared that not more than one half the members of the House of Commons were attending. The queen herself sent to complain of it and ordered the roll to be called to indicate who were the offenders. The total number voting is frequently scarcely more than a hundred out of the four hundred and sixty members. In the House of Lords the attendance was apt to be as poor as it is three hundred years later. Burghley at one time made a motion that such lords as were absent without sending proxies and those who neglected attendance should be admonished.[22]

Although voluntary resignations were not permitted, members were frequently allowed by vote of the House to return to their homes to attend to business considered necessary or on account of serious illness of themselves or members of their families. Vacancies occurred from time to time. At the beginning of each parliament it became evident that, in the absence of party machinery for nominations, the same man had been elected for two or more constituencies. He must choose for which of them he would serve and a new election must be held to fill the vacancy. Defective returns, deaths, " phrensy " or other illness making a man incapable of serving, all gave occasion for bye-elections, though these could not then serve their major modern use of indicating changes of popular political sentiment. Every effort was

[22] D'Ewes, 430, 439, 453, 528.

made to keep the membership intact and to secure attendance. Yet after all the work of parliament was done by a minority of interested and hard-working members.

Good order was then as now regularly insisted on though not always secured. The Speaker at one time complains that three or four members often continued standing at the same time, though they all knew which had risen first, each hoping that he would be called upon to speak first by acclamation of the House, " growing for the most part to a great confused noise and sound of senseless words." He urged members to consider that they were as judges in the highest court in the land and should respect the honor and gravity of the House. At another time the Speaker noticing some members whispering together called them to order on the ground that none should speak secretly in the House but all should use public speech only. A member complains in the parliament of 1593 that he is being constantly interrupted and the ancient customs of the House not observed. In 1601 when a certain lawyer in a debate on the subsidies expressed absurdly high royalist doctrine, that the queen might take all the lands and goods of all her people if she liked, " all the House hemmed and laughed and talked." Even after the Speaker called them to order and the debater proceeded to declare " all your hemming shall not put me out of Countenance," and quoted rather musty twelfth and thirteenth century precedents, " the House hemmed again." When in a debate on pluralities in November, 1601, an old doctor of the civil law was both long-winded and inaudible " the House hawked and spat and kept a great coil to make him an end."

This parliament of 1601 was, it is true, the most disorderly of the queen's reign. More than once the members got out of hand and cried out their desires in opposition to the Speaker's decision; those who supported his authority were hissed, debaters were coughed or cried down, and even the privy councillors got scant attention. Cecil at one time quite lost his patience and declared that in the seven parliaments of which he had been a member he had never seen so much levity and disorder. The behavior of the House, he said, was "more fit for a Grammar School than a Court of Parliament." The next day he apologized, though he could not help reminding his hearers that Demosthenes had called the clamors of the Athenians puerile, an analogy satisfactory, it may be presumed, to all concerned. Once when there was a close vote, two men on one side and one on the other were pulled back by their coats when they were about to go out on division and thus prevented from voting. In fact the disorders of this parliament were spoken of outside and became a matter of general scandal. At least one pamphlet describing its disorderly proceedings was printed and publicly circulated. Yet these disorders must not be exaggerated or considered typical. They occurred infrequently and mostly in connection with the few questions on which the spirits of the time were most stirred or in the somewhat anomalous session of 1601. They were always rebuked by the more dignified members. The very attention these instances awakened strengthens the abundant direct testimony, which is that the usual proceedings of both the House of Lords and the House of Commons were conducted with gravity and decorum.[23]

The privileges which the Speaker had claimed and obtained at his appointment were not by any means an empty formula. It is true that his plea for personal pardon for failure in interpretation was merely formal and was never questioned. Nor was the privilege of access to the queen frequently made use of or ever denied, though at least once it gave the members small comfort. In 1589, when word had come to the House of Commons that the queen was much offended with their proposed legislation on certain matters she considered in her own province, the House asked the vice-chamberlain of the household, one of their members, to arrange for a time when the Speaker and a

[23] D'Ewes, 434, 481, 487, 633, 640, 653, 684; Sir Thomas Smith, *De Republica Anglorum*, 169–81.

committee could appear before her to explain their action.
Although their first appointment had to be postponed because the queen had taken cold, she gave them audience the
next day and in characteristic fashion sent them away graciously scolded and politely informed of her objections to
their action rather than given an opportunity to deliver their
message. The much more important and more satisfactory
interview at court in 1601 between the members of the
House of Commons and the queen concerning the monopolies was rather of Elizabeth's seeking than theirs. An account of it will fall more properly in a later section.[24]

The privilege of freedom of speech was a more difficult
matter. If it meant simply, as the queen described it in
1593, that the expressions used by any individual member
in the course of the debates should be unrestricted, there
was during this period no case of limitation or punishment,
at least by the queen, though there was some unofficial criticism by individual ministers. But if freedom of speech included permission to any member or to the House as a whole
to introduce and to discuss any measure he or they thought
fit to initiate and consider, such privilege was far from being
admitted. Elizabeth felt herself free not only to veto bills
which had been passed but to limit both in general and in
detail parliament's proposals for legislation. This claim in-
volves in fact the whole question of the extension or limitation of the queen's prerogative, which, culminating as it did
in the last parliament of her reign, will be treated there
rather than in its occasional emergence in these earlier
parliaments.

Of the four traditional privileges, it was, however, neither
the pardon of the Speaker, access to the queen, nor freedom
of speech that interested or occupied most the Elizabethan
parliaments, it was the freedom from suits and arrests of
themselves and their servitors, with the various ramifications
and implications of this privilege. In that litigious age the
possibilities of involvement in the law seem to have been al-

[24] D'Ewes, 442–4; Townshend, *Historical Collections,* 261–6.

most infinite, and exemption from this, even during a couple of months once in four years, was a tempting monopoly for members of parliament, quite apart from the dignity of that body and high theories of their representative character. Much of the time of their sessions was spent in enforcing this right. They were in no danger at this time of arrest by the government for political objects. The suits, arrests and subpoenas from which members claimed exemption were of a civil kind. What may be considered a typical instance was brought up in the House of Commons Thursday, March 5, 1593, five days before the close of the parliament of that year. Francis Neal, one of the burgesses from the borough of Grantham, Lincolnshire, complained that on the preceding Sunday afternoon he had been arrested for a debt by a bailiff named John Lightburn on a warrant sworn out by a brewer named Wesselen Weblen. He had paid the debt, but to preserve the liberties and privileges of parliament made this protest.

The House was quick to take up the matter and ordered the serjeant to summon the two offenders, the brewer and the bailiff, to appear at the bar the next day. They did so and were " charged by the Speaker very deeply and amply with their contempt against the Authority and Jurisdiction of this Most High Court of Parliament." They acknowledged their fault with great humility, as occurred in every similar case of which we have record during this period. Once placed at the bar of the House there seems to have been none who was not awed by its dignity and repute. In this case, after considerable comparing of notes among the members, the heinousness of the fault of the culprits was declared to them and they were sent to the Tower of London to remain during the pleasure of parliament. The pleasure of this particular parliament had no long continuance, for its dissolution was, as has been said, to come five days later. So after a detention of three days the dignity of the House was considered to be preserved, and Lightburn and Weblen were released, after paying their fees. The fact that a parliament, however powerful during its continuance, had but a limited life, and went out of existence immediately on its dissolution, in contrast with the administrative and judicial sides of government, which had a continuing life, deeply affected the character of Tudor government, weakening the influence of parliament as an institution and at the same time increasing the self-assertion of any particular parliament during the few weeks or months in which it did exist. It was this shortness of its life, probably, quite as much as the fact that by being troubled by suits a member would be " withdrawn from his service in the House, both in his mind and in his person," that made the House so sensitive to violations of this ancient privilege, and the substantial advantages of the exemption added vigor to their repeated assertions of it.[25]

Questions of freedom from arrest were apt to be combined with disputed elections. For instance in 1593 a Thomas Fitzherbert, who had been outlawed for debt according to the formalities of an ancient writ, and was therefore, on a strict interpretation of the law, incapable of serving in parliament, was arrested for debt during the few hours between his election and his certification by the sheriff. Did his privilege of parliament exempt him from arrest? This case filled hour after hour of debate, into which the Speaker himself was drawn, and was closed finally by a compromise that did little but make more clear the claim of the House of Commons to be judge of its own disputed elections.[26]

This frequency of questions of dispute about elections and privileges seems to have given rise to the first regular standing committee of the House, an institution which had but a temporary life in England but was destined to a long and influential career in numerous offshoots of the English parliament. Committees had been appointed from time to time in earlier parliaments to consider election disputes and claims of members that their privileges had been invaded.

[25] D'Ewes, 518–9, 612; Tanner, 554–65.
[26] D'Ewes, 393, 396–9, 502–3.

But each of these was for a particular case. In 1589 a further step was taken. Thursday, February 6, the very day on which the Speaker was accepted by the queen, a motion concerning the privileges of the House was made, and on the next day a committee of ten was appointed to examine into all matters of privilege that should come up during the session of parliament and report from time to time to the House. The next day, Saturday, Sir Edward Hobby called attention to the many abuses in the election of knights and burgesses, some places that should send representatives not having done so and some that had not before sent them now doing so, two sets of claimants appearing for some places, and one representative sometimes elected for two places. The House thereupon appointed another committee of ten who should with the clerk of the crown go over the returns of the sheriffs as to elections and compare them with the official roll of members.[27]

In the next parliament, that of 1593, one committee for the two purposes was appointed when, immediately after the organization of the House, a member moved for the investigation of a contested election case and another for a committee on the liberties and privileges of members of the House. This committee was a distinguished one, including all privy councillors, Ralegh, Bacon, Drake, Yelverton, Moore and Wroth, the movers of the two resolutions, and others. It was ordered to remain in existence during the whole session of parliament to consider and report on all cases of election and all cases of privilege that might come up, and it proved to have much work to do.

In the next parliament the appointment of such a standing committee on elections and privileges seems to have been taken for granted for the Speaker reminded the House of the matter at its first meeting and a committee of some forty members was thereupon appointed and served through the whole session. In the parliament of 1601 the same action was taken, and in the first parliament of the next reign

[27] D'Ewes, 417, 429-30.

it is spoken of as " a usual motion in the beginning of every Parliament." [28]

Many of the cases brought to the attention of the House were subpoenas to testify rather than actual arrests in a suit. On the second day of the parliament of 1597 Sir Thomas Knyvet, one of the members from Westminster, reported that he had been served since the opening of parliament with a subpoena to testify in the Chancery, and appealed to the privileges of parliament. The matter was referred to the standing committee upon privileges and elections. They took it very seriously and found a precedent of the time of Queen Mary where two members of the House were sent to the lord chancellor requiring him to revoke a subpoena. This precedent was followed and Sir Edward Hobby and a Mr. Brograve were sent to Lord Keeper Egerton requiring him to revoke the writ recently sent out. The Lord Keeper balked at the word " require," and asked them whether the House had used that word advisedly. On their insisting that this was the form of their commission he pointed out that by withdrawing the subpoena under these circumstances they would be restraining the judicial power of the queen, and he would have to consider further before giving his consent.

The decision in this particular conflict between privilege and prerogative is not recorded; but parliament certainly did not give up its claim, for later in the same session when a member complained that he had been served notwithstanding his protest with a subpoena to testify in the Chancery, and two other members rose to say that they had the same day received subpoenas to testify in the Star Chamber, the House immediately summoned all concerned to the bar. Numerous cases occurred in the next parliament in which those who served the writs were arrested, brought to the bar and remanded to the custody of the serjeant for three

[28] D'Ewes, 471, 479, 489, 552-3, 556, 558, 570, 572, 622, 666, 684; J. F. Jameson, *Origin of Standing Committees, Polit. Science Quarterly,* ix, 250-2; Townshend, 194, 282, 285, 290, *Commons Journals,* i, 149, 934.

and five day periods. The usual punishment for such infringement of privilege consisted only in the humiliation of arrest and a scolding by the Speaker, the discomforts of a few days imprisonment, and the expense of the payment of the fees attached to arrest, custody and discharge.

The claim of privilege in these cases did not pass without opposition. An official of the Chancery who was also a member of the House declared that the subpoenas of 1601 had come out of his office and ought to be obeyed by those that received them because the hearing of a case was appointed for a certain day and if the witnesses were not there, the litigant might fail of justice. This doctrine did not appeal to parliament, several speakers took a contrary view and the House decided by a formal vote that a member of parliament could not legally be served with a subpoena as witness.[29]

Sometimes it was jury duty that was in question. When it was reported that a certain member of the House, Sir John Tracy, was being held at the Court of Common Pleas for jury duty the serjeant with his mace was despatched to transfer him with a high hand to his duties in parliament. A long dispute between the two Houses occurred in 1601, when the attorney-general, himself formerly a Speaker of the House of Commons and therefore especially familiar with its claim of privileges, at the request of the earl of Huntingdon brought information in the Star Chamber against a member of the House of Commons. The case is obscure, involving an election dispute already referred to, but the final result was an order from the House exonerating their member from any charge and declaring that he must not be molested. Members upon whom writs of nisi prius were served in connection with suits to be tried in various parts of the county during the session of parliament asked for and were regularly granted writs of supersedeas.[30]

[29] D'Ewes, 431, 532, 537, 552–4, 564, 637, 647, 651, 655–6, Tanner, 578–91, 595–7.

[30] D'Ewes, 426, 612, 666, 669, 672–3, 677–8, 688.

It was more often the servants of members, however, than members themselves who were disturbed by suits, and over whom for their masters' sakes the mantle of parliamentary privilege was thrown. It was the well nigh universal custom of the time for any who claimed to be of the rank of gentlemen to have one or more personal attendants. Members, these attendants and sometimes their attendants crowded Westminster and London during parliament time, adding to that congestion so often referred to, and created debts and mingled in disputes which gave abundant occasion for suits at law. When a melée occurred among some lawyers' and scriveners' clerks near Temple Bar, and the servant of a member received a beating, the question came up whether privilege covered this case. A precedent was, as usual, discovered, and the assailants were brought to the bar and condemned to five days imprisonment and payment of the usual fees. November 6, 1601, it was reported that a servant of one of the burgesses of Westminster had been arrested and was now lying in Newgate " to the great indignity and contempt of the Priviledges and Liberties of this House." The serjeant was immediately sent to Newgate and brought the jailer and his prisoner both before the House. The prisoner was by order of the House discharged from custody and the person who brought the suit rebuked at the bar.[31]

A servant of one of the burgesses from Beaumaris journeying with his master through Shrewsbury was arrested for debt. When he said that he was with his master and on his way to parliament the local officers of the law seemed inclined to respect his privilege and let him go, but the creditor refused, saying to the bailiff, " I care not for that. Keep him fast. I will be your warrant." When this incident was reported all the House cried out, " To the Tower to the Tower with them. Send for them, send for them." But Shrewsbury was a long way off; the serjeant did not

---

[31] *Acts of the Privy Council*, xiv, 342, xxviii, 43; *Cal. State Papers, Dom.*, 1601-3, 111; *Hatfield House MSS.*, iii, 189; D'Ewes, 560, 657.

feel inclined to go or send there at his own expense, and while other plans were under discussion the whole matter slipped by and parliament was dissolved. Indeed one of the members complained, though with much exaggeration, that " many complaints were made, but none punished, many sent for but none appeared "; another declares " our own lenity is the cause of this contempt." Yet in the seven weeks of the parliament of 1601 there were sixteen cases of at least a theoretical enforcement of this particular privilege of parliament.[32]

In the House of Lords there were similar complaints of the arrest of servants of the peers. Two bailiffs who arrested Edward Barston, servant of Lord Chandos; the knight marshal's man who arrested John York, the archbishop's servant; those who arrested a servant of the earl of Shrewsbury and others were at various times summoned to the bar of the House of Lords and sent to the Fleet prison or to Newgate, whence they were released after a few days in each case. A very considerable part of the time of both houses of parliament during the few weeks of each of these sessions was devoted to the preservation of this not very worthy privilege and the punishment of those who invaded it. A justification may be found for the preservation of all possible prestige for parliament only in the light of later events when all its traditional powers and immunities would be needed in its great contest with the crown.[33]

In addition to the privileges which parliament claimed and obtained from the queen there was one other, self-asserted yet none the less valued and enforced. This was their right to secrecy in their deliberations. The parliaments of Elizabeth had but little sense of responsibility to an outside public. Its members once chosen were a law to themselves. No reference to the opinions of their constituents except perhaps once or twice in connection with

[32] D'Ewes, 629, 643, 647, 651, 655.
[33] Ibid. 530, 532, 604, 607, 608.

taxes is found in the debates; no expectation of being held to account for their action in parliament is seriously felt by its members.   No persons not members are therefore allowed to be present during its deliberations.   When a lawyer's clerk is found in the House he is arrested by the serjeant, brought to the bar and sent to ward until he can be examined by two appointed members as to his reasons for being there.   Though they reported two days afterward that he wandered into the House from " mere simplicity and ignorance," he was brought to the bar again and made to take the oath of supremacy and pay the fees before being discharged.   The same investigation and the same disciplinary measures followed the discovery that a servant of the earl of Nottingham, having a message for a member of the House, entered and sat waiting there, " not thinking any harm, nor knowing the danger thereof."   It is possible that greater attention was given to this case from the fact that a nobleman's servant had sat all forenoon in the House of Commons just when a somewhat bitter dispute was in progress between the two houses and he might be looked on as a possible spy or at least an informant of his master of proceedings in the other House.   But this could hardly be true of a certain Matthew Jones, gentleman, described as " a simple, ignorant old man," who was found sitting in the House a week or so later, brought to the bar and forced to apologize, remain in ward over night and pay the usual fees.[34]

It is a not infrequent matter of complaint by members that what they have said in parliament has been repeated outside.   The Speaker on every such occasion issues a warning against breach of the privacy of their discussions.   Parliament is as much a secret body as is the privy council. Once elected as representing their constituencies the members look upon themselves as personally entrusted with all the responsibility and the privileges of legislation.   At one time a member moved that " for the freedom of the House

[34] *Ibid.* 486, 488, 491, 511, 566.

it might be concluded amongst them a matter answerable at the Bar for any man to repeat anything of any Speech used or matters done in this House "; and another member declared that those men had been injured whose names had been noted to the queen as opponents of a measure in which she was interested. Cecil agrees to the right of the House to secrecy against the outside public but protests that the claim that speeches must not be repeated to the queen is not a valid one. All that can be claimed is that nothing shall be repeated to her in *malam partem,* a doubtful theory which was to be a subject of contest in another reign.[35]

Procedure, strictly so called, the daily practice of parliament, was already developed essentially in its modern form. A seasoned parliamentarian would probably feel himself equally at home, so far as parliamentary custom and rules of order go, in a parliament of the sixteenth and of the twentieth centuries. Bills could be initiated in either house and either by private persons or by representatives of the administration. They were much less frequently introduced by the latter than might have been supposed. Although some, and those perhaps the most considerable, were brought in by privy councillors, far the greater proportion were introduced by unofficial members. All bills had three readings, on different days, in each house, with the single exception of the queen's bill of pardon, which was only read once. At the second reading the bill was either " dashed," that is to say rejected, or committed to a group of members for report or elaboration. The persons to whom the bill was committed were called the " committees," or, as the expression was already becoming a collective noun, the " committee."

The committees of the time were very large, often including in the House of Lords from fifteen to twenty-five members, in the House of Commons fifty, sixty or more. A bill in the House of Lords for the preservation of pheasants and partridges, certainly not a matter of high impor-

[35] *Ibid.* 432–3, 464–5, 487–8.

tance, was referred for consideration to a committee consisting of the archbishop of Canterbury, Lord Burghley, the
earls of Nottingham, Northumberland, Derby, Worcester,
Pembroke and others.   In the House of Commons a certain
bill in 1597 was referred to a committee consisting of all the
privy councillors, all the knights of the shire, the burgesses
from all the port towns, Rochester, York and Derby and
thirty-nine others, certainly more than a hundred members;
a chance bill to abridge the penal laws, in 1601, was referred to a committee including the four privy councillors
in the House, six doctors of the civil law, some fourteen
knights and others, in all fifty-one.   There was some difficulty in finding rooms for these large committees.   Then
as now the large Exchequer Chamber was in constant use
for committee purposes.   Star Chamber was used when it
was not term time; the Court of Wards, the Council Chamber at Whitehall, and sometimes the House itself in the
afternoon when no sitting was being held, the halls of
Lincoln's Inn, Gray's Inn, Serjeant's Inn and the Middle
Temple were made use of, sometimes the Rolls House in
Chancery Lane and occasionally even the Guildhall of
London.[36]

It was observed then as it has often been observed since
that committees were not attended in proportion to their
numbers.   On November 22, 1597, Sir Edward Hobby complains that only four members of a committee in which he
was interested met at the appointed time, although it included all the privy councillors and all the lawyers in the
House and others, certainly twenty or more.   This neglect
of committee work is a common complaint, although it
might seem that the privilege of serving on the same committee with Francis Bacon, Sir Walter Ralegh, Sir Francis
Drake, Adrian Gilbert, Sir Robert Cecil and Sir Robert
Sydney, as might often have been the opportunity of members of the parliaments of 1593 and 1597, would in itself

---

[36] *Hatfield MSS.*, vii; D'Ewes, 422, 602, 622, etc.; Redlich, *Parliamentary
Procedure*, i, 22–43; Tanner, 541–50.

be of sufficient interest to guarantee good attendance. But the glamour of Elizabethan England was not so visible to contemporaries as it is to us and many members of parliament evidently found greater interest elsewhere than in the hard work of committee discussions no matter how clearly destined to later fame their fellow members.[37]

Much the same ceremony surrounded the dissolution of parliament as occurred at its opening. The queen seems always to have been in haste for the close of the session and often brought it to an end while measures of importance were still under discussion. Nothing suggests that this hurry to close parliament had any political significance; it is probably to be explained by the queen's impatience at being restricted in her movements for any length of time to Westminster or its vicinity by the needs of communication with parliament. When she had determined on the day of closing word was sent beforehand to the House of Commons and, usually at two or three o'clock in the afternoon the queen with some of her attendants and greater officials appeared in her robes in the House of Lords and took her seat. The Commons, who had in most cases long been waiting in the lobby, were then informed of the queen's presence and came thronging in behind their Speaker who took his stand at the bar. After the usual three ceremonial bows to the queen he proceeded to make a somewhat lengthy address, closing usually with thanks to the queen for her general bill of pardon, a request for her consent to the laws framed by the two houses and a presentation of the bill of subsidy. The bill of subsidy was a material object, as much so as the money which was its eventual fruition, however different in character, and it was received by the clerk of the crown from the hands of the Speaker with some ceremony and is described on one occasion as being deposited reverently by the clerk on a green table flanked by candles, standing in front of the queen.

The lord chancellor after a short conference with the

queen replied to the Speaker in a speech carefully prepared beforehand, thanking him in her name for the subsidies and usually improving the occasion by urging the country gentlemen and burgesses on their return to their homes to pay more attention to their work of local government. Sometimes the queen " with her own mouth concluded with a princely and eloquent speech."

The titles of the acts were then read by the clerk and the willingness or unwillingness of the queen to accept them reported by him in the old French formulas, *La Reine le veult* or *La Reine s'avisera*. There is some uncertainty about this matter of approval or disapproval. After the parliaments of 1589, 1593 and 1601 all acts laid before the queen were approved and appear on the statute book. At the close of the parliament of 1597 the seventeenth century compiler of the records of parliament reports that the queen accepted forty-three and rejected forty-eight bills. This is certainly a mistake, due to his misinterpretation of an earlier record, and not more than ten acts can have been vetoed. In the absence of the official journals, which have been lost for this period, it is even uncertain whether any acts were rejected by the queen, and it may be that her influence over legislation was exerted only at earlier stages of procedure. After the reading of the titles of the acts the lord chancellor stepped forward and in a traditional Latin formula declared the parliament dissolved. The Speaker of the Commons and those who were with him then made their three bows to the queen and scattered to their homes and other occupations.[38]

Such being a somewhat shadowy composite picture of the organization and procedure of the parliaments of the period, it remains to chronicle in still slighter detail the specific actions of the parliament of 1589. The deposit of actual legislation it left on the statute book was not large

[38] D'Ewes, 427, 455, 465–7, 521, 546–7, 505–6, 618–9, 689; J. E. Neale, *Queen Elizabeth's Quashing of Bills in 1597/8, Eng. Hist. Rev.*, Oct., 1919, 585–8; *Hist. MSS. Comm., Rutland MSS.*, i, 315.

or important. Of the sixteen laws enacted three were the regular subsidy acts and the act of the queen's pardon; six were government bills concerning procedure in the courts and three were either for the continuance or revival of old laws. The laws against horse stealing, embezzling war munitions, erecting cottages without agricultural land, unregistered brewers' measures and abuses in the election of fellows in the universities scarcely reach the higher levels of interest. An examination of the journals of its thirty-four sessions during more than seven weeks however indicates that many more bills were introduced and debated than were passed. Scarcely one of the questions troubling the time was left untouched and most of those subjects on which later laws were passed were at least under discussion at this time. Forestalling, excess in apparel, the regulation of grammar schools, disorder in taverns, multiplicity of lawsuits, retail trade carried on by aliens, the false packing of hops and a dozen other every day difficulties were brought on the floor of the House in bills which were introduced by members only to be " dashed " by an adverse vote or to fall by the wayside in their progress. Much time was given to debate on private bills and, as has been said, to cases of privilege. Members were constantly trenching on the dangerous ground of the queen's prerogative either in ecclesiastical or civil affairs to be warned off by privy councillors, or occasionally by the queen herself.

Just at the close of the session the two Houses unitedly ventured into a field where though not exactly intruding on the prerogative they were at least treading on unfamiliar ground. It has already been remarked that the whole Elizabethan war with Spain was fought without any declaration of war on either side. The queen and her councillors doubtless had their own reasons for this restraint. But some parliamentary expression of opinion in the matter was apparently wished for. On the morning of the last day of the session the Lords asked the Commons to send a conference committee to meet their representatives. At this meeting

Lord Burghley suggested that the Commons unite with the Lords in an appeal to the queen for a declaration of war against Spain, pointing out that they had in their subsidy act granted a liberal supply of money and had offered their lands, bodies and lives for her defense. The committee reported favorably to the House, all the privy councillors made speeches, and it was determined to ask the queen " to denounce open war against the said King of Spain." The Speaker was ordered to include this request in his closing speech. Whether he did so or not and whether any reply was given is not recorded; we have only a brief account of the arrival of the queen in the House of Lords on Saturday March 29th, summons sent to the Commons in the midst of their debates, their appearance before the queen led by their Speaker, and the dissolution of the parliament of 1589 announced by Lord Chancellor Hatton. Certainly no formal declaration of war against Spain followed.[39]

[39] *Statutes of the Realm,* iv, pt. 2, 798–839; *State Papers, Dom., Eliz.,* ccxxiii, 34; D'Ewes, 428–55.

CHAPTER XXXIV

THE PARLIAMENT OF 1593: FINANCE:
THE PENSION ACT

THE primary object of the parliaments of this time was not general legislation but, as is practically true of all parliaments of all time, the provision of income for the needs of the government. Those needs were becoming steadily greater. Military and naval operations were a source of growing expense notwithstanding the fact, perhaps owing to the fact, that the defensive position of the country had become more unfavorable. As has been more than once pointed out the defeat of the Armada in 1588 was the beginning not the close of the great duel between England and Spain. Rumors of a new armada constantly reached England, and over and over again hurried measures were taken to defend the coasts and to arm against invasion. It will be remembered that, from mixed motives of defense and aggression, successive expeditions under Drake and Norris, Cumberland, Frobisher, Howard and Hawkins were sent to the Spanish coasts and islands in 1589, 1590, 1591 and 1592. Four successive bodies of English troops and numerous reinforcements for them had been sent to France during the same four years to support Elizabeth's principal ally and to keep the Spaniards further from her shores. Troops were constantly kept in the Netherlands. The year 1591 was, as has been described, a specially warlike year, with from ten to fifteen thousand English troops in France, the Netherlands, Ireland and at sea.

The expense of these operations had been enormous and yet the danger from Spain seemed to become greater rather than less. In January, 1590, Philip had signed his treaty with the Holy League against Henry and his English allies;

since October of that year the Spaniards had possessed a fortified base at Blavet in Brittany just across the Channel and were in control of most of the Breton harbors. Parma had twice shown his ability to march from the Spanish Netherlands half way across France, once to the relief of Paris, once to that of Rouen. During the year 1592 reports of the dispatch of an invading armada were especially numerous and insistent, the Spanish troops in Brittany were reinforced and the English troops in France met disaster under the walls of Craon. Negotiations for Spanish alliances hostile to England were reported from France, Scotland, Ireland, Denmark, Poland and the Hanse towns.

The old theory that the regular income of the sovereign from permanent and personal sources, such as crown property, feudal dues, the traditional import and export duties, profits of purveyance, fees and fines of the courts and a few other forms of fixed income, should cover the expenses of government had long ceased to be more than a theory or a reminiscence. Certainly these sources were inadequate for present needs. Direct taxes periodically authorized by parliament were now a necessary part of the system of government finance. The connection between the approaching exhaustion of the last grant of such taxes and the summons of a new parliament was always close, and at no previous time had it been more so than when the queen and her councillors determined to summon a parliament to meet in 1593. The financial work of parliament may therefore be taken as the particular phase to be discussed in this chapter, though this, like procedure, can be made more clear by drawing from the records of the other three parliaments of the period. Nor must it be forgotten that the parliament of 1593 did other work besides the grant of taxes, and preceding and succeeding parliaments also granted taxes.

The calling of a parliament, generally distasteful both to the queen and her subjects, was sometimes avoided by other financial devices, especially by borrowing. In fact there had been plans for the summons of a parliament in 1590 but they had been put aside in favor of efforts to reduce expenses and to increase the productivity of old taxes and by a loan. The queen may have had still other possibilities in mind. At about this time a Dutchman named Rodenbaugh, formerly a member of the States of Holland, handed to the queen a written series of proposals for getting rid of the constant appeals to parliament for funds by creating what he called a " chamber of accounts," to consist of twelve financial officials. Into the hands of this body should be paid certain new and bizarre taxes, and it should have the profitable administration of certain property. For instance, into the chamber should be paid the first year's salary of each appointive officer of the government and one fifth of each later year's salary. One per cent of all property conveyed at a marriage should be paid into the chamber and a legacy should be made to it by everyone leaving property by will.

A shilling per head might be collected from the whole population of England, for no one would grudge a " poor single shilling " to the queen. Since the author of the plan estimated in one paragraph that there were 60,000 cities, towns and villages in England, and in another that there were 72,000, with an average of 200 households in each and four persons in each household, a neat sum of £2,400,000 or £2,800,000 would accrue yearly from this source alone. His further suggestion that any surplus of annual income might be put out at usury, the income to strengthen the general fund, was probably not intended jocularly, however beyond the bounds of financial good fortune it may have seemed to the treasury officials. All church property might be taken into the hands of the chamber, and such stipends paid to ministers as should be thought meet. All pardons for crime should go through the hands of the chamber, with suitable payments. The author was doubtless correct in his claim that if this plan could be carried out " it would create great strength and wealth and authority to the state and no enemies would come against it." However, although the queen had promised M. Rodenbaugh that her vice-chamberlain would give him an answer and if the plan were adopted she would grant him one thousandth part of the proceeds for his trouble, and although after long waiting and repeated appeals to the vice-chamberlain M. Rodenbaugh sought Burghley for advice and assistance and received a certain amount of comfort and attention, nothing naturally came of such a revolutionary proposal.[1]

A more substantial source of income was the sale of crown lands. The Tudor sovereigns had acquired vast amounts of land in the exigencies of sixteenth century history; it had long been their policy to dispose of these lands to advantage and land, especially woodland, was now in great demand. As a matter of fact Elizabeth derived large sums from this source. From November 14, 1589, to November 26, 1590, for instance, sales of land by her commissioners amounted to £126,305 5s. 11d; and an item of court gossip in a letter written just ten years later is that " the queen sells land still." [2]

Yet this was not enough and in default of an immediate summons of parliament the queen as usual fell back on the ancient device of borrowing. The wealth of London now made this possible without going abroad. In November, 1589, one hundred and thirty-one London merchants loaned the queen £15,000 for a year at 10%, taking as security for this and some other loans a mortgage on thirty-six royal manors situated in thirteen counties. At another time nine merchants, at still another fifteen, are named as being able to lend the queen £500 each for three months or more. In 1598 the queen is planning to borrow £150,000 from the city merchants in amounts from £2000 downwards, though the correspondent who records the fact thinks it unlikely she

[1] *State Papers, Dom., Eliz.*, ccli, 35, 36.

[2] *Ibid.* ccxxxviii, 30; *Chamberlain's Letters, Camden Society*, 120; F. C. Dietz, *English Government Finance, 1485–1558*, 39–40, 149, 153, 198; *Cal. State Papers, Dom.*, 1591–4, 483.

can obtain it, trade being so bad, especially that of the Merchants Adventurers.[3]

In addition to the native merchants were the numerous and wealthy Dutch merchants living in London whose enjoyment of the "Intercourse" or favorable conditions of trade established by old treaty with the Netherlands and their enjoyment of freedom of conscience seemed to the queen to give her a right to demand loans of substantial amounts and without interest. This she declared to be the more justifiable since the produce of these loans would go in good part to the expenses of her troops in the Netherlands. In 1600 a list of one hundred and fourteen such Dutch merchants was drawn up from whom the loan of sums from £2000 downward could be expected.[4]

Such loans, indeed all acknowledgments of debt and promises to pay on the part of the crown, were represented by what were known as "privy seals" or "letters of privy seal." Privy seals were small strips of tough paper signed and sealed in the name of the queen by the clerk of the privy seal, one of the exchequer officers, with her smaller seal, which was however at this time a substantial disc of wax more than three inches in diameter. Such an acknowledgment was given to a person possessing a claim on the queen or making a loan to her and was payable at the exchequer at the term indicated on it or in a document accompanying it. Privy seals were being constantly issued for all sorts of purposes; for, as lord treasurer Buckhurst wrote in 1602, "to pay her majesty's money without warrant of privie seale nevar was done nor can be done."[5] In eight weeks between September 6 and November 2, 1596, twenty-six privy seals were issued for various purposes; in

---

[3] *Lansdowne MSS.*, xxxii, 14–34; lx, 18 fo. 35; *State Papers, Dom., Eliz.*, ccxxxv, 55; *Eliz. Addenda*, xxxiii, 99, 100; *Cal. State Papers, Dom.*, 1598–1601, 13; Chamberlain to Carleton, Dec. 8, 1598.

[4] *State Papers, Dom., Eliz.*, cclxxviii, 8–15, 124 I–II; *Cal. State Papers, Dom.*, 1598–1601, 500, 538–9, 597.

[5] *State Papers, Dom., Eliz.*, cclxxxiii (a), 69.

another three months of the same year privy seals were
given to the amount of £48,874, including acknowledgments
of something more than a thousand pounds for the expenses
of the troops in Ireland, a subsidy of £3000 to the king of
Scots, £2,185 for the equipment of the troops sent to France
under Sir Thomas Baskerville, to Hugh Kayle, her majesty's
goldsmith, for jewels and plate to the value of £2,065, to
Lady Hunsdon and her daughter to pay for the funeral of
the late lord chamberlain, and other uses. Privy seals were
regularly given for the subsidy of five shillings per ton
granted for the building of ships in English ports.[6]

Although practically all payments due by the crown
passed through the intermediary of a privy seal before they
were paid, far the most interesting privy seals were those
wholesale issues which were made by queen Elizabeth from
time to time to a large number of her subjects as security
for the repayment of comparatively small sums which she
asked them to loan to her. Though not unknown at other
times they were especially characteristic of her reign. They
were practically small-denomination, short-term, non-inter-
est bearing bonds, issued as a means of tiding over a short
period of special expenditure or an interval till a parliamentary grant could be obtained.

It may be of interest to trace briefly the history of such
an issue from its inception to its repayment. Among the
records of the year 1588 is an order headed " By the
Queen," extensively corrected and interlined in her own
hand and sealed with her signet. It is addressed to the
lord treasurer, states her reasons for asking for a loan from
her subjects, acknowledges that it is reasonable for lenders
to have her letters signed by her privy seal as an assurance
of repayment, and requires him to have as many such letters
prepared and sealed as should be determined upon by him
in agreement with five other members of the privy council.
This personal order from the queen initiated the loan. Ac-

[6] State Papers, Dom., Eliz., ccxxii, 84; cclx, 107, 120; Cal. State Papers,
Dom., 1591–4, 449; 1595–7, 97, 178, 306, 496.

companying it was the form of the privy seal, also approved by the queen and in this case also corrected in her own handwriting. The letter of privy seal explained to the lender her need and her belief in the willingness of the person to whom the letter was directed to loan her money, " which is not refused between neighbor and neighbor "; it requires him to pay the amount named to the collector; and assures him that that amount will be repaid on presentation of the letter of privy seal at the exchequer one year from the date of his making the loan. Nothing is said of interest and none was of course paid.

The second step in the loan was the issue and distribution of the letters. They were prepared in the exchequer, signed by the clerk of the privy seal, at this time a man named Thomas Kery, and sealed with the privy seal which was in his charge. Blank spaces were left for the amount of the loan, the name of the lender and of the collector. A few original letters of this date with the seals attached still remain. One is made out in the name of Thomas Lawley of the Coppice, Shropshire, for £25, dated February 20, 1589, payable at the exchequer a year from that date. Another is in the name of Humphrey Hill of Seton in the same county, for £50. Still another is made out to Roger Columbell of Darley Hall, Derbyshire, for £25, dated on the day of the receipt of the money by the collector, April 12, 1589. These however are chance survivors from the two or three thousand such letters prepared and issued in the years 1588 and 1589. November, 1590, a similar collection was similarly initiated, the record of which is still preserved in a handsome manuscript volume giving all the forms, the names of thirty-six collectors, one in each shire, all prominent knights or gentlemen and many if not all deputy lieutenants. Similar loans took place at least in 1597 and 1598, perhaps in other years.[7]

At each of these times great sheaves of such letters were

---

[7] *State Papers, Dom., Eliz.,* ccxxii, 84; ccxxxvi; *Cal. State Papers, Dom., Add.,* xxxi, 3; Thomas Wright, *Queen Elizabeth and her Times,* ii, 361.

sent to each county. The selection of the men who should be asked to make the loans was placed in the hands of the lord lieutenant and his deputies in each shire. The choice of the lord lieutenant, a military official, instead of the sheriff, the usual financial and judicial officer, to administer this work may be explained possibly on the ground that the loans were professedly for the military defense of the country, possibly because the lord lieutenant and his deputies had a better knowledge of men of estate in the county than anyone else. Whatever the cause, we find the earl of Shrewsbury for instance being asked in December, 1588, for a list of the men in the three counties under his lieutenancy who might lend the queen reasonable sums. Lord North, lord lieutenant of Cambridgeshire, two years later sends to Burghley a list of 120 names of men in his county, not one of whom, as he says, was called on to lend money to the queen the year before, yet all of whom could without sacrifice lend sums of £100, £50, or £25, and would do so " with as reasonable contentment of the subject as may be looked for from men who parte with their money." These sums were the usual amounts of the privy seals. They were never more than £100, never less than £20; most usually they were £50 or £25.

Those to whom the letters were directed were addressed as " esquire," " gentleman," " widow," " merchant " or " yeoman "; they were never nobles and very seldom knights. It was evidently plain people from whom the queen made these popular loans. Those of higher rank were reached in other ways. The number of lenders was considerable. In 1590, 175 privy seals were sent to Essex, 200 to Oxfordshire and about 600 to London. The lists of possible lenders in Cambridgeshire contained, as has been said, 120 names. Perhaps 2500 to 3000 persons were appealed to for any one general loan of this kind. Cambridge and Derbyshire in 1590 were expected to provide £2000 each, Dorsetshire £1900, Essex, one of the richest counties, £6500; Gloucester £4000, though an abatement of £1000 was asked for by the lord lieutenant of that county on account of the murrain among cattle and the bad condition of the cloth trade. The total amount produced by one loan seems to have been some £50,000 or £60,000.[8]

Collectors for the respective counties and for London were appointed either directly by the privy council or by the lord lieutenants. They were invariably knights or well-known gentlemen who were or had been sheriffs, and were usually deputy lieutenants. To these collectors the bundles of letters of privy seal filled out with the proper names and amounts were sent, and by them they were delivered by messenger to the individuals honored by this opportunity to loan money to the queen, with the request that they come in promptly with the money. On doing so their letters were countersigned by the collector, the sum paid receipted for and the date of payment entered upon the document, a proceeding necessary to its validity.

To the earlier loans little or no opposition is recorded, and there is little delay in making payments. Although the actual issue of the privy seals of 1588–9 did not apparently begin till January, 1589, by the middle of June £46,925 had been collected. In the levy of 1590–1, we hear of more reluctance to pay, but even in this the collector for Derbyshire, who was appointed in January, 1591, was able to send on July 9, £933 of the £2000 demanded from that county. To the loans of 1597 and 1598 there is, judging from the records of at least one collector, a constant series of protests, excuses on account of poverty, and neglect of payment. Although appointed in January, 1597, he is able to make his first payment only in September and that is but £815 out of £2000 called for from his county. There is constant pressure from the privy council, but the collector is told at the same time that the queen has " forbidden oppression." This is one of many indications that either the country was poorer or the government less popular as the reign of the queen approached its end.[9]

As to repayment, the requirement was that the letter of privy seal should be presented at the exchequer one year after it had been countersigned by the collector. In the few actual instances preserved the document was assigned to a business relative of the country lender and collected by him, as in the case of the assignment of the privy seal of Thomas Lawley to his brother Robert Lawley, Merchant of the Staple. Robert presented and received payment for it ten days after the expiration of the year for which it was issued. Another is repaid to two merchants, assigns of the lender, four days after the expiration of the year.

May 1, 1598, the queen, explaining that the first payment of the subsidy recently granted by parliament would not be due until the next February and that preparation against her enemies had exhausted her funds, deferred the repayment of all outstanding privy seals for six months. This seems to have been the only default in the payment of such a loan in the queen's reign and she took pride in this relative promptitude, however far in arrears some of her other debts may have been.[10]

The loans of Elizabeth on privy seal were scarcely distinguishable in their nature or perhaps in their form from the benevolences of earlier times and the forced loans of Henry VIII except by the fact, a very significant one, however, that they were always repaid. Due perhaps to this they do not seem to have been generally unpopular. The only opposition recorded is the occasional protest of an individual that he is unable to find the money. Nor can it be said they were a serious imposition upon the people. The small amounts, widely distributed, drawn from a class who were presumably comfortable, and repaid after a short

[9] State Papers, Dom., Eliz., ccxxiv, 96; ccxxxviii, 10; cclxxxv, 65; Rutland MSS., i, 277, 286–90, 293, 300–3, 336–42; Lansdowne MSS., xxxii, fo. 204.

[10] State Papers, Dom., Eliz., ccxxii, 84; Additional, xxxi, 3, 4; Rutland MSS., i, 345–7.

period, even though they bore no interest and were collected with some severity, can hardly have been an unfair share of the common national burden.

The ultimate repayment of these loans, as well as the heavy expenses of these war years, made the summons of a parliament sooner or later a necessity. Parliament alone could provide the government with funds adequate for its needs. It is true that the queen on her accession had been granted once for all import and export taxes which amounted now to almost £100,000 a year. She had also, as already indicated, other sources of income.[11]

But the old conception of parliamentary grants as something additional, a free gift to the queen from the people whom parliament represented, of a different character from all other forms of government income, still persisted in full vigor. Parliamentary grants are invariably spoken of as gifts. The queen indeed carefully avoids, in form at least, asking for them. The privy councillors and other speakers in parliament, while pointing out the necessity for taxes for the protection of the country, base their argument for a grant on the queen's services in protecting the country from its enemies and freely spending her money in doing so. Her liberality in spending her own income for the good of her people, to preserve England in peace, or at least in security, is constantly adverted to as a reason why her people should, both by way of reimbursement and by way of addition to her means, make her a free gift from their possessions. The lord keeper at one time says, " we her Majesties subjects must with all dutiful consideration think what is fit for us to do, and with all willingness yield part of our own for the defence of others and assistance of her Majesty in such an insupportable charge. Were the cause between Friend and Friend, how much would we do for the relief one of another? But the Cause is now between our Sovereign and our selves." When the queen has reason to think that the subsidies have been given reluctantly she orders

[11] *State Papers, Dom., Eliz.,* cclxxxv, 65; *Hatfield House MSS.,* v, 393.

the lord keeper to say that " for this offer of three subsidies her Majesty most graciously in all kindness thanketh her subjects; but except it were freely and willingly given she did not accept it; for her Majesty never accepteth anything that is not freely given," a statement of somewhat doubtful truth. On the same occasion she herself said, " The Subsidy you give me I accept thankfully, if you give me your good will with it; but if the necessity of the time and your Preservation did not require it, I would refuse it.[12] The gratuitous character of this parliamentary taxation came out even more clearly in the ceremonies at the dissolution of parliament, when, as already described, the Speaker of the House of Commons advanced to the bar of the House of Lords, where the queen occupied her throne, holding in his hands the actual bill of subsidy and, as the main part of his speech, declared that he was deputed to present to her a free gift from the loving hearts of her people.

Yet notwithstanding all these formalities nothing is more clear than that these grants were taxation pure and simple, made for public and national ends and measured in amount partly by the need of the government for funds, partly by the willingness of members of parliament to make sacrifices on their own part and that of their constituents. The personal element was only an ancient reminiscence and subservience on the part of parliament to forms from which it could not free itself.

In the parliament of 1589, a week after the opening, Sir Walter Mildmay, chancellor of the exchequer, brought up the question of some aid to be given to the queen; other speeches were made; the matter was referred to a committee which held various sessions and made a report that resulted in the grant of two subsidies and four fifteenths and tenths. Although this was twice as large a sum as had ever been appropriated before the danger of its being taken as a precedent was thought to have been avoided by a clause skilfully drawn up by Francis Bacon, and it was accepted

[12] D'Ewes, 457–8, 466–7.

by the two houses and presented to the queen as already described.[13]

In the parliament of 1593, now under consideration, as already intimated the matter of subsidy was more fully and sharply debated than in any other of Elizabeth's reign. It was the principal subject of the opening addresses in the House of Lords. On the very first working day of the parliament three of the privy councillors in the House of Commons and two other prominent members, Bacon and Sir Edward Stafford, made long set speeches on the subject of finance, and this was but the beginning of debates that filled at least one half of the working time of the seven weeks of the session. These discussions resulted in the grant, notwithstanding Bacon's efforts to prevent the creation of a precedent in 1589, not of a double as then but of a triple subsidy, with its usual accompaniments of tenths and fifteenths.

The difficulties and occasions of expense connected with the war with Spain and the dangers threatening England were rehearsed to parliament by the lord keeper in the queen's opening address, by the privy council members and others in the debates in the House of Commons, and by the lord treasurer in a conference between committees of the houses. Secretary Wooley declared that the wars with Spain had cost the queen more than £1,000,000 and Burghley stated still more specifically that the queen "in these defensive wars expended of her own Treasure alone £1,030,000" since parliament four years before had made its grant of £290,000. Chancellor of the exchequer Fortescue, restricting himself, as he said, to matters of his own calling, explained that the financial burden of four kingdoms, England, France, Ireland and Scotland, had rested on the queen, besides the defense of the Low Countries, which alone cost her yearly £50,000. She had done all this to free England from war at home. "As for her own private expenses they have been little in building; she hath con-

13 D'Ewes, 425, 427, 431, 433, 440–1, 447, 454.

sumed little or nothing in her pleasures. As for her apparel it is Royal and Princely, becoming her calling, but not sumptuous nor excessive."

It was not, however, in these financial details, nor even in the patriotic and more or less candid interpretation given to recent events nor in the measure of the queen's habits of expenditure that the members of parliament must have been most interested. That which was really a condescension was the glimpse given them of foreign relations, shut out as they ordinarily were from all the diplomatic information which was the current knowledge of the privy council. When Cecil spoke of the reported use of Spanish gold in building up a pro-Spanish party in Scotland and of the efforts of the king to arrest Bothwell and Huntley, and said that " though it be not talked of in the Exchange, nor preached at Paul's Cross, yet it is most true and in Scotland as common as the highway," he was giving to the members of the House of Commons an insight into the relations of the two British kingdoms to which they had no other access. Under ordinary circumstances foreign affairs, war and peace, all matters of state in the higher sense, were exclusively in the knowledge and control of the queen and her appointed ministers and councillors. When these were communicated to parliament that body was correspondingly appreciative, and expressed their thanks for the momentary confidence reposed in them.[14]

All the discussion of foreign affairs was not left to the initiation of the privy councillors. In the course of the debate the old proposal of a declaration of war against Spain which had borne no fruit in the parliament of 1589 was again brought up. Sir Henry Knyvett, a military man, approved the proposed subsidies but expressed his desire " First, that it might be lawful for every Subject to annoy the King of Spain that would; that weak Forces might not

[14] *Harleian MSS.*, 6265, fos. 111–4, quoted in Neale, *The Lord Keeper's Speech in the Parliament of 1593*, *Eng. Hist. Rev.*, Jan., 1916, 130–2·; D'Ewes, 472: 35 Eliz., c. xiii, Preamble.

be sent against him but a Royal Army; that we should not wrastle with him on our own ground but abroad." A lawyer, Serjeant Harris, asked to have it set down that the subsidies about to be granted should be " to maintain a War impulsive and defensive against the Spaniard," for " whether it be War or no War as yet we know not." Ralegh seconded this speech, declaring that he knew many, though he does not claim that he was one of them, who did not think it lawful in conscience, under the circumstances, to " take from the Spaniards." He stated his belief that if lawful and open war were declared, more volunteers would go to sea against them than the queen should need. Speaking from his personal knowledge of European affairs he suggested a far-reaching military and naval policy. Other members proposed that all this should be inserted in the preamble of the bill, and also a statement that the specially large grant was made to resist the power and prevent the malice of the king of Spain. The subsidy act bade fair to become an appropriation bill. But the privy councillors took no part in this phase of the discussion, there is no record of the queen's paying any attention to it, and in the long preamble of the subsidy act, as finally passed, though there is much about the necessity for defense against the Spaniard, there is no mention of a declaration of war, no restriction of the purposes to which the grant was to be put and no particular form of campaign indicated. Possibly the queen's learned council who put the act into form saw to it that there was no intrusion of parliament into the administrative sphere.[15]

Another question of general interest sprang up in the debate on the parliamentary grant of 1593, a question which reached a definite settlement only after the expiration of three hundred and eighteen years, in the parliament act of 1911. This was the relation of the two houses in the grant of taxes. The speeches of the privy councillors on the open-

[15] D'Ewes, *Journals*, 477–8, 484, *Statutes of the Realm*, Vol. IV, pt. 2, 567, 867–83.

ing day of the session were all alike closed by a proposal
for the formation of a " grave committee " to consider the
provision of treasure for the queen's needs in her wars. The
committee consisted of all the privy councillors, all knights
of the shires and some fifty others, making more than a
hundred members. They reported through the chancellor
of the exchequer in favor of the same grant as in the parliament of 1589, two subsidies with the accompanying tenths
and fifteenths. During the debate a message reached the
Commons from the House of Lords reminding them of the
recommendations in the lord keeper's speech, expressing
their surprise that the Commons had so far done nothing
about the finances, and asking for a conference on the subject. The Commons at first accepted this proposal willingly
enough and sent a large committee to a conference in the
room adjoining the upper House with the committee of
twenty appointed by the Lords. Lord Treasurer Burghley
in the name of the House of Lords told this committee that
the product of the subsidies was now so small and the needs
so great that the House of Lords would not agree to any
less grant than three subsidies, half as much again as the
grant in the last parliament, and as they had doubtless
learned the House was proposing again to grant.

When this was reported in the Commons, Bacon, who had
been on the committee but took an independent view of the
question, protested that quite apart from the amount of
the grant it would be a derogation from the privileges of the
House of Commons to accept the initiative of the House of
Lords in matters of contribution of money and therefore
proposed that a courteous reply should be made to the
Lords, thanking them for their interest and promising to
consider the matter promptly, but explaining that further
conference with them on this subject was impossible without prejudice to the privileges of the House of Commons.
There was much debate; the privy councillors and courtier
members of the House advocated conference, others opposed. The large sum proposed evidently frightened many,

and procedure, principle and amount became inextricably mingled in the debate. Though on occasion the Speaker could assure the queen that " Our Lands, our Goods, our Lives are prostrate at your feet to be commanded," yet the Commons had no inclination in actuality to lose control of their property. Finally when one of the members found what seemed a clear precedent for a similar refusal of conference with the Lords, only one hundred and eighty-five years old, the House, as usual, seized upon this easy form of argument and by a vote of 217 to 128 refused to enter into further conference and sent a committee to the Lords to report their refusal. The Lords, reluctant like their successors to allow taxation to pass entirely from their control, accepted the reply grudgingly but urged speedy action and questioned the precedent.[16]

This was on Saturday; in the next forty-eight hours there was evidently some heavy pressure brought to bear on members of the House of Commons to reverse their action. On Monday Mr. Beale, the discoverer of the precedent of the time of Henry IV, rose to state that he had been mistaken in the question at issue, that his precedent did not really apply and that he saw no objection to a general conference with the House of Lords. Heneage, Wooley and Cecil of the privy council returned to the attack, and although there was some bitter complaint that the House had been unfairly represented as being opposed to the suggested subsidy, and that the names of speakers against the conference had been reported to the Lords and the queen, when Sir Walter Ralegh proposed as a compromise that there should be a general conference with the Lords on the dangers of the state and the necessary provision of funds, the House reversed its former decision and agreed without a dissenting voice to a new conference.

It was now proposed, in order to avoid any appearance of dictation from the Lords and to secure for themselves due thanks from the queen, that the House of Commons should

[16] D'Ewes, 465, 472-86, *Cal. State Papers, Dom.*, 1591-4, 322.

itself decide upon the three subsidies before the conference took place, so that the conference committee might report the grant to the Lords as a *fait accompli*. This proposal brought the discussion back to the amount of the grant. Few debates of the period brought more eminent men to their feet. Three privy councillors, Heneage, Fortescue and Cecil, spoke repeatedly, Bacon, Drake, Ralegh, full of references to general conditions, Fulke Greville with a philosophical and eloquent speech, Sir Henry Unton, late ambassador to France, Sir Edward Stafford, Sir Thomas Cecil, Sir Francis Hastings, Sir Henry Knyvett, Sir Francis Godolphin, Sir John Hart, late lord mayor of London, Heyl, Lewis, George Moore, expressed themselves at length for or against the three subsidies, or proposed other plans. The wealth and the poverty of the people were both asserted and denied. Bacon fears that if such a large subsidy is collected in any short period gentlemen must sell their plate and poor men their brass pots, that the queen may lose the hearts of her subjects, and that later princes may use this as a precedent to impose similar taxes upon the English people, of all nations the most impatient of taxation. Mr. Heyl on the other hand declares that he is familiar with all England from St. Michael's Mount to London; he is sure the country is many thousand pounds richer than ever before and that it is able and willing to pay. More than one member proposed an exemption of poorer men from the levy, what they would have paid being added to the charge against the richer. Others proposed new forms of taxation; one that there should be a general survey of all men's lands and property in England and a levy of £100,000 a year made on it for the queen's wars, another that each of the 10,000 parishes of England should provide a certain number of men for the wars and pay their expenses at the rate of £12 a year per man. But Sir Thomas Heneage replies to these proposals that he has served the queen many years, knows her disposition well, and has besides heard her say only lately that she loves not fineness of device and novel inventions but likes rather to have the ancient usages followed.

The next conference with the committee of the Lords took place amicably enough, but was of little interest or consequence since before it occurred the subsidy bill, as the clerk records, " after many days' agitation did at length very difficultly pass the House, by reason of the greatness thereof," and the Lords could only express their satisfaction with the action of the lower house and join in its grant. Bacon's reluctance in this parliament to allow the interposition of the lords in money matters and his expressed doubts of the wisdom of placing so heavy a burden on the people were evidently distasteful to the queen and influenced unfavorably, notwithstanding his excuses, his prospects of personal advancement in the service of the crown.[17]

The grant of 1597 followed the precedent of 1593: there was the same report by the privy councillors of danger from Spain, the same statement of the expenditures of the queen far beyond her means, and in response a repetition of the triple subsidy and accompanying tenths and fifteenths, payable this time one part in each of the three succeeding years, instead of being spread over four years as before. On the parliament of 1601 the Spanish acquisition of a foothold in Ireland and the desperate siege of Ostend then in progress made a great impression. Ralegh called attention to the fact that they had granted three subsidies in fear that the Spaniards were coming, now they were actually on land in the queen's dominions and reinforcements for them daily expected. Financial conditions were shown to parliament more fully and freely than ever before. It was pointed out that the first subsidies had been already exhausted for almost a year and the temporary loan then made had not yet been repaid. The queen needed £300,000 before next Easter; the question was how this money should be raised. The chancellor of the exchequer had no hesitation in proposing

---

[17] D'Ewes, 486–8, 490–6, 499; James Spedding, *Letters and Life of Francis Bacon, Occasional Works*, Ed. 1861, i, 212–26, 232–4.

the grant of four subsidies. This was four times as much as had ever been granted before 1589, twice as much as in that year and one third more than the largest grant made since. There was much presentation of figures and debate through a four hour afternoon session of a committee of the whole house till it was " dark night." There were references as in 1593 to poor men who would have to pawn their pots and pans to pay the subsidy and replies that "neither pot nor pan nor dish nor spoon should be spared when danger is at our elbows." Ralegh and others again urged exemption of poor men, and a progressive property tax was proposed. Finally the bill for four subsidies was passed in its old form, to be paid in four annual payments, destined, as it proved, to extend beyond the queen's life-time and into a period when all questions of taxation took on a new significance.[18]

A tabulation of these parliamentary grants would show, what has already been intimated, that notwithstanding all the appearance of voluntary gifts, all the contrast drawn between them and the more purely personal sources of the queen's income they were not less regular, indeed were more so, than income from crown property and other ancient resources and claims. Irregularity of parliamentary procedure conceals their regularity of recurrence. In every February except one from 1589 till the queen's death, either a half or a whole parliamentary subsidy was paid into the treasury, and either in June or November of every year except one a further payment of either a single or a double parliamentary fifteenth and tenth was made.

Fifteenths and tenths and subsidies were the only forms of taxation by parliament during this period. A fifteenth and tenth was an old form of taxation dating from the fourteenth century. It derived its name from the fact that it purported to be one fifteenth of the value of the personal property of all residents of the open country, one tenth of that of all residents in cities and boroughs. The assessment, however, early became fixed both in amount and distribution, and from about 1344 forward the grant by parliament of a fifteenth and a tenth meant the levy upon each subdivision of the country of a certain set sum. The decay of many of the towns in the sixteenth century led to their exemption from the payment of this tax, the reduction by the close of the century amounting to £6000. The total value of a fifteenth and a tenth was, during our period, after all deductions had been made, about £30,000. Burghley estimated it in 1598 in a private memorial to the queen at but £26,000, but according to his own accounts it averaged somewhat above that, and went slightly beyond £30,000 in 1596 and 1597. As this was such a small sum the custom had arisen of granting two or more fifteenths and tenths at a time, making a corresponding increase of the amount payable from each district. The payment was sometimes to be made all at once, sometimes distributed over several years. The act of 1589, for instance, provided for the payment into the treasury on November 10, 1589, of the first of the four fifteenths and tenths then granted, the second on the same date of 1590, the third in 1591, and the fourth in 1592. In the grant of 1593, the first and second fifteenths and tenths were both payable November 1593, the third and fourth on the same date of 1594, the fifth in 1595, the sixth in 1596. Collectors of the fifteenths and tenths were appointed in each county or town by the members of parliament from that district, put under bonds by them to pay in the amount due from that district, remunerated for their services according to custom and discharged from their bond only on payment into the treasury of the full sum for which they were responsible at the time due or within one month afterward.[19]

---

[19] *Statutes of the Realm*, IV, Pt. 2, 819–20; *Cal. State Papers, Dom.*, 1598–1601, 2, 22, 63, 154; *State Papers, Dom., Eliz.*, cclxiv, 169; cclxvi, 154; Prothero, *Select Statutes, Introduction* (c–4); *Hatfield House MSS.*, iv, 339.

A fifteenth and tenth was an inflexible and relatively un-
productive tax. It took no cognizance, except in the exemption of certain towns, of changes in the distribution of
population, nor, except in the crude way of duplications,
of increase in the amount of wealth in the country. It was
proportioned to personal property only not to income from
land. Finally, its method of collection was an inheritance
from a period when parliament not only granted but itself
controlled the levy and tried to control the use of the funds it
appropriated, not consonant with the strong administration
that had grown up in the later fifteenth and the sixteenth
century. To overcome these defects another form of parliamentary grant, which shared with several other forms of
taxation the name of "subsidy," had grown up. A parliamentary subsidy, as it had already, like the fifteenth and
tenth, become stereotyped, and as it is described in almost
identical terms in each of the four subsidy acts of this
period, was a levy of two shillings eightpence on each
pound's worth of personal property of every person or corporate body in England possessing property worth three
pounds or above, or, as an alternative, four shillings from
every pound of income from land from every person having
as much as a pound of such income. The choice was with
the taxing authorities to collect on personal property or on
income from land, whichever was largest, but no one was
required to pay on both his personal property and his land.
It will be observed that the subsidy on personal property,
two shillings eightpence, is two fifteenths of a pound and
that the subsidy on income from real estate, four shillings,
is two tenths of a pound so that a subsidy is in a certain
sense a double fifteenth and tenth, although on a new and
wider and more productive assessment. This perhaps suggested the practice of granting two fifteenths and tenths
with one subsidy.

There were various modifications and exceptions to the
subsidies. Aliens living in England paid double; personal
property in pawn and debts owed were excepted from the

valuation of personal property; ornaments in churches dedicated by gilds and other corporations were exempted from the assessment of those bodies; clergymen were assessed only on their lay not on their ecclesiastical income and possessions, inhabitants of Ireland, Jersey, Guernsey, the counties of Northumberland, Cumberland and Westmoreland, the bishopric of Durham, the towns of Berwick-on-Tweed and New Castle-on-Tyne, of the Cinque Ports and Romney Marsh were not included in the subsidy acts; the property both real and personal of the colleges in the two universities, of Winchester and Eton, of all free grammar schools, of the knights of Windsor, of all hospitals, and the personal property of scholars, schoolmasters, graduate students and officials residing or holding any connection with any of these educational or charitable institutions — doubtless an exiguous exclusion — were exempted from the subsidy.

Apart from including these exemptions and a few special provisions the lengthy labors of those who drew up the statute resulted in a most detailed series of provisions for the assessment, levy and collection of the subsidy. Its administration was not by members of parliament as were the fifteenths and tenths but immediately under the crown. It was taken charge of primarily by a group of commissioners for each shire and other principal divisions. They were appointed by the lord chancellor, lord treasurer, lord admiral, lord steward and lord chamberlain, or any two of them, and were usually noblemen, gentlemen or town officials. These commissioners with certain local co-adjutors appointed assessors and instructed them, the high constables and local officials to give a full statement of the value of the lands and personal possessions of every inhabitant of their districts. Peers and peeresses were assessed at the parliamentary rates by the lord chancellor, and the commissioners assessed themselves and the subordinate assessors. High collectors were appointed for the larger divisions and they in turn appointed sub-collectors. Tax bills were made out in accordance with the assessments, for the payment of which the collectors and their heirs were given powers of distraint and were held responsible. Sixpence in each pound, two and one half per cent, was withheld from the treasury for expenses; twopence of this went to the commissioners, twopence to the high collectors and twopence to the sub-collectors; the original assessors seem to have been required to serve without pay. Every means of inquiry, even the most minute and inquisitorial, including the requiring of an oath from each taxpayer, was provided for the discovery and report of property and the prevention of evasions, and every form of authority was invoked for collection of the tax.[20]

Notwithstanding all this detailed and cumbrous machinery the unproductiveness of parliamentary subsidies was a commonplace of the time. The lord keeper complained in 1593 that the grant of a subsidy " is with such slackness performed as that the third part of that which hath been granted cometh not to her Majesty. A great show, a rich grant and a large sum seemeth to be made, but it is hard to be gotten and the sum not great which is paid." " Howsoever it seeme a greate helpe in wordes, it proveth but little in deedes, promised with full mouth, and payed with more than half emptie hands." With all the possibilities of direct assessment, centralized administration and choice of either landed or personal property, and with its double rate, a subsidy produced only about two and a half times a fifteenth and tenth, about £80,000 as against £30,000. From 1593 to 1596 subsidies averaged £74,760. The lord treasurer reports in 1593 that the double subsidy and four fifteenths and tenths granted in 1589 had all together produced only £280,000. Cecil reports the same amount in 1601; the last single subsidy had produced ap-

[20] *Acts of the Privy Council*, xxxii, 464; *State Papers, Dom., Eliz.*, ccxliv, 51; cclxxxiii, 33; *Lansdowne. MSS.*, xxxii, 25, 27; lix, 50; *Rutland MSS.*, i, 316–29, 355, 382–5; Robert Hudson, *Memorials of a Warwickshire Parish*, 115–7.

proximately £80,000, the double fifteenths and tenths £60,000.[21]

The reason for the unproductiveness of the subsidy lay without doubt in the inadequacy of the assessments. The queen was reported as saying that the wealthier sort of men charged the payments upon the poorer sort and these were not able to satisfy the charge. The estimates of income of the well-to-do classes were indeed absurdly small. A member once moved that justices of the peace should be assessed, according to the statute, at £20 income from land, saying that there were few justices now placed at more than £8 or £10. Yet it is probable that few justices had less than several hundred pounds income. Burghley declared that the subsidies were imposed on the meaner sort of her Majesty's subjects, and that he knew one shire where there were many men " of good living and countenance," yet none in the subsidy of 1589 assessed at more than £80 a year. He declared that in London where most of the wealth of the realm lay there was no one assessed at more than £200 in goods and only four or five of these. This statement Sir John Harte, formerly lord mayor of London, was able to controvert and to point out that four Londoners had each been assessed at £400 of personal property, eight at £300 and thirty-two between £200 and £300. But even these amounts are far too small for merchants a group of one hundred of whom paid subscriptions averaging £300 apiece for the first voyage of the East India Company, and who were regularly investing hundreds and thousands of pounds in other commercial ventures. Complaints of the losses of merchants by piracy and other mischance are constantly estimated in thousands of pounds. Noblemen, gentlemen, merchants and officials are frequently fined or charged with damages in the Star Chamber of hundreds, sometimes thousands of pounds;

[21] *Harleian MSS.*, 6265, fos. 111-4, quoted in Neale, *The Lord Keeper's Speech to the Parliament of 1593, Eng. Hist. Rev.*, 1916, 133; *State Papers, Dom., Eliz.*, cclxiv, 169; *Cal. State Papers, Dom.*, 1591-4, 322; D'Ewes, 458, 483, 630.

dowries and jointures are frequently of similar sums. As to country gentlemen, John Evelyn describes his father as having at this time an income from land of £4000 a year, in the very county in which Burghley states no one was estimated on the subsidy books as having an income from land of more than £80. A chance character in a play written about 1600 says, " I am a Northamptonshire gentleman born to a thousand pound land by the year." Yet there is little probability that any gentleman in Northamptonshire in 1600 was rated on the subsidy books at an income of more than £50 or £60 a year. When Ralegh is pleading in opposition to Bacon for an exemption of poor men from the subsidy of 1601 he says that a three pound man's estate is perhaps little better than he is set at, " when our estates that be £30 or £40 in the Queen's books are not the hundredth part of our wealth." Essex in 1598 testifies that there is luxury everywhere in England, surfeit in diet, costly furniture, prodigality in dress, all proving that England could well pay more taxes.[22]

What is the explanation? At a time when incomes were in hundreds and thousands of pounds, the estimates for the subsidy were in tens or scores; why the discrepancy between these actual incomes and the official statements of the subsidy books? A closer examination of Elizabethan finance or a more penetrating analysis of Elizabethan policy will have to be made before this question can be satisfactorily answered. One thing, however, is evident, that the subsidies had become, notwithstanding the machinery for new assessment, approximately as stereotyped as the fifteenths and tenths. The " subsidy books " were little more than traditional lists of incomes and possessions whose amounts were not changed by the assessors in spite of the portentous requirements of the statute. Indeed, in the innovating parliament of 1601 one of the members moved in all seriousness that the subsidy be gathered by a new levy and not by

[22] John Evelyn, *Diary, Calendarium;* D'Ewes, 458, 483, 496, 633; Heywood, *The Wise Woman of Hogsdon,* Act. ii, Sc. 2: Essex, *Apology,* E. 2.

the old roll.[23] Even now, in a much more rigorous period, there is as we know a constant tendency for estimates and valuations to become fixed. Under the ineffective administration of the Tudors the difference between demand and performance is a matter of constant wonder to the student. Moreover it is to be remembered that the whole social and political system of England at this period rested on the good will of the well-to-do middle classes, and these classes are under all systems and at all periods the most sensitive to the burdens of taxation. It may be that the government connived at a habit of underestimate rather than enter into a contest with the classes on which it relied for its support.

We must include in the financial action of parliament their confirmation of the clergy's grant to the queen. This was a purely formal proceeding. Convocation, which was called at the same time as parliament, regularly imposed on the spiritualities of the clergy a tax analogous to the taxes imposed by parliament on their temporal possessions. This subsidy was usually four shillings on the pound of the value of benefices as this had been estimated in 1534, less what was already paid regularly to the crown as annates and such special payments of first fruits as should fall due. Such a subsidy was reported by Cecil in 1601 as amounting to about £20,000, a quarter the amount of the regular parliamentary lay subsidy at the same period, but like other taxes it was incompletely collected. During the last four years of this reign it amounted successively to some £12,000, £18,400, £17,700, £17,500. The number of subsidies granted by Convocation and the period of time over which their collection was spread corresponded approximately, though not exactly, to the parliamentary grants. During the early years of this period, from 1589 to 1593, half such a subsidy was payable yearly, for the remaining years a full such subsidy. Detailed provision for levy and collection were made by convocation similar to those already described for lay grants, and the queen was notified by the archbishop of the fact

[23] D'Ewes, 632.

and the amount of the grant. All this was in order to assert the control of parliament over taxation and perhaps to strengthen the hands of assessors and collectors of the tax. It was embodied in a special act of ratification and passed by the two houses of parliament, although without debate or consideration of details.[24]

All this is the parliamentary history of the grants; the processes which the subsidy acts set in motion, the actual assessments, collections, personal judgments, estimates and actions in the country at large would make a more varied story and one which if it could be followed out would give much insight into Elizabethan England. Nor is material for it lacking. Every collection of contemporary manuscripts contains subsidy books, lists, orders, appointments and other documents connected with the levy and collection of these taxes. A whole division of the Public Record Office is devoted to the " Exchequer Lay Subsidies," the originals or duplicates of assessment and collection lists, many of which still lie rolled in their neat little bags of soft leather, probably never unwrapped and seldom otherwise disturbed for centuries. Many assessment lists have been printed. No attempt can of course be made here to coördinate these records but a few instances may be suggestive.

The nobles were assessed, as has been said, by the lord chancellor. Their incomes were estimated in 1596 from £700 for the earl of Shrewsbury, through £600 and £500 for the earls of Pembroke and Cumberland and £400 for the marquis of Winchester, down to £100 each for the earls of Kent and Oxford. There were eighty-seven on the list, and noble ladies were not excluded, Susan, countess dowager of Kent, Lettice, countess of Leicester, and others being assessed at incomes of £200 or thereabouts. The relation of these amounts to their real incomes may be judged from a survey of the lands of the earl of Derby in 1601 showing a

[24] 31 Eliz., c. 14, 35 Eliz., c. 12, 39 Eliz., c. 26, 43 Eliz., c. 17; *Statutes of the Realm*, iv, pt. 2, 812–8, 860–6, 930–7, 984–91; *State Papers, Dom., Eliz.*, cclxiv, 169; cclxvi, 54; cclxxxii–iii, 53; Tanner, 610–9.

rent roll of £4035, 10s. 8d. He was assessed at £400, about one-tenth of his real income. Nearness to the queen was reflected in favorable assessments, the earl of Essex in 1596 paying on only £100, the lord admiral on £166, and Burghley both in 1585 and 1590 on £166. Precedence of rank yielded to economic status, a number of mere barons being credited with larger incomes than earls or the marquis. On these estimates of income the members of the nobility paid toward an ordinary subsidy all together between £3000 and £4000; individually their payments were such sums as £60, £50, £20 or £17. These correspond in modern values approximately to $1800, $1500, $600 or $450, which would certainly be easy returns to the income tax from the wealthiest men in England, though it must be remembered that this was only one of many burdens then incumbent on the nobility.[25]

The five country gentlemen of Derbyshire who acted as commissioners for the subsidy of 1593 and who must by law assess themselves, estimated their annual income, though urged by the privy council to set a good example to others, only at £80, £40, £30 and £20 respectively. An estimate of the incomes of 981 Londoners ranges from one at £400 down to 255 at £50 a year, making a total assessment for the city of £55,380 of income. The city is divided into two groups of wards, over each of which there are two collectors. The total collection from the city for the subsidy of the year 1589 amounts to £7191, of the year 1593 to £9240.[26]

A subsidy book for the county of Devon gives a list of 1163 persons assessed to the tax, the highest with an income of £45, but far the greater number from £30 down to £10. The numbers are strangely few; there are only seven who pay the subsidy in Plymouth, the wealthiest assessed at an income of £10. In Totnes, however, there are twenty-

[25] Lansdowne MSS., xxxii, 25; xliv, 55; lxiii, 10; State Papers, Dom., cclxv, 56; cclxxviii, 18.

[26] Rutland MSS., i, 316; Acts of the Privy Council, xxxii, 464; Lansdowne MSS., lix, 55 fo. 140, 56 fos. 149–51; State Papers, Dom., Eliz., Additional, xxxiii, 100.

four and in Tiverton twenty-eight. In many parishes there is only one taxpayer; in some none at all. Assessments for local taxes were more thorough. In the village of Lapworth, Warwickshire, the assessors can only find four persons to pay subsidies while at the same time twenty-six are levied upon for the repair of a bridge. On the other hand a subsidy book of Suffolk shows 8490 names, the whole shire paying £2160, and even in country parishes there are from six to eighteen on the list.

The assessments were evidently quite conventional. In a chance subsidy roll of two of the hundreds of Worcestershire in the last year of the queen, while there are often fifteen or twenty persons listed in even a small village, they are in groups, ten with £3 worth of goods, four with £4, one with £5; in a small town, twenty-one persons have the same amount of property, while the three knights in the district are each assessed at £20. At Havering-at-Bower in Essex in 1596 far the greater number of taxpayers are assessed at either £3 or £4, very few at any larger or smaller sum. The fifteenths and tenths are naturally still more conventional as they remain the same in total amount from year to year. Thomas Knight, collector of the first fifteenth and tenth from thirty-four parishes in the wapentake of Wirkworth, Derbyshire, for the year 1589, and the third and fourth, granted in 1593, collects the same sum, £48 9s., each year; the collector for the hundred of High Peak collects the same sum, £89 5s. 8d. for the first fifteenths and tenths of the three grants of 1589, 1593 and 1597. These tax collections of the tenths and fifteenths are often of minute sums; from one parish 23 shillings; from Upper Lamborn, Berkshire, in 1593 £4 17s. 5d.; from Chorleton £3, 4½d.; from nine whole hundreds £65 11s. 1¾d.[27]

From such scattered payments parliamentary grants in

[27] *Harleian MSS.*, ccclxvi, 103–28; *State Papers, Dom., Eliz.*, cclx, 53; *Public Record Office, Exchequer Lay Subsidies*, 74/265, *Particulars of Accounts of Fifteenths and Tenths, Derbyshire*, 31 Eliz., etc.; J. Amphlett, *Lay Subsidy Roll of Worcester of 1603;* S. H. A. Hervey, *Subsidy Roll of Suffolk in 1568;* Robert Hudson, *Memorials of a Warwickshire Parish,* 115–6.

their three forms, fifteenths and tenths, lay and clerical subsidies, were made up, and from these sources parliament
provided the queen from 1589 to 1594 with a sum varying
from £80,000 to £100,000 a year; from 1594 to the end of
her reign with a much larger sum.   An account dated October, 1597, endorsed in a shaking hand by the old lord
treasurer but a short time before his death, shows income
from parliamentary grants of £72,492 for 1593, £158,507
for 1594, £159,523 for 1595, £104,404 for 1596 and £82,270
for 1597; with a total of £636,504 for 5½ years, or an average of something more than £100,000 a year.   Another account of receipts at the exchequer annotated by the same
weakening hand at about the same time shows a total from
all sources for practically the same period of £1,895,723
with an average of something more than £300,000 a year.
Parliamentary grants of property taxes, therefore, provided about one third of the income of the government.   A
contemporary but unfortunately anonymous statement of
the finances of the whole of the queen's reign credits to parliamentary grants £3,519,574, and points out that this provided more than three quarters of the cost of all her wars,
which amounted to £4,978,054.   Whatever doubt there may
be of the accuracy of these figures it is evident that parliamentary taxation was an absolutely indispensable part of
the queen's income, and its periodical grant is a trustworthy
clue to the summons of the Elizabethan parliaments, certainly in these later years of her reign.[28]

But small space remains for any account of the non-
financial activity of the parliament of 1593.   A member of
the House of Commons once complained that " the granting
of this subsidy seemed to be the Alpha and Omega of this
parliament," and another expressed the hope that the queen
would not dissolve parliament till some acts had been passed,
even though the subsidy had been granted.   Secretary Cecil
rather resented these remarks, declaring that the queen was
just as " respective " concerning her laws as concerning her

[28] *State Papers, Dom., Eliz.*, cclxiv, 169, 172; cclxxxvii, 59.

money, but it is to be noted that he goes on to speak of her interest in the amendment of the old law rather than in new legislation. Outside of parliament also some surprise was expressed that parliament still remained in session after the subsidy act had been passed.[29] Yet many laws were introduced and considered and two or three of much importance passed. Of this general legislative work of the parliament of 1593 much must be disregarded and some postponed. The laws passed for the restraint of Roman Catholics and Separatists can be left for consideration in connection with other religious matters; the abortive efforts to legislate on the church courts was part of the long struggle against the prerogative which will be more fully discussed in the history of a later parliament.

Another question was pressing for more immediate solution. The problem of the sick, the maimed and the disorderly ex-soldier had been forcing itself more and more on attention since the outbreak of the war with Spain in 1585. Every campaign on the continent or in Ireland, every expedition at sea had, in addition to the loss of those who never returned, brought its harvest of those who returned incapacitated by illness, wounds, the bad moral effects of their experience or other causes from settling down and supporting themselves in ordinary civil life. As early as November, 1586, the lord mayor of London was ordered by the privy council to call before him the men who had been noticed begging in the most crowded streets of the city declaring that they had been hurt in the queen's wars in the Netherlands. If this proved to be true a general contribution was to be taken up at the sermons at Paul's Cross and elsewhere to send them back to the counties they had come from.

The difficulty still continued for in July, 1589, the lord mayor wrote to the privy council of the " soldours and

---

[29] D'Ewes, *Journals*, 458, 524, 633; *Cal. State Papers, Dom.*, 1591-4, 328; *Harleian MSS.*, 6265, fos. 111-4, quoted in Neale, *Eng. Hist. Rev.*, Jan., 1916, 134.

mariners which do resorte in great numbers to the city,"
of their recent reinforcement by those returning from the
Portugal voyage, of his efforts to induce them to return to
their home counties by advancing them funds, and of their
abuse of this kindness by taking new names and remaining
till they were given new advances. The privy council could
only advise him to seek the help of the nearest justices of
the peace in putting in force former statutes and orders for
sending masterless men and vagrants home to the counties
where they belonged. In fact the court was suffering from
the same trouble. Soldiers landed at Plymouth from the
Portugal fleet, without pay and in many cases already infected with the plague, formed themselves into disorderly
troops and marched toward the queen's court, which was
now at Nonesuch, demanding their pay. In July and
August proclamations were issued forbidding this and ordering the mariners to go to the admiralty, the soldiers to the
lords lieutenant of their respective counties for payment
or relief. Officers were also to guard the roads to prevent
their reaching the court.[30]

In November the disorders remained as great: " loose,
vagrant and masterless men," claiming to have been soldiers,
were dispersed through London and the nearby counties
begging up and down the streets and committing many disorders and outrages. The remains of Willoughby's army
were expected back daily to reinforce them. The queen
thereupon issued a proclamation, giving all " vagrants and
ill disposed persons calling themselves soldiers " two days
in which to secure passports from the nearest justices of the
peace, after which they were to return to their native
counties at least as rapidly as twelve miles a day. Pressed
men if able to work were to be reëmployed by their former
masters under pain of prosecution in Star Chamber, those
unable to work were to be relieved by their parishes. Since
they claimed, whether truly or not, to have been soldiers

[30] *Acts of the Privy Council*, xiv, 253, xvii, 453; Steele, *Proclamations*,
Nos. 814, 817; Dyson, *Proclamations*, No. 275.

they were given the benefit of the doubt and put under martial law, a system of discipline which had been recently applied rigorously to pressed men deserting from the expeditions to the Netherlands and Portugal.[31]

This proclamation was followed by the issue of commissions under the great seal to the lord mayor of London and the lords lieutenant of the seven southeastern shires authorizing them to appoint provost marshals for their shires, similar to those appointed for the military forces of the time. The provost marshal in each shire was to be provided with ten mounted men chosen for their knowledge of the country and paid from funds to be raised by the justices of the peace. He was to apprehend and execute by martial law disorderly soldiers and mariners and those not provided with passports and, by an astonishing extension of his powers, "other vagrant and masterless persons and sturdy vagabonds." The sheriffs and justices of the peace were to set watches on the highways from sunrise to sunset each day and to make searches late at night once a week in each town, village or hamlet where disorderly persons were likely to be.

All this was to continue only for three months. At the end of this period, however, there were still many complaints of the "mysdemeanors, insolences and enormyties dailie commytted by soche as had ben emploied in the warres in forraine partes." In some places such men assembled in great numbers "very royottislie and tumultyouslie." The appointment of provost marshals was therefore continued till the queen should order otherwise, though there was much complaint of its expense.[32] In 1591 and 1592, with the new expeditions to France and the constant ebb and flow of the Netherlands troops, we hear again that "many vagrants claiming to be soldiers are wandering abroad committing

---

[31] Steele, *Proclamations*, Nos. 805, 809, 818.

[32] *Acts of the Privy Council*, xvii, 237, xviii, 214, 221, 229, 236, 267, 420, xix, 34; *Cal. State Papers, Dom.*, 1581–90, 629, 630, 633, 1591–4, 119–20, 123, 1595–7, 335–6.

crime," and renewed efforts were made to meet the difficulty. Two new proclamations were issued, instructions were given to local officials to advance money to soldiers who landed in their localities to reach their homes, special sessions of the justices were held to examine those who claimed to have served and to indict those who had no passports, and new commissions were issued for the appointment of provost marshals with authority to punish offenders by martial law. It is evident that the underworld of London and the men of the highroads used the claim that they had served the queen in France or Holland to secure sympathy for their poverty and indulgence for their disorders, and the authorities therefore had the double task of distinguishing the unfortunate from the criminal among the ex-soldiers and at the same time finding whether the claim of military service was true or not. This may be the explanation of the fact that the use of martial law, which had been protested against by the judges in 1572, was connived at in its successive extensions during this period. Somewhat later provost marshals were authorized to " execute on the gallows " disorderly London apprentices and servants " not reformed by ordinary justice," those attempting to rescue prisoners, and in fact any disorderly elements among the lower classes, even when they made no claim to have been soldiers.[33]

In the course of time the disorderly soldier became less prominent, the sick or maimed soldier more so. Not only commanders of returning expeditionary forces, but mayors, justices of the peace and other officials at places where troops landed were given stringent orders to see that they were given the means of reaching their homes. In October, 1592, among the charges of the expedition to Normandy is a credit of 5s. apiece given to 152 poor and sick soldiers to carry them back to the counties whence they were levied; in September, 1593, two local justices in Sussex who took charge

[33] Steele, *Proclamations*, 840, 849, 861, 864, 867, 870, 873, 874, 916; *State Papers, Dom., Eliz.*, cccxl, 61; *Cal. State Papers, Dom.*, 1591–4, 119, 120, 123, 132–3; Camden, Ed. 1688, 199.

of 88 sick and wounded soldiers from Dieppe, although relieved of the expense of two by their death immediately on
landing, allowed the remainder two days' rest at the government's expense because of their miserable condition and then
dispatched 77 to their various homes with £34, 18s. for their
traveling expenses. They were only expected to make eight
miles a day. The remaining nine were so sick and weak
they had to keep them for a while longer at an expense of
more than £5. Another group were given from 2s, 6d to
7s, 6d according to the distance of their homes.

It is evident that these payments would give a sick man
but slight incentive to tramp through winter weather to a
distant home, and many drifted aimlessly about. Some of
those whose misfortunes were brought to the special attention of the queen or council were recommended to almsmen's
positions in various ecclesiastical establishments. When
there were no vacancies, pressure was exerted on these
bodies to support the poor soldiers till such a position became vacant. The cathedrals of Norwich, Chester, Peter-
borough, Durham and Rochester, Trinity College, Cambridge, Christ Church College, Oxford, Thornton College,
Lincolnshire, and others had maimed soldiers successively
thrust upon them. But claimants were many and unoccupied positions few and the poor soldier found himself often
with only a reversion to a position with five or six, in one
case eleven, other appointees preceding him. The council's
requirement to provide him a pension in the meantime was
hard to enforce, and not infrequently he was consoled with
a permit to beg. There are instances of government pensions for life given to a soldier. The dissolution of a certain
decayed hospital was opposed on the ground that it furnished pensions for a certain number of maimed soldiers,
and one of the few hospitals dating from this period was
established especially for this purpose.[34]

[34] *Acts of the Privy Council*, xxiv, 46, 67, 68, 88, 132, 150, 168, 181, 184;
Cal. State Papers, Dom., 1591–4, 326, 1595–7, 8, 306, 308, 503, 1598–1601,
15, 505; *Docquet*, July 1, 1597, July 19, 1597.

But all these methods were inadequate; the ravages of war could not be repaired by such tentative methods, and by the time the parliament of 1593 met the evil was as flagrant as it was familiar. Sick and maimed soldiers begging on the highways are constantly referred to in the debates of that parliament. In the discussion of the subsidy bill, when the multitude of beggars is mentioned as a proof of the poverty of the country, Ralegh denies this and points out that men of the " broken " companies from Normandy and the Low Countries when they come home do not return to their own towns where changes in industry have deprived them of their old occupations but remain in London or take to the highway. A strong impression was made upon the country gentlemen and burgesses from distant towns by the sight of more than a hundred maimed soldiers, acknowledged to be such, besides the usual crowds of mendicants, begging in the streets of Westminster and London.

The subject was soon brought into discussion in parliament; a proposal was made that a general subscription should be taken up in the two houses for their relief. In the House of Lords the bishop of Worcester moved that every earl should contribute forty shillings, every bishop thirty shillings and every baron twenty shillings " for relief of such poor Souldiers as went begging in the Streets of London "; this was agreed to. Later it was determined that those who had not attended the session and therefore were not subjected to the expense of living in London should pay double and those who had attended less than half the time should pay a third more. The bishop of Worcester and the queen's almoner were appointed to collect the contribution from the prelates and Lord Norris from the lords temporal; the earl of Essex and Lord Willoughby to distribute the fund. In the House of Commons a similar contribution was made of thirty shillings from every member who was a privy councillor, twenty shillings from every knight and serjeant at law and five shillings from every burgess, those who had departed without license to pay double. Pressure was applied to make the payment general and when one burgess refused to pay more than two shillings sixpence, on the ground of lack of means, the Speaker threatened to put him into custody for disobedience to the orders of the House. The House generally, however, were against such drastic action " and so he escaped." [35]

Similar subscriptions were made by the lower clergy in Convocation. One hundred and twenty pounds was collected from the London butchers who had been given license to kill and sell meat during Lent; a public subscription was opened in the Guildhall, and the mayor, aldermen and heads of Companies were urged by the privy council to contribute freely, so that " the citie shall be eased of the clamour and trouble those lame, maymed and poor creatures do give goinge up and downe the streets abegginge." As soon as these collections were made the privy council appointed eight well-known military leaders with half a dozen lawyers and prominent Londoners to meet on a certain day at the Sessions House at Newgate to take the names and record the claims of applicants. A week later, doubtless on their report, credentials were given to some sixty or seventy maimed soldiers authorizing them to receive two shillings every Saturday for twenty weeks, by which time it was expected that further arrangements should be made, and giving them a penny or twopence a mile, according to their state of health, to reach their respective home counties. Letters were sent to fifteen lords lieutenant asking them to appoint one of their deputy lieutenants to attend to the local distribution and putting in their hands the necessary funds. A proclamation was then issued through the lord mayor requiring all ordinary beggars, according to the old statute, to go to their own native parishes for relief and all maimed soldiers to present themselves to be supported from the voluntary contribution for the twenty weeks provided

[35] D'Ewes, 462, 463–4, 492, 503, 507; *State Papers, Dom., Eliz.*, ccxliv, 118.

for by the contribution. Persons falsely claiming to be soldiers were to be whipped and returned to their parishes as vagrants. Sir John Hawkins was asked to make the payments to the twenty-nine mariners who were put on the list, and three city men distributed the fund to soldiers whose homes were in London, Southwark and Westminster.[36]

This voluntary collection, however, like the other devices described, was but a makeshift. It was with a more states-manlike view that Cecil in a speech in the House of Com-mons urged a general consideration of the whole problem of poverty; pointing out that there were three general classes of those whom they daily met begging, first, and with the best claims to relief, the maimed and sick soldiers, second, poor, aged and diseased honest people, and, lastly, stout idle rogues. Each of these classes needed attention. The whole subject was referred to a distinguished committee, including in addition to Cecil and the other privy councillors, Francis and Nathaniel Bacon, Ralegh, Drake, Sir Robert Sydney, Sir John Wingfield, Sir Conyers Clifford, Sir Fernando Gorges, Sir Thomas Baskerville, Sir Francis Vere, Sir Francis Hastings, and some forty more, including in fact all the well-known men of the House. The subject of pro-vision for the poor as a whole was left to be attended to in the next parliament and this committee gave its principal and in fact its only attention to the first class referred to by Cecil, soldiers injured in the wars. It was at first agreed to recommend that a fund be raised for their relief through a tax of four shillings a year on inn-keepers and other re-tail dealers in wine, and of two shillings on alehouse keepers, victuallers, dealers in grain, butter and cheese and cattle drivers. But the bill formulated on these lines seems to have been unsatisfactory and was withdrawn and it was not until the next month that a more far-reaching bill, drawn

---

[36] *State Papers, Dom., Eliz.*, ccxliv, 118; *Acts of the Privy Council*, xxiv, 159–60, 170–1, 178–80, 191–6; *Cal. State Papers, Dom.*, 1591–4, 340; *Hatfield House MSS.*, iv, 300.

up by a new committee, was introduced by Bacon, debated, several times amended and finally passed by both houses.[37]

Although there had been some attempt to make this bill more inclusive, as passed it was purely a military pension act, applying to poor, sick and maimed soldiers only. It provided for the levy for their relief of a weekly tax in every parish in England, the incidence of the tax within the parish being left to the inhabitants themselves or to their petty officials, or in case of their neglect to the nearest justices of the peace. The amount to be paid by each parish should be decided yearly by the justices of the peace of the county in quarter sessions, but should not be less than a penny nor more than sixpence weekly in any parish. The money should be collected by the churchwardens, paid over to the high constables of the hundreds and by them to one or two of the justices of the peace elected by their colleagues to act as county treasurers for the administration of the fund. A soldier injured in the wars might present himself to the treasurer of the county from which he was drafted, or, if he was a volunteer, of the county where he was born or where he had last lived for three years, and must show a certificate of his service from his former officer. According to the nature of his injuries and the commendation of his services in his testimonial the treasurer or the justices of the peace in quarter session established a rate of pension for him payable quarterly as long as the law should remain in force. Ordinarily common soldiers were not to receive more than £10 a year, officers under the grade of lieutenants not more than £15 and lieutenants not more than £20; no provision was made for higher officers. Arrangements were made for conveying such soldiers from the place of their discharge from county to county till they reached their home county; fines were imposed upon administrators of the fund failing in their duty, and it was stipulated that maimed

---

[37] D'Ewes, 492, 499, 503-4, 507, 509, 513, 514, 516, 518; *Hatfield House MSS.,* iv, 295-6, 298, 300.

soldiers who begged after being granted a pension should be deprived of it and whipped, like other vagrants.[38]

With the hesitation characteristic of the legislation of the period, the law was to come into force only two months after the close of this parliament and to endure only to the end of the next parliament, which proved to be a period of about four years. In the next parliament, however, the law was reënacted, with some increase in the maximum that might be assessed in each locality, and in 1601 it was reënacted with a still further increase in the maximum, corresponding to the increase in the number of maimed soldiers and sailors, the sad effect of the long continued wars.[39]

Thus the existence of a pension law for disabled soldiers became a settled part of the national policy through the remainder of Elizabeth's time and down into the reign of James. The enforcement of the law was however quite a different matter, and although it forms no part of parliamentary history, it may be noted that there was constant difficulty, and it may be doubted whether it gave serious relief to the soldiers or ease to the government. Immediately on its passage the privy council wrote letters to the sheriffs and justices of the peace of all the counties and to the presidents of the Councils of the North and the Marches of Wales urging a prompt carrying out of its provisions. A royal proclamation was issued reminding all officials of their duties under it, and the mayor of London issued sharp orders for all soldiers to leave the city. But complaints soon came in that in most counties the law was a dead letter; justices of the peace sent applicants from the places where they had been impressed to those where they had been born and from the places where they had been born to those of their impressment, refused to sign their certificates, and did not keep registry books as required by the statute. One justice of the peace complains that no one knows of the

---

[38] 35 Eliz., c. 4. *Stat. of the Realm*, IV, ii, 847–9.

[39] 39 Eliz., c. 21, 43 Eliz., c. 3, 1 Jac. I., c. 25; *Stat. of the Realm*, IV, ii, 923–4, 966–8, 1050.

existence of the law because it was promulgated through the sheriff not through the justices. There are constant demands by the council on county authorities and their complaints in turn that their payments for this purpose have already reached their legal limit; pensions are cut off by new treasurers; allowances are given to officers and denied to men. Towns and counties neglect their assessed dues for many years and it is only occasionally that we get records of regular payments, such as that of Cornwall of £39 6s. a year for many years for this purpose. It was to the authorities of Cornwall that Thomas Benson, a cannoneer who had been wounded on the Revenge in the famous fight under Grenvylle, was referred for relief.

The privy council still find it necessary to appoint old soldiers to bedesmen's places in the church and universities, or provide for them by special pensions. Nor is order any more completely attained. Discharged soldiers still remained or became beggars and riotous vagabonds. In 1598 and 1599 provost marshals are still being appointed to enforce martial law and the queen is still annoyed on her walks by the sight of men who have become sick or maimed in her service.[40]

All sixteenth and early seventeenth century parliaments devoted much of their time to economic legislation. The parliament of 1593 discussed bills " for clapboards and cask," " concerning salted fish and salted herring," " touchinge the bredthe of pluncketts, azures and blewes," " concerning overlengths of broad cloths," " for the true assizing of bread," " concerning brewers," concerning Devonshire kersies or dozens, for the assizing and marking of timber, to restrict further building in already overgrown cities, and

[40] *State Papers, Dom., Eliz.*, ccxliv, 124, 125, cclxviii, 54, cclxxxviii, 36; *Cal. State Papers, Dom.*, 1591-4, 340, 1598-1601, 209, 210, 214, 215, 244, 1601-3, 313; *Acts of the Privy Council*, xxiv, 193-6, 278-301, xxv, 9, 16, 148, 188, 249, 291, xxvi, 24, 74, 115, 146, 165, 177, 348, 375; Steele, *Proclamations*, No. 858; *Hist. MSS. Comm., Rutland MSS.*, i, 315, 316, 377; Strype, *Annals*, iv, 408-9; Bateson, *Leicester*, iii, 397, 403; W. F. Cobb, *Churchwarden's Account of St. Ethelburga*, 11.

on a dozen similar subjects. This was not different, however, from what was true of earlier and later parliaments. But there was one trade proposal in the parliament of 1593 that has an added interest from the fullness with which it was debated, the information it gives on internal conditions in England, and the light it throws on prevailing habits of thought. It was somewhat clumsily entitled "An Act against Aliens born to sell by way of Retail Foreign Wares brought into this Realm." It was debated at length on three separate days, passed by a close vote in the House of Commons, and debated but finally defeated in the House of Lords.

It seems that among the many foreigners in London, there were some forty Dutch or Flemish Protestant merchants, the remnants of those who had originally come to London as refugees from religious persecution in the Netherlands. Many had returned to their homes in the more quiet times that followed, at least in the north, but those who remained became successful retail merchants, dealing in velvets, lawns, linens, cambrics and other fine textile goods. They made a community of their own in London with their own church, language and customs. As one of the speakers said " they will not converse with us, they will not marry with us, they will not buy anything from our countrymen." They made use of their family connections in the Netherlands to buy to advantage the articles they imported and sold and thus were able to undersell English dealers, and their goods were better. Notwithstanding the fact that they ranked as retailers, not importing or exporting merchants, they carried on a large business, £7000 at one time being paid by them for customs, some of them doing a business of £10,000 or £12,000 a year. Foreigners were always unpopular; there had recently been petitions from Colchester against a similar settlement of Dutch artisans there, and libellous placards threatening attack on these strangers were during this summer put up on the wall of the Dutch churchyard in London.

The city of London presented a petition to parliament

asking to have a bill passed forbidding these aliens to sell at retail. It was considered by a committee; a lawyer of the Middle Temple was allowed to speak at the bar representing the city, and two from Lincoln's Inn appeared in the interest of the strangers, a very unusual parliamentary proceeding. More than a dozen members took part in the debate. Ralegh spoke twice, as well as serving on the committee, and Cecil was drawn into the discussion, although, as he said, he had promised himself to keep silent on the bill because " it speaks of Trades, wherein I have no skill." Defenders of the strangers pleaded that charity and honor required that they should protect those who had fled to England for refuge. England " was accounted the refuge of distressed nations," which was a great honor. It was not so long since, in Queen Mary's day, many Englishmen had been exiles for religion's sake; England should not now withhold that liberty which was then allowed their citizens; " they are strangers now, we may be strangers hereafter, so let us do as we would be done with." All great cities, such as Venice and Antwerp, had become great by permitting strangers to live and trade in them; goods were made cheaper by the retail trade of these foreigners; they set a good example to Englishmen by their thrift and the industry to which they brought up their children. Such arguments might have been heard in the Councils of Delft or Leyden a generation later, when persecuted Englishmen were again to sojourn as strangers there.

Other speakers argued that these foreigners by their advantages were driving Englishmen out of their trades, that sixty English retailers formerly prosperous were now beggars, that prices were higher than they had formerly been because of the absence of native competition, that they carried coin out of England, that charity begins at home and the " *patres conscripti* " of parliament should have respect to the interests of London, on whose flourishing estate the whole kingdom depended. Ralegh took high nationalist and royalist ground, declaring that it was baseness in a nation to give to any other nation privileges which its citizens did not receive in return, that the strangers had forsaken their own king, and that although they might now return freely to the lands from which they had come, so far as religion was concerned, they preferred to stay in England, though "disliking our church." They were vacillating, "now under Spain, now under Montfort, now under the Prince of Orange, but under no governor long." They were by nature mercenary, considering only their own profit. They were getting the trade of the whole world into their hands. They were secretly providing Spain with the materials with which she equipped her fleets against England. He saw no charity, no honor and no profit in giving relief to the Dutch strangers. This was not the magnanimous and generous spirited Elizabethan Ralegh speaking, but the English nationalist, fearing competition and displaying a hostility to the Dutch anticipatory of the antagonism of a later age.

The arguments used in the House of Lords are not recorded. It may be surmised that the arguments of trade did not appeal so much to the territorial magnates as they did to the Commons, where there was so large an intermixture of merchants and other city men. Whatever the cause the bill failed in the Lords, as already stated, and the foreigners retained their foothold in the great city. April 10, 1593, the queen dissolved this parliament.[41]

[41] D'Ewes, 463, 489, 504–5, 507–11; *House of Lords Journal*, i, 463; *House of Commons Journal*, 505–6; *Acts of the Privy Council*, xxv, 200, 222; *State Papers, Dom., Eliz.*, ccxl, 115, ccxliv, 104, 105, 106; *Cal. State Papers, Dom.*, 1591–4, 337, 343, 349.

CHAPTER XXXV

THE PARLIAMENT OF 1597: ENCLOSURES:
THE POOR LAW

T HE years immediately following the close of the parliament of 1593 were, as has been described in an
earlier chapter, largely years of dearth, high prices, poverty
and turbulence. There was no improvement visible by
1597; indeed another bad season, a continuance of the trade
war with Germany and the extension of the rebellion in
Ireland made matters worse. There was continued unemployment and consequent poverty in the clothmaking districts and in London. Prices of food were higher than in
1596. Vagabondage, suffering and complaint were widespread. Whipping, imprisonment and execution of the tur-
bulent by martial law, enforced selling of grain by farmers,
compulsory payment of wages by manufacturers and such
charitable relief as was available for the poor had not suf-
ficed to introduce order or seriously to reduce destitution.
Administrative authorities national and local had reached
the limit of their powers. To parliament alone could
thoughtful men look for constructive measures to increase
prosperity or at least to diminish want.

On the other hand, the meeting of a new parliament was
at this period not popular with the people nor desired by
the queen. It was burdensome to many of those who attended and expensive to their constituents, either directly
through the wages of the members or indirectly through
their grants of taxes. The queen was often annoyed by the
debates and apprehensive lest legislation should be pressed
upon her to which she was not willing to agree. To avoid
a meeting of parliament as long as possible was therefore

looked upon as an advantage to all. In his opening speech to the parliament of 1593, the lord keeper had in the queen's name declared how loth she was to call the people to a parliament, how infrequently she had actually done so and with what regret she would change her practice. There seem to have been plans for a parliament in the spring and again in the winter of 1595, but it was postponed again and again until by some period early in 1597 the queen had settled in her mind that it must be called in the fall of that year. Essex, who was about to start on the Islands Voyage, was anxious it should not meet till his return and Cecil in his interest urged the queen to postpone it as late as possible. It was finally summoned August 13, to meet October 25, 1597, just four years and a half from the dissolution of its predecessor.[1]

This long intervening period gave opportunity for many official changes. Lord Keeper Puckering had died in 1596 so this parliament was opened by a new lord keeper, Egerton. Mason, who had long been clerk of parliaments, a permanent crown office, died early in 1597 and was succeeded by Thomas Smith, already clerk of the privy council. He introduced, to our great advantage, better order and fullness into the parliamentary records. According to the letters of the privy council sent out in September the old members of the House of Commons should as far as possible be reëlected; there were nevertheless many changes. As to the House of Lords there was the usual series of letters asking to be excused from attendance sent by various lords and bishops who were in bad health or, as they thought, more usefully employed in other service, as the bishop of Durham and Lord Eure on the Scotch border and the earl of Pembroke presiding over the Council of Wales. Essex,

---

[1] Camden, *History of Elizabeth*, Ed. 1688, 471, 541; Stow, Ed. 1631, 769–70, 785–6; *Hatfield House MSS.*, vii, 352, 359, 366; *Harleian MSS.*, 6265, fos. 111–4, quoted in Neale, *Eng. Hist. Rev.*, 1916, 130; *State Papers, Dom., Eliz.*, cclxiv, 5; *Cal. State Papers, Dom.*, 1595–7, 12, 449, 505; *Sydney Papers*, i, 374; *Parliament Pawns* No. 15; Mountmorres, ii, 87.

also, for all his desire to have parliament postponed till his return from his naval expedition had nothing but failure to bring back with him, and received a cold welcome from the queen. He was met also with the news of the advancement of Lord Howard, his colleague and rival at Cadiz, to an earldom. He retired to the country in chagrin, and, his summons to parliament by some means delayed, sulked under pretense of ill health until during the Christmas holidays he was made earl marshal, which gave him precedence over Howard. His health immediately improved and in January he reappeared at court and resumed his usual activity in the House of Lords.[2]

On the other hand the approach of this parliament stirred various noblemen and gentlemen to " rake up the cinders of their long buried titles, claims and demands to places of honor." Lord Hunsdon, still only a baron notwithstanding his kinship to the queen and his father's long service, brought up his claim to an English earldom under the Irish title of Ormonde. Sir Richard Fiennes asserted his right to the title of Lord Say, temporarily inhibited to his father; and after the opening of parliament Lord de la Ware sued for and obtained a higher seat in the House of Lords in the half forgotten right of his grandfather. These matters would have little claim to our notice did they not, along with many other evidences, indicate a steadily increasing valuation placed on membership in either house of parliament and a growing interest in its actions.

Even before the meeting of this parliament the public interest in social questions showed itself and it was evident that, although the queen's need for money might be the crucial reason for its summons, an attempt would be made to pass some far-reaching laws to alleviate poverty. As a matter of fact problems of high prices, insufficient production and above all of destitution almost monopolized the

[2] *State Papers, Dom., Eliz.,* cclxiv, 134; *Cal. State Papers, Dom.,* 1595–7, 497–8, 505; *Acts of the Privy Council,* xxvii, 361; *Hatfield House MSS.,* iv, 467; vii, 299, 359, 366–7, 383, 385, 410, 415, 422, 429, 431.

attention of this parliament from its very beginning. Two members were early appointed to make a general collection from their colleagues for the poor, and several important laws for social relief were placed on the statute book.

It was in this parliament that the last serious attempt to limit enclosures was made, and the poor law as it has been known in English history is the national code formulated in the parliament of 1597. Although the government had been struggling with the rising mass of pauperism for more than half a century, and although some changes were made later, it is nevertheless true that the poor law as passed in 1597 and renewed in almost the same words in the next parliament remained practically the same for two centuries and a half, and indeed is still the foundation of the English system of dealing with the problem of pauperism.[3]

The formal motion always made in the House of Commons on its opening day to indicate that parliament is actually in session was on this occasion the introduction of a bill against forestallers, regraters and engrossers, an attempt to make food cheaper. Soon afterward Francis Bacon arose and in a carefully constructed speech introduced another phase of the same subject, one that was to occupy much of the time of the session. Surrounded by the teeming population of London and Westminster and remembering the solitudes being artificially created in old farming regions as he believed by evictions of tenants to introduce sheep farming, he declared that " the overflowing of the people here makes a shrinking and abate elsewhere," and introduced two allied bills, one " Against Inclosures," the other " Against Depopulation of Towns and Houses of Husbandry and Tillage." He had, he said, read the preambles of all the " former moth-eaten laws " on the subject back to the time of Henry VII. He still believed that enclosures

[3] Cal. State Papers, Dom., 1581–90, 575; 1595–7, 509–11, 518, 531; Acts of the Privy Council, xxviii, 43; Cal. Hatfield House MSS., iii, 395, vii, 383, xi, 43; D'Ewes, Journals, 551, 566; E. M. Leonard, Early History of English Poor Relief, 67–80.

and evictions lay at the basis of national impoverishment; leading to idleness, subversion of houses, decay of tillage and of charity and greater charges to the poor. He was not in a position to quote the description by a future and still more famous essayist of the scene of depopulation when " some traveler from New Zealand shall, in the midst of a vast solitude, take his stand on a broken arch of London Bridge to sketch the ruins of St. Paul's "; but he did quote Ovid's " Reeds grow where Troy once stood," and reminded his auditors that they might see in rural England " instead of a whole Town full of people nought but green Fields, a Shepherd and a Dog." Chancellor Fortescue supported his motion and a large committee was immediately appointed and ordered to meet the same afternoon in the Exchequer Chamber. Bacon fought for his two bills in one form after another through the whole session and they appear on the statute book as the first fruits of the labors of this parliament, chapters 1 and 2 of 39 Elizabeth. Their influence on the diminution of poverty and on the progress of enclosure is however more doubtful. It requires a stronger government than that of Tudor England to reverse the direction of economic change.[4]

Other members were impressed with other phases of the problem of poverty. Immediately after the speeches of Bacon and Fortescue on the first day of parliament a Mr. Finch rose and called attention to the two evils long familiar but imperfectly distinguished from one another, the ill-doing of the idle and vagrant and the " miserable estate of the Godly and honest sort of the poor Subjects of this Realm."

This matter was referred to the same committee as the bills on enclosure and tillage. One after another within the next two weeks bills were introduced by various members " for the extirpation of beggars," " for the erection of houses of correction and punishment of rogues and sturdy beggars," " for the building of work houses and the extension of hos-

---

[4] D'Ewes, 551, 558, 560, 562, etc.; 39 Eliz., cc. 1, 2, *Statutes of the Realm*, iv, ii, 891–6; Bacon, *Works, Spedding*, Ed. 1862, ii, 79–83.

pitals," "for the employment of the poor," "for the relief of the poor, aged, lame and blind in their parishes," "for those impoverished by casual losses," "for the relief of the poor out of church livings," and other approaches to a settlement of the great problem of beggary and disorder. Altogether there were seventeen bills presented in the House of Commons on this general subject in this parliament.

It was early complained that Bacon's committee was giving all its time to enclosure and tillage and none to rogues and the poor. Several of the proposals on this subject were thereupon referred to another committee, nine bills in one day, the 22nd of November, till the committee was in the unprecedented condition of having eleven bills under consideration at the same time. Some of the proposals were rejected at an early stage, others were referred to subcommittees. Finally there was so much confusion that new committees were appointed and a new distribution of the work made so that there were, so far as the somewhat confused records allow one to be sure, three committees, each in charge of one of the three main divisions of the subject, tillage, vagabondage and involuntary poverty.

They were all large committees with much overlapping. They included many prominent members: all the serjeants at law and all the readers of the Inns of Court in the House, all the knights of shires and citizens of cities, Francis and Nathaniel Bacon, Robert, Thomas and William Cecil, Sir Francis and Sir Edward Hastings, Knyvett, Hobby, Horsey, Knollys, Gilbert, Sandys, who had been on a committee on the same subject twenty years before, and Sir Thomas Wroth, who continued his interest and made the motion for the renewal of some of these bills in the next parliament. There were but few days before the Christmas recess in which one or other of these committees did not make some report or in which there was not some mention of these subjects. The discussions in the committees and speeches in the House are unfortunately not recorded, except for the outline of Bacon's introduction and one nameless speaker's address on the bill against enclosures. There was evidently however much difference of opinion in each House and between the Houses. Bacon anticipated opposition to his bill against enclosures from the Lords, and it was at one time proposed to exempt from its provisions the northern counties where powerful nobles were the enclosers; but Cecil opposed this and the dean of Durham, who had just come from the rich fields of Kent to the poorer North and had found " 500 ploughs decayed in the last fifty years " and " great villages dispeopled," protested that there more than elsewhere the prohibition of enclosing was needed.[5]

In the House of Lords, December 8, a large committee, containing Archbishop Whitgift and six other bishops, Lord Burghley, Lord Admiral Nottingham, four earls and several barons, was appointed to consider the bill sent up from the House of Commons for the building of houses of correction and the punishment of sturdy beggars, and a bill for the relief of the poor in times of extreme dearth of corn, apparently initiated in their own house. Four of the judges and the attorney general were summoned to attend this committee to give advice. A number of amendments were proposed, there was considerable controversy between the two houses, complicated by questions of procedure, and the amendments of the Lords to their bill were finally disapproved by the House of Commons by a vote of 106 to 66. A new bill was then drawn up by the House of Lords itself on the subject of punishment of rogues and vagabonds, passed, sent to the House of Commons and finally accepted there. On the other hand a bill for the maintenance of hospitality, " whereby the Poor shall be much relieved," was rejected on second reading as late as February 1st. Successive conferences between committees of the two houses and the sending of amendments to and fro continued through the session, the bills got through slowly, and it was not until a few hours before the queen arrived

[5] D'Ewes, 551–93; *Hatfield House MSS.*, vii, 541; *Cal. State Papers*, 1595–7, 247, 348, 542.

to dissolve parliament that the bill against decaying of Towns and Houses of Husbandry, the first to be introduced, was finally passed as amended by the House of Lords.[6]

All these discussions were of course intermingled with the multifarious other matters that interested parliament, though this session was even more than the meeting four years earlier and that which was to take place four years later devoted to economic matters. The actual legislation of this parliament on matters concerning the poor is to be found in the first six acts placed upon the statute book at the close of its session. The first two, as already stated, were an attempt to renew in more skillfully drawn terms the old effort to prevent the substitution of sheep raising for grain raising and its effect in evicting tenants, " decaying " villages and houses and reducing the production of grain. The first law is directed to the keeping up of the number of farms and farm houses, the second to the prevention of conversion of land from tillage to pasture. The former defines a " house of husbandry " as one that has or has had for three years at a time since the accession of the queen as much as twenty acres of arable land, meadow and pasture attached to it. All such houses with their attached arable lands are to be preserved. Any which have within the last seven years been pulled down or allowed to go into disrepair must now be rebuilt and twenty to forty acres of land attached to them. Any owners or heirs of owners who pulled down such houses of husbandry or allowed them to go into disrepair more than seven years ago but since the beginning of the queen's reign must rebuild half as many as there were before, but need not attach to them less than forty acres. This was a concession apparently to the increasing average size of farms at this period, as compared with mediaeval practice, even when used for arable not pasture. Purchasers of lands on which such houses have been since the beginning

---

[6] D'Ewes, 551, 555, 557, 558, etc.; *Cal. State Papers, Dom.*, 1598–1601, 4, 9, 19.

of the queen's reign need rebuild only one quarter the old number. There were many exceptions, penalties and provisions for enforcement. The anticipation of this law was that there would gradually be reconstructed within the next few years a very considerable part of those rural villages and village farm houses which had gone to decay in the last half century or more, and that they would be reoccupied by their old yeomen inhabitants.

The law for the maintenance of husbandry and tillage was another method of securing the same end. Its preamble calls attention to the dependence of the country for its defense, food supply and the prosperity of its people on " the Plough and Tillage," and to the fact that from 1536 to the last meeting of parliament, there had always been laws forbidding any alteration in the proportionate amount of the country occupied in tillage as compared with sheep runs. The repeal of these laws in 1593 had been followed by an unprecedented depopulation and conversion of arable land to pasture. It was now provided that, with some exceptions, all land which had been since the accession of the queen converted to sheep pasture or to the grazing of cattle, after having been for twelve years or more before used in tillage, should now be restored to tillage, and that none now in tillage should be converted to pasture in the future. Provision was made for the use of sod as part of a rotation of crops, for feeding cattle for domestic use, in reclaimed grounds, and, being a parliament made up largely of nobility and gentry, for deer parks and rabbit warrens. It was anticipated that in this way the sheep-raising districts would again revert to the old-fashioned grain raising with its greater opportunity for occupation and self-support of the people on the land. The old houses being rebuilt, small farms available and labor in demand, the old days would return and the springs of vagabondage and pauperism would be dried up.[7]

[7] 39 Eliz., cc. 1 and 2, *Stat. of the Realm,* IV, ii, 891–6; *Hatfield House MSS.,* vii, 498, viii, 278–9.

Existing disorder and poverty were attacked more directly in the third and fourth statutes of the series, " For Punishment of Rogues, Vagabonds and Sturdy Beggars," and " For the Releife of the Poore." With laws for punishment Tudor England was familiar, and offenders of this kind were now attacked with simple and direct savagery. For simplicity's sake all former statutes on the subject were repealed. Justices of the peace in quarter sessions were authorized to levy a tax, and build and administer one or more houses of correction in each county, city or town in addition to the old jails. The same ten classes of persons as had been enumerated twenty-five years before, in the law of 1572, were again declared to be rogues, vagabonds and sturdy beggars and subjected to the penalties of the new law. They included " all persons calling themselves schollers going about begginge," all seafaring men claiming that they had been shipwrecked, all fortune tellers, all persons claiming to be collectors for prisons or hospitals, all bearwards, minstrels and common players, except those authorized as players by some nobleman, all wandering craftsmen, as tinkers and pedlars, all artisans and other workmen refusing to work for legal wages, all persons on parole from jails begging for their fees, all wanderers claiming losses by fire or other accident, and all wanderers calling themselves Gypsies. Every person of any of these classes arrested by any justice of the peace or parish officer shall, with the approval of the minister and one other of the parish, " be stripped naked from the middle upwards and shall be openly whipped until his or her body be bloodye." After the whipping a testimonial is to be signed and sealed by the justice of the peace, constable and minister or any two of them, giving the date of the punishment and requiring the person whipped to go by the most direct route and within a prescribed time to the parish where he was born, where he had last lived for a whole year, or through which he had last passed unpunished, according as either of these could in due order be discovered. If the requirements of this testimonial were in any respect disobeyed, the whipping should be repeated in every parish until the culprit had returned to his legal dwelling place and "put him or her selfe to labour"; or in the case where a legal dwelling place was not discovered he must be sent by the authorities of the last parish through which he went unwhipped to the local house of correction or to the common jail of the county for a year or until he should be placed in service, or, "not being able in body," placed in some almshouse.

If any rogue or vagabond apprehended should be considered by the justices of the peace in quarter sessions to be a leader of the lower classes of the people and therefore dangerous, or incorrigible, he might be banished to parts beyond the sea and his return would be a felony punishable by death. Or he might be sent to the galleys for life. The "parts beyond the sea" to which such dangerous characters were to be sent were to be decided upon by at least six members of the Privy Council, of which the lord chancellor or lord treasurer must be one. This was apparently an anticipation of the regular system of transportation adopted long afterwards and was perhaps suggested by the contemporary attempts to plant colonies in America and the plans for using paupers and criminals for their early colonists. The alternative of the galleys is referable either to foreign practice or to contemporary projects for the greater use of galleys, suggested however rather than carried out to any appreciable extent. The whole fabric of this law, moreover, with its definiteness of requirement, exceptions, extension and provisions must be looked upon in the light of the interval between promise and performance, between legislation and actual administration so characteristic of the time and to which reference has so often been made. It is true that forms for testimonials to whippings are given in manuals of local government, as indicated in a later chapter in this volume, and that our few remaining local records are full of evidences of harsh punishment. Nevertheless there is no reason to believe that the objects of the law were really fulfilled. The population of England was not reduced to the fixed, plodding and servile body contemplated by a parliament of landlords, employers and zealots for the unremitting drudgery of the lower classes.[8]

Even with the wandering paupers disposed of it was obvious that there were many beggars who remained in their own parishes, some who had work and many who were unable to work. It was for these, the children, the unemployed and those described in the law for the relief of the poor as " the lame, ympotente, olde, blynde . . . poore and not able to worke " that the most constructive and permanent results were accomplished by this body of legislation. The pith of the new law was the appointment in each parish of four overseers of the poor who, along with the church wardens, had the power of compulsory taxation of landholders and others of the parish, and of using the funds thus obtained for binding poor children out as apprentices, buying raw materials with which to put the unemployed to work, the support of the very poor and for building cottages on the commons for their occupation. To carry out these purposes the overseers of the poor and the church wardens were to meet once a month on Sunday afternoons, keep careful accounts of the sums they levied, collected and spent, and give licenses to poor persons to beg though only within their own parish limits and only for food. Although much of this work was to be carried out under the general oversight of the justices of the peace of the county, the machinery of parish taxation and administration thus created was a powerful element of decentralization, and it introduced a special type of poor relief which reacted on the whole system of local life and government in England. In 1601 the law was reënacted with slight changes, as has been said; its further development belongs to a later period; but the plan of 1597 did much to solve the problem it was intended to solve and notwithstanding minor changes re-

[8] Vol. I, pp. 361-72; 39 Eliz., c. 4, *Stat. of the Realm*, IV, ii, 899-902; *Eng. Hist. Rev.*, January, 1921.

mained, as has been said, the basis of the English poor law system.[9]

No begging for money being now allowed, the law made provision for the collection from the people of each parish of a small sum weekly to be used for certain other charitable purposes. It was to be paid quarterly to the high constable and by him to certain of the justices of the peace elected treasurers for the county. This money was to be paid partly to the hospitals and almshouses of the county, partly to the poor prisoners in King's Bench and Marshalsea prisons in London. This contribution was analogous to the provision of money by the parishes for the support of sick and wounded soldiers passed in the last parliament and renewed in this. Men claiming to be soldiers but not having any credentials and therefore not having any claim for a pension, were ordered by another law of this session to betake themselves to some service and to cease wandering, on pain of punishment by death for felony. If an ex-soldier did not either obtain a pension or go into service he should be arrested, tried, condemned and executed, unless some competent freeholder would agree to take him into his service for a year and give bonds to return him to the justices at the expiration of that time. On the other hand, if an ex-soldier were sick, or unable to find work, or even extremely poor he might, as an exception to all others, obtain a license from a justice of the peace to ask for such alms as might be given him.[10]

The two remaining laws making up the poor legislation of this parliament need not detain us. One gave facilities for ready incorporation and endowment by private persons of hospitals or other dwelling or working houses for the poor; the other provided for commissioners to examine into the misapplication of the revenues of charitable foundations already existing.[11]

[9] 39 Eliz., c. 3, 43 Eliz., c. 2. *Stat. of the Realm,* IV, ii, 896-9, 962-3; E. M. Leonard, *Early History of English Poor Relief,* chaps. 6-14.

[10] 39 Eliz., c. 17, *Stat. of the Realm,* IV, ii, 915-6.

[11] 39 Eliz., chaps. 5 and 6, *Ib.* pp. 902-4.

The tendency during this period to codification, to organization of scattered provisions into a systematic whole covering some one large field of interest has already been referred to. The statutes of both the universities were gathered and reissued, the thirty-nine articles of religion were promulgated, the old statutes of laborers were codified and enacted as the statute of apprentices of 1563. In the same way, now after seventy years of experimentation and the trial of many plans, after long discussion by some of the best minds of the age, a system of provision for the poor had been adopted. It was intended to bring about an entire cessation of wandering and begging. So far as the law was concerned the last crevice through which open country-wide begging could leak in or out had been closed. All poor men had been confined to their own parishes and there either set to work or supported. Soldiers were on a pension. There was to be no more begging and no more actual destitution. It need hardly be said that these ends were not attained. Yet there was a measurable improvement. A considerable body of surviving records seem to show that the next generation was less troubled by either vagabondage or unrelieved poverty than that which had passed.

This parliament granted to the queen the same subsidies, tenths and fifteenths as the last; it debated, though ineffectually, the subject of monopolies, passed many private and regulative acts, continued a number of acts passed for a restricted period by former parliaments, and after a continuance of three and a half months was summoned before the queen on the afternoon of the 9th of February, 1598, and dissolved.[12]

[12] D'Ewes, 546, 595–6

CHAPTER XXXVI

THE PARLIAMENT OF 1601: THE PREROGA-
TIVE: MONOPOLIES

THE parliament which met October 27, 1601, and was
dissolved December 19th, after a session of eight
weeks, had marked characteristics. Thanks to a private
journal of its debates and occurrences, kept by a young
member from a Shropshire borough, we have fuller and
more intimate knowledge of it than the official records are
apt to give us. It was more disorderly than its immediate
predecessors. Interruptions and personalities in debate,
disputes between the two houses, recrimination between lay
and ecclesiastical office holders, disorderly behavior of the
pages on the stairways, intrusion of outsiders constantly
interfere with the progress of business. Yet it was a busy
parliament. Thirty-nine bills were introduced into the
House of Commons and twenty-three into the House of
Lords within its first week. Altogether more than a hundred
bills were read and discussed. It was more jealous of its
privileges and more assertive of the interests of its constituents than any other parliament of the sixteenth century.
Its activities however were not creative; the new laws actually placed upon the statute book apart from extensions
of old statutes were few and unimportant. It was religious,
indeed puritanical, bills being introduced and debated for
the better keeping of the Sabbath, against the holding of
markets and fairs on Sunday, against blasphemous swearing, to suppress the sin of adultery, against neglect by the
clergy of their religious duties and for the better payment
of clergymen; yet not one of these laws was passed. Division of opinion apparently was too great.

It was more outspoken and headstrong than usual. The privy councillors had the greatest difficulty in guiding the course of debate and securing legislation, and they did not themselves work well together. Indeed it was to the future rather than to the past or even to the present that this parliament looked. It was as if the approaching dissolution of the queen was casting its shadow before. The opening of the session saw the incident already described of a large number of members of the Commons excluded by carelessness from the ceremonies. Although in its midst occurred a moving interview of the queen with a great representation of the House come to thank her for her quick response to their wishes, at its close, her last public appearance, as it proved, before the representatives of her people, she was less gracious than she might have been, and the members of parliament were somewhat lacking in their usual shows of loyalty and personal respect. The end of the reign of Elizabeth and of an era was approaching.[1]

The most notable occurrence in this parliament was undoubtedly the crisis on the question of patents or monopolies. But this was from a parliamentary point of view only a conspicuous instance of a familiar conflict, frequently recurring and in 1601 as before and until long afterward, left unsettled. How far did the powers of parliament extend? Were they unrestricted, or must these country gentlemen, burgesses and officials, when they met for a few weeks every four years accept the condition that there were certain subjects that they were not at liberty to legislate upon or even to bring up for discussion? How far did the prerogative of the queen limit the freedom of parliament? Many conflicts on this question occurred in earlier parliaments but their culmination was in the parliament of 1601. The views of the queen were perfectly definite and were

---

[1] D'Ewes, *Journals*, 624, 626, 629, 633, 639, 642–3, 648, 666, 682; Heywood Townshend, *Historical Collections*, 173–336; J E. Neale, *The Authorship of Townshend's Historical Collections*, *Eng. Hist. Rev.*, January, 1921, 96–9.

repeatedly expressed. During the parliament of 1593 she sent for the Speaker and directed him to carry to the House of Commons this direct message in her own words: " It is in me and in my power to call parliaments, it is in my power to end and determine the same, it is in my power to assent or dissent to anything done in parliaments." From the last clause she proceeded to draw the logical inference that she could decide what matters should be propounded in a parliament, reminded the Speaker and members that the objects for which this parliament had been called had been clearly stated by her in the chancellor's speech at its opening and had especially excluded " matters of state or causes ecclesiastical "; and closed by forbidding the House to discuss matters of state and of reformation of the church and the Speaker on his allegiance to read to them any bill on such matters presented to him. It is of interest to note that the queen used the expressions " this parliament " and " parliaments," as indeed was practically universal contemporary usage. She hardly conceived of " parliament " as a permanent institution. There was not in her view a coördinate branch of the government known as parliament; rather from time to time a special assembly known as a parliament was called. The permanent continuous government was the queen, her privy councillors, judges and other officials. In the parliament of 1597 she had expressed the judgment already quoted that freedom of speech does not permit a parliament " to frame a forme of Relligion or a state of Government as to their idle braynes shall seeme meetest. She sayeth no king fitt for his state will suffer such absurdities." [2]

This view of the limited sphere of parliament was occasionally controverted by some bolder spirit who found his proposals excluded from consideration, but was on the whole supported by the leaders and acknowledged by the great

[2] D'Ewes, 478–9; *State Papers, Dom., Eliz.*, ccxliv, 51–4; Neale, *The Lord Keeper's Speech in the Parliament of 1597, Eng. Hist. Rev.*, Jan., 1916, 136.

body of members of the parliaments of the time. Peter Wentworth had in 1571, 1572 and 1576, deprecated influence being exerted over the House by rumors of the queen's liking or misliking measures under debate and protested against her prohibition of their discussion of matters of religion except as these were put before them by the clergy. In 1587 he had propounded in the form of a series of questions to the Speaker eight principles asserting the most complete liberty of parliament to discuss without interruption or restriction and to act on all matters " touching the service of God, the safety of the prince and this noble realm." But the Speaker declined to put these questions and the House itself sent the propounder of them to the Tower till the end of the session. Coke, who as Speaker manfully asserted some of the lesser claims of the House, as of privacy of its bills till they were ready to lay before the queen, and was no partisan of royal claims, not only yielded to the queen's positive commands not to submit to the House bills on prohibited subjects, but drew up a written acknowledgment of the ineffectiveness of parliamentary action as against the power of the crown.[3]

Although individual members occasionally brought up in the House matters which they knew to be distasteful to the queen, and courageously insisted on discussing them, they never failed to acknowledge her possession of a prerogative power which enabled her, if she wished, to make their actions nugatory. Elizabeth in relation to the parliaments of her time was a possessor of authority to restrict or disregard them, limited only by her reluctance to override long established custom, respect for a body representing her people, and recognition that from them alone could be obtained adequate means for carrying on her government. Parliament's attitude to the queen on the other hand was of recognition of her supreme power, modified by great self-esteem, a firm, if somewhat vague, conviction that it also

---

[3] D'Ewes, 410; *State Papers, Dom., Eliz.*, ccxliv, 52–4; cclxxvi, 81–3; J. E. Neale, *Peter Wentworth, Eng. Hist. Rev.*, Jan., 1924, 40–54.

shared in the government of England, and a claim alternately asserted and ignored to discuss and even legislate upon all matters that interested them. These two conceptions were inconsistent, and although in the friendly relations of the time serious friction seldom occurred, the parliaments of this period found themselves at one time or another prohibited by the queen from discussing many subjects that arose in their midst. There were four classes of such cases, the regulation of administrative departments of the government, the succession to the crown, the church and, above all, patents of monopoly.

Early in the parliament of 1589 two bills, apparently innocuous, had been introduced, one by Sir Edward Hobby, knight of the shire for Berks and an active parliamentarian, for the abolition of certain exactions in the exchequer, the other by John Hare, a burgess from Horsham in Sussex, for reforming disorders of the purveyors for the royal household. Both bills immediately became centers of unusual attention. Hobby had reason to complain that his speech in the House in introducing the bill had been repeated and misrepresented outside, had been used as "table talk," as he expressed it, and he had been rebuked by "some great lord," probably Burghley, for criticizing the administration of one of the queen's offices. Both bills were nevertheless referred to committees of which the privy councillors were members, and were, as a matter of fact, put into shape in consultation with exchequer and household officials. Both were eventually passed by the Commons.

Everything seemed to have been done regularly and with no serious objection. Immediately after they had been sent to the House of Lords, however, came a message from that house that two lords, members of the privy council, had brought them a message from the queen declaring her mislike of both bills on the ground that they were an interference, the one with the conduct of her household, the other with one of her courts of revenue, and that she was quite able to attend to the reformation of any ill-doing in either of them herself. The House, somewhat discomfited at this rebuff, after much discussion decided it would be most in consonance with their liberties and their honor to send their Speaker and as many of their members as the queen would receive to explain their action, to state their entire freedom from disrespect and withal to beg her to allow the bills to be passed. The interview at court, at which the Speaker and ten members, two of whom were privy councillors, were present, followed. The Speaker and his committee could only report to the House that the queen assured them of her love and care for them " yea more than of her own self, or than any of them have of themselves." She intended to redress of herself all their grievances in these two respects, for their greater ease than they would have had if they acted without her and thus deprived her of the " Honour, Glory and Commendation " of the reforms.

However within a few days the queen had changed her mind on the matter and sent word through the Speaker that if the Commons would send four of their members to confer with some of her privy councillors and household officers and thus obtain her views the two bills might be proceeded with. This conference took place and there was more or less further discussion of the matter, but in the midst of a busy closing fortnight of the session nothing was brought to completion and the statute book bears no impress of reform of administration by legislation at this time.[4]

This dispute did not interest the queen seriously; her opposition to the action of parliament was probably due to the protest of some official, Burghley or someone else, against outside interference with his office. In the next parliament, however, was brought up an old subject on which she was far more sensitive. This was the succession to the crown. The main parliamentary struggle on this question had occurred early in the queen's reign; on no subject up to that time had parliament been more insistent and on none

---

[4] D'Ewes, 410, 432, 434, 436, 437, 440, 442–4, 446, 448, 450; *Stat. of the Realm*, IV, ii, 798–839.

had the queen resisted its intrusion more steadily. Almost twenty years had passed since these early contests when they were brought up again by the action of the Peter Wentworth just mentioned. He was a country gentleman of learning, wealth and position, connected by marriage with more than one of the queen's council, a Puritan and a member of every parliament but one from 1571 to this of 1593. He early became convinced that a settlement of the succession to the crown was necessary in order to avoid civil war on the death of the queen and that if she would not herself take the initiative, parliament was bound to force it upon her. About 1587 he wrote, though he did not publish, a pamphlet or small book which he called *A Pithie Exhortation to her Majestie for Establishing her Succession to the Crown.* He seems to have planned to bring the matter up in the parliament of 1589, and made several attempts to interest Burghley in the project, but was rebuffed, though with courtesy.

In the fall of 1591 when it was anticipated that there would be a new parliament, Wentworth called some of his friends into conference at his home in Oxfordshire and put his little book before them. In some way this meeting and a copy of the book itself became public and he was summoned and placed in confinement by the privy council, and all his papers, especially such as concerned the succession and were intended to be brought up in parliament were seized. He wrote an earnest and manly letter to Burghley declaring his pleasure that God had brought it about that his book would in this way come to the eyes of Burghley and the queen. He knows that the queen will be angry at first but trusts that after she has read it she will herself be convinced that she is tempting Providence by leaving the succession unsettled, now that she is fifty-six years of age. He appeals to Burghley to use his influence with the queen to call a parliament and allow this question to be settled there, and not to turn back from so great a work which God has given him to do. He was soon called before the council, where a second manuscript copy of his essay was shown him and the lord chancellor charged him with making the matter of the succession a subject of discussion in " cobblers' and taylors' shops." He was held under restraint for six months, until February, 1592. Notwithstanding his appeal to Burghley to induce the queen to call a parliament for this special purpose, none was called till 1593 and the lord chancellor's warning at its opening against any discussion of matters of state presumably was directed against any attempt to raise the question of the succession.[5]

Notwithstanding the prohibition laid upon Wentworth in 1591 and now upon the whole parliament in 1593, he came to London fully determined to bring the matter up again and provided with a bill already formulated and a speech of introduction already written out. During an interval of three days between the opening of parliament and its first working session Wentworth discussed the matter with a number of his friends, mostly newly elected members of the House of Commons, and called a meeting at Lincoln's Inn to decide on procedure. Whether the bill was actually presented or not is not clear. Certainly no action was taken upon it, for the conference and plans were learned of by the council. Wentworth and later Sir Henry Bromley and two others were arrested and examined and Wentworth sent to the Tower, the others to the Fleet.

Formally the queen and council had not imprisoned these men for anything they had said or done in parliament, but practically the freedom of parliament to choose its own subjects of discussion was as much invaded as if the arrest had been made a few days later. Parliament itself resented the intrusion, for two weeks later a member of the House of Commons moved that the House make humble suit to the queen for the release of its four imprisoned members, on the

---

[5] *Acts of the Privy Council*, xxi, 392, 440; *State Papers, Dom., Eliz.*, ccxl, 21, 21.i; D'Ewes, 458; Neale, *Eng. Hist. Rev.*, xxxi, 134-7, xxxix, 36-8, 175-86.

ground partly that the constituencies whose representatives were absent from parliament might complain if taxes were imposed on them by a body in which they had no representatives, partly on the general consideration that " an Instrument taking away some of its strings cannot give its pleasant sound," and that parliament deprived of some of its members was such an instrument. All the privy councillors, however, defending on this occasion the most extreme conceptions of royal power, declared that the queen had committed the offenders to prison for causes best known to herself and would no doubt soon of her gracious disposition yield what they proposed to ask, and would be more pleased to have it so left to herself. Left to her, however, nothing was done. The members remained in prison during the whole session; Wentworth indeed remained in the Tower till his death four years afterward, a sacrifice to royal statecraft, indecision or mere tyranny. During these years, in answer to Dolman's book advocating the claims of the Infanta, Isabella, he wrote two more pamphlets which were printed, along with his earlier essay on the succession, in 1598 after his death. Thus the writings of Wentworth may have influenced the succession to the crown though not through the intervention of parliament.

The other victims of the queen's determination not to allow parliament to intrude upon this question were ordered to remain in London for some time after the close of the session, for fear they would disseminate in the country copies of the proposed parliamentary proceedings. The matter was not brought up again, though the next year an official said to Mrs. Wentworth that, " if the gentlemen of Englande were honest, there woulde be five hundred in prison for her husbandes opinyon." In preparation for action by the parliament of 1601 a bill was drawn up, apparently by some privy councillor, to prohibit writing or publishing any book concerning the succession to the crown, but it does not seem to have been introduced. Thus notwithstanding the widespread interest and the undoubted apprehension of many patriotic Englishmen, after 1573 the subject of the succession was not actually raised in parliament during the queen's reign.[6]

Another subject, however, the reorganization of the established church, would not down, however strongly the queen insisted on reserving such matters to herself or in restricting parliament's action to that which was laid before it with the previous approval of the clergy. During the later years of Elizabeth's reign, it is true, the tide of attempted church reform did not flow so strongly as during the period from 1572 to the year of the Armada. Whether the national danger had made men more patient of what they did not like, or whether the more aggressive Puritans were quietly awaiting the demise of the obstinate queen, or whether the tide was simply flowing beneath the surface, or whether the hand of authority had really repressed the spirit of innovation, certain it is that efforts to change the forms or the doctrines of the church were not so vigorous now as they had been twenty years before. Yet not even these later parliaments of the reign passed without attempts at further reform by act of parliament and instances of the queen's suppression of debate on the subject. February 25, 1589, a Mr. Davenport made a speech calling attention to the need of altering certain parts of the ecclesiastical law which were now being administered injuriously to the queen's subjects, and asked the Speaker to read the written statement he had prepared. Secretary Wooley immediately rose to remind the House of the queen's direct instructions, at the opening of the session, not to deal with ecclesiastical causes and to express his own belief in the incompetence of the House to take up such a question against such inhibition. The Speaker held the manuscript for three weeks and then handed it back to its author without bringing it before the

---

[6] *State Papers, Dom., Eliz.*, cclxxxii, 31; D'Ewes, 470, 471, 497; Birch, *Memorials*, i, 96; *Cal. Hatfield House MSS.*, vi, 284, 288, 289, vii, 286, 303–4, 324–5, *Acts of the Privy Council*, xxiv, 269; Strype, *Annals*, iv, 334–5; Neale, *Peter Wentworth, Eng. Hist. Rev.*, xxxix, 186–99.

House at all. Another Puritan submitted to Walsingham about the same time a petition to the queen against the profaning of the Sabbath and a proposed bill to suppress all cathedral churches in England, but there was no echo of this in parliament.[7]

In 1593 the quarrel about the *ex-officio* oath, which had already been in progress for almost a decade, made its way into parliament. This was the claim of the church authorities, in the use of their disciplinary powers over the lower clergy, to force them to give answers on oath to questions which might incriminate them. When clergymen refused to take such an oath they were sent to prison and kept there as if they had already been proved guilty of an offense. The matter had created much public interest, Burghley was known to have protested to the archbishop against it, and lay lawyers were generally opposed to the practice. At the very beginning of the session of 1593 James Morice, attorney of the Court of Wards, a civil lawyer, introduced two bills directed against this practice. An animated debate immediately sprang up in which two privy councillors took opposite sides and a third spoke favorably of the bills, though he warned his fellow members of the queen's probable anger at their discussion of ecclesiastical matters against her prohibition. After some hours of discussion, as it was approaching closing time, the Speaker, Sir Edward Coke, interposed to ask the House to let him take the bills home with him to read in private before laying them before parliament. The matter in some way reached the ears of the queen; Morice, who was an official, was summoned to court and committed to the custody of one of his colleagues, Sir John Fortescue, chancellor of the exchequer. She also sent for Coke, who had read the bills between twelve and two o'clock and, although she respected his promise not to let anyone see them while they were in his hands and only required him to say what was in them, gave him the sharp prohibition of further discussion of ecclesiastical matters

[7] D'Ewes, 438; *Cal. State Papers, Dom.,* 1581-90, 578.

and vigorous asseveration of her right to control debates in parliament that has already been quoted. Coke, who felt as much overwhelmed by the critical nature of the conflict as his successor, Lenthall, did on a somewhat similar occasion fifty years later, nevertheless conveyed the queen's instructions to the House of Commons as he was bid. Morice sent a manly letter of protest to Burghley from prison but was kept there till the end of the session, and the matter dropped.[8]

The queen was less insistent on parliament refraining from discussion of another matter of ecclesiastical regulation, legislation against pluralities. Such a bill was introduced in the parliament of 1589, debated at length and, notwithstanding desperate appeals to the queen by the clergy, allowed to pass the House of Commons without reprimand. It failed, however, in the House of Lords, doubtless due to the influence with their colleagues of Whitgift and the other bishops. It seems to have been introduced again in 1597 and withdrawn at the demand of the queen, though the history of this debate is obscure. In 1601, however, it was twice debated at length and with some bitterness, and without royal disapproval or any objection except on the part of one of the queen's serjeants, who insisted that debate on this subject was violation of an established custom of the House to refrain from meddling with matters which touched the queen's prerogative. The bill passed second reading but got no further. The queen expressed no objection to discussion in parliament of bills against bishops giving long leases on their lands, against profane swearing, against neglect to observe the Sabbath day and against absence from church.[9]

The limits to which parliament might go before being met

[8] *State Papers, Dom., Eliz.*, ccxliv, 51–4; *Cal. State Papers, Dom.*, 1591–4, 322; *Hatfield House MSS.*, iv, 290; D'Ewes, 474–9; Lodge, *Illustrations of British History*, ii, 443.

[9] *State Papers, Dom., Eliz.*, ccxxiii, 15; *Cal. State Papers, Dom.*, 1581–90, 569, 1601–3, 115; Townshend, *Collections*, 174, 182, 185–7, 194, 206, 218–20, 224, 227–8, 273–8, 287, 317.

by the insuperable obstacle of the queen's prerogative were tested most clearly by its repeated efforts to nullify gifts of special trade privilege made by the queen, the so-called " monopolies." These were grants of sole powers, rights or advantages, usually secured to their possessors by letters patent under the great seal and therefore also known as " patents." They were of many kinds. Some were special licenses to export or import goods in which trade was forbidden by statute, as, for instance, a license given in 1578 to some persons living in London to export a certain quantity of hides and leather " anye act, statute, provision, commandment or other thynge before made, proclaymed or given to the country in any weyse notwithstanding "; such a license was called a *non obstante,* and by high legal authority, although perhaps at a later time, was recognized as well within the royal prerogative powers. " Anything prohibited by any penall statute the king may by the laws of the Realme grant a license or dispensation to one or more persons with a clause of *non obstante.*" Similar to these in principle were those privileges given to the Merchants Adventurers and to certain courtiers to export cloth undyed and undressed, although the law required all cloth to be finished before exportation, and a great number of other royal licenses. In fact the royal charters given to companies or groups of men to utilize and control the trade between England and some special region or in some special kind of goods amounted to letters patent for the sole enjoyment of a special privilege.[10]

Others were grants for the carrying out of general licensing laws, such as Ralegh's patent, dated August 9, 1588, to last for thirty years, to regulate the grant of licenses to taverns. He made this profitable by charging a substantial fee to each tavern keeper for his license and it was his duty to keep an oversight of their good behavior.

---

[10] *Patent Rolls,* 18 Eliz., pt. i, mm., 28–9, 30–1; *Cal. State Pap., Dom.,* 1594–7, 329, 332; *State Papers, Dom.,* cclxxvi, 81, § 1; Townshend, *Collections,* 239.

Thomas Bedingfield asks for a similar right to open houses in London and Westminster himself or by deputy where it will be legal to play dice, cards, bowling and tennis, and to receive the fines from those who keep such houses illegally. He promises to admit only noblemen, gentlemen, merchants and those rated in the subsidy books at as much as £10, to close Sunday forenoon and during service in the afternoon, and to carry on only a reasonable number of such houses.[11]

A closely allied group of such patents were those for obtaining the fines or other income from enforcing the laws, or within certain limits of giving dispensation from them, as that given in 1576 to Sir Edward Dyer to enforce or dispense with the law for the tawing of leather, or that given in 1597 to William Carre allowing him for nine years to license any person to brew beer for transport beyond the seas. Others were for the sole right to draw up certain documents, as that given Sir Thomas Gorgas to make writs of subpoena for the chancery. Others were of a more familiar kind, such as a license to manufacture drinking glasses, or for the sole printing of the Psalms of David and others analogous to our modern patents and copyrights.[12]

These grants were outside known law, both common and statute; in fact they were in many cases in derogation of the law. They were privileges drawn directly from the reserve or prerogative powers of the crown. This was not anomalous in the sixteenth century. The spheres of the statute and common law and of the powers of government were by no means coterminous. Nor was the fact that each such grant gave a monopoly to one or a certain group of individuals strange. The roots of special privilege were deep in the soil of the middle ages and it still flourished freely in that of the sixteenth century. Monopoly existed everywhere in Elizabethan England; unrestricted freedom of individual action, especially in matters of trade, com-

---

11 *State Papers, Dom.*, ccxliii, 58.

12 *Cal. State Papers, Dom.*, 1591–4, 212; 1598–1601 (Nov. 10, '99); *State Papers, Dom., Eliz.*, cclxxxii, 28.

merce and manufacture, was extremely rare. Indeed with
the increasing centralization of government and with the
extension of economic opportunity characteristic of this
period, the demand for and advantages of grants to priv-
ileged individuals or groups steadily increased.

Another occasion for this demand was the scramble for
office or emolument, perhaps more general, perhaps only
more familiar at that time. The queen and her ministers
were, as has been pointed out in an earlier chapter, constantly under siege from all who could put forward any
claim, the most personal or the most tenuous, for any kind
of office, appointment or means of gain. When a young
Frenchman has been teaching French in England for some
years, and has presented the queen with some verses and
a little book on the state of France, he and his patron write
to Cecil reminding him that the queen " promised him something," and ask in fulfilment of her promise the privilege
of exporting 1,000 tons of beer in exception to the statute.
Captain John Clarke spent £1200 in the queen's service,
then £5000 more at court in suits extending through fourteen
years for its repayment. In 1596 he asks by way of
reimbursement a monopoly of all the forfeitures due from
engrossers and forestallers of grain for the next nine years,
and it is to be noted that both Burghley and Coke recommend the grant, though the latter urges that the patent be
so carefully penned as not to do harm to the people. A
William Hunter, apparently a spy, obtains as a gift in
recompense for the risk of his life and his long imprisonment in Spain in the queen's service a license for the export
during a time of restraint of 500 quarters of wheat.[13]

Grants were made with particular frequency to courtiers;
they were constantly on the ground to ask and often had
more or less valid claims. One petitioner in 1596 enumerates six forms of possible court favor and dismisses each as
unsatisfactory except the one for which he asks, a lease of

---

[13] State Papers, Dom., Eliz., ccxlv, 94; Cal. State Papers, Dom., 1591-4,
550; 1595-7, 327.

crown lands. His condemnation of monopolies is that they
are " scandalous." They are nevertheless being constantly
asked for and given. John Spilman, the queen's jeweler,
is given in 1597 a patent for fourteen years for the sole
setting up of paper mills and gathering linen rags for the
manufacture of paper. The famous monopoly for the importation of playing cards was obtained by Edward Darcy,
groom of the privy chamber. The three Bassano brothers,
queen's musicians, obtain in 1598 a patent for the exportation of 6000 bundles of calfskins at a favorable export duty.
A gentleman usher of the queen is given the monopoly of
the purchase in Devon and Cornwall of tin for export. Two
gentlemen pensioners are given a monopoly of the export
of rabbit skins.[14]

They are often given to very humble dependants of the
queen. A grant of the monopoly for making a certain kind
of glass is given to two footmen. An equerry of the stable
after twenty-five years' service asks to have a patent requiring all refiners of sugar to obtain his authorization
before selling their product. Two household servants of the
queen, Thomas Weber and John Andrews, obtain a patent
for the sole making of black, white and red lead. Mrs.
Carr, who after the death of her husband secured the
license for the export of beer already referred to, was a
woman of the bed-chamber of the queen.[15]

It was natural that requests of this kind should be somewhat freely granted. They cost the treasury nothing; they
often took the place of salary or a pension. The familiarity
or the fondness of the queen was apt to be involved. They
were " her old servitors," as she afterwards told parliament.
The patent for salt was given to Sir Thomas Wilkes, secretary of the Privy Council, " in some reward of his service."
Frequently the grant brought an income to the crown.

[14] State Papers, Dom., Eliz., cclxxvi, 5; Cal. State Papers, Dom., 1591-
4, 561; 1595-7, 348-9, 450; 1598-1600, 65, 90, 554; 1601-3, 46; Lansdowne
MSS., lxxxi, 6, 7, 8.

[15] State Papers, Dom., Eliz., clvii, 78; ccxlv, 48; Cal. State Papers,
Dom., 1581-90, 675, 1594-7, 97, 304, 307, 359-60; Lansdowne MSS., lix, 77.

"Advantageous to the country, not burdensome to those affected, profitable to the queen and a source of some slight profit to the petitioner," was almost an established formula. The number and variety of such letters patent, each giving the possession of some monopoly, great or small, was almost incredible. They were scarcely known before the middle of Elizabeth's reign, but some fifty were given in its last eighteen years.[16]

There is reason to believe that the queen's addiction to such grants was not entirely approved of by her advisers. Lord Burghley sometimes advises a grant but insists on so guarding it as to protect the public interest. He interposed many objections and finally introduced several restrictions in the patent to William and Bridget Carr for brewing export beer. The patents for the refining of sugar and for the making and importing of black, white and red lead were granted only after Burghley had secured a careful report from the port officers of London on these matters. The salt monopoly of Sir Thomas Wilkes was only obtained after overcoming Burghley's opposition. Sometimes, as in the case of the patent asked for by Edward Darcy for the search of leather, the conditions attached were so onerous as to make it valueless to its possessor. As early as 1585 a monopoly of the tanning and export of certain kinds of leather was repeatedly asked for but never granted, due to Burghley's objections. Sir Francis Drake wrote freely to Cecil in 1593 protesting against the enforcement of a grant to Henry Warner of the sole right to salt, dry and pack fish in Devon and Cornwall, on the ground that it was grievous to the whole country, the inhabitants having withstood its introduction and sent up to London to ask for its revocation. Coke's acknowledgment of the queen's prerogative in this respect required that the grants should be for the public good. In parliament, when the subject was brought up, all the privy councillors deprecated the existence of the monop-

[16] *Acts of the Privy Council*, xiv, 395; xxiv, 369; xxv, 16, 517; xxvi, 426; xxx, 132, etc.; W. H. Price, *Patents of Monopoly*, 17.

olies, stoutly as they might maintain the queen's right to give them.[17] Nevertheless, the queen gave them more and more freely. Twenty-three seem to have been given in the year 1593, twenty-four in the four years between 1598 and 1601. It seems that the queen, used as she was to refusal, could not refuse a request for a grant of privilege in some field of profitable monopoly. The Docquet books are loaded with such entries. They correspond in the case of the more humble officials to grants of lands, wardships, offices and other benefits to the higher courtiers.[18]

Of all this variety of privilege it was only certain kinds which roused serious resistance from private men or interested parliament and against which attempts to legislate were directed. One type well described by Bacon met with little or no opposition. " If any man out of his own wit, industry or endeavor find out anything beneficial for the Commonwealth, or bring in any new Invention, which every Subject of this Kingdom may use, yet in regards of his pains and travel therein her Majesty is pleased to grant him a Priviledge to use the same only by himself or his Deputies for a certain time. This is one kind of monopoly." Such monopoly rights granted for useful inventions, such as dredging machines, iron furnaces or the manufacture of white soap, had been granted, along with less useful privileges, with increasing frequency since the beginning of Elizabeth's reign. When a man obtains in 1588 a grant of the sole right " to use for 21 years the trade of a new instrument devised by him for the cutting and making of iron into small rods," or two others ask for the sole benefit of " publishing and practicing " a mill which they have

---

[17] *Lansdowne MSS.*, xliv, 27–30, 33–5; lix, 66–70; lxxxi, 6–8; *State Papers, Dom., Eliz.*, clvii, 78; ccxlv, 48; ccliii, 119; cclxxvi, 81, 84–8; *Cal. State Papers, Dom.*, 1581–90, 675, 710; 1591–4, 187, 376; 1595–7, 327, 458; *Hatfield House MSS.*, xi, 506, Townshend, *Collections*, 238, 240, 244, 253, 258.

[18] Hewins, *English Trade and Finance, Intro.*, ii; D'Ewes, *Journals*, 648, 650; Townshend, *Collections*, 243–5; *State Papers, Dom., Eliz.*, cclxxxii, 28, 29; Lodge, *Illustrations of English History*, iii, 159–62.

invented for grinding corn and pumping water without wind or water, no one grudged them the privilege. These were merely patents in the modern sense. They paid 6s. 8d. for the document they received, a nominal charge for an official license. Nor was there any more objection to the grant to Richard Watkins and James Robert of the sole right "to print Allmanacs and prognostications from the 12th day of May, 1588, for twenty-one years next ensuing. This was a copyright.[19]

The vexations that stirred the Commons to protest and to attempts at legislation, notwithstanding the known opposition of the queen, were practical not theoretical burdens. Increase of prices, interference with individual liberty, intrusion into private affairs, arrogance of possessors of monopolies and their agents and inability to sue in the ordinary courts naturally brought about resistance to the existence of favored individuals possessing monopolies of the purchase or sale or importation or exportation or manufacture of some kind of familiar goods.

Private resistance was tried. Charles Snead, a gentleman of Kent, declares his determination to continue the manufacture of starch, as the laws of England give him a right to do, notwithstanding the monopoly of the starch manufacture possessed by John Pakington, and is informed against to the privy council. Osmund Withers and his family resist the search of his house at Taunton by Capt. Moffatt and William Lyons, messengers from the privy council, on suspicion of the same unlawful manufacture of starch. Withers is arrested but rescued by his friends, the bailiff of Taunton giving scant help, then rearrested by a constable and brought before the chief justice and remanded, but escapes still again. The monopoly of the manufacture and sale of starch was a fruitful source of trouble. Some forty citizens of London join in a complaint of their losses, injuries and op-

---

[19] D'Ewes, 644; *Lansdowne MSS.*, cvii, 77, fos. 126–205; *Docquet, Signet Office,* Nov., 1588; W. H. Price, *English Patents of Monopoly,* 5–9; Cecil T. Carr, *Select Charters of Trading Companies,* lvii–lxiv.

pressions due to its enforcement. One was arrested in his own shop by a messenger of the Council, and carried away to prison till he entered into bonds and paid certain damages. Another had two hundred pounds of starch taken forcibly from his shop, " It being my own proper goods, which I suppose is contrary to law "; and others have similar complaints of wrongs, imprisonments and rigorous treatment from agents of the holder of this monopoly or pursuivants from the Council acting in his interest.[20]

" Contrary to law " had little or no meaning in the case of grants made by prerogative. When a citizen of London brought suit in the Court of Common Pleas against the holder of one of these patents the privy council sent in the name of the queen a letter to Chief Justice Anderson and the other judges informing them that the queen will not let her prerogative be called in question in a court of law and ordering them to stay the suit. Sufferers from the patents had little if any recourse. Holders of the patents on the other hand had the powerful, if we may suppose somewhat reluctant, support of the privy council in enforcing their chartered rights. In January and February, 1596, six merchants are successively summoned before the privy council for selling without permission of the patentees and ordered, according to the usual disciplinary practice of the council, to give daily attendance till they are dismissed.[21]

Complaints of intrusion on their rights are frequently made to the privy council by patentees and are answered by summons to the offenders to appear before the council or writs of assistance directed to crown officials ordering them to secure obedience to the terms of the patent. In an early case, the officers were directed to go to a glass factory set up by a certain John Smith in defiance of the patent for

[20] Cal. State Papers, Dom., 1581–90, 634; State Papers, Dom., Eliz., cclxxvi, 84.

[21] State Papers, Dom., Eliz., cclxxxii, 8; Acts of the Privy Council, xxvi, 434.

making and selling drinking glasses given to a certain Randall, and there to deface the furnace and warn the infringers against any further contempt.[22]   Another complaint somewhat later exemplifies most of the elements in the contest. John Spilman, who had received the grant for setting up paper mills before referred to, sends a petition to the privy council stating that other men are setting up rival mills and collecting rags.   He has procured an order from the justices of Bucks ordering these men to cease manufacturing, but they have treated the warrant slightingly, received his messenger with a refusal and with unseemly words and gestures, and continue to disregard her Majesty's license.   Having no other recourse he flies to the council for protection and assistance, asks that the intruders be summoned and punished and points out the bad effect such resistance will have on all other patentees.   Here is an old servant of the crown, provided with a monopoly by patent which he is carrying out by deputy, resisted, given scant support by the authorities and forced to appeal to the council for official protection in the enforcement of his claims.[23]

Of all the observed results of these grants none were more vexatious than the intrusion of the deputies, "substitutes," as they were then called, the officials and servants of the monopoly holders.   There may well have been several hundred, possibly several thousand such persons engaged in the inquisitorial and offensive work of spying out violations of the rights of their employers or expelling those formerly engaged in the lines of business now monopolized.   One member of parliament speaks of his town of Warwick as "pestered and continually vexed with the substitutes or vicegerents of these monopolies."   Another describes the representatives of the patentees by virtue of their letters of assistance from the privy council searching houses for un-

[22] *Acts of the Privy Council*, x, 431, xii, 246, 336–7, xxvii, 8–9, xxx, 443, xxxi, 333–6.

[23] *State Papers, Dom., Eliz.*, cclxxvi, 5; *Cal. State Papers, Dom.*, 1595–7, 450; 1600–3, 43, 108.

licensed playing cards, and if they found a few carrying the offenders by pursuivants fifty miles or more and threatening them with imprisonment unless they ransomed themselves. The substitutes of the patentees for drinking glasses are said to hold masters of ships in port till they give bonds not to bring any in from beyond the seas. Ingenious rogues proclaimed themselves representatives of patent holders and levied blackmail on persons violating their monopolies. Cecil asserted when they were about to be given up, far from truthfully, however, that letters of assistance had been used principally against poor cottagers or " desolate widows " who were frightened into conformity with the requirements of the representatives of the monopolists. The queen herself later acknowledged that she had heard that the substitutes of the patentees had used great oppression. A representative of the patentee for vinegar came to Warwick and served notice on all dealers in the town that unless they made terms with his employers within two months they would be summoned before the privy council, and made them give bonds in the meantime. Many other instances are recorded. The pursuivants acting on letters of assistance from the privy council must have been practically indistinguishable from employees of the patentees.[24]

It might be supposed that injury was felt only by those engaged in lines of business in which a patent of monopoly had been given. But vexation with the grants evidently extended very much more widely. A popular sense of injustice, as in the case of modern trusts, strengthened the belief that prices were raised, quality lowered and other losses and waste brought about. For the increase of prices actual statistics were given. It was said that salt in the eastern counties had been raised in price after the monopoly was obtained by Sir Thomas Wilkes from one shilling fourpence to fourteen shillings a bushel, but the government interposed to put an end to this extortion. Starch

[24] Townshend, *Memorials,* 230, 231, 241, 248, 249; Bateson, *Records of Leicester,* iii, 291; *State Papers, Dom., Eliz.,* cclxxxii, 29.

was said to have risen from eighteen to fifty shillings a hundred-weight, steel from twopence half penny to fivepence per pound, and drinking glasses from one shilling fourpence to five shillings a dozen. Calfskins had risen from ten to sixteen shillings a bundle and poor people's shoes therefore cost fourpence more per pair since a license for export had been given to three Italian merchants.[25] Opposition to the practice of making such grants showed itself in parliament early if but momentarily. April 7, 1571, after Sir Francis Knollys, chancellor of the exchequer, had made a long speech concerning subsidy, a member named Bell remarked that collections would be hard to make as the people were being so galled by " licenses and abuses of promoters." If these were remedied the subsidies would be paid much more willingly because " although by licenses a few are enriched the multitude are impoverished." Several members, including Popham, later chief justice, two other lawyers and Peter Wentworth, expressed their agreement, and a committee was appointed to consider these griefs and certain petitions on the subject and ordered to meet in the Temple Church the next Monday. Sir Humphrey Gilbert, a strong upholder of royal rights, was the only opponent of this proposal. But the next day the Speaker read parliament a little lecture from the queen on wasting their time in motions and long speeches, referring, in the opinion of the reporter, no doubt correctly, to Mr. Bell's speech concerning licenses, " wherein he seemed to speak of her prerogative but quietly and orderly." When members seemed inclined to press the matter the Speaker said further that the queen had told him she intended to take order for licenses, that she had been careful about them in the past and would be more so in the future. The matter was allowed to lie in committee; nevertheless in the lord keeper's speech at the end of the session a month later, he says that the queen considers some of the members have " shown themselves audacious, arrogant and

---

[25] Townshend, 238, 240–1; *State Papers, Dom., Eliz.*, ccl, 19. Cecil T. Carr, *Select Charters of Trading Companies, Selden Society*, lvii–lxviii.

presumptive, calling her majesty's grants and prerogatives into question." [26]

Less sensitive about her promises than about her prerogative, the queen continued to grant licenses and other monopolies more and more freely, but it was more than twenty years before the matter was heard of again in parliament. In the parliament of 1597, however, it was evidently very much in the minds of members, for it was brought up in the most concrete form on one of the earliest working days of the session. Francis Moore, an active and influential member, introduced a motion " touching sundry enormities growing by patents of privilege and the abuse of them." Then and during the next three days they were under constant discussion, speeches being made on the subject by Cecil and two other privy councillors suggesting delay, and by various other members urging immediate action. It was finally referred to a large committee, including all the well known men of the house, under the chairmanship of Francis Moore who had brought the matter up. While it was lying in the hands of the committee Cecil's brother, Sir Thomas, moved as a substitute for the proposed bill that a petition to the queen to take some action on the monopolies be drawn up and presented to her by the Speaker; after some debate this was referred to the same committee as the bill. The matter had now been before parliament for a month. The queen evidently felt that it was time to take some notice of it and must have intimated her intention to reform the monopolies, for December 14th, the chairman of the committee instead of reporting either the bill or the petition, presented a form of humble thanks to the queen for her gracious care in the repression of the inconveniences of monopolies and patents. This was adopted by the House and delivered to the Speaker to be used as part of his speech to the queen at the close of the session, as it eventually was, word for word as the House had drawn it up. Just what the queen had promised and in what form does not appear,

[26] D'Ewes, 151, 157, 158, 159, 175.

but she announced her acceptance of the thanks of parliament, none too graciously, but at least with less ill humor than in the lord keeper's speech of 1571. She hoped the Commons would not take away her prerogative, which was the chiefest flower in her garden and principal and head pearl in her diadem, but would rather leave that to her disposition. Her intention of providing a remedy, however, was stated definitely enough. She had already through her law officers brought some of the monopolies before the judges, and would continue to do so till all were " brought to the touchstone of the law." [27]

This promise if fulfilled would doubtless have deprived the monopolies of half their sting. The " touchstone of the law " was just the test that had previously been denied sufferers, and just the remedy that parliament wished, as was seen afterward, to apply. But the queen did not keep her promise. Patents continued to be given, as has been seen, through the remainder of 1597 and in the three following years. But one or two private suits seem to have been tried, and during these years none is recorded as initiated by the law officers of the crown, notwithstanding the claims of Bacon that *quo warranto* proceedings had been brought in the exchequer. Instead the privy council continued to give writs of assistance to the patentees, and it was only two weeks before the opening of the next parliament, October 7, 1601, as has before been mentioned, that when one of the patents was impugned in the Court of Common Pleas the queen ordered the privy council to write inhibiting the judges from hearing the suit, on the ground that her prerogative should not be called in question by examining into the validity of the grant. The queen's promise of 1597 had intimated that her own law officers would bring the monopolies to a test before the courts and she may have resented private suits. But it was not till more than three years had passed away and an early session of parliament had been determined upon that she gave

[27] D'Ewes, 547, 554, 570, 573; *Cal. Hatfield House MSS.*, vii, 476–7.

orders to the attorney and solicitor general to bring any such suits, and at that time the confusion connected with Essex's rising prevented any action from being taken.

The ambiguous position of the government in the matter and the appreciation by some of the most astute of the queen's councillors of the rising tide of popular opposition was indicated by a proposal of Lord Buckhurst made in August, 1601, shortly before the calling of parliament, to hold a meeting of the council so that the queen might call in some of the monopolies before parliament opened. The queen herself was not ignorant of the popular discontent, for petitions against the monopolies were presented to her personally, according to old custom, on her way to chapel and in her walks; but like Pharaoh, she still hardened her heart.[28]

All these stored up vexations and belated proposals for remedy asserted themselves soon after parliament met in October, 1601, and brought an assault against the prerogative unequalled by any other incident in the relations between the queen and her parliaments. Wednesday, November 18, a member rose and declaring that many commodities which should be for public benefit were monopolized by patents from her majesty, presented a bill "Against Patents," though he confessed its full title was a much longer one. Immediately another member, also a lawyer, presented another bill which he claimed was only twelve lines long, — no more lines than there were words in the title of the first bill. His bill was entitled "An Act of Explanation of the Common Law in Certain Cases of Letters-patent." This bill became the centre of a long and bitter controversy. Its wording has unfortunately not been preserved, though Bacon acknowledges that it was "in few words but yet ponderous and weighty." A fair guess may be made that it provided simply that all charters and patents

---

[28] Townshend, *Collections*, 232, 236, 238, 248; *Acts of the Privy Council*, xxxii, 237; *State Papers, Dom., Eliz.*, cclxxxii, 8; *Hatfield House MSS.*, xi, 324.

should be left to be tested for their validity in the common law courts; though there seems to have been a proviso exempting municipal charters.[29]

Although by the influence of Cecil the Speaker postponed its consideration for a day or two the interest in the subject could not be kept down. One member after another rose to complain of the excesses of the patentees' agents, of the increase in the price of salt, of steel, of starch, of playing cards, of glasses. Lists were passed around among the members and read to the House enumerating patents for currants, iron, powder, cards, horns, ox shin-bones, train oil, cloth lists, ashes, bottles, glasses, bags, shreds of gloves, aniseed, vinegar, seacoal, steel, aquavitae, brushes, pots, saltpetre, lead, " accidence," oil, transportation of leather, calaminth stone, blubber oil, smoked pilchards and others. One member rose to ask sarcastically whether bread was not on the list. Even Cecil read a sort of official list of patents granted since 1574. Altogether twenty-two members are named as having participated in the debate, apart from the discussions in the committee.

It was recognized from the beginning of the debate that the subject involved the queen's prerogative. One speaker referred to the part he had taken in the debate in the last parliament and the good reason he had to remember that this bill also might touch the prerogative royal, another of his recognition that he " must walk warily." But all protested that they had no intention of questioning the queen's supreme power; one spoke only " out of grief of heart " at the sufferings of his fellow citizens, another that the queen herself might not lose the love of her subjects. Yet disguise it as they might, implicit in a bill to prohibit patents or to submit the validity of royal grants to the common law was a restriction of the queen's prerogative, an assertion of the supremacy of parliament. One bold member even urged, " let us do Generously and Bravely, like Parliament Men, and ourselves send for Them and their Patents, and Cancel

[29] Townshend, 224, 231, 238.

them before their Faces, Arreign them as in times past, at the Bar, and send them to the Tower." But he laughed as he said it, and Cecil charged him with making the proposal in mere bravado.[30]

On the other hand early in the debate Bacon, somewhat disingenuous as usual, gave an unduly favorable description of patents, exaggerated the number which had been repealed or vacated, called parliament to witness that he had protested against any questioning of the prerogative, and ended with the familiar suggestion that a petition rather than a statute be laid before the queen. The debate oscillated between a discussion of the evils of monopolies and of the relative propriety of approaching the queen by petition or by a bill. Against a petition it was pointed out that this action had been taken last parliament, and that a favorable answer had been given, but no relief had followed. There were some bold speeches. The introducer of the bill said, in apologizing for introducing an old precedent, " Far be it from this Heart of mine to Think; this Tongue to speak or this Hand to write any Thing in Prejudice or Derogation of Her Majesty's Prerogative Royal and the State "; yet, urging a committee on the bill, declared: " Mr. Speaker, as I think it no Derogation to the Omnipotence of God to say he can do ill, so I think it no Derogation to the Person or Majesty of the Queen to say so." Another member bluntly called the solicitor general's attention to the fact that he had waited four years to begin prosecution, that many of the patents had a clause of reversion and might have simply been called in, and nevertheless the monopolies were " worse than ever they were." On the other hand, in repeated speeches Cecil, though he evidently disliked the patents and won commendation for the length he went in criticism of them, urged delay and a petition, recited some pretty bad constitutional history in disposing of a precedent of Edward III, and rebuked the Speaker for disobeying the command of the queen given at the opening of the session

[30] *Ibid.* 231–44.

not to receive bills of this nature. Bacon's speeches were equally frequent but more subservient to the queen and disparaging to parliament, while others declared their indifference to the method of action so long as their grievances were removed. Townshend, the reporter of the debates, proposed as a compromise that the queen be petitioned to allow them to present a bill.

After the debate had progressed almost continuously for a week, on the morning of November 25th, the Speaker rose and amidst general silence " everyone marveling why he stood up," announced that he had been summoned by the queen the previous afternoon, and proceeded to deliver a gracious message from her to the House. She wanted to express to them her hearty thanks for the subsidies which she heard had been granted to her, so liberal and so promptly decided upon, and to assure them of her appreciation of their loyalty and her life-long devotion to their interests. She had learned, to her surprise, partly from her councillors, partly from private petitioners to her, that some of the patents she had granted were grievous to her subjects and that the agents of the patentees had been oppressive. She had never assented to any that she supposed to be injurious and she was highly indignant with those who had abused her grants. She had had the matter in mind notwithstanding recent troubles, and she would immediately now and not *in futuro* provide for the repeal of some and the suspension of others till their lawfulness might be tested in the courts. The Speaker then called upon the privy councillors who had been present at his interview with the queen and were now in the House to correct or amplify his statements. Cecil, Knollys, Stanhope and Herbert whispered together, then Cecil rose and in a reassuring and even jocular speech corroborated the Speaker's report, assured the House that a proclamation would be immediately issued, that no more letters of assistance would be issued by the privy council, that men might now " eat their meat more savourly," as the salt patent would be called in, that those who had weak stomachs should have their vinegar set at liberty, that " those that desire to go sprucely in their ruffs " might do so more cheaply, for "starch which hath been so much prosecuted shall now be repealed," and so through a dozen or more monopolies which had long been grievances.

All this being interpreted doubtless means that knowledge of the rising storm in parliament had been brought to the queen and she had bowed to it. Neither the hectoring of Bacon nor the appeals of Cecil nor the counsels of submission of lesser men had checked the evident intention of parliament to obtain some more definite action on the patents of monopoly than in 1597. Cecil explained that the queen's decision was due not to any plan pressed upon her by her councillors, and expressed his fear that it resulted from private and personal information of the course of events in parliament, though he had done his best to " salve the sore." He had inquired for the betrayer of the secrets of their House, and suspected they were not secret among themselves. He gives a curious glimpse of sixteenth century relations between parliament and people by complaining that " Parliament Matters are ordinarily Talked of in the Streets." He had himself heard as he rode in his coach " these words spoken aloud: God prosper those that further the Overthrow of these Monopolies! God send the Prerogative touch not our Liberty." He acknowledges that this is a great scandal and does not mean to wrong his hearers by intimating that any one of them so expressed himself outside, but, like all administrative officers in all ages, he believes that " the Time was never more apt to Disorder," and warns members that " whatsoever is subject to a Publick Exposition cannot be Good," hoping that " whatsoever is here spoken may be Buried in these walls." [31]

The response of parliament to the gracious message of the queen was prompt and enthusiastic. Speeches of gratitude were made and a motion carried that the privy councillors

[31] *Ibid.* 249–51.

should arrange for an interview with the queen and the
Speaker should attend her with a number of members of the
House to express their thankfulness. The next day but one
several members, apparently remembering that in the preceding parliament the promise of the queen had been asked
for and given only in the last hour of parliament, proposed
that now it be recorded in the journal of the House, and
that the privy councillors should urge speed in the issue
of the proclamation. But this time the queen had kept
her word. Not only could the comptroller of the household
rebuke the doubting Thomases and the Speaker express
his entire faith in the queen's gracious intention and wish
her a long life, " to which the whole House cried Amen,"
but Cecil could assure them that he had already seen
the draft of the proclamation and indeed had it in his
hands.[32]

This was true, and the next day, Saturday, as Cecil
pointed out, the proof that the queen had kept her promise
was before them for the proclamation was in print and
"extant in every man's Hand." It was dated November
28th. It was headed " A proclamation for the reformation
of many abuses and misdemeanors committed by patentees
of certain privileges and licenses, to the general good of all
her Majesty's loving subjects." After explaining that the
queen had been misled into granting these privileges and
licenses by the assurance that they would be for the common good, and that letters of assistance for the enforcement
of them had been issued by the privy council " upon like
false suggestions," and that she had now been informed of
the grievances that had lighted upon her people by them,
she enumerated two groups of grants and made corresponding provision for them. Those concerning salt, vinegar, al-
cohol and liquors containing it, salt fish, train oil, fish-livers,
pots, brushes, butter and starch were declared void, the
letters patent revoked, and the patentees forbidden to put
in force anything contained in them, under pain of punish-

[32] *Ibid.* 252–3, 258.

ment as breakers of the queen's commandments. This sudden assertion of the royal prerogative for purposes of destruction rather than support must have carried consternation to the holders of this first class of grants and their small army of agents and " substitutes," for some of the most lucrative to their possessors and burdensome to the people came thus to an abrupt end.

Holders of the second class of grants were left to the cool consideration of the courts of common law, unprotected by extraordinary royal protection for either plaintiff or defendant; persons aggrieved by grants for saltpeter, Irish yarn, new makes of cloth, calf-skins, pelts, cards, glasses, leather, steel and some others were permitted and even encouraged to seek remedy in the ordinary courts of law, notwithstanding any special provisions in their grants. No writs of assistance for the enforcement of either of these classes of grants should hereafter be issued by the privy council, nor should writs already in existence be put in execution " seeing that they have served for pretexts to those that have had them to terrify and oppress her people." Nor should any messengers of the queen's chamber or any officer of hers attempt anything against any of her subjects in execution of those grants or anything contained in them.

But the queen had no mind to yield her general prerogative along with her special grants. It will be noted that nothing in her message to parliament acknowledged its right to legislate on the subject. It simply thanked them for bringing the matter to her attention and announced her intended action upon it. Cecil had warned the House that the queen did not mean to be "swept out of her Prerogative." The proclamation accordingly, along with its deprecation of grants in the future praises her people for their obedience to the grants in the past, " being under the great seal of England," and threatens dire punishment to any who " shall seditiously or contemptuously presume to call in question the power or validity of her prerogative royal annexed to her imperial crown." Her proclamation was a means of preventing parliament extending its legislation into this field, not permission to do so.[33]

On the afternoon of Monday, November 30, only ten days after the great debate on monopolies had begun and five days before the close of parliament, the Speaker with about a hundred and fifty members of the House by arrangement of the privy councillors appeared at the door of the council chamber at Whitehall and after the queen had taken her seat under the cloth of state entered the room. The Speaker after three low reverences, made a speech in which ascriptions to the queen and to the deity can hardly be distinguished, and in which flattery goes beyond that recorded in any speech by any courtier. All then knelt to hear her answer. The " golden speech " of the queen, as it has often been called, and as in several slightly variant forms it has been preserved, was in reality a noble and yet a characteristic address. It was self-centred, it is true, but it was raised to dignity by the intensity of Elizabeth's sense of closeness between herself and her people. " Though God hath raised me high yet this I account the glory of my crown that I have reigned with your loves. This makes me that I do not so much rejoice that God hath made me to be queen as to be queen over so thankful a people, and to be the means under God to conserve you in safety and preserve you from danger. . . . In governing this land I have ever set the last judgment day before mine eyes, as so to rule as I shall be judged and answer before a higher judge, to whose judgment seat I do appeal that never thought was cherished in my heart that tended not to my people's good. . . . Though you have had and may have many mightier and wiser princes sitting on this seat yet you never had nor shall have any that will love you better." Midway in her address the queen ordered the members to rise from their knees and they listened to the rest of her speech standing. It was the shifty, politic queen that professed to thank parliament for opening her eyes to the evils of the monop-

[33] W. H. Price, *Patents of Monopoly, Appendix J.,* 156–9.

olies. " For had I not received knowledge from you I might have fallen into the lapse of an error only for want of true information. Mr. Speaker, tell the House from me I take it exceeding grateful that the knowledge of these things are come unto me from them." But it was nevertheless the high-hearted queen, in words not to be heard from the throne again for many a long year, perhaps never again, who says, " What dangers, what practices and what perils I have passed, some if not all of you know, but none of these things do move me. . . . For myself I never was so much enticed with the glorious name of a king, or the royal authority of a queen, as delighted that God hath made me his instrument to maintain his truth and glory and to defend this kingdom from dishonor, damage, tyranny and oppression." In dismissing the assembly she asked the councillors to see that all those present were brought to kiss her hand on the dissolution of parliament before they should leave for their distant homes.[34]

This was the climax of the recognition of parliament by the queen, and it is to be noted, as a prophecy of things to come, that this recognition came not from submissiveness or yielding to the persuasion or pressure of Cecil, Bacon or other crown advocates, but as a result of parliamentary self-assertion. It was, like so many occurrences of these later years of the queen, an anticipation of the future claims and power of parliament, and through it of the people, the germ of ultimate self-government. On the other hand it furnished no immediate settlement of the questions of either monopolies or the prerogative.

It is no part of the history of parliament, but some of the later steps in the history of monopolies may be briefly mentioned. Grants of the first class mentioned in the proclamation presumably ceased immediately to be enforced, while those of the second class had to run the gauntlet of the courts, if their validity was questioned. A test of this kind

---

[34] Townshend, 263–6; Price, *Patents of Monopoly*, Appendix K, 160–2; *Somers Tracts*, i, 244–6.

was soon made in the case of the monopoly of the manufacture and importation of playing cards, so often alluded to already. This patent was originally granted to Ralph Bowes and Thomas Bedingfield, two gentlemen pensioners, in 1578. It was superseded by a new grant in 1588 to Ralph Bowes for twelve years, on condition of making certain yearly payments to the crown. In May of 1598 some time before its expiry this was regranted to Sir John Pakington in consideration of an annual payment of £40 and of £500 toward a certain debt. This seems again to have been transferred in August of the same year to Edward Darcy, groom of the queen's chamber. The successive holders of this patent evidently had great difficulty in enforcing their rights. Writs of assistance were sought and obtained by its first holders. Later several persons who infringed the patent were summoned by name. In May, 1601, Darcy obtained a specially detailed letter of assistance from the council.

Immediately after the proclamation of November, 1601, it seems to have been taken for granted by various haberdashers and other dealers that Darcy's patent was forfeited, but in June, 1602, he sought and obtained an order from the privy council declaring that his grant must be considered valid until it was tested in court. Notwithstanding this order and the fact that Darcy had during the summer some 4000 gross of cards manufactured, at an expense as he claimed of £5000, a London haberdasher named Allen had 80 gross of cards made, and sold half a gross to a certain grocer for 13s. 4d. Darcy promptly sued him in the court of Queen's Bench and a long contest followed which has become famous as Darcy vs. Allen, or the Case of Monopolies. Darcy's case was presented by Coke, the queen's attorney general, and Fleming, solicitor general. Their principal arguments gathered around the assertion that card playing was not a legitimate field of beneficent trade; but a vice or at best a vanity, involving the misemployment of time and the deception of masters by their servants, and that the queen might by virtue of her prerogative either suppress, limit or tolerate such unprofitable occupations. By granting a patent of monopoly she was simply laying down the conditions of toleration. Fuller, counsel for the defendant, opposed to these arguments the fact that the plaintiff had already contended that his trade was " for the necessary use of the subject," claimed that the queen could not take away from her subjects their moderate recreation any more than she could their money, and that the importation, manufacture and sale of cards were forms of industry, whatever might be true of their use, and that this should not by the common law be monopolized. The judges agreed with him and gave their decision against the monopolist Darcy. It was declared that the queen had been deceived in her grant and the patent was contrary to common law. This decision was in 1603, after the death of the queen. Notwithstanding this leading case and the queen's proclamation monopolies still remained an abuse and were one of the many problems handed on by Elizabeth to her successor. The early part of the reign of James was filled with appeals, contests and concessions, and the subject remained an unsettled question through the next three reigns and indeed till after the Revolution.[35]

This concession on monopolies did not close the controversies involving the royal prerogative during this session. The day after the queen's speech a discussion arose in the House of Commons concerning losses suffered by the seaport towns from the ships of the half-piratical, half-hostile ports of Dunkirk and Niewport. Burgesses from Yarmouth, Sandwich and elsewhere rose to complain of the depredations of privateers from across the Channel. Among the explanations given was the readiness with which these

[35] Steele, *Proclamations*, 801, 897; J. W. Gordon, *Monopolies by Patent*, 2; *State Papers, Dom., Eliz.*, cclxxix, 93; cclxxxiv, 47; cclxxxvi, 47, 48; *Cal. State Papers, Dom., Eliz., Add.*, 371; Coke, *Reports*, xi, 84; Moore, *Reports*, 671, 672, 674, 675; Price, *Patents of Monopoly*, 35–49, 129–32, *Appendices* L–R; W. R. Scott, *Constitution and Finance of Joint Stock Companies*, i, 149, 173–9, 236; Cecil T. Carr, *Select Charters of Trading Companies, Selden Society*, xxiv, lxvi–lxxxi.

marauders could arm themselves with cannon cast in England. According to existing law no ordnance nor metal for ordnance could be exported from England. But since 1592 Sir Henry Neville had held a grant from the crown, valid for twenty years, to export iron cannon. This license was not mentioned by name in the queen's proclamation and no one had sufficient interest to test its legality. There seem to have been other specific licenses for the casting and export of cannon. Certainly it was an active industry. During the debate a ship was lying in the Thames ready to sail with thirty-six pieces of ordnance aboard, and it was stated that the queen's annual income from customs export duty upon ordnance was £3000. The result was that English ordnance was sold as familiarly in France and the Netherlands as in England, and Dunkirk or Niewport privateers readily bought it and turned it against English merchants and shipping.[36]

It was but natural that as a result of this discussion a bill should be introduced, as it was December 8th, " for prohibiting transportation of iron ordnance beyond the seas." There seems to have been no opposition to the object desired. Fifteen members including three privy councillors took part in the debate and all agreed on the undesirability of the practice and the probability that its cessation would gradually put a stop to the guerilla warfare in the Narrow Seas which was so destructive to English shipping and so baffling to the efforts of the admiralty. But the old question rose, was such a bill an invasion of the queen's prerogative and should parliament approach her by petition or by the passage of the bill? Every day but three from the 8th of December till the dissolution of parliament on the 19th it was debated. The privy councillors and the Speaker tried to give other subjects the precedence, but numbers of the members called out "Ordnance, Ordnance! " The bill was considered by a large committee and a new bill finally

[36] D'Ewes, *Journals*, 665-6, 668, 670-2, 677; 21 Henry VIII, c. 10; 2 and 3 Ed. VI, c. 37.

substituted for the original. It was then resolved that the privy councillors be requested to move the queen by petition, but that in the meantime the bill be proceeded with. No report came from the former, so the bill was passed by the House of Commons and sent to the House of Lords, December 15. There it lay unacted upon and two days later messengers were sent by the lower house begging that their bill be expedited. The afternoon of the day before parliament was to be dissolved attention was called to the delay, and next morning two members moved, since their bill had "fallen into an everlasting sleep" in the other house, that the Speaker be directed to say something on the subject in his final speech to the queen. He promised to do so, but from forgetfulness, policy or fear he did not say a word on the subject, "which was greatly murmured at and spoken against amongst the Burgesses, that the House should be so abused and that nothing was done therein." Though no echo from their bill reached the Commons from House of Lords, privy council or queen, the hint seems to have been taken and three months after parliament was dissolved a proclamation against the exportation of cannon was actually issued. So with a multiplicity of large questions and small left unsettled, the last parliament of Queen Elizabeth drew to its end and its members scattered to their homes or their non-parliamentary duties.[37]

[37] D'Ewes, 670, 676–8, 681, 687, 688, 689.

Part VIII
Local Government

Part VIII

Local Government

CHAPTER XXXVII

THE JUSTICES OF THE PEACE

TO the ordinary Englishman public authority was embodied not in the great ministers of the queen, an active privy council or the central courts at Westminster, nor in the occasional meetings of parliament, but in local officers, exercising power either directly in the name of the queen or according to the ancient custom of the locality. These officials, so far as their share of activity was the shire or county, the most important local division of the country, were named and their services briefly described in somewhat stilted but accurate terms by a contemporary writer. " There are in every county certain *eirenarchae* or justices of the peace, settled by king Edward III, and these take cognizance of murders, felonies, trespasses and many other misdemeanors." " Every year some one inhabitant of the lesser nobility is set over the county and called *vice-comes* . . . and in our language he is called sheriff." " In each of these counties, in troublous times especially, there is appointed a deputy under the king by the name of lieutenant." The three chapters that follow will be little more than an amplification, with evidence and illustrations, of these statements of Camden in his *Britannia*.

The local representatives of central government whom Camden places first and undoubtedly the most active officials were the justices of the peace. In each county of

England and Wales from twenty or thirty to fifty or sixty or even, in one or two counties, as many as eighty of the leading gentry served as justices of the peace. In a list compiled in 1580, in which year there were 1738 in all England, the smallest number in any county was in Rutland, where there were thirteen, the largest number in Kent, where there were eighty-three. The forty-seven of Sussex or the fifty-six of Suffolk were about average numbers. They were drawn from that great class of country gentry which has played so prominent a part in English history and with which we shall be especially frequently concerned in the study of local government in the Tudor period, the " country squires " of later literature. In fact they formed that class. The list of the justices of the peace in any shire is practically identical with the list of the landed and well-born families in that county. In Devonshire, for instance, it included Careys, Courtenays, Paulets, Gilberts, Raleghs, Stukeleys, Grenvilles, Tremaines and Fortescues; on the other side of England, in Essex, it included Grays, Mildmays, Waldegraves, Harveys, Darrells and Capels; in the far north, in Northumberland, Suttons, Ratcliffes, Calverlys, Darcys and Herons, and so throughout England.

The members of these families enjoyed, along with the nobility, the possession of most of the land of England and many other advantages and distinctions, but in return they had imposed upon them by the diligent but not very well-equipped Tudor government a large number of public duties and services. The justices were the men-of-all-work of the queen and the privy council. Occasionally it is true nobles, prelates and high officials were placed on the commission of the peace. In 1592, for instance, of the fifty-five justices in Devonshire, one was an earl, one a bishop, twenty-three either then or subsequently knights; the remaining thirty were undistinguished esquires or gentlemen. In Lancashire, somewhat later, the list of justices of the peace included two earls, two barons, several judges, seventeen knights and fifty-one esquires. But the noblemen and high officials took little part in actual work of this kind, and it was in the main true that this with certain other local offices was the characteristic field of public service of the country gentry. These other offices which were filled by the rural gentry were those of sheriffs, deputy lieutenants, coroners and vice-admirals of the shires and high constables of the hundreds. As has been pointed out in a previous chapter the gentry also provided commissioners performing many duties, mostly of a local character, especially imposed upon them by the government, and they made up the largest single element in the House of Commons when parliament met.[1]

A succession of text-books on the duties of justices of the peace, the more important of them appearing in many successive editions, prove the intelligent interest of the country gentry in this part of their work, as well as the need for their instruction. Marrow's classical work appeared in 1503, and in 1619 was still spoken of as " in many hands to be seen." Fitzherbert, originally published in 1538, was re-edited and extended by Crompton in 1583 and reported as " everywhere to be had." Lambard's *Eirenarcha* was, as he himself stated, after it had become a well-known book, " first gathered 1579, published 1581. and now fourthly revised, corrected and enlarged in this forty and one year of the peacable reigne of our most gracious queene Elizabeth, 1599." In the early years of the seventeenth century appeared Michael Dalton's popular manuals, " The Country Justice," " The Duty and Power of Justices of the Peace in Their Sessions," and " *Officium Vicecomitum*," which went through many successive editions. One of Dalton's works, as will be noticed, is devoted to the duties of sheriffs, and other works concerning that office followed somewhat later. The office of coroner is described in a separate division of one of these works, the duties of churchwardens and

[1] Camden, *Britannia*, i, ccxxviii; *State Papers, Dom., Eliz.*, clxv; *Liber Pacis, 1596, Ibid.* Case F.; A. H. H. Hamilton, *Quarter Sessions from Queen Elizabeth to Queen Anne*, 3; Sir Thomas Smith, *De Republica Anglorum*, Book ii, c. 19.

constables in another, and much is incidentally included concerning high constables. The offices of deputy lieutenant and vice-admiral demanded mainly the fulfilment of specific orders, and therefore called forth no general treatises.

The contents and implications of these books give valuable insight into the training, character and occupations of the Elizabethan gentry and local office holders. Marrow, Fitzherbert, Lambard and Dalton are not easy reading. The men who bought and read them were evidently not uninterested in their work or entirely inadequate to its performance. The career which is described in them is one of busy and not unintelligent activity. The services expected of country gentlemen were evidently varied and difficult. The books were however entirely practical; they devoted but little attention to legal principles; they were judiciously edited, and intended, as one of them declares, " to further the good endevor of such gentlemen as bee not trained up in the continuall study of the Lawes."

On the other hand the literary character of the text-books, the occasional Latin documents the Elizabethan country gentleman must read, or at least sign and swear to, the manifold and complicated duties urged upon him by the statutes and the central government, must not create an exaggerated opinion of his legal learning and his official character. We have still the contemporary portraits of Justice Silence and Justice Shallow and the requirements of clever Dorothy Osborne for a husband, " He must not be so much of a country gentleman as to understand nothing but hawks and dogs, and be fonder of either than his wife; nor of the next sort of them, whose aim reaches no further than to be Justice of Peace, and once in his life High Sheriff, who reads no books but statutes, and studies nothing but how to make a speech interlarded with Latin that may amaze his disagreeing poor neighbors, and fright them rather than persuade them into quietness." The fact is that, as the queen and privy council constantly complain, a great proportion of the gentry neglected the public duties

they were sworn to perform, and almost all must have inter-
spersed them liberally with hunting, looking after their
estates, attention to family and social interests and occasional visits to London and abroad; while in these later
Elizabethan days of military and exploring expeditions on
sea and land many detached themselves from their country
homes for long periods to take part in voyages, the wars or
distant naval expeditions.[2]

The justices of the peace were appointed by the lord
chancellor, who from time to time issued under the great
seal a joint commission, naming the whole list of justices
of a county. The " commission of the peace " from which
the justices thus drew their powers, was a well known
formula, the product of long tradition, constantly quoted
and made the basis of discussion and reference. It had been
modified, added to, and indeed corrupted, repeatedly. It
was now, in 1590, revised and formulated anew by Sir
Christopher Wray, chief justice, with the advice of all the
other judges of the time, and approved by the lord chancellor, and has not been changed from that day to this.
This commission was not issued at any special time for the
whole country or any locality, but when some change or
need in any particular county, the desirability of adding or
dropping a name or other cause gave occasion for the issue
of a new commission for that county. When a commission
of the peace was signed, the men named in it, after taking
an oath before appointed officials to perform faithfully the
duties devolving upon them and the oath of supremacy became the magistrates of that county and remained such until
they were either removed by the issue of a new commission
in which the names of any of them might be omitted, or
until the sovereign died. Usually a man after being once
placed on the list of justices remained on it for the rest
of his life, though he might be removed by a special writ

    [2] Lambard, *Eirenarcha, Ed. 1599, Proheme,* 1; Henry IV, Act iii, Sc. 2;
Letters of Dorothy Osborne to Sir William Temple, Everyman Ed. 152;
Bertha H. Putnam, *Treatises on the Justices of the Peace.*

or, as already intimated, simply dropped from the list in a new commission.[3]

In making his appointments the lord chancellor relied in his choice of men for the most part apparently upon the reports of the justices of assize who went on circuit in the various counties, though his personal knowledge and that of other men on the council with whom he consulted must have gone far toward giving him means of making up the list. Not infrequently the queen herself intervened and ordered the inclusion of certain men and the exclusion of others from the list. Toward the end of her reign she became convinced that the number of the justices of the peace was too great. Lord Keeper Puckering in a speech in Star Chamber at the close of Easter term, 1595, told how the queen had shown her interest in the subject. " For that the number of justices of the peace are grown almost infinite, to the hindrance of justice, the one trusting so much unto another that there are more justices than justice . . . and of these many insufficient, unlearned, negligente and undiscreete, Her Majesty therefor, like a good huswyfe looking unto all her household stuffe, tooke the booke in her owne handes, and in the sight of us the lord keeper and treasurer went throughe and noted those justices she would have continue in commission and whome she thought not meete, and willed us to consyder of the reste."

In addition to this utilization of her personal acquaintanceship with her rural gentry the queen somewhat later laid down certain tests of suitability for the office of a justice of the peace. None should be appointed who were retainers of any one else, who did not live in the county, who were not of sufficient living and countenance, thereby to be a discredit to the rest, who were unlearned or negligent in their places. These requirements were largely a restatement of the old laws. A more personal statement is given in her instruction to the chancellor in 1599, to remove

[3] Lambard, *Eirenarcha*, 26, 44; Dalton, *The Countrey Justice*, c. 5, 16–20; J. R. Tanner, *Tudor Constitutional Documents*, 452–63.

" those that be drones and not bees," and in 1602 those who
" as they do no ill so they do no good." [4]

Influential noblemen sometimes nominated suitable gentlemen for justices of the peace, or more often protested
against the choice of individual candidates or classes of
men. Leicester complained at one time that notorious pa-
pists, base men and " mere attorneys " were put on the commission. Some of his charges were however unfounded,
though his influence seems to have been responsible for the
exclusion of a considerable number of justices because of
their wives' recusancy. At another time Burghley urges
that the old legal restriction be enforced, that no person
retained in any one else's service should be a justice. Other
critics laid more stress on insufficiency of estate as a bar
to being a justice. The law required that a justice of the
peace must have lands and tenements to the value of twenty
pounds a year, the traditional amount necessary to make a
man a knight, but the change in the value of money and
the increase in the wealth of the gentry as a class had long
made this standard insignificant, so that men of little financial ability might legally be appointed.[5]

There was evidently considerable dissatisfaction with the
character of the justices appointed. In a spirited speech
by a Mr. Glascock in the House of Commons, Dec. 16, 1601,
two classes of justices are described as equally undesirable,
the one " who from base stock and lineage by his wealth
is gotten to be within the commission," the other " a gentleman born, virtuous, discreet and wise, yet poor and needy,
and so only for his virtues and qualities put into the commission. This man I hold unfit to be a justice though I
think him a good member in the commonwealth. Because
I hold this for a ground infallible . . . that no poor man
ought to be in authority. My reason is this: he will so bribe

---

[4] Hawarde, *Les Reportes del Cases in Camera Stellata*, 19–21, 106, 108–
9, 159–60; Strype, *Annals*, Ed. 1824, iii, pt. 2, 449–66.

[5] *Cal. State Papers, Dom.*, 1581–90, 69, 240–2, 440, 449; 1595–7, 47;
18 Henry VI, c. 11.

you and extort you that the sweet scent of riches and gain
taketh away and confoundeth the true taste of justice and
equity." It must be said, however, that these strictures
were bitterly resented by members of the House, many of
whom were themselves justices, and the speaker was forced
to apologize for some of his expressions.

By others it was complained that " with us these magistrates have been so unsuitably appointed that a county justice is made a jest in our comedies and his character the
subject of buffoonery and laughter," an obvious reference
to the worthies who have been named above. It is dangerous to make too serious inferences from contemporary
comedies, for certain types then as now soon became stock
characters and ceased to have any close relation to real life.
Still one can hardly disregard Jonson's picture of the
truculent knight who was " so hung with pikes, halberts,
petronels, calivers and muskets that he looks like a justice
of peace's hall," as testimony to the military interests of the
country justice. On the whole such actual records as we
have left show the justices of the peace by no means wanting in dignity or ability, although there may have been unprofitable members, and although they may have somewhat
slighted the unpaid duties the government demanded of
them.[6]

These duties and the accompanying powers were so numerous, considerable and varied as to tax the ability of an
Elizabethan text-book writer to reduce them to simplicity
of statement or to the compass of five or six hundred pages
of enumeration and explanation. Many of these powers
were general, arising from the very nature of the office,
which was established " for the conservation of the peace."
But the great mass of their duties were imposed upon them
by statute. Ten early laws which they were to enforce are
enumerated in the commission itself, before coming to the

---

[6] D'Ewes, *Journals*, 660, 663, 664. Heywood Townshend, *Historical Collections*, 953–4; *Diary of Walter Yonge, Camden Soc.*, 57; Carey, *English
Liberties*, 275; Ben Jonson, *The Silent Woman*, Act iv, Sc. ii.

inclusive requirement "and cause to be kept all other ordinances and statutes made for the good of our peace and the quiet rule and government of our people." From the middle of the fifteenth century forward, the enforcement of the greater number of new laws was placed primarily in the hands of the justices of the peace. As time passed legislation became more and more minute and inclusive. Few interests in human life escaped the paternal attention of government under the Tudors and this great mass of enactment it became the duty, nominally at least, of the groups of country gentry of the counties and of the corresponding civic magistrates of the towns to put into force. A writer of the time enumerates two hundred and ninety-three statutes passed previous to 1603 by which justices of the peace are given some jurisdiction or duties. Under Elizabeth alone some seventy-eight were passed, ranging in subject from a law " for the preservation of the spawne and frie of fish," to one " against fond and fantastical prophesies." Although many of these laws were repetitions, others temporary, local or insignificant; yet, on the other hand, some of them opened up whole new fields of activity. Of such a character were the act of apprentices of 1563, the recusancy acts, the poor law and the law for the relief of injured soldiers. Around these statutes grew up whole codes of law, procedure and precedent and they provided the justices of the peace with a corresponding multiplicity of duties.[7]

The justice of the peace performed some of his duties as an individual, acting separately, almost privately, as circumstances required or as it proved convenient to himself. Other powers could be exercised only when two or more justices acted together and concurrently. Still others, and those by far the most important and dignified, they performed in a body at their " quarter-sessions." Some statutes provided that the offenses prohibited in them might be punished by any justice whose attention was drawn to

[7] Lambard, *Eirenarcha*, Ed. 1599, 36–40.

them or when occasion should arise. For instance, it was the right and duty of any justice to arrest and commit to prison rioters or those committing any disorder or making any show of force if these actions came under his own observation. He must when the matter came to his knowledge notify dwellers in infected houses to remain within them; he must arrest anyone he hears using slanderous words against the queen, or any disturbers of preachers, and he may seize the goods of any gypsies that appear in his neighborhood, retaining half for himself and handing over the other half to the queen. Enforcement of the fierce aristocratic detestation of the time of idleness on the part of the populace is provided for by clothing a single justice of the peace with power to enter any place where common men are engaged in playing bowls, quoits, tennis, football, dice or cards and putting keepers and players alike under bonds to refrain from such unlawful games. The still greater sixteenth century antagonism to vagabondage and the familiar predilection for whipping as a form of discipline are reflected in the regulation that " any justice of the peace may appoint anye person to be openly whipped naked untill his or her body bee bloodie that shall be taken begging, wandering or misordering him or herself." Sometimes the justice acts only on complaint of others, as when he binds over " for good abearing," that is to say to keep the peace, anyone who threatens another; or when he binds over for trial offenders who are brought before him on complaint; or when he forces the restitution to claimants of horses acknowledged to be stolen.[8]

Some powers it seems to have been felt unsafe to leave to a single justice, and two or more must combine to exercise them. For instance, two justices together might require any laborer who had departed before the end of his term of service to return to his master, or imprison for ten days the master who paid more than the statutory wages

[8] Lambard, *Eirenarcha*, Ed. 1599, 118–26, 185, 196, 199, 200, 206, *Precedents*, No. 37.

to his servant, or they might authorize the compulsory binding out as apprentices of children of poor parents, or, under certain circumstances, they might impose payments upon the people of a part of their county.[9]

The conception of the office of a single justice of the peace, or even of two or more acting informally together, was primarily that of police officials rather than of magistrates. Far the greater part of their older duties at least were in this way connected directly or indirectly with the keeping of order. But the separation of the powers of government is seldom complete; certainly it was not so in the case of the Elizabethan justice of the peace. His name suggests a connection with judicial activity, and among the various duties imposed upon him by law and by special order some certainly crossed the line that separates the official from the judge. A justice of the peace could, even acting alone, make original inquiries concerning felonies, fine violators of the labor, game, and enclosure laws, send men to the workhouse or to jail and, as has been seen, order them to be whipped.[10]

All the higher judicial and administrative functions of the justices of the peace were carried out not singly or in small groups but in the general assembly of the justices of the county. These assemblies were known as " quarter-sessions " or " general sessions." They had been re-modelled in 1545. Quarter-sessions, as the name indicates, were meetings held four times a year, at which all the justices of the county were supposed to be present. The meetings should by law be held within the weeks after Michaelmas, Epiphany, Easter and the translation of St. Thomas, respectively. This brought them in October, January, the early Spring and Midsummer. But this was the old rule rather than current practice. In the county of Middlesex full regular legally appointed sessions were held only twice a year, but both there and elsewhere additional sessions might be held at other times when there was spe-

9 *Ibid*. Book iii.   10 *Ibid*. 195, 202, 206, 207, 290, 297, 325, 339–41.

cial occasion, and variations from the strict law had grown
up everywhere. Sessions were sometimes adjourned from
one town to another, or held at different times in two or
three different parts of the county for the convenience of
the people. As a matter of fact sessions of greater or less
formality were held much more often than four times a year.
In Middlesex in one year the justices of the peace had
actually twenty sessions; in the West Riding of Yorkshire
there were in 1598 ten sessions; a contemporary writer remarks that in many counties they were held usually six
or eight times a year, sometimes as often as sixteen times.
Of the only too few surviving records of the proceedings
of quarter sessions those of the West Riding, which was
treated, like the other two sections of Yorkshire, as a separate county, are probably the most full, unless they are those
of the county of Middlesex outside of the cities of London
and Westminster. In the West Riding, in the typical year
1599, sessions were held on the 8th, 10th, and 12th of January at Doncaster, Wakefield and Wetherby, respectively;
on the 17th of April at Pontefract, on the 10th of July at
Halifax; and on the 1st, 7th, and 8th of October at Knares-
borough, Wakefield and Rotherham respectively. The practice of meeting in various localities, as indicated here, may
have been the origin of the " petty sessions," which are
heard of frequently in Elizabeth's time but began their regular development early in the next century and played such
an important part in the local government of later times.
Their development was so embryonic in the reign of Elizabeth that they hardly require consideration here.[11]

The time and place of the next meeting were regularly
decided upon by the justices present at each meeting and

[11] *Ibid.* 573; 2 Henry V, c. 4; John Lister, *West Riding Sessions Rolls,*
1598–9, *Yorkshire Archaeological and Topographical Association, Record
Series,* iii; J. C. Jeaffreson, *Middlesex County Records;* Hubert Hall, *Reper-
tory of British Archives,* i, 110–4; *State Papers, Dom., Elizabeth,* ccxix, 74;
Acts of the Privy Council, ii, 431; Hamilton, *Devonshire Quarter Sessions,*
65–71; S. & B. Webb, *English Local Govt.,* 297–8. *Cal. State Papers, Dom.,*
1598–1601, 519.

the sheriff ordered by warrant of two or more justices to give public notice thereof. By ancient law a meeting should continue for three consecutive days if there was any need, but as a matter of fact, notwithstanding the press of business, sessions seldom lasted more than a day, and a contemporary writer complains that, " in these days of ours . . . many do scantly afford them three whole hours, besides that time which is spent in calling of the country and giving of the charge." The law contemplated the attendance of all the justices of the county at each quarter-sessions, and when efforts were being made near the close of Elizabeth's reign to strengthen the system the lord chancellor in the name of the queen gave instructions to the justices of assize to discover and report the absence of any justices of the peace from quarter-sessions in order that they might be punished or removed from the commission. Absence from the Easter sessions, where the rates of wages of artificers for the year were drawn up, was especially forbidden under penalty of £5 fine. But law and royal injunction alike were of the type of so many legal and administrative proceedings in Tudor times; they were promulgated but not enforced. As a matter of fact the attendance at sessions was extremely irregular and incomplete. In the West Riding between 1597 and 1600, of the fifty-seven justices there were usually only about six or eight present; in a period of great interest, 1601 and 1602, at eight successive sessions there were present at one as many as twenty-two, usually but ten or eleven, and once only four. At a chance meeting of Lancashire sessions at Manchester in 1608 eleven justices were present out of the seventy of the county. The text-book writers are at great pains to show that a meeting was legal and could proceed to most forms of business if only two justices were present. It is obvious that the great proportion of the justices of the peace were much like other country gentlemen and came riding up to quarter-sessions when it suited their convenience and remained away when it did not. On the other

hand among the names on the records some occur at nearly
every meeting, and it is evident that a comparatively few
regular attendants, perhaps six or eight in each county,
made up the usual quarter-sessions and did the greater part
of the work.[12]

Of those who made up quarter-sessions one at least must
be " of the quorum." A clause of the commission giving
the justices power to inquire and determine by the oath of
jurors concerning felonies and other offences and to punish
them, after naming for a second time all those to whom the
commission is directed, says, " *quorum aliquem vestrum,
A, B, C, etc., unum esse volumus*," " of whom we wish some
one of you, A, B, C, etc., to be one," naming a shorter list.
Those so distinguished were presumably such as had some
knowledge of the law or were otherwise especially trustworthy or competent. To be a justice of the peace and of
the quorum was therefore to be one of a select list of the
justices. John Evelyn records in his Diary that his father,
Richard Evelyn, was " justice of the peace and of the
quorum," of Surrey. However, the distinction was not very
great for usually a third or even a half of the list of those
on the commission were named also in the quorum, and they
did not hold any precedency over the others except for
the requirement of their presence at the judicial work of
quarter-sessions.[13]

Conspicuous among the justices at quarter-sessions was
one, " especially picked out either for wisdom, countenance
or credit," the *custos rotulorum* or keeper of records of the
sessions, — the " *custalorum* " of Justice Shallow. The
custos was regularly indicated by name in the revised form
of the commission of 1590, and was understood to be in a
special sense the personal appointee of the lord chancellor.

[12] 12 Richard II, c. 10; 5 Elizabeth, c. 4, § xii; Lambard, 367, 586;
West Riding Sessions Rolls, 23, 28, 44, 63, 80, 182–225; Hamilton, *Devonshire Quarter Sessions*, 8, 65; *Hist. MSS. Comm., MSS in Various Collections*, i, 167.

[13] Lambard, 37, 369, 371; John Evelyn, *Diary*, Chandos Ed., 17;
Tanner, 463–9.

He was a man of prominence. A list of the *custodes rotulorum* of all the counties of England that has come down from Queen Elizabeth's time shows eleven noblemen, eighteen well known knights or government officials and twenty less conspicuous esquires and gentlemen. The *custos* could be and probably was generally represented at the quarter-sessions by an appointed deputy. A more important if less dignified officer of sessions than either the *custos* himself or his deputy was the clerk of the peace, also an appointee of the *custos*. He was usually an attorney, familiar with the law, and his knowledge of precedents and procedure must often have stood the unlearned justices in good stead. He was a sort of county attorney. He drew up and read indictments, wrote orders, kept lists of licences and tables of wages and prices, and carried on the necessary correspondence with the central courts. In fact his office tended to absorb all the practical duties of the *custos rotulorum*, leaving to that official his honorary distinction alone. When the clerk of the peace wished to be represented, as almost any officer in Tudor times was apt to be represented, by a deputy, he had to provide one familiar with the law, as well as satisfactory to the *custos*. The office seems to have been of some value, more than £100 a year in one chance case recorded. The hand of the clerk is recognizable in all the records of sessions that still exist, and if his official standing as actual custodian had been legally recognized we would probably now possess far fuller files of documents and a far clearer knowledge of the procedure of these courts than we can obtain from the surviving fragments.[14]

Quarter-sessions was a veritable court of law with all the organization and formality of a judicial gathering. In addition to the clerk, the *custos* and such other justices of the peace as were present, the sheriff or his deputy to empanel juries and execute process must be present, the gaoler

[14] 3 Ed. VI, c. 1, Lambard, 373–80; Peck, *Desiderata Curiosa,* 77; *Merry Wives of Windsor,* Act 1, Sc. 1; *Cal Hatfield House MSS.,* v. 153, 356.

ready to produce his prisoners, all jurors and witnesses who
had been summoned by the sheriff, all persons who had been
bound over by individual justices to appear at quarter-
sessions, all high constables and bailiffs of hundreds and the
coroner.   The sessions were held in a room in a royal castle,
when one existed at a convenient place in the county, sometimes in a chapter house of a cathedral, sometimes merely in
an inn or even in an inn-yard.   In Devonshire the regular
meeting place was in the old castle at Exeter, though sometimes it was in the chapter house; sometimes sessions were
held at Totnes or Ottery St. Mary.   In Cambridge they sat
in the castle.   In 1595 ten justices of Hampshire petitioned
Burghley to have the decayed north aisle of the hall of
Winchester castle repaired, as it was the only suitable place
in the county for holding sessions.   The justices of Middlesex met sometimes at Westminster, sometimes in the manor
house at Finsbury, most frequently in the old castle at St.
John's Clerkenwell.   In Leicester they met in an old building of the dissolved college of Newark.   The justices of
Suffolk met earlier in Elizabeth's time in the Angel Inn at
Bury but in 1596 they were engaged in building for themselves a sessions house in connection with the jail at
Ipswich.[15]

Quarter-sessions was evidently sometimes a crowded,
often a disorderly occasion.   A medical writer advises those
who have the falling sickness not to go to sessions or other
places where there is a great resort of company.   A special
statute of the University of Cambridge forbade students
being present at the crowded quarter-sessions in the town.
The rogue in " A Winter's Tale " soliloquizing about his
thefts declares that " every lane's end, every shop, church,
session, hanging, yields a careful man work."   The justices
coming to sessions were followed by their servants, and op-

[15] Lambard, 371-82; Jeaffreson, *Middlesex County Records,* i, xxiv;
Hamilton, *Devonshire Quarter Sessions,* 29; Strype, *Annals,* III, ii, 175;
Cooper, *Cambridge,* ii, 494, 500; *State Papers, Dom., Eliz.,* ccli, 422; *Cal.
Hatfield House MSS.,* x, 89, *Acts of the Privy Council,* xxvi, 38, 402.

portunities for the settlement of local feuds between followers of rival gentlemen, as well as for casual conflicts,
were provided by this concourse. We hear concerning Sir
William Hollis of Haughton in Nottinghamshire that he
never went to sessions at Retford, four miles from his
manor house, without thirty proper fellows at his heels. A
regular form of indictment is provided in a legal handbook
of the time " For a Riotous Affray at the Quarter Sessions
of the Peace." [16]

That this was not mere pedantry may be judged from a
Yorkshire incident that has been preserved from the year
1598. While the justices of the peace were in session on
Tuesday, April 25th, at Pontefract, a quarrel broke out
between a certain John Ogleby, one of the servants of a
gentleman of the region, and a servant of Richard Gargraves, one of the justices. The quarrel spread to their
respective friends and adherents and the uproar became so
great that the mayor of the town made a proclamation from
the market cross ordering all to keep the peace and disperse.
But this was ineffective and the mayor was forced to call
upon the justices in their court for assistance. They sent
out the sheriff, who was able to awe the rioters into temporary order. But in the afternoon as the justices and their
followers were mounting their horses to ride homeward the
conflict broke out again, one of the friends of the first ag-
gressor giving " a box of the Eare to Gargraves' servant,
both being on horseback." Mr. Gargraves and his followers
seem to have been worsted and forced to take refuge in a
house in the town, riding home later that night. The justices met again the next morning, bound the ringleaders, all
of whom are described as " gentlemen," each in £200 bail
to keep the peace, and appointed three of their own number
as a committee to investigate the circumstances, call witnesses and report at the next sessions. But the matter was

---

[16] Andrew Borde, *Dyetary of Helth, Early Eng. Text Soc.*, 294; *Statutes of the University of Cambridge*, i, 484; Lambard, *Eirenarcha, Precedents*, No. 45; Aikin, ii, 319.

presumably made up, as the next sessions were busy with
the punishment of a man who had opened an ale-house without a license and had committed an assault there, fining a
number of parishes for not maintaining the roads and lanes
running through them, ordering relief for the poor, fining
a man six shillings and eight pence for tracking a hare
through the snow and killing it, and summoning before them
a certain Mistress Ramsden who had taken in a maid servant fleeing from the employ of Sir Robert Gibson and had
declared in most scornful manner to a constable who came
to serve a warrant issued by Sir Richard Mauleverer that
she cared not for Sir Richard nor for Sir Robert. Nothing
was said of the riot of the last sessions day.

Conflicts between "town and gown" in the university
towns were traditional, but one that occurred at Cambridge
in 1591 was especially connected with quarter-sessions. The
justices of the county were gathered on Friday, October 1,
in the castle in Cambridge. Among the servants of those in
attendance was a certain Richard Parish of Chesterton, a
suburb of the University town and within the limits of its
academic privileges. Parish had some weeks before attacked a student while on the ferry to Stourbridge fair,
resisted arrest, been seized by a University official, then
rescued by men of the fair. He had stayed away from
Cambridge until, taking advantage of the enforced order
of the period of sessions, he returned for the day. The
University authorities hearing of his presence gave a writ
for his arrest to two fellows of Trinity College. They
waited till sessions were over, then attempted to arrest him
in the street. But his fellow-servants in the employ of
Lord North and Sir John Catts rescued him and an affray
broke out which involved several hundred persons and
led to a long controversy between the University and the
justices. There were serious disorders at Oxford also at
quarter-sessions in the year 1586.[17]

[17] Lister, *West Riding Sessions Rolls*, 76–87; Cooper, *Annals of Cambridge*, ii, 494–508; Wood, *Annals of Oxford*, ii, 229.

There was no distinct precedency among the justices who gathered at sessions, even of the *custos* or of those of the quorum, and the presidency seems to have been a very indefinite matter. Nevertheless the court was opened with the usual judicial formalities, juries of presentment were made up, culprits were indicted, petty juries empanelled, and a regular if not technically formal trial took place. Quarter-sessions had no power to hear civil suits, and treason, forgery and a few other high crimes were excluded from their competence. Apart from these restrictions, however, it is hard to see how their jurisdiction differed from the criminal jurisdiction of the king's great courts of law at Westminster or of that of the judges as they went on circuit through the country. The justices of the peace in their sessions tried persons accused of murder, assault, burglary, theft, horse-stealing, witchcraft, disorderly conduct, pocket picking, cheating, keeping nuisances, violation of industrial laws, failure to attend church, religious dissent, and almost all the other varied crimes and misdemeanors of which sixteenth century Englishmen were capable. The offences most usual at the time, taking England as a whole, seem to have been robbery in its different shapes and various forms of incontinency. In some parts of the country certain crimes and misdemeanors especially prevailed, or were especially prosecuted. In Yorkshire, for instance, invasions of rabbit warrens and game preserves and disorders connected with illegal hunting evidently occupied a great deal of the time of the justices.[18]

The records of the sessions for the county of Middlesex outside of the city of London show an astonishing number of murders, bloody fights and assaults on women and girls. Men with iron-shod staves are constantly attacking for purposes of robbery servants delivering goods; hasty quarrels

[18] Hawarde, *Cases in Camera Stellata*, 166; *Hist. MSS. Comm., MSS. in Various Collections, Records of Wiltshire and Worcestershire Quarter Sessions*, i. 68, 72, 73, 80, 87, 285, etc. Lister, *West Riding Sessions Rolls*, 26, 29, 33, 45, 64, 67, 183, etc.

in private houses and taverns lead to blows and death; men, even common men, fight as the result of insulting words, sword in the right hand and dagger in the left. Pistols are by no means unknown, and in addition to murders committed with firearms, deaths of that familiar kind in which those who used them were " unaware that the weapon was loaded " already appear. Even women fight viciously, often in set contests. Witchcraft exercised against men, women and children, horses and cows is also specially characteristic of Middlesex, though by no means unknown elsewhere. But these records are doubtless far from typical. The suburbs of the great city were probably more disorderly than any other part of England, even than London itself.[19]

Charges were brought at sessions, according to the law, against scores and hundreds of recusants, in addition to the discipline to which they were subjected by the individual justices in their homes. Punishments for infractions of the act of apprentices fill a large part of the time of the justices. William White of Rotherham has for the past eleven months set up and exercised the trade of pewterer although he has not served an apprenticeship of seven years in that art and mystery as required by law. Henry, Robert and John Wilson, laborers, have been carrying on the trade of butcher at Gisbourn although they have never passed an apprenticeship to it. Three nailers have carried on their trade contrary to the rules established by the justices in their sessions. A carpenter of Edgeware although not in service refuses to work when offered twelve pence a day, the legal rate. Such are familiar examples of violation of the sixteenth century attempt to organize industry, and each is appropriately punished. There are occasional instances in which masters or mistresses are punished for undue hardness to their apprentices, or apprentices released from their

bonds because of cruel treatment. There are innumerable
instances in which men and women "strong and fit for
labour, but having neither masters nor lawful vocations
whereby to get their living" were adjudged to be vagrants
and ordered to be whipped and then "burnt through the
gristle of the right ear" according to the law as it existed
from 1572 to 1597. In two months in the early winter of
1591 seventy-one such poor laborers were whipped and
burned through the ear in Middlesex.[20]

The punishments that followed upon conviction were, as
in the instance just given, and as in other criminal courts
of England in the sixteenth century harsh to the border of
ferocity. The mildest punishment was the stocks. Flog-
ging was extremely common, especially for first offences,
lesser crimes and the misdemeanors of women. The lash
was a ready and constant accompaniment of justice, so-
called, both central and local. Offenders were occasionally
sent to row in the galleys which were at this time being
experimented with in the queen's navy in rivalry with those
of Spain and France. Sometimes this was treated as a
commutation from continued punishment in the jails.

Hanging was extremely common. In Devonshire in the
midwinter sessions of 1598 out of sixty-five culprits who
were tried eighteen were hung; in the spring sessions out of
forty-five twelve were hung; at midsummer out of thirty-
five eight were hung, thirteen flogged, seven acquitted, and
seven on account of their claim of benefit of clergy branded
and released. Although only one was hung at the autumn
sessions, with the thirty-five who suffered the same year
by order of the assize courts, seventy-four men and women
altogether were put to death in one county in this one year.
In Middlesex although no actual statistics during Elizabeth's reign are available the number was enormous. It
is startling to read in the scattered sessions records in-

[20] 5 Elizabeth, c. 3; 14 Elizabeth, c. 5; Lister, 23–5, 50, 203; Jeaffreson,
43, 101, 109, 190, etc.; *Hist. MSS. Comm., MSS. in Various Collections*, i,
County of Wilts, 71, 103.

stance after instance in which relapsed vagrants, both men and women, a thief who had stolen a sheet worth eight shillings, three robbers who took a dagger away from a man in Marylebone, a man who consorted with gypsies, a woman who had sheltered a priest in her house, a man who hid a felon, burglars, murderers and other offenders in a long line are alike condemned to be hung. In the fifth year of the next reign fifty-five men and women were put to death in Middlesex; in 1614 ninety-eight, and altogether in the first ten years of that reign seven hundred and four. Life was evidently as cheap in the eyes of the law as it was in the minds of the reckless thieves, brutal assailants, and unhappy mothers of bastard children whose bloody and fatal acts darken the records of the time.[21]

Although quarter-sessions was primarily a judicial occasion, the meeting of the justices was also taken advantage of for the carrying out of many of those general labors imposed upon them by the law and by special instructions from the privy council which they could not or did not perform singly at their own homes. Some of these general duties, the settlement of wages, the repair of bridges, the licensing of taverns, the binding of apprentices, and some other varied duties may be here glanced at. Perhaps the most exacting duties at the close of the reign, the payment of pensions to maimed soldiers and the enforcement of the new poor law, have been already described. By the statute of apprentices they must yearly at their Easter sessions establish wages for the ensuing year for laborers and artificers of all kinds, and report the rates decided upon to the lord chancellor for approval and confirmation. This duty was more or less consistently carried out. By a law passed in the middle of the reign of Henry VIII, and by later legislation, the justices of the peace were bound to keep an over-

[21] Lister, 45, 58, 76, 128, etc.; Jeaffreson, i, 9, 32, 103, 207, 209, 214, ii, xvii; Hamilton, 20–33; Camden, *Annals*, Ed. 1706, 641; Stow, *Chronicle*, s. a. 1601; *Acts of the Privy Council*, xxiv, 487; *MSS. in Various Collections*, i, 71–88, 284–298; *Shrievalty of William Farington*, Chetham Soc., 23–7, 38–9.

sight of bridges. When any bridge was found to be in decay
it was their duty to decide which hundreds, parishes or persons were bound to repair it, to levy a tax upon the responsible parties and see to its effective expenditure upon
the work. There are numerous records of the appointment
of individual justices or subcommittees of justices for the
laborious work of collecting the money for and overseeing
bridge repairs. There was some similar work on highways
but most legislation for this purpose came later.[22]

It was incumbent upon the justices to grant licenses to
ale-houses, to keep an oversight over these houses and to
withdraw their licenses if they proved to be disorderly. Ale-
houses were very generally looked upon as " nurseries of
naughtiness," and the misbehavior of tipplers at them was
a constant worry. The justices were also much occupied in
binding out apprentices, a duty which they were required
to perform by several statutes and by constant reminders
from the privy council. The justices of Norfolk early in
the seventeenth century report that they have within the
last year put out as apprentices some five hundred poor
children; those of the West Riding of York somewhat later
that they have apprenticed two hundred; and those of Somerset four hundred. The children of paupers and in fact all
children of the working classes who were not apprenticed by
their parents were provided for in this way by the justices,
and employers of sufficient substance were compelled to
take such apprentices as the authorities saw fit, or were fined
for refusing to do so. The justices were being constantly
ordered by the privy council to list, arrest, impose special
services upon or otherwise discipline their recusant neighbors, a task which frequently disclosed sympathy or connivance with the Catholics which awakened the vexation, as
it did the apprehensions of the central government.[23]

[22] 22 Henry VIII, c. 5; 5 Elizabeth, c. 4, §§ xi; Lambard, 352, 594;
Hamilton, 12; Lister, 38, 74, 129, etc.; *MSS. in Various Collections*, i, 161–8.

[23] Lambard, 195, 343, 519, 552; Lister, 46; *Hist. MSS. Comm. Rep.*, 13,
App. iv, 463, *Rutland Papers*, i, 347, *MSS. in Various Collections*, i, 79,
285; Leonard, *Early History of the English Poor Law*, 215, etc.

Apart from these general responsibilities the position of leadership in which the justices of the peace stood required them to act in many public and private emergencies and to give or authorize special relief in many particular cases. If a man's thatched cottage was burned, the nearest justice might authorize him to make appeal to his neighbors for help; if a whole village or town suffered from a more extensive fire, the justices in sessions quartered the homeless people on various parishes, announced a collection, and called constables and leading villagers before them, exhorted them to liberal voluntary gifts and appointed a committee to administer the funds for relief. If a pestilence appeared, a tax rate for immediate assistance was levied and the justices enforced the quarantine and supported the sick. If food became scarce and high priced, the justices forbade the export of grain or its conversion into malt, and even enforced what amounted to a maximum market price for it. When weavers or other artificers were out of work, the justices induced masters to employ them or urged merchants to buy their goods, or as a last resort levied a rate for their support. If news came of the capture of a number of English sailors or merchants by Barbary pirates, collections were taken up by the justices of the maritime counties for their redemption.[24]

In the discharge of their varied duties the justices were not allowed for any long time to forget that they were under the control of the privy council. Not only were such specific requirements constantly made of them by letter or messenger as have been already indicated, but this pressure grew steadily stronger in the closing years of Elizabeth's reign. The personal interposition of the queen in the selection of the justices has already been mentioned. In October, 1592, soon after the remodelling of the commission, a circular letter was sent by the council to a few prominent noblemen and gentlemen in each shire ordering them to summon a

[24] Hamilton, 19, 63; *Hist. MSS. Comm., MSS. in Various Collections,* i, 68; Tanner, 469–507.

special session of the justices and cause them to take anew, or if they had previously neglected that duty, to take now the proper oath of the justices and the oath of supremacy. Any who declined and any who remained absent and did not seek opportunity within twenty days to take the oaths were to be deprived of their powers as justices. The immediate object of this requirement was doubtless to purge the lists of all recusants or sympathizers with recusants, but its peremptory character gave it the effect of a reminder of the superior powers of the central government. The duties imposed upon the justices in the effort of the government to keep down high prices during the scarcity years from 1594 to 1598 have already been described.

In 1598 vigorous letters were sent by the privy council to the various counties, calling the attention of the justices to the recently enacted poor law and requiring them to take all necessary steps for seeing it put into execution. Attempts at discipline of the justices and instances of narrow oversight of their actions were becoming constantly more frequent, more detailed and more drastic. This movement of centralized control came to a head, so far as this particular period is concerned, in a series of special instructions sent to all the counties by the privy councillors shortly after the queen's death. These orders threatened punishment to any justices who were absent from quarter-sessions or the proposed new special sessions, and required reports from other local officials and the royal judges on circuit concerning the fulfilment by the justices of their various duties.[25]

If the justices of the peace were in many ways merely the local representatives of the queen and council in each county, in some other respects and to a slight degree at least they represented local interests as against the control of the

---

[25] Hamilton, 2, 324; *Acts of the Privy Council*, xxvi, 80, 95, 151, 154, 188, 226, etc.; *Cal. State Papers, Dom.*, 1595–7, 337; *Orders Considered fit to be put in Execution*, Greenwich, June 23, 1605, Hamilton, 67; Leonard, 143.

central government. They possessed and frequently exercised the power to give local, individual or temporary dispensations from some of the drastic general laws so characteristic of this period, such as the prohibition by a statute passed in 1593 of the erection of any new houses in England unless accompanied with the possession of four acres of land.

Much effort was made by the justices to reduce or at least to limit the exercise of the right of purveyance. This was the privilege possessed by the crown to purchase at a fixed and generally at an inadequate price provisions for the consumption of the queen's household. The body of a thousand or more persons described in an earlier chapter of this work as making up the queen's household, consuming a vast amount of meat, bread, beer and other heavy forms of food, was kept provided with these by a household department known as the " green cloth." The emissaries of this office, utilizing the queen's ancient claim to purveyance, still came into every county demanding cattle and grain at prices established by themselves, or required the county officials to deliver these provisions at the queen's court wherever it might be. During this period an earnest effort was being made by the justices of the peace to reach a " composition " as it was called; that is to say, an agreement for a fixed annual provision of beef cattle and other provender by each county and town at an agreed upon price. In 1588 eighteen counties were at " composition," in this way, each furnishing a certain number of steers, calves, sheep, lambs, or hogs, or a certain amount of wheat, bacon, butter, or poultry, at a price previously agreed upon in each case. Eight counties had formerly made composition but had broken it and fallen back on the old system of submission to purveyance by direct and forced purchase through officials of the queen's household. Composition was preferred, however, even by the royal officials. During the remaining years of Elizabeth's reign pressure was brought by the ministers of the household to force the counties to compound and almost all came into the newer system, though there was much dispute with Somerset, Lincoln, Kent, Wiltshire and certain other counties.[26]

The general method of composition may be understood from the case of Devonshire. By old established custom the household officials had the right of compulsory purchase yearly in that shire of a number up to 40 oxen for beef and 300 sheep for mutton. In 1593 the justices of the peace made composition with the household through the privy council. In consideration of the fact that the provisions for many of the naval expeditions of the time must be purchased in Devonshire to provide the fleets fitting out in Plymouth harbor, and that it was not a cattle breeding county, the number of cattle required was reduced to 10 oxen and 150 sheep; the former were to weigh at least 600 lbs. apiece, the latter 46 lbs. apiece. These the justices agreed to deliver at the gates of the court at two periods of the year and to accept for the oxen £4 apiece, for the sheep 6s. 8d. apiece. In return for this the officers of the green cloth agreed not to send any purveyors into Devonshire, unless in the exceptional case of the queen coming on one of her progresses within twenty miles of the borders of the shire. The privy council also authorized the justices to distribute among the different divisions of the shire and to impose upon their inhabitants the costs of this arrangement and promised to arrest and punish anyone refusing to pay his share. The composition could be abrogated on six months' notice either by the justices or by the officers of the green cloth. Since at this time oxen were worth about £6 and sheep about 12s and the cost of driving them to the vicinity of London fell upon the county it is evident that the arrangement would cost the county at least £100 more than they would receive from the officers of the green cloth, and this they would have to pay for the privilege of escaping the petty exactions of

[26] *State Papers, Dom., Eliz.*, ccxviii, 58; *Cal. State Papers, Dom.*, 1591–4, 364; 1595–7, 70, 135, etc.; *Acts of the Privy Council*, xxv, 80, 83, 408; Hawarde, *Cases in Camera Stellata*, 58; *MSS. from Various Sources*, i, 81, 294, 296, etc.; *Hist. MSS. Comm. Rep. 13, App.* iv, 155, 157.

purveyors. As a matter of fact the justices found a contractor who undertook to purchase the necessary cattle in the county at market prices and pay all necessary expenses and deliver them at the queen's court, receiving there the agreed upon price, for a lump sum, £103, to be paid him by the county. Notwithstanding many disputes and much subsequent negotiation between the justices of the peace and the privy council this composition continued in force, at an annual cost to the county ranging from £103 to £106, until the whole system was terminated in 1622 by an agreement of the county to pay to the crown a lump sum of £140 a year in money in lieu of purveyance, the crown officers in future buying the necessary provisions wherever they could best procure them, and at such prices as they would have to give.[27]

The waves of the rising tide of opposition to monopolies reached the counties before they finally broke in parliament, and this local opposition was led by the justices of the peace. As early as 1599 a general contribution was taken up by the justices of Devonshire to fight in the law courts and oppose before the council a certain grant of a monopoly of salting fish. Instances are not unknown of the justices leading in a tentative, though in all cases a futile opposition to the forced loans and benevolences of the period.[28]

But these were simply modest efforts at self-defence of a local gentry whose interests in many cases were the same as those of the lower classes of their neighborhood against the strong hand of the central power. Any opposition to the form of government of England was still far in the future, and the justices at the close of the queen's reign were, as has been indicated, more completely subordinated than ever before to the control of the crown and the privy council. Indeed when it is considered that the justices of the peace were independent landed gentlemen of rank and dignity, called upon to perform laborious duties requiring much sac-

[27] Hamilton, *Devonshire Quarter Sessions*, 6-12, 35-41.
[28] *Ibid.* 24-6, 42-55.

rifice of time and comfort and bringing no reward and little satisfaction, the discipline imposed upon them and the harsh tone of reproof so frequently used toward them by the queen and the privy council are a matter of constant wonder. This control gives no slight testimony to the high claims of Tudor despotism, just as the neglect of their duties by the justices testifies to its ineffectiveness.

CHAPTER XXXVIII

THE SHERIFF

FROM among the justices of the peace or at least from the same class of rural gentry was chosen each year a county official still more closely connected with the crown and performing duties of a more directly administrative nature. This was the sheriff. His social and political position has been already described in a quotation that will bear repetition. " Every year some one of the gentlemen inhabitants is set over the county wherein he dwelleth." Elsewhere he is spoken of as " Her Majestie's chief mynyster and officer in that countye." He might or might not be a knight. There was in the sixteenth century little or no real difference in rank between a gentleman who had been knighted and one who had not; knighthood was a matter of opportunity, almost of chance, not of birth. Of the thirty-five sheriffs who in 1588 represented the queen in the various counties of England and Wales, thirteen were knights, twenty-two merely esquires or gentlemen. A list of the successive sheriffs of Cheshire in the first half of the next century shows twenty-three who were knights, twenty-three without that title. The selection of the sheriff from among the justices of the peace of the county was not uncommon. Of the fifty-five justices of the peace in Devonshire during the early years of the seventeenth century, twenty-eight were at one time or another in their lives appointed sheriff. Commissions of the peace were constantly being renewed to omit or reinstate one of the justices who had been appointed to serve as sheriff. The list of sheriffs in any county for a succession of years was, like the list of justices of the peace, much the same as the list of the landed families of the county, omitting the nobles. In Humphrey Gilbert's proposed Academy for the queen's wards and sons of the gentry, he provided for a teacher of the common law who should give instruction in the duties of justices of the peace and sheriffs.[1]

The sheriffs were in a special sense the immediate appointees of the queen, although nominated to her by ministers of state. November 1 every year a meeting was held in the exchequer, presided over by the lord chancellor or the lord treasurer and attended by the chief justices and other judges or councillors, where a list of some of the leading men of each county was made up. This list was laid before the queen, who made her choice from among the nominees, "pricking," as it was called, from the list one to be sheriff of each county, much as the ceremony is still performed. The sheriff's office was only for one year and he could not be re-appointed till after the expiration of two more years. There were a few anomalies in the system. London had two sheriffs of its own, apart from the sheriff of the county of Middlesex. Bristol, Southampton and several other towns each had one. In these towns the sheriffs were elective officers. Again, certain pairs of adjoining counties, Surrey and Sussex, Somerset and Dorset, Essex and Hertford, and some others were traditionally placed under one sheriff, and although most of these had been separated in 1566 and 1575, Surrey and Sussex and Cambridge and Huntingdon still had only one sheriff for each pair of counties.[2]

His appointment announced to him, it was the sheriff's duty to go or send to the exchequer at Westminster, give bonds to answer his pecuniary responsibilities to the crown, obtain the patents which clothed him with his powers for the year, appoint an attorney to represent him in each of the

---

[1] P.R.O. *Lists and Indexes,* ix, *Sheriffs for England and Wales;* Camden, *Britannia,* Ed. 1637, 160; *Acts of the Privy Council,* vii, 335; Hamilton, *Devonshire Quarter Sessions,* 330–45; *Cal. State Papers, Dom.,* 1591–4, 124, 179, 191, 197, 200; King, *The Vale Royal,* 233.

[2] Sir John Fortescue, *De Laudibus Legum Angliae,* c. 2; Michael Dalton, *Officium Vicecomitum,* 6; 8 Eliz., c. 16, *Statutes of the Realm,* IV, i, 499.

courts, and take the traditional oath of his office and the oath of supremacy either before one of the masters in chancery or, after his return, before one of the judges of assize in his county or two of the justices of the peace clothed with special powers from the chancery to administer the oath. The newly appointed sheriff could conform to all of these requirements by deputy without actually appearing at Westminster in person, and he must often have done so, but there was no way in which he could avoid the payment of the multiplicity of customary fees which burdened a sheriff's year in office. In a typical county the fees for entry on the sheriff's office amounted to about £15; for the settlement of his two accounts of the year about £50, and for leaving his office about £40. There were fees to barons of the exchequer, masters of the chancery, attorneys and marshals and clerks and criers and tipstaves and the men of all these; for patents and writs and petitions and warrants and tallies and views of account, " with many others which to record would be long, and so he is quit." Twenty-four separate fees were to be paid at Michaelmas, twenty-three at Easter. The unpaid or almost unpaid hordes of attaches of the chancery, exchequer and law courts swooped down upon the sheriffs or their representatives at these two periods of the year at Westminster as hungry for fees as it will appear were the gentlemen and their servants for dinners and suppers at the sheriff's expense in their counties.[3]

At the first county court after his appointment it was the duty of the sheriff to read out his patents and the more important writs put in his hands and to name his under-sheriff, county clerk and at least four bailiffs. These subordinate officials must be of his own county but, like the sheriff himself, could not be appointed after one year of service until two more years had passed; nor could a sheriff appoint the sheriff of the preceding year as his under-sheriff.

[3] John Wilkinson, *Office and Authority of Coroners and Sheriffs*, 82-4, 145; Dalton, 7-10.

Special care was apparently taken that none of this group of local officials should stay in office continuously enough to obtain any undue control or exert any long continuing abuse over their neighbors. Once having received his appointment and taken his oaths the sheriff was bound to remain in his county for the year of his appointment, unless he received a special summons or license from the queen. A dramatist of a somewhat later period opines that the women of his time " would rather marry a London jailor than a high sheriff of a county, since both are bound to their place of employment, but the former is at least in the city." [4]

It was the duty of the sheriff to represent his county during his year of service in such hospitality as might be called for by visits of the queen, the passage of foreign ambassadors or other distinguished visitors from abroad through his county, the stay of commissioners coming from court and of the justices of assize on their semi-annual visits to the county town. The special choice of a gentleman for sheriff must have depended largely on his ability to meet such expenses. The father of John Evelyn, who has been mentioned before as a justice of the peace, in the year in which he was made sheriff of the combined counties of Surrey and Sussex had an estate worth about £4000 a year. He must, however, have made inroads even upon this large fortune, for during the year, " he had one hundred and sixteen servants in liverys, every one livery'd in green sattin doublets." Many of these servants, it is true, were friends or relatives or their servants who came as a matter of civility to wait upon him. But much expense was nevertheless unavoidable. A William Farington, sheriff of Lancashire, was not only attended by a retinue of seventy-six gentlemen and servants in livery, but kept up during his term of office the following astonishing household: a steward, a clerk of the kitchen, two yeomen of the plate cup-

[4] 4 Henry IV, c. 7; 1 Henry V, c. 4; 23 Henry VI, c. 8; Wilkinson, 79, 84, 125; Wycherly, *The Country Wife*, iv, i.

board, a yeoman of the wine cellar, two attendants in the sheriff's chamber, an usher of the hall, two chamberlains, four butlers and butlers' assistants, eight cooks, four scullions, a porter, a baker, a caterer, a slaughterman, a poulterer, two watchmen for the horses, two men to attend the docket door by turns each day, twenty men to attend upon the prisoners each day by turns, — altogether a household of fifty-six servants. Thirty or forty men were sometimes spoken of as the proper retinue of the sheriff.[5]

During the visits of the justices of assize the sheriff was expected not only to perform the legal duties of his office but to entertain the judges and more dignified officers of the courts. Farington spent at the Lent assizes of his year a little short of £100 for the personal entertainment of the judges and their trains and of his own followers. Besides this his stewards spent well on to £200 for special luxuries, fees, presents and other requirements, while the clerk of his kitchen purchased several barrels of ale, poultry and rabbits by the score, sheep and geese by the dozen, " forty-eight venison pasties " and all the solid substance and luxury of Elizabethan times, for use at dinners and suppers for the five days of the sitting of the court, altogether costing several hundred pounds. It is no wonder therefore, that the sheriff was required to be one who had land in the county " sufficient to answer king and people." [6]

If the queen visited the county during his year of incumbency, the sheriff was expected to see to her protection, attendance and, in default of other provision, her entertainment. The chronicler Stow tells how the queen " entered into Hampshire and upon Chilchester Heath was received by the sheriff of that shire, Francis Palmer, accompanied by many Gentlemen of accompt in the same shire, for Hamp-

    [5] Evelyn, *Diary*, s. a. 1634; *The Shrievalty of William Farington*, 17; King, *The Vale Royal*, 233.

    [6] *The Shrievalty of William Farington*, 5–22; 9 Edw. II, c. 2; 4 Edw. III, c. 9; 5 Edw. III, c. 4; *Cal. State Papers, Dom.*, 1595-7, 124; *Hist. MSS. Rep.* 7, *App.* i, 3, 9, 25; Rep. 12, i, 414.

shire is well inhabited by ancient Gentlemen civilly educated
and who live in great amity together." Scarcely had
Palmer left the queen after attending her to Basing House
where she was to spend two weeks of hunting, riding and
enjoying the hospitality of the Marquis of Winchester in
that beautiful region, when news came of the approach of
the Duc de Biron, ambassador of France, and he was
summoned in haste to the border of his county nearest
London to receive him with his train of four hundred and
twenty French nobles, gentlemen and servants, and to lead
them to the country house that had been prepared for
Biron's occupancy during his visit to the queen. Palmer had
busy times during the ensuing festivities until two weeks
later he was permitted to hand the queen and her train over
to the sheriff of Surrey on the border between the two shires.
However, he won the royal commendation and with nine
others was knighted when she left. As a special mark of
favor also he was permitted to leave his shire in order to
make a visit to the bishop of Winchester at Farnham in
Surrey. Shortly afterward we get a view of still another
ambassador of France riding down from London to his
place of embarcation at Margate attended by the sheriff and
gentlemen of Kent.[7]

Apart from the duty of representing the hospitality of
the shire, the sheriff's functions fall into two main classes,
judicial and financial. In both of these he must have relied
largely upon his principal official, the under-sheriff, for,
country gentleman as he was, he could seldom have had
the legal and financial knowledge required, even with the
aid of the numerous manuals of his duties that were in
print. Indeed the term so constantly used, high sheriff,
without any special signification other than the simple term
sheriff, was probably intended to distinguish him clearly
from the under-sheriff. This official was the sheriff's own
appointee, though a candidate was sometimes recommended

[7] Stow, *Annals* (Ed. 1631), 797; *Cal. State Papers, Dom.*, 1595-7, 276.

by the crown or the council, as in the case of all other offices. It was customary for the sheriff to make a written agreement with the under-sheriff that the latter should do practically all his legal and financial work, under his protection and guaranteed by him against loss. The sheriff was recommended in the legal text-books to take security from his under-sheriff, " if he will sleep quietly and take his repose in safety." He is urged again to appoint his own household clerk as under-sheriff, when he can, in order that his office may be in his own home.[8] The under-sheriff's place, in fact, although a minor appointment and exercised presumably by a country lawyer, was one of much influence, dignity and consideration. In the formulas he is always described as esquire and is treated as a man of some position. At one time the privy council takes up for consideration a dispute between an under-sheriff and a gentleman of his county; at another he attends the courts at Westminster to receive his superior's writs; at another he sends out in his own name summons to certain persons to appear before the lord lieutenant. His position is also indicated in an incident of the year 1603, when a defendant in Yorkshire who opposed the under-sheriff in executing a writ was fined £50 by the Star Chamber, ordered to pay damages, to be imprisoned, to give a bond for good behavior and to confess his fault at the next assizes.[9]

Yet the sheriff could not divest himself entirely of his individual responsibilities. He was bound to preserve order and to keep at least a general oversight of judicial and some other matters in his own person. Like everyone else he was subject also to the constant supervision and specific orders of the privy council and the great officers of state. Moreover no really clear cut distinction of functions existed under the Tudor system, especially in this time of war; and duties

[8] Wilkinson, 88, 91–4; *Hist. MSS. Comm., MSS. at Montague House,* i, 226.

[9] Hawarde, *Cases,* 125–9, 167; *Acts of the Privy Council,* xxvi, 29, 221; *Cal. State Papers, Dom.,* 1581–90, 662–3, 1591–4, 135.

and services, many of them of a military nature, were imposed upon the sheriff, as will appear later, far removed from what might be considered the normal duties of his office at this period.[10]

The sheriff's financial duties consisted in the collection of certain old and not very profitable forms of royal taxation, of debts due the crown in his county, including fines imposed on the men of his county by the courts at Westminster and on circuit, in helping officers of the household and the justices of the peace to enforce the queen's right of purveyance and in the levy and collection of certain special imposts. He must account for these amounts of money at the exchequer or in such other way as he was ordered by the treasury. For the year ending at Michaelmas 1592, for instance, the sheriffs of twenty-five counties and thirteen cities and towns were charged with the collection of £6100, 8s, 3d. in various fines, fees and other requirements. In the year 1596 the sheriffs accounted for £3806, 11s, 8d. as the queen's " post fines "; the next year, when there was a general pardon, some £1500; and in 1598, £5124. The sheriffs were frequently ordered to pay salaries of royal officials or other expenses of the government in their respective localities out of money in their hands. For such payments they received tallies or other receipts which they presented when they settled their accounts at the exchequer in November. The account of the sheriff was ordered to include not only the actual collection of fines, regular payments and special impositions which may have been entrusted to him, but an account of the condition of the queen's debts in his county, unpaid purveyance charges, waifs, felon's goods and all other possible profits, even if they were not immediately available. The sheriff's primary financial duty was evidently to conserve and collect those small forms of income in the shires that were either survivals from an earlier and half-forgotten system or products of judicial sentence, which could never compete in amount

---

[10] Camden, *Britannia*, i, ccxxviii; Wilkinson, 79, 97.

with parliamentary taxation or the proceeds of the custom house.[11]

The most ancient and the most interesting, if not the most important, duty of a judicial nature performed by the sheriff was his presidency over two ancient, indeed antiquated courts, the "sheriff's tourn and leet," and the "county court." From time immemorial it had been the duty of the sheriff to pass semi-annually through one division of the county after another, the so-called hundreds or wapentakes, holding a petty court in each. This "tourn" or "turn" or circuit of petty court sessions ought by old law to be held in the months following Easter and Michaelmas. A jury should be empanelled in each hundred and there was an ancient list of queries which the sheriff should submit to each of these juries for answer. It should also take cognizance of petty misdemeanors and violations of the law which should be voluntarily brought up. But this duty was much neglected. Even a pedantic text-book writer, much interested in legal requirements and full of musty lore as to the duties of "douzaines" and "vills" at such gatherings, acknowledges that "this court is now almost out of use," and again that "these ancient courts are not kept as they might be." Coke in his exhaustive list of contemporary courts gives but a vague and passing mention of the sheriff's tourn and leet.[12]

The other ancient local gathering under the presidency of the sheriff, the county court, had preserved a somewhat greater vitality. It met once a month at the county town. No criminal matters were punishable there, nor could civil suits for a greater sum than 40 shillings be taken cognizance of. The change in the value of money characteristic of the sixteenth century had reduced this maximum limit to very insignificant proportions. Moreover, the frequency of assizes in each county, the comparatively easy and safe

[11] *Cal. State Papers, Dom.*, 1581–90, 113, 118, 544; 1591–4, 124, 325. 561, 562, 565; 1598–1601, 456–9; Wilkinson, I, 97, 136.

[12] Wilkinson, 122–4, 125; Coke, *Fourth Institute*, c. 53.

travel which made a journey to Westminster so much more
practicable than of old, the absence of lawyers and the
amateur nature of the justice dispensed had no doubt combined to make the civil jurisdiction of the county courts but
a drop in the ocean of Elizabethan litigation. Nevertheless
at these courts were still brought suits for small debts, for
damages resulting from breach of contract, for non-payment
of wages, for not returning borrowed or pledged articles
and numerous other petty causes. The sheriff was not
the judge in the county court as he was in his tourn; the
free-holders of the county who attended were the judging
body, the sheriff was only the presiding official. He
was bound to use the meetings of the county court for
various other purposes. He must proclaim certain ancient
statutes, and it was there that new laws and ordinances
were publicly announced. At the county courts writs
of outlawry and certain other ancient writs must be
declared.[13]

One use of the meetings of the county court which has
already been referred to in another connection occasionally
rose far above all its other functions in prominence, in dignity and importance, and when it occurred gave the sheriff
for the time great influence. This was the election to parliament of the knights of the shire. Forty or fifty or more
successive old-fashioned monthly sessions of the county
court might be held, when suddenly the gathering in each
shire was galvanized into life by orders from the queen.
When a parliament was summoned it was to the sheriff that
the writ for the election of members of the House of Commons was sent. The writ was read in the next county court,
it was there that the election took place and it was thence
that the sheriff directed instructions to the mayors and
bailiffs of cities and boroughs in their counties to hold their
separate elections and send the returns of their elections to
him. The election in the county should by old law take

---

[13] Wilkinson, 84, 115, 120; Coke, *Fourth Institute*, c. 55; Greenwood;
Fitzherbert, *Natura Brevium*, 28; Mitten's Case, 25 Eliz.

place between eight and eleven o'clock in the morning, but many irregularities had grown up and sheriffs exercised much liberty in the conduct of elections. To the court where such an election was to be held the gentlemen and freeholders of the county often came in a great throng, and the petty disputes of poor suitors and reports of obscure officials gave place for the time to the excitement of a political or personal contest. More or less successful pressure was exercised upon the electors by an influential sheriff or by candidates who were possessed of credentials from great officials, the privy council or even from the queen. A long series of statutes had checked the abuses connected with the sheriff's influence, but even yet lack of uniformity in the process of election gave opportunity to the sheriff. Sometimes the members were elected by acclamation, sometimes by poll; sometimes the sheriff postponed the election or refused to accept the candidates insisted on by the electors, or threw out votes which he claimed were not properly given, or closed the election when the candidate he preferred was in a temporarily advantageous position. The journals of the House of Commons at a period slightly later than that under consideration are filled with the records of contested elections, and sheriffs are repeatedly found standing at the bar of the House to receive censure or pardon for acts concerning elections. The privy council also kept its hand on parliamentary elections by letters sent to the sheriff. When the parliamentary service of the knights of the shire was over, writs were sent to the sheriff for the payment of their wages and travelling expenses and these were assessed upon the hundreds and the townships within the hundreds at the next county court.[14]

The position of the sheriff in the county court during elections for parliament was administrative rather than

[14] *Journals House of Commons,* i, 511, 556, 801, 854, 884, etc. *Hist. MSS. Comm. Rep. 14,* App. ii, 208; *Acts of the Privy Council,* vii, 74, xiv, 222, 241; Wilkinson, 105, 110–11; Coke, *Fourth Institute,* Ed. 1809, 48; 6 Henry VI, c. 6; 23 Henry VI, c. 11.

judicial. We have still to consider his duties in connection with the assize courts and the courts of quarter sessions, which were, as before stated, his most conspicuous duties. Apart from meeting the justices of assize on their semi-annual visits and entertaining them, it was his duty to arrange the room for their sessions, to have ready a panel of grand and petty jurymen, to bring prisoners from the jail, and to return them thither, and to see that the punishments imposed by the judges were carried out. The court could hardly proceed without the presence of the sheriff to impanel jurymen and he should by law have them ready at least four days before the opening of the session. He must also certify to the justices the names of prisoners in jail for felony or bound over for appearance in a " Kalendar."[15]

The responsibility for the keeping of the jail also fell upon the sheriff, although, just as he transferred most of his financial and legal duties to the under-sheriff so he deputed the oversight of the prisoners in the jail to a keeper and the execution of sentences to still another deputy. In that period of harsh punishments a session of the assize court seldom passed without a series of hangings following upon it. William Farington, who has already been alluded to as holding the shrievalty of Lancashire at a somewhat later time, had to make himself responsible for the execution of twelve men and women after the Lent assizes in his year of service, besides nine who were released on account of benefit of clergy. At the opening of the August assizes of the same year there were some forty who either remained in jail under postponement of trial or reprieve or had been bound over by justices of the peace in the meantime. Some of these were declared guilty of felony and presumably executed; the others were whipped, placed in the pillory or fined. Most of these offenders were charged with robbery in one or other of its forms, although one was charged with murder, two with clipping the coin, and ten were held as " witches." When prisoners were acquitted it was the duty

[15] 3 Henry VII, c. 3; Wilkinson, 114.

of the sheriff to give them letters under his seal allowing
them to beg for their fees for a period of six weeks.

The duty of the sheriff to attend at the quarter sessions
of the justices of the peace has already been stated. There
was the same necessity for the empanelling of juries, for the
production of prisoners, for the carrying out the orders of
the court as at the assizes. But the justices were, like the
sheriff himself, local squires, not judges coming directly
from the queen and her central courts, so there was not the
same formality or ceremony and the sheriff was usually, in
all probability, represented by the under-sheriff. Over and
over again in the Yorkshire roll, we find such entries as
this, " At this term appeared William Cartwright, gentleman, under-sheriff of Robert Swift, esquire, sheriff of the
county of York, to attend the court in the place of the
sheriff aforesaid." Occasionally there were disputes, some
of the justices ordering the sessions to be held at one town,
the sheriff attending with the remaining justices at another.
In that case the former group begged him at least to
empanel a jury so that they could go on with their work.
The under-sheriff was of course available for many such
duties, but the fuller dignity of the sheriff himself was
desired at all courts.[16]

A quasi-judicial activity of the sheriff was his extensive
work in the service of writs. Generally speaking all writs
issued by the queen's courts at Westminster and by the
justices of assize and of quarter sessions in the counties,
which were very numerous, must be served by the sheriff
or his under-sheriff or bailiffs. To see to the proper return
of these writs each sheriff had an attorney at Westminster
to represent him in each of the three great courts and in
the chancery. His four bailiffs must also be present with
him at assizes and quarter sessions to serve or report the
return of writs. The sheriff did not always perform this

[16] Lambard, *Eirenarcha*, Book iv, c. 3; Lister, *West Riding Sessions Rolls*, 28, 44, 64, 80, 170, 194, 208, etc.;*Cal. Hatfield House MSS.*, iv, 312, 318–9; Wilkinson, 119–20.

work efficiently. Complaints are constant that, influenced by neighborly feeling or family connection, or from fear or indolence, the service of writs was not fulfilled or was resisted or obedience neglected or judgments not followed up. The result was that additional orders, special messengers, the appointment of special commissioners and other devices were made use of that would certainly not have been necessary if the sheriffs had been more efficient or more submissive.[17]

Certain powers of an irregularly judicial nature the sheriff should exercise of his own initiative. When he heard of a riot or an unlawful assembly he must raise the county and apprehend such malefactors, he must arrest " Egyptians," men whom he suspects of being thieves or doing evil of any kind, workmen bearing arms, servants wandering abroad, and recusants. Numberless instances of his performance of this last duty are recorded in the history of the Catholics and of other non-conformist bodies.

On one side the sheriff was occupied with ancient, traditional and local duties, on another side he was, like the justices of the peace, under the constant direction of the newer, more active and aggressive central government. He was very generally addressed along with the justices of the peace by the privy council in their numerous missives requiring some local action. He was frequently required to give his aid to persons holding writs of assistance, in the carrying out of commissions of piracy and other commissions for local action. In cases where the more modern provisions for the military protection of the country were not applicable, the privy council, as will be explained later, fell back on the sheriff as the head of a " commission of musters." Military capacity was one of the considerations in the choice of a suitable sheriff. Burghley in the midst of a long attack of the gout in 1595 writes to his son, " I strained myself to be this day at the chequer with the lord-

---

[17] *Acts of the Privy Council*, xxvi, 29–30, 338; *Cal. State Papers, Dom.*, 1595–7, 31, 413; Wilkinson, 79, 102, 125.

keeper and justices for nomination of men to be sherifs the next yeare, finding great lack of martiall men, though otherwise hable for wealth and knowledge. And so retorning forthwith to my howse, I am laid down with grcat paine, not being hable to sett upp." [18]

One sheriff is ordered to help the justices of the peace of his county to apprehend certain impostors and send them up to be questioned by the privy council; another is called upon by the lord treasurer to seize and hold some goods obtained from pirates; still another reports his efforts to discover the men who had found a " treasure." In the troubled years of dearth all the sheriffs are joined with the justices of the peace in watching over the supply of grain, requiring its sale at a fair price and arresting all those who refuse to conform. The sheriff of Oxfordshire is ordered to bring up to London the rioters of 1596, and the sheriff of Hampshire to prepare for the execution in public and for the putting up placards concerning the seminary priests in the Isle of Wight in 1586; in the same year the sheriff of Somerset is ordered to require master clothiers to set their unemployed spinners to work and to watch over the beacons. In 1589 the sheriff of Oxford on his own account orders the justices of the peace to prevent rioters taking down Maypoles. Instructions are sent down in 1596 to the sheriffs of every county in England to order all public officers having seals to present them on a certain day at the mint in London to have them examined and new ones engraved and given out. Sometimes the sheriff is raised in power above the justices, as in a certain case where the privy council, out of patience with the neglect of the magistrates to obey the proclamations against forestalling, bids the sheriff take their duties out of their hands. It is noticeable also that the sheriff was under the protection of council as " a chief officer of her majesty," and when in one case the sheriff of the county was arrested and sent up to London by the justices of the peace on suspicion of treason he was imme-

[18] Peck, *Desiderata Curiosa*, Ed. 1779, i, 169.

diately released and a rebuke administered to the justices
for their readiness to consider light testimony against an
officer of such great dignity.[19]

Yet, notwithstanding the dignity of the office, it was apparently in most cases an unwelcome honor. We hear of
special charters of exemption from appointment as sheriff
being sought on grounds of physical incompetency or of
other services, and of relief being secured in individual instances through personal influence. Sir Frances Coke writes
to Sir John Coke "to keep my loving neighbor and friend
Edward Revell of Brookhill from being sheriff this year,"
and Roger Manners, who is at court in November, 1582,
writes that "my cousin Francis Leek is by my means escaped." Three petitioners write to Burghley in the same
year, begging for exemption from appointment, Sir W.
Malorye because he "is in every way unmeet for it," Cotton
Gargreaves because he is greatly overburdened with his
father's debts, and Sir George Cary, speaking for his father-
in-law, Sir John Spencer, that he may be relieved from serving as sheriff of Northamptonshire because he has been
sheriff three times, because he wants to live this year in
Warwickshire and because he has many lawsuits in progress.
Somewhat later, in the next reign, a gentleman at court
writes to his friend in the country that "The next news I
heard was that your name was the first of three which were
presented to the king. When laboring to get you off, I
perceived that my lordkeeper distasted you, having resolved
that you should be sheriff. Many journeys I made, yet
find the matter difficult." Later, when bribery had brought
success, he writes, "I have given Mr. M. ten pieces for
the good office he did you, and have taken his promise to
keep you off hereafter for nothing." There was much interest in the yearly appointments and they were sometimes

[19] *Acts of the Privy Council*, vii, 164, xiv, 58, 62, 93, 128, 174, 278–80,
370, xxvi, 12, 67, 73, 81–3, 153, 196, 208, 250, 331, 365, 413, 424, 432; *Cal.
State Papers, Dom.*, 1581–90, 588, 1595–7, 26, 153, 313; Wright, *Queen
Elizabeth and her Times*, i, 441; Wilkinson, 103–5, 117.

delayed past the proper time in the effort to procure a list satisfactory to the sovereign or the council.[20]

Presumably the reluctance to accept service was due to its expense. It is true that the office brought in many fees. A long list of customary payments for the service of writs and the performance of various actions by the sheriff is given in the manuals of the time. But the fees he receives are given in pence or at most in shillings while those that he must pay for induction into his office and for the auditing of his accounts are given for the most part in pounds and only occasionally in shillings. The court fees for his entrance upon and discharge from his office have already been mentioned. The salary of the under-sheriff was a serious item, amounting in one chance recorded case to £352, 18s. 6d. If to these costs is added the expense of the social requirements of his position the comment of a contemporary law writer is doubtless quite justified: " The sheriff is at much charge which is laid out and disbursed during his sheriffwick, as experience will inform him." [21]

[20] *Cal. State Papers, Dom.*, 1595–7, 48, 124; *Hist. MSS. Comm. Rep.*, vii, App. iii–ix, 25, Rep. xii, App. i, 414, App. iv, 144, 145, 155; *Chamberlain's Letters,* Camden Society, 166; *Trevelyan Papers,* Camden Society, iii, 196; *Hatfield House MSS.,* ii, 524, 530.

[21] Wilkinson, 139–48.

CHAPTER XXXIX

THE LORD LIEUTENANT AND HIS DEPUTIES; THE VICE-ADMIRAL; THE CORONER

IN considering the lord lieutenant we must step for a moment outside the circle of that rural gentry from which, as has been seen, county officials as well as so many others engaged in the work of government were drawn. The lord lieutenant was always or almost always a nobleman. His office was a comparatively new one, representing a more centralized monarchy than the more ancient offices of the sheriff and justice of the peace. It is heard of only in few and irregular cases before the middle of the century with which we are dealing. It is however provided for in statutes of 1550, 1555 and 1558; it becomes more usual and more systematic as time goes on until by the end of a decade after the accession of Elizabeth lords lieutenant of the counties are almost as regularly and generally appointed as the older officers of the shires.[1] The events of Elizabeth's reign tended to make the office constantly more conspicuous. The Rebellion of the North in 1569 led to a filling up of the list and a complete distribution of the counties, singly or in groups, among the greater nobles. The earl of Shrewsbury had charge of Derbyshire and Nottinghamshire, the earl of Huntingdon of Lincolnshire and Rutland, the earl of Derby of Lancashire and Cheshire, the earl of Bedford of Devon, Cornwall and Dorset, the earl of Pembroke of Somerset and Wilts; the marquis of Northampton and the earl of Warwick were lords lieutenant of the important

[1] G. W. Prothero, *Select Statutes and other Constitutional Documents*, cxx; E. F. Jackson, *Office and Actions of the Lord Lieutenant*, University of Pennsylvania Ph.D. Thesis, Written 1916, Published 1923; Gladys Scott Thomson, *Lords Lieutenants in the Sixteenth Century*, 1–42.

shires from which they respectively drew their titles; Viscount Hereford was lord lieutenant of Staffordshire, Lord Wentworth of Norfolk and Suffolk, Lord North of Cambridge and Lord Grey of Bucks. In several cases lord lieutenancies and court appointments were combined, as in the case of Lord Buckhurst, who was treasurer of the household and lord lieutenant of Middlesex and Southampton, Lord Hunsdon, who was lord chamberlain and lord lieutenant of Surrey, Lord Clinton, who was lord admiral and lord lieutenant of Lincolnshire. In a few cases the charge of counties was given to men of less than noble rank but distinguished by being already in the direct service of the queen, as in the case of Oxford which was under Sir Francis Knollys and Hertfordshire which was under Ralph Sadler. There was in fact a distinct connection between the group of lords lieutenant and the regular service of the crown, seventeen out of the thirty lords lieutenant being at this time also members of the privy council.

There were, as in the case of the sheriffs, some irregular-, ities. As will be seen, very generally two counties were placed in charge of one lord lieutenant; on the other hand in some cases two or more nobles or gentlemen occupied jointly the lieutenancy of one county, as in the case where Lord Mountjoy and Sir William Paulet were together placed over Dorsetshire. With series of appointments or reappointments of 1569, special letters were sent out urging upon the lords lieutenant the fulfilment of the duties of their office.[2] After this time lord lieutenancies became again less regularly filled. The degree of attention paid to appointments may perhaps be inferred from the list of successive commissions to the earl of Bedford to be lord lieutenant of the three counties of Devon, Cornwall and Dorset; these were dated 1557, 1559, 1567 and 1574. Somewhat later but ten lords lieutenant, the marquis of Winchester, the earls of Leicester, Sussex, Pembroke, Derby, Shrewsbury and Rutland and Lords Hunsdon, Cobham and Howard, held com-

---

[2] Haynes, *Burghley State Papers*, 559–60; *Hatfield House MSS.*, i, 443.

missions and a number of counties had no oversight of this kind. It was evidently not yet felt that every county must have a lord lieutenant, as it had a sheriff or as it had justices of the peace, all the time.[3]

It was not until the inception of the war with Spain that the office of lord lieutenant was given the full importance that it held during the warlike later years of Elizabeth and for a long period afterward. As the disputes with Spain became more intense, in 1584 and again in 1585, the privy council wrote to the lords lieutenant warning them of the queen's urgency " in these times of jelousie " to put the realm in a state of defense. On the seizure of English vessels in the harbors of Spain, May 29, 1585, which may perhaps be considered the first overt act of the Spanish war, the queen immediately issued a warrant to the lord chancellor, the form of which remains to us corrected in her own hand, requiring him to issue a commission under the great seal appointing certain noblemen to the lieutenancies of such counties as had been allowed to lack military governors, and to introduce various changes in their distribution.[4] From this time forward during the next three years, up to the actual approach of the Armada, a constant series of instructions, reminders, requests and suggestions goes from the privy council to the lords lieutenant; and almost equally numerous reports and other communications come up from the counties to the council. A series of sixteen "orders to be observed by all lords lieutenant " is formulated by the privy council, and the replies of the earls of Rutland, Derby and others still exist reporting that they have fulfilled these duties. The death of the earl of Bedford left Dorsetshire unprovided for and the marquis of Winchester was immediately given charge of it, in addition to Hampshire. The approach of the Armada led to a still more complete military organization and after that cam-

---

[3] *State Papers, Dom., Eliz.,* clxxix, 46, 52, 58.

[4] *Cal. State Papers, Dom.,* 1581–90, 169, 243, 248–9; *State Papers, Dom., Eliz.,* clxxix, 47, 52, 53; *Acts of the Privy Council,* xiv, 199, xvi, 14–5.

paign the privy council sends a special letter of thanks to all the lords lieutenant for the great care they have taken in the public service committed to their charge.[5]

It is evident that by this time a form of commission to a lord lieutenant had been established as familiar as that to the justice of the peace or the sheriff. In an Elizabethan patent roll a model commission of lieutenancy is already given under the date 1585. A commission given to the marquis of Winchester and the earl of Sussex to be joint lords lieutenant of Hampshire, dated June 15, 1585, corresponds almost exactly to this form, and a few years afterward we hear of the keeper of the great seal sending to the clerk of the crown for a copy of the usual lord lieutenant's commission in order to make a new appointment. Commissions given to Lord North for Cambridge and the Isle of Ely and to the earl of Hertford for Somerset and Wilts are practically identical in wording with these. The general duties of the office were evidently by this time well established. More specific instructions were issued in March, 1590, and these were still further defined and the commissions renewed at the time of the threatened attack of the Spaniards and their momentary success in ravaging part of the coast of Cornwall in the summer of 1595. The queen ordered the council to look into the whole condition of the lord lieutenancy in July and August of this year. The investigation showed that twenty-nine counties were at that time under seventeen lords lieutenant. It was even more exclusively a body of noblemen than in the early years of the reign, the only lieutenants who were not noblemen being Sir Walter Raleigh, lord lieutenant of Cornwall, and Sir Francis Knollys who was joined with Lord Norris in the lieutenancy of Oxford. Since there were at this time in England only one marquis, nineteen earls, two viscounts and forty-one barons, one quarter of Elizabeth's nobility were in service in this capacity. Some of them had wide spheres of control, the earl of Huntingdon having the lieutenancy of the three northernmost shires and two in the midlands, the earl of Pembroke having Somerset, Wiltshire and three shires on the Welsh frontier, while Burghley had Essex, Hertford and Lincoln, and Howard, Surrey and Sussex. There was the same close connection with the council already spoken of, nine of the seventeen lords lieutenant, and those the most powerful, being members of the privy council.[6]

Notwithstanding this careful arrangement, however, there were, three years later, eight counties without lords lieutenant. In several cases the incumbent had died and no successor was immediately appointed. It is just possible that this avoidance of regular appointment was intended to prevent the growth of an ancestral, almost an hereditary claim on the office, a shadowy revival of hereditary ealdormanships, sheriffdoms and other local governorships of a long past period. The Stanleys, earls of Derby, for instance, were lords lieutenant of Lancashire and Cheshire for several generations. Lord Chandos in 1595 claimed that no one not an ancestor of his had ever occupied the lieutenancy of Gloucester, and protested against his rumored removal from the office. The earl of Bath was appointed lord lieutenant of Devonshire in succession to his father, although he was a mere boy and his duties had to devolve upon others.[7]

During such an interim the queen and privy council fell back on earlier custom and imposed on the sheriff and a group of carefully selected gentry of the county, under the name " commissioners of musters," the duties that otherwise would have been placed in the hands of the lord lieutenant. This practice was regularized by the grant from the queen

---

[6] Prothero, *Select Statutes*, Ed. 2, 156–8; *Cal. Hatfield House MSS.*, v, 382, 523; *State Papers, Dom., Eliz.*, cclxxxiii (a) 85, *Add.* xxiv, 49; Thomson, Appendix B.; Lodge, *Illustrations of English History*, ii, 104–11.

[7] *Cal. Hatfield House MSS.*, v, 340; *Lancashire Lieutenancies*, i, 16; *Acts of the Privy Council*, xiv, 243.

on the 28th of August 1595 of a commission to the members.of the privy council in case of a vacancy in the lieutenancy of any county to appoint the sheriff and some gentlemen of the county to exercise for a year all the powers of a lord lieutenant. This commission was renewed the next December a year and frequently made use of by the council. It is evident that the duties of the lord lieutenant had become so insistent that no actual vacancy could be allowed, even if the exigencies of personal claim made some delay desirable. It is possible also that the crown disliked the grant of such extensive powers to an individual and was seeking some other means of having the necessary work accomplished. Once appointed no hereditary claim or dignity gave any authority to an Elizabethan official as against the over-mastering power of the queen and council. The lord lieutenant was as apt to receive positive orders and as bound to fulfil the duties of his commission and to perform the instructions sent down to him by the council as were the justices of the peace and the sheriff.[8]

A description of the military system of which the lords lieutenants were by their commissions and instructions placed in principal charge will be postponed for the moment until their assistants and some other phases of their duties are described. In carrying out his duties the lord lieutenant was given the assistance of a small group of deputy lieutenants. This practice probably arose from the fact that the lord lieutenant was in many cases a privy councillor or otherwise in the direct service of the crown so that he could not be expected to be continually in his county. His actual duties must therefore often be performed for him by gentlemen of the locality. At one time an attempt was made to require the lord lieutenant to spend nine months of the year in his shire, just as the sheriff must spend the whole year of his service, but this was given up. There is, however, no mention of deputy lieutenants earlier than 1585 and it is not unlikely that their appointment began with the

[8] *Lancashire Lieutenancies,* ii, 104–11; Thomson, 69–72.

more thorough organization of the lord lieutenancy in that and the immediately succeeding years. Before the end of the queen's reign it was judicially decided that there must be at least two deputy lieutenants in each county. Usually there were more. Under the ten lords lieutenant in office in 1585 there were thirty-six deputy lieutenants. In 1587 Sir R. Jermyn and six others were deputies under Lord Hunsdon in Suffolk. In 1590 there were four under Sir Christopher Hatton, lord lieutenant of Northamptonshire. Sometimes at the request of the lord lieutenant or on the petition of those already appointed the usual number was increased to meet increasing demands on their time and labor. There seem to have been altogether in the fifty-two counties of England and Wales about the middle of this period some two hundred deputy lieutenants.[9]

With the deputy lieutenants we return to the familiar class of the rural gentry, although they were almost always knights, perhaps a reflection of their prevailingly military duties. However a country gentleman was frequently at the same time a deputy lieutenant and a justice of the peace, sometimes a deputy lieutenant and sheriff. A more nearly typical case is that of Sir George Trenchard, deputy lieutenant of Dorsetshire, made sheriff in 1596 and relieved for the time of his military duties, "that he may the better attend to the charge of his office of Shryvalty.[10] Although the deputy lieutenants were under the orders of the lord lieutenant and serving as his assistants and must frequently have been nominated by him, their names appeared in the lord lieutenant's commission by direct appointment of the queen, and their powers and duties were defined in the same commission. Further commissions were often given by the lord lieutenant to his deputy lieutenants. When Burghley was made lord lieutenant of Hertfordshire in 1587, for instance, he issued commissions to his four deputy lieuten-

[9] Hawarde, *Cases*, 116; *Rushbrook Parish Register*, 215.
[10] *Acts of the Privy Council*, xxvi, 367; *Lancashire Lieutenancies*, i, 3 n., 38 n., 45 n., 53 n., ii, 107, etc.

ants of that shire; when in 1590 Essex and, later in the same year, Lincoln was added to his charge, he gave commissions in the one case to two deputies, Sir Thomas Mildmay and Sir John Petre, in the other to four, and divided the charge of the shire between them. In 1590 when Sir Christopher Hatton was made lord lieutenant of Northamptonshire, he appointed Sir Thomas Cecil, Sir Richard Knightly, Sir Edward Montague and Sir George Farmer, whose names were already in his commission, to be his deputies.

On the death of a lord lieutenant it was his late deputy lieutenants who were habitually joined with the sheriff of the shire as commissioners of musters and who took over all his powers until a new lord lieutenant was appointed. The privy council frequently communicated directly with the deputy lieutenants, receiving reports from them, giving them instructions and answering questions which they had raised. The three deputy lieutenants of Dorset in 1587, for instance, certify that there are 3220 armed men in the shire, and those of Essex that there are 12,000 men able for military duties in their shire; those of Norfolk ask for relief for the citizens of Norwich from certain restrictions, in order that they may perform their military duties more effectually; the deputy lieutenants of Northamptonshire receive as an answer to their request of September 17, 1595, that the musters be postponed until spring, on account of the lateness of the season, that it is probable " there will be the usual Michaelmas summer to serve the purpose." [11]

A set of orders issued by the lord lieutenant of one county to his deputy lieutenants in 1590 well sums up their duties. They must muster the able men of the shire, select the

[11] Prothero, *Select Statutes,* 155; Hawarde, *Cases,* 116; *Acts of the Privy Council,* vii, 360, 371; xiv, 40, 181, 200, xxvi, 52, 123, 358; *State Papers, Dom., Eliz.,* clxxix, 17, cclxxxiii, 85, Addenda xxxiv, 49; *Hatfield House MSS.,* v, 381, 403; *Hist. MSS. Comm., Papers of the Duke of Buccleugh and Queensberry at Montague House,* 226; *Cal. State Papers, Dom.,* 1581-90, 306, 307, 436, 441, 447, 1595-7, 124.

soldiers for the trained bands, list all armor, weapons, etc., "as well private as common," see to the supply of powder, bullets and slow match, compel all gentlemen of good living to furnish horsemen, require captains of lances and light horse to muster their bands at least once a quarter, see that all these horsemen have cloaks of the same color, pay attention to fire-arms, keep up the beacons, select and oversee captains of the trained bands, and see that no officers or members of these bands leave their parishes or shires without permission. The soldiers often refused to carry their arms and armor to the place of training, so that the constables and owners of armor were forced to carry it in carts or in sacks on horseback and much of it was bruised or broken. The deputy lieutenants were in this document authorized to offer them in addition to the eighteen pence a day wages during training, a penny a mile to carry their own armor. Recurrent threats of invasion by the Spaniards and frequent calls for the levy of troops to be sent abroad between 1585 and 1603 made the position of the deputy lieutenants a busy as well as a responsible and honorable one, and there is scarcely any group of documents more familiar in the period than those connected with their office and activities. The more technical parts of their work as time passed came to be performed by muster masters and the provost marshal.[12]

The provost marshal for the county, though provided for in the lord lieutenant's commission and occasionally mentioned as actually in existence, seems to have played but a small part until from 1589 onward the discharged soldiers returning from the expeditions to France, the Netherlands and Ireland, began to become a disorderly element in the community. The queen insists repeatedly on the appointment of provost marshals, especially for the counties near London and the court, not so much for the trial of soldiers

---

[12] *Cal. Hatfield House MSS.*, iii, 297; *State Papers, Dom., Eliz.*, ccxxi, 47; *Hist. MSS. Comm., 15 Rep., App.* 7, 2–54; Grose, *Military Antiquities*, 79–80.

committing crimes when in actual service, as was the primary intent of the office, as for the punishment of vagrants, pretended soldiers and other wandering ill-doers who might in some way be brought under martial law and thus punished, as has been already explained, more expeditiously and more severely than was practicable under common or earlier statute law. The muster masters are rather employees than officials.[13]

So far in this discussion the duties attributed to the lord lieutenant, his deputies and other assistants have been of a military character, and probably all the others sprang from the same origin, though their connection was in some cases a remote one. When the lord lieutenant of a county was ordered by the council to find out what gentlemen of the county were maintaining their sons abroad as Catholics, and other matters of recusancy, it was doubtless suggested by the military dangers from the Catholics. When they were required in 1600 to collect ship money it was presumably because this was considered a form of military expenditure. Their duty to enforce the observance of Lent, set fair prices for corn and make out lists of those who should lend money to the queen on privy seals can have had but little military significance, unless possibly the loans were always looked upon as being for military defense, as indeed during this period of threatened attack all taxation was so excused. The responsibility of the lords lieutenant in connection with privy seals has been discussed under the head of parliamentary finance. It may simply be observed here how convenient it must have been to collect such loans through appointed administrative officials, independent of the meetings and claims of parliament.[14]

Much more characteristic, however, are the instructions

---

[13] Prothero, *Select Statutes*, 155; *Hist. MSS. Comm., 14 Rep.*, App. vii, 4, 5.

[14] *Cal. Hatfield House MSS.*, iv, 12, 52, 449; *Cal. State Papers, Dom.*, 1598–1601, 406; *State Papers, Dom., Eliz.*, ccxxii, 128; Strype, *Annals*, iii, pt. 2, 40; *Papers of Sir Nathaniel Bacon, Camden Soc.*, 95–106.

to the lieutenants and their deputies, spread all over the records, for the muster of the men of their shires, the levying of troops to be sent abroad, the purchase of pikes and corselets, the watching of the beacons and the other military duties of the period. According to the lord lieutenant's commission he must put his county into the best condition of military defense he could and keep it so. For this purpose he had authority to call together all persons in his county fit for military service, arm them, drill them, lead them against rebels or invading enemies, "subdue, slay, kill and put to execution of death" his opponents, "to use the law called the martial law," and to appoint a provost marshal as a sort of sheriff to execute its mandates. He could in case of rebellion or invasion go outside of his county to any place in England to resist the queen's enemies. All other local officers were required to obey and assist him.

In the fulfilment of these services he took the leading part in the somewhat cumbrous military system of the period. He was in the first place to find out by inquiry or "muster," that is a show or trial, how many men between the ages of sixteen and sixty fit to perform any kind of military duty were in his county. The returns from these inquiries, notwithstanding their frequency and the detailed exactitude insisted upon by the queen and privy council are even more unsatisfactory than most Tudor statistics. The totals varied enormously. One made almost in the middle of Elizabeth's reign gives a total of men of military age for all England of 589,981, another somewhat later, of 182,929, still another 158,509. Probably the terms were used in different senses at different times. Though there seems no possibility of discovering the correct number of men of military age in the whole country, local reports are more satisfactory. In one of the six divisions of Wiltshire there were 3698 "young striplings" below military age, 3676 "able men" from 18 to 50, 1316 "old men" above 50. In Lancashire there were reported to be just 6000 men of military age, though the even figure suggests approximation rather than exactitude.[15]

There were to be selected, in the next place, from this total a " convenient number " of men fit for training; they were to be arranged in companies, sufficient armor and equipment provided for them, captains and lieutenants selected from the local gentry, and they were to be put through a considerable amount of military drill. These were the trained bands or militia of the time. What purports to be a list of the militia of all England gives about 12,000; another list gives 9672. In 1577 Lancashire had 300 in its trained bands; ten years later it had 600.[16]

It will be remembered that the lord lieutenant was authorized by his commission to appoint suitably trained officers to act as organizers and drill masters for the militia. These " muster masters," as they were called, were as a matter of fact usually appointed, like the deputy lieutenants, by the queen or privy council. Captains returning from service in the Netherlands or France are constantly being sent down into the counties with letters directing the lieutenants or deputy lieutenants or justices of the peace to take them into their service as muster masters. Sometimes the local officials, confident in their own powers and anxious to avoid expense, try to resist this intrusion, but the council is pressing and they have to yield. By 1595 the system seems thoroughly established. Essex in a memorial to the queen in that year recommends that muster masters be sent down into all the counties to see the people armed and trained. In September, at the queen's special commandment, a list of captains was made out and they were sent as muster masters to every county with orders to the lords lieutenant to establish them in their positions and to procure for them payment of their traveling expenses and a

---

[15] *State Papers, Dom., Eliz.*, clxxix, 17, cclxxxiii (a), 85, *Add.* xxxiv, 49; Peck, *Desiderata Curiosa*, Ed. 1779, 75; Grose, *Military Antiquities*, ii, Appendix. Baines, *Hist of Lancashire*, i, 522.

[16] *Lancashire Lieutenancies*, i, 32, 91–2, ii, 98, 184; Peck, 75–7.

suitable monthly salary. Even the details of how much powder was to be used by the men with calivers or muskets, how every man should be taught to handle his piece, how large the bolts should be and how long the range for archers at their practice were defined by privy council.[17]

After the trained bands had been selected out, the remainder of the able men of the county, or as many of them as practicable, were supposed to be grouped into companies, called out four times a year, furnished for the time with arms and subjected to some slight training. In times of threatened invasion the equipment and drill of these " able men " was taken more seriously. In Lancashire, for instance, at the close of the reign, although the trained bands numbered only 600, there were in the county 3585 men organized and furnished with arms, besides 2415 not furnished with arms. In Devonshire, in 1586, where there were 400 militia, 2000 men were ordered to be armed and trained " or more if there be arms." The next year, in the shadow of the approaching Armada, the county was required to respond to a possible demand for 4000 men, and in 1598 the lord lieutenant ordered that there should be six regiments of 900 serviceable men each, a total of more than 5000 men. In 1595 there were 1500 in the trained bands of Hertfordshire, and altogether in that county 4000 men with some degree of organization.[18]

These trained bands and occasionally mustered men were all footmen. It was the duty of the lords lieutenant or commissioners of musters to list the gentry of the county and to require them either voluntarily or as a result of assignment each to agree to keep ready and to send to musters or to provide for needed service one or more horsemen mounted and armed. The gentry were also very gen-

---

[17] *Cal. State Papers, Dom.,* 1581–90, 256, 1595–7, 99, 325, 399, 1598–1601, 355; *Additional,* 1580–1625, 382. *Cal. Hatfield House MSS.,* v, 523; *Hist. MSS. Comm., Kenyon Papers,* 14 Rep., App. iv, 593–4; Birch, *Memorials,* i, 293.

[18] *Cal. State Papers, Dom.,* 1595–7, 124, 134.

erally required to have on hand a certain amount of equipment for the footmen of the shire, besides that which was kept in stock in public possession either in certain storehouses of the county or by the constables of the parishes.

In addition to the regulation of this, which might be called the defensive force of each county, it will have been seen from our previous narrative that from time to time orders came down to the county officials from the privy council to levy, arm, equip and hand over to appointed officers special bodies of men intended to be sent to Ireland or the Netherlands or France for some one of the frequently recurring campaigns in those countries. In making up such troops it was usually required that the trained bands be left intact, although there are instances where as a matter of special concession some of these well drilled soldiers were allowed to be sent away. In each such case a levy was made of its proper proportion of the musketeers or archers or billmen or pioneers, as the case might be, on each hundred in the county and, within the hundreds, on each parish. The willingness or unwillingness of the men to go was regarded but little, sometimes not at all. Conscription was frequent, the exigencies of the government allowing but small consideration to private objections, and compulsion being a perfectly familiar practice of the time in most spheres of life.[19]

Much of this military procedure was merely a perpetuation of the old " assize of arms " under somewhat new conditions. It is not a matter of surprise therefore that the sheriff and justices of the peace, the older officials, were frequently given concurrent military responsibility with the lord lieutenant. Indeed the long and detailed order for mustering and training the people sent out by the privy council in 1572 makes no special mention of the lord lieutenant, all the provisions for its enforcement being placed

---

[19] Peck, *Desiderata Curiosa*, 76; *Lancashire Lieutenancies*, i, 34–61, 62, ii, 188; *Cal. Hatfield House MSS.*, v, 262; *Duke of Somerset MSS., Hist. MSS, Comm.*, *15 Rep., App.* vii, 3, 26, 37, 51–3, 55.

in the hands of the justices of the peace acting as commissioners of array. Not only were orders for special musters, levies and provision of equipment frequently issued jointly to all the shire officers but even the prelates were given military responsibilities. From 1585 onwards the higher clergy were required by the queen to provide or equip a certain number of horsemen; letters for this purpose were usually sent directly from the privy council to each bishop defining the number for which he was to be responsible or calling upon him for the payment of £25 apiece to provide them.[20]

But this mixture of functions became less as the period progressed. The increase of the control of the lord lieutenant and his deputies over military matters as distinguished from the military activity of other county officers is clearly recognizable. The succession of expeditions of attack sent out of the country, the recurring threats of invasion by the Spaniards, and the rising danger in Ireland made constantly more need for perfecting means of internal defense and gave constantly more frequent occasion for equipping bodies of troops for service outside of England. The officers whose duties were more purely military became consequently more prominent. The regularity of appointment of the lieutenants or their substitutes in the later years of Elizabeth has already been noted. After 1595 they and their deputies are much more in evidence than at any earlier period. In 1596 the number of deputy lieutenants is increased in several of the counties and from that time onward the instructions from the privy council to both the lieutenants and deputy lieutenants are especially detailed.[21]

In this outline account of the local military system under Queen Elizabeth it remains to discuss its financial aspect. There is absolutely no clear division of expense between

[20] Grose, *Military Antiquities*, Ed. 1801, 12–19, 79–90; Peck, *Desiderata Curiosa*, Ed. 1779, i, 153, 155, 160–2.
[21] *Acts of the Privy Council*, xxvi, 474, etc.; *Cal. State Papers, Dom.*, 1581–90, 441, etc.; Thomson, 84–116.

the central and the local government. Generally speaking the keeping of the local militia should have been at local expense and its use for offensive or distant defensive purposes at the expense of the crown. As a matter of practice taxes are constantly being imposed in the counties, hundreds and parishes for military purposes and demanded by local authorities indiscriminately for local and national uses. Instances are numerous. In 1592 the earl of Derby, lord lieutenant of the county of Lancashire, with the agreement of the justices of the peace orders a general taxation of £26 to be laid upon the shire for the expense of providing arms and weapons, for the repair and watching of the beacons, and for the equipment of " 600 trained and 700 selected soldiers " for the queen's service on the Scotch borders and in Ireland. In the Armada summer of 1588, one of the hundreds in Lincolnshire is required to tax its sixteen townships £5 9s. 4d. for watching the ancient beacon on Riven Pike for 82 days, certainly a local duty; at another time four parishes in the same county with their thirteen included townships are taxed by the deputy lieutenants £48 18s. 11d. for the expenses of the eleven soldiers which were their quota of a levy of 200 for service in Ireland, certainly an external service. The people probably recognized little distinction in the nature of their military burdens. The lord lieutenant and deputy lieutenants of Devonshire complained to the privy council that for the eight months between March and November, 1596, they had been required to spend £7,743, 6s. 9d. for military purposes. This fell upon the whole population. At another time in another county three hundred and fifty-eight nobleman, knights, ladies, and well-to-do yeomen were required each to furnish for military use a certain amount of armor, a corselet, a steel cap, a caliver, a pike, a long bow, a sheaf of arrows or some number or combination of these accoutrements, besides the armed horsemen which the more wealthy of them had to provide.[22]

[22] *Kenyon MSS., 14 Rep. Hist. MSS. Comm.*, App. iv, 583–4, *MSS. of Duke of Somerset, Ib.* 15 Rep., App. vii, 27; *Lancashire Lieutenancies*, i, 34–57, ii, 147, 208; Grose, *Military Antiquities*, i, 88.

When the practice of appointing skilled muster masters to assist the deputy lieutenants in the drilling of the trained bands was introduced it was apparently the intention of the crown to bear the whole weight of the expense itself. In 1585, £700 was set apart by queen and council for this purpose and some £600 was spent in the next two years. Late in the year 1587, £500 is drawn from the exchequer to pay captains for this work. In the same year Ralegh with his usual good sense suggests that the expenses of training be divided, the queen contributing one half, the county one half, and a short time afterward a part at least of the expense is imposed upon the localities. Within the next year the counties are required to provide at their own expense experienced muster masters, and there are numerous local complaints of the burdensomeness of the charge. The privy council generally defined the amount of their wages, ordering the county authorities to see that twenty pounds or some such sum yearly is paid to them. Yet as late as 1596 the queen herself agrees to pay twenty-six captains six shillings a day for a month to drill the trained bands and twenty-seven are similarly engaged the next year.[23]

" Coat and conduct money " was a customary payment by the crown for the cost of uniforms and the transport of soldiers when they were levied for service outside of their counties, and for their support until they entered regularly into the pay of the crown at their place of rendezvous. But the queen's allowance of coat money was only four shillings a man, while it was estimated in 1590 that it cost on the average 14s. 10d., leaving the county to provide more than 10s. for the cost of equipping each man. At one time the queen offers to various lords lieutenant good coats made for the soldiers at London for 12 shillings apiece, of which she would pay four shillings, the other eight to be paid by the respective counties from which the soldiers came. At another time the estimate of what the queen will pay is only

[23] *Acts of the Privy Council*, xiv, 372–3, 378, 382, etc.; *Cal. State Papers, Dom.*, 1581–90, 444, 467; Thomson, 109.

three shillings for each coat though four shillings is spoken of as the " ancient rate." [24]

As time progressed and the state of war became a more settled one, and as the financial condition of the central government became worse, the costs of equipment were more and more regularly imposed on localities and individuals. A government engaged in a long war can appeal constantly more vigorously to the patriotism and the instinct of self preservation of its people, and when parliaments were infrequent this meant direct local contributions of men, equipment and money for military expenses. Moreover it probably made little difference to the country gentry who controlled these local arrangements whether the expenses of the war were met by the direct contributions of themselves and their neighbors, or indirectly through loans on privy seal and subsidies which they had to pay to the queen for the same purposes. Whatever opinion may have been, before the end of Elizabeth's reign practically the whole expense of the defensive military force and much of that, of equipment of expeditions going abroad was provided through local levy of funds by local officers.

The regular allowance for conduct money was a half penny per mile, which was considered " marvelous little," by one of the queen's commanders in 1589. As the distance to the sea-side or other point where the troops were ordered to assemble of course varied the total sums required were different. Two shillings and sixpence and other sums up to five or even eight shillings per man are mentioned. The payment of conduct money by the crown practically amounted to taking soldiers into the royal service as soon as they were levied, although, as twelve miles was a common limit of a day's march, the allowance would only be sixpence a day instead of the usual wages of soldiers, which were at this time eightpence a day. Both coat and conduct money were usually paid in the first place by the county

[24] *Acts of the Privy Council,* xxi, 222, 307, 308, etc.; *Cal. State Papers, Dom.,* 1581–90, 16, 1591–4, 76, 245, 265, 362.

officers, then the agreed upon amount reimbursed to them, when it was reimbursed at all, by collectors of loans, port officers or other officials of the exchequer. This still left to the crown the cost of transport abroad, the food, wages and cost of returning the surviving troops to their homes, but in these expenses no question arises of local expenditure.[25]

The uniform of troops was still in an embryonic stage, though there are numerous instances of its use. The privy council in sending an order to the county authorities of Berkshire in 1581 to prepare troops for Ireland uses a figure of speech that might well have had only too literal a meaning to the soldiers, considering how few ever returned from an Irish campaign. They were required to provide for the troops levied in their county " coates of some dark, sadde colour, as russett or such like, and not of so light colour as blewe and redd, which heretofore hath commonly been used." Troops to be sent from Cheshire to Ireland three years later were ordered to be clad in " a cassocke of some motley or other sadd grene collor, or russett." A body of archers from Lancashire were furnished with coats of blue cloth, faced with white. Cavalry to be sent to the Low Counties were ordered to be " furnished with cassocks or redd clokes, lined, without sleeves and of length to the knee." Another body of troops were to have red coats made " Galonie fashione tyed under the armes with white ducke or tape." In Devonshire the coats of horsemen were to be " red of colour." There was already a tendency to use red as a military color, a practice explained by a contemporary continental writer as intended to prevent the soldiers being discouraged by the sight of blood from their wounds upon their clothes, a suggestion which could hardly have been based upon observation of blood spots. But troops of different counties and even of the same county at various times differed completely in the color and design

[25] *Cal. State Papers, Dom.*, 1581-90, 524, 525, 620, 621, 623, 1591-4, 21-7, 31, 52, 60, 76, 78, 116, 198, 362, 547.

of their clothing. An approximate uniformity in one particular band at one particular time is all that existed and this not at all invariably.[26]

In each of the counties bordering on the sea was a quasi-royal officer whose name would indicate a military or naval office but whose functions in fact were mainly financial and judicial. This was the vice-admiral. His appointment came not directly from the crown but from the lord admiral, and his commission was not under the great seal but under the seal of the admiralty. He was either a courtier friend of the lord admiral or a local magnate or a country gentleman of the same class as the greater number of the county officers. At the time of the Armada Lord Hunsdon was vice-admiral of Hampshire; during the closing years of the century Lord Cobham, and then Sir Edward Hobby, nephew of Burghley, were vice-admirals of Kent; the earl of Derby was vice-admiral of Lancashire, Sir Edward Winter of Somerset, Sir John Stanhope of Yorkshire. Sir Walter Ralegh was vice-admiral of Devonshire during the long period from 1585 to 1600, as his father had been before him in the early part of Elizabeth's reign. Frequently these vice-admirals acted through deputies or sublet their offices, and sometimes the lord admiral retained one or more counties in his own hands, himself appointing a deputy. There were the usual exceptions to regularity, two counties being placed under one vice-admiral, two or more men being joined in one vice-admiralty or a part of the coast, not a whole county, being placed under one vice-admiral. The office was not an old one, scarcely older than that of lord lieutenant, having been instituted, apparently, in 1525. It was, however, destined to last for three centuries. The admiral seems usually to have granted the office for life, although sometimes only during pleasure. Each vice-admiral had a court analogous to the court of the judge of

[26] *Lancashire Lieutenancies*, i, 23, 67, ii, 121; Peck, *Desiderata Curiosa*, 156; *Cal. State Papers, Dom.*, 1581–90, 621; Julius Ferretus, quoted in Grose, *Military Antiquities*, Ed. 1601, i, 326–7.

the admiralty, to which litigants could appeal. These courts were, like their great representative at London, usually presided over by a doctor of the civil law. The great object of the appointment of vice-admirals was the collection of wreck, salvage and other perquisites granted to the lord admiral by his patent, and the settlement locally of disputes connected with them. The vice-admiral usually received half of these profits, turning over the other half to the lord admiral through the judge of the admiralty.[27]

Although the vice-admiral was directly an officer of the lord admiral, not of the crown, the queen and the privy council had no hesitation in giving him direct orders and imposing upon him duties exactly analogous to those performed by officials directly appointed. Early in Elizabeth's reign, as one step in the long continued struggle against pirates which has been traced in an earlier chapter of this book, letters were sent to the vice-admirals of all the western counties calling attention to the numerous piracies recently reported, to the fact that many suspected men had been arrested but none executed, and ordering them with other persons named to hold sessions of oyer and terminer for the trial of pirates and cause the guilty to be executed "upon sum cliffes nere to the sea side, to the example of others that shall presume hereafter to commytt the like."

When the general issue of letters of reprisal of 1586 was determined upon the duties required of the vice-admirals were set down by the lord admiral, put into print by the queen's printer and sent down to them for execution. They are ordered by the privy council from time to time both before and after that date to stay pirates and give information concerning them, to forbid men to go to sea in warlike manner, to stay all ships arriving in their harbors until it shall be seen whether they will be needed for naval pur-

[27] R. G. Marsden, *The Vice Admirals of the Coast*, English Historical *Review*, xxii (1907), 473, 474–5, 477, xxiii (1908), 736–52; *Names of all the Vice Admirals in England*, Cal. State Papers, Dom., Eliz., 1581–90, 427, 437; *Cal. Hatfield House MSS.*, iii, 222; *Statutes and Ordinances for All Vice-Admirals of the Coast*, Cal. State Papers, Dom., Eliz., 1598–1601, 515.

'poses, to impress seamen, to enforce embargo, to see that prizes are not unloaded until an inventory is made of their cargo, and to do a hundred other general and specific services connected with maritime control.[28]

Various and ill-defined as were the duties of most county officers, of one they were simple enough. This was the coroner. Although his full title, *custos placitorum coronae* suggested a broader field, his usual functions had already settled down to the one duty of investigating sudden deaths and binding over for trial persons strongly suspected by the jury to have been responsible for the death. The number of coroners in a county varied. In some there were as many as six, in others four, in still others two and frequently only one. Bacon speaks of them as regularly two. He says "two other officers there are in every county called coroners, by inquest to inquire concerning violent deaths." They were of the class of gentry though probably not from among its most distinguished representatives; no instance has been met in the records of this period of a knight filling the office of coroner. He was, as already remarked, elected by the freeholders of the county court, and was therefore in a certain sense more purely representative of the locality than the appointive county officials.[29] He took a traditional form of oath administered by the county clerk. There seems to have been no definite period for which the coroner was elected. The probability is that the office was accepted with reluctance and laid down when opportunity offered. It was nevertheless an office of some dignity and prominence. The coroner's power to swear in a jury, to take the depositions in writing of sworn witnesses, to require the attendance both of witnesses and jurors, to bind over any person suspected of complicity and to pronounce judgments of outlawry, were powers of no mean extent and distinction.

[28] *Acts of the Privy Council*, vii, 141, 181, 182, 312, 374, xiv, 54, 203, xxvi, 55, 196; *Cal. State Papers, Dom., Eliz.*, 1581–90, 312; Marsden, *Eng. Hist. Review*, xxii, 475; Chap. XXIII.

[29] Greenwood, 258; Sir Francis Bacon, Ed. Spedding, 1892, vii, 780.

There was apparently much occasion for the activity of the coroners and their juries of inquest. The frequency of murders and fatal affrays in this period has already been adverted to. Deaths by misadventure were not unusual, infanticide of base-born children sadly familiar, fatal outcome of the " pining sickness," a constant result of sojourn in the jails. The verdict of the coroner's jury varied correspondingly from murder to " divine visitation." For each case of indictment for murder following on a coroner's inquest the coroner received by law a fee of thirteen shillings fourpence payable from the slayer's goods, if convicted and if he possessed any; if not from the township which was responsible for his escape. Otherwise there is no record of fees being payable, and the coroner therefore, like the other county officers, probably served as a matter of public duty. In a few cases the coroner had other duties. In case a protest was made and sustained against the fairness of the sheriff in drawing a jury, upon the coroner devolved the duty of returning a new jury, and in case of certain other malfeasance of the sheriff, the coroner was required to execute the writs of the queen and courts in his place. As a result of the fact that he was elected not appointed, he was the only county officer whose term of office did not terminate with the death of the sovereign.[30]

It might seem that the connection between the central government and the government of the county was made sufficiently close and effective by the constant instructions sent by letter and messenger to the justices of the peace, sheriff and other local officials, and by the commissions which were so frequently issued to gentlemen in the county for the performance of special duties. There was, however, one other and more personal means of influence. This was through the justices of assize. Twice a year two judges or other immediate appointees of the crown were sent into every county of England and Wales to hold court

[30] Jeaffreson, *Middlesex Co. Records,* i, xliii–xlvii, 1–6, 13, 47, 127, 137, 171–2, 176, etc.; 3 Henry VII, c. 2; 1 Henry VIII, c. 7.

at the county seat and incidentally to exercise a supervision over local affairs. When the twelve judges finished up the work of Hilary term in the middle of February and again at the end of Trinity term they were divided into couples, or in some cases one was provided with a serjeant of the law as a companion, and they went, in the words of the lord keeper of the great seal, as he gave them their charge in June 1599, " to traverse all the realm in their several circuits for the common justice of the realm." [31]

During Lent therefore and for some weeks of the long vacation in June and July the judges were administering the law not at Westminster but in the various counties of their respective circuits. There were six circuits, the Home circuit, including Middlesex, Kent, Essex, Surrey and Sussex, the Midland, Western, Northern and what was often called the Oxford circuit, including that shire and the seven lying to the westward of it. Wales was reorganized in the middle of Elizabeth's reign into four separate circuits under special justices. The judges were allowed a certain amount of freedom in their choice of circuits. It was not considered seemly for a judge to go into the county in which his own home lay, and unpleasant experiences of one kind or another sometimes led to the avoidance of a particular sphere of action, as when Judge Yelverton changed his circuit after a humiliating altercation with the President of the Council of the North in Yorkshire. Circuits were deliberately changed sometimes by the council to prevent personal rulings on the part of the judges.[32] There were, as in the case of other offices, some irregularities, some of the judges being occasionally retained in London for one reason or another, while other legal officials were, as already indicated, specially appointed to go on circuit with judicial powers. After the rising of the earl of Essex in 1601 all the justices were held back for some

---

[31] Hawarde, *Cases,* 100.
[32] *Acts of the Privy Council,* xiv, 5–6, xxx, 785; 18 Eliz., c. 8; *Chamberlain's Letters,* 152.

time from their circuits. Into the Northern circuit the judges went but once a year. There were instances where only one judge was sent and others where there were apparently three. The queen sometimes interested herself in the choice and distribution of the judges of assize and regularly instructed her councillors to give them special directions as to their duties in their circuits. Each group of justices took with them four commissions. That from which they took their name, the commission for granting assizes, was now but seldom made use of. The *nisi prius* commission gave them charge of certain civil suits. But their greatest duties were those provided for by their commissions of oyer and terminer and of gaol delivery. In 1595 a custom was reintroduced, after it had passed out of use for some time, of holding a meeting in Star Chamber on the last day of its Hilary and Trinity sessions at which the judges who were about to be sent on their circuits, such justices of the peace as were in the vicinity of the court and a considerable number of ministers and others were present to listen to a speech from the lord chancellor or lord keeper, often relating what the queen had given him in direct charge to say. The justices were required not only to perform their strictly judicial functions but to see that various old laws were enforced, that rogues, vagrants, idle persons and those who " made profession to live by their swords and by their wit " were punished, that wine and ale houses were kept in order, that slanders and libels were repressed, that excess of apparel on the part of the wives and daughters of all classes in town and country were restrained, as being a waste of their patrimony and " a pestilent Canker in the commonwealthe, the Confusyon of all degrees." [33] The ever-repeated requirement that no animals should be killed and no meat eaten in Lent was also disseminated by means of the justices of assize. They were supposed to restrict unnecessary litigation, to warn country gentlemen not to spend their

[33] Hawarde, *Cases,* 19–21, 56–8, 101–2; *Chamberlain's Letters,* 77; *Cal. Hatfield House MSS.,* v, 270; *Acts of the Privy Council,* xiv, 5.

time in cities and borough towns but to keep hospitality and
attend to their duties in the country, to prevent forestalling
and regrating of food, and generally speaking to exercise on
their circuit that oversight of the good order and the manners of the country that the queen and council wished to
have effective throughout the whole kingdom. The justices
of assize were also expected to exercise observation and
some disciplinary powers over local officials, especially over
the justices of the peace, and to bring home to the lord
chancellor information that would help in their selection.
Along with the justices of assize went various clerks and
attendants, a clerk of assize, attorneys, sometimes, on special circuits, the attorney general or solicitor general himself.

Arrived at the county seat of one of the shires in his
circuit the justices were met, as already described, by the
sheriff and accompanied with much ceremony into town to
their lodgings or to the place where the assizes were to be
held. The expenses connected with their entertainment
which have been spoken of in another connection were a
matter of much concern at this time. Notwithstanding the
fact that much of the expense fell upon the sheriff it was still
a serious burden to the crown and in any case was felt to
be a bad example of unnecessary expenditure. In 1578 the
privy council tried to establish a limit for such expenditure; the arrangement made with the local authorities in
Lancashire being that a common table should be provided
for the justices of assize, sheriff and justices of the peace of
the county from Monday noon to Thursday afternoon of
assize week and that each should pay twelvepence for each
meal for himself and eightpence for each of his servants;
the sheriff had only to find venison and wine at the summer
assizes and wine at the Lent assizes. But neither here nor
elsewhere were these restrictions effective. In July, 1585,
the expense to the exchequer of the two justices on the home
circuit was £102 12s., for the midland circuit £152 16s.,
sums equal in modern values perhaps to $2,500 and $3,500.
In the famine winter of 1596–7 a letter was sent to all the

justices of assize as they were about to start on their Lenten journey, directing them to urge upon the sheriffs of the counties in their several circuits moderation in their entertainment and a restraint of their " feastinges and prodigall expenses." Nevertheless a few years later, when a sheriff of Lancashire in a well-meant effort to reduce the extravagance of the entertainments of assize week invited the justices to stay at his own house, instead of providing a continuous feast for them at the castle, they were deeply offended and before the next assizes took occasion to impose upon him fines of more than £200, for fanciful or unproved offenses on his part.[34]

The length of the sitting in any one county seems to have varied from one to three days. We hear of a case where the assizes closed in one day where it had been expected they would last three, and another, in Westmoreland, where the court sat for only one and a half days where formerly it had sat for two and a half. There must have been much time lost in getting from county seat to county seat, and as there were from five to eight shires in each circuit, the round could hardly have been completed in less than three or four weeks.[35]

In addition to the instructions given to the justices of the assize at the beginning of their circuit, the privy council forwarded a constant series of letters urging upon them certain actions, restraining them from others, transmitting to them petitions and warnings that had come directly to the council, and reminding them of the desirability of attention to recusants, the grain supply and other matters. The actual sessions cannot have differed very greatly from quarter sessions, though there was doubtless a larger concourse of persons, more ceremony and more excitement. In their commissions of gaol delivery a large number of other officials and local personages were conjoined with the justices,

[34] *Cal. Hatfield House MSS.*, iii, 100; *Acts of the Privy Council*, xxvi, 481–3; *Farington Papers*, Chetham Society, 4–5, 528–53.
[35] *Cal. State Papers, Dom., Add.*, 1580–1625, 363.

and their criminal jurisdiction was perhaps restricted to more serious offenses than the more petty of those taken up at quarter sessions.

The civil jurisdiction exercised by the justices introduced another element in addition to that which came within the competence of the justices of the peace. Presentments and reports from local officials were or should be called for in the fulfilment of the duties of the justices of assize as being the most direct representatives of the queen and council. The justices seem frequently to have allowed liberty on constantly renewed bail to recusants whom they considered harmless, and a great number of the prisoners who were declared guilty were remanded without sentence until the recommendations of the justices for a pardon from the crown could be acted upon. June 25, 1599, eleven poor persons were pardoned at one time at the suggestion of the justices of assize of one circuit, and six months later twenty-five were similarly pardoned at the recommendation of two other justices of assize. Nevertheless, as has been seen, this occasional extension of mercy rather than judgment was not so extensive as to diminish seriously the rigor of the Elizabethan criminal courts.[36]

As one reflects upon county and other local government in England in the later years of Elizabeth and in the early years of the seventeenth century two considerations impress themselves with constant insistence. The first is the minute, constant and overbearing control or attempted control of the queen and council over all local life, the other the vast amount of laborious service and pecuniary sacrifice demanded from the local nobility. and gentry. As to the former, no general statement can give so strong an impression as the record of proceedings of the privy council, the correspondence of ministers and officials and the reports of local officials from which a few scattered extracts have been given for purposes of illustration in these chapters.

[36] *Cal. State Papers, Dom.*, 1581-90, 84, 1595-7, 122, 306, 347, 353, 455, 475, 1598-1601, 14, 219, 337, 382, 387, 391.

The hand of the council was never taken off, its attention never flagged; no pride of noble birth, or opposition of rural inertia, or disinclination to local expense was allowed to stand in the way of the requirements of the queen's government, or to deter the privy council from rebuking neglect or demanding obedience. The autocratic spirit of government in the sixteenth and seventeenth centuries is in no way better illustrated than by the relation between the central and the local governments.

The second observation, the vast amount of unpaid work done by the rural gentry, bears a close relation to the first. The gentry, and indeed the nobility also, were the unremunerated agents of this absolute government. If the amount of time, the sacrifice of comfort, the expenditure of effort and money by the nobility and gentry of Tudor and early Stuart times for public purposes be compared with that given by the corresponding classes in modern times, the contrast is almost startling. The modern rich, even the wealthy landed classes of an old social system like that of England, are practically freed from all personal burdens except such as they may choose to assume or for which they may be paid, or such as are involved in the payment of taxes. The average well-to-do landholder of Elizabeth's time was expected, indeed compelled, to give a very large part of his time, his labor and his income to military, civil and administrative work for which he received no remuneration. His personal services have already been sufficiently explained. In addition to taxation in the form of subsidies payable by act of parliament to the crown, and in addition to frequently recurring loans to the queen on privy seal and more or less regular local rates for the support of the poor and the repair of roads and bridges, the nobility, gentry and clergy had imposed upon them the provision and support of all the mounted forces of the crown, and, along with their neighbors, frequent payments for the fitting out of troops for the defense of their own county, the protection of all England, and assistance to England's foreign allies; and for the fitting out of shipping. One of the most constant, as it must have been one of the most ungracious of all the duties of justices, sheriffs, lords lieutenant and deputy lieutenants and of the lower officials whom we have still to consider was that of laying a rate upon their fellow-citizens for payments insisted upon by the crown. It is striking how frequently the estates of Elizabethan officials, general and local, became involved. The great wealth that was certainly sometimes amassed during this period was generally the result either of a very exceptional amount of royal favor, especial good fortune, trade or the general advance in the wealth of society. Certainly the nobility and gentry, whatever may have been true of city men, obtained no more than a moderate share of new wealth, and the deductions in the form of money or service from their uncontrolled use of it were so great as to make not an unfavorable balance between their privileges and their duties.

CHAPTER XL

THE HUNDRED AND ITS HIGH CONSTABLE

MIDWAY between the county and the parish, the ultimate unit of England for purposes of local government, there still existed at the close of the sixteenth century in a considerable degree of vigor and significance the ancient division known as the hundred, or more commonly, in seven of the midland and northern shires, the wapentake. Its size differed very much in the different parts of the county, so that there were from four or five to sixty or eighty in a shire. There were between seven hundred and eight hundred hundreds or wapentakes in all England. The old use of the hundred as the primary division of the country for judicial purposes had fallen into desuetude, or existed merely, as already described, for the sheriff's tourn and leet, as the sphere of the duties of the sheriff's bailiffs in the service of writs and occasionally as a " liberty " possessed by the successor of some feudal lord and valued because it gave excuse for the collection of a few petty traditional fees. On the other hand the hundred was still constantly used as a subdivision of the shire for purposes of taxation, of military levy and equipment, of purveyance and the oversight of public order.[1]

The only officer or officers whose sphere of action was coterminous with the hundred, except, as just stated, a sheriff's bailiff, a quite inferior official, was the high constable, or as he was often called when there was no danger of confusion with the local petty constable, merely constable. There were usually two high constables for each

---

[1] *Hist. MSS. Comm., Rep. 14, App. iv,* 356; *Cal. State Papers, Dom.,* 1628–9, 502; *Reports Deputy Keeper of the Rolls,* xliii, 109; Chancey, *Hertfordshire,* 163.

hundred, though frequently there was only one and in some hundreds by old custom there were three or even more. On the other hand occasionally two or more hundreds are placed under the charge of one high constable. Bacon declared that the high constables " ought to be of the ablest free-holders and substantialest sort of yeomen, next to the degree of gentlemen." But there is frequent reason to observe in Bacon's writing that he was not very familiar with the local institutions of his time, and as a matter of fact to the names of all high constables actually mentioned in accessible records the name gentleman is attached, or suggested, and they were evidently men of position, means and influence. A list of the thirteen high constables of the six hundreds of Lancashire in 1612 includes many well-known family names of that county and each is described as a gentleman. The justice of the peace and the high constable are conjoined as equals in a bill at one time introduced into parliament.

An instance in the records of Worcestershire of a kind un-fortunately only too familiar is that of Gerald Purshall, of Purshall Hall, gentleman, who was put under bonds of £100 for his appearance at next quarter sessions to show to the justices of the peace his accounts as high constable and to make restitution to certain parishes in the hundred of the money he had wrongfully collected from them. A high con-stable of Norfolk was fined £500 in 1597 and otherwise punished in Star Chamber for ingrossing grain and convert-ing thirteen farmhouses into tenements. There is no doubt that the high constables were generally drawn, and they are the last group of officials that we shall have to name as being drawn from that same important class of gentry in the country and the corresponding class in the towns that furnished sheriffs, justices of the peace, deputy lieutenants and coroners, although perhaps from its lower ranks.[2]

[2] Dalton, *chap. 28;* Chancey, *Hertfordshire,* 304, 527; Axon, *Manchester Quarter Sessions,* 38, 112, 141; *Hist. MSS. Comm., MSS. from Various Sources,* i, 306; Bacon, *Answers to Questions Propounded by Sir Alexander Hay,* Spedding Ed. 1892, vii, 751; *Lancashire Lieutenancies,* ii, 254; *Journals House of Commons,* i, 101; Hawarde, *Cases,* 76.

The high constables were appointed, theoretically at least, yearly, by the justices of the peace at quarter-sessions or by the judges at assizes. Their position was an unpaid office and evidently undesired. At the sessions held at Pontefract, Yorkshire, in April, 1598, William Hall, gentleman, one of the high constables of the wapentake of Osgodcross " upon his humble suit into this Court is discharged of his place." It was immediately ordered that Thomas Maples of Raucliffe should serve in his place. At next sessions, at Barnsley, John Saville, of the wapentake of Strafford, gentleman, was excused on account of his age and services already performed; but when the justices chose Robert Mote, who was present in court, in his place, the latter objected strongly and " obstinately and in contemptuouse maner without shewing any just cause refuseth both to be sworne and also to execute the same place." But before the year was over, Mr. Mote yielded and took his oath to fulfill the duties of the office. Sometimes the outgoing high constables were required to recommend a list from which the justices of the peace should select their successors. The fact that the incumbency usually only lasted for a year and that it involved apparently no considerable payments such as those of the sheriff must have made it less burdensome though of course also less honorable.[3]

The high constables were at this time primarily tax collectors. When a tax of a certain amount was to be imposed upon a county by the crown, by the justices of the peace or the lord lieutenant, the usual practice was to divide this sum among the hundreds in proportion to their supposed means. Within the hundreds it was in the same way divided among the townships or parishes, and ultimately it was levied upon individuals. The collection was done by the high constables directly or through the township officers. For instance, in 1598, when the West Riding of Yorkshire was required, in an early instance of the imposition of ship

[3] Axon, *Manchester Quarter Sessions*, vii, 38, 112, 141; Lister, *North Riding Sessions Rolls*, 80, 98, 130.

money, to contribute £400 " toward the setting forth of a ship by the inhabitants of Yorke and Hull for her Majesty's service," the justices of the peace of the Riding at their quarter sessions divided this sum among the fourteen hundreds in varying amounts, appointed a group of assessors in each hundred and ordered the high constables to collect the sums under their direction. At the same session the sum of £33 6s. 8d. was assessed upon all the hundreds of the Riding for the relief of the plague stricken people of Richmond and Gisborough. Payments for the repair of bridges, for the maintenance of sick and maimed soldiers, for the relief of prisoners and for the payment of the expenses of composition for purveyance were all as a usual thing divided among the hundreds, collected by the high constables and paid over by them to the respective higher authorities.

Military affairs in the county were so largely looked after by the lord lieutenant and deputy lieutenants that money for such expenses passed less frequently through the hands of the high constables. The hundreds nevertheless had considerable military significance. They were the usual divisions for military equipment and the levy of troops, and the money for these payments was often collected by the high constable. When the descent of the Armada was imminent the hundreds were made the units of local defense, the trained bands were usually made up of men drawn from particular hundreds and the high constable was often made responsible for their summons and payment. He was regularly given charge of keeping up the beacons. In Devonshire, so important for defense against possible invasion by the Spaniards, the duties of the high constables were interwoven inextricably with those of the more purely military officials, and the division of the county into hundreds was closely connected with its military organization. It was divided into three parts, the Eastern, Northern and Southern, for the muster and support of the trained bands. The first two of these divisions each included five hundreds, the Southern division had eight hundreds. The high constables of these hundreds are being constantly ordered to warn the trained men and the gentlemen who are bound to provide horsemen to present themselves to the deputy lieutenants. They are occasionally ordered to levy new troops, to certify deficiencies in equipment, and from time to time to collect money for the payment of the bands and their exercising. At the other end of England, in Lancashire, the high constables and their hundreds were being utilized in much the same way. The hundreds were the units regularly utilized for the impressment of soldiers in cases of compulsory levy.[4]

Another usage connected with the military position of the high constable is suggested somewhat later by the case of a certain Rowe, high constable of Tavistock, who was convicted in Star Chamber of billeting too many soldiers upon a certain enemy of his, of extortion and other offenses, fined 500 marks, disabled from the constableship forever, ordered to pay back £110, the amount of his extortion and as damages and to acknowledge in the parish church his offense to the man he had injured. A whole gamut of misdeeds is run through in another case, in Yorkshire, in 1598. Robert Rigge, who is described, rather inconsistently with Elizabethan usage, as both a draper and a gentleman, and who was at that time high constable of the hundred of Barkstone, collected twenty marks composition money for purveyance of beef and mutton which he did not pay to the purveyor, making it necessary for the county to pay it over again the next spring. He had collected money for the training of soldiers when no muster took place, added some thirty pounds to the taxation of various townships beyond that which had been authorized by the justices, summoned more men than were required for soldiers and let them go home again for bribes, and collected money for the repair of

---

4 Grose, *Military Antiquities*, Ed. 1801, i, 82; *MSS. of the Duke of Somerset, Hist. MSS. Comm.*, 15th Rep., App. vii, 2, 3, 6, 12, 19, 24, 26, 33, 36, 38, 44–7, 53, 55; *Lancashire Lieutenancies*, i, 2–14, 15, 19, 21, 23, 34–57, 87–8, ii, 180–5, 199, 215.

Friston causeway but left the laborers unpaid and the causeway little better than it was before. The two uses of the hundred, as a taxation and a military unit, are well indicated in the following yearly accounts of musters and payments for the hundred of Berkeley in Gloucestershire in the first quarter of the seventeenth century. At general muster, 2064 able men; for subsidies, 400 subsidy men paying £164; of purveyance, it pays £33 3s. of the £440 payable by the whole county of Gloucester; for release of poor prisoners, £17 3s.; for pensions of soldiers, casual fires, etc., £17 6s. 8d. The collection of all these funds and the preparation of these lists were done by the high constable.[5]

In the enforcement of the law the hundred and the high constables were made use of, in some cases at least, because they were nearer to the individual offenders than the officials of the county at large. When a daylight robbery occurred, if the hue and cry were duly raised and yet the robber not arrested or discovered, the person robbed might bring suit against the hundred for the amount of his loss. In 1597 the hundred of Benhurst, Berkshire, which included only five villages and three hamlets but was traversed by two great roads, complained that £255 had been collected from it in the last year and the hundred was being impoverished by this means. In a contemporary diary an interesting account is given of the hanging at Bedford of two brothers, the elder with an estate of £500 a year, the younger, a high constable with an estate of £100 a year. It is remarked that they had been robbing for years, obtaining great sums such as £200 or £300 at a time, but robbed " between sunne and sunne " so that the hundreds were sued and required to pay the losses.[6]

In the more general conservation of the peace the high constables were also utilized. They were bound to attend the courts of quarter sessions and assize, and to report there

[5] Lister, *West Riding Sessions Rolls*, 207, 222; Smyth, *Description of the Hundred of Berkeley;* 15 *Rep. Hist. MSS. Comm.*, App. 2.

[6] 27 Eliz., c. 13; 39 Eliz., c. 25; Dalton, 84; *Diary of John Rous, Camden Soc.*, p. 83.

any violation of law of which they knew, to act on grand juries, and to return any warrants which might have been sent them for service. In 1599 Coke drew up a set of eighteen articles which were to be submitted at each assizes to the high constables for answer. According to these they were required to report on a long series of violations of law within their hundreds, ranging from vagrancy to " dove-houses maintained by any other than lords of the manor or parsons." The justices of the peace as well as of assize constantly appealed to the high constables for help in carrying out the law, as well as for information in regard to its violation. From time to time they were commanded by the justices to choose a certain day or night and with the parish officers make a general search through their hundreds for rogues, vagabonds and idle persons. These were to be whipped, or, if seemingly dangerous characters, to be brought before the justices for more serious punishment. They were also used by the justices as intermediaries to give notice to parish officers of their duties and of meetings of the justices which the parish officers should attend. They had also a general oversight of parish constables. It is evident that, half-forgotten relic of earlier conditions as it was, the hundred was still a convenient subdivision of the county and its principal officer an official useful because of his local knowledge and the practicable size of the region in which he served.[7]

[7] *Cal. State Papers, Dom.*, 1598–1601, 519; Dalton, chap. 174; Coke, *Fourth Institute*, Ed. 1809, 267.

CHAPTER XLI

*THE PARISH; THE CONSTABLE, THE CHURCH
WARDENS, SURVEYORS OF ROADS AND
OVERSEERS OF THE POOR*

A FIFTEENTH century law writer makes the following
statement, which is certainly sufficiently concrete:
" England is divided into counties, counties are divided into
hundreds, which in some parts of England are called wapentakes, and hundreds are again subdivided into vills." By
using the word vills, or, in his Latin, *villas,* he was able to
evade one of the greatest difficulties in the description of
English local government in his own time and in the next
two centuries; that is to say the confusing and conflicting
use of terms for the smallest subdivision of civil government and life in England. Vill is a generic term used without very exact definition or connotation for one of those
groups of people, living somewhat close together, which
made up the rural population of England, with the territory
on which they lived. If only its appearance was concerned
we would call it a village and have done with it.

As a matter of fact, vill, town, township, tithing, manor,
parish, and certain other less usual terms are used in the
language of Queen Elizabeth's time almost, though not quite,
indiscriminately. This confusion of nomenclature arose
from several causes. In the first place, since the ultimate
units of political organization had grown up largely without the coördinating power of a strong central government,
much diversity in different localities actually existed. Secondly, local organization as it existed in the sixteenth and
seventeenth centuries was the residuum of several systems
of custom and law which had existed successively, and contained elements and survivals from each. Thirdly, the union

of church and state, the mutual interpenetration of the ecclesiastical and the civil system served to complicate still further the organization of the body that was the smallest division of each. As a result the use of terms varies from locality to locality, and is often loose and inconsistent. It it therefore difficult to make correct generalizations and it is still harder to give an inclusive and accurate picture of universal normal local administration.

The various terms mentioned above, although all in use and all of significance, were of varying degrees of familiarity. The word vill itself, a direct translation of the Latin, was used, especially in legal parlance, but not very commonly. The oldest term was undoubtedly town or township. Although, presumably, town originally referred to the village and the land about it, township to the people who lived upon the land, there was no distinction in the use of the two terms at the close of the sixteenth century. Over and over again we find the same locality spoken of at one time as a town at another as a township.[1]

The term manor may be largely disregarded, because by the close of the sixteenth century it was fast becoming a forgotten or disregarded institution; but a number of words still in familiar use can only be explained by their connection with it. The manor was a stretch of land with the people settled upon it, so far as they were connected with and dependent upon a lord of the manor who had certain economic and judicial rights over them and their land. The most characteristic of these rights was that of holding manor courts, that is to say courts baron and courts leet. These are described in a contemporary manual as follows: " The court baron may be kept every three weeks or, as sometimes, oftener, if it please the lord; but a court leet is not kept oftener than twice a year . . . the leet, called also a law-day and a view of frank-pledge." The

---

[1] Fortescue, *De laudibus legum Angliae,* chap. cxxiv; Lister, *West Riding Sessions Rolls,* 40–1; Simpson, H. B., *The Office of Constable, Eng. Hist. Rev.,* x, 625–41; 39 Eliz., c. 41.

court baron was, as suggested in this definition, a gathering of the people of the manor at frequent intervals to settle questions connected with rights of the lord of the manor as a landlord and with the agricultural interests of the inhabitants. It was, however, now held in but few places, at irregular times and almost solely for the purpose of making land transfers of certain kinds.[2]

The court leet was a somewhat more formal assembly, although of the same people, held by the lord of the manor in imitation of the sheriff's tourn and leet, usually twice a year. It had somewhat greater powers, including the election of certain petty officers, and drew its authority, in theory at least, from a direct grant from the king. Combined with the court leet is almost always to be noticed in legal records the expression view of frank-pledge. This refers to the ancient practice by which the great body of common people of England were organized locally in groups of ten for purposes well described by old Lambard: " Everie one of those ten men of the companies should bee suretie and pledge for forth-coming of his fellowes; so that if any harme were done by any of those ten against the peace then the rest of the ten should be amerced, if he of their company that did the harme should flie and were not forthcoming to answer to that wherewith he should be charged." [3] It was a system of joint personal bail. The enforcement of this enrolment with such rights of imposing fines and such duties of administration as it involved was possessed by the same lords of manors as held the court leet, so that view of frank-pledge and court leet became inseparable from one another, as they both were from the very conception of a manor. The number of persons in a manor or vill was in most cases small and it may well be that the exact number of ten as the unit for the view of frank-pledge would not be insisted on, the whole population of

[2] Sheppard, *Court Keeper's Guide*, chap. 7, § 3, quoted in Coke, *Fourth Institute*, fo. 264.

[3] Lambard, *Duties of Constables, Borsholders, etc.*, Sects. 7, etc.

the village being treated as one frank-pledge group. But courts leet were now only infrequently held and view of frank-pledge seldom enforced, by many lords of manors not at all.

The traditional name of tything, or group of ten, however, gave rise to another form of local nomenclature. One of the frank-pledge group spoke for or represented it; he was therefore called the tythingman or head of the tything. Each of its members moreover was a "pledge," or, using the old Anglo-Saxon word, a *borh* for the others. The tythingman was therefore the chief pledge or the "borhs-older" of the group, from *borh,* pledge, and *ealdor,* chief or head. Other forms in use, borough-head, head-borough, etc., are equivalent in meaning to borhsolder though the etymology of the older expression was forgotten and its spelling has even more than usual sixteenth century variations. The boundaries of the manor and the township were very generally the same, and the manorial group of people and those of the township were therefore practically indistinguishable. The manor in such cases had simply been superimposed upon the older township. If as in some cases township and manor were not coterminous, there was nevertheless a tendency toward their identification. Vill, township, tithing and manor were therefore in all essentials indistinguishable. The tythingman, chief-pledge, borhsolder and constable in such a township were four different names for the same official, and as a matter of fact these names are often used as alternatives in laws, proclamations and legal decisions. Where the term tythingman or one of its direct equivalents is applied to an assistant or subordinate of the constable, as sometimes occurs, it probably means that that particular township was so large as to be divided into several tythings, and to only one of the tythingmen was the special term constable applied.[4]

However familiar these ancient terms for local officers

---

[4] Blackstone, *Commentaries, Intro.,* Sect. 4, § 2.; Lambard, *Duties of Constables,* etc., Ed. 1633, 67, 69.

may have been, there was another name for the locality
itself which was fast superseding all the others. This was
the term parish. Notwithstanding the ecclesiastical connotation of the name, the local body which was habitually
sued, taxed, fined, bequeathed property, or ordered by the
government to perform various civil duties was the parish.
It is the parish that at this time naturally comes to the
mind of the draughtsman of a statute or a royal proclamation when he wishes to make provision for local services,
duties or powers. All the terms properly applicable to
township, manor or tithing are habitually used at the end
of the sixteenth century in connection with the parish. We
hear of the constable of a parish, although strictly speaking
he was an officer of a township; holders of copy-hold land
and attendants at a court to be held every three weeks in a
certain parish are spoken of, though these relations were
properly manorial. Inaccurate as these expressions were
they were common and they indicate the contemporary tendency to substitute the parish for the older terms and conceptions that might have been more exactly applied to the
units of local government. The parish was a sort of residu-
ary legatee of the functions of the other local bodies and
of the official terms applicable to them.

The difficulties connected with the inconsistent and in-
exact use of words in this connection can therefore be
reduced to smaller proportions by using, in accordance with
Elizabethan practice, the word parish as a general if not
always an accurate term for the smallest group of the people who carried on any form of political life as an organized
body. An exception ought perhaps to be made for the
northern shires, where the parishes were usually very large
and the town or township was still a well known and frequently mentioned subdivision of the parish, as for instance
" the township of Fishwick in the parish of Preston in
the county of Lancashire." [5]

---

[5] Lister, *West Riding Sessions Rolls;* Saalkeld, *Reports,* iii, 98; *Archaeological Review,* iv, 344; *Hist. of Preston, Lancashire.*

No surveyed boundaries existed for the parish; its limits were a matter merely of tradition. To preserve this tradition and to impress on the memory of fleeting generations the special trees, marked stones, hill-tops or water-courses that indicated the parish boundaries, the practice known as perambulation was kept up. From time to time, usually once a year, a procession was formed which went the round of the outer boundary, stopping from time to time at well marked points for various commemorative exercises. In pre-reformation times the ceremony had been a religious one, the priest leading and the parishioners following with cross, banners, bells, lights and sacred emblems, successive points being blessed and sprinkled with holy water. When at the reformation religious processions were forbidden this ceremony came under the condemnation of the law, but after a period of neglect Queen Elizabeth found it necessary, in order to reach so useful an end, to direct by proclamation a certain form of renewal of the processions. " The people should once in the year, at the time appointed, with the curate and substantial men of the parish, walk about the parish, and at their return to the church make their common prayers. And the curate in the said perambulation was at certain convenient places to admonish the people to give thanks to God in the beholding of His benefits, and for the increase and abundance of his fruits upon the face of the earth, with the saying of the one hundred and third Psalm." Whether in this form or with less religious accompaniments the practice long survived, indeed in some remote districts is said to be still preserved. One of the rogation days, in the spring or early summer, was often chosen as the time of the ceremony, and the perambulation was therefore often called " the rogation." Conversely, rogation days were sometimes called " gang days." Boys were taken along as those whose life and memory would naturally be the longest, and the poorer boys were sometimes especially included since it was looked upon as something of a festivity. Among the churchwarden's accounts for the parish of St. Clements,

Ipswich, is the item " ffor bread and beare given to the
boyes when they wente the boundes of the parishe, 12s."
In those of Chelsea, Middlesex, is the entry " Spent at the
perambulation dinner, £3 10s." No material obstacle was
allowed to interfere with the progress of the perambulators.
They could by law enter all dwellings on the boundary, and
pass through and even break down all enclosures which lay
across it. Private persons whose houses lay in the line of
march of the perambulators sometimes provided food and
drink for them, and this became so usual that efforts were
made, though unsuccessfully, to enforce the custom by law.[6]

Within the bounds of the parish there was a little world
of economic, social, religious and political activity, not by
any means detached from the larger spheres of hundred,
county and nation, and yet to a considerable extent self
centred. It is to the last phase of this life alone, the
political, that we must devote our particular attention,
though here as elsewhere the various aspects of human
interest are more distinctly separated in scholars' descriptions of them than they are in reality. There was at the
period of this study a periodical meeting of the inhabitants
of the parish known as the vestry. The actual administration of the parish was, however, carried on by four officials
or groups of officials, the constable, the church wardens, the
overseers of the poor, and the surveyors of roads, and by
certain holders of still more humble offices. In describing
this local population and these officers and their functions,
we pass at last entirely away from the body of gentry who
fulfilled the duties of county and hundred government.
Harrison in the invaluable *Description of England,* written
in the later years of Elizabeth, from which we have had
occasion to quote so frequently, after describing the nobility, the gentry and the well-to-do merchant class, goes on to
say: " The fourth and last sort of people in England are

[6] Burn, *Ecclesiastical Law,* ii, 133–4; Gibson, *Codex,* 213; *East Anglian*
iv, 2 Series, 5; Toulmin Smith, *The Parish,* 473; S. L. Ware, *The Elizabethan Parish, Johns Hopkins Univ. Studies,* xxvi, 7–8, 27.

day laborers, poor husbandmen and some retailers which
have no free land, copyholders, and all artificers, as
tailors, shoemakers, carpenters, brickmakers, masons, etc.
This fourth and last sort of people therefore have neither
voice nor authority in the commonwealth, and are to be
ruled and not to rule others; yet they are not altogether
neglected, for in villages they are commonly made churchwardens, sidesmen, aleconners, and now and then, constables, and many times enjoy the name of headboroughs." [7]

The constables, or petty or parish constables, as they were
generally called to distinguish them from the high constables, and who were " now and then " according to Harrison, made from such common material, were the oldest
and in many ways the most conspicuous officers of the
parish, or more properly, of the township which was so generally identified with it. Their position and power were
probably already lower than they had been at an earlier
period when the constables had more fully represented the
whole body of the village community. As to their social
rank, Bacon says " petty constables are now of inferior,
yea of base condition, but this is a degeneracy from earlier
times." There was usually but one constable, though in
certain parishes there were two, and even three are not unknown. The constable was regularly appointed by the
court leet, where this gathering was still held; in other
cases, where other manorial courts were held, by the steward
of the lord of the manor; in still other parishes by the
vestry. Where none of these practices was the custom, the
appointment of constables, like so many other residual
duties of government, was made by the justices of the
peace.[8]

Normally the constable seems to have been an elective
officer chosen by and especially representing the people of

[7] Ed. 1587, Book ii, c. 5.

[8] Bacon, *Answers to Questions, etc.*, Spedding Ed. 1892, vii, 749-51;
Simpson, H. B., *The Office of Constable, Eng. Hist. Rev.*, x, 633-4, 639;
Lambard, *Duties of Constables;* Lister, *West Riding Sessions Rolls,* 58.

the village, not the government. His duties were in connection with the internal administration of the parish or township and with the courts leet and baron of the manor. His office, like that of his higher colleagues of the hundreds, was an annual one. Its duties were so fully and clearly expressed in a form of oath that seems to have been well established at this period that it may well be printed in approximate entirety. "You shall swear that you shall well and truly serve our sovereign lord, the king, in the office of a constable. You shall see and cause his majesty's peace to be well and duly kept and preserved, according to your power. You shall arrest all such persons as in your sight and presence shall ride or go armed offensively, or shall commit or make any riot, affray, or other breach of his majesty's peace. You shall do your best endeavor to apprehend all felons, barrators, and rioters, or persons riotously assembled; shall levy hue and cry and shall pursue them until they be taken. You shall do your best endeavors that the watch in and about your town be duly kept for the apprehending of rogues, vagabonds, night-walkers, eavesdroppers, and other suspected persons, and of such as go armed and the like. . . . You shall well and duly execute all precepts and warrants to you directed from the justices of the peace of the county or higher officers. In time of hay or corn harvest you shall cause all meet persons to serve by day for the mowing, reaping, and getting in of corn or hay. You shall in Easter week cause your parishioners to chuse surveyors for the mending of the highways in your parish. . . . And you shall well and duly, according to your knowledge, power, and ability, do and execute all things belonging to the office of a constable so long as you shall continue in this office. So help you God." [9]

Among the most fundamental of these duties was the arrest of criminals or at least the raising of hue and cry when it was demanded by any sufferer from violence. That is to say, if any one were assaulted or robbed and appealed

[9] Dalton, *The Countrey Justice,* chap. clxxiv.

to the constable of the parish in which the injury occurred the constable must summon out his neighbors, whether it were day or night, to seek the culprit. If he was not captured notice must be given to the constables of the adjacent parishes, who were similarly to raise the hue and cry in their neighborhoods. If the offender was not then discovered the person who suffered the loss might bring suit for its recovery, as already stated, from the whole hundred in which the attack occurred. The constable might, like a justice of the peace, of his own accord order any disorderly persons to desist from their trouble making and on their refusal arrest and carry them before any magistrate. He might even search houses in which he suspected criminals were being harbored, or in which it was apparent that violence was being committed. In practice this local responsibility for the capture of ill doers seems to have been rather ineffective. Harrison says " I have known by my own experience felons being taken to have escaped out of the stocks, being rescued for want of watch and guard; that thieves have been let pass because the covetous and greedy parishioners would neither take the pains or be at the charge to carry them to prison, if it were far off; that when hue and cry should have been made, even to the faces of some constables they have said, ' God restore your loss. I have other business at this time.' " [10]

Some of the constables' responsibilities for criminals were those which were handed down to him, since it was his duty to inflict minor punishments and collect petty fines imposed by the justices of the peace of a more purely local character than those coming under the charge of the sheriff. As a typical instance, when a certain poor woman, Elizabeth Armistead, was convicted of petty larceny at West Riding Sessions, in 1598, it was ordered by the justices that " she shall nowe be delivered to the constable of Keerbie, and he

---

[10] Dalton, *The Countrey Justice,* chaps. lxxxiv, clxxiv; Bacon, *Answers to Questions, etc.,* Spedding Ed. 1892, vii, 1750; Lambard, *Eirenarcha,* Ed. 1599, 135; Harrison, Camelot Ed., 247.

to cause her to be stripped naked from the middle upward and soundly whipped thorowe the said town of Keerbie, and by hym delivered to the constable of Kirkby and he to see like execution within his town, and the next markett att Weatherbie to delyver her to the constables of Weatherbie, and they to see like punishment of her executed thorow their towne." [11]

The constable must also make arrests and execute any other requirements of the justices of the peace in summoning parties before them. Apart from criminals proper a large part of the duty of the constables was, according to a well-known contemporary authority, " to comprehend vagrom men." Since vagrants, according to the laws of 1572 and 1597, were a varied and numerous class, the requirement of the law that the constable must, with the approval of the minister of the parish, whip all such and start them, with a testimonial to the whipping, on the direct road to their native villages, must have been no sinecure. Two contemporary testimonials of this kind furnish no mean illustrations of the constable's duties and of the manners of the time. " A.B., a sturdy Rogue, of tall Stature, red haired and bearded, about the age of thirty years, and having a wart neere under his right eie, born (as he confesseth) at East Tilberie in Essex, was taken begging at Shorne in this county of Kent the tenth of March, 1598, and was then and there lawfully whipped therefore, and hee is appointed to goe to East Tilberie aforesaid, the direct way by Gravesend, over the River of Thamise: for which hee is allowed one whole day, and no more at his peril: subscribed and sealed the day and yeare aforesaid. By us," signed by the minister, the constable or borhsolder and a parishioner. " John at Style, a sturdie vagrant beggar, of low personage, red-hayred, and having the nayle of his right Thombe cloven, was this sixt day of Aprill in the fortie and one yeare of the Rayn of our Soveraigne Ladye Quenne Elizabeth openly whipped at Dale in the said Countie, for a wandering Rogue, according to the

Law, and is assigned to passe forthwith from parish to parish by the Officers thereof, the next straight way to Sale in the Countie of Middlesex, where, as he confesseth, he was borne." It is no wonder that constables are advised " in every corner to have a readie hand and whip." [12]

The constable was not only a disciplinary officer, he must give to the justices of the peace, the high constables and even the sheriff such information as they might need concerning conditions in his parish and the means or character of individual inhabitants. He was the instrument through whom the county and hundred authorities obtained such knowledge as they needed or wished concerning parish details. He reported at quarter sessions the condition of the ale-houses, of the bridges and highways, of vagrancy and recusancy, and the degree of adequacy with which other officials performed their duties. He handed in lists of offenders or persons under suspicion. Such reports of constables were not in themselves indictments, or at this time even official presentments, but they might well be the basis upon which such presentments were made. It was incumbent upon the constable to sign testimonials for all laborers properly leaving the parish, to see that inn-keepers refused lodging to no travelers, to require road supervisors to be chosen by the people of the parish every year, to force all otherwise unoccupied laborers to serve in the fields in time of harvest, and to fulfill various other duties imposed upon him by statute or by his oath.[13]

All the duties of the constable were not invidious. For instance he was regularly the warder of the arms and armor which every Elizabethan parish was supposed to keep ready for use. To quote Harrison again: " The said armour and munition likewise is kept in one several place of every town, appointed by the consent of the whole parish, where it is

[12] Lambard, *Duties of Constables, etc.*, Sect. 45; *Eirenarcha* (Ed. 1599), 206; 14 Eliz., c. 5.

[13] *Hist. MSS. Comm.*, 14 Rep., App. 4, lxix, 67; Lambard, *Duties of Constables, etc.*, § 45; 11 Henry IV, c. 41; 22 Henry VIII, c. 5; 32 Henry VIII, c. 13; 2 and 3 Philip and Mary, c. 8; 14 Eliz., c. 5; 27 Eliz., c. 13.

always ready to be had and worn within an hour's warning. Sometimes also it is occupied when it pleaseth the magistrate either to view the able men, and take note of the well-keeping of the same, or finally to see those that are enrolled to exercise each one his several weapon, at the charge of the townsmen of each parish, according to his appointment. Certes there is almost no village so poor in England (be it never so small) that hath not sufficient furniture in a readiness to set forth three or four soldiers, as one archer, one gunner, one pike and a billman at the least." This system of the preservation of arms by the parish must have been exceedingly unsatisfactory, and even the additional provision kept by the gentry in their manor houses was quite inadequate. It was one of the unfulfilled projects of the time to substitute a central storehouse in each large town for this local preservation by the constables.[14]

These relatively varied and responsible duties made high demands upon an uneducated and untrained class of villagers, and it is no wonder that they frequently failed in the performance of them. It is not unusual for constables to beg exemption from appointment, as did those selected for higher office. Sometimes it is because they could not read or write and are obliged to go to the minister or others to get their warrants read. Often they are fined for incompetency or failure that must have been largely the result of sheer ignorance or stupidity.[15]

Yet the constable himself sometimes had subordinates. In many cases, as already explained, the term tythingman or its practical equivalents, chief pledge, headborough or borsholder, was the same as the constable. In other parishes however there was a constable and one or more tythingmen below him. The official duties of these personages must have been petty indeed. There were in some parishes still

[14] Harrison, *Description of England*, Camelot Ed., 224-5; Toulmin Smith, *The Parish*, 473; *Cal. State Papers, Dom.*, 1595-7, 134, 136, 1598-1601, 390.

[15] *Middlesex Sessions Rolls*, ii, 36, 41, 139.

other inferior officers, some which were of an ecclesiastical nature, such as sidesmen, synodsmen, swornmen, questmen, beadles and sextons, others whose economic duties can be at least partly inferred from their names, such as haywards, waywardens, ale-conners, and mole-catchers, others whose duties have left no explanatory record. Analogous duties to those devolving upon the mole-catchers were however raised into greater prominence by two laws of the earlier years of Queen Elizabeth. A tax was by these statutes to be levied each year upon the inhabitants of every parish " for the destruction of noisome fowle and vermine," and two men were to be appointed to pay bounties from it for the heads and eggs of crows, rooks, starlings and many other birds and for evidence of the killing of any of a long list of four-footed beasts. A fox was worth a shilling to its destroyer, a mole a halfpenny.[16]

Like the beadle and the sexton, the title of church-wardens suggests ecclesiastical duties, though of a higher dignity. But the functions of those officials were far wider than the name intimates, at least in modern usage. In some ways they were even more truly the embodiment of local political life than the constable, for they were chosen almost invariably by the whole body of parishioners at a vestry meeting in Easter week, and they were more occupied with the purely internal affairs of the parish and less with services imposed upon them from outside of the parish than were the constables. There were two, three or four church-wardens in each parish, according to local custom, with occasional variations, as usual, some parishes having only one, some having several. Custom also varied as to the manner of their appointment, though, as just stated, they were most generally at this time elected by the parishioners. On the other hand a custom was growing up, which the church authorities strove to enact into law the year after Elizabeth's death, by which one churchwarden was always

<hr>

[16] Lambard, *Office of Distributers, etc.*, 92; *Hist. MSS. Comm. Rep.* III, App. 331; v, 597; 8 Eliz., cxv, 14 Eliz., cxi.

chosen by the minister of the parish, the other by the vestry. As a matter of fact the outgoing churchwardens usually nominated their successors, and, like other burdensome offices, the few suitable inhabitants of the parish felt it incumbent upon them, or were compelled by their neighbors, to serve in some kind of rotation. Their principal duties were in connection with the church, but in days when every man and woman of the neighborhood was a member of the church and required by law to attend its services, to be baptised and married, if married at all, at its chancel, and buried ultimately in its churchyard, the distinction between ecclesiastical and temporal life was not a marked one. An indication of the ecclesiastical connection is to be found in the fact that the wardens took their oaths of office to the archdeacon or the bishop's official when he appeared next in the parish after their election. But this oath could not be refused any claimant by the clerical officer. Decisions exist to the effect that " the church-warden is a temporal officer, he has the property and custody of the parish goods," and the great contemporary authority Coke declared that " the office is mere temporal." [17]

The churchwardens were a sort of continuing corporation for the holding of all the property that belonged to the parish. The most important forms of this property were the church buildings, the churchyard and the furniture and ornaments used in the church service, and these they were bound to keep in good order and replace when necessary. But there was other property in the possession of many parishes. Bequests were made to the parish for various purposes, and these funds were administered by the churchwardens. Ilkley, a parish in Yorkshire, for instance, had, a short time after the close of our period, £53 3s. 4d. which was regularly loaned in small amounts to various well-to-do men at about seven and one half per cent interest, the in-

<hr>

[17] Canons of 1604, 89; *Morgan vs. Archdeacon of Cardigan, Reports of Cases by William Saalkeld*, i, 165 (quoted in Webb, *Hist. of Local Govt.*, 23 n.); Lambard, *Duties of Constables*, Sects. 57–60, *Duties of Churchwardens*, Sect. 1.

come being applied to the support of the poor. They had
also land belonging to the parish which was rented out for
the same purpose. Instances of parishes having lands and
tenements bringing in from £10 to £20 a year are numerous.
Occasional instances existed of the bequest of cows or sheep
to the parish authorities. These were hired out at a regular
rent and presumably were replaced in due time.[18]

Even in these days of imminent puritanism, church ales,
Hock-tide games, Easter games and festive parish gatherings of various kinds were still held and made the occasion,
indeed were largely intended, for the collection of small
sums of money which were regularly taken in charge and
expended by the churchwardens. When funds were not
available the churchwardens had a right to levy a church-
rate for any proper purpose, and when this had the sanction
of the vestry it could legally be collected even if it involved
seizure and sale of the property of such people in the parish
as refused or neglected to pay the sums assessed upon them.
In the numerous surviving churchwardens' accounts the
local life of the sixteenth century goes by us in a long and
varied procession. In the parish of St. Martins-in-the-
Fields, which lay on the high road between London and
Westminster, payments are constantly recorded for ringing
the church bells when the queen passed on her way from
Somerset House to Whitehall, or went to open parliament,
or on her birthday or accession day, or when the news came
of the defeat of the Armada, or of the battle of Ivry. Elsewhere payments are made for buying prayer books and
washing surplices, for keeping the clock in order and mending the bell rope and for entertaining the magistrates. The
wardens " paid the carpenters five shillings for a barrow to
carry the people that died of the sickness to church to bury
them "; " for a coat for the whipper, and making, three
shillings," " for two payre of glovys for Robin Hode and
Mayde Maryan, threepence." They " received for the May-

18 Ware, *The Elizabethan Parish*, 60–9; Collyer and Turner, *Ilkley,
Ancient and Modern*, 187, 188, etc.

pole, £1, 4s." They "paid Robert Warden, the constable, which he disbursed for carrying away the witches, eleven shillings." [19]

The offices of constables and church wardens, and several of the more petty and obscure offices which have been named came down from a remote antiquity. The active legislation of the sixteenth century added others which soon came to vie with them in prominence. The earliest of these was that of the overseers or supervisors or surveyors of highways, a product of the awakened interest in the improvement of the roads. A law of the reign of Queen Mary provided that every year on Tuesday or Wednesday of Easter week the constables and churchwardens should summon the parishioners to come together and choose two surveyors for work on the highways in their parish. Six days were also then to be appointed and announced in church on the next Sunday, in which every person occupying land was to send a team and two men, and every other person to come himself or send a man to work under the direction of these supervisors. It is interesting to note that eight hours was declared to be a day's work on such occasions. [20]

Notwithstanding the extension of this plan by later statutes, the services of these overseers can hardly have been very effective. Favoritism must have vied with inefficiency, and the kind of road-making ability that could be found in an ordinary rural village was probably not greater than the readiness to give time to such work. A writer whose lateness of date may be excused by the weight of his authority on the subject, Macadam himself, looking back on the almost steady degeneracy of the roads down to his own time says, "The greater part of the evils were occasioned by the dishonesty and incapacity of the surveyors." Another eighteenth century writer speaks of "those spiritless, ig-

[19] J. V. Kitto, *St. Martins in the Fields; Ilkley, Ancient and Modern*, p. 187; Ware, *Elizabethan Parish*, 70–8; Toulmin Smith, *The Parish*, chap. vii, § 12, 465–72, etc.

[20] 2 & 3 Philip and Mary, c. 8; Lambard, *Office of Supervisors of Highways*.

norant, lazy, sauntering people called surveyors of the highways." [21]

The overseers of the poor were also new officers, but they had to meet a more insistent problem and were kept more steadily to their work by the privy council and the justices of the peace. Collectors of alms for the poor had been appointed from time to time in some parishes from an early period. In the long course of experimentation with the ever more pressing problem of pauperism which fills the middle years of the sixteenth century by 1572 parliament had come to the conclusion that special officers, to be known as collectors or overseers should be appointed in each parish. But the definite establishment of the office of overseer of the poor as it was known for the next two centuries and a half appears for the first time in the great poor law of 1597. This has already been described in another connection and its principal local implications there stated. The overseers of the poor carried on the main part of their work in conjunction with the churchwardens, forming with them and the minister of the parish and sometimes with the nearest justices of the peace a sort of local board of direction for the affairs of the poor. But the detailed work of levying funds, keeping oversight of the very poor and watching for vagrants was largely in the hands of these newly appointed officers, as already described.[22]

Nothing has been said in this connection of the incumbent of the parish, whether rector, vicar or curate, nor need there be. Some of his early semi-public functions had been lost during the changes of the Reformation period, and others that were to come later had not yet been imposed upon him. He is scarcely mentioned in the administrative legislation of this period; and apart from his keeping of the register of

[21] Macadam, *Observations on the Management of Trusts for the Care of Turnpike Roads*, 15, quoted in Webb, *Local Government*, 67; Richard Bacon, *History of the Poor Laws*, Ed. 1764, 239.

[22] Chapter XXXIX; 39 Eliz., cc. 3, 6, 17, 21; 43 Eliz., cc. 2, 34; Leonard, *Early History of the English Poor Law;* Tanner, *Tudor Constitutional Documents*, 469–507.

births, deaths and marriages, his habitual signature, along with the constable or church wardens, of certain testimonials, and his voluntary attendance at vestry meetings, his duties were only religious and their description belongs elsewhere.

According to our modern conceptions all this action of local officials, so far as it was not based upon authority from the national government, should have rested upon the authorization of some kind of local assembly or representation of the people. Such a body indeed existed in the form of the vestry, but it existed in so crude, inadequate and unassertive a form that it is hard to ascribe to it, as it was in the sixteenth century, any very significant powers. The vestry of the parish is scarcely mentioned in the laws or the law books of the time and seldom adverted to in other contemporary documents. The record of proceedings in the parish is the record of the churchwardens; the reports to the justices and other authorities are those of constables, churchwardens and overseers of the poor; local authority seems to reside in the parish officials themselves rather than in the people of the parish, and to be passed on through the successive occupants of the office, not granted to them from time to time by the people. Nevertheless vestry meetings were sometimes held and the inhabitants at large, all who held or occupied house or land on any kind of tenure, had the right of attendance at them.

This gathering of the people of the parish took its name apparently from the practice of meeting in the part of the church in which the vestments were kept, although it was not especially concerned with church affairs.[23]

Vestry meetings were summoned in many parishes regularly at Easter and occasionally at other times. The parishioners met in the church, normally they heard the report of the expenditures of the outgoing church wardens, elected their successors and approved the church rate, if any had been laid. They fined those who refused to accept parish offices, and had by common law or old custom a right to

[23] 5 Coke's Reports, 66-7.

adopt by-laws binding on all the people of the parish on matters concerning the common lands and the petty general interests of the parish. But all was indeterminate, unsubstantial and irregular. The knowledge that there was vigorous control from above and official authority apart from that dependent on the support of vestry meetings made them apparently a shadowy and alien element in the midst of what was essentially a centralized administrative system. The fact is that the typical rural parish had seldom more than one or two hundred inhabitants; often much fewer, perhaps ten or twenty, or at most thirty or forty grown men. At least two thirds of these were poor laborers, leaving not more than five, ten or twenty substantial personages, such as farmers, an innkeeper or two, a miller, a weaver or blacksmith, besides the minister and perhaps the squire. Among these few men must be distributed the offices of constable, churchwardens, overseers of the poor, surveyors of roads and perhaps parish clerk and some still smaller offices. It was to this little body, with the overwhelming influence in it of its few well-to-do members, that proposed church rates and by-laws must have been submitted. It is no wonder that it was not self-assertive, and that in the face of the centralized power and unceasing activity of the privy council and of those with whom the council constantly corresponded, it showed no ambition or capacity to act as it might have done as a little parliament for its locality.

Looking at the parish, as at the county, we get the same impression of Elizabethan administration, an assertive national authority taking up and trying to solve all problems of internal national life, including local defense and good order, obedience to the established church, the succour of the poor, the encouragement of industry, the keeping up of roads and bridges, the payment of taxes, and the provision of men and arms for foreign military and naval adventure. It tried to do all this by means of the unpaid and untrained services of local officials closely connected by birth, property and relationship with their own immediate neighborhoods.

It is no wonder that the results were not ideally effective. There were of course different degrees of local ability and local ineptitude, ignorance and neglect, from the relatively high training and capacity of justices of the peace who had been long in office down to the half-hearted services of an innkeeper or small farmer who was grudgingly serving his year as constable or surveyor of the roads. Reluctance, transiency of appointment, the sense of being kept from private interests, and lack of professional training were true of all local officials high and low. And yet the very absence of a trained body of paid employees of the central government did its part in preserving to England a kind of popular liberty, and guaranteed to the masses of the people a localization at least of whatever oppression they suffered from.

The control of their own affairs must have been much greater in that phase of local government which we have not yet considered, the government of the cities, boroughs, market towns and other municipal bodies which had especial privileges of their own, either by charter or old custom. In the case of these even such generalizations as to their government as have been made for the rural regions of England are impossible. It can only be said that there was a certain assimilation of urban to rural divisions and officials. The mayor, aldermen and other officials of cities and boroughs were also in general justices of the peace of those towns, with the same rights and duties as justices of the peace of the counties. Sixteen of the cities and boroughs had sheriffs of their own, the others were subject, except for their special franchises, to the authority of the sheriffs of the counties in which they lay. A number of the larger towns had coroners of their own. City and borough parishes had much the same organization as those outside of the walls and chartered boundaries. It was undoubtedly true that life was more highly organized in the town than in the country, and common property, held from antiquity or obtained by bequest, such as we have noticed in the possession of rural parishes, existed in much larger amounts in the possession of London and other city parishes. The vestries were also perhaps more influential. The city governments themselves were an instrumentality for local legislation, administration and judicial enforcement of local custom that had no correlative in the country. But these were different in every chartered town. Therefore unless this chapter were to be carried into an undue amount of detail and particularity of study of individual local divisions of England, its statements must be restricted largely to the government of rural regions, of the people of the counties, hundreds and parishes, — those not living in the larger towns. This rural population, however, must have included, in the later years of Elizabeth, at least four-fifths of the people of the country. It is also true that the government of rural England was attracting greater attention and going through a more active development than was that of the towns. Although many new charters were given at this time and many towns became corporations which had previously been chartered but never incorporated, the new charters were more verbose than pregnant; they are characterized rather by greater length than by more extended powers of self government. The central government of the Tudors and the Stuarts was as jealous of town independence as it was of all other rival power.

In three large sections of England, those groups of counties which lay within the administration of the Councils of the Marches of Wales and of the North and of the Wardens of the Scottish Marches, local government was very different from that of the rest of the country. But after all they were exceptional; the main outlines of county, hundred and parish government as described in the preceding chapters, with the varied activities of lords lieutenant and their deputies, sheriffs, justices, coroners, constables, churchwardens and overseers, include all that was characteristic of local political life at the close of the sixteenth century.[24]

[24] Tanner, 314–35; C. A. Coulomb, *The Administration of the English Borders during the Reign of Elizabeth;* Rachel R. Reid, *The King's Council in the North;* Caroline S. J. Skeel, *The Council in the Marches of Wales.*

Part IX
The Fall of Essex

Part IX

The Fall of Essex

CHAPTER XLII

THE ISLANDS VOYAGE OF 1597;
THE YEAR 1598

IF the earl of Essex had been born a king he would have been a gracious, popular and reasonably happy monarch. Adventurous, alert-minded, quick to reward merit, appreciative of devotion, affable, liberal, he would have rejoiced in the popularity it was so easy for him to win. Born a subject, as he was, under the repressive authority of the queen and restricted by the rival influence of other statesmen and courtiers, his limitless ambition, his desire for glory and applause, his inefficiency, gave him no rest or satisfaction in life. It is true when he returned from the Cadiz expedition, at the end of the summer of 1596, he held as distinguished a position as a subject could attain to, at least under Queen Elizabeth. He was then at the highest point of his brilliant, but, in his own eyes at least, somewhat dolorous fortunes. A picture has come down to us from those months of the queen's towering passion against Burghley for his unwillingness to accept her view of the proper division of the spoil of Cadiz, and of the lord treasurer's recourse to Essex, begging him on his knees to befriend him with the queen in her anger. The unedifying spectacle of the aged minister, dignified by character, learning and a lifetime of devoted state service, kneeling before the young nobleman whose strength lay only in the fondness of the queen, his high birth and popular favor shocked Essex himself. It serves none the less to indicate his political and personal position at that time. Francis Bacon, the clearest head and the coldest heart of that age, in a letter to Essex of October 4, 1596, refers to his supremacy in England, next to the queen, as a matter of general acknowledgement. It was this prominence that permits the following of the fortunes of Essex as the most satisfactory clue to the occurrences of the next four years.

His career and the general history of England were inseparable. In midwinter, 1596-7, he was ill and angry because of the criticism of the Cadiz expedition and some other matters, and for two weeks stayed sullenly away from court, while the queen, wishing to " breake him of his Will and to pull down his great Hart," delayed giving him the comfort and favor he desired. But in March she abandoned the attempt, charging his obstinacy to his maternal inheritance, added the office of master of the ordnance to his mastership of the horse and other positions, and he was again on affectionate terms with his royal mistress. He was still reported occasionally to be " malincholy," but this was part of his temperament. His wide correspondence with the rulers, statesmen and scholars of his time, the stories of his gallantry at Cadiz, current on the Continent as well as in his own country, the good opinion of the common people and their conviction that he would in some way at some time serve their interests were added to the favor of the queen and the kindly feeling toward him of most of his colleagues on the Council and at the court. A Moroccan prince writes to a nobleman in Portugal that he has heard much of the fame of this English lord and wants to be told about him, his age, his rank, his personal character, his religion. The estates of the Netherlands declare that they are willing to enter into a certain enterprise though costly and dangerous, if Essex is placed at the head of it. According to the bright little contemporary poem " The Robin," with its transparent reference to Essex,

The larke and lynnett singeth well
The thrissell dowe his best,
The Robyn beares away ye bell
And passeth all the rest.[1]

The year 1597 was marked by an apparently complete cessation, at least for the time, of the jealousies, antagonisms and factional contests in which Essex was more or less involved. Sir Robert Cecil, whose influence with the queen, now that he was secretary, was steadily increasing, made every effort to conciliate him, and they two together in April dined with Ralegh, made up all differences, and agreed that Cecil should make an effort to secure Ralegh's restoration to the favor of the queen, long denied him on account of his intrigue and later secret marriage with Elizabeth Throgmorton. This was accomplished shortly afterward, Ralegh resumed his duties as captain of the guard and his regular appearance in the queen's chambers; Cecil was, according to a private letter from the court, "in greatest credit with the queen, passing most part of the day in private and secret correspondence with her Majesty"; and as to Essex, "there is not a day passes that the queen sends not often to see him, and himself every day goeth privately unto her." The queen rejoiced in these good relations among her favorite courtiers. In midsummer, when Essex was away, Cecil wrote to him, "The queen is so disposed now to have us all love you as she and I do every night talk like angells of you"; while Ralegh with Essex and the army in a letter to Cecil at about the same time writes that he has given the secretary's kind messages to Essex, and promises for himself "I will ever be yours, it is all I can say, I will perform it with life, with fortune." Cecil writes as Essex is about to start on the Islands expedition "If you bring home something we shall thank you, but bring home yourself and take my word, we will never chyde you."

[1] *Sydney Papers*, ii, 18–20, 23–7, 31; Birch, *Memoirs*, ii, 281–3, 296, 334; Devereux, *Lives of the Devereux, Earls of Essex*, i, 294–401, 403; *Ancient Biographical Poems*, Camden Soc. *Miscellany*, iii, 21; *Hatfield House MSS.*, xiv, 15, 26, 50, 57, 79, 81.

Good relations extended even more widely. Essex at the beginning of the summer's campaign called Ralegh and Vere before him and made them shake hands, for fear there remained between them " some grudge of the last year's falling out," and he did his best to have Sir Robert Sydney raised to a peerage. Cecil expressed to Francis and Anthony Bacon, who were supposed to be his rivals, his desire to do what he could for them, and Francis was specially graced at Christmas by the queen. Cecil and Cobham after long estrangement made friends in February. Some of these agreements were perhaps not of flawless sincerity, as they were certainly not of permanent endurance, and among lesser men there were undoubtedly divided allegiances; but in the main and for the time the queen's radiant affection for Essex, her dependence on Cecil's abilities and her recognition of Ralegh's gifts of body and mind were reflected in their cordial and confidential relations to one another.[2] In the middle of 1597 Essex might consider himself happy in the sunlight of the queen's favor, the respect of his colleagues and the affection of the people. Later the clouds of misfortune which he complained were always sweeping across his sky settled into the leaden covering which was never again lifted till the final storm broke over him.

For the present, however, his fortunes were happy and apparently susceptible of still further advance. The expedition for the invasion of Spain which was placed under his command in 1597 would, if it succeeded, not only give England a permanent advantage over Spain but raise still higher his own prestige and influence. In the outcome its almost complete failure deeply involved his standing, especially in that direction which was most important to him, the favor and support of the queen.

The Islands Voyage, as this expedition came to be called, was in point of policy a repetition of the Portugal expedition

---

[2] *Sydney Papers*, ii, 17, 18, 22, 42, 54; Birch, *Memoirs*, ii, 241, 281-3, 345, 348, 351, 353; *State Papers, Dom., Eliz.*, cclxiv, 5, 10, 57; Vere, *Commentaries*, 45-8.

of 1589, Lord Thomas Howard's voyage of 1591, that of Hawkins and Drake to the West Indies in 1595, the Cadiz expedition of 1596 and other similar projects; that is to say, an effort to destroy the Spanish war navy in its own harbors or at sea, and at the same time to inflict some further injury upon Spain or to gain some advantage for England. This ulterior advantage might be the capture of the East Indian or West Indian fleet or some of her trading ships at sea, the creation of a troublesome diversion for her, or the ravaging or even capture of some of her territories. It was sometimes clearly planned, sometimes obscurely anticipated and sometimes merely hoped for from chance. Some ulterior plan was always in existence, yet the hope of destroying the means by which Spain might invade England was always, and with entire military justification, given precedence.

The Spanish fleet and army which had been so hastily and inefficiently organized for the invasion of the queen's dominions in the autumn of 1596 had as already described been scattered by storm and driven back into harbor, but it had not been destroyed, and it lay in Ferrol and Corunna through the winter, a constant threat and danger to England. Even Burghley declared " I think nothing so needful as to attempt some enterprise against the Spanish army in Ferrol." An attack directly upon it by the ships of the Channel fleet under Lord Thomas Howard and Sir Walter Ralegh was planned, apparently, in midwinter. Later, in January, 1597, both Essex and Cumberland laid plans before the queen for a surprise attack on the fleet; but both these projects were rejected. It was ultimately decided to organize for the spring of 1597 an expedition on a larger scale and with more ambitious aims. The plans and preparations gradually took shape. It was to be a more purely government enterprise than those which had preceded it, the whole cost being a public charge. In February the Netherlands estates were asked to contribute twenty ships, a number later reduced by ten, but this reduction was to be compensated for by permission for a thousand English troops to be temporarily withdrawn from the cautionary and garrison towns.[3]

The queen, as usual, at one time doubted the wisdom of sending out this expedition and is reported as being angry with her counsellors who were urging her to it. But in April she ordered ten more ships of the royal navy, in addition to the ten originally planned for, to be equipped, and from this time preparations advanced rapidly. A general restraint was placed on all shipping and seamen, followed by the usual press of mariners and vessels for the transport service. The results of the press were an even more unsatisfactory body than usual. They were " taken up by the press-masters in mariners' clothes, but shall not know any one rope in the ship." It was complained that the press-masters let the good men go " for twenty shillings apiece," while competent sailors engaged on privateers " made a jest of the press." Nevertheless the sailors, the queen's ships and the transports were ultimately collected in the Downs, Sandwich, Weymouth and Plymouth.[4]

Six thousand troops, later reduced to four thousand, were ordered to be levied to make up, along with those brought from the Netherlands, a land army. Essex does not seem to have asked for the leadership of this expedition. During this winter he was again half inclined, as once before, to give up martial service and seek his greatness in civil influence in the government. His plans for an expedition in midwinter had only been made in response to the queen's order. His best friends deprecated both his absence from court and his possible achievement of military glory which might create jealousy in the highest quarters. Francis Bacon followed up the letter of advice of the preceding October by another carefully worded letter to the same

[3] Birch, *Memoirs,* ii, 266, 278–9, 344; *State Papers, Dom., Eliz.,* cclxii, 16; *Cal. State Papers, Dom.,* 1595–7, 350; *Acts of the Privy Council,* xxvii, 101–7.

[4] *Acts of the Privy Council,* xxvi, 60–2, 65; *State Papers, Dom., Eliz.,* cclxiv, 11, 12, 20; *Sydney Papers,* ii, 52: Corbett, *Successors of Drake,* 153–6, 158–60.

effect, and others of his own adherents urged that the command of this expedition must at least be pressed upon him not sought by him. In April it was rumored that he was to be sent with it and in May he was definitely appointed to the command of the expedition. He was to be sole commander. The evils of divided control had been made sufficiently obvious at Cadiz, at Lisbon and in the West Indies, and the lord admiral, being sixty-one, had become according to sixteenth century standards, so old a man that he might be excused from the rigors of a sea journey.[5]

The formal commission was issued June 4. It includes the usual complaint of the aggressive intentions of the king of Spain, followed by a declaration of the queen's intention to withstand attack by all means defensive and offensive. Essex, adorned with his seven titles of nobility and three of office, is endowed for this occasion with the additional office and title of lieutenant general and governor of the army and fleet about to be sent out. He is empowered to appoint officers, regulate and control men, enforce martial law, grant knighthood, invade and carry on warfare wherever the army and navy under his command shall go by land or sea, until the queen revokes his commission. His instructions, issued June 15, limited somewhat these high powers by requiring that they should be exercised in conformity with the advice of six councillors, Lord Thomas Howard, Ralegh, Vere, Sir George Carew, Lord Mountjoy and Sir Ferdinando Gorges. The objects of the expedition were stated more definitely than usual. Its primary duty was the destruction of the Spanish fleet; if this was found on the coast of Spain it should be attacked there, if it had left it must be followed up and destroyed. Yet, by a curious restriction, none of the queen's ships were to be seriously endangered. Later, the fleet and army might lie in wait to intercept carracks or

[5] *Acts of the Privy Council*, xxvi, 60–2, 65; *State Papers, Dom., Eliz.*, cclxiii, 102, cclxiv, 11, 12; *Sydney Papers*, ii, 53: Birch, *Memoirs*, ii, 281–2, 296, 327, 334, 345; Devereux, *Lives of the Devereux*, i, 394–410, 404; Essex, *Apology*, B. 2, 3.

galleons and if desirable go to the Azores for that purpose. If Terceira, the stronghold of the Azores, was taken and all the council agreed, Essex might retain it and leave a garrison there, though it was made clear that the queen's consent to this bold policy was reluctant and doubtful. As before, a printed " Declaration of the just causes moving the queen's majesty to send a navie and armie to the seas and toward Spain " was issued as an appeal to the critical judgment of the world.[6]

By the 25th of June the fleet with its transports was gathered and at anchor in the Downs with 2000 of the soldiers aboard. There they were joined by the Dutch contingent and the 1000 English soldiers from the Netherlands garrisons. Vere reported to Essex at Sandwich. The other principal leaders were already aboard and during the next two weeks the fleet was working along the south coast against adverse winds, stopping to take on more troops at Weymouth. Essex was fretting about the depletion of the food supply, only prepared for a three months' voyage, receiving letters from the queen and replying to them from almost every port. These letters to the queen reached the very acme of flattery and subservience. Yet they secured a promise of another month's supply of food for the troops, and July 8 ships, sailors and soldiers were all at their rendezvous at Plymouth. There were nineteen of the queen's ships, nine armed merchantmen, the fleet of ten Dutch warships, and some fifty or sixty transports and victuallers, besides the usual swarm of irregulars sailing along in hopes of plunder. As volunteers also came the earls of Rutland and Southampton, Lords Grey, Cromwell and Rich and many knights and gentlemen. To a number of others the queen had refused permission to go. Among the queen's ships were the St. Matthew and St. Andrew which had been captured at Cadiz the year before. Altogether the fleet was about the same in number with those which had gathered in

---

[6] *Egerton Papers, Camden Soc.*, 239–44; *State Papers, Dom., Eliz.*, cclxiii, 102.

the same harbor the year before for the attack on Cadiz, and in 1589 for the expedition to Lisbon.[7]

By what seemed at the time unusual good fortune the wind was favorable and on Sunday the 10th of July the expedition sailed, ranged in four squadrons, respectively under Essex, Lord Thomas Howard, Ralegh and the Dutch admiral Duvenvoord. The good weather, however, was deceptive. The northeast wind developed the next day into a gale which swept them out of the mouth of the Channel only to be met by a southwestern storm that battered the ships up and down between Scilly and Ushant until for the most part they gave up the fight and ran back for Plymouth and nearby ports. There seems little doubt of the unusual severity of the storm. The letters of the various commanders to the queen and the secretary vie with one another in their florid descriptions of their experiences, and John Donne, who was one of the gentlemen volunteers on the expedition, in his poem *The Storm,* of which it was the subject, declares:

> " Compared to these storms death is but a qualme,
> Hell somewhat lightsome and the Bermuda calme."

In a letter to a friend he gives testimony to the unusual piety of the sailors. It was " so very bad wether that even some of the mariners have been drawen to think it were not altogether amiss to pray, and myself heard one of them say, ' God help us.' "

Howard's squadron alone, either missing the worst of the storm or exercising better seamanship, reached the coast of Spain, showed itself off the harbor of Ferrol and along the coast of Asturias and Galicia and finally, on hearing of the return of the rest of the expedition, came back to Plymouth. It brought the significant news that although the adelantado's fleet had seen them and must have recognized their inferiority in numbers, it had not ventured out to attack

⁷ Oppenheim, *Monson's Tracts, Navy Records Society,* xxii, Pt. 2, ii, 38–52; *Sydney Papers,* ii, 54–5; Birch, *Memoirs,* ii, 344–5, 348, 351; Camden, *Annals,* 530; Devereux, *Lives of the Devereux,* i, 413–22.

them. This reluctance of the Spanish fleet to come out to fight had an undue influence on the judgment and policy of Essex and his councillors through the whole remainder of the campaign.[8]

At Plymouth the fleet all gathered again and while it was being refitted and awaiting a favorable wind, various changes of plan were suggested. Ralegh urged that they should wait till winter weather should complete the immobilization of the Spanish fleet at Ferrol, then make a run for the West Indies to seek the treasure fleet before it sailed. The queen and privy council on the other hand questioned whether the ill fortune of the expedition at the outset did not indicate the desirability of giving up the voyage altogether. In the meantime supplies were being exhausted, a number of noblemen and other distinguished volunteers, disgusted by seasickness and delay, were slipping off home, and there was much illness among the troops. Early in August Essex and Ralegh rode up to court to urge on the queen a quite different plan. This was to conserve supplies and get rid of a sickly army by discharging all the land troops except the thousand from the Netherlands, and to start again for the coast of Spain under new auspices, making the expedition mainly if not entirely naval.

Without an army, of course Ferrol could not be captured, but neither the queen nor Essex proposed leaving the Spanish fleet unimpaired. According to the latter a forlorn hope might be sent into the harbor to destroy the fleet and then escape as it could. Essex wished himself to lead this dash, anticipating that if it were successful he could afterwards sail up and down the Spanish coasts and go adventuring to the Azores or elsewhere almost at will. The change of plan was approved in its general outlines, but the queen refused to risk any of her war vessels in the harbor of Ferrol and forbade Essex to lead such a dangerous attack in person. It was planned therefore that Ralegh should

[8] *Relation*, Purchas, *Pilgrimes*, xx, 24–6; Gorges, *Ib.* 34–44; Oppenheim, *Monson's Tracts*, ii, 50–2; Devereux, i, 429–33; Camden, *Annals*, 530.

take in the two galleons lately captured from Spain, with
some merchant and fire ships, while Essex with the remainder of the fleet should lie outside the mouth of the
harbor to lend succor and prevent the escape of the Spanish
fleet.

It was a full month before the fleet actually sailed from
Plymouth for the second time. There was an occasional
gracious letter from the queen to Essex and to " good
Thomas and faithful Mountjoy," but more than once she
was smitten with doubts. At Greenwich, Sunday, July 25,
during morning service, she wrote with her own hand the
sketch of a letter to Essex ordering him on no account to
attack Lisbon while on the voyage, called Cecil to her and
handed it to him, and later in the day corrected and signed
a formal copy and had it sent. When Cecil expressed a
doubt whether this warning was necessary she told him that
Essex had once said to her that he could have taken Lisbon
the year before if he had been let alone. Cecil sent Essex
the queen's original draft as well as the fair copy, thinking
he would be interested in it, and the two still lie folded
together among Essex's confiscated papers with the great
" Elizabeth R." at the top and the signet at the bottom of
the more formal letter.[9]

Even when the risk of recall had passed, the wind turned
to the north and east and the expedition finally got off only
on the 17th of August. Even now the weather was scarcely
more favorable. They soon reached the Spanish coast, but
heavy easterly winds kept them standing up and down off
the bay at the head of which Ferrol lies; the St. Matthew
lost her foremast and went limping home by way of France;
the St. Andrew, the other " old cart," as Essex called her,
became separated from the fleet; his own ship sprang a leak
and he had to lie to to mend it, and Ralegh, his main yard
broken, with his squadron of twenty vessels following him,

[9] State Papers, Dom., Eliz., cclxiv, 54, 60; Essex, Apology; Cottonian
MSS., Otho, E., ix, fo. 377; Hatfield House MSS., vii, 349, 352, 361; Oppenheim, 52–6; Corbett, 176–86; Devereux, I, 445–6.

drove before the wind far to sea and could do no better than make for the next rendezvous, Cape Roca. Essex with such members of his council as could be reached decided that the adverse wind, the lack of the principal vessels appointed for the adventure, and the absence of Ralegh made an attack on the Spanish fleet in its harbor without the support of landing troops impracticable. Thus the main original purpose of the expedition was rather lightly abandoned. Yet Essex can hardly have given up the effort to destroy the Ferrol fleet without regret and misgiving. To go with his fleet wherever he would with no threatening enemy behind him would have been liberty indeed; to leave the Spanish armada undestroyed made certain the fear and probably the anger of the queen. Yet an Elizabethan fleet was after all somewhat the sport of chance. It was limited in its ability to sail into the wind, powerless before a storm, always insufficiently equipped with food and water and information, and often indefinite in its objective. It is seldom a naval expedition sailed undeviatingly on its course as did the Cadiz fleet in 1596; and it will be remembered that even that fleet was subject to endless vacillation once its first object was attained. So Sir Robert Knollys was sent home to make out the best case he could for the abandonment of this part of the plan, the absence of Ralegh with his squadron being made, as was afterwards acknowledged, somewhat more than fair use of as an excuse.[10]

The next few days were spent by Essex with his three squadrons sailing up and down the northerly section of the coasts of Spain and Portugal, Ralegh with the remaining squadron doing the same somewhat farther south, both watching for the possible though improbable emergence of the adelantado's armada or the much more probable arrival of carracks from the East or galleons from the West Indies. August 30 Ralegh picked up an English privateer from Southampton who reported that he had heard that the adelantado had sailed from Ferrol, evaded the whole English

---

[10] Oppenheim, 57-8; *Hatfield House MSS.*, vii, 368, 371, 383-4, 465.

fleet and was now on his way to the Azores to meet and
convoy home the treasure fleet from the West Indies. Improbable as this report was Ralegh believed it and sent the
news to Essex. With the agreement of the whole council
both branches of the fleet now abandoned the Spanish coast
and sailed away for the Azores. By September 15 they had
all gathered at their rendezvous at Flores, the westernmost
of the Islands. On the way Essex looked into Angra roads
in the island of Terceira, the natural stopping place of a
Spanish fleet, found the harbor empty, and soon learned that
the story of the armada's departure from Ferrol for the
Islands was false. But it was too late or too uninviting to
return to the coast. To get fresh water and food, to plunder
the scattered islands, to watch for carracks from the East
Indies, the fleet from America or the chance merchantmen
that habitually stopped there before starting on the remaining long run for Cadiz, Seville, Lisbon or Corunna was a
much more attractive and possibly an equally profitable
task, since the adelantado seemed inclined to stay quietly in
harbor at Ferrol.[11]

To the chief men of Flores who immediately came aboard,
submitted themselves humbly, insisted that they were poor
men, natural subjects of the Portuguese and only by tyranny
under the crown of Spain, Essex with his usual good nature
granted a written letter of protection, and issued orders to
the fleet that everything taken must be paid for. They
spent a happy week refreshing themselves at Flores. The
other islands were divided among the captains for seizure
and plunder or enforced contributions. The admiral and
Ralegh were to take Fayal, Howard and Vere Graciosa,
Mountjoy and Blount St. Michael, while Pico, with its
famous wines, was left to the tender mercies of the Dutch.
The capture of Terceira, if it should be undertaken at all,
was reserved for the joint efforts of the whole fleet. In the
meantime scout vessels were sent to the north and south

[11] *Relation*, Purchas, xx, 26; Gorges, *Ib.* 44–61; *Hatfield House MSS.,*
vii, 361, 369, 371, 386; Corbett, 184–94.

to watch for the possible coming of the Indian fleet, though the probability of its arrival was weakened in the credulous soul of Essex by a chance report from a captured pinnace from the West Indies that it would not sail this year.[12]

Three incidents in the attempt to carry out these plans may serve to differentiate this expedition from those that preceded it and to measure its success or failure; the capture of Fayal, the escape of the West Indian fleet and the indecisive operations at St. Michael. Intermingled with these major but unprofitable operations was the capture of five Spanish merchantmen which not only inflicted corresponding loss upon Spain but might under more careful administration have paid the expenses of the expedition.

Essex, who with the main body of the fleet had arrived at the rendezvous earliest, impatient to begin the plunder of the islands, interrupted Ralegh and his squadron still engaged in the work of watering at Flores with midnight orders to sail for Fayal, where he would find him with the main fleet. Ralegh in accordance with these orders with his rear-admiral's squadron arrived before Fayal the next day. But in the meantime Essex had been led off on an obscure search for the Spanish fleet and for four days Ralegh lay before Horta in Fayal watching the inhabitants carry their goods inland and hesitating whether he should attack without waiting for his chief. He was tempted still further when two Portuguese islanders swam out to his ships in the harbor in the night, assured him the inhabitants would gladly receive him if he would land and gave valuable information as to the defenses. The necessity for watering, the provocative action of the Spanish garrison and the genuine doubt as to what action Essex would wish him to take at last led him to land troops and occupy the city, the shore and the lower forts. The next day Essex appeared with his fleet. Stirred by advisers unfriendly to Ralegh, who went immediately to meet him, the general received him coldly, and even threatened to courtmartial

[12] *Relation,* Purchas, xx, 27–8; Gorges, *Ib.* 67–74; Oppenheim, 62–3.

and execute him for violation of the rules of warfare in making a landing and capture without orders from the head of the expedition. Ralegh explained the circumstances, claimed that he was not an ordinary officer but one of those in commission as a principal leader of the expedition, and intimated to his friends that rather than submit to court-martial he would betake himself to his squadron and either leave the earl or resist him by force.

The interposition of Lord Thomas Howard, vice-admiral, Essex's recognition of the danger of having to report at home that he had courtmartialled the only officer who had so far achieved a victory, his own placable disposition and his recent renewal of intimacy with Ralegh healed the breach. Ralegh made a formal apology for his precipitate action, Essex accepted it readily and with all the principal officers came aboard Ralegh's flagship, the Warspite, to dine with him. As a matter of fact the news of Ralegh's successful seizure of Fayal reached court promptly and was given perhaps more than its full weight by his friends there, while there was no news of the fleet as a whole except its ineffective sailing to and fro. The discovery of the bodies of an English gentleman and a Dutch sailor with their throats cut by the Spanish garrison during its retreat led to the burning of the town and the ravaging of the surrounding country; then, some supplies being taken aboard, the distribution of the islands among the commanders apparently disregarded, the whole fleet stood away northward to Graciosa.[13]

Here again a letter of protection was granted on the appeal of the inhabitants, as at Flores, and preparations were made for landing and refreshment; but the statement, mistaken and calamitous as it afterwards proved, of Essex's shipmaster, that the anchorage here was not good, led to the sailing of the whole fleet far to the eastward, to St. Michaels, leaving, with incomprehensible carelessness, the whole sea

[13] Gorges, Purchas, xx, 74–98; *Monson's Tracts, Navy Records Society,* ii, 24, 64–5; *Sydney Papers,* ii, 68, 74.

open and unguarded to the westward. If the Indian fleet should come now it might easily reach a safe harborage in Terceira without ever meeting the English fleet. Something very like this happened. One vessel of Essex's fleet, the Rainbow, under Sir William Monson, was for some reason sent by the southern rather than the northern route around Terceira in going from Graciosa to St. Michael, and in the middle of the first night suddenly found itself in the midst of a fleet of twenty-five sail. Uncertain whether this was a detached English squadron or in truth the long sought Spanish fleet, Monson with true Elizabethan bravado, after giving his shipmaster stringent orders to keep the weather gauge of the fleet, had himself rowed in a small boat close enough to hail some of the strange vessels. Receiving the reply that they were Spaniards bound for Seville he called out that he was English, that the galleon from which he had rowed was one of the queen's ships, and dared them to chase and capture him, hoping thus to lead them in a long pursuit till they should come up with Essex and the main fleet. The Spaniards, however, too sea weary or too well disciplined, simply " gave him some shot and ill language " and sailed on for Angra Roads in Terceira. Shooting his ordnance and displaying his lights as signals Monson and the Rainbow sailed after their escaping booty, hoping that the main fleet would hear them or that they might themselves make some captures. But a stern chase is a long chase and by the close of the next day the Spanish West Indian fleet was safe in a well-protected harbor.

Never probably during the course of these wars did the English come so near a definitive victory. Six of the Spanish galleons were loaded with silver bullion, this and other treasure aboard amounting to 10,000,000 pesos. The transfer of this money into the possession of Elizabeth or even the destruction of the fleet would have enriched her or impoverished Philip and crippled his merchants beyond the possibility of recuperation within any short period of years. But the failure was complete and unalterable. It is true that the earl of Southampton on the Garland and Vere and Brooke on the Mary Rose and Dreadnaught came up in time to join in the chase, but they lost valuable time in the side pursuit of a stray Spanish frigate, and although Monson made his way into the harbor of Angra, past the entrance forts, and tried to cut out the newly arrived galleons, he was soon forced by a change of wind to make the best of his way out again. The other three English ships remained outside and by the time Essex and the main fleet had been summoned back from St. Michael, the shore forts had been so strengthened by cannon and men from the Spanish fleet and the vessels warped so close in under the defenses that the English, baffled of their prey, could only look helplessly in from the sea and grieve over their ill fortune or ill judgment. It seems certain that if the fleet, according to the advice of the most experienced captains, had only remained to the westward of Terceira, above all if it had patrolled the open sea to the westward of all the islands, instead of scattering like landsmen for refreshment or plunder, they would have gained an overwhelming victory. The West Indian fleet, ignorant of their presence, was almost in sight beyond the western horizon when they left Flores, and must almost inevitably have sailed into their arms as had the German hulks into those of Drake before Lisbon in 1589.[14]

Without an army and with scanty supplies Essex and his councillors could not hope to capture Terceira, thus reinforced, and the whole English fleet accordingly sailed back to St. Michael to join the detachment of Ralegh's ships which had been left to beleaguer that island. The main town was so situated that it could not be captured directly, but Essex and his principal officers and troops soon landed at Villa Franca, a small town from which he hoped to control the whole island. But an unusually vigorous and re-

[14] *Relation*, Purchas, xx, 28–31; Gorges, *Ib.* 74–103; *Hatfield House MSS.*, vii, 438; Fernandez Duro, *Armada Española*, quoted in Oppenheim, *Navy Records Society, Monson's Tracts*, ii, 66–7.

sourceful Portuguese officer was in command and has left us his own account of the English attack and his defense, in which the invaders naturally do not show so favorably as in most of our records of the time. Even his own record leaves something to be desired in chivalry if not in frankness. A boat sent in by Essex with a flag of truce he ordered to be fired on, so that his men would not be dispirited by the thought of surrender; to a later communication he replied that if the English wanted the water and provisions for which they asked they must come ashore at their own risk and take them. From the rough country inland he kept up such a careful watch and continuous attack on the forces at Villa Franca that they could neither forage in safety nor extend their lines away from the shore.

In the meantime the season was becoming late and the danger of such open harbors in case of storm was great. The food supply on the ships would not enable them to stay at sea long if at such a time all should sail out for safety, and the troops might have to stay ashore all winter if the ships alone went out and could not return. It was therefore determined to sail for home. Essex could not refrain from his habitual ceremony of knighting some of his comrades, though in this case he used praiseworthy restraint, the number not exceeding eight, including certain young noblemen who would presumably soon be knighted in the ordinary course of events. There are the usual stories of chivalry and tolerance on his part during the occupation of their foothold on St. Michael. Five women found when the town was occupied were placed by the commander in a house under guard to protect them from insult, and fed from his table " as if they had been women of a different rank "; and the churches and shrines were left so completely uninjured that the governor believed Essex must be secretly well disposed toward Catholicism, as indeed had been suspected under similar circumstances the year before at Cadiz.[15]

[15] *Relation*, Purchas, xx, 31–3; Gorges, *Ibid.* 108–19; Gonzalo Vaz Cou-

Six sea prizes had been captured altogether during the harrying of the islands, the pinnace from the West Indies captured at the first at Flores, a frigate plundered and then sunk by Monson during the pursuit of the great fleet south of Terceira, a large and valuable vessel belonging to the governor of Havana, accompanied by two frigates, sailing in the wake of the main fleet, and captured by Essex on his way from St. Michael to Terceira, and a small but rich ship loaded with sugar from Brazil which sailed in among the English guard vessels off St. Michael and was captured shortly before they left the islands. But here, as so often during these raids, the best of their possible booty escaped them by a hair's breadth. Not only had they seen the main fleet escape into Angra roads, but as they lay at anchor before St. Michael a great carrack of 1500 tons came unsuspectingly sailing toward them. She had been driven out of her course in attempting to round the Cape of Good Hope the year before, had gone instead to Brazil, and was now bringing home a cargo of sugar. In a half hour she would have been in their possession when an impatient Dutchman weighed anchor and sailed to meet her. Perceiving that she was among enemies she turned and ran herself ashore under the castle, unloaded much of her cargo and ordnance, then, when the English seemed inclined to follow her up, set herself on fire and burned to the water's edge.

The English fleet left St. Michael, the southeasternmost of the Azores, October 15, just a month from their arrival at Flores, the northwesternmost island. Their embarcation and departure were carried out with none too much dignity, safety or unity. There was a rear-guard conflict with the Spanish garrison in which there was some loss; Essex sat on horseback, smoking a pipe of tobacco, surrounded by a group of nobles and gentlemen on foot while the troops were embarking; discontent was felt by many if

tinho, *Hist. do Succeso que na Ilha de St. Miguel ovoe con Armada Ingresa*, Lisbon, 1630, quoted in Oppenheim, *Monson's Naval Tracts*, ii, 68–72.

not expressed; several cannon, horses, boats and water casks were left ashore as the invaders retired, and the Spanish garrison as it reoccupied Villa Franca fired farewell salutes of derision. After its departure the fleet scattered widely; haste, depression, want of provisions and northeast gales keeping its members apart until they reached, some Irish ports, some the Bristol Channel, some, among them Essex himself, their original Channel points of departure, the latest ships creeping in on the very last days of October. The commander's report of his arrival on the coast was dispatched to court, October 21, and he himself landed at Plymouth, October 26.[16]

Yet, scattered, weatherbeaten and disappointed as they were, they were more fortunate than they knew at the time. They had escaped a still greater danger. The same gales from which they had suffered had scattered and driven back the Spanish armada, which had taken advantage of their absence in the Azores to leave Ferrol with the hope of intercepting the returning English fleet, dispersed as they expected to meet it, and of making a landing on the English coast. Philip had never reconciled himself to the failures of previous years and had not ceased to urge the refitting and departure of his battered fleet of 1596. In August he had sent 4000 Italian soldiers from Cadiz to reman it, and when the news of the English departure from the Spanish coast for the distant islands came the opportunity seemed too good to be lost. The adelantado therefore, reluctantly enough, two days before Essex left the Azores, though the movements of each fleet were unknown to the other, sailed out of Ferrol harbor. He had instructions to seize, fortify and garrison the peninsula on which Pendennis castle stands, near Falmouth, then to take his station off the Scilly islands and watch for the return of the English ships from the Azores and destroy as many of them as possible. If successful he should land again at Falmouth, where he would

[16] Corbett, 203–11; Oppenheim, *Monson's Naval Tracts,* ii, 70–2; *Hatfield House MSS.,* vii, 437, 443–5.

be reinforced, march eastward and capture and hold Plymouth. This ambitious and indeed well-nigh impossible plan was to be carried out by an army of some 5000 carried in a fleet of something like a hundred and forty vessels. These were of the most varied origin, including forty-four royal ships of war and twenty-seven Levantine and Easterling ships of 400 or 500 tons apiece, all together scarcely less in strength than the great armada of 1588. The fleet carried horses, oxen, carts, mills, landing rafts and material for fortification, but was only slenderly supplied with victuals and war munitions.

Yet the English fleet as it came in from the Azores was almost defenseless. Not only were its vessels making their way homeward singly or in small groups, but on account of the bad weather and their confidence that there would be no more fighting many had unshipped their larger cannon and stowed them in the hold so that the vessels might ride better. Still there were other English ships at sea and troops ashore, and the contest must have been a bitter one. Fortunately for both parties, probably, none of these things were tested, for again, as the year before, scarcely had the Spanish fleet emerged from Ferrol when the Biscay gales caught it and buffeted and scattered it during three days. Some of the Spanish vessels were sunk, some took refuge, as the lesser of two evils, in ports in Ireland and the Bristol Channel; the greater part succeeded in getting back to Spain, though humiliated and demoralized.[17]

This whole series of events was unknown to Essex and to the English government until the storm was over, the danger past and the adelantado back in Spain. The returning vessels of the English fleet were surprised to hear as they entered port rumors of Spanish vessels seen off the coast, and in one or two cases to find disarmed Spanish ships in English ports when they made their own way in. During the last few days of October the government, at last

[17] *State Papers, Dom., Eliz.*, cclxv, 26; Gorges, Purchas, xx, 104, 118–25; *Hatfield House MSS.*, vii, 428, 494–5.

apprised of the danger, was taking hurried measures of defense by land and sea. Lord Chamberlain Hunsdon was ordered to the west to resist with local levies the Spaniards if they landed and all country gentlemen were ordered to go to their homes. Essex on his arrival at Plymouth and discovery that the Spanish armada was at sea declared that he and his crews would sail again immediately if the queen would allow them, " though we eat ropes' ends and drink nothing but rain water," food and drink equally unpalatable presumably to an Elizabethan ship's crew. He made a hasty trip to London to secure the queen's consent and instructions. The consent to go out again he received readily enough, but the instructions reminded him that the Spanish fleet had recently sailed while he was absent with the queen's fleet and forbade him to leave the English coast, even to go as far as Ireland, unless absolutely certain that the Spanish fleet had gone thither ahead of him. At the same time orders were issued to Palmer and Gilbert to take the Channel squadron of small warships westward. Ralegh went ashore to raise the levies of his counties of Devon and Cornwall if they should be needed. Some laggards of Essex's fleet as they arrived reported being in action with Spanish ships, but these were evidently themselves stragglers, and the complete dispersal of the Spanish fleet was soon learned. The English ships were recalled, the Dutch fleet with its English soldiers went back to the Netherlands, and before Christmas all extra forces of the year by sea and land were discharged.[18]

As to costs many thought that if the captures had been carefully exploited and all the plunder honestly turned over to the government the expedition would not have ended with a deficit, indeed might have shown a profit. A careful officer, like Gorges, according to his own narration was able on his return to pay off his sailors and soldiers from the sugar,

[18] *State Papers, Dom., Eliz.*, cclxiv, 153; Gorges, Purchas, xx, 118–25; Oppenheim, ii, 72–9; Corbett, 219–27; *Hatfield House MSS.*, vii, 428, 433–4, 445, 449–57, 462; *Sydney Papers*, ii, 72, 74.

logwood and other things he had captured from the enemy and sold by auction for £500 in Bristol. Gorges acknowledges that he was personally unfortunate in that a captured Spanish gentleman who had been given him by the General to be ransomed and with whom he had much interesting talk while they were at sea, when they reached port bribed the captain of a pinnace in which he was being taken ashore and escaped, " without even bidding me farewell "; but others were more fortunate in their ransom money. The finances of these campaigns are an almost unsolvable puzzle, as already indicated in the study of earlier expeditions, even when traced with the greatest skill and care.[19]

As to the three original objects of the expedition, to destroy the Spanish war fleet in the harbor of Ferrol or at sea, to capture the treasure and merchant fleets from the West and East Indies on their way to Spain, and to seize a foothold in the Azores, these, according to the acknowledgment of Essex and his fellow commanders themselves, had " failed of successe." The effect of this failure on the fortunes of Essex, which is just now our special interest, does not seem to have been serious if only his colleagues and the populace are considered. The good relations between the earl, Ralegh and the quietly influential Cecil still remained cordial. The privy council wrote as a body congratulating the commander on his safe return, and several of the other statesmen and courtiers took occasion to write him letters of confidence and reassurance. The lord admiral, recently made earl of Nottingham, when it was expected that Essex would again go to sea wrote, " I would give half my land that I were with the Tryumphe and the Ark with you to serve under you." Burghley in an affectionate letter written with his own hand, October 29, and closing, " From Westminster, with a weak hand and sore eyes, besides other infirmytyes," expresses his joy at his safe return and commiserates his losses as being due to the

---

[19] Gorges, Purchas, xx, 122, 126–9; Oppenheim, *Monson's Tracts*, i, 239, 267, 292–5, ii, 13–5. *Hatfield House MSS.*, vii, 454; *Sydney Papers*, ii, 74.

winds, " against which no creature can contend but with loss." There are many indications of his continued popularity with a large circle of lesser friends and adherents and among the mass of the people.[20]

With the queen, however, it was different. By her Essex was received coldly. She held him personally responsible for the failure to destroy the armada and to capture the West India fleet and lent a ready ear to adverse criticism. However exaggerated the charges of intrigue among men of higher rank and position at Elizabeth's court may be, it is certain that a crowd of lesser men habitually sought the favor and advantage of their respective patrons by petty depreciation of their supposed rivals, and the queen was not uninfluenced by this incessant stream of detraction. On the other hand, when Sir Francis Vere, who had broken with Essex as a personal friend and follower but who still felt a debt of honor to him as his longtime leader, visited court and found the queen in so censorious a mood, he defended the actions of the earl point by point and indeed spoke in so loud a voice as to attract the attention of the whole court and to induce the queen to summon some of the critics of Essex and force them to listen to Vere's explanations. Her irritation was somewhat reduced, but even yet she showed her dissatisfaction by complaining of the " humors and ambition " of Essex.[21]

Dissatisfaction was not all on the side of the queen. Essex himself was deeply vexed with his cold reception and with the course of events. A few days after his return to court he is reported as " disquieted "; he kept to his room and delayed taking his seat in parliament, which had opened a few days before his return. He was quick to complain to his friends that those who go to the field of danger receive no benefits, while those who stay snugly at home

[20] *Relation*, Purchas, xx, 24; *State Papers, Dom., Eliz.*, cclxiv, 159, 160, 161.

[21] Vere, *Commentaries, An English Garner*, iii, 133–4; *Sydney Papers*, ii, 74; Birch, *Memoirs*, ii, 361–2.

obtain commendation and offices and advantages for themselves and their followers. As a matter of fact court influence had not favored the earl in recent years as he had hoped. His advocacy of Davidson for the Secretaryship two years before had been unsuccessful as against the claims of Cecil; he had urged the choice of Bacon for attorney general only to have Coke given the appointment; his efforts for Sir Robert Sydney as Warden of the Cinque Ports had failed before the queen's personal preference for the young Lord Cobham. Now on his return to court he learned of two more recent and unwelcome appointments. One was the lucrative chancellorship of the duchy of Lancaster given to Cecil in October without consultation with him. The other was still more distasteful. On Sunday, October 23, while the fleet was still at sea, though approaching the English coast, the queen had handed to Lord Admiral Howard, according to old custom, as she came out from chapel, his patent as earl of Nottingham. Every mark of distinction accompanied his installation. The earl of Cumberland carried the new earl's sword, Sussex his cap and coronet, Shrewsbury and Worcester attended him, the queen made a speech acknowledging his services, Lord Treasurer Burghley was present and Secretary Cecil read aloud the patent. He was at the same time given the honorary office of Lord Steward, the ministrations of that official being just then necessary to the organization of parliament.[22]

The pride of Essex could ill bear the thought of this ceremony in honor of another noble during his short absence, and his pique was raised to hot anger by two circumstances. In the first place the new earl would take his place above him in parliament, in the council and at court; for although the holders of the great honorary offices like that of Lord Admiral regularly took precedence over all others of the same rank in the peerage, the earldom of Essex had previously raised him above Howard, Cobham and

22. *Sydney Papers*, ii, 41, 42, 54–5, 64, 68–70, 74, 75; V. G. A. Tressler, *Die Politische Entwickelung Sir Robert Cecils*, 37, 49, 57.

Hundson, who although great officers were only barons. Now as both earl and admiral Nottingham would be above him.

Secondly, the terms in which the patent of Nottingham was couched seemed to give him the principal credit not only for the great victory over the armada in 1588, but for the destruction of the Spanish fleet at Cadiz in 1596. Upon this point Essex took hold and against these terms he entered a bitter protest. He demanded that the wording of the patent should be altered, but this Howard utterly refused to agree to. Then Essex urged that right should be done him either by the appointment of a special commission to examine the circumstances of the capture of Cadiz or by the queen taking the whole matter into her own hands and giving a decision, which he agreed to accept unquestioningly. In default of either he wants to fight with Nottingham himself or with one of his sons or with anyone of his blood and name, and thus prove which of the two leaders really won the Spanish city.

The whole court was filled with the conflict. Under the claim, probably not all pretense, of ill health, Essex withdrew to his country seat of Wanstead. His best friends urged his return. There remain two kindly letters from Burghley written at this time, again in his own hand, appealing to the earl to come back to court, and one no less urgent, though less personal, being signed merely " ab Ignoto," expostulating with him for his absence from parliament. The queen was much troubled. Impressed by the justice of Essex's protest or by her fondness for him, she seems at one time to have sent Greville and Killigrew, two gentlemen of the court, to him with a form of words she proposed to introduce into Nottingham's patent. Eventually she employed Ralegh to bring the quarrel to a settlement. Either at his suggestion or possibly on the intervention of Cecil a way out was found by giving Essex the honorary office of earl marshal, vacant since the death of the old earl of Shrewsbury in 1590. Since a law passed in the time of

Henry VIII had made the order of precedence of these offices, chamberlain, constable, marshal, admiral and steward,
this appointment again gave Essex his superior position to
the lord admiral and to some extent soothed his feelings.
Nothing more was said of the terms of the patent. He returned to court, showed himself more in public, and January
11, 1598, took his seat in the House of Lords next below
the earl of Oxford, lord chamberlain, and above the
earl of Nottingham, lord admiral and steward. Howard,
on the other hand, soon laid down his white staff as
lord steward and retired to his house at Chelsea, where,
according to a court correspondent, " he intends to be
sick." [23]

Notwithstanding the blowing over of this storm, the year
1598, during the whole of which Essex remained in England,
was a period of scarcely less estrangement at court than
the preceding and the ensuing year, during so much of which
he was abroad. Although his personal relations with Burghley, Cecil and Ralegh remained for some time pleasant
and confidential, other conditions both private and public
created opposition and strained his relations with the queen.
There was much difference of opinion on the question of
peace or continued war with Spain. Henry IV, urged by
the pope, pressed by strong influences in his own country,
and considering the attitude of Spain now favorable, determined to make peace, and invited his companions in the
alliance of 1596, England and the Netherlands, to join him
in the negotiations. The queen deprecated a treaty at this
juncture, especially as it was practically sure to exclude
the Netherlands, and sent Cecil, Herbert and Wilkes to
France to try to divert Henry from entering into it. They
were in France for more than two months, but were unable
to prevent or even delay the signature of the Peace
of Vervins, which took place May 2, 1598. The queen

[23] *Sydney Papers,* ii, 77, 87; Camden, *Annals,* 535–6; *State Papers, Dom.,
Eliz.,* cclxv, 6, 10, 14; *Hatfield House MSS.,* vii, 506, 520, 526–7; Birch,
Memoirs, ii, 365; 31 Henry VIII, c. 10, § 5, *Stat. of the Realm,* iii, 729;
Townshend, *Collections,* 90.

thereupon sent Vere to Holland to draw closer the bonds between the two remaining members of the old Triple Alliance.[24]

These actions did not, however, definitely settle England's attitude toward a more general peace. The treaty between France and Spain had specifically set apart a period of six months in which negotiations might be taken up between England and Spain. One party in the English council, among them Burghley, fast approaching his death, favored a treaty; other members, among them Essex, favored a continuance of the war. The same division of opinion extended through the country. Although the sixteenth century gave little opportunity for popular opinion to express itself, not only did Burghley draw up formal " Considerations for a Treaty of Peace," but the chronicler Camden finds it possible to sum up the reasons for and against wanting the war brought to an end that he had heard publicly argued. The former are of particular interest; England would be relieved of the aspersion that she was the disturber of the whole world, the assassination of the queen would be less likely, there would be an end to war taxation, the Irish rebellion would die out, Spain, Flanders and Germany would again be open to English trade, the risks of ultimate failure in so widespread a war as that in which England was now engaged would be avoided, she would no longer be supporting self-seeking and democratic allies in the United Netherlands, " England would take Breath and lay up Wealth against future Occasions."

As a substitute for what Camden says he heard pleaded against a peace may be given a synopsis of the striking " Apology of the Earl of Essex against those who falsely and maliciously tax him to be the only hinderer of the peace and quiet of this kingdom," which was an appeal made at this time to warlike public opinion, though given as a personal defense. It was written in the form of a letter to Anthony Bacon, was circulated at the time in manuscript and was printed two years later. As disproof of the charge that he had preferred and encouraged war rather than peace Essex sets his own original " bookishness," and his private losses by the wars, especially the death of his brother. He declares " I have ever thought warres the diseases and sickness, and peace the true, natural and healthful temper of all States." He claims that he has had little to do with the initiation of the expeditions by land and sea in the carrying out of which he has taken a part, and that he has done his best to make each one of them the occasion for bringing the long war with Spain to an end. He defends especially his actions in the Islands Voyage of the preceding year. He acknowledges that as far as England is concerned, "the people itselfe growes wearie of the charge and miserye of the warres." On the other hand, he defends the soldiers as the protectors of the country, he pays eloquent tribute to the military men with whom he has served, and acknowledges that he loves them. . . . " I love them for their virtues sake and for their greatness of minde."

But the question, in his opinion, is not the desirability of peace but its possibility, and the wisdom of embracing the present offer. By a long line of argument, since become familiar, he urges the impracticability of a negotiated peace, warns against defeatists and in eloquent terms appeals for confidence in the army and navy of England and in the strength and good feeling of her confederates, the Low Countries. Notwithstanding the suffering of the poor and the deep drafts which have been recently made upon the queen's treasury, the luxury everywhere visible in England shows her wealth. The fact that Spain is now weak indicates that it is the time for war against her, not for a peace that will give her time to recuperate and which with papal sanction she can disown at any time. There is danger that the English nation will then have become unwarlike, " in love with the name and bewitched with the delights of peace," and that her military men will have been scattered or " consumed in a beggerly and miserable Irish warre." Such was an eloquent and public statement of the arguments that doubtless influenced the queen and postponed peace for five more years. When the same arguments were used once in private discussion, the aged lord treasurer silently handed Essex a copy of the psalter and pointed to the twenty-third verse of the fifty-fifth psalm, " The bloody and deceitful man shall not live out half his days," as sad a prophecy of his fate as it was an unfair description of his character.[25]

The " miserable Irish warre " which Essex deprecates gave occasion for another and more serious dispute characteristic of this period of Essex's fortunes. Although the condition of Ireland was well nigh desperate and the lord lieutenant, Lord Burgh, had died in 1597, no successor had yet been appointed. About the middle of the summer of 1598, probably in July, at a conference with the queen at which were present Essex, Howard, Cecil and Windebank, clerk of the signet, the queen proposed the appointment as lord deputy of Sir William Knollys; Essex urged the appointment of Sir George Carew, who was generally considered unfriendly to him and whom he was suspected of wishing to remove in this indirect way from the court. When his arguments for Carew seemed to make no impression on the queen Essex petulantly turned his back on her. In no mood to take such an affront, either as disparaged queen or insulted lady, Elizabeth with quick resentment, according to the chronicler, " gave him a box on the ear and bade him get him gone and be hanged." Essex put his hand to his sword, and when the lord admiral interposed, swore with an oath that he could not bear such an indignity, that he would not have taken it from King Henry

[25] Camden, *Annals*, 550–5; *An Apology, etc., State Papers, Dom., Eliz.*, cclxix, 71; *An Apology, etc.*, London, 1603; Strype, *Annals*, iv, 451; Hume, *Great Lord Burleigh*, 493; Birch, *Memoirs*, ii, 384.

VIII himself; and so rushed from the queen's presence and from the court.[26]

Months passed with Essex absent and angry. Since August 8 the moderating hand of Lord Treasurer Burghley had no longer lain on the country or controlled court conflicts. But Lord Keeper Egerton, Sir Henry Leigh, Sir William Knollys and other courtiers and friends of Essex wrote letters of friendly expostulation. They received in reply only arguments of his powerlessness at court, the justice of his sense of outrage and his determination to remain in retirement till the queen herself summoned him again into her service. August 29, he was one of the most conspicuous of the five hundred mourners at the funeral of Lord Burghley. A correspondent who was present said he carried the heaviest countenance of anyone there, but questions whether this was due to his sorrow for the lord treasurer or to his own disfavor. We who are more detached in time can be more charitable and readily believe that the loss of his boyhood's guardian and kindly mentor may have drawn tears from the eyes of the impressionable earl as naturally as the loss of her aged minister and friend is said to have done from those of the queen.

But after the funeral Essex went back to Wanstead and the queen was reported to have said that he had played upon her long enough and she would now stand upon her greatness as he upon his stomach. There are, however, some suggestions of approaches by the queen, and the earl as time went on made some show of submission, at first unsatisfactory to the queen. Early in September he is back in London, at Essex House on the Strand, not recalled to court, but enjoying the ministrations of the queen's own physician and replying occasionally to messages from her sent through her gentlemen. The steps in the healing of the breach are not recorded but by the middle of September, 1598, Essex is again at court.[27]

[26] Camden, 555-6.
[27] Birch, *Memoirs*, ii, 384-92; *Cal. State Papers, Dom., Eliz.*, 1598-1601,

Periods of disfavor of the earl with the queen were evidently becoming more numerous and prolonged, those of favor less so. Early in the year his friends at court were apprehensive that the queen would hear of his renewed attentions to Elizabeth Bridges, one of the maids of honor, which had caused an outbreak and a good beating at the queen's own hand for the lady concerned the year before; but nothing further is heard of that matter except some reported disquiet on the part of the countess of Essex, pregnant at the time. In May Essex was mildly disciplined by the queen for his share in the unauthorized marriage of the earl of Southampton.[28] These were small affairs compared with the dissatisfaction about Cadiz, the Azores, and the governorship of Ireland and the resulting periods of alienation, but they were significant. In more than one of the letters of advice that were sent to Essex the possibility is mentioned that although the queen might find it necessary again to use his services she might no longer give him her affection. A nobleman of such high rank, so popular, so experienced and so assertive could hardly be disregarded by the queen either at court or in military or civil appointments. But he might be looked on by her with coolness, and a certain amount of estrangement certainly marked the relations of the queen and her former favorite from the close of the year 1597 to his final fall.

The existence of a " favorite " was normal in royal courts of the sixteenth and seventeenth centuries. A servant or friend or minister whose relations with the monarch were more personal than the mere official, more influential than the mere courtier, seems to have been an object of natural and overmastering desire on the part of the autocratic ruler of the period, whether it was Elizabeth or James, Mary Stuart or Philip III. Essex had succeeded

88–90, 95; Chamberlain, *Letters, Camden Soc.*, 19–20; *Lansdowne MSS.*, lxxxvii, 15, 52, 53, 71.

[28] *Sydney Papers*, ii, 38, 89, 90, etc., Oppenheim, ii, 93 n.; Violet A. Wilson, *Queen Elizabeth's Maids of Honour*, 222–3.

Leicester; there were indications that young Lord Herbert, son of the earl of Pembroke, or Sir Henry Carey, son of Lord Hunsdon, with their requisite qualities of youth, good looks and vivacity, might fill the void in the queen's affections that the moody, erratic and over-ambitious earl was creating by his neglect, inconsiderate behavior, independence and frequent absence. A few months later both of these young men are spoken of at court as seeking and being pushed for the position of favorite.[29]

The word fear seems inapplicable to Elizabeth; she was personally fearless. But there may have been a certain amount at least of apprehension in her attitude to Essex. She complained to Vere, as will be remembered, of his "ambition" as well as his "humors"; the hand on the sword hilt at the interview in the summer may have remained in her memory as emblematic, if not threatening; the story that the queen and Essex "had each threatened the other's head," a court rumor reported by a London merchant to an Italian correspondent a few months' later, is probably the merest gossip, but even as such it is not without significance. The frequent indications of the popularity of the earl with the masses of London must have wakened the jealousy if not the suspicion of the queen. Moreover, as we have already seen, under the surface of Tudor subservience was always the dreaded possibility of a recourse to popular or baronial violence.[30]

So the year 1598 passed away. It had seen the death of Philip II and Burghley, the burial in Westminster Abbey of Edmund Spenser, the peace of Vervins, the establishment of the half-Spanish, half-Flemish archdukes on the throne of the Netherlands, the recession of Calais and Blavet by Spain to France, the fruitless discussions of peace with Spain, a new treaty between England and the Dutch, by which a beginning was made of the repayment of Elizabeth's loans, and other occurrences in the field of inter-

[29] *Sydney Papers*, ii, 120–2.
[30] *Cal. State Papers, Dom., Eliz.*, 1598–1601, 225.

national policy. But in certain nearer but equally troubled waters there was no policy but drifting. Unless Ireland was to drift away from England altogether some action must be taken there. It was the ill fortune of Essex during the next year, with inadequate means, unsuited abilities, deficient perseverance and little encouragement from home to try to save for England and the queen that derelict dependency.

CHAPTER XLIII

ESSEX IN IRELAND, 1599

IT is impossible to discuss the events of the year 1599 in Ireland without some consideration of the course of events for some years preceding. These gather largely around the personalities of two remarkable men, Hugh O'Neill and Hugh Roe O'Donnel. Hugh O'Neill was head of one of the two branches of the numerous clan of the O'Neills, which occupied the central and eastern portion of the old kingdom of Ulster, — the modern counties of Tyrone and Londonderry and the northern parts of Armagh, Fermanagh and Monaghan.

His branch was the elder of the two lines but was weakened by the illegitimacy of its origin, and his cousin Turlough, head of the younger branch, therefore bore the title of The O'Neill. Hugh was however favored by the English as a makeweight against the holder of the native title, who was to that extent more independent. For six years, from 1568 to 1574, when he was a young man of twenty-two to twenty-eight, he was in England, attached it would seem to the household of the earl of Leicester, certainly forming acquaintance with him, Walsingham and other English public men, and waited upon by attendants and servants, living the life of any young noble or gentleman. He was again in England in 1590. He was short of stature, but well-built, hardy, active, and as an Englishman who knew him testifies, " of a high, dissembling, subtle and profound wit." The chronicler Camden, who deplores the necessity of paying so much attention to his activities, nevertheless concedes that " his understanding was very great, his soul large and fit for the weightiest business. He had much knowledge in military affairs and a proud dissembling heart." He was well educated, and, whether arising from what seemed to the Englishman his " proud, dissembling heart," or from some native Celtic charm, he had a winning manner that not only gave him eventually unmeasured sway over his own people, but captured the hearts and obscured the judgment of many who would naturally have been his enemies. This was true not only of successive lords deputy from Fitzwilliam to Essex, but of veteran soldiers like Norris and Lee, not to speak of Philip of Spain and the great queen herself, who, notwithstanding her years of loss and exasperation at his hands, and reluctantly enough, but three weeks before her death granted him pardon on favorable terms.[1]

For twenty years after his return from England in 1574 Hugh was acknowledged and supported by the English government as one of its intermediary chieftains relied upon to secure the obedience of the still unconquered tribes. He held under his direct control, with the lord deputy's approval, most of what is now Armagh, and was expected in return to preserve order among the native population, to keep the highways open for peaceful men and, if there was occasion, to see that English troops might freely occupy a certain blockhouse on the Blackwater and pass from the Pale through Dundalk and Newry into the far north. In this capacity and in occasional conflicts with rebellious native septs, he was in command of a troop of horse and for a time was provided with six companies of foot made up of natives but paid by the English government. After his rebellion it was charged that O'Neill had made frequent changes of these soldiers, so that more of his own countrymen might be habituated to the use of muskets and English discipline. Many other native Irishmen at the same period in the English service or as volunteers in the Netherlands or

---

[1] Richard Bagwell, *Ireland under the Tudors*, iii, 74–7, 118–9, 161–5, 174–94, 218–25; Fynes Moryson, *Rebellion of the Earl of Tyrone*, 7; Camden, *History of Queen Elizabeth*, Ed. 1688, 446.

Spain learned the use of improved weapons. In the battles musketry appears regularly on both sides.

This was the period in which a handful of English officials, from one to three thousand English soldiers and perhaps as many English and mixed settlers, established among perhaps a million or more natives, were pursuing the traditional policy of divide and conquer. Conditions were particularly favorable to the success of such a policy, for with that dangerous, possibly fatal, proclivity for dissension of the Irish race inter-tribal and inter-family conflicts were constant. The harryings by natives of other native districts were equally frequent and equally barbarous with the incursions, hangings and beheadings of natives by the English military, though the latter were explained, if not justified by the effort to enforce an alien domination with inadequate force on a stubbornly resisting native population. The successive lords deputy expected to keep and extend English control in Ireland and to preserve some sort of order by ruling the Pale according to the English system of local government, by keeping garrisons in the towns and the few small fortified places beyond the Pale, and by the intermediation of friendly native chieftains like Hugh O'Neill. Until 1593 he acted with reasonable loyalty, as the English officials defined loyalty, and more than once when this had been questioned had come in to Dublin to reassert it. Nevertheless the English could not help but realize that his native claims, his Catholic religion and his position on the border of Ulster, beyond which English rule and the English type of culture had as yet no influence, made him a dubious servant of the crown, and, if his obedience should slacken, a dangerous opponent. In 1585 the Irish parliament at Dublin acknowledged his English titles of baron of Dungannon and earl of Tyrone, in succession to his grandfather Con O'Neill, the first earl, and in 1587 this was confirmed by the queen by letters patent. This seemed to set the seal to his English connection, but early in 1593 he entered into an agreement by which his cousin Turlough, now old and infirm, withdrew from the leadership of the clan and allowed the native title of The O'Neill to be transferred to Hugh. Sitting in the old stone chair in an open field at Tullaghogue, eight miles north of Dungarvan, in which with curious rites of ancient ceremony each successive principal chieftain of Ulster was solemnly consecrated to his office, Hugh became head of his clan. He thus united the two incongruous and as it proved incompatible positions of an appointed earl bound by allegiance to the English queen and an elective Irish chieftain subject to the passionate desire for independence of his race. This action involved almost necessarily a closer alliance with the other Irish chieftain who has been named.[2]

Hugh Roe O'Donnel, who held much the same native position in Tyrconnel or Donegal, the western part of Ulster, that O'Neill held in Tyrone, its eastern, central and northern region, was the son and grandson of two successive Hughs, chieftains of that race. His mother was Ineen Dubh, daughter of James MacDonnel, Lord of the Isles, and of Agnes Campbell, daughter of the earl of Argyle. This parentage on the mother's side drew in a Scottish connection not without influence on later struggles. " Dark Agnes," as Ineen's familiar name might be translated, like Hugh's own surname, Roe, or the Red, calls attention to the mixed dark and rufous strains which run through the Celtic peoples. Ineen is spoken of as a woman of dignity, of shrewdness and persistence, and it is evident that she had much influence on the remarkable though short and tragic career of her son. In contrast with Hugh O'Neill, Hugh O'Donnel was never in England, never subject to English influence, and, so far as appears, was educated in the manner of native Irishmen of the higher ranks in such Latin and native lore as the monks and bards at the convent of Donegal gave him.

The most important crisis in his life came early. As he grew up rumors of his personal qualities and certain old

[2] Bagwell, iii, 9, 124, 129, 140, 146, 170, 197, 218, 233, 244–6, 258; Cal. State Papers, Ireland, 1588–92, Preface, 452–597.

prophecies that one Hugh who should succeed two others in direct descent in the line of the O'Donnels would drive all foreigners out of Ireland reached the ears of Sir John Perrott, then lord deputy. There were at the same time reports that the O'Donnels were becoming restive under the misuse they charged upon an English official named Willis, who, with a supporting force, had been lately imposed as sheriff upon a section of their country. The lord deputy therefore proceeded in 1587, the year in which O'Neill received his earldom from the queen, to apply the policy so often used by the English in Ireland of seizing scions of the greater houses and holding them in ward as pledges for the obedience of their relatives. It was no easy matter to secure possession of the popular young chieftain, now sixteen years old, dwelling among his people in the forests of the most distant corner of Ireland, but Perrott succeeded through an ingenious though dishonorable trick. A vessel was loaded with wine and manned, besides her crew, with fifty soldiers. She sailed from Dublin up the east coast and into Lough Swilly and anchored off Rathmullen castle. Her crew went ashore and offered their wine for sale, at first on the beach, then on the ship. The news of the wine merchants soon spread through the country and after a little manoeuvring, young O'Donnel and some of his companions were induced to come aboard. As they were being entertained in the cabin the hatches were suddenly closed down, they were hustled into an inner cabin, and the vessel sailed away to Dublin where the young men were put in irons in Dublin castle. After more than five years imprisonment, Hugh with two or three other hostages escaped on the night of Christmas, 1591, and after bitter exposure, from which one of the party died and Hugh Roe suffered for the rest of his life and after many adventures in passing through the Pale, he reached first O'Neill's country then his own.[3]

Twenty-one years of age, embittered against his captors,

[3] Lughaidh O'Clery, *Life of Hugh Roe O'Donnell*, Ed. and translated by Denis Murphy, 5-33, 43; Bagwell, iii, 221-3, 226-8, 235-40.

in the midst of his own clan, he scarcely waited recovery from the sufferings of his escape before, gathering a number of fighting men about him including some Scotch mercenaries brought in by his mother he attacked the nearest body of English soldiery and officials. He then drove out a garrison which had lately seized the monastery of Donegal and an adjoining stronghold belonging to the O'Boyles and was using them as a base for establishing shire government and incidentally plundering the people and seizing hostages. In the spring of 1592 a meeting of the various branches of the O'Donnels and their subordinate clans was called at which Hugh's father, old and unable to settle the dissensions that had arisen, voluntarily gave up the headship, Hugh Roe was acknowledged as The O'Donnel and at the rock of Kilmacrenan took the oath, was handed the white rod and the " book of laws," and thus became head of his clan and native ruler of Tyrconnel.

His harrying of the lands of the branches of the O'Neills which did not yet accept Hugh O'Neill, his joining with Maguire and some other chieftains of Fermanagh and Monaghan in an attack upon the English garrisons at Ballyshannon and elsewhere are not an essential part of this narrative, except as they constituted a definite breach with the English government and resulted in the new chieftain being proclaimed a rebel. Within the next year Hugh O'Neill joined him in a secret confederacy to strengthen themselves against the English government and to ask for help from the king of Spain. The two chiefs were already closely allied by marriage ties. O'Donnel had married O'Neill's daughter and there were other bonds of blood and fosterage between the two families. Their position in Ulster was much the same. They were the respective heads of the two most numerous and powerful native Irish races remaining unsubdued. The break of O'Donnel with the government forced upon O'Neill, or Tyrone, as it may be well, conforming to English usage of that period, to call him, a decision whether he would support the English government

or his racial allies, and in the year 1593 he definitely, although for some time covertly, adopted the latter policy.[4]

The possibility of the intervention of Spain in Ireland
was at this time a factor of growing importance. The advantages of support from that great power, if the Irish
chieftains were to make a bid for independence, were obvious. Moreover Spain had already more than once
interested herself in Irish affairs. As early as 1578 while
the sovereigns of England and Spain were still nominally
at peace there was an interchange of charges and denials of
encouragement of rebellion in Ireland and in 1580 Spaniards
were among the victims of the massacre at Smerwick.
After war had broken out, in 1588, in the wake of the
Armada some hundreds of Spaniards had suffered almost
indiscriminately from the storms, the English and the
natives on the wild west coast of Ireland. The idea of
making trouble for Elizabeth by giving aid and encouragement to the hostile Irish Catholic chieftains and fomenting
rebellion among them was as natural to Philip as the same
policy in the Netherlands and in Portugal was to Elizabeth.

The way for a closer connection was now facilitated by
the presence at the Spanish court of a number of Irish
gentry and ecclesiastics exiled on account of their participation in the Desmond rebellion ten years before, or driven
out of Ireland by the slowly advancing wave of Protestant
ecclesiastical organization. It was to some of these exiles,
James, Thomas and Maurice Fitzmaurice, sons of the earl
of Desmond, James Eustace, viscount Baltinglass, and other
noblemen, and to James O'Hely, archbishop of Tuam, and
Cornelius O'Mulrian, bishop of Killaloe, both of whom had
been frequently to and fro between Ireland and Spain, that
O'Donnel sent a letter from Donegal, April 8, 1593. He
wrote in his own name and in that of a confederacy of northern chieftains, which he explained had been formed, appealing to his fellow-countrymen in Spain to influence the king

---

[4] O'Clery, *Hugh Roe O'Donnell,* 33–59, 60–89; Bagwell, 222, 227,
254, 260.

to give them aid in their struggle against England. At the same time, the Catholic bishops in Ireland authorized those in Spain to assure the king of their approval of the proposed rising. Letters were thereupon sent by the Irish noblemen and bishops in Spain to Philip appealing to him to send the desired aid to their countrymen. They pointed out that he would by so doing compel the queen to withdraw her forces from the Netherlands, France and the coasts of Spain, himself obtain the rule over Ireland and thus gain an entrance into England, and at the same time defend and extend the Catholic faith. The ease of the undertaking, the excellence of the opportunity, the justice of the cause and the advantages that would ensue to Christendom were all put forward with the familiar force of Celtic persuasiveness.

On the margin of the original letter of the archbishop of Tuam to Philip can still be seen an annotation in the king's own hand that would probably have discouraged rather than heartened the Irish leaders if they could have seen it and realized how fully it represented Philip's policy. It reads, " If what they say is true it would be a pity not to help them. We will see what is the smallest possible support required. If it is small enough for us to spare we will help them." [5]

There was further correspondence in 1593, 1594, and the early part of 1595, but the letters were either lost or intercepted on the way. In 1594, Philip seems to have decided definitely to give help in Ireland, and Archbishop O'Hely, Thomas Fitzmaurice, John Lacy and a Spanish captain were sent over with 100 Spanish soldiers on a merchant ship, but the vessel with all her crew and passengers was lost. Later in the year another vessel was sent over with some money, but this also was lost. Nevertheless some Spanish funds must have reached Ireland for bids were made for mercenaries by the northern chiefs, even Tyrone at last venturing to show his hand. Late in the year 1594, he took the field

---

[5] *Simancas Archives, Inglaterra*, No. 839, quoted in O'Clery, l-iii; J. B. Kelso, *Die Spanier in Irland, 1588-1603*, 16-8.

openly against the English, united his forces with those of Maguire, MacMahon and O'Donnel, and on June 28, 1595, as a result, a proclamation was issued in the name of the queen declaring him, along with O'Donnel and their con-federates, traitors.

The significance of this defection of Tyrone and the danger to English supremacy in Ireland were clearly rec-ognized at the time. The queen was bitterly angry with her representatives in that country who were held respon-sible for the " treason," and the author of a contemporary *Discourse* says of Tyrone; " His rebellion will be more dangerous and cost the queen more crowns than any that have foregone him since her Majesty's reign; for, educated in our discipline and naturally valiant, he is worthily reputed the best man of war of his nation. Most of his followers are well-trained soldiers in using weapons and he is the greatest man of territory within that kingdom." The union of the two great Ulster houses in the leadership of a native rising was a new and ominous danger for the English, even apart from the burning patriotism of O'Donnel and the skill, experience and influence of Tyrone.[6]

The rebellion ripened slowly. Destructive but indecisive skirmishes and mutual ravaging took place on the borders of Tyrone and Tyrconnel. The queen's forces were not nu-merous enough to occupy hostile territory or put an end to the rising; the Irish leaders on the other hand could not make good their independence by shaking off the incubus of English military and civil pressure, and no army came from Spain to bring the conflict to a decision. A series of negotiations therefore took place. " Cessations " or sus-pensions of fighting were entered into and extended from time to time. In January, 1595, English commissioners met Tyrone and O'Donnel in an open field near Dundalk, and there was much subsequent correspondence to and fro. The

---

[6] O'Clery, *Hugh Roe O'Donnel*, 89–91, 117–19; *Cal. State Papers, Ireland*, 1592–6, 341; *Cal. Carew MSS.*, 1589–1600, 87, 97, 100, 105, 109, 111, 122–3; Kelso, *Die Spanier in Irland*, 18–9.

points of dispute were many. Religion was perhaps the most fundamental. The Catholics sought liberty of worship. Elizabeth would not listen to such a demand, although the lord deputy avoided bringing the matter up in the Irish council for fear there would be a party among the English officials themselves in sympathy with it. The queen replied to the demand of Tyrone, " He may be sharply told that the request for free liberty of conscience is unreasonable and disloyal, it being a request to have liberty to break laws, which her majesty will never grant to any subject of any degree." This was almost word for word Philip's answer to the Protestant Netherlanders, the two religious systems being reversed.

Almost equally prominent among their demands and almost equally distasteful to the government was that English officials should not be allowed to intrude into the regions under the sway of the native chieftains. There were questions of pardon, reimbursement, disputed territorial claims of rival native families defying compromise. But the English commissioners wanted the form at least of submission and peace and the Irish wanted time to see whether they were to obtain any actual help in Spain; so by May, 1596, most of the conflicts seemed settled or the demands withdrawn, and O'Neill and even O'Donnel had formally, though somewhat vaguely, agreed to accept the queen's pardon, to keep the peace and to hold no intercourse with the king of Spain or any other foreign ruler. A pardon for Tyrone and his adherents was signed by the queen on May 12, and sent to him a few weeks later.[7]

This agreement must have been quite hollow and disingenuous on the part of the two Irish leaders, for the months from September, 1595, to May, 1596, when these negotiations were in progress were marked by an actively renewed correspondence with King Philip and others of influence in Spain. On September 25, 1595, Tyrone and O'Donnel wrote

[7] *Cal. Carew MSS.*, 1589–1600, 140–70; O'Clery, lxix, lxxi, lxxv; Bagwell, iii, 265–7.

joint letters to the king and Don Juan d'Aquila, and Tyrone a separate letter to Don Carlos, the king's son, appealing for 3000 men, money and arms before the succeeding summer. These letters were intercepted and handed over to the lord deputy by the spy Piers O'Cullen.

By May 1, or a few days afterward, there arrived in Ireland, not troops or munitions, it is true, but an envoy from Philip, Don Alonzo de Cobos, with three small vessels, each with sixty musketeers aboard, and a sheaf of letters of encouragement for the Irish leaders. Cobos landed at Killybegs on Donegal bay early in May and immediately pushed on to Lifford, between Tyrconnel and Tyrone, where O'Donnel then was and where O'Neill may have secretly joined him. Cobos delivered his letters to them May 15 and to O'Rourke and some other Irish leaders in the next few days. The king's letters encouraged them in their good service to the Catholic cause and gave somewhat vague assurances of support. The letters had been written in January and named no date or circumstances of the relief for which the Irish leaders longed, but they grasped at the possibility, and when Cobos left, after but a few days on land, sailing from Killybegs, "with the first breeze of wind from the northeast," fearing that he might be captured by the English, he carried back with him a whole batch of letters in reply from the Irish nobles. They begged the king to rescue them from the bondage in which they were held by the English who had taken their patrimony away from them and were persecuting the Roman Catholic faith.

Most of the letters exchanged between Spain and Ireland at this time were in Latin, although occasionally a chieftain writes on his own account in his own language. In this correspondence the most important was a long Latin letter to the king signed by both O'Neill and O'Donnel on the 16th of May, four days after the date of their pardon by the queen. They excuse themselves for their recent negotiations with the English government, of which he must have heard, promise not to agree to any treaty with the queen and to renew war upon her as soon as they can. They accept the king's offer, made perhaps through Cobos or perhaps only dictated by their hopes, to send them 6000 soldiers with arms for 10,000, lead, powder and cannon. They beg him to send someone " to rule over and live among us," and express a preference that this should be the archduke Charles of Austria, formerly viceroy of Portugal and recently appointed governor of the Netherlands. Similar letters were sent to the crown prince, begging his support in their plea, to the secretary Don Juan de Idiaquez, and to others in Spain. The leaders were not able to wait till all the chiefs of the confederacy had gathered, but Cobos wrote and signed in their presence while at Lifford a statement to the king of his conviction that all the northern Irish lords were united and determined to rise and join with the king of Spain if he would send them help.[8]

The agreement of the chieftains that they would have no intercourse with the king of Spain, they had obviously violated in their conferences with Cobos and in the letters they had written in May. Nevertheless, they were not yet ready to throw off the mask, so they wrote with apparent frankness to Norris, commander of the English troops, that they had held a conversation with a Spanish gentleman, a messenger from the king of Spain, but had told him they had been received into the favor of their own prince and could accept no foreign aid, " and so dismissed him." Tyrone even showed to Captain Warren, who had been carrying on the negotiations for their reconciliation with the queen, the letter he had received from King Philip. Warren urged him to allow the letter to be shown to the lord deputy, and Tyrone, after the English officer had taken his oath that the letter would either be returned as it was or destroyed in his presence, allowed Warren to take it with him to Dublin.

---

    8 O'Clery, 117–9; *Simancas Archives, Inglaterra,* 839, quoted in O'Clery, lxxviii, lxxx, lxxxiii; *Cal. State Papers, Ireland,* 1592–6, 514, 517, 522–3, 527, 529–31; 1596–7, 10–11, 32, 35, 53, 62, 92; *Cal. Carew MSS.,* 1589–1600, 122–3, 128–9, 131.

When the letter was shown to the Irish Council, however, on May 31st, the lord deputy, with the agreement of all except Norris and Fenton, the earlier commissioners for the peace with Tyrone, determined, against the protest of Warren, to " stay " it, and sent the letter to the queen. She, in order to convict Philip of negotiations with her rebels and to prove that they had submitted to her, sent it on to Philip himself. Philip was very angry, but influential Irishmen at his court suggested that Tyrone might have sent the letter to the queen merely from policy, which was not far from the truth, and begged him not to allow this to prevent his sending help to the Irish patriots. The loudly expressed anger of Tyrone at this violation of a promise honorably made and honorably accepted and his threats to appeal from the lord deputy directly to the queen were also doubtless " policy." The betrayal of the given word served, as so often in the government of Ireland, to put England in the wrong, and to give an excuse to the two Irish leaders to withhold the pledges they had promised while awaiting the hoped for Spanish support.[9]

These negotiations of the Irish leaders, open and secret, with the English and the Spanish authorities were in progress during the critical months in which the attack upon Cadiz was being planned, prepared for and consummated. Before the end of July news of the catastrophe in Spain reached Ireland but it seems to have had no depressing effect on the Irish, for Tyrone, O'Donnel and others had a secret conference of several days in Donegal in the middle of August, where they discussed the best landing place for the Spanish army, whose early coming they hoped for and urged in the usual batch of letters to Spain. A month later, they received new encouragement through the arrival of Cobos for his second visit in the year 1596. He sailed from Corunna on the 6th of September, reached Killybegs on the 16th and immediately sent messengers summoning O'Donnel,

[9] Bagwell, iii, 267–8; *Cal. State Papers, Ireland,* 1596–7, 150, 158, 166; O'Clery, 517, 519, 526, 527, 532.

O'Neill and other leaders of the clans to a conference. This was held in the old monastery in Donegal from the 26th to the 29th of September.

Cobos read letters from the king, described, with some reservations, the sack of Cadiz, and assured the Irish of continued Spanish sympathy and intention ultimately to send assistance. Then he held a separate interview with each of the chiefs, and obtained their advice as to the best place for a landing, whether at Waterford in the south, at Galway in the west or at Carlingford in the northeast. It was probably at this time that a Spanish captain with some sixty foot soldiers was seen by English spies traversing Ulster, apparently surveying the country; and that the examinations of the harbors were made from which were drawn the maps that still lie in the archives at Simancas. The Spaniards had good reason to remember from 1588 the terrible west coast of Ireland, and if ships and soldiers were to be sent there it was well to know more of the coast beforehand. Cobos returned early in October carrying letters with still more urgent appeals for aid in the struggle which was now imminent. Apparently still another envoy came and obtained further letters to the king from O'Neill and O'Donnel late in October.

The position of Philip in Ireland was not substantially different from that of Elizabeth in the Netherlands. There was the same patriotic native race, the same sympathy of religion, a weak English garrison in Ireland just as there was an inadequate Spanish garrison in the Netherlands. Philip promised to be a strong foreign ally of the native cause in Ireland as Elizabeth was in the Netherlands, and the same political supremacy was offered to both rulers in return for their support. Nor were native leaders wanting in either case. Tyrone and O'Donnel were very different personalities from the princes of the house of Orange, but they were gifted and capable men. They had numbers and the benefit of position, and one of the best of the English captains, who knew both the Netherlands and Ireland, testifies to the training in modern warfare Tyrone had given to his tribes-men during the last three years. If a Spanish fleet and a Spanish force had reached Ireland in 1596 as they did five years afterward, when the fires of rebellion had been well-night smothered and its original force exhausted, the story of Spanish intervention would certainly have been a differ-ent one and it is difficult to see how English rule in Ireland could have withstood the storm.[10]

Although Spanish help did not come, through the remain-der of 1596 and the years 1597 and 1598 the native rebellion constantly spread, rooted itself anew in one part of the island after another and attained some unity and univer-sality. The Counter-reformation gave the whole struggle a religious as well as a patriotic support. A confederation of most of the native chiefs of Connaught was formed to resist the English. Negotiations were held with the clans of Munster, humbled by the crushing of the Desmond rebellion but not seriously weakened in number or in resources of food. These resulted in a new Desmond rebellion, under a rival earl set up by O'Neill as a substitute for the boy whom Elizabeth was holding in captivity in the Tower of London. Shocking barbarities accompanied the expulsion of the Eng-lish settlers from their holdings. Edmund Spenser was only one of many impoverished and driven into flight by the na-tive rising. In Leinster several half-outlaw clans were wast-ing the province and the bulk of the population were grad-ually turning from submission to the English to dependence on the northern chieftains. Even in the Pale there was much sympathy with native ambitions and readiness for defection if this center of English rule should be strongly invaded. In distant Connaught the governor, Sir Conyers Clifford, one of the few attractive characters in this tragedy, in 1598 with a little band of a hundred and twenty English and a few hundred Irish soldiers and with " not one barrell of

---

[10] Bagwell, iii, 267; O'Clery, lxxxiii; Kelso, *Die Spanier in Irland*, 32–6; *Cal. State Papers, Ireland*, 1596–7, 67–76, 86–98; *Ralph Lane to Essex*, Oct. 23, 1596, *Cal. State Papers, Ireland*, 1596–7, 151.

gunpowder " for his musketry, was holding the province precariously by a mixture of policy and force against the almost irresistible influence of the adjacent northern rising.

In the middle of the summer of 1598, August 14, there was a disastrous defeat near Armagh in which almost a thousand English troops, with thirty officers, including the marshal of the English army, were cut to pieces by the Irish under Tyrone himself. Danger pressed close to the gates of Dublin. Burning and spoiling reached to within three miles of its walls; one internal conspiracy after another was discovered, and a sudden advance of the native armies might any day capture the city and dissolve the government. There were left under English control in all Ireland only the towns and the few points held by small bodies of troops scattered here and there through the country. Even in the towns, although they were for the most part engaged in commerce and therefore favorable to the English connection and were controlled by English officials and small detachments of troops, there was much restlessness and readiness for revolt. The troops scattered through the country or engaged in military operations were unpaid, ill-equipped, dissatisfied and untrustworthy because of the many Irish among them, who were secretly in sympathy with their rebellious fellow countrymen, and were in many cases ready for mutiny or voluntary disbandment. A contemporary observes, " It is strange that Englishmen become traitors among these Irish rebels." It was hardly strange. Of the 8000 or 9000 soldiers supposed to be in the queen's service in Ireland all were scattered, many were sick, ill clothed, ill fed and ill paid and many were daily deserting.

The queen and the privy council were keenly interested in Ireland and were spending much money there. Yet although they felt that they were continually sending over men and supplies only to be swallowed up, as it were, in the Irish bogs, the English officers there, so great was their need, felt that their appeals for victuals, ammunition, men and money were being scarcely more favorably answered by

Elizabeth than the appeals of the Irish leaders by King Philip. They write warning of " these storms which break out and rage above our strength." As the winter draws on they appeal for supplies, not only to keep the soldiers from cold and starvation but to prevent the complete dispersal of the army.

The pardons granted to the Irish leaders in May, 1596, were soon withdrawn and they were anew declared to be traitors. Whether traitors or not they bade fair to wear out the strength of successive deputies and provincial commanders. Sir William Russell was recalled as lord deputy in May, 1597, and Lord Burgh took his place, but died in September. Sir John Norris, President of Munster, died in August of the same year worn out by his campaigns, and his brother, Sir Thomas, who succeeded him, died of a wound received in a skirmish two years later. Sir Henry Norris, the third brother of that warlike family, was killed at about the same time. For more than a year Ireland was without a lord deputy, its troubled civil affairs being administered by two lords justices, while military responsibility was placed in the hands of the earl of Ormonde, head of the old Norman Irish family of the Butlers, with the title of lord lieutenant, though this title was at other times generally used as synonymous with lord deputy. The Irish council alternately supported and thwarted the policy of these higher officials, or wrote to England in querulous protest against their actions. Divided counsels paralyzed effective action even where it was otherwise possible. Unless Ireland was to slip out of English hands altogether a new and more vigorous lord deputy with much more concentrated powers and much greater resources must be sent over. The lords justices themselves repeatedly plead with the queen and privy council to send over " a deputy to take upon him the management of the whole." In June, 1598, Sir Geoffrey Fenton, one of the most experienced and outspoken English officers in Ireland, writes to Cecil of the necessity for " settling the government in one sufficient man's hands."

and in November repeats that, " it is most requisite to send over a deputy with all possible speed." Captain Reade begs for the speedy appointment of " some worthy personage fit to manage the present state of this distempered kingdom." [11]

Various men of distinction were mentioned during the year 1598 for the vacant position, Sir Walter Ralegh, Sir Robert Sydney, Sir William Knollys, Sir George Carew, Lord Mountjoy. None were anxious to go. Moreover the opportunity for distinction and the need for service could hardly escape the boundless ambition and restless desire for achievement of Essex. Ireland was already the grave of reputations; his father had lost his life and his fortune there, twenty years before, and the son might well have taken warning. But the position of Essex at court was extremely unsatisfactory, his state of mind depressed and almost any field of activity, adventure or power attractive. Nor can a conscientious desire to be of service to his country and his queen be denied to him. He believed he was called to great duties and had an incorrigible, however unjustified, reliance on his destiny, or as he, like Cromwell, would have put it, on the guidance of Providence.

Whether Essex asked definitely for the appointment does not appear, but as it became evident how serious the crisis was he seems more and more to have looked upon himself as the destined restorer of Irish obedience. He criticized the suggested appointment of Mountjoy on the ground that that nobleman was too inexperienced, too slender in fortune and prestige and too literary in his interests. Bacon, who was now the mentor of Essex, first advised for, then against his taking up the task; some who wished him away from court urged his undertaking the service. In November Cecil writes to the English ambassador in France that it is likely Essex will be sent, and to the lord lieutenant in Ireland that the queen has resolved to appoint a deputy

[11] J. T. Gilbert, *Account of Facsimiles of National MSS. of Ireland*, 205–18; *Cal. State Papers, Ireland*, 1598–9, 117, 189, 327, 338, 341, 375; J. P. Kelso, *Die Spanier in Irland*, 46–9, 52–4.

and that the earl of Essex was named though there was not yet a certainty that he would go.[12]

This uncertainty was doubtless closely connected with Essex's insistence on an adequate army, sufficient supplies and a comparatively free hand. There was abundant advice from Ireland as to what was requisite. One estimate of what the queen should " afford him that shall be sent to recover Ireland," made by an official there in November, 1598, names 12,000 foot, 1,000 cavalry, 12 pieces of artillery, proportionate amounts of powder, tools and arms, planks for building, some small vessels to command the coast, money, food and apparel to support the army for a year, reinforcements to keep up its complement and extra pay to encourage the higher officers. Besides new equipment every correspondent from Ireland insisted that funds should be sent for the payment of arrearages and for the settlement of other long-standing debts. The troops already in Ireland were of small value and the new should, according to all advice, be either veterans from the Low Countries or " the best that be in England." One correspondent gives 13,000 foot as needed for the conquest of Ulster alone, and still another makes the requirement 18,000 foot and 2000 horse. Another says that three armies are necessary, one for the north, one for the south and another for Leinster and the Pale. The queen on the other hand, angry at what she considered the negligence of her representatives there and hoping to reduce such waste of treasure in Ireland, was disinclined to " pour out water enough from England to quench the fire in Ireland." [13]

Before the end of the year, however, she had agreed to most of the requirements, resolved to place Essex in command and made up her mind to give him an army of 12,000 to 14,000 men and 1000 horse. This would be the largest

[12] *Chamberlain's Letters, Camden Soc.,* 6–8; *Sydney Papers,* ii, 72, 94–5, 96–7; *Cal. State Papers, Ireland,* 1598–9, 304, 308–10, 316, 326, 322, 330–1, 333–5, 337–8, 341, 350, 353, 357; Camden, 542–5, 555–6, 565–7, 567–8.

[13] *Cal. State Papers, Ireland,* 1598–9, 307, 328, 344–5, 383, 401, 404; Sir John Harington, *Nugae Antiquae,* ed. 1804, i, 173.

military force sent out of England in the queen's reign. Ultimately the number of forces in Ireland, new and old, was set at 16,000 foot and 1300 horse. The expense of these for the next year, along with the regular Irish establishment of officials high and low was estimated at £277,782, as compared with £250,963 of total expenditure for the previous fifteen months. Two thousand recruits were to be sent over every three months to repair losses, but arrangements for supplies were left indefinite and no money was provided for the payment of old debts. The troops necessary to fill up this establishment were rapidly transported to Ireland. Levies of money and men, purchase of victuals, impressment of transports, and all the hurried preparation usual for a foreign expedition now busied the new deputy and the English officials. The advance guard of the expedition, consisting of two thousand veterans brought from the Netherlands under the command of Sir Henry Docwra, who reached Ireland in February, did not find the Irish climate in midwinter healthful. Many fell sick and they were soon reported to " die apace." Recruits were ill cared for and those in a position to know best feared that the new governor would find his army a great disappointment.[14]

The appointment of Essex was, however, received with acclamation in England and with almost unalloyed satisfaction in Ireland. Even Tyrone let it be known that he would try to speak with Essex immediately after his arrival, hoping to gain his grace and favor; and it was thought by some that a large number of the common Irish would gladly enter into the service of the popular earl if he would or could pay them wages. Indeed Essex himself had some hope that his prestige would go far toward quieting Ireland. With this anticipation, on the 25th of January, a proclamation of the usual somewhat turgid Elizabethan eloquence was issued to the people of Ireland, enumerating their offenses, explain-

[14] *Cal. State Papers, Ireland,* 1598–9, 406–7, 427, 449, 452, 457–8, 472, 485, 492, 503, 1599–1600, 1; Fynes Moryson, *Itinerary,* ii, 221–9; *Stowe MSS.,* clxvii, fo. 87; *Acts of the Privy Council* xxix, 736–7.

ing their misguidance, regretting that the queen has had to repair to "the last but worst of all remedies, the sword," appealing to them to "prostrate themselves to our mercy," and stating that she had appointed the earl of Essex as the minister of both her justice and mercy to them.[15]

The earl's commission was signed at Westminster, March 12, 1599. It appointed him "Lieutenant-General and General Governor of Ireland," and gave him the extensive powers of punishing or pardoning offenders, levying troops, making war on rebels and granting knighthood, customary in commissions of such high lieutenancy at the time, and the additional powers, peculiar to a governor of Ireland, of calling and proroguing a parliament, though the queen's permission was to be specially sought for this at the time. These extensive and general powers were somewhat limited and certainly made more definite by his formal instructions, given him two weeks later, when the queen was at Richmond. He was directed to go immediately to Ireland, deliver the queen's letters to the Lords Justices and Council there, take the oath and receive the sword of office. He was to reform abuses in the administration and in the comissariat, put an end to the spread of Popery in the obedient districts, remove native Irish from the queen's forces, and reduce the whole military and civil establishment to the numbers and wages provided for. He was to be careful in giving rewards, not bestowing lands or granting pardons except for adequate services. He must confer knighthood only upon men who have performed notorious services and have sufficient living of their own, not immoderately as he has done before. He must give due consideration to the judgment of the Irish Council of State. As to Tyrone, the principal rebel, he must require from him, if he asks the queen's mercy, complete submission; but if he seems desperate he is to promise him his life, and if he refuses all conditions and Essex has no time to consult further with the queen, he is to "take him in upon such conditions as you shall find

---

[15] *Cal. State Papers, Ireland,* 1598–9, 449, 472, 503, 1599–1601, 4.

good and necessary for our honour and safety of that kingdom." [16]

No official going into distant service at that period could disregard the question of the time and conditions of his return. Long suit and powerful influence was sometimes necessary, and often ineffective, to secure permission to return, as was found by Sir Robert Sydney, governor of Flushing, Sir Henry Wallop, Treasurer at War in Ireland, and many others. Essex, therefore, as one of the main points of his freedom of action, sought and obtained from the queen on the 27th of March a warrant giving him permission to return to England when he saw fit, without waiting for special permission. This freedom was made dependent on Ireland being in a sufficiently settled state not to be endangered by his departure and on his appointment under the great seal of Ireland of two capable persons to take the government temporarily, and indeed, as will be seen, was later withdrawn altogether.[17]

The departure of the earl from London, March 27, 1599, with a great train of nobility and gentry amidst the plaudits of the people, though marred by a thunder storm from a clear sky, ominous to many, was one of the famous scenes of the age. The " Chorus " in Henry V has preserved for us an allusion to the high hopes that accompanied him.

> " Were now the general of our gracious empress,
> As in good time he may, from Ireland coming,
> Bringing rebellion broachèd on his sword."

In *A Prayer for the Prosperous Proceedings and Good success. of the Earle of Essex,* written and published by John Norden, he is compared to Moses, Josiah, Gideon, David, " and the rest that have fought under thy protection."

But the farewell to the earl and prayers for his support were popular, not royal compliments. There was little of

[16] *Cal. Patent and Close Rolls of Chancery in Ireland,* ii, 520–1, 531; *Cal. Carew MSS.,* 1589–1600, 292–5.

[17] *Cal. Carew MSS.,* 1589–1600, 295; *Cal. Patent and Close Rolls of Ireland,* ii, 531–2; *Cal. State Papers, Ireland,* 1598–9, 502; Laura H. Cadwallader, *Later Career of the Earl of Essex,* 100–1.

the favorite now in his position. His official relations were all with the privy council, not with the queen, or in so far as she sent direct messages to him, they were to rebuke his actions, to blame his policy or to reverse his decisions. He wished to take Sir Christopher Blount, his step-father and a tried soldier, with him as marshal of the army and a member of his council in Ireland. The queen agreed to the former but objected to the latter appointment. When Essex proposed in that case to leave Blount home, the queen insisted on his going, as an officer only, not as councillor. The earl yielded, but appealed again from Ireland for the admission of Blount to the Irish council, receiving only an angry refusal from the queen. A similar personal dispute gathered around the earl of Southampton. He was an intimate friend and old companion in arms of Essex and had been promised by him the generalship of the horse on this expedition. He was, however, still in disgrace with the queen because of his disorderly behavior at court and unauthorized marriage to Elizabeth Vernon, one of the maids of honor, during the last summer. Essex waited until the signature of his commission gave him the right to make all appointments, then announced that of Southampton, but the queen forbade it and reversed the appointment. Waiting again till he reached Ireland he made Southampton, who had accompanied him as a volunteer, general of the horse, but the queen sent peremptory orders through the privy council for his removal from command, and during the remainder of the campaign he was only leader of a small cavalry troop. The young earl of Rutland had begged to go on the expedition as a volunteer and Essex had pleaded with the queen in his favor, but unsuccessfully. Nevertheless, Rutland, like Essex himself ten years before, slipped away from court and joined the earl in Ireland. A positive message from the queen soon brought him back.[18]

[18] Stow, *Chronicle*, 788; *Cal. State Papers, Ireland*, 1599–1600, 1–6, 20, 34–5, 61–2, 100–2; *Stowe MSS.*, clxvii, 7, 8; Violet A. Wilson, *Queen Elizabeth's Maids of Honour*, 231–8; Birch, *Memoirs*, ii, 395–7.

These personal conflicts would be unimportant, except that they indicate alike the persistent self-will of Essex and the unconciliatory attitude of the queen toward him. She yielded neither to his judgment nor his wishes. He left on his difficult mission with the least possible encouragement or favor from the highest quarter. Whatever may have been true of the opposition to his plans which he charged to courtiers and privy councillors, the queen of her own motion then and later construed harshly all that he did. After a hard ride to Beaumaris, and a stormy passage across the Irish Sea, Essex landed at Dublin, April 13, and on April 15 was invested with the sword of state with all ceremony.

Elizabeth and Essex alike had anticipated an immediate attack upon the " arch traitor " Tyrone in his stronghold of Ulster. The queen could no longer bear the thought of the continued defiance of the Irish chieftain. That one whom she called " a base bush kern " should have defeated her armies, brought her power in Ireland to decay, and boasted in Spain and elsewhere of his successes against her filled her with exasperation. Essex himself had criticized earlier deputies for their failure to strike directly at the root of the troubles in Ireland, and in a boastful moment, even after his appointment, he wrote to a friend, " I have beaten Knollys and Montjoy in the councele and by God I will beat Tyrone in the feilde." [19]

But when the new governor had to face the actualities of his position, he was forced to recognize that there could be no such simple and prompt solution of the problem. His Irish councillors pointed out that there was no forage for the horses in Ulster so early in the season as April and May, the cattle which were the universal reliance for the food supply of an army in Ireland could not be collected at once from Leinster, Munster or Connaught, which were for the most part in the possession of the rebels, and they were moreover too weak to be driven and too thin to be eaten after

---

[19] *Nugae Antiquae*, i, 246; L. Pearsall Smith, *Life and Letters of Sir Henry Wotton*, i, 307.

their long winter fast; draught-horses or wagons to carry grain for food did not exist in Ireland in any sufficient numbers. Probably the dispirited Irish councillors were influenced, even if Essex was not, by the knowledge that Tyrone had an army of 6000 men actually under arms and his confederate O'Donnel 4000 more, and that a pitched battle might mean destruction to the English governor and later to the garrison. It was evident that the war in Ireland, as has proved to be the case in India, America and in other countries where England has fought, must be fought under local conditions, not in accordance with preconceived ideas.[20]

Essex spread the queen's proclamation widely, and added his own promise of grace on submission, but there was no appreciable response. The tide of native success was running too strong to be checked by words of either threatening or mercy. Hopes of help from Spain and Scotland were still alive. While Elizabeth and her councillors insisted on addressing the native Irish as " rebels " and " traitors," O'Neill appealed to a wavering fellow countryman on the ground that " it is lawful to die in the quarrell and defence of the native soil," and that " we Irishmen are exiled and made bond-slaves and servitors to a strange and foreign prince." What the queen and her councillors, including Essex, called " their barbarous revolt," and they called " resistance to oppression," seemed on the eve of success. They could look forward with some hope to driving out the invader and regaining their own lands, religion and customs. It is no wonder therefore that Essex had to complain that " not one capital traitor hath sought or made show of conformity." If the reputation of the new governor counted for something it was merely to extract some fair speeches and possibly fair intentions from Tyrone, it could not suppress a rebellion or, at this stage of the contest, induce even a compromise.[21]

There seemed nothing for Essex to do but postpone the

---

[20] *Cal. State Papers, Ireland,* 1599–1600, 16–8.
[21] *Cal. State Papers, Ireland,* 1598–9, 358; 1599–1600, 18.

Ulster expedition till mid-summer, begin the restoration of Irish obedience nearer home, and in the meantime put his government into such order as possible. To this last task he gave " extreme toil," and in fact did much in these early weeks to lessen the confusion into which the administration had fallen. He began the work of auditing accounts and putting a stop to speculation and neglect in the distribution of supplies. He strengthened weak garrisons in the Pale, sent Sir Conyers Clifford, who had come to Dublin to meet him, back to Connaught with a substantial force of 3000 men, and appointed Sir Arthur Chichester, the later lord deputy, governor of Carrickfergus and sent him there by sea. He placed three other small garrisons on the borders of Ulster to keep communications open and hold back Tyrone. The establishment of a garrison on Lough Foyle, in the rear of Tyrone, recommended by every Irish adviser, recognized as necessary by Essex himself, and later found to be the crucial step toward the defeat of the " great bear Tyrone in his own den," as Clifford described O'Neill in Ulster, was, however, not carried out. This may have been either because no sufficient transports were available, as Essex later claimed, or because it was looked upon as a part of the proposed Ulster campaign which had now been postponed.

The most recent extension of rebellion had been to the south and west of Dublin, a region which had long been the most orderly and profitable to the English crown of any outside the Pale. Here the Irish council unanimously advised, as they had constantly before recommended, that action should first be taken. Into Leinster and Munster, therefore, Essex planned a campaign which was intended to pass through the principal disturbed districts to the south of Dublin, and to last perhaps a month. The queen approved this plan, though reluctantly, and with an army of 3000 foot and 300 horse, May 9, a little more than three weeks after his landing, and, as a matter of fact, before the queen's letter of permission had been received, Essex marched out from Naas, his rendezvous. Soon afterwards he was joined by Ormonde with his force of 700 foot and 200 horse, which had been carrying on such fighting as had been in progress in recent months, and a week later was met by Norris, President of Munster, with a small body of troops which he had withdrawn from their garrisons. He marched through Athy, Stradbally, Maryborough and Kilkenny in Leinster, then through Clonmel and Tipperary in Munster to Limerick, the principal city of that province. After relieving the castle of Askeaton, near Limerick, he turned eastward to Waterford, then northward through Wexford, Enniscorthy, Ferns and Arklow to Wicklow, and thus back to Dublin.

There was little fighting. At most places the rebels withdrew to their fastnesses in the woods and mountains or scattered through the country. At certain passes between wood and bog, the traditional points of attack in Ireland, there was some opposition, and at Cashel, Ballyragget, and Adare considerable fighting was necessary on the part of Essex to make his way through the wooded paths. Several strongholds of rebellious Kavanaghs, O'Mores, O'Byrnes, McFeaghs, O'Connors and other septs were reconnoitred; in some cases these surrendered, in two cases they were captured. Others were found so well defended at all approaches that another route of march was chosen. A number of wavering Irish made their submission, two or three influential chieftains were taken to Dublin in custody and certain captured leaders were hung. There was also, as usual, much burning and destruction of crops. The rebel army of Munster, said to consist of 4000 to 5000 men, hung in the distance but evaded the engagement Essex would gladly have entered upon. Even after the detachment of troops for garrison duty and losses by fighting and sickness had reduced his army to 1200 men, he offered what promised to become a pitched battle with the rebel forces of Leinster, but it proved to be only a skirmish though marked by a picturesque rescue of the English foot by the cavalry. In military operations, Essex, as a result of his campaigns in France and the Azores, an experienced military commander, made careful and judicious arrangements of his forces, and his losses were few compared with the toll of deaths imposed upon the natives.[22]

In the main this campaign was a success; the power of the government had been shown and there was no serious resistance to the governor and his armed forces. Soon afterward, though not immediately, several of the Leinster chieftains, Donnell Spainagh, so called because in his youth he had been in Spain with Stukeley, Brian McDonough, Ownie McRory, chief of the O'Mores, the sons of the old outlaw Feagh McHugh, several of the O'Molloys, Kavanaghs, O'Connors, and McGeoghans and a number of lesser persons " came in " and received their pardons. As part of a systematic and carefully planned effort to reconquer Ireland the Munster campaign would have been well worth while; but as for immediate results, the waters of Irish disobedience closed in again behind the army much as they had been before. The queen's description of the campaign as *via navis in mare*, though used by her in another sense, was by no means inapt.

In some respects the journey had been as much a " progress " as a campaign. Orations in Latin and English were recited before the governor at Kilkenny, Clonmel and Limerick, and rushes were scattered before him in the streets of those towns. His military discipline on the other hand was rigorous. Lord Grey for attacking the rebels against the orders of his superior officer was imprisoned for twenty-four hours and thus made his enemy for life. A considerable body of troops detached under Sir Henry Harington for some special service who were seized with panic and ran away from the enemy were all tried by court martial and one of the officers and every tenth private hung for cowardice, the rest cashiered or reduced to lower service. The cowardice of the English foot soldiers, so constantly com-

[22] *Cal. State Papers, Ireland,* 1598-9, 335; 1599-1600, 77; Birch, *Memoirs,* ii, 398-418.

plained of in these Irish campaigns, was due to the circumstances of their levy, their forced service and difficult sur-
roundings, not to any laxity on the part of their commander.
The courage of the English officers and cavalry, on the other
hand, was conspicuous, and in fact called for a firm hand
to repress its excess.[23]

Essex brought back to Dublin an army weakened by all
the usual losses of a prolonged campaign through a difficult
country, and depleted by detachments left in garrison as he
passed through the two provinces. He was himself wearied
and in bad health. Soon after his arrival he received as his
only comfort for his losses an angry, captious and sarcastic
letter from the queen, the first communication from her
since his departure from London. She scolded him for re-
appointing Southampton, complained of the small results
of his Munster campaign, charged him with general mismanagement and waste of her men and treasure and ridi-
culed his personal complaints against her councillors. However unreasonable and petty some of the protests of Essex
in his letters home may have been, certainly never did any
commander in a difficult enterprise receive less encouragement from his sovereign, and never did Elizabeth show more
personal acrimony and greater lack of statesmanship than
in these affairs of Ireland. With that curious sensitiveness
to foreign opinion to be felt by so national a sovereign she
speaks in this, as in many other letters of the period, of her
sense of humiliation in the eyes of foreign rulers at being
defied by such a poor enemy as O'Neill, and at his boasts
abroad of having forced her to such great and yet such futile
exertions.[24]

As a matter of fact the expedition through Leinster and
Munster had taken almost two months instead of one; it
was now July and although Essex continued to speak of the

[23] Cal. Patent and Close Rolls of the Chancery in Ireland, ii, 517–37;
Nugae Antiquae, i, 271, 275, 278; Cal. State Papers, Ireland, 1598–9, 117;
1599–1600, 37–91, 140–1.

[24] Cal. State Papers, Ireland, 1599–1600, 98–101; Devereux, ii, 61–4,
73–5.

Ulster expedition as only postponed he must have felt less and less hopeful of entering promptly upon it. The season was now ripe, but sufficient forces were wanting. To march into Ulster and attack Tyrone with the little army now at his disposal and with only such supplies and equipment as were now available would be purposeless self-destruction. The 3500 men left in Munster, 3300 in Leinster and 3000 in Connaught, however necessary for purposes of defence, left but 6000 for the north. These should be divided into two for the two places of entry and drawn upon for convoys and guard. All this and the reinforcements and changes of plan necessary to make the campaign practicable were set forth in a long letter from Essex and the Irish Council sent to the Privy Council in England a few days after his return to Dublin.

While waiting for the queen's decision on these points, Essex made a rapid campaign into King's and Queen's Counties, the Leix and Offaly of the Irish, the scene of the earliest English colonization, which had just been swept by revolt. But there was no need for long waiting; the letter of Essex and the council which reached the queen July 28 was promptly and sharply answered by her July 30. She yielded on some of the minor points, but on the main question gave Essex a peremptory order to enter upon the Ulster expedition with such equipment as he had without further delay or discussion. More important for his personal fortunes, as it proved, she withdrew quite clearly and positively, at least for the time, his permission to return home. A rapid journey to court, as in earlier cases, to explain matters to the queen or to renew affectionate relations with her, was a matter of common expectation by courtiers and was already in the mind of Essex himself. Now in words as positive and formal as the original warrant itself, he was forbidden to make use of it " till the northern action be tried " and till he had informed the queen of his arrangements for the government during his absence and obtained her approval of them and a renewal of his license to return.

This and many acts of the queen in regard to Essex it is difficult to explain without supposing some continuous influence unfavorable to him being exerted upon her. Nor can there be much doubt that this influence was the cold, steady, effective pressure of Sir Robert Cecil. Indeed his brief endorsement upon his copy of this letter, " To command him not to come over," perhaps gives the clue. There seems no reason to believe that Cecil now or later had any personal hostility to Essex. But the statesman, filled with purely political conceptions, with less of the milk of human kindness than his father, may have felt it his duty to keep the queen up to her work of government, and in his constant interviews with her have checked any inclination on her part to treat Essex in a more personal relationship. In these later days of her life the queen was evidently losing her equanimity, and yielding more readily sometimes to her personal vexations, sometimes to the pressure of the few courtiers and ministers who had access to her.[25]

Stung by the tone and compelled by the direct orders of this letter and others from the queen and the privy council which followed it, Essex determined to proceed as quickly as possible to Ulster. The Irish council expostulated with him and urged the danger to Leinster and the Pale if he took his army north. The people of the Pale begged him not to carry away their small local supply of grain and beef. Eighteen colonels and captains, after a council of war, signed a letter of protest, pointing out that the army, dreading a northern campaign, was deserting in crowds, feigning sickness, and was thoroughly unreliable, that the general would be far overmatched in numbers and forced to fight on unfavorable ground, and that they could not advise or assent to a northern campaign under these conditions. In the second week of August news came of a severe defeat of the Connaught army in trying to cross the Curlew Mountains to relieve O'Connor Sligo, still considered faithful,

[25] *Cal. State Papers, Ireland,* 1599–1600, 91–5, 105–7, 111–12, 137; *Sydney Papers,* ii, 114–15, 120.

with the death of the governor, Sir Conyers Clifford, and Sir Alexander Ratcliffe, one of the captains. Some two hundred and forty men were killed and as many more wounded. The attack had been by the forces of O'Rourke, with O'Donnel himself on foot ready to follow up the victory. The English in Connaught had to withdraw for safety to Athlone, where they were for the time powerless.[26]

The Ulster expedition was nevertheless finally entered upon. August 28, a little more than four months from his arrival in Ireland, Essex wrote to the privy council, " I am even now putting my foot into the stirrup to go to the rendezvous at the Navan, and from thence I will draw the army so far and do as much as duty will warrant me and God enable me." This proved to be, as all who knew anticipated, not very much. The rendezvous was between Navan and Kells, some twenty-five miles north of Cavan, and there the forces, which nominally amounted to 4950 foot and 450 horse, but actually only to some 2500 foot and 300 horse, were gathered. Three days were spent in waiting for supplies to be sent from Drogheda, in a council of war as to whether a garrison should be placed in Cavan at the risk of Tyrone's passing Essex's flank and invading the Pale, and in reconnoitering Lord Dunsany's country, through which they must pass; three days more were passed in slowly marching to the actual frontier of Ulster.

At last on September 3 Tyrone was seen with his army, somewhat more than twice the size of that of Essex, a mile and a half away across a little river and a stretch of woods. Then began a series of efforts on the part of Essex to bring his adversary to battle and a determination on the part of the Irish commander to block his advance without entering into a contest. With his inequality of forces and disadvantages of position, it was evidently impossible for Essex to storm trenches, enter woods or cross river-valleys in the face

---

[26] Cal. State Papers, Ireland, 1599–1600, 113–25, 126–7, 127–37; Hatfield House MSS., ix, 263–7, 270–7, 289–90, 294; O'Clery, Life of Hugh Roe O'Donnel, 211–9; Fynes Moryson, ii, 244–6.

of his enemy. All he could do was to draw up his little army on successive hillsides, as he marched parallel to the border, hoping that his adversary would come over and fight. Tyrone, an old commander, his army well in hand, of superior numbers and well equipped, on the other hand was entirely master of the situation and could afford to play with the English forces. He had heard through his correspondents in Scotland that Essex was " mightily crossed in England," and " would make no great stay " in Ireland, and was evidently wearing out the time, planning to secure one of his usual treaties, or perhaps, under the circumstances, a more favorable and more permanent one.[27]

It was doubtless with this hope that he sent a series of messages to Essex asking for a parley. The way was somewhat prepared by a visit to Tyrone's camp made by Sir William Warren, who obtained permission from Essex to negotiate with the Irish commander for the release of a brother officer, Captain John Moore, recently captured by the Irish in Offaly.[28] Tyrone used this opportunity to send word to Essex that he wished to make his submission to him. September 5, the second day after the two armies came in sight of one another, Henry Hogan, Tyrone's closest friend and councillor, appeared in Essex's camp asking for a parley. Essex refused to parley with a rebel, as he had refused all such proposals since he had been in Ireland, and sent word he would meet Tyrone the next day at the head of his troops; but the next day Tyrone kept his foot forces in the forest and withdrew his horse successively from every hill as Essex occupied it, one of his horsemen riding back calling out that Tyrone did not wish to fight but desired a conference with the English general.

The next day, September 7, while Essex was marching toward Drumcondra, a quite ineffective march so far as the occupation of Ulster was concerned, Hogan appeared again

---

[27] *Hatfield House MSS.*, ix, 330; *Cal. State Papers, Ireland*, 1599–1600, 136, 137, 142, 144–5; *Nugae Antiquae*, 293–6.

[28] John Dymmok, *A Treatise of Ireland*, 48.

with the still more urgent message that Tyrone desired her Majesty's mercy and begged the governor would meet him at the ford of Ballaclinch two miles to the right. Fords play a large part in the early history of Ireland. Open places where such highroads as there were crossed the rivers, clear of trees and brush, they are constantly mentioned as places of attack, of defense, of conference. Essex hesitated, sent two gentlemen to survey the place of the proposed meeting and finally, influenced by some unexplained change of feeling or policy, yielded and rode down alone, though in sight of his army, to the edge of the ford, while Tyrone, whom he met in person now for the first and only time, rode into the water on the other side up to his horse's belly. The Irish chieftain saluted the queen's representative " with great reverence," and there the two leaders talked quite alone for half an hour.

Just what was said in this conference is unknown. Tyrone refused to " open his heart " to Essex till he was promised that his conditions should be delivered to the queen orally, not put in writing for fear they should be sent to the Spanish king, as the letter entrusted to Sir John Norris had been three years before. Later Essex told the queen and the privy councillors " where the knot is which being loosed he hath protested that all the rest shall follow," but what the " knot " was is not recorded. It may have been Catholic predominance in Ireland, as indicated in earlier and later demands; it may have been the land question; it may have been more purely personal. There is no adequate evidence either external or internal that the twenty-two demands of Tyrone for religious equality, economic freedom and Irish self-government, procured for Ormonde in writing by a spy in the English service a month or two later and endorsed by Cecil " Eutopian," were the exact conditions presented to Essex. Though they are not an unfair statement of the concessions long desired by Irishmen and indeed granted by England three centuries later, they are certainly not conciliatory in their tone as presumably were the terms offered by Tyrone, and may well have been what he presented to his confederates, not to the queen. The conversation was doubtless an intimate one. There could hardly fail to have been some natural sympathy between the young commander smarting under the harsh displeasure of the queen and the old chieftain, superior for the time in military position but weary of conflict and apprehensive of ultimate defeat. They were both men of sensitive disposition and personal charm, and they had already heard much of one another. In their half hour's confidential talk they may have discovered not only a congeniality of disposition but a common desire to bring the long and destructive war to an end. Elizabeth afterward told Essex that although she would not suspect him, yet to talk thus to a traitor without witnesses and for so long a time was incautious and unwise, and that Tyrone's doffed hat and inclined head were rather a " forme of greatness " than sign of submission, so long as he kept part of the stream between them and did not cross and throw himself humbly on the mercy of Essex and herself.[29]

The relative positions of Essex and the traitor, however, were different from the queen's fantastic conception of them, and it was in conformity with this reality that the private interview was immediately followed by another in which the principal officers with Essex, Southampton, St. Leger, Bourchier, Wingfield and others, and Tyrone's brother Cormac, the heads of the Maguires and Maginnises, Ever McCooly, Tyrone's secretary, Henry Hovenden, and a Spanish-Irishman familiarly known as " Owen " were present as equal conferees. The next morning there was another still more formal conference at a neighboring " castle," hostages for the safety of the commissioners being sent in by the Irish. Essex gave written instructions to his four representatives

[29] *Hist. MSS. Comm., Buccleugh Papers at Montague House,* i, 29; *Cal. State Papers, Ireland,* 1599–1600, 145–6, 279–80; Dymmok, 48–50; Gilbert, *Account of Facsimiles of National MSS. of Ireland,* 249–50; Laura H. Cadwallader, *Later Career of the Earl of Essex,* 59, 107–8; *Nugae Antiquae,* i, 297–9, 302–5; Winwood, *Memorials,* i, 119.

at this conference. His secretary, Henry Wotton, was one of the commissioners and drew up the proposed agreement or truce. This was to the effect that there should be a six weeks' cessation of arms of the kind long familiar in Ireland, and so from six weeks to six weeks, from the next day, the 8th of September, till the 1st of the succeeding May, unless either party should give two weeks notice of its close. Each party was to give immediate notice of the conclusion of the truce to their respective adherents, and if any of the Irish, as was likely to be the case with O'Donnel and the rebels of Leinster and Munster, were to refuse to be bound by the agreement, Tyrone was to give them no support. There was to be no extension of the territory occupied at the time by the English; and all men on both sides were to have liberty to pass freely anywhere through Ireland. To this agreement Essex gave his written, but otherwise unsupported, assent, and Tyrone, as a form of special respect, took his oath. Those who were present believed that Tyrone intended to keep this oath, and, if he could control his colleagues, to make a permanent peace. He was growing old; there was much dissension, as always, among the native Irish themselves, he was losing faith in help from the Spanish king, and he knew the English power to be irresistible if the queen should once make up her mind to let it be used without stint.[30]

A retreat by the English had really begun two days before when Essex, on the advice of his officers, had marched from Louth toward Drumcondra, parallel with the borders of Ulster, instead of making an attempt to force the trenched passes and wooded defences of Tyrone and so precipitate a battle in the forest and bogs. If he had done the latter there is no reason to doubt that his army would have been overwhelmed and Essex himself probably have lost his life then on the battlefield instead of later on the scaffold. The whole policy of a rapid campaign, leaving all other centers of dis-

---

[30] *Cal. State Papers, Dom.*, 1599–1600, 144–7, 154–5; *Nugae Antiquae*, i, 298–301; *Trevelyan Papers*, ii, 101–3.

affection untouched, and concentrating a massed attack on Tyrone, as the queen in her ignorance and at a distance conceived it, was as futile as a similar policy on a greater scale proved to be three hundred years later in France, even when calculated with supreme military skill. The immediate successor of Essex testified that that commander did as much as any general could in a single campaign, and his own successful policy required three years and the crisis of a Spanish invasion, in addition to the preliminary work of Essex, to bring it to completion.

As it was, the army of Essex was now distributed to its earlier stations and he himself went to Drogheda and after a few days to Dublin to recuperate. The constant bowel trouble from which he suffered he attributed largely to depression due to the hostile influences which he believed were being exerted against him at home, and to the harshness of the messages from the queen which constantly reached him in Ireland. A long, nagging and intolerably severe letter of this kind anticipating the failure of the northern campaign and ordering the deputy and Irish council to submit military plans for the rest of the year for her consideration and approval or disapproval, was sent from Nonesuch, her favorite palace, where she spent the whole of this summer, a few days after the agreement with Tyrone. But before this and still another, written after she had received news of the armistice, reached Essex, he had taken and immediately acted upon a fatal resolution. Whether he had read Elizabeth's letter of Aug. 30 too carelessly to recognize the peremptory character of its prohibition of his return, or relied on his old ability to make her forget his disobedience in the joy of his presence, or took some other chance, he fell back on the original warrant permitting him to return to consult the queen when he thought fit, conformed to its requirements by putting civil authority in the hands of two lords justices and military authority in the hands of the earl of Ormonde, assured the officials and soldiers of his early return, drew ahead on his salary, and September 24, with

Southampton, Danvers, and others of his personal attendants, left Ireland for London.[31]

From the point of view of statesmanship, the journey of Essex to England was wise. To explain Irish affairs personally to the queen, to make her look at them more realistically, was most important. To induce her either to accept the submission of Tyrone in good faith, yielding what was absolutely necessary, or else to agree to what was ultimately granted to his successor, the carrying on of a more deliberate and prolonged campaign, and then to return to carry out the agreed upon policy, would have been well worth the few risks involved. But from a personal point of view his hasty and unauthorized return was to put himself in the power of his enemies, if he had any, or at best of his rivals, and to trust all his fortunes to the chances of the queen's doubtful affections.

Before tracing the unhappy working of these chances, a rapid survey may be made of the almost equally unhappy outcome of the rebellion of Tyrone, the declining fortunes and final failure of which fill in the remaining days of the queen's reign. The armistice agreed upon between Essex and Tyrone, September 8, 1599, was kept by both sides for the first six weeks' period, but it had scarcely entered upon its second six weeks when a series of attacks by certain Irish allies of the English in the south on their native opponents, involving the killing of some two hundred men, brought angry protests from Tyrone. Sir William Warren, an old intermediary, was sent to him by the lords justices and council with explanations, but he now complained further of the imprisonment of Essex, with whom he had made the treaty and whom alone he declared he trusted, saying that he could not rely upon the Irish council or longer hold back his adherents from avenging their injuries. November 8 he gave the required two weeks' notice of the cessation of the

[31] *Cal. State Papers, Ireland,* 1599–1600, 156–7, 160–1, 165, 176, 189–90, 243; *Lansdowne MSS.,* lxxxvii, 73, 74, 75; Fynes Moryson, *Itinerary,* ii, 246–53.

truce and at the end of that period resumed warfare. At the same time he renewed his appeals to Spain for aid, asking especially for artillery with which the Irish cities, the principal centres of English strength, might be captured.[32]

With the excuse of making a pilgrimage to Holy Cross Abbey Tyrone went immediately with a body of followers into Munster and there spent the greater part of the winter in strengthening his own party and overawing those still inclined to obedience to the English. He claimed to be the representative of the national independence of Ireland and of the predominance of the Roman Catholic church. In one of his letters of protest to Lord Lieutenant Ormond he says, " I wish you would command your secretary to be more discreet and to use the word Traitor as seldom as he may. By chiding there is little gotten at my hands and they that are joined with me fight for the Catholic religion and liberties of our country." He might well protest against being treated with contempt in the winter of 1599 for at no time during this whole period did his fortunes stand higher or was he nearer to uniting all Ireland in a determined and successful attempt to obtain freedom from England.

In carrying out his policy in Munster Tyrone established himself at Inniscarra on the river Lee and received messages of support and hostages from many previously doubtful local chieftains both of English and of Irish blood. On the other hand he ravaged much of Westmeath, the barony of Delvin and other districts, and burned every house on the island where Queenstown now stands, the property of Lord Barry, a prominent southern noble on the queen's side.[33]

In the meantime Essex was in disgrace, the queen had evidently made up her mind not to send him back to Ireland, and the office of lord deputy was unfilled. She hesitated whether or not to accept Tyrone's offer of sub-

[32] *Cal. State Papers, Ireland,* 1599–1600, 154, 157–61, 170, 241, 261–2, 337, 405–6; Kelso, *Die Spanier in Irland,* 53–5; *Cal. Carew MSS.,* 1589–1600, 337–50.

[33] Camden, 575–6, 580; Gilbert, *Natl. MSS. of Ireland,* pt. iv, App. 16; *Carew MSS.,* 362–3; Bagwell, iii, 352–4.

mission which Essex had brought with him, and gave ambiguous directions to the lords justices and council in Ireland concerning him. Early in 1600 she seems to have decided definitely to continue the war, appointed Charles Blount, Lord Mountjoy, to the lord-deputyship and, almost equally important as it proved, made Sir George Carew President of Munster. The new commanders arrived in Dublin February 26, 1600, with reinforcements bringing the army practically up to its standard under Essex. Their first effort was to intercept Tyrone when he attempted to return to the North, but in this they were unsuccessful. With a picked force the Irish leader by a rapid march reached his own province late in March. Carew then left with one quarter of all the forces for the South.

Mountjoy and his officers, left more freedom of action by the queen, who had perhaps learned by the experience of the previous year, thereupon proceeded to establish a series of better fortified and better garrisoned posts in Ulster and Connaught. On the island of Derry, on Lough Foyle, amidst the ruins of two churches, an old abbey, a bishop's house and a castle, a garrison was established under Sir Henry Docwra, one of Essex's old captains, while Mountjoy marched to the borders of Ulster to relieve him from too great pressure by Tyrone while he was strengthening this foothold. A new castle was then built in a strong position near Armagh and named Mountnorris after the old general. Little by little the borders of independent Ulster were pressed backward by spade warfare and Tyrone's territory was hemmed in by a line of fortified stations with small garrisons.[34]

In the centre of Ireland also small fortified posts were gradually reëstablished. In order to prevent Irish raids upon these the governor not only burned the native villages, drove away the cattle and cut down all the growing crops, but harrowed up the young grain so that it could not grow

[34] Bagwell, iii, 355; Camden, 580–2; Kelso, 61–3. *Carew MSS.*, 1589–1600, 339–49, 356–62, 374–6, 387; 1601–3, lxiv–lxvii.

again during the year. When the soldiers could not carry away all the cattle they captured they hacked and mangled and drowned as many as they could of the rest. An English captain, Flower, under orders of the President of Munster burned all the grain in a belt ten miles wide from Kinsale to Dunmanus Bay and killed great numbers of the peasantry. Carew writes to the privy council of the exploits of his forces in Munster. "No day passeth without report of burning, killing and taking prey. . . . Infinite numbers of their cattle are taken, and besides husbandmen, women and children, of weaponed men there hath been slain in the province since my coming above 1200." On the other side Hugh Roe O'Donnel with several other chiefs ravaged the whole of County Clare, burning, it was claimed, every house.[35]

In the miserable devastation that cursed Ireland during this period there is little if anything to choose in barbarity between Irish and English; but in intrigue and betrayal the English were in a position to excel and used their opportunity unscrupulously. The absence of any standard of honor, excused as they claimed by the falsity of their enemies and justified by the extremity of their position, was everywhere apparent. Docwra put up a gibbet on the ramparts of Derry and hanged a number of hostages given by one of the Ulster chiefs whom he suspected of leading his soldiers into an ambuscade. The policy of setting brothers and other near relatives in antagonism to one another by secret offers of support in claims of inheritance, the sowing of mutual distrust among the natives by causing counterfeit letters to be written and then intercepted and the use of native spies, were relied upon for weakening the native clans both in Ulster and Munster. Sir George Carew suborned a pardoned rebel to murder one of the native chiefs, as he seems from his own account afterward to have connived at the murder of the earl of Tyrconnel. Docwra offered £2000 for Tyrone alive or £1000 for his dead body, and Carew

[35] Bagwell, iii, 377, 379; *Pacata Hibernia*, i, chaps, iv, xii.

offered £1000 for the kidnaping of the native earl of
Desmond.[36]

So, little by little, through 1600 and the first three
quarters of 1601, by hard fighting, by the steady pressure
of a more concentrated and skilful military system, by skilful manoeuvring, by intrigue, by outrage, the extent of territory under English control was increased, old fortified
places were repaired, country houses in Leinster and Munster, originally captured from the Irish and given to English
captains, gentlemen and courtiers, then within the last three
years recaptured by the Irish, were in turn again captured
by the English and made places of support for English garrisons. Mountjoy, although in general following the same
policy as Essex, followed it with more deliberation, persistency, and skill, and above all was allowed more time and
more freedom of action and was given more encouragement
from home. Though soon after his arrival Elizabeth wrote
him a letter of rebuke for the dishonor of allowing Tyrone
to get back from Munster to Ulster unfought with, and although she certainly knew something of his secret correspondence with James of Scotland, her letters to him were
almost always kind and often jocular and reinforcements
were sent regularly.[37]

Native resistance was being steadily if slowly worn down
when in September, 1601, the Irish rebellion was suddenly
brought to a crisis by the arrival at last of the Spaniards in
force. The anticipation of Spanish support, as has been
shown, had been continuous since the first rising of O'Neill
and O'Donnel. The arrival from time to time of a vessel or
two with letters, money and ammunition had kept up the
hopes of the Irish. Early in 1600 as an earnest of more
serious support Oviedo, a Franciscan monk, came from
Spain with the title of bishop of Dublin with a small com-

[36] Bagwell, iii, 363-4, 365, 371, 372, 374, 377, 390, 426; *Docwra's Narrative, Cal. State Papers, Ireland*, 1601-03, 92-7; Fynes Moryson, ii, 330, 333,
338, 350, 354, etc.; *Carew MSS.*, 1601-3, 241, 245, 350-1.

[37] Bagwell, iii, 361-95; Camden, 582-4, 638.

pany of other Spaniards. In April a conference was held at
the cloister of Donegal at which Tyrone, O'Donnel and some
sixty Irish nobles were present, where Oviedo turned over to
the cause £6000, and agreed to join in a new appeal to
Philip for 6000 men and more artillery, to be sent before
the end of the year. Tyrone at this time sent his son to
Spain as a sort of hostage. Philip would willingly have sent
the troops immediately, but the Spanish council decided that
for financial and other reasons it was impossible, and the
whole year 1600 passed without aid from Spain, beyond the
arrival in Donegal in November of two small ships with
some money, arms and ammunition, which was divided between Tyrone and O'Donnel.

Through the winter of 1600–01, however, a Spanish fleet
and army were being collected. Much difficulty was experienced. Service in Ireland was as unpopular in Spain as it
was in England and there was much resistance to the levy
of troops. The preparations were well known in England
and a descent constantly anticipated. Finally, early in September, 1601, the fleet, consisting of some 33 ships with 4500
soldiers, six field cannon, and some equipment for fortification, sailed from Lisbon. It was driven westward past Cork
harbor, where it had intended to land, but September 22
was sighted entering Kinsale bay. The next day the army
disembarked, meeting no opposition, the little English garrison with most of the well-to-do inhabitants retreating to
Cork, the rest welcoming the Spaniards. The Spanish fleet
after landing its troops and equipment sailed away for Spain.
Don Juan d'Aquila, the Spanish commander, with his little
army left to its own devices, did everything possible to
strengthen his position and conciliate the Irish. He issued
a proclamation as " Master General and Captain General of
the Catholic king of Spain in God's war for maintaining the
faith in Ireland," declaring that the queen was a mere
usurper in Ireland, that the Irish people owed her no allegiance and should support the Catholic cause, paid in money
for everything he took from the country, distributed arms,

gave the people permission to come and go in the city as they chose, and sent messengers to Tyrone and O'Donnel urging them to hasten to his support.[38]

Within a few days, Mountjoy and Carew from Dublin, Tyrone and O'Donnel from Ulster were marching to the south with such troops as they could collect to fight out their battle respectively for the capture and the relief of Kinsale. The English arrived first, ravaged the surrounding country in order to deprive the Spaniards of supplies, and established camps to the north and west of the city to prevent the entrance of the Irish forces. The Spaniards were at a disadvantage from having no cavalry. They had brought over saddles but no horses, anticipating that these would be provided by their Irish allies. The English on the other hand had a great advantage in their sea connections. Two successive fleets with supplies, cannon and reinforcements arrived within the next few weeks. A small Spanish supporting fleet also appeared but was prevented from entering Kinsale harbor and forced to sail farther west where it was almost destroyed by Sir Richard Leveson, but not before it had landed 700 men and some cannon and occupied the towns of Baltimore, Dunboy and Castlehaven.

By November the main body of the Spaniards were closely besieged in Kinsale, the outlying posts had been captured by the English, the frequent sorties made by the Spanish garrison were being regularly driven back, and a constant cannonade was being kept up upon the city. On the other hand the English were between two fires, for Tyrone had arrived and been joined by O'Donnel and many of their clan chieftains and they now surrounded the English to the west, north and east. Through December there was much disease and suffering in the English camp and their condition became critical. The contest seemed to be settling down to one of endurance, with the advantages on the whole in favor of the Irish, who had the open country behind them,

[38] Kelso, 55–6, 57–9, 64–71; Camden, 638–41; Bagwell, iii, 376, 398–401; *Sloane MSS.*, xxv, 4; *Hibernia Pacata*, ii, 357–60.

when Mountjoy was released from his dangerous position,
as many another worried commander has been, by the pre-
cipitancy of his opponent. The Irish decided to make a
night attack on the 23d of December. The plan was betrayed to the English by a traitor in the Irish camp and
early in the morning of the day before Christmas the Irish,
already badly disorganized by rivalry among themselves
and misled by their guides, found themselves in the out-
skirts of the English camp, faced by an English army
prepared to receive them and the attacked instead of the
attacking party. A confused conflict resulted in an overwhelming victory for the English and the disastrous retreat
of the Irish. A great number were killed, many after they
had been taken prisoners. On Christmas day a council of
the Irish took place and it was decided that O'Donnel should
sail immediately for Spain to seek reinforcements, that
Tyrone and the other Ulster chieftains should return to
the north to strengthen the resistance there, and Tyrell, one
of the best of the Irish leaders, should keep up the war in
Munster.[39]

But the climax of the rebellion had come, and disintegra-
tion rapidly set in. The Spaniards in Kinsale recognized
the hopelessness of their position and after a week more of
conflict under the walls entered into negotiations with
Mountjoy for surrender. The governor was glad to give
them easy terms. January 2, 1602, the capitulation was
signed, and D'Aquila entered upon such cordial relations
with Mountjoy as angered the Irish and led to his own arrest
when some weeks later he followed his troops back to Spain.
Through the next year there were constant rumors of another Spanish invasion but none occurred, and the Spanish
forces in the three western towns eventually withdrew, leaving the native Irish to their own efforts. Through the succeeding spring, summer and autumn there was a series of
petty conflicts in Munster, Leinster and Connaught and on

[39] Fynes Moryson, ii, 450–66; iii, 1–96; *Cal. Carew MSS.*, 1601–3,
179–204; Bagwell, iii, 398–415; Camden, 642–4; Kelso, 70–83.

the borders of Ulster, which worried Mountjoy and required the continuance of the queen's charges and the constant impressment of new troops. The remains of the resistance in Munster were stamped out with considerable difficulty by Carew in a campaign that extended to the remotest capes and islands of the southwest and was stained by almost indiscriminate hanging of captives, soldiers, civilians and priests. The governor himself late in the fall went to the westward and secured the submission of many of the Connaught chiefs.[40]

In Ulster Tyrone and his adherents were gradually forced into a region of glens and forests not more than ten or twenty miles square, but the wintry weather at Christmas time apparently made his actual capture impossible. More destructive than military conquest, however, was stark famine. It had been the deliberate and consistent policy of Mountjoy to starve the Irish into submission, to make resistance impossible by making starvation universal. The winter of 1602–1603 saw the success of this policy. The stories by English observers of swollen bodies lying in the ditches, their mouths green with the nettles they had eaten before they died, of children eating the bodies of men and women who had died of starvation, of dogs and wolves fighting over corpses, of the killing of children by women for their flesh, go beyond the decencies of history to record, if they were not an essential and truthful part of the history of this war and the time and country. The exhaustion of the country fell upon the invaders as well as upon the natives, and the English armies had to be supported entirely by food brought from England.[41]

From the middle of the summer of 1602 Tyrone sent to Mountjoy successive offers of submission, but always with conditions, returning more than once to those he had dis-

[40] Bagwell, iii, 419–24, 430; *Cal. State Papers, Dom.*, 1601–3, 154, 191–2, 197, 198, 222; Camden, 645–7.

[41] Bagwell, iii, 418–9, 429, 432–3; Manningham, *Diary*, 172; *Cal. Carew MSS.*, 1601–3, 366–74, 376, 382–3.

cussed with Essex in 1599. While these were being considered there was no cessation of efforts for his capture. His
lands were ravaged, the old stone chair of investment of the
O'Neills at Tullaghogue was broken down, he was forced
for refuge into the woods at the lower end of Lough Erne.
Finally, just before Christmas, 1602, and a year after the
defeat before Kinsale, he wrote to the lord deputy that
" without standing on any terms or conditions I do hereby
both simply and absolutely submit myself to her majesty's
mercy."

All the influences that surrounded the queen favored her
grant of this mercy, and that of her best advisers urged that
it be exercised generously. The war in Ireland was the
heaviest expense to which her government was now subjected, service there was the most unpopular to officers and
the common soldiers. The danger of Spanish intervention
was still imminent, the possibility of new outbreaks among
the Irish people still threatening. On the other hand the
eight years of Tyrone's defiance of her power had exasper-
ated her almost beyond endurance, and the determination to
punish him had become one of her most constant obsessions.
It was therefore a bitter requirement that was urged upon
her by Cecil and Mountjoy, and it was only with the greatest
reluctance that she yielded. February 6, 1603, she wrote
to Mountjoy authorizing him to promise Tyrone his life, and
on the 17th she extended this to liberty and pardon, with an
intimation through Cecil that further favors and eventual
reinstatement would be given him.

In consequence on April 1 an interview was arranged at
Mellifont where Mountjoy was lodging. Commissioners
were sent to Tyrone who willingly accompanied them. He
appeared in the lord deputy's chamber, knelt humbly at
the threshold and again as he drew nearer, and declared his
penitent submission. He then signed a written agreement,
in which he abjured the name of O'Neill, renounced all dependence upon Spain, promised to bring his son back if he
could, and agreed to accept such estates as the queen would

grant him and behave for the future as a faithful subject of the English crown. Mountjoy in return promised him the queen's pardon and a patent for most of the lands he had held before his rebellion. April 4 he accompanied the governor to Dublin expecting to go with him immediately to make his submission to the queen in person, but before April 4 the queen was dead, and it was another sovereign who received and pardoned Tyrone in London some months later.[42]

The Irish rising against England has already been compared with the contemporary Dutch rising against Spain. There are as a matter of fact many forms of parallelism. The different outcome in the two cases is due to many causes, but there are three that stand out with special prominence, the superior economic resources, the better political organization and training and the greater proximity of England to Ireland than of Spain to the Netherlands. England had men, munitions, food and money sufficient to overwhelm a poor country like Ireland, while Spain before the contest with the Netherlands was over was inferior to them in all the requirements for war; secondly, England was better governed than Spain, and, decentralized as the Dutch state was, it was superior in its powers both of resistance and aggression to Ireland still organized, or disorganized, under the tribal system. Finally, England was able from her geographical position to pour troops and supplies into Ireland far more easily than Spain could send them to the Netherlands. The English government was thus able to bring to bear upon the neighboring island all her superior resources, and to drive those deep rifts through Irish unity which made Ireland and her people helpless before her in this as in later struggles.

[42] Harington, *Nugae Antiquae*, Ed. 1804, i, 340–1; Bagwell, iii, 434–9; Camden, 656–8; *Cal. State Papers, Ireland,* 1601–3, 566–84; Chamberlain, *Letters,* 179–80; Fynes Moryson, iii, 289–304.

CHAPTER XLIV

THE DISGRACE, REBELLION AND DEATH OF ESSEX, 1599–1601

THE argument of the last act in the tragedy of Essex, since it opened at court, may be taken from a letter of a courtier. Rowland Whyte writes from Nonesuch to his absent patron, Sir Robert Sydney, September 29, 1599, " Upon Michaelmas Eve, about ten o'clock in the Morning, my Lord of Essex lighted at Court Gate in post, and made all hast up to the Presence and soe to the Privy Chamber, and staied not till he came to the Queen's Bed Chamber, where he found the Queen newly up, the Hare about her face; he kneeled unto her, kissed her Hands, and had some private Speach with her, which seemed to give him great Contentment, for coming from her Majestie to goe Shifte himself in his Chamber, he was very pleasant and thancked God, though he had suffered much Trouble and Storms abrod he found a sweet Calm at Home." This calm survived through another interview an hour later, when Essex had washed the mire from his face and the queen's ladies had brushed the straggling and graying hair from hers, and they were both in more seemly costume. " As yet all was well and her Usage very gracious towards hym," so he was merry at dinner. But when he went to her again after dinner all was changed. Her kindness of the morning was a last flickering of the ancient fondness. Now she was again the harsh critic, questioning why he had left his post, and the angry queen, sending him from her presence to that of his fellow-councillors. It was the last time she ever saw him. He conferred with the lords for an hour in the afternoon and at ten in the evening the queen sent an order for him to confine himself in his chamber.

The next day a full meeting of the council was called but
Essex did not attend till he was summoned, and, although
the lords all rose and saluted him when he appeared, he remained standing during the interview. From this time forward he was a culprit rather than a minister. The complaints that Cecil then presented in the name of the queen
against him were, with one or two later additions, in essence
the same as were charged in all later proceedings, till they
were superseded by the offences connected with the actual
outbreak of rebellion. Indeed they were all that could be
charged against him, either as unsuccessful general, disobedient subject or minister disgraced. They may be
summed up as, first, his unauthorized return and " over-
bold " intrusion into the queen's chamber; second, his mismanagement of affairs in Ireland, disobeying the queen's
repeated injunctions to proceed directly and immediately
against Tyrone; third, his insistence on the appointment of
the earl of Southampton as general of the horse; fourth, the
making of an excessive number of knights; fifth, the pre-
sumptuous tone and expressions used in his letters; and,
lastly, an offence which was only named later but which took
continually increased proportions in the mind of the queen,
his private and apparently friendly interview with Tyrone.
One day of consideration of his answers to these charges
and apparently of rising anger on the part of the queen intervened, then, Monday, October 1, Essex was ordered into
confinement in charge of Lord Keeper Egerton at York
House. He was sent in the earl of Worcester's coach from
the court at Nonesuch, where his early interviews with queen
and council had taken place, to Westminster.[1]

It was the expectation of the court and the opinion of
even the councillors closest to the queen that the confinement of the earl would last but a short time, perhaps for
a few days. As a matter of fact almost six months passed
away before he was given even the freedom to live with a
keeper in his own house instead of with Lord Keeper Eger-

[1] *Sydney Papers*, ii, 123–33; Winwood, *Memorials*, i, 118–9.

ton in his; and it was almost a year before he was actually released. Why was he kept so long a prisoner? Of the charges against him only the first and the last could be taken very seriously. The others were at most errors of judgment or of manners, not offences deserving punishment. It is true that in pursuance of the fourth of the charges named above, in October a proclamation was drawn up reciting the restrictions on the grant of knighthood imposed on him and declaring the new titles of some thirty-eight of the sixty he had knighted in Ireland null and void. But this proclamation, for fear it would bring discredit upon action taken under the great seal, was never issued. Notwithstanding the personal disgrace of Essex on the whole the queen followed his recommendations. She confirmed the six weeks' truce with Tyrone and its renewal. The half promise of her pardon given by Essex she decided ultimately also to confirm, with conditions little less definite if somewhat less ingenuous than those he had required. Essex had promised that he would ask the queen to give Tyrone her princely word that if he showed " true penitency and dutiful endeavours to do service hereafter " she would forgive him " in her heart as well as in parchment, and by an open pardon." The disgrace of Essex and his retention in England of course prevented any further personal negotiation, but the queen directed the lords justices and Ormonde to let Tyrone know that on his sincere repentance he would find her a gracious and merciful sovereign. She thus connived at the prospect of a full pardon.[2]

The return of the earl in spite of the Queen's prohibition was a clear instance of disobedience of orders, and though not always differentiated from the other charges, left him in the wrong and without excuse for resentment at her anger. In fact Essex was an unsuccessful general, a fallen minister, and, most serious of all, a displaced favorite. His fellow members of the privy council seem not to have been seri-

---

[2] *Cal. State Papers, Ireland,* 1599–1600, ix, 217, 218, 219, 220; *Sydney Papers,* ii, 204; Chamberlain, *Letters,* 86; *Cal. Carew MSS.,* 343.

ously dissatisfied with his answers or his behavior. They are reported by one of the best of court observers to have united on Sunday, October 21, to urge the queen to release him, commending his explanations of his policy in Ireland and his submission since his return and declaring it inconsistent with her honor and clemency to continue to hold him in confinement. But the queen, though she declared in a letter to the council in Ireland that she was merely laying " some public shadow of our displeasure upon him," by restraining him to the house of one of the privy councillors as a warning to him and others against disobedience, was really mingling, as usual, personal with official motives. It was to bring down the high heart of Essex that she allowed day after day and week after week to go by without giving the word for his release, some sense of injury or desire for his further humiliation still rankling in her mind, or possibly some obscure personal influence being exerted to keep her displeasure alive and keen. It is just possible, but not likely that it was genuine fear rather than jealousy, fear of the popularity of Essex as a danger to her throne, that compelled her action. Whatever the reason, every few days it was rumored that Essex would be set free; every conference of the queen with her councillors was expected to result in his release, but there was no change in his situation.[3]

This policy of confinement without charge and without period soon entered upon a vicious circle. Friends and admirers of Essex showed their sympathy, murmured against his imprisonment and indulged in surreptitious criticism of the government; the queen, angered and perhaps alarmed by this agitation, hardened her heart and prolonged his confinement. From Ireland came news of the protests of Tyrone against the retention of Essex in England, his refusal to trust anyone else, his complaints that he had been deceived again, and finally in December his denunciation

---

[3] *Sydney Papers*, ii, 132; Winwood, *Memorials*, i, 118; *Cal. State Papers, Dom.*, 1598–1601, 407.

of the truce and entrance again upon active warfare. Elizabeth found it hard to brook that the Irish rebel should trust the good will of one of her subjects rather than her own authority or power, and was consequently jealous of Essex. The English soldiers in Ireland who wanted him back cried, " Essex or none; Essex out of hand or all is lost," and English officers there continued to write as though expecting him back to complete what he had begun.

In London when Sir Christopher St. Lawrence, one of the officers who had returned with him from Ireland, drank at a tavern to the health of Essex and the confusion of his enemies, he was summoned before one of the privy councillors, who " did schoole him," but nothing else was done. Men passing York house cheered Essex under the windows, special prayers for his health and restoration to the queen's favor were recited in the London churches, and there were repeated expressions of sympathy for him in popular sermons at Paul's Cross. Written libels against the enemies of the earl were put up in public places and scurrilous pamphlets published and circulated in the country and city and at court itself. " Railing speeches " at taverns and elsewhere were reported to the council.

Much umbrage was taken by the queen at a certain *History of the Reign of Henry IV*, compiled and published by a Dr. Hayward just before Essex sailed from Ireland. It was very popular; according to the printer " No book ever sold better." It was dedicated to Essex in such fulsome terms that the archbishop of Canterbury, as chief censor, ordered the dedicatory letter to be removed; but the remainder of the edition was soon sold and a second edition of 1500 printed. Now that Essex was in prison attention was called to its seditious tone; in it the popular sentiments of Henry IV were praised, and the dethronement of Richard II seemed to be excused. The author seemed to consider present conditions analogous and to give to Essex the rôle of the popular duke of Lancaster. In July, 1600, the author, printer and censor of the book were questioned repeatedly, but without result, in an effort to find whether Essex or any of his adherents had influenced its writing or publication, and if it was intended as an attack on the government. Hayward was held in the Tower six months. The queen herself asked Bacon whether the book did not contain treason. According to his own account the witty lawyer replied that he saw no treason in it but much felony, for the author had stolen many of the sentences of Tacitus and put them into his text. The queen was also offended by the publication about this time of Essex's *Apology* which had been current now for two years in manuscript and had been translated into French: its printing, however, was found to be only a publisher's venture and its suppression was the only penalty.

Some of the more extreme of the friends of the earl, fearing that he might be removed to more rigorous imprisonment in the Tower offered aid in securing his escape to France, but he refused his consent. Essex had no liking for the life of an exile. He had no connection with the manifestations that have been described; he had no previous knowledge of the publication of Hayward's book, deprecated agitation in his favor and even discouraged attempts of his friends to visit him. One of his servants who was a Catholic tried to draw him into a statement favoring that party but without success. Lord Keeper Egerton in a spirit of kindness wrote him a letter warning him that he was being watched and urging him to carry himself with integrity so that his friends might do their best for him, but he found no occasion now to speak of any such defiance of the queen as he had warned him against two years before. According to all testimony his bearing during these months was quiet and dignified. He was in poor health, requiring frequent attendance of the doctors, spent much of his time in reading, and showed to his unwilling host all letters that reached him. The more prudent of his partisans, such as Southampton and Rutland, went abroad, and after their return avoided going to court, passing away the time in London according

to a correspondent " merely in going to Plaies every Day."
His sister, Lady Rich, and cousin, Lady Southampton, went
into the country to avoid the sympathetic company that
gathered around them. Even his servants were afraid to
make merry, for fear it would give offense at court.

In the court itself Cecil seems, notwithstanding the suspicions of Essex, to have done what he could for him, short
of pressing for his return to power, and Bacon, who was now
special legal adviser and confidant of the queen, professes
to have worked hard in his favor. Certainly some of the
court ladies did so. Lady Scrope, the queen's cousin and
one of the oldest court ladies, for a time wore black and
" ventured far " in urging his restoration to favor. Lady
Walsingham, his mother-in-law, begged the queen in his
early imprisonment to allow him to write to his wife, who
had just given birth to a daughter; and although this was
refused at the time later Lady Essex was allowed to write
him and eventually to visit him daily. Lady Warwick, an
old friend of his mother, and Mary Radcliffe, one of the
queen's ladies, secretly offered to arrange an opportunity,
if Essex would take the risk of breaking his captivity, and
throw himself again before the queen as she walked in
the park; but the days for such an appeal were over.[4]

An increase in the number and violence of anonymous
pamphlets and veiled criticisms of the queen concerning the
" Comyttment of the Earl of Essex " in November led the
councillors to use the occasion of the public ceremony in
Star Chamber at the close of Michaelmas term to justify
the actions of the queen in regard to Ireland and Essex, —
one of the few contemporary instances of an appeal to public
opinion. It will be remembered that it was the usual prac-

---

[4] *Cal. State Papers, Ireland,* 1599–1600, 165–9, 171, 178, 186, 209, 216,
218, 219–21; *Cal. State Papers, Dom.,* 1598–1601, 347–8, 352, 387, 404–5;
Cal. Carew MSS., 1589–1600, 336–7, 339–40, 343–8; *Sydney Papers,*
130–9; *Hatfield House MSS.,* ix, 392–3; Camden, 574–6; *Nugae Antiquae,*
309, 356; Birch, *Memoirs,* ii, 434–40; Francis Bacon, *Apology;* Violet A.
Wilson, *Queen Elizabeth's Maids of Honour,* 250–2; Laura H. Cadwallader,
Later Career of the Earl of Essex, 59–64.

tice for the lord chancellor or lord keeper on that day, in instructing the judges about to go on their circuit, to make public announcement of matters of general interest and to convey some of the queen's wishes to her people. On this occasion the lord keeper, lord treasurer, lord admiral, lord chief justice, Secretary Cecil and some lesser members of the court and council successively made speeches expressing their abhorrence of the libels and slanders of the queen that were prevalent, their disapproval of the discussion of politics in taverns and the pulpit, their deep appreciation of the constant care of the queen for her people and for her kingdom of Ireland, the failure of Essex to recognize the " unspeakable wisdom " of the queen and to follow her instructions and utilize the means she had provided him with while there. It was an unconditional justification of the recent actions of the queen. There was naturally much that was exaggerated, much that was unfair, a certain amount that was untrue in these speeches. Cecil was anxious to defend himself from personal aspersions, and to place all the responsibility upon Essex; the lord treasurer dilated on the vast and ineffective expenditures; but on the whole the councillors were rather more interested to defend the queen than to condemn the earl, and they left the reasons for his confinement as much unexplained as before.

In December Essex became desperately sick, taking communion on two successive Sundays and so weak and suffering that he was not expected to live. The queen sent permission for his wife to visit him in the day time, allowed a consultation of eight physicians, and when they reported the desirability of his mind being quieted, sent him some broth and a half promise she would go to see him. Courtiers thought " she had water in her eies when she spoke yt." There was general expectation of his death, special prayers were said for his recovery and in fact a mistaken report led to the tolling of the bells in London churches, for which the bishop of London was much blamed by the queen. But a scandalous attack on Cecil written on the white walls of the court gave the queen occasion to believe she was being deluded, and improvement in the earl's health soon brought all relenting to an end. So the year 1599 ended with Essex still under restraint by *lettre de cachet*. All the courtiers were watching, most of them hoping for the restoration of Essex to favor. Even those he considered his opponents, Nottingham, Cecil, Ralegh and Cobham and their followers, including Bacon, were doing little more than setting their sails to the prevailing wind. They would not be sorry to see fairer weather.[5]

On the opening of Hilary term, January 23, 1600, the rumor spread, and indeed was well founded, that the long uncertainty of the charges against Essex was to be brought to a conclusion by a trial in the Court of Star Chamber. Everything was prepared for Wednesday, February 8. A rail was built across the room to keep the populace from pressing upon him and multitudes of people crowded the chamber early to hear his trial. But he did not appear. Cecil and Buckhurst, who may well have recognized the difficulty of formulating any charge against the earl that would have met even the easy requirements of a Star Chamber bill of complaint, had visited him, told him of the prospective summons and urged him to write a submissive letter to the queen, asking not to be brought to this public and ruinous humiliation. Such a letter, begging that " this cup may pass from me," was written, delivered to the queen by the secretary, who gained for himself much credit by this kindly and judicious intermediation, and late on Tuesday night Elizabeth reluctantly sent orders to stay the Star Chamber trial. The next day Essex sent another letter of humble gratitude.[6]

" Out of sight out of mind " justified itself by a gradually increasing court neglect of the earl. The reception of for-

---

[5] *Sydney Papers*, ii, 146–8, 152–6; *Cal. State Papers, Dom.*, 1598–1601, 347–54, 361–5, 375; Hayward, *Cases in Camera Stellata*, 394–5.

[6] *Sydney Papers*, ii, 164, 166–7, 169; *Letters of John Chamberlain*, 65, 67; *Cal. State Papers, Dom.*, 1598–1601, 392–4, 412–3.

eign ambassadors, vague negotiations for a peace with Spain, manoeuvres for office and favors, petty factional disputes, routine court formalities, private sorrows in the household of the lord keeper, who had by March been reluctant jailer of the earl for six months, and the slow development of events in Ireland, filled the time of the queen and courtiers. Essex was less and less mentioned or thought of. Therefore his transfer from York House in Westminster to his own house in the Strand, March 20, 1600, attracted but little attention. It was in itself no great step toward ultimate release though it brought out as usual a letter of too humble gratitude from Essex to the queen. He was placed under the care of a keeper, Sir Richard Barkley, who carried the keys both of the Strand and the River gates, and no members of his household except servants were allowed to visit him except by special permission on each occasion from the queen. In April he was given somewhat greater freedom from the supervision of his keeper and we catch a pleasant glimpse of him and Lady Essex on her daily visits walking in the garden " now he, now she reading one to the other." [7]

Yet it was evident that Essex could not be kept indefinitely in confinement without some formal sentence. He must either be given his freedom or brought to some form of trial. The common charge that he was being condemned unheard could not be allowed to continue even under Elizabeth's autocratic rule. During Easter term and again in mid-summer term the queen seems to have proposed again to have him brought before the court of Star Chamber, either *ore tenus,* the information being based on his own confessions, or charging him with responsibility for the current libels. But Bacon, according to his own statement, dissuaded her from this. He told her plainly that although the earl's faults might be termed contempts because they were disobedience of her orders, there were many grounds

[7] *Sydney Papers,* ii, 172–82, 187; *Letters of John Chamberlain,* 69, 70-2; Birch, *Memoirs,* ii, 443–4; *Cal. State Papers, Dom.,* 1598–1601, 407.

of defense he could plead: the ampleness of his commission, the distance of Ireland, the support of the Irish council, his good intentions. His eloquence and the favor of his hearers would also plead for him. A public hearing might not be to the queen's honor.

Elizabeth finally decided on a more private but scarcely less formal trial. June 5, 1600, just eight months after his arrest, he was ordered to appear before a commission consisting of eighteen councillors, noblemen and judges. They met at York House, the residence of the lord keeper, where Essex had been so long a prisoner. It was a dignified assembly, the commissioners including the archbishop of Canterbury, the lord keeper, lord admiral, lord treasurer, lord chamberlain, two other household officials, Secretary Cecil, five earls and six judges. An invited company of about two hundred persons of quality of various professions served to give the court an appearance of publicity. All the queen's learned counsel, the attorney, solicitor, queen's sergeant and Bacon as special counsel were also present, the part each was to take in the prosecution appointed beforehand by the privy councillors.[8]

There was no doubt of the position of Essex. As he entered and knelt at the end of a long table about which the commissioners sat, no one lifted his cap or gave any other sign of courtesy or recognition, and it was only after some time that he was given a cushion on which to kneel, and later, as the session lasted for almost eleven hours, a stool on which to sit. It was a lawyer's occasion. Yelverton, Coke, Fleming and Bacon, each in turn, with the ingenuity, exaggeration and rhetoric demanded by their duty to the queen, the traditions of their profession and their respective hopes of advancement, rang the changes on the old complaints against the earl, — his appointment of Southampton as general of the horse against the orders of the queen, his campaign in Munster when he had been ordered to go to

---

[8] Camden, 597, 601; Birch, *Memoirs*, ii, 439-40; *Life and Letters of Bacon*, Spedding, Ed., ii, 175; *Acts of the Privy Council*, xxx, 351.

Ulster, his making of knights so much more freely than the restrictions of the queen would warrant, his conference with Tyrone, his unauthorized return. No servility of form in the letters of Essex can compare with the servility of spirit of these prosecutors, so keen to fulfil the wishes and justify the anger of the queen. The speech of Coke especially was not only prolonged and beyond measure severe but it had all a public prosecutor's disingenuousness, and as he quoted from Cicero's diatribes against Catiline and hinted at similar ulterior objects on the part of Essex, that nobleman gave evidence of being stung beyond endurance. When the accusations were over and had been supported by the reading of some of the earl's letters and others of the queen and council, he replied with much passion that he would enter into no contest with his sovereign and would not excuse or justify himself; he would only insist on his absolute loyalty, his " faithful, unspotted heart and unfeigned affection." Notwithstanding this self-renunciation, however, induced, according to the chronicler, by the " oversharp speeches " of his accusers, he was later led to enter upon a defense of his actions which seemed to him, as it does to the modern scholar, so easy and so reasonable. But the lord keeper in a friendly, if scarcely an elevated spirit interrupted him to say that he would gain more by appealing to the queen's mercy alone, which would seem greater and doubtless be given more readily the greater his offenses.

As a matter of fact the " censures " of the lords and judges, which were then successively expressed, as in Star Chamber and similar bodies of equity judges, were mild enough and given with evident reluctance and with the full anticipation that the queen would finally nullify his conviction by her pardon. As lord keeper Egerton remarked when beginning his sentence, since the throne of kings is based on justice and mercy and the queen had appointed them to apply the former, she herself would no doubt by the inspiration of God use the latter. After much testimony to the queen's wisdom, recapitulation of the earl's mistakes, restatement of his disobedience and rejoinder to his defense, the lord keeper gave as his judgment that the earl should be suspended from his offices of privy councillor, earl marshal and master of the ordnance, and should remain prisoner in his own house till the queen should remit this and the remainder of the sentence. The mastership of the horse, his earliest and most personal court honor, was left to him, it was said, at the command of the queen herself, as though she would not cut him off entirely. All the rest agreed, Cecil joining with the lord keeper in explicitly acquitting the earl of any disloyalty and treating him with much courtesy, though he took occasion to dilate on the queen's careful attention to Irish affairs, the absolute wisdom of her judgment as to how the campaign should have been carried on and the errors Essex had fallen into by deviating from that infallible guidance. Cumberland demurred somewhat to the severity of the sentence, knowing as he said " how easily a general commander might incur the like," but, confiding in the queen's mercy, agreed with the rest. Lord Zouch was inclined to require him to do only that which Essex himself would doubtless do, that is, refrain from the execution of his offices and remain at home till the queen released him from her disfavor. As a matter of fact Essex was so ill at the time that he returned at once to his home and remained as secluded as before. His keeper was soon afterward removed and August 26 he was again summoned to York House, where Egerton, Buckhurst and Cecil told him from the queen that he was now free to go where he would, except that he should seek no access to court.[9]

Yet it was this access which had been the burden of his letters, his hopes and the efforts of his friends, ever since his banishment from the face of the queen the day after his return from Ireland. Attendance at court and personal ap-

[9] Camden, 517–602; *Cal. State Papers, Dom., Addenda*, 1580–1625, 399; *Sydney Papers*, ii, 199–201; Winwood, *Memorials*, i, 250; *Hatfield House MSS.*, x, 178; *Hist. MSS. Comm., Rutland Papers*, i, 361–2; *Letters from Cecil to Carew*, Camden Society, 23.

pearance before the queen were the indispensable conditions of all influence in the government of Elizabeth and of all royal favor. Those who were with her most constantly achieved the greatest success; those who had no intimacy with her accomplished nothing. Men and women schemed and plotted and waited just to get within the purlieus of the court. Those who were there could obtain favors for themselves and their friends; those who were not could get nothing, and were besides at the mercy of their enemies or rivals. Essex was especially dependent on such intercourse. A courtier all his adult life, raised to greatness by the personal favor of the queen, subjected to danger and disgrace by its loss, he was both unhappy and unsafe till his position at court was regained. The periods when he had been away, in France, at Cadiz, at sea, in Ireland, were periods when his fortunes had sunk and those of others more constantly at court had risen. All courtiers feared to be away from court. Even Cecil when he went to France on the embassy of 1598 had found it desirable to secure a promise beforehand from Essex not to displace him with the queen.

To remain in retirement and obscurity in the country, where he spent the next few weeks, would for a more philosophic and less highly placed man, such for instance as Sir Francis Vere, have been quite possible; for Essex it would be to eat his heart out as much as if he were actually in confinement; and absent from court trouble of some kind was sure to gather around him. If nothing else demanded the completion of his restoration to court favor, his debts would require it. From the day of his return from Ireland and the gathering of the clouds of royal disfavor his creditors had been pressing him. They were almost the only visitors who intruded upon his privacy at York House and Essex House. Essex had always been in debt. He had inherited debts from his father and his way of life had never allowed him completely to lift that load or to avoid creating new liabilities. Many of these were practically national expenditures, incurred in connection with those semi-public, semi-private military and naval expeditions of which he had been sole or joint commander. He supported a horde of volunteers or private followers who ate at his table and travelled and fought largely at his expense. Sudden military exigencies were met from his personal means or by mortgaging his personal credit. Now these all rose up against him. A liberal gift from the queen on occasion of his departure for Ireland was charged against him as evidence of the queen's favor to him, but this appears to have been nothing more than a remission of certain debts nominally due the crown, but expended by his father or himself for crown purposes and never collected. Practically all public men of the time were in debt; the peculiarity in the position of Essex was his powerlessness so long as he was in disgrace.

Yet he had, like other favored courtiers, — more, probably, than any other courtier, unless it were Ralegh, — received profitable grants from the queen. His principal source of free income had long been the monopoly of the collection of customs and licensing of dealers in sweet wines, that is to say all wines but those of France and Germany. This license, which his father-in-law, Leicester, had had before him, and which had been granted in 1590, would extend only to September 2, 1600, and as the date of its expiring approached Essex, though neither he nor others believed that the queen would really fail to renew it, became apprehensive. Its continuance would be taken as a more complete restoration to favor, its withdrawal as his ruin. A week before its expiration he wrote to the queen apologizing for appealing to her on this ground, but pointing out that the patent was not only his chief maintenance but his only means of compounding with his " hungry creditors," and taking occasion to make suit again that she would " look with gracious eyes " upon him. But no attention was paid to his letter except a jibe from the queen that she had received from the earl what began as a letter of affection but was really only an appeal for money. The day passed and it was not granted; a month passed by and it was announced that the grant would not be reissued but put into the hands of the treasury officials.[10]

Even yet, in four more letters written through October, he begs for her favor, and declares that the loss of his wine patent was forgotten in the craving " to hear your natural voice of grace," and in the desire " to prostrate myself at your feet." Twenty-two letters written by Essex to the queen during the period of his imprisonment remain, mostly in his own handwriting. They are written in a tone of excessive humility. This style is due partly to the time, partly to the relation of subject and sovereign, partly to the personality and position of Essex. Apart from this blemish they are not unworthy of the best literature of a great age. Humble they may be, but they are never obsequious, and they are always lucid, always grave, always eloquent. He " kisses her fair correcting hand "; he prays to her " on the knees of my heart "; he would hear her comforting words " though all the world besides should ring alarms "; he begs an answer " before he that sends this enjoins himself eternal silence." He complains that " the prating tavern-haunter speaks of me what he lists; the frantic libeller writes of me what he lists; they print me and make me speak to the world, and shortly they will play me upon the stage "; " you have refused to hear me, which to traitors you never did." The appetite was certainly jaded, the mind warped or the heart hardened that made no response to any one of these letters spread over a full year.[11]

One last letter of appeal for favor Essex wrote on the queen's birthday, November 17, and it was even rumored that he would enter the usual masked tournament on that

[10] *Sydney Papers*, ii, 220; Winwood, *Memorials*, i, 271; Birch, *Memoirs*, ii, 458, 472–3; *Letters of John Chamberlain*, 90–93; Camden, 602–3, Devereux, *Lives of the Devereux*, ii, 125; *Cal. State Papers, Dom.*, 1598–1601, 468.

[11] *Cal. State Papers, Dom.*, 1598–1603, 393, 394, 418, 444, 457–8, 463, 465–6, 468, 473, 475, 479, 483; Devereux, *Lives of the Devereux*, ii, 96, 110, 114, 125; Birch, *Memoirs*, ii, 436–7, 443–5.

day, in the hope doubtless of rousing her memory of earlier times; but he did not come to the running and his letter of congratulation, like all others, remained unanswered.

This was the close of the period of Essex's hopes and appeals. During more than twelve months he had preserved an attitude of submission, even penitence; he had talked little and avoided companionship, except of his wife and nearest relatives; and after his release from confinement had nevertheless kept the gates of Essex House shut. No fault was found by anyone except some of his warmest adherents with his dignified retirement and silence. They had been of no avail, and his financial grant had been cut off. He seems now to have given himself up to discouragement and to have oscillated between bitter complaints of his fate and religious devotion. Sir John Harington, whose opportunities for knowledge and whose acute observations have been so often made use of in this work, said of him at this time, " The man's soule seemeth tossede to and fro, like the waves of a troubled sea "; he " shyftithe from sorrowe and repentaunce to rage and rebellion so suddenlie as well provethe him devoide of goode reason or right mynde "; " his speeches of the Queene becomethe no man who hath *mens sana in corpore sano.*" One remark he made about the queen at this time has come down to us and may have reached her, that she had become an old woman and her mind was as crooked as her carcase. A few such observations might readily explain her implacability after this time, though no such words had escaped him, or even probably passed through his mind before December, 1600.[12]

The fact is that the queen, if her intention was only to punish disobedience and rebuke pride, had overdone her work. She was reported to have said when Essex had made public confession of his sorrow for his actions before the York House court, " I must have some time to make proof of his humility." But she had already then had eight months'

<hr>

[12] *Nugae Antiquae,* i, 179–80; Birch, *Memoirs,* ii, 473; Camden, Ed. 1688, 605.

proof of his submission. When she refused the renewal of the wine patent she said, " An unruly horse must be abated of his provender that he may be the easier managed." But the provender of Essex, the prosperity and popularity and royal favor and opportunity for service on which he lived, had already long been of the most exiguous proportions and bade fair to reduce him to starvation or desperation rather than to docility. The year's resistance of the queen to his reinstatement in some degree of dignity had been too long. She had said early in his imprisonment that her object was to reform not ruin him, and he and others had frequently reminded her of this saying, but his ruin seemed now imminent. She may have been induced, as was contemporaneously believed, to have prolonged so far beyond measure her disfavor to him by those at court who dreaded his return; but this supposes a responsiveness to suggestion almost incompatible with the independence of a long experienced queen.

There remains the possibility that she was under the influence of fear, the nemesis of autocratic rulers, in this case fear of the popularity of Essex. Violence, although long unknown or quickly suppressed in England, was always in the background of the minds of the age. While Essex was still in Ireland Bacon had told the queen that to put arms and power into his hands, as she had, and then " discontent " him by her sharp letters was to tempt him to " prove unruly." He himself later said that if he had wished to do ill he might have done it when he had an army at his back; and it was later charged, probably without basis, that he had contemplated bringing his army back with him, as though the Irish sea were the Rubicon.[13]

Whatever the explanation of the queen's behavior, that of Essex after the early days of December became reckless and provocative. The gates of Essex House, which had so

[13] *Reliquiae Wottonianae*, 188; Fulke Greville, *Life of Sir Philip Sidney*, 157; Birch, *Memoirs*, ii, 432; Camden, 599, 603; *Cal. State Papers, Dom.*, 1598–1601, 575; Laura H. Cadwallader, *Later Career of Earl of Essex*, 73, etc.

long been closed, now seemed open to all comers. " Men of
the sword," officers on leave or recently discharged, and soldiers of lower rank, the men whom in his *Apology* he acknowledged that he " entirely loved " frequently visited him.
Puritan preachers under the disapproval of the authorities
of church and state came to him for comfort and gave lectures or sermons daily in his house; and this provided occasion for the gathering of many hearers. One of his confidants
he knew to be a Catholic and others were so in secret. His
self-assertive sister, Lady Rich, in disgrace at court because
of her alienation from her husband, her favor to Lord
Mountjoy and her outspoken appeal to the queen for her
brother's restoration, was there daily. He received many
visits now from his close friends, Southampton and Rutland.
There was probably much said in conversation that was
foolish, much that was dangerous. Essex was believed at
the time, and indeed later acknowledged, that he was much
influenced by one of his secretaries, Henry Cuffe, a learned
man long in his service, who carried under his scholar's
gown a restless and proud and challenging spirit, restive
under the humiliation of his master and convinced that a
bolder policy would secure better conditions. Removed in
the summer from the earl's personal service because of this
aggressive attitude, Cuffe was allowed by Sir Gelly Merrick, the earl's steward, to remain in obscurity in the household and was afterwards restored to the earl's service by the
influence of Southampton. Incitements to some bolder action were no longer so distasteful to Essex and were certainly not without influence. Sir Christopher Blount, Sir
John Davies and Sir Charles Danvers, old Irish officers and
all out of favor at court, were more favorable to active protest than to a long and fruitless course of submission.[14]
In the middle of January an occurrence of a kind not
unusual at the time, except in the rank of the principals,
played a part in the rising spirit of those who gathered at
Essex House. This was an attack in the open street by Lord

[13] *Reliquiae Wottonianae*, 180-1; Birch, ii, 462-3.

Grey and a group of his followers on the earl of Southampton, his personal enemy. Grey was sent to the Fleet for a couple of weeks as a nominal punishment. It was not a very serious affair; there had long been bad blood between the two nobles and a duel had only been avoided by the absolute prohibition of the queen. A letter writer describes it as a " little bickering in the Strand on horseback," and some doggerel verse of the time says:

> " Littel Graie, littell Graie,
> He made a ladies' fraie
> Turned his heels and ran away."

But it was a bad example of the settlement of private grievances by personal violence. Essex was much moved by the assault on his friend, and afterward claimed that the inability of the queen to protect men from such attacks suggested to him his own danger from his enemies. Soon afterward another adherent, Sir Ferdinando Gorges, whom Essex had asked up to London to give him advice, was invited by Ralegh to meet him at Durham House, where Ralegh intended to discuss with him the risk he was running in leaving his captaincy of the fort at Plymouth without special permission. Essex and his friends citing the case of Southampton warned Gorges of his danger in putting himself in Ralegh's power and induced him instead to make a later appointment to meet Ralegh in a boat on the river.[15]

It had long been the conviction of Essex that his troubles were due in the last resort to his enemies at court. The mind of the queen was poisoned against him by the hostile influence, untrue reports and malicious suggestions emanating especially from Ralegh and Cobham. With them came more and more to be associated in his mind Secretary Cecil and, more remotely, the other privy councillors. In these beliefs he was no doubt partially correct, though their influence with the queen, apart from her own inclinations, was

---

[15] *State Papers, Dom., Eliz.,* cclxxviii, 23; *Cal. State Papers, Dom.,* 1598–1601, 588; *Letters of John Chamberlain,* 100; Birch, *Memoirs,* ii, 462–3; Camden, 602–3; Jardine, *Criminal Trials,* 328, 330, 338, 348, 355.

certainly much less than he supposed, and their hostility, apart from the care of successful office holders to keep out a dangerous rival, much less bitter than he believed. His conviction of their malevolence became an obsession. An instance of this was his belief in a Spanish plot. Easily deluded as he had always been, relying on some chance gossip and on a coincidence, he convinced himself that Cecil, the lord treasurer and lord admiral, who were under his influence, Cobham and Ralegh, who were related to him, were engaged in a scheme to hand over the succession to the English crown to a Spanish candidate. He was deeply impressed with the fact that the treasury, the fleet, the Cinque Ports and the Island of Jersey, all the requirements for a Spanish occupation, were in the hands of this coalition.

Perhaps with the idea of gaining some influence over the general course of events, perhaps simply to throw discredit upon his opponents, he opened negotiations with King James of Scotland, or, rather, renewed some obscure negotiations in which he and Mountjoy had been engaged with the king the year before, telling him of his suspicions of a Spanish plot and suggesting that he should send envoys to England to make more sure his own succession.[16]

In Essex's belief there was only one cure for all his troubles, — personal access to the queen, a direct appeal to her in person against the misrepresentations and plottings of his enemies. Yet this was forbidden. Gradually there grew up in his mind the determination to accomplish by force what apparently could not be obtained otherwise. He could count on the absolute devotion of the earls of Southampton and Rutland; the persuasions of other friends had long been for action; and there lay in the background his widespread popularity. Just when or how far he had determined on a definite policy does not appear, but in January he wrote or sent messengers to Sir Ferdinando Gorges, Danvers and Blount asking them to come up to London by

<hr />

[16] Birch, *Memoirs*, ii, 463, 470–3; *Correspondence of James VI*, Camden Society, Appendix iii, 81–4; Hardwicke, *State Papers*, i, 372–6.

February 1 to give him advice and help. As each appeared he told him he had determined to "stand on his defense," to "stand upon his own strength," and "put himself again into the court."

After various individual interviews a meeting of five friends of the earl took place at his request February 3 at Drury house, the London dwelling of the earl of Southampton. Essex himself was not present but he sent, written in his own hand, a list of a hundred and twenty nobles, knights and gentlemen, whom he considered members of his party who could be depended on, and a series of "projects." These were heads of proposals for the seizure of the court, for the forcible entry of the earl into the presence of the queen, for the removal of his enemies. The court buildings of Whitehall, where the queen was then staying, might be seized. Ralegh, Cobham and Cecil might be arrested, then Essex and his principal adherents, "nine honorable persons," he afterwards testified, would throw themselves at the feet of the queen, declare their grievances and demand the removal of their enemies from her service. A parliament might then be called, the arrested courtiers and ministers given a fair trial, general reforms carried through, and possibly "an alteration of the state," whatever that may have meant. All should be without violence and without injury to the queen. It was a harebrained scheme. Apart from all other difficulties and inconsistencies, they all knew Elizabeth and could hardly have imagined her submitting tamely to such control. They should rather have pictured her "lionlike rising," as when she had once been insulted by a foreign ambassador, her Tudor blood aroused, and either daunting them by her royal resoluteness or yielding, if she yielded at all, only to actual physical force. And who would have suddenly taken up the daily duties of Cecil, and what reason was there to believe that Nottingham and Buckhurst, Egerton and the judges would connive at such a disorderly interference with the dignity of government, undisturbed now for half a century? The plan was a dream of disordered minds.

This appeared when the conspirators at Drury House discussed the actual steps of their adventure. It was easy to make the general plan; for Sir John Davies to take ink and paper and write down that Sir Christopher Blount when the day came should quietly take possession of the outer gate and some one else of the water gate; that Sir Charles Danvers with some of his servants should slip unobserved from the hall into the guard chamber and get between the dozen or so unsuspecting guards and their halberds piled up against the wall; and that Davies himself should take possession of the larger presence chamber; then at a signal Essex and his friends, who would have come quietly down the Strand from Essex House and secreted themselves in the stables, would enter without interference into the presence of the queen. But there must evidently be some force back of this action or reaction would quickly follow. The city might not like their proceeding. Should they seize the Tower to bridle London, and, if so, before their occupation of the court or at the same time? These points were discussed vaguely by the conspirators. Gorges objected that an attempt to seize the Tower with so small a force was absurd, and, according to his own testimony, misliked the whole proposal. Eventually this, and perhaps a later conference at Drury house, broke up, everything being left to the earl with nothing actually settled.[17]

Such gatherings as the rendezvous at Esséx House and such discussions as those at Drury House do not go unobserved by a watchful and suspicious government, and all these nebulous plans were suddenly broken in upon by a summons to Essex on Saturday, February 8, from the privy council. Dr. John Herbert, the recently appointed second secretary, appeared at Essex House with a message in the name of the queen ordering the earl to appear immediately before the council, which was assembled at the house of the lord treasurer, who was ill. The councillors declared after-

---

[17] *Cal. State Papers, Dom.*, 1598–1601, 545, 548, 552, 557, 565, 571–5, 577–82, 599–600; Jardine, *Criminal Trials*, 322, 327, 330–5, 338–41, 349–50.

ward that their only intention was to admonish him to be more careful in his speech and behavior. Fearing, however, that he was to be committed to the Tower, and warned at the same time by a secret note to beware of his "private enemies," Essex pleaded sickness, refused to go, and determined immediately upon the use of either defensive or offensive force. A council of a few of his most intimate friends was held at Essex House that evening. An invasion of the court that night was suggested, but, courtiers as they all were, they hesitated at such a disturbance of the queen. There was besides a rumor that the court guards had been doubled and were on the watch. Some thought that the game was up and that it would be better for them all to save themselves by flight. But the arrival of a messenger from London with the statement that Sheriff Smyth, who had command of a regiment of a thousand men of the trained bands, had declared himself devoted to the cause of the earl brought anew to their attention the possibility of obtaining overpowering support for their plans from the adjacent city.

With the vaguest of anticipations therefore, except that the earl should in some way try out the Londoners the next day, Sunday, the gathering broke up, and Essex proceeded to send letters and messengers to Southampton and Rutland, Lord Sands, Lord Monteagle and other members of his faction who were not already present, and to certain adherents in the city. Essex testified afterwards that he received another warning that day that his life would be openly attempted, or that his house might be beset in the night and he be killed in his bed by Cobham and Ralegh. A watch by some of Essex's and Blount's servants against such a night attack on Essex House and garden was thereupon set and several gentlemen, informed by the earl that his life was threatened, asked to stay all night.[18]

Confusion between public and private grievances, be-

18 Camden, 607; Speed, 1212; Jardine, 321, 324, 331, 343, 346; Spedding, *Life and Letters of Bacon,* ii, 295–6, 306–9.

tween self-protection from personal enemies and violent removal of them from the position near the sovereign that gives them their power, is perhaps inseparable from life under a personal monarchy like that of Queen Elizabeth. But the over-credulous mind and excitable temperament of Essex made him blind beyond all reason to realities. The power or the inclination of Cobham and Ralegh to carry out such a plot did not strike him as incredible: and neither he nor Southampton seems to have seen any essential difference between protecting themselves by their servants against attack by a band of desperadoes and inducing the populace to aid them in over-aweing the queen and so forcing her to punish their rivals. They had not thought of treason.

Some of their party, however, evidently played with more dangerous thoughts. Essex took dinner quietly with his sister and four of his friends, but a group of eight or ten gentlemen of his faction, after dinner at a tavern on the Strand, went early across the river to the Globe on the Bankside, where the lord chamberlain's players were acting, and induced the manager by a gift of forty shillings to substitute " King Henry IV and the deposing and killing of Richard II " for the play they had intended to give. Whatever may have been true of the publication of Hayward's Henry IV, the connection of this incident with existing conditions could hardly have been a coincidence. But of all this Essex knew nothing.

The London dwelling of the earl of Essex consisted at that time of a group of buildings and gardens lying just west of the Temple, and extending from the Strand to the banks of the river. Enclosed within its walls was a considerable stretch of ground, now covered by a tangle of narrow streets, courts and buildings many of which still bear one or other of the family names. Here early Sunday morning, February 9, 1601, a great company began to gather. One after another as they arrived they were admitted through the wicket in the gate on the Strand. The usual household, numerous enough, was soon swelled, it was said, to three hundred persons, more than a hundred of whom were nobles, gentlemen and their personal attendants. The confusion in the courtyard extended to the street outside where crowds gathered. Rumors spread inside that armed men were preparing to attack the house. Gorges went out by the watergate to keep his engagement with Ralegh, but after an altercation in which Ralegh urged his kinsman to leave a sinking ship and Gorges threatened him with " a bloody day," their boats were pushed apart and Gorges returned to the house.[19]

It was perhaps through Ralegh, perhaps through some Londoner who had heard the messages sent to the city by the earl, perhaps through a spy that word of the gathering at Essex house reached the court. Prompt action was taken. Sir Thomas Gorges, a brother of Sir Ferdinando, was sent to London by the council with a warning to the mayor, whom soon after ten o'clock he found at sermon at Paul's Cross; and at about the same hour, in the midst of the confusion at Essex house, Lord Keeper Egerton, Lord Chief Justice Popham, the Earl of Worcester and Sir William Knollys, comptroller of the household, appeared at the gate saying that they came with a message from the queen. They were admitted through the wicket, though without their servants. They found the earl in the court yard and the lord keeper asked him the cause of this tumultuous assemblage, assuring him from the queen that if he and his friends had any particular cause of grief it would be heard and they should have justice. Essex thereupon made his usual complaint that his life was being sought and that he had been perfidiously dealt with, adding that counterfeit letters had been sent in his name and declaring that he and his friends were assembled to defend their lives. The councillors assured him again that if he knew of any such thing or had any private offense against anyone they would declare it faithfully to the queen and justice would be done, whomever it concerned.

[19] Jardine, 327, 330–1, 346.

No messengers more favorable to the earl could have been sent; Knollys was his own uncle, Worcester a relative, Egerton and Popham, as he himself testified, " ever my best friends "; their message was also conciliatory. But his hands were forced. The confusion was great; cries arose, " Away my lord, they abuse you, they delay you! " a man afterwards described as wearing a white satin doublet but not otherwise identified cried out " kill them, kill them "; others proposed to seize the great seal and throw it out of the window. The lord keeper suggested to Essex that they go inside the house for a more quiet discussion of his grievances, and, putting on his hat as a sign of official authority, in a loud voice though without effect commanded the rest of the company on their allegiance to the queen to disperse. Essex led the councillors through the house to his study; but instead of entering into further discussion with them ordered the doors to be locked, put them under charge of Sir Charles Davies, with some musketeers at the door, and when they protested, begged them to be patient for awhile as he was going into London to take order with the mayor for the city, but would be back in half an hour. Instead of a half hour they were as a matter of fact held captive for more than four hours, and although Davies brought the ladies of the family down to entertain them they insisted again and again upon their release or at least that some one of them should be allowed to go to the queen and report their position.[20]

In the meantime Essex had proceeded with his appeal to the city. A messenger was sent galloping ahead to the house of Sheriff Smyth to announce his coming, and his steward, Sir Gelly Merrick, was placed in charge of Essex House with orders to allow no one to pass in or out. Then with a body of about 200 noblemen, gentlemen and their followers, all unarmed except for their usual swords and

[20] *Cal. State Papers, Dom.*, 1598–1601, 548, 552, 557, 585–7, 1601–3, 4; Spedding, *Life and Letters of Bacon*, ii, 306–9; Howell, *State Trials*, i, 1340–2.

rapiers, Essex mounted his horse and passed out of the gate into the Strand. Even yet there was a momentary hesitation as to their plan. Some called out "To the court." If they turned to the left it was but a mile to Whitehall and the queen; if they turned to the right it was a still shorter distance through Fleet Street to Ludgate and the city. To the city they went, Essex crying as he and his friends made their way up Ludgate Hill and along Cheapside, "for the queen, for the queen; there is a plot against my life." To those to whom he spoke individually he repeated his complaint that Ralegh and Cobham intended to murder him and that he came to the city for his own safety, for the good of the queen and the maintenance of religion. He was evidently hard put to it to give an excuse for a city rising, and therefore added that England was being sold to the Infanta of Spain referring doubtless to his suspicions of Cecil, and that they were all betrayed by atheists, the old charge against Ralegh.

As he rode "triumphing down Cheapside," there were general plaudits from the citizens and boys in the street; there was no doubt of his popularity. But no one appeared with weapons, even when he asked them to arm themselves, explaining that otherwise they would be of no use to him. His first object was to reach the house of Sheriff Smyth, who lived in Fenchurch Street near the Exchange; but when he arrived there he found the whole report of Smyth's armed support a fiction or a misunderstanding. Smyth, like most of the city aldermen, was an admirer of Essex but had had no communication with him for nine years, had sent no messages, so he said, and could not if he would bring together an armed band in this time of confusion.

While Essex with fifteen or twenty of his followers at the sheriff's invitation went into the house and upstairs for rest and refreshment, and beer was being brought out to those in the street, Smyth and another alderman went out by the back gate and made their way to meet the lord mayor, who by this time was engaged in putting the city

into a condition of defense. Within the next hour or two
while mayor and aldermen were closing and placing guards
at the gates and drawing chains across the principal streets,
Essex, taking a few halberds for his men, left the sheriff's
house, rode again through Cheapside, then walked to and
fro alone in Paul's churchyard for half an hour uncertain
what to do. The failure of the populace to rise and the
refusal of the city authorities to give him support had destroyed his dream of popular backing for the advance on
the court. As a matter of fact Essex represented no public
cause, his grievances were only personal. Why should the
people rise?

But his invasion of the city was worse than a failure, it
was a challenge to the queen's chosen ministers, indeed to
the queen herself. The defiance was promptly accepted.
Close on his heels, as he had come through Ludgate, had
come Lord Thomas Burghley accompanied by a herald who
bore direct orders from the queen. In Cheapside, in accordance with these orders, Essex was proclaimed a traitor
and all his followers ordered to disperse. Sir Thomas
Gerard, Knight-marshal of the court, made the same proclamation at other places. Essex might scornfully declare
that the first herald, Dethick, was a man of ill-fame, and
that a herald would do anything for two shillings; and the
gentlemen in his company might, as they did, press with their
rapiers so hard on Burghley's train that these had to fall
back. None the less his more apprehensive followers began
to drop from him and find excuses to retire into shops, to
go to their homes or even to seek means to offer their services to the queen. When the mayor with his train, about
two o'clock, met Essex and his party in Gracechurch street
he stopped his horse some sixty yards away and sent
Sheriff Smyth to urge the earl to surrender and put himself
on the queen's mercy, promising to place a city guard over
him in his own house, to let him have some of his own people
with him, and not to yield him to anyone except on the
orders of the queen herself. The earl seized the bridle of

Sheriff Smyth's horse and held it for a quarter of an hour while he recounted his injuries and dangers, the dangers of the country, and then, " looking wildly up and down," declined to go into any man's house and declared he would remain in the open street. Smyth seized the opportunity to return to the mayor, with whom he spent a busy day putting the city into a state of defense.

Although no one attacked Essex, all the forces of the city were gradually surrounding his diminishing band, and recognizing his desperate position he turned westward to go again through Ludgate to his house, hoping perhaps to make use of the imprisoned councillors to secure his desired interview with the queen independent of the city. It was too late. A chain had been drawn across Ludgate not far from St. Paul's defended by a file of city soldiers under Sir John Leveson, placed there by the earl of Cumberland under orders from the queen. Notwithstanding the protests of the earl and his doubts whether Cumberland would thus oppose him, Leveson refused to let him pass and Essex finally drew his sword and gave the order for an attack, the first actual violence of the day. Some of the principal gentlemen charged the defending soldiers; Sir Christopher Blount killed his opponent, an old enemy, and was himself wounded; a page of Essex, a soldier and a citizen were killed, and Essex was grazed by a musket ball. But the fight was one of swords and rapiers against pikes and muskets and was hopeless from the beginning. Essex with perhaps fifty or a hundred followers gave up the effort to break through, turned back through Watling Street and Friday Street, but finding the mayor holding Cheapside, turned down through Bow churchyard and Bow Lane to the river at Queenhithe, where as many as could find boats returned by the river to Essex House.[21]

Here he was doomed to a severe disappointment. The

[21] Camden, 608-10; Stow, 792-3; *Cal. State Papers, Dom.*, 1598-1601, 547-50, 558-62, 573-5, 577, 579-81; 1601-3, 3-5, 8-11, 13, 16, 22, 24-5, 26-7, 38-9, 50.

privy councillors had been in a certain sense hostages, and might for their safety have secured for him the desired interview with the queen, fruitless as it must now more than ever have been. But Sir Ferdinando Gorges, always half-hearted in the enterprise, and at last perhaps taking to heart Ralegh's advice to leave a sinking ship, had slipped away from Essex in London, reached Essex House and in the name of the earl offered freedom to the lord chief justice. When he refused to go without the lord keeper the councillors were all released. There was nothing left to the returning earl and his companions but to defend themselves as best they might. Resistance was in fact hopeless. Overwhelming force was on its way against them. Already in the morning the court gates had been barred, and a barricade of coaches drawn across the street between Whitehall and Charing Cross. Such troops as were available from Westminster, the surrounding country and London were gathered, to the number of 2000, and the lord admiral placed by the queen in command. She herself, it was said, could hardly be restrained from taking horse and going with the troops to meet the " rebels." All the nobles and gentlemen from the court came thronging down the Strand, and by the time Essex and his friends had entered the watergate the house was fully beset.

There was some fighting with muskets over the gateways from within and through windows and doors from without, and Captain Owen Salisbury of Essex's party was killed. The earl himself after burning some papers which he took from a casket and a little black bag he carried around his neck, containing either a diary of his recent life, a list of his adherents or some correspondence which might bring other people into trouble, proposed to his companions that they should sally out and lose their lives fighting. They did not agree, however, and as the short February day came to its close, Nottingham, Sydney, Lincoln, Compton, Ralegh, Stanhope, Cobham, Greville, Cumberland, Grey and the rest of the court forces were in possession of the garden and banqueting house, and two pieces of artillery and some petards were on the way from the Tower to batter the house itself. So Essex on the roof and Nottingham in the garden parleyed in the darkness. Essex asked for hostages for the safety of his party if they should surrender, but was refused; Nottingham on the other hand offered an opportunity for the women of the household to leave. Finally, about ten o'clock, Essex announced his surrender, asking only that they might have honorable treatment, a fair trial and the company of a clergyman in prison, which Nottingham assured to him. The three earls then came out, handed over their swords and were sent with six other lords and gentlemen to the Tower. The inferior members of the little company were distributed to various prisons; the stormy Sunday was over, — a planless, hopeless, meaningless rising.[22]

Camden, the annalist, who was himself in the midst of this rising testifies ten years later " to this day there are but few that ever thought it a capital crime "; and the earl of Lincoln, one of the captors of Essex House and later one of the judges of Essex, afterwards declared that it was a riot not a rebellion. But such was not the attitude of the government at the time. There can be little doubt that the direction of events of the days immediately following the rising fell into the hands of Cecil, and that he had reached a determination to have done with Essex, to remove him permanently from his path and from all influence in the government. His authority over the queen was almost complete. The French ambassador says, a few weeks later, that the English peers are more afraid of this little man than of either their consciences or the queen. A contemporary satirist has left among his sketches of the courtiers this of Cecil and his brother:

[22] *Manuscript account of the rising, uncatalogued, lying in Brit. Mus. pamphlet,* E. 1940, 2 (1); *State Papers, Dom., Eliz.,* cclxxviii, 23; Camden, 610–2; Stow, 792–3, *Declaration of the Practices and Treasons of the earl of Essex.*

Littel Cecil tripping up and downe,
He rules both court and crowne,
With his brother Burlie clowne,
In his great fox-furred gowne;
With the long proclamation
He swore he saved the town.

The "long proclamation," of which the original draft corrected by Cecil still remains, was issued in print the day after the rising. In it the queen is made to charge Essex and his confederates with traitorous plans extending back into Ireland and to supposed treasonable negotiations with Tyrone, gives a statement of the violent actions of the preceding day and their failure, thanks the citizens of London for remaining faithful and warns them against any calumniators of her government or her ministers. Apart from the exaggeration usual in such a document, of its ten statements at least three were untrue and must have been known by Cecil to be untrue, but he was one of those statesmen who believe that the test of statesmanship is its effectiveness rather than its sincerity. It is probable that to his political mind the removal of the earl was an essential factor in the safety of the state, and the earl must be made odious in order to secure his removal.

This policy was made still more manifest in the "Directions for the Preachers," a series of headings given to the London clergy for their sermons on the Sunday after the uprising. In extreme exaggeration and in deliberate untruth these excel what one would have believed of the subserviency of the clergy and the credulity of their hearers. It is taken as proved that Essex had been plotting treason for six or seven years, that he had reconciled himself with the Pope, that he was scheming to set the crown of England on his own head, that he had connived at the printing of Hayward's book in order that he should be looked upon as another Henry of Bolingbroke, that he had agreed with Tyrone that the latter should bring an Irish army of 8000 men into England, that he had planned a rebellion which would have been the worst that England had ever experienced. Some clergymen are reported to have amplified these instructions beyond all probability, while others resented the fact that they were made to preach what the government was afterwards not willing to charge against Essex on his trial. The sermon of Dr. Barlow, drawn up under Cecil's instructions and preached at Paul's Cross three weeks later, was published and is still extant.[23]

Before the day of the rising was over seventy-five persons were under arrest and during the next few days arrests continued to be made, until about a hundred were under more or less rigorous detention in various prisons. Members of the privy council were busy calling before them the more prominent members of the conspiracy and subjecting them to examination. Lower government officials examined lesser suspects and material witnesses. No torture was used to extract confessions, nor indeed was any necessary. All participants seemed willing to acknowledge their various parts, the lesser men making only such judicious reservations or modifications as would show their own relative innocence and complete ignorance of the earl's intentions. Those most active in the conspiracy, since all were examined privately and separately, could hardly deviate very widely from the truth for fear the others might have betrayed it. All this testimony was put in written form ready for use in the trials of the principals.[24]

If vigor was needed for the prosecution it was increased by the action of Captain Thomas Lea, a man of good family, an old soldier in the Netherlands and Ireland, the recipient of many favors from Essex and devoted to him body and soul. He made a plan by which with half a dozen confederates he believed he could seize the door of the queen's private chamber while she was eating supper with only a

[23] State Papers, Dom., Eliz., cclxxvii, 23, 30; cclxxviii, 63; Dyson, Proclamations, No. 382; Cal. State Papers, Dom., 1598–1601, 545–6, 584, 598–9; Winwood, Memorials, i, 299; Hudson, Star Chamber, Collectanea Judicales, 85; Letters of John Chamberlain, 105.

[24] State Papers, Dom., Eliz., cclxxviii, 31–43; Hist. MSS. Rep., Rutland Papers, i, 366–9.

few ladies in attendance, force her to sign a warrant for the release of Essex and his companions, and induce some one of the ministers to take it to the Tower and secure their delivery rather than have the queen kept longer in durance. He took two gentlemen of the court into his confidence but they revealed the plan to the council. In the meantime, about nine o'clock on the evening of Thursday, he took his place at the door from the kitchen to the private chamber, whether to test the practicability of the plan or to attempt to carry it out alone is not clear, was discovered and arrested, examined during the next two days, arraigned for treason on Monday, and hung at Tyburn on Tuesday, declaring to the last that he only intended " to vex the queen for half an hour that she might live the merrier all her life after." [25]

The preachers were not the only mouthpiece of the government for impressing on the people the greatness of the catastrophe they had escaped and the wickedness of those who had plotted it. On the Friday after the rising, the last day of the term, just as fifteen months before the councillors had made in Star Chamber their first public declaration of the offenses of Essex, now in the same place they gave a public description of the calamitous events to which their own and the queen's mismanagement of those offenses had led. They were deeply perturbed, perhaps panic-stricken, by the events of the preceding Sunday, the ramifications of the plot they had discovered or thought they had discovered, the suspicious actions of Captain Lea the night before, the personal outrage to which four of them had been subjected, and the general atmosphere of exaggeration they themselves threw around the whole set of occurrences. Only notes of their speeches survive. The lord keeper, detailing the series of events, including his own imprisonment, and dilating on the wickedness of the plot and the danger to the queen, is said to have spoken in great

[25] *Cal. State Papers, Dom., 1598–1601*, 554–6, 562–4, 568, 583–4, 589–90; *Letters of John Chamberlain*, 104; Camden, 612.

agitation and finally broke off in tears; the lord admiral was especially impressed with the fortitude of the queen under circumstances of danger, and Knollys with the disrespect shown to him and his fellow councillors at Essex House. Cecil made the same extreme claims concerning the objects of the plot that had already been given in the intructions to the clergymen. There is no possibility that Cecil was sincere in his statement of belief that Essex had been "devising five or six years to be King of England," that he wanted to be himself both secretary and admiral, that he intended to summon over Tyrone with his army of 8000, and that England and the queen would then be a prey to Irish kerns while Essex should become king and give toleration to the Catholics. The only explanation of these exaggerations is that already given, that Cecil was determined to destroy Essex and his reputation among the people.[26]

The latter was no easy task. We are told that "The sermon at Poules is verie offensively taken of the common sort, but the preacher, Dr. Barloe, one of his confessors, ript up, oratorlike, the sinnes of his youth." Murmuring against his arrest still continued, and ten days after the rising a second proclamation was issued by the government directed against base and loose persons remaining in the city "spreading rumors and tales," and ordering all such to "get them down into the country" under pain of death by martial law. Two months later, April 5th, there was another proclamation offering a reward of £100 to the discoverers of the authors or dispersers of seditious libels against the government. At least one man, a lawyer's clerk, was hung for this offense in Smithfield.[27]

The excitement in London and the country made it desirable that action should be as prompt as possible. The mass of testimony that had been obtained was put in the hands of attorney general Coke with instructions from

---

[26] *Cal. State Papers, Dom., 1598–1601,* 553–7, 582–5.

[27] *Hist. MSS. Comm., Rutland Papers,* i, 370; Dyson, *Proclamations,* 383, 386; *Cal. State Papers, Dom., 1601–3,* 88.

the Council to put it into order for the prosecution of the earls of Essex and Southampton. Rutland was not prosecuted. The depositions to be read and the parts of them to be omitted still show annotations by the hand of Coke, and the alterations and interlineations in his long speech of accusation show the care with which it was prepared and its close correlation with the written evidence he had chosen to submit.

The trial of Essex and Southampton is one of the earliest state trials of which we have anything like a full report. Little can be given here except its outline and result. It was set for Thursday, February 19th, ten days after the rising. A large square was railed off in Westminster Hall, with a chair and canopy at one end for the lord steward, Lord Buckhurst, benches on the sides for the nine earls and sixteen barons who were to make up the court, and at the lower end other benches for the eight judges and seven queen's counsel. Back of them was a form for the two prisoners. The invincible fondness of the age for ceremony was gratified by the presence of the king-at-arms, a gentleman usher with a white rod, two clerks of the crown and Sir Walter Ralegh with forty of the queen's guard. Seven sergeants at arms with maces preceded the lord steward as he took his place, then as the court was organized and the prisoners summoned, Lord Howard, constable of the Tower, entered, then the lieutenant of the Tower and finally a gentleman porter, carrying the axe with its edge turned away from the two earls, who followed him. The ceremonies lasted from nine in the morning till nearly seven at night. The French ambassador, who was present, says that the peers ate biscuit and drank beer during the trial, and the earl of Cumberland and some others smoked tobacco, circumstances, however, not mentioned in any English record, perhaps because of their familiarity. Certainly some nourishment was necessary during a ten hours' session.

The queen's commission for the court and for Buckhurst as its presiding officer and the indictments were read and pleas of not guilty entered. Yelverton and Coke delivered their rhetorical invectives, the carefully prepared confessions and examinations were read, there were interruptions, speeches, protestations and answers from the defendants; Cecil stepped forward to protest against Essex's charges against him of a pro-Spanish policy, and Essex was forced to acknowledge that he had spoken from misinformation; the events of the preceding months and of the day of the rising were told and retold in various forms. Essex learned much about his confederates that he should have known before and apparently told the simple truth as to his own actions and intentions. Southampton somewhat too humbly pleaded ignorance and an undue affection for his friend.

Of all the complaints made against the earl in the proclamations, in the pulpit and in Star Chamber, the law officers of the crown saw fit to choose only three definite charges, the plot to seize the court formed at Drury House, the imprisonment of the queen's councillors at Essex House and the attempt to rouse London. These with their implications were made the bases of charges of treason, and the judges being formally asked declared that each of the three was a treasonable act. There was little doubt or denial of the main facts of the uprising or of the preparation for it; the only question was the degree of criminality involved. This was a matter of law, which the judges must expound. They did so with all the resources of the sixteenth century law of treason, so that Essex himself acknowledged, " since I have committed that which hath brought me within the compass of the Law, I may be counted the Law's Traitor in offending the Law, for which I am willing to die," though he continued to assert, " I never had any treacherous or disloyal intentions towards her Majesty."

It was not an unfair trial for that age. Defendants in state trials in those days were helpless, without counsel, without previous knowledge of the indictments, without opportunity to bring witnesses in rebuttal. The peers who must give the judgment, although probably not unsympathetic, were in the hands of the lawyers. Grey and Cobham, Ralegh and Bacon had no means of foreseeing that they themselves would later be involved in the same toils of the law, nor Coke that he would be sacrificed in his turn to the exigencies of state policy. So the peers when asked whether Essex and Southampton were guilty of treason rose one after another and laying their hands on their breasts replied " Guilty "; the lord steward recited the familiar formula. " They shall be returned to the Tower of London, and from thence through the city of London they shall be drawn to Tyburn, and there they shall be hung, and living their entrails shall be removed from their bodies and burnt, and their heads shall be cut off and their bodies divided into four parts, and their heads and these parts shall be placed where the queen shall assign." The lord high steward then broke his staff, the sergeant at arms dissolved the court, and the officials of the Tower led the two earls back to their prison, the gentleman porter following with the edge of the axe turned toward the victims.[28]

The carrying out of the sentence was not long delayed, and only for these few days because of the possibility of obtaining further information from Essex concerning the plot, if such there were. There seemed some hope of this, for the strain of religious mysticism in the character of Essex now took full control of his mind. The dean of Norwich, sent to him by the council the day after the trial to urge a further acknowledgment of his offenses, had little success, it is true, but his own chaplain, Ashton, by a mixture of religious threats and unctuous appeals, not improbably suggested by authority, so wrought on him that he sent for the lord keeper, lord treasurer, lord admiral and Secretary Cecil to come to the Tower to hear his further con-

[28] *State Papers, Dom., Eliz.,* cclxxviii, 98–100, 101, 102; *Baga de Secretis,* Pouch lvi, m. 7; *4 Rep. Dep. Keeper of the Rolls,* App. ii; Baschet, *Transcripts,* Bundle 32; Jardine, *Criminal Trials,* 310–66; *The Arraignment, Trial and Condemnation of Robert, Earl of Essex, Feby. 19, 1601,* Printed 1670; Winwood, *Memorials,* i, 299; Camden, 613–20; *Chamberlain's Letters,* 104–6.

fession. This he gave to them during the next two days, Friday and Saturday, orally and afterward in writing, but though they stayed with him through the latter of those days from nine in the morning to eight in the evening what they obtained included nothing more than had been testified to at the trial. His mind, as he said, was eased, but apparently only by the opportunity to take a position of resignation rather than opposition, and to ask the forgiveness of the councillors he had aspersed or injured.

This confession, such as it was, enabled Cecil to say that he had acknowledged and begged forgiveness for his treason. He was reported also to have expressed the opinion that the queen was not safe as long as he lived, and to have asked that his execution be in private for fear the people would give evidence of their love for him and his spirit be filled thereby with undue pride. The French ambassador, however, reports exactly the opposite, that he had asked that his execution be public, but that this request was refused. These confessions and petitions were well worth two days' delay. His asserted request for a private execution was widely reported by the government, though his written confession was never published and is not known to exist. Two days are still unaccounted for, unless they represent a period of vacillation shown by the queen in sending Edward Carey to countermand the warrant already signed, then Darcy to command her ministers to fulfil it, reported by Camden, but by no other contemporary. Tuesday morning a servant of the Order of the Garter was sent to the Tower to take away his George and in the evening came the executioners, two, in case one should falter, and the queen's final warrant for the execution. At some time after his sentence must have been sent the queen's commutation for his execution in the Tower instead of at Tyburn, and for the remission of all the details of his death for treason except his beheading. From one of these days also survives a pathetic letter from Lady Essex to Cecil appealing to him for " the not urginge if you may not to the hinderinge of that fatill warrant for execution, which if it bee once signed I shall never wish to breath one howre after." [29]

Early in the morning of the 25th of February, Ash Wednesday, the earl emerged from his lodgings in the Tower dressed in a suit of black velvet and satin, a black felt hat and small ruff, and walked with three clergymen to the scaffold in the court yard. Sitting on a bench on the ground were the seven noblemen whom the queen had appointed as witnesses, and standing were perhaps a hundred lawyers, citizens and others who had been admitted to the Tower. Among them was Ralegh, present, so it was said, to oppose any charges Essex might make against him in his last speech; but on the protest of those around that his presence was unseemly, he being a professed enemy of the earl, he withdrew to the armory and watched the events that followed, as he himself claimed, with tears in his eyes. He might well have felt sympathy if he could have looked forward some ten years and seen the wraith of his own form on the same scaffold, dying with the same unheeded claim of a misunderstood loyalty on his lips.

The speech of Essex had little, however, to do with political matters. The Tower officers and the clergymen had strict orders to interrupt him if he entered upon these, but there was no need. He removed his hat and greeted courteously the lords and others present. As on all other occasions there was a certain distinction and originality in what he said, but his speech now was concerned principally with his early surrenders to the world, the flesh and the devil, with the perennial conflict between the good a man would do and the evil he would not that Paul had observed, with his devotion to the faith in which he had been brought up and in which he was ready to die. Only incidentally he acknowl-

---

[29] *Lansdowne MSS.*, lxxxvii, 53, lxxxviii, 28; Boissise au Roi, March 7, *Baschet Transcripts*, Bundle 32; Ellis, *Original Letters*, First Series, iii, 57–8; *Cal. State Papers, Dom.*, 1598–1601, 587–8, 591–2, 594–5, 597–9; 1601–3, 90; Birch, *Memoirs*, ii, 445, 475–81; Jardine, 379; Camden, 620–2.

edged or is said to have acknowledged the justice of his recent trial and his regret for this last " bloody, crying and infectious sin " of which he had been guilty. He asked pardon of the queen and the councillors and prayed for their prosperity and wisdom and asked for himself the prayers of all; he forgave his executioner, recited the Creed and the Lord's prayer, then removed his gown, ruff and doublet, disclosing a scarlet undervest, and with a prayer for mercy upon his prostrate spirit, lay down on the scaffold with his neck on the block. It was severed in three blows, though the first deprived him of all consciousness.

This pious and submissive death seemed to some, like Marshal Biron, himself destined to death on the scaffold little more than a year later, contemptible, and more like the end of a clergyman than of a soldier. But one would have a poor comprehension of the complex character of the earl of Essex, if he failed to perceive that it included the devotee and the dreamer as well as the soldier, the courtier and something of the statesman.[30]

It was perhaps these more ardent phases of his personality and character that endeared him to his close friends and to the people and alienated from him colder natures, such as Cecil, Bacon and Ralegh, and, after her affection had once cooled, the queen. He was by all testimony the best loved man of his time. Tall, somewhat stooping, not graceful, rather reserved in his manner, inattentive to his dress, even when he was to appear before the queen, open — " he carried his love and hatred always on his brow," — sober in his eating and drinking, yet incontinent, except when his religious scruples beset him, his most marked characteristic was the eager abandonment with which he threw himself into whatever interested him at the time, a campaign, a letter, an intrigue, a game of tennis, a speech, a poem. He had a habit of stopping in the midst of his eating to think

---

[30] Birch, *Memoirs*, ii, 481–92; Camden, 622–4; Stow, 793–4; Winwood, *Memorials*, i, 296–9; *Cal. State Papers, Dom.*, 1598–1601, 592–6, 598; *Hist. MSS. Comm., Rutland Papers*, i, 373.

out a problem of action or policy. He acknowledged with
evident enjoyment and with no caution the people's applause
on his every appearance. The executioner on his way home
from the Tower was set upon by the populace, beaten, and
would have been murdered but for his rescue by the sheriff.

The people's affection died slowly after his death. *A
Lamentable Ditty composed upon the Death of Robert
Lord Devereux, late Earl of Essex,* with its refrain

> " Sweet England's pride is gone
> Welladay, welladay ";

*A Lamentable new Ballad upon the Earle of Essex his death.
To the Tune of Essex's Last Good Night,* with its appeal

> " All ye that cry O hone O hone
> Come now and sing O Lord with me.
> For why? Our Jewell is from us gone,
> The valiant knight of chivalry ";

Honor's Fame in Triumph Riding, with its complaint

> " Though Law strict course of justice kept,
> The most and best of all sorts wept ";

and a whole anthology of popular verse and prose were
tributes of the common people to his kindly soul. A
greater poet had already dedicated to him the first three
books of the *Faerie Queene* and eulogized his victory at
Cadiz in the *Prothalamion,* while Essex had in turn paid
the expenses of his friend's burial in Westminster Abbey.

At Oxford, two months after his execution, a bachelor of
arts of Christ Church made a fervid oration in Latin in
the hall, recounting the career and condemnation of Essex,
bitterly reproaching his enemies and appealing for the tears
of his hearers for his fall. The University authorities heard
of it, the offender was arrested and although he tore his
manuscript to pieces and wrote another less compromising
speech the last we hear of him is a month later as a sup-
pliant writing from one of the London prisons to Cecil for
pardon. The council continued to complain that " wicked
and seditious libels are thrown abroad," and that " the dregs

of these treasons . . . do yet remain in the hearts and tongues of some misaffected people." A visiting German nobleman more than a year later heard sung through the country *Essex's Last Good Night,* a song in which he is supposed " to take leave of the queen and the whole country and in which also he shows the reason of his unlucky fate." It was not till 1633 that his one time secretary Sir Henry Wotton gave more measured but hardly less vivid testimony to the interest and attractiveness of his character in his *Parallel* between Essex and Buckingham. Certainly England was the poorer and the queen and her ministers less loved and trusted ever after the execution of the Earl of Essex.[31]

The council, troubled by widespread criticism, made every effort to explain and justify their action. The proclamation the day after the uprising, the instructions to the preachers and the declarations in Star Chamber have already been mentioned. Cecil wrote immediately to the lord lieutenant of Ireland and the English officers in the Low Countries enclosing the proclamation and describing the rebellion; form letters were drawn up for distribution by a " conveyer of information," a forerunner of the modern publicity manager, in Cecil's service. The day after the rising Elizabeth told the French ambassador that Essex had no one to blame but himself and made merry over the failure of his attempt on London. After the trial full particulars of the whole affair were sent to the English envoy in France, which he was to " dilate to such persons as are worthy of satisfaction." Five prayers " fit for the time " were set forth by authority against " Disloyall subjects who have risen up against thine Anoynted." But the most formal and extensive defense of the government was *A Declaration of the Practices and Treasons attempted and*

[31] Stow, 794; Speed, 1214; Birch, *Memoirs,* ii, 486–9; Camden, 623–4; *Cal. State Papers, Dom.,* 1601–3, 35–6, 44; *Declaration of the Practices and Treasons of the Earl of Essex;* Trans. Royal Hist. Soc., New Ser., vi, 14–5; *Reliquiae Wottonianae,* Ed. 1672, 161–83; Roxburghe Ballads, i, nos. 184. and 185.

Committed by Robert, late Earle of Essex, and his Complices, drawn up at the queen's command by Francis Bacon. Minute instructions were given him for its compilation, his first draft was gone over and much altered by the council, then by the queen, and after this had been printed the early copies were suppressed and a new form printed in which, by order of the queen, all formal expressions of respect such as " My lord of Essex " were changed to " Essex " or " the late Earl of Essex." [32]

This official account, in which certainly nothing is extenuated and much set down in malice, with the compiler's part in the examination at York House, and still more conspicuously his speeches at the trial, are the traditional foundations of a charge against Bacon of pusillanimity and betrayal of his friend and patron. On the other hand he has himself given a labored defense of his actions, and there have not been wanting defenders of the great lawyer and thinker. Without entering into this controversy it is perhaps germane to point out that as early as July 20, 1600, a month after the York House trial and while Essex was still a prisoner, though in his own house, Bacon in a letter to Cecil declared his love for the secretary, his devotion to him, and his desire to do him any service possible. No man could serve two masters in the time of Cecil and Queen Elizabeth, especially if he wished to rise in public life, and all the more if he had no native repulsion to servility, and Bacon looked for advancement to Cecil and the queen.[33]

Little consistency is discoverable in the punishment of the other members of the conspiracy. There was a general desire to excuse the action of the other four earls, for the earl of Bedford had joined the Essex party after they had

[32] *Cal. State Papers, Dom.,* 1598–1601, 546–7, 549–52, 582–5, 597–8; 1601–3, 16; Baschet, *Transcripts,* Bundle 32; Winwood, *Memorials,* i, 299–303; Birch, *Memoirs,* ii, 499–500; Bacon, *Apology,* 1604, William Rawley, *Resuscitatio,* Ed. 1671; Spedding, ii, 247–274; *A Declaration of the Practices, etc.,* 1601.

[33] *Lansdowne MSS.,* lxxxvii, No. 79, fo. 210; W. H. Dixon, *Personal History of Lord Bacon,* 126–51; Spedding, ii, 122–365.

entered the city. Southampton, who had been declared guilty along with Essex, was kept in the Tower unsentenced till the death of the queen, when her successor released him and restored him to his blood and fortune. Rutland and Bedford were after some months released on payment of fines. The other noblemen were also ultimately fined and pardoned. The more personal servants of Essex, Cuffe, his secretary, and Merrick, his steward, were tried for treason and hung, drawn and quartered at Tyburn. Cuffe is reported to have said on the scaffold " I am here adjudged to die for plotting a plot never acted, for acting an act never plotted, but greatness will have the victory." Of the four Drury House conspirators Blount and Danvers were beheaded on Tower Hill; Davies after a year's imprisonment was pardoned, and Gorges, as the price of his defection from Essex, still earlier, though his public career was diverted to a very different sphere of interest. Thirty-eight altogether of the prisoners were finally released without trial after being fined amounts varying from £30,000, in the case of Rutland, down to £40 each for a number of military and personal followers of the earls, the larger sums being reduced, however, one third or even one half. Many, like Sir Henry Neville, were examined, held for a while and released without punishment. Others, like Lord Mountjoy, who was certainly conversant with some of Essex's plans for reaching the queen by forcible means, and who at one time contemplated flight to France, unwilling, as he said, to put his neck under the file of Attorney Coke's tongue, were, because of their value in public affairs, their prestige or their influence with Cecil never questioned. Examinations were still in progress in the succeeding autumn and at least one culprit was indicted, though not tried, a full year after the rising.[34]

[34] *State Papers, Dom., Eliz.*, cclxxix, 106; *Cal. State Papers, Dom.*, 1601–3, 5–10, 14–5, 16, 17–8, 26, 36–9, 45, 50, 55, 88–91, 93, 109–11, 114, 120, 145–6, 162–3; Camden, 624–30; *Hist. MSS. Comm., Rutland Papers*, i, 364–77, 188; Birch, *Memoirs*, 492–7; Gorges, *A Breefe Answer, etc.*, Prince Society, xix; Fynes Moryson, *Itinerary*, ii, 354–7.

Part X

The Last Days of the Reign, 1601–1603

Part X
The Last Days of the Reign, 1601–1603

CHAPTER XLV

RECAPITULATIONS

IT remains to complete the narrative of the two years of
the queen's reign after the death of Essex. Some of the
occurrences of these two years have been already described.
The activities of the chartered commercial companies and
the beginnings of intercourse with America have been
brought down in earlier chapters to the death of the queen.
The actions of the last parliament of the reign, anticipated
in 1600, promised by Essex in February 1601 as part of his
scheme of reform and meeting finally in October of that
year, have been told in some detail. Many of the illustrations of the working of local government and finance in the
chapters devoted to those subjects are drawn from these
last two years and throw some light on their events.

Before entering upon a rapid survey of the remainder of
the history of the years 1588–1603 excuse must be made for
the apparent neglect of two fields of interest larger perhaps
than any that have been included. These are the intellectual
and the religious aspects of the history of this critical period.
They are of the greatest interest and importance. But they
are as extensive as they are interesting, and notwithstanding
the attention given to them in existing literary and church
histories there is much that would require prolonged re-
search and detailed narration, for neither of which is there
time or space in these two volumes. These subjects must

therefore, though with reluctance, be omitted or at least postponed. Nor are English relations with Scotland and the other countries to the north and east of her told with anything like the fulness of her relations with the countries to the south and with Ireland; this omission also must be excused on the grounds of time and space.

As the reign draws toward its close a thread for public affairs is less and less easily to be found. Apart from those movements that have been already mentioned and one or two lesser lines of policy, much of the work of the privy council, the occupation of officials and the interest of the queen had fallen into a somewhat meaningless routine or disintegrated into petty personal ambitions. It would almost seem that the government of England was awaiting the close of one reign and the opening of another for any effective activity. A fairer impression of such a period may perhaps be obtained by looking at it through the eyes of some observant contemporary than by a more systematic procedure. Such a source of information exists. John Chamberlain who describes his time in a series of letters for his friends' benefit and ours was the son and principal heir of a wealthy London merchant. His frail health made his period of study at Cambridge short but apparently not unfruitful, and drew him into a life of quiet social interests and observations reflected in a long series of familiar letters. As it happens twenty-five of his letters, addressed to Dudley Carleton, a rising young diplomat stationed successively at the Hague and Paris, remain from these last twenty-five months of Elizabeth's reign, though unfortunately not quite so evenly distributed. His news was gathered partly among his intimate friends in their homes, but more largely in casual conversation in various parts of London, especially in St. Paul's, the great contemporary exchange for information. He complains at one time of " a new devised order to shut the upper doores in Powles in service time, whereby the old entercourse is cleane chaunged, and the trafficke of newes much decayed." Notwithstanding this, however, he remarks soon afterward that " Powles is so furnisht that it affords whatsoever is stirring in Fraunce." His intelligence is naturally somewhat gossipy, and his personal predilection in news is for births, deaths and marriages. On the other hand few of the larger matters of the day fail of mention in his letters, and when they are insufficiently detailed there for our purpose they can always be pieced out from the abundant material left by the busy pens of Robert Cecil and other letter writers, or from the never failing chroniclers and state papers.[1]

In a letter written soon after the death of Essex, Chamberlain mentions to his friend, then in Paris, that the queen is entertaining " your Frenchmen." These Frenchmen were Marshal Biron and some other noblemen and their attendants. The curious similarity in the personality and fate of Biron and Essex attracted the attention of Chamberlain, as it did of the dramatists and the historians of the time, and might well have served the purposes of an Elizabethan Plutarch. They were both soldiers, both royal and popular favorites, both gifted and amiable men, both high born, both young at their death, both charged with and formally at least guilty of treason, and they were convicted and executed within little more than a year. The death penalty was imposed upon each to the regret of his sovereign and the resentment of the populace.

Now, however, Biron was in England as the trusted personal representative of his king. Henry being at Calais had taken the opportunity to send over this embassy to congratulate the queen on her safety after Essex's rebellion. They found her on progress, stopping at Basing House in Berkshire, and they were brilliantly entertained there by her, by Ralegh and other courtiers and, as already told, by the sheriff. Ralegh rode all night to London to get himself a plain black silk suit to conform to the French fashion.

---

[1] *Letters Written by John Chamberlain during the Reign of Queen Elizabeth,* Edited by Sarah Williams, Camden Soc., *Introduction,* 120, 127, 162, 176.

The sheriff gathered a body of local mounted gentry to attend them on their arrival and departure. Elizabeth's advice returned to Henry in reply to his congratulations, not to be too lenient with aspiring and restless subjects, as she had been with Essex, but to bring them to execution as soon as they showed signs of disloyalty, must have sounded ominous in the ears of Biron, already meditating the actions which within a few months led him into the same position and to the same retribution as Essex. He left the queen after a few days and returned to London and so back to France, having been in England about a month. Going through Kent he and his train came into conflict with the people and were harshly treated by the customs authorities at Dover. Even a present of a valuable pearl sent after him by the queen, and the usual freely expressed admiration of the Frenchmen for the English ladies did not prevent persistence of bad feeling between them and the English populace. One of the objects of another French embassy, six months later, under the duke de Nevers, was to remove the unpleasant remembrance of the disorders of Biron's followers.

His own later history was short and tragic. Although a peer and marshal of France, a duke, governor of Boulogne, trusted friend and companion in arms of the king, his boundless ambition made him impatient of Henry's refusal to give him still higher station, and he fell into the net of a widespread malcontent French-Spanish plot against the king. Henry learned of it through one of the nobles, sent for Biron to come to Fontainebleau May 14, 1602, and urged him to confess everything. Biron stood on his dignity and refused, and the next day was arrested by the captain of the guard and placed in the Bastille. He was tried before the Parlement of Paris, without the attendance of the peers, July 28, convicted and condemned to death. Like Essex he was beheaded inside of his prison, nominally to

---

[2] Chamberlain, *Letters*, 116, 126; Camden, *History of Elizabeth*, 635; *Cal. State Papers, Dom.*, 1601–3, 94, 97, 107, 113.

avoid the humiliation of a more public execution, really in fear of demonstrations of sympathy from the people. In Chamberlain's letters are conflicting rumors of his offenses, then of his pardon and finally of his execution, and the observation that in his case also as in that of Essex, " a great part of the world rests unsatisfied in their deaths." The comment of a prudent English correspondent writing from Paris is much the same. " Statesmen justify the king, but the multitude speak very ill of his proceedings. I do not presume to censure Prince's actions." [3]

In Chamberlain's letter of May 27, 1601, he makes the remark that the earl of Mar has returned to Scotland leaving behind him " the report of a courtly and well-admired gentleman." The stay of the earl of Mar in England was significant. He had arrived in March on the summons and in the interest of Essex; he left in May an avowed partisan of Cecil. He carried to James messages that initiated a policy concerning the succession by which two years later, to use Cecil's own figure of speech, " the king's ship was steered into the right harbor without crosse of wave or tyde that shall be able to throw over a cockboate." The secret negotiations of Essex, Mountjoy, Southampton and their associates with the Scotch king from 1598 to 1600 had contemplated compelling the queen to acknowledge him as her successor by a display of force on the northern border, supported possibly by the landing of an army from Ireland. The imprisonment of Essex and the Irish responsibilities of Mountjoy in 1600, however, had reduced this ambitious plan to a suggestion to King James made by Essex in a letter written about Christmas 1600 that he send an ambassador into England to look out for his interests and to bring pressure to bear on the queen in the period of change which Essex and his party anticipated. This letter was sent to James through Lord Willoughby, governor of Berwick, and thence by John Norton a London bookseller with business

[3] Chamberlain, *Letters*, 123, 139, 146; *Cal. State Papers, Dom.*, 234, 235, 244; Lavisse, *Histoire de France*, vi, 2, 38-43.

in Edinburgh. The reply from James seems to have been the letter carefully preserved in the little black silk bag Essex carried around his neck and burned along with his other private papers during the siege of Essex House. This bag was known about by the queen, demanded from him by Admiral Howard immediately after his capture, and searched for in vain on his person by his jailer in the Tower the day before his execution. Essex testified that the bag held but a single sheet of paper not more than six or seven lines long, but he would not say by whom it was written or what it contained.[4]

For the instruction of the Scotch ambassador when he should arrive Essex had prepared a statement of his theory that Cecil and other councillors were engaged in a plot for the succession of the Spanish Infanta, declaring his own devotion on the other hand to the interests of James. About the middle of February the earl of Mar and Edward Bruce, lord of Kinloss, with about forty attendants, left Edinburgh for London. Before they had crossed the border, however, Essex had been tried and executed, the myth of a plot in favor of the Infanta had been exploded and they found a new political world when they arrived some time in March. The king already knew of the course of events at London and had sent new instructions to his envoys. They were well received publicly by the queen and her ministers but Cecil also made use of their presence to enter into a series of private negotiations of his own with their master. At a secret interview with the ambassadors at the office of the Duchy of Lancaster, of which Cecil was chancellor, he received from them assurances of the king's transfer of his confidence from the party of Essex to himself, and a letter from the king offering to trust Cecil's advice in all matters concerning the succession, to carry on a secret correspond-

---

[4] Chamberlain, 107–10; *Cal. State Papers, Dom.*, 1601–3, 2–3, 19, 25, 41, 42; Camden, 605, 631; *Correspondence of King James of Scotland with Sir Robert Cecil*, Camden Soc., xxi, xxviii, 80–90, 96–8, 102–7; *Boissise au Roi*, Feb. 21, 1601, Baschet, *Transcripts*, Bundle 32.

ence with him directed to that end, and that, "quhen it shall please god that the king shall succeide to his richt," Cecil should receive as great or greater favor than the queen had bestowed upon him in her time. To this Cecil replied in a long letter with much assurance of his own devotion and much good advice to the king not to be impatient for the queen's death and not to interfere with her policy or seek to strengthen his own future position by encouraging the formation of a popular party in his favor in England. If he followed this policy James might *dormire securus,* knowing that his interests were being perpetually and faithfully watched over.[5]

This correspondence continued for two years, until the death of the queen and the accession of James, and knowledge of it was extended to include in each country perhaps half a dozen councillors and confidants respectively of the king and the statesman. It was quite independent of the more open diplomatic relations between the two countries. Its secrecy was due professedly to the necessity for considering the queen's dislike of the question of the succession, but doubtless also to the preference of Cecil and James for this secret diplomacy. In none of the letters is there any suggestion of haste for the termination of the queen's reign or any lack of loyalty and respect for her. Indeed there is nothing in the whole correspondence that need have given her offence, and it is not impossible, such was the tortuous policy of the time, that it was all laid before her.

The question of the succession was hard to keep down. A contemporary remarks, "No man almost can be found so symple never to have thought of it." A bill was introduced into the parliament of 1601 prohibiting the publication of books on the subject, and as has been seen prompt action was taken against members proposing a parliamentary settlement of the succession. It was nevertheless increasingly in men's thoughts and while Cecil and James were corresponding many others were secretly writing on

---

[5] *Correspondence of King James with Cecil,* xxix–xxxvi, 1–8, 82–4.

the matter or discussing it. The written opinion of Father Parsons had been circulated on the Continent in 1599. During the early summer months of 1601 Thomas Wilson, an English correspondent of Cecil in Italy, was composing, apparently for his own satisfaction, a statement of the claims of twelve possible competitors, and in the next year Sir John Harington wrote, though naturally he did not publish, a thoughtful essay on the succession to the crown, advocating the claims of James.

One foreign correspondent reports in July 1601, a general belief that the king of Spain is preparing for an immediate attempt to secure the crown of England for himself; another, a Catholic, suggests that all of that religion agree to accept such ruler as shall be nominated by the pope, "when God shall call the Queen out of this life." Two women, the Infanta of Spain and Arabella Stuart, are each occasionally spoken of as a possible successor to the great queen and the suspected designs of the latter were a constant source of vexation to the queen and councillors. Even the king of France is suspected of having an eye on the throne of England and some reported that the queen favored his claim. On the other hand, a letter written in April 1602 reports a belief abroad that after the queen's death the people of England intend "to Govern the Kingdom by States, as they doe in the lowe Countries." Ralegh himself is said to have held that after the queen's death the English people should keep the staff in their own hand and establish a commonwealth. When the Venetian ambassador arrived in London in January 1603 he found the subject so generally talked of that he sent home a full report of the claims of the different candidates, and as the queen lay on her death bed a courtier wrote, "Matter of succession is now ordinarie discussion both in Courte and Countrey, but no appearance of any likely to prevayle but the king of Scottes, uppon whome the farre greater part of the Realme seeme to have fixed theire hopes; many have utter aversion that way and would be opposite had they any

potent competitor. In the meane is continual postinge be-
twene London and Scotland." Five days before the queen's
death Cecil sent to James a secret draft of the proposed
proclamation announcing her death and his accession which
was reported to be " musicke that soundeth so sueitly in the
ears of the king that he can alter no nots in so agreeable ane
harmonie." That there was no serious competition for the
crown of the dying queen was undoubtedly due in fullest
measure to the judicious and subtle policy of Cecil. It had
protected her during these two years from impatient interference by James, built a bridge over which the king of
Scotland was to pass easily to his new throne, and secured
to England a peaceful change of dynasty. It showed Cecil
at his best.[6]

Peace with Spain receives the least mention in Chamberlain's letters of all the major interests of this period, though
efforts to attain peace were almost constant between 1598
and the close of Elizabeth's reign, and a near approach to
the signature of a definite treaty was made in the summer
of 1600. The queen was on the whole an advocate of peace.
Peace was desired by both nations. The policy of Burghley
in his later days and of Cecil during his whole administration was in favor of peace, and the declining fortunes of
Essex were not unconnected with his opposition to that
policy. As early as 1598 a series of " Considerations for
the Peace now in Speach," apparently written by Burghley
shortly before his death, advocates peace on religious, political and economic grounds and " to avoid the scandal that
England is the cause of wars in Christendom." In August
1599 an observant courtier declares, " A Peace is generally
desired here, and not without good cause, for our countrey
is not able to endure the Charges of warre. They that are

----

[6] *State Papers, Dom., Eliz.,* cclxxxii, 31, cclxxxiii, 79, cclxxxvii, 50; *Cal.
State Papers, Dom.,* 1598–1601, 211–3, 413, 424–5, 438, 442, 484, 1601–3, 60,
62, 180, 225–6, 282; *Venetian,* 1592–1603, 539–42; *Correspondence of King
James with Cecil,* xxxviii–xlvii, 9–46, 47, 48–76; Ralegh, *Works,* Ed. 1829,
viii, 737, 740; Sir John Harington, *Treatise on the Succession to the Crown,*
1602, Pub. by Roxburgh Club.

in greatest authority seem to affect it. . . . Peace, Peace, is hartily desired here of all the World, and blessed be the Peace Makers yf we may have a safe, honorable Peace."

The statement of the President of the North in July 1601, "I pray God sende us peace, or ells I dare assure you it wyll brede great discontentment in these northe partes," was echoed from all parts of England and from all classes of the people during that and the next two years. "I know not what pollycye may persuade but I fynde what necessetye dooth urge," writes one of Cecil's correspondents. The new Spanish rulers of the obedient Netherlands had every interest in the attainment of peace and every desire for it. After much diplomatic discussion a conference between representatives of England and Spain actually met at Boulogne in May 1600 and sat for some weeks, but dissolved in July with nothing accomplished. Approaches to a resumption of negotiations were made in the next year and there was an exchange of letters through a Portuguese merchant, Fustado, in March 1602. The long, tortuous and ineffective course of these peace efforts has recently been traced in a special study of the subject and need not therefore be retraced here. The overweening pride of Spain, the suspicions of England, the divergent interests of the Netherlands and of Scotland from those of England, and perhaps some deficiency in diplomatic skill, combined to bring all attempts at a definite treaty to failure. So the war, purposeless, inglorious and unprofitable from the beginning, drew out its weary length through the remainder of the queen's reign in a series of minor conflicts in the Netherlands, in Ireland and on the sea.[7]

[7] *Cal. State Papers, Dom.*, 1598–1601, 12, 279, 374, 375, 377, 379, 461–2; 1601–3, 75, 93, 95, 119, 138, 151, 156, 275–6; *State Papers, Dom., Eliz.*, cclxxxi, 28; *Sydney Papers*, ii, 114, 119, 120–4; Chamberlain, *Letters*, 70, 75, 93, 95; *Lansdowne MSS.*, lxxxvii, 7–9, 49, fos. 139–41; *Stowe MSS.*, clxvii, 27, 87, 106–221, 312–4; Harington, *Nugae Antiquae*, i, 176, Grimestone, 2 Ed., 1040–2; *Cal. Hatfield House MSS.*, ix, 246–7; Nathan G. Goodman, *Efforts for Peace between England and Spain, 1597–1603*, University of Pennsylvania, Ph.D. Thesis, 1925.

These were matters mentioned in Chamberlain's letters of such importance in the history of these years as to claim special attention. There is no lack of notice of minor matters of public interest. May 8, 1602, he notes the departure of Weymouth in the service of the East India Company with two well equipped ships seeking a shorter passage to India by the northwest and October 15 their return " *re infecta.*" The May 8 letter is also full of news of Shirley's trading expedition to the South Seas, of Sir Richard Leveson's last naval expedition against the Spaniards, and about the same time there is a report of the capture of three Spanish prizes by Sir John Gilbert and of three Lubeckers on their way to Flanders. A Portuguese carrack, one of the most valuable of the prizes of the Elizabethan war, was taken in the same month. On the other hand we hear of the capture by the Spaniards of a Levant Company's ship. So steady is the alternation of captures that it is hard to compute the gains and losses of the Spanish war.[8]

There is rather frequent mention of Russia. In the middle of 1601 the coming and departure of a Russian ambassador is noted, in 1602 four Russian boys are reported to have come to study English and Latin and to have been sent respectively to Eton, Winchester, Cambridge and Oxford. In another letter the queen is reported as having given audience, Sunday, February 6, 1603, to an ambassador from Venice. This was Giovanni Carlo Scaramelli, the first Venetian envoy sent officially to England in the queen's time. Both parties hoped for much advantage from the resumption of diplomatic relations, but the rapidly failing powers of the queen made the visit of little significance for her reign; the envoy's request that a Venetian lieger should in future reside regularly in England was refused by the council for fear they might thereby be entertaining a Spanish spy, and his demands for the punishment

[8] Chamberlain, 24, 127, 130–3, 140–4, 157; Camden, 646; *Cal. State Papers, Dom.*, 1601–3, 198, 206, 210.

of English pirates in the Mediterranean were but evasively answered.[9]

Internal affairs receive quite as frequent mention as foreign. In July 1601 we hear of the establishment of Bodley's Library at Oxford with 3000 or 4000 books as its nucleus, and a year later of its being opened "with great applause." Sixteen Catholic boys, sons of good families, are arrested at Tilbury Hope, on their way to enter the college at Douai. The Catholic controversy between the Jesuits and the secular clergy and the renewed Puritan controversy that sprang up around the publication of Hooker's *Ecclesiastical Polity* are matters of frequent mention. There is a slight earthquake on Christmas day 1601. The queen's progresses in August and September 1601 and in July and August 1602 are duly chronicled.[10]

The council were much worried at the increase of building in London and in June, 1602, ordered rooms newly constructed over stables, in gardens and other odd corners pulled down. They might well dread the congestion of population in old London: it has already been frequently referred to; Chamberlain describes the "six-penny dole" given to the populace at Leadenhall at the funeral of the charitable Lady Ramsey in November, 1601, where the number of beggars was so great that seventeen were trampled to death and many more severely hurt. There are numerous instances of disorder, varying from duels between courtiers to the breaking up of the chairs and destruction of the curtains and hangings of the Bankside theatre by the mob disappointed in their expectations of a play. The plague and smallpox break out from time to time. Chamberlain reports, half-sceptically, half-credulously, that a snake eight feet long with two heads was taken from the body of O'Donnel after his sudden death in Spain; that an apparition of "great troupes of horse and foote in battell

[9] Chamberlain, 110, 160, 178; *Cal. State Papers, Dom.*, 1601–3, 211–300; *Venetian*, 1592–1603, 514, 526–69.

[10] Chamberlain, 107–10, 111–2, 115–8, 125, 143, 146–7, 150, 178; *Cal. State Papers, Dom.*, 1601–3, 232; Camden, 559–60.

array " was seen for a moment on a mountain in Wales then suddenly vanished; that Dr. Dee has delivered a noble-woman of a devil; that two hundred whales were seen in one school in the Narrow Seas, and the probability that they were a portent of something more than merely the tempest that followed.[11]

We get occasional glimpses of some of the harsher practices of the time. April 26, 1602, " here were three seminarie priests hanged and quartered the last weeke, but what is that among so many? " On the twelfth of February, 1603, an English Catholic priest named Richardson, educated in Spain, was betrayed to the authorities in London. He was treated with so much harshness by the chief justice at his trial, and himself showed such mildness and dignity that general compassion was expressed for him and it is remarked even by our good Protestant letter writer that " Such spectacles do nothing to increase the Gospel." He was hung, drawn and quartered at Tyburn only four days after his arrest. In May, 1602, a lawyer is placed on the pillory and loses both his ears for plotting against a fellow lawyer; in June four men, convicted in Star Chamber of slandering the lord treasurer, are condemned to be whipped, placed on the pillory, lose their ears and to be imprisoned for life; and early the next year a puritanical youth of Merton College for libelling the vice-chancellor and certain members of the privy council is sentenced by Star Chamber to be carried on horse-back with his face backward, to be whipped and to have his ears cut off, part of his punishment to be at London, part at Oxford. The last part was remitted by the queen on the petition of one of the court ladies.

In April, 1602, the efforts of Vere to raise volunteer troops for the Netherlands resulted, notwithstanding the authority of the council and " with drumming and all they could do," in getting only two men in three days. The council thereupon authorized a press of 3000 men, but of these a quarter

[11] Chamberlain, 142, 150, 159-60, 163-4, 171, 173; *Cal. State Papers, Dom.*, 1601-3, 213.

ran away before they reached the port of embarcation, others were " thrust together under hatches like calves in a stall," and there was so much violence on the part of the press masters and so much objection on the part of employers to the drafting of their serving men that the whole matter became a scandal and protests were lodged with the council. But a year later the press gang was still using such harshness in seizing men in the streets of London as to attract the surprised attention of the newly arrived ambassador of Venice. Suicides and murders come not infrequently under our correspondent's notice. Most of his observations are, however, of a more personal, kindly or humorous nature. He and his correspondent frequently send one another pamphlets that have recently appeared in the two countries. He has much detail of " wiving and childing " among their common acquaintance. February 10, 1603, he with his friends, like their more distinguished literary contemporaries, take supper at the Mermaid tavern on Bread Street and drink as he acknowledges more than is good for them. At the Oxford commencement the cutpurses are so numerous that many of the visitors lose money, jewels, scarfs and gloves, and one thief shows his skill by stealing a lady's slipper from her foot.[12]

So Chamberlain tells his story, writing from one of his friends' houses or another as he passes from Ascot to Knebworth, to Englefield, to Little Britain, to their country places in Hampshire, Hertfordshire, Bedford and Huntingdon, then back to London, giving to Carleton his chronicle of private and public events. It is not on the whole such a story as to make life in late Elizabethan England especially attractive. Like all contemporary testimony it pictures a society active-spirited but materialistic, intellectual and sometimes religious, but permeated with much conflict, much intrigue,

[12] Chamberlain, 102, 107–10, 112, 117, 125, 126, 131–2, 134, 135, 144, 151, 179; *Trevelyan Papers*, iii, 39–40; Manningham, *Diary*, 42–3; Camden, 652; *Cal. State Papers, Dom.*, 1601–3, 144, 300–1; *Venetian*, 1592–1603, 534.

much hypocrisy, much distress, much injustice. The milder, kindlier, more genial and more enjoyable life that undoubtedly existed is largely hidden under the hard, sordid, unhappy and repellent details of which we have a full record.

The last of these letters in the time of Queen Elizabeth is dated on the 28th of February, 1603, and is full of news of death in high places, suits for office, Irish affairs, the capture of Spanish fugitives, the arrest of a pirate and other familiar matters. There is no mention, however, of the most important fact in Chamberlain's world, a fact of which he was probably unaware, that the queen was on her deathbed, and that a crisis in English history was approaching.

CHAPTER XLVI

THE DEATH OF THE QUEEN

ELIZABETH'S health throughout her life had been reasonably good. Her habit of asserting greater freedom from bodily infirmities than she actually felt, and her persistent opposition to the ministrations of the doctors gave her the appearance and the reputation of a vigor that more intimate knowledge sometimes belies. Yet as a matter of fact she had seldom been really ill. The year 1602 saw more frequent alternations of sickness and health. In January she has rheumatism in her arm. In February the "crasiness" of the queen is noted with apprehension in official correspondence. In March the French ambassador notes that the pain in her arm prevents her from riding and she is therefore taking less exercise than usual. In April, on the other hand, she danced a gaillard with the duke of Nevers at a ball given at the court in his honor. The next month she went a-maying at Sir Richard Buckley's at Lewisham, three miles from the court at Greenwich. In June a slight indisposition prevented her receiving the French ambassador. In July the Scotch ambassador was permitted to see her dancing privately in her room before a mirror, a scene doubtless intended as a lesson in patience to his master. Early in August she was unwell, though she insisted on walking publicly in the garden to prevent anyone taking notice of it. Later in the month she is reported as very weary, but she might well have been so for on that day she had ridden ten miles on horseback and had afterward gone hunting.[1]

[1] Medical Record of Elizabeth, Frederick C. Chamberlin, *Private Character of Queen Elizabeth*, 41–76; Opinion of Medical Experts, *Ib.* 77–104; *State Papers, Dom., Eliz.,* cclxxxiii (a), 34; cclxxxiv, 97, *Cal. State Papers, Dom.,* 1601–3, 153–4, 232; Chamberlain, *Letters,* 126, 133, 163; Baschet, *Transcripts,* Bundle 33; Lodge, *Illustrations of English History,* ii, 578; Wilbraham, *Journal,* Camden Soc. Misc., x, 58.

The 7th of September the queen entered upon her seven-tieth year, but she seems to have been quite well, for on the 19th a courtier writes of her pleasure in watching the new country dances performed by her maids in her privy cham-ber, and on the 23d Greville writes to the countess of Shrewsbury that he has not seen the queen in better health for many years. On the 26th the visiting duke of Stettin saw her walking in her garden at Oatlands " as briskly as though she was eighteen years old." October 22 she is re-ported as being at Richmond and very well, but a few days later we hear a contrary report. On the anniversary of her coronation, November 17, she was merry at the antics of the clown, Gerard, who appeared at the running, disguised, pro-vided with a device and shield and mounted on a horse " no bigger than a ban-dog." On the other hand it was reported that when she had been on horseback for an hour it made her so weary that she had to rest for the next two days. She wrenched her foot as she was leaving the house of Secretary Cecil after dinner, December 12, but seems to have felt no ill effects of it afterwards.[2]

The festivities at court at Christmas were not markedly less lively than usual. The new comptroller set a good ex-ample by appearing every day freshly attired in white and there were plays, dancing, bear-baiting and much card play-ing, at which it was noted that Secretary Cecil played es-pecially deeply and lost £800 in one night. There is ample evidence, however, that this gayety but poorly reflected either the physical or mental condition of the queen. Eliz-abeth's favorite godson, Sir John Harington, to whom we are beholden for so many intimate glimpses of her life and character, came to court just at this time. He was shocked, as he wrote to his wife, at the queen's " most pitiable state," at her " show of human infirmity," and of its ill bodings for

[2] Lodge, *Illustrations*, ii, 582; Chamberlain, *Letters*, 157, 172; *Trevelyan Papers*, 42; Manningham, *Diary*, 99–100; Baschet, *Transcripts*, Bundle 34; *Diary of the Duke of Stettin's Journey through England in the year 1602*, Trans. Royal Hist. Soc., New Ser., vi, 50–1.

England. He told how in his interview with her in her
private chamber she held a cup in her hands and occasionally put it to her lips, but did not drink, and complained
that she had " eaten but one ill tastede cake since yester-
nighte." She dismissed from her presence in anger some
men whom she had summoned but had forgotten for what
purpose. Harington tried to divert her by reading some
verses he had recently composed and she smiled once but
soon stopped him, saying, " when thou doste feele creepinge
tyme at thye gate these fooleries will please thee lesse. I
am past my relish for suche matters." Another courtier
reports her at the time as " by fitts troubled with melancholy." [3]

The Christmas festivities of 1602 were as a matter of fact
the last flickering of the brilliant court life of which Elizabeth had so long been the centre, but in which she now
scarcely shared. There was much desertion of old courtiers.
We hear that Sir Edward Norris was keeping a " great
Christmas " at Englefield, that Sir Walter Ralegh had taken
Lord Cobham, Lord Compton and others away with him to
Sherborne for the holidays, and that Sir John Harington
had invited the earls of Rutland, Bedford and Pembroke,
Sir John Gray, Sir Henry Carey, Sir Robert Sydney and
other gentlemen and ladies to spend Christmas with him at
his country house in Rutlandshire. A series of banquets
given to the queen in November and December by the
lord admiral, lord chamberlain, Secretary Cecil and Lord
Thomas Howard at their town houses in London were professedly for the object of inducing her to remain longer at
Whitehall, where presumably business could be more con-
veniently carried on, before she should go, as she intended,
to Richmond. [4]

The increasing melancholy of the queen which Harington

[3] Chamberlain, *Letters*, 172; Harrington, *Nugae Antiquae*, Ed. 1804, i,
320-3; Manningham, *Diary*, 146.

[4] Chamberlain, *Letters*, 163, 166, 167, 170, 171-2, 174, 175; Manningham, *Diary*, 99-100.

and others noticed was no doubt primarily physical in its origin; but there was much in her position at this time to cause depression. The scandals that continued to circulate both in and outside of England can scarcely fail to have reached her ears. In 1601 an official of the Merchant Adventurers reports having heard at Frankford an Englishman declare that the queen was an atheist and that he could not therefore find it in his heart to pray for her, that she had a daughter married to the Prince of Condé whom she was plotting to have succeed her, that a London midwife had confessed on her deathbed to a midnight delivery of the queen at a palace in Hampstead and the subsequent murder of the child. A correspondent of Cecil at Hamburg writes in March, 1602, that a Latin work has been lately published there so scandalous in its statements about the queen and her ministers and courtiers that he has bought up all copies he can find and is shipping them to England to be destroyed. Scandal was generally, but not always, kept under in England. The words of the earl of Lincoln were comparatively harmless. He was charged with having said at his own table, after Essex's rising, that he had seen the queen kiss the earl twenty times and did not believe she would send to execution one with whom she had been so familiar. The " lewd words " about the queen for which men are constantly being brought before the council are not always to be understood in the modern sense of that expression, but they must often have been highly offensive in their nature. Without repeating the long and mostly mendacious chronicle of scandal that had run like a foul though narrow stream parallel with the career of Elizabeth from her girlhood, we may yet well realize as we trace her last darkening days that her knowledge that these stories still circulated must have been bitter to her.[5]

[5] *Cal. State Papers, Dom.*, 1601–3, 23–4, 166, 224, 230–1; Manningham, *Diary*, 146; Chamberlin, *Private Life of Queen Elizabeth, passim; Acts of the Privy Council*, xxvii, 338; xxviii, 26, 28, 118; xxix, 7, 186, etc.; Speed, *Chronicle* (Ed. 1632), 1216.

Her councillors were increasingly unpopular. Cecil, her ablest and most trusted minister, was girded at by the populace for his persecution of Essex: by one Englishman abroad he is described as a " Machiavellian "; a rumor is reported by another that, fearing a change of government in England, he has placed funds in Italy for his support if he has to flee. Such casual contemporary expressions as " the growing tyrannies of the queen," " the sundrie causes of discontentment in the great part of her people, needful to be qualified by one means or another," the reported unpopularity of the " present government," the " widespread hatred of ministers," charges that the soldiers are only paid half their wages, that the government connives at the immunity of Catholics from punishment; the popular odium of those nearest the queen on which Essex had counted, the complaints made in the parliament of 1601, criticism by foreign governments, fault-finding on the part of her courtiers, must have filled her when she heard of them with regret for the loss of the love and confidence of her people, perhaps her strongest sensibility.[6]

The expenditure of government in Ireland, the Netherlands, Scotland and at home, on the fleet, officials, diplomacy and the household, remained heavy; the queen's advances to France and the Netherlands had not yet been returned; income from some sources was less than it had been, and although parliament had been liberal in its grants there was difficulty in making collections. The treasury was frequently entirely empty, many royal debts remained unpaid, and the city of London was pressing for reimbursement of the £60,000 loaned the government some years before. The finances were scarcely in better shape in the last than in the first year of Elizabeth's reign, and this was a constant source of vexation to her. Religious disputes, although not so insistent as at some other periods, were still unsettled. Al-

[6] *Cal. State Papers, Dom.*, 1601-3, 2, 25, 27, 37, 62, 115, 116, 166, 183, 239, 261, 262, *Ven.*, 1592-1603, 558; *State Papers, Dom., Eliz.*, cclxxvi, 97; Camden, 659.

though the long rebellion in Ireland had been quenched and
the royal authority momentarily restored, this had necessi-
tated so wide an exercise of the pardoning power as to have
left the queen with a burning sense of humiliation.

Whatever Elizabeth may have known or not known of
the secret correspondence between Cecil and James, she
knew that the succession was being discussed, she was ex-
asperated by the rumors of the marriage of Arabella Stuart
and the earl of Hertford's son and its influence on that
question, and she realized, as she told some of her courtiers,
that the eyes of men were turning from her to the northward. Vexed by her powerlessness in this respect she cried,
"They have yoked my neck. I have none whom I can
trust; my condition is strangely turned upside down." Even
Harington, sincere as was his affection for the queen and
deep as was his sense of gratitude toward her, sent to James
as a Christmas present some congratulatory verses, a letter,
and a curiously wrought lamp, with the apposite if not entirely reverent motto, "Lord, remember me when thou
comest in thie kingdom." [7]

To Elizabeth, as to all who endure old age, the shrinking
of the circle of those who surrounded her in earlier life must
have made the world seem constantly poorer. Death had
been busy in her court of recent years. Hatton, Hunsdon,
Burghley, Knollys, Cobham had dropped away from her
closest group of ministers and courtiers; Catherine Hunsdon, countess of Nottingham, wife of the lord admiral, her
cousin and former maid of honor and her oldest woman
friend, was soon to follow; the earls of Huntingdon and
Pembroke, Lords Willoughby and Norris were only the best
known of her nobles outside of court who had died since
1598. She had no near relative. A different generation
surrounded her from that she had known at her accession;
she had seen practically the whole body of the nobility and
a large part of the knighthood and gentry of England pass

---

[7] *Cal. State Papers, Dom.*, 1601–3, 154, 298–9, 301, 302, 304; Camden,
659–60; Harington, *Nugae Antiquae*, i, 325–35.

away and give place to successors whom she did not know so well.

The loss of Essex stands apart. Her last favorite, the cherished object of the attachment of her old age, the willful boy whom she had seen grow up to the self-willed man, the victim of her suspicion, hardness and anger and of the supposed requirements of state, as much as of his own foolishness, she grieved for him constantly. On Ash-Wednesday, the second anniversary of his execution, when she remembered what day it was she burst into tears and lamentation, according to a foreign visitor, " as if for a sin she had committed." She refused to allow Dr. Barlow, the preacher of the St. Paul's sermon against him, to come into her presence though she had herself at the time approved the outlines for the sermon drawn up by the privy council. When Harington said something that reminded her of Essex she cried and beat her breast. When she was urged for reasons of state to pardon Tyrone she exclaimed that it was shameful to ask her to pardon a rebel who had made seven years' war upon her when they would not permit her to spare Essex " for one day's delict." " And upon this when she reflects she falleth into great passion." Weak and inconsistent all this was but none the less human and natural. A lonely, ailing old woman, kept up to her work of government and her show of majesty a little longer by habit, a sense of duty and the urgency of her ministers, Elizabeth watched the year 1602 out. It was looked upon by her courtiers as a sad omen that soon afterward she caused to be filed from her finger her coronation ring, long so grown into the flesh that it could not be removed otherwise.[8]

The queen with her court removed from Whitehall to Richmond January 31, 1603, " in very fowle and wet weather." During February there was no marked decline

---

[8] Camden, 659; Ant. Rivers to Giacomo Creveleto, March 9, 1603, *State Papers, Dom., Eliz.,* clxxxvii, 50; *Cal. State Papers, Ven.,* 1592–1603, 554, 557; Manningham, *Diary,* 51, 159; Chamberlain, *Letters,* 165; Harington, *Nugae Antiquae,* i, 322; *Beaumont au roi,* June 10, 1602, Baschet, *Transcripts,* Bundle 33.

in her condition. She was well enough to give audience to the Venetian ambassador on Sunday, February 6, in full panoply of taffeta and jewels, necklaces and bracelets, sitting on a chair of state on a raised platform and surrounded by her councillors, ladies and musicians. The ambassador had been told on all sides that she was in the best of health and congratulated her on it, congratulations which however she received in silence. Through the rest of the month he was expecting a second audience and its postponement was nominally on quite other grounds than the condition of the queen's health.[9]

Soon after the first of March, however, she became ill. It was at this time that the countess of Nottingham died, and a waning in the queen's strength and spirit became evident to all. The melancholy which had before been intermittent now settled down upon her like a heavy cloud. She scarcely left her chamber. She complained occasionally of a sore throat, of aching in her bones and cold in her legs, but her principal troubles were sleeplessness and depression. She would scarcely eat; she sat silent, hours at a time, her eyes directed to some one object. But her mind was not seriously clouded; we hear from one courtier that she was ready at any time to respond by word or gesture to the religious discourse of her chaplains, from another that she showed pleasure in hearing " old Canterbery tales " read to her by her attendants. She was testy, however, and although all the privy councillors were staying at court she would speak to none of them but the archbishop and Secretary Cecil. She would take no medicine, though the doctors declared her free from any special disease and her constitution so sound that if she would take their remedies she might live for many years. But, as one of them said, " princes must not be forced." She herself said " I am not sick, I feel no pain, and yet I pine away." When asked the cause of her sorrowing, she replied with her old spirit that

<hr>

[9] Camden, 659; Chamberlain, *Letters*, 174, 178; *Cal. State Papers, Ven.*, 1592–1603, 528, 529, 531–4, 551, 553–4.

she " knew nothing in the world worthy to trouble her."
On the 6th of March she insisted on going into the garden,
but on the 9th she was so ill that the courtiers despaired of
her recovery, and the next day she fell into a partial stupor.
On the 11th however a small abscess in her throat opened
and although she was almost strangled by the discharge she
felt better afterward and slept naturally a few hours on each
of the following nights, and ate and drank something.[10]

The improvement was only temporary. Already on the
15th she was worse again, sleepless and miserable. Her
grandnephew Sir Robert Carey tells that when he went into
her room a day or two later " she tooke me by the hand and
wrung it hard and said, ' No, Robin, I am not well,' and
then discussed with me of her indisposition and that her
heart had been sad and heavy for ten or twelve dayes, and
in her discussion she fetched not so few as forty or fifty
great sighes." Publicly she still asserted her activity. Saturday evening the 20th of March she gave orders to prepare
the great chapel for public service the next day, but the
courtiers awaited in vain until eleven o'clock her appearance there. She then sent word that she would hear service
in the small chapel, but finally gave up attendance even
there and had cushions laid on the floor of her privy chamber near the door whence she could hear the service outside.
Here on her cushions she remained for three days and nights
refusing to go again to her bed.

The councillors had now given up hopes of the queen's
recovery, and fearing disturbances as rumors of her illness
spread through the country sent orders to the lords lieutenants and other officers of the shires and to Ireland to take
measures to prevent any disorders or unauthorized assemblies, ordered the queen's guards and gentlemen pensioners

[10] Camden, 660; *Rutland MSS., Hist. MSS., Comm.,* i, 387; *Beaumont au roi,* 19 and 24 March, Baschet, *Transcripts,* Bundle 35; Rivers to
Creleto, *State Papers, Dom., Eliz.,* cclxxxvii, 50, 51; Caron to Aersens,
March 15th, 1603, *Cal. State Papers, Dom.,* 1601–3, 302; *Venetian,* 1592–
1603, 554, 557–8, *Cottonian MSS.,* Julius C., iii, fo. 14b; *Sloane MSS.,*
718; Manningham, *Diary,* 146.

to be on the watch, hastened the press of vagrants in the streets of London to be sent as soldiers to the Netherlands, so as to diminish the danger of rioting, summoned horse-troops to guard the exchequer, and ordered the fleet to keep watch in the Channel. The mayor of London also set watches, and citizens living in the suburbs began to bring their plate and valuables into the city or to the exchequer for safety. A public prayer for the recovery of the queen was hastily composed by the bishop of Winchester, her almoner, printed and distributed.

It was not until Wednesday the 23d, apparently, that the privy councillors summoned up the necessary courage, or hardness, to require of Elizabeth the last of her duties as queen. The contemporary accounts of her deathbed advocacy of the claims of James as her successor, after her years of silence on the subject, are too favorable to the plans of those who surrounded her at the time and had already determined on his succession to be accepted without some hesitation. Nevertheless the testimony to some such nomination is conclusive. Howard seems to have declared to his fellow councillors that Elizabeth had herself opened up the matter by remarking to him during the recent removal from Westminster to Richmond, " My throne has been the throne of kings, neither ought any but he that is my next heir to succeed me." Asked now by the lord keeper and the secretary, as she was evidently approaching death, whom she would have to succeed her she answered " No base person, but a king." Questioned directly whether she meant the king of Scots, according to one account she answered with gasping breath, " I will that a king succeed me, and who should that be but my nearest kinsman the king of Scots"; according to another she merely lifted her hand above her head and moved it in a circle to indicate a royal crown.

By this time she had become speechless, her finger hung in her mouth, her open eyes were fixed on the floor, she was unresponsive to anything that was said. Partly by the persuasions of Howard, partly by force she was on Wednesday the 23d carried from her cushions to her bed. As she lay in her inner chamber almost unconscious, Dr. Parry, one of the chaplains, read the usual Wednesday morning service and preached in her chapel before the lord keeper, the lord treasurer, the archbishop of Canterbury, Lord Admiral Howard, the earl of Shrewsbury, the earl of Worcester, Secretary Cecil, Lord Grey, Sir William Knollys, Sir Edward Wotton and others and prayed so fervently for her that, we are told by one who was present, few eyes were dry. About six o'clock in the evening she roused from her lethargy and made signs to her women attendants for the archbishop and chaplains to come to her. With some of the more intimate of her courtiers they went into her chamber and found her lying in her bed, one hand on the covers, one stretched over the side. The archbishop spoke to her of her faith and reminded her that she was about to appear to give her account before the king of kings. She moved her hand and eyes in acknowledgment. Then he prayed for a long half hour; as he was about to rise she signed for him to continue, and this occurred still again. By this time the hour had become late and all left her but her women. She fell asleep and between two and three in the morning passed quietly away. The privy councillors gathered once more for a few moments around her dead body, then passed to the secretary's chamber to make preparations for the proclamation of her successor.[11]

The queen's body was brought immediately from Richmond, where she died, to Westminster, by water and at night, surrounded by torches and followed by some of her household in barges; but her funeral was postponed, as was

[11] *Memoirs of Robert Carey,* Ed. 1759, 136–46; Manningham, *Diary,* 145–7, 170; Wilbraham, *Diary,* Camden Soc. Misc., x, 53–5; *Rutland MSS., Hist. MSS. Comm.,* i, 388; Camden, 660–1; *State Papers, Dom., Eliz.,* cclxxvii, 58; Thos. Ferrers to Sir H. Ferrers, March 25, 1603, *Cal. Stowe MSS.,* i, 127–8, No. 57; *Cal. State Papers, Ven.,* 1592–1603, 558, 565–6; 1603–7, 15–6; *Certain Observations concerning the Reign of Queen Elizabeth, Sloane MSS.,* 718.

not unusual at that time, for some weeks. The proclamation of King James, in English and French, at the palace gate in Whitehall and in Cheapside in London early in the morning of March 24 and in various parts of the country in the next few days, the hurried messages of notification of the queen's death sent to the new king in Edinburgh, the journeys of many courtiers to meet him in the north, his orders that this flow should cease and that the councillors and officials should retain their positions and proceed with their duties until his arrival, and his approval of the arrangements for the queen's funeral all took place while her body lay wrapped in its cere cloth, soldered in a leaden coffin covered with purple cloth, strewn with flowers and herbs and watched over by her ladies in the palace of Whitehall. Her body was not opened, as was usually done, it was said by her request in her lifetime, and was not seen by anyone after it was taken from Richmond.

As this work opened with a procession, the triumph for the defeat of the Armada, so it may close with another procession, the funeral of the queen. Between them lay fifteen long years, with many similar ceremonials and all the thronging events that have now been so inadequately recorded. The funeral took place April 28. It made a deep impression at the time. The foreign ambassadors wrote home full accounts; the chroniclers describe it. Several detailed lists of the personages as they walked in order in the procession from Whitehall to Westminster, two series of pictures by contemporary draughtsmen, one giving what appear to be silhouette portraits of the principal officials, foreign representatives, heralds with their banners and groups of lesser participants, the other, said by old tradition to have been drawn by the chronicler and herald-at-arms Camden, and more than one written narrative are all in general correspondence as to the appearance of the funeral procession.[12] There were more than a thousand

---

[12] *Expicedium, A Funeral Oration written by Infelice Academico Whereunto is added the true order of her Highnes' Imperiall Funerall,* London,

persons in line. First came bell ringers and knight marshal's men with truncheons to open a way through the crowd. The first section of what must have been at best but a straggling column consisted of two hundred and sixty poor women and sixteen poor men dressed in black walking four by four as mourners. They were followed by a crowd of artisans and servants and messengers of the various household offices, — the laundry, the buttery, the scullery, the woodyard, the stable, many of them driving the empty carts used by the household in its ordinary routine. After these came the menial servants of noblemen, knights and gentlemen connected with the court. Two horses, one covered with black cloth, the other with black velvet, each led by two equerries, presumably represented the queen's stable. Trumpeters blowing blasts walked at intervals in the line and sergeants at arms with maces kept it in order.

So far this could hardly have been distinguished from the funeral of any other great lady or nobleman of that age, so given to ceremonial displays, except that the appearance in the early ranks of the procession of various pursuivants at arms, the standard of the Dragon carried by Sir George Bourchier, its hereditary bearer, the standard of the Greyhound carried by a brother of the earl of Pembroke, the standard of the Lion carried by Somerset, the portcullis and other heraldic emblems would have indicated to anyone versed in heraldry that it was some member of the Tudor family, perhaps of the royal line of England that was being so honored. But as the principal clerks, the musicians, apothecaries, physicians, marshals, clerks of the council, privy seal, signet and parliament, the cofferer, the chaplains and the subordinate secretaries appeared, accompanied by the gentlemen and children of the chapel in their copes and surplices, all " singing in a mournefull tune," and followed

1603; *Additional MSS.*, 35, 324 (7); *Cal. State Papers, Venetian*, 1603-7; 22-3; *Hist. MSS. Comm., Rutland MSS.*, I, 389, Speed, *Chronicle*, Ed. 1632, 1217; *Sloane MSS.*, 718; *Stowe MSS.*, 1847; *Vetusta Monumenta*, Pub. by Society of Antiquaries, iii, Plates xviii–xxiv.

by Lord Zouch carrying the banner of Chester and Lord Herbert carrying the banner of Cornwall, the royal character of the procession became clearly predominant. The mayor, recorder and aldermen of London and their officers, the law officers of the crown, the judges, the personal attendants of the queen, including the band of gentlemen pensioners holding their pole-axes heads downward and wrapped in black, were followed by the Lancaster herald and by the banners of Wales and Ireland carried respectively by Viscount Bindon and the earl of Clanricard. Secretary Cecil, represented in one of the drawings, as he was in reality, as small, round-shouldered and with pointed beard, marched in a position that but poorly represented his power in the government alongside the chief justice and higher household officers and the resident agent of the Netherlands and somewhat lower in dignity than the nobles in their own right. Then came Lord Keeper Egerton carrying the seals in a bag over his shoulder, Whitgift, archbishop of Canterbury, in his flat cap, and the French ambassador, as in the Armada procession, a gentleman carrying his train, which is described and indeed pictured as being more than six yards long. This section of the procession was closed with the great embroidered banner of England carried by the earl of Pembroke assisted by Lord Howard of Effingham surrounded by a crowd of heralds — Somerset, Richmond, York, Chester and Norris.

After an interval came the central figure, no longer as in 1588 the triumphing queen but merely a waxen image, " the lively picture of her Majesty's whole body in her parliament robes with a crown on her head and a Sceptre in her hand, lying on the Corpse inshrined in lead and embalmed, covered with purple velvet, born in a Charriott drawn by four horses trapt in black velvet." The canopy over this royal hearse was carried by six earls, and six banners were borne alongside by twelve of the lesser nobles. The earl of Worcester, master of the horse, followed leading the queen's palfrey where Essex had walked in the procession of fifteen years before. Our historian, William Camden, Clarencieux, and William' Dethick, Garter king-at-arms, closed the display of heraldry. The marchioness of Northampton, the highest noblewoman in England, followed on foot, as chief mourner, her train held up by two countesses. She was followed by the lord treasurer, Buckhurst, the aged lord admiral, Howard, two earls, fifteen countesses, the queen's ladies and maids of honor and women members of the families of the nobility. Sir Walter Ralegh, still captain of the guard for all the intrigues that were so soon to bring about his downfall, with his men walking five and five, their halberds held downward, closed the line, garbed, as were all who participated in the funeral, in hoods and customary suits of solemn black. The procession passed slowly over the short space which has been the scene of so much royal and memorial solemnity between crowds that thronged the streets and covered the roofs and cornices, some sobbing and lamenting, others discussing the virtues and weaknesses of the great queen. After a brief service and sermon the body of Elizabeth was placed in its tomb in Westminster Abbey.

INDEX

INDEX TO VOLUME II